FOURTH EDITION

MIDDLE AND SECONDARY CLASSROOM MANAGEMENT

Lessons from Research and Practice

CAROL SIMON WEINSTEIN

Rutgers, the State University of New Jersey

INGRID NOVODVORSKY

University of Arizona

Mc Graw Hill

Connect
Learn
Succeed™

MIDDLE AND SECONDARY CLASSROOM MANAGEMENT: LESSONS FROM RESEARCH AND PRACTICE
Published by McGraw-Hill, a business unit of The McGraw-Hill Companies, Inc., 1221 Avenue of
the Americas, New York, NY 10020. Copyright © 2011, 2007, 2003, 1996 by The McGraw-Hill
Companies, Inc. All rights reserved. No part of this publication may be reproduced or distributed
in any form or by any means, or stored in a database or retrieval system, without the prior written
consent of The McGraw-Hill Companies, Inc., including, but not limited to, in any network or other
electronic storage or transmission, or broadcast for distance learning. Some ancillaries, including
electronic and print components, may not be available to customers outside the United States.

This book is printed on acid-free paper.

1 2 3 4 5 6 7 8 9 0 DOC/DOC 0

ISBN-13: 978-0-07-337861-9
ISBN-10: 0-07-337861-5

Vice President, Editorial: *Michael Ryan*
Publisher: *David Patterson*
Senior Sponsoring Editor: *Allison McNamara*
Managing Editor: *Meghan Campbell*
Developmental Editor: *Beth Kaufman*
Marketing Manager: *James Headley*
Production Editor: *Jasmin Tokatlian*
Designer: *Laurie Entringer*
Production Supervisor: *Laura Fuller*
Composition: *Laserwords Private Limited*
Printing: *45# New Era Matte, R. R. Donnelley & Sons/Crawfordsville, IN*

Cover image: © *BananaStock / PictureQuest*

Library of Congress Cataloging-in-Publication Data

Weinstein, Carol Simon.
    Middle and secondary classroom management : lessons from research and practice /
    Carol Simon Weinstein, Ingrid Novodvorsky.—4th ed.
        p. cm.
    ISBN 978-0-07-337861-9
    1. Classroom management. 2. Education, Secondary. 3. Education, Elementary. 4. Classroom
    environment. I. Novodvorsky, Ingrid. II. Title.
  LB3013.W46 2011
  373.1102′4–dc22
                                                                                    2009031679

The Internet addresses listed in the text were accurate at the time of publication. The inclusion of
a Web site does not indicate an endorsement by the authors or McGraw-Hill, and McGraw-Hill does
not guarantee the accuracy of the information presented at these sites.

www.mhhe.com

ABOUT THE AUTHORS

Carol Simon Weinstein is professor emerita in the Department of Learning and Teaching at Rutgers Graduate School of Education. She received her bachelor's degree in psychology from Clark University in Worcester, Massachusetts, and her master's and doctoral degrees from Harvard Graduate School of Education. Dr. Weinstein began her research career by studying the impact of classroom design on students' behavior and attitudes. She pursued this topic for many years, writing about the ways that classroom environments can be designed to facilitate teachers' goals and to foster children's learning and development. Eventually, her interest in organizing classroom space expanded to include classroom organization and management in general. She is the author (with Molly Romano and Andrew J. Mignano, Jr.) of *Elementary Classroom Management: Lessons from Research and Practice* (McGraw-Hill, 2011), as well as numerous chapters and articles on classroom management and teacher education of students' beliefs and expectations. In 2000, Dr. Weinstein was recognized by the American Federation of Teachers for "Bridging the Gap between Theory and Practice in Effective Classroom Management." Dr. Weinstein also co-edited (with Carolyn Evertson) the first *Handbook of Classroom Management: Research, Practice, and Contemporary Issues* (Lawrence Erlbaum Associates, Inc., 2006), a compendium of 47 chapters written by scholars from around the world.

Ingrid Novodvorsky is Director of the College of Science Teacher Preparation Program at the University of Arizona. Dr. Novodvorsky earned a bachelor's degree in Physics and Mathematics, and master's and doctoral degrees in Secondary Education, all from the University of Arizona. Before joining the university community, she taught high-school physics and mathematics for twelve years. During that time, Dr. Novodvorsky mentored beginning science teacher colleagues and hosted student teachers in her classroom. As part of the teaching faculty of the Teacher Preparation Program, she created and teaches a course on classroom management, recognizing that this is a critical aspect of preparing teachers. Her current research is focused on preservice teacher thinking about assessment and activity selection.

DEDICATION

Once again—to Sandy, Christina, Fred, and Donnie:

You continue to teach and inspire all who read this book.

CONTENTS

PART III   ORGANIZING AND MANAGING INSTRUCTION   187

PREFACE

In the years since the first edition of *Middle and Secondary Classroom Management,* the challenges of classroom management have grown dramatically. Classes are more heterogeneous than ever, with students from a wide range of cultural and linguistic backgrounds. Students with disabilities are educated in classes with their nondisabled peers, and teachers may be working in co-teaching arrangements that require collaboration and coordination. Increasing numbers of adolescents come to school with emotional and psychological problems. The recent economic crisis has increased the incidence of poverty and homelessness and created a climate of uncertainty, anxiety, and fear. Now more than ever, teachers need to know how to establish classrooms that are supportive, inclusive, caring, and orderly.

Unfortunately, beginning teachers frequently report that their teacher education programs did not prepare them for the challenges of classroom management. They call for more preparation in areas such as communicating with parents, responding to inappropriate behavior, working in diverse, multicultural settings, and helping students with special needs. They complain about courses that are too removed from the realities of schools and crave examples of real teachers dealing with the challenges of real students in real classrooms.

PROFILES OF REAL TEACHERS

Middle and Secondary Classroom Management: Lessons from Research and Practice is designed to address these concerns. As the subtitle of this book indicates, we have integrated what research has to say about effective classroom management with knowledge culled from practice. This is done by highlighting the thinking and the actual management practices of four real teachers: Fred Cerequas (social studies), Donnie Collins (mathematics), Sandy Krupinski (chemistry), and Christina Lugo Vreeland (English). Readers will come to know these four teachers—to hear their thinking on various aspects of classroom management and to see the ways they interact with students. Their stories provide real-life illustrations of the concepts and principles derived from research.

These four teachers not only teach different subjects, they also work in school districts that differ substantially in terms of race, ethnicity and socioeconomic status. For example, Fred's suburban district is predominantly European American (64 percent) and Asian American (20 percent), and only 12 percent of the students are eligible for the federal free or reduced-price lunch program. In contrast, Donnie's urban district is 54 percent Latino and 41 percent African American, and 80 percent of the students are eligible for the federal lunch program. Donnie and Christina teach basic skills classes, while Sandy teaches an advanced placement course, and Fred teaches an elective entitled "Institute for Political and Legal Education." Because of differences like these, their ways of managing their classrooms often look very different. But all of the teachers are able to create productive, respectful, and orderly classrooms, and all of the teachers enact the same basic principles of classroom management.

THE FOURTH EDITION: WHAT'S THE SAME? WHAT'S NEW?

As in earlier editions, this edition of *Middle and Secondary Classroom Management* provides clear, practical guidance for organizing and managing classrooms. Our goal has been to write a book that is based on actual research findings, yet is accessible, even enjoyable to read. We have tried to balance the goal of providing breadth and depth of coverage with the need for a book that is easy to use and reasonable in length. We hope that we have succeeded in producing writing that is clear, lively, conversational, and engaging. (It should be noted that, for the sake of readability, we consistently use "we" and "us" even when describing incidents that involved only one of the authors.)

This edition continues to address the ongoing management tasks that teachers face—from organizing physical space, creating community, and teaching norms to responding to problem behavior and preventing violence. We also include topics that are often omitted in classroom management texts but that are crucial, such as working with families and using time effectively. In addition, we discuss strategies for motivating students and managing the instructional formats commonly used in middle and secondary classrooms (e.g., independent work, small-group work, recitations and discussions), topics more commonly found in general methods books. Throughout the text, we emphasize the importance of positive teacher-student relationships for effective classroom management.

This edition retains several pedagogical features that instructors and students have found useful. In almost every chapter, readers can find the following:

- *Pause and Reflect* boxes to promote engagement and comprehension.
- *Activities for Skill Building and Reflection* that are divided into three sections: "In Class, "On Your Own," and "For Your Portfolio."
- An annotated list of books and articles in *For Further Reading*.
- A list of *Organizational Resources* describing agencies that can provide additional information.

- *Practical Tips* boxes that contain useful classroom management strategies.
- Marginal icons that alert readers to content focusing on cultural diversity.

In addition, this edition contains two new features. First, an introduction to each section provides an organizing framework for the chapters to come and summarizes their contents. Second, *Meet the Educator* boxes highlight the work of well-known speakers and writers whom beginning teachers are likely to meet during inservice workshops or lectures. All of these educators have widely disseminated classroom management programs or have done work that has relevance for classroom management (e.g., Alfie Kohn, Harry Wong, Jane Nelson and Lynn Lott, and Spencer Kagan).

In response to feedback from the users of the third edition, a few chapters have been reordered to better mesh with the way classroom management courses are organized. We have also improved coherence by moving some material from one chapter to another, eliminating redundancy, and streamlining discussions. Finally, all chapters have been updated to reflect recent scholarship and current concerns, with more than 70 new references. New or expanded material addresses topics such as:

- The importance of being both warm *and* assertive.
- Presenting yourself professionally.
- The norms and values of middle-class White culture.
- Learning about students' lives.
- The developing adolescent.
- Working with students who are poor or homeless.
- Dealing with the inappropriate use of electronic devices.
- Positive behavioral supports.

 This text is available as an eTextbook at www. CourseSmart.com At CourseSmart you can save up to 50% off the cost of a print textbook, reduce your impact on the environment, and gain access to powerful web tools for learning. CourseSmart has the largest selection of eTextbooks available anywhere, offering thousands of the most commonly adopted textbooks from a wide variety of higher education publishers. CourseSmart eTextbooks are available in one standard online reader with full text search, notes and highlighting, and email tools for sharing notes between classmates. For further details contact your sales representative or go to www. coursesmart.com.

ELEMENTARY CLASSROOM MANAGEMENT: A COMPANION TEXT

This edition of *Middle and Secondary Classroom Management* parallels the fifth edition of *Elementary Classroom Management: Lessons from Research and Practice* (Weinstein, Romano, & Mignano, 2011), so that instructors teaching courses with both elementary and secondary teacher education students can use the two books as a package. While the principles and concepts discussed are the same, the teachers on which the companion book is based all work at the elementary level, and the "lessons from research" are based largely on studies conducted in kindergarten through sixth grade.

ACKNOWLEDGMENTS

As always, we express our gratitude to the teachers featured in this book. They allowed us to observe in their classrooms and shared their wisdom, frustrations, and celebrations during countless hours of interviews. In the interest of full disclosure, one point about the structure of the book needs to be made explicit. The portraits of Christina, Donnie, Fred, and Sandy are composites derived from material that was collected over a number of years, starting in 1993. In other words, we have created a portrait of each teacher by describing incidents that occurred in different years with different students at different grade levels as though they had all occurred in the same academic year with the same class. Christina and Sandy are still working in their schools, so they were able to contribute to this new edition; however, Fred and Donnie retired several years ago.

We are also grateful to the district administrators who agreed to this project and to the school counselors who took the time to speak with us and shared their perspectives. To our students, many thanks for allowing us to use your journal entries and for providing us with feedback on everything from confusing content to printing errors. It should be noted that in some cases, details from the journals have been changed to avoid embarrassment to anyone, and at times, composite entries have been created.

We express our deep appreciation to the individuals who reviewed the earlier edition: Eileen Austin, University of South Florida; Linda V. Neiman, Cardinal Stritch University; Gail Richmond, Michigan State University; and Jill Freund Thomas, Illinois State University. If there are any errors or misstatements, the fault is entirely our own.

Finally, a special thank you to Neil, from both of us, for putting up with long authors' meetings in his home! We would also like to acknowledge our mutual friend, Ginger, who introduced us and got our collaboration started. Thank you to Chris for providing unfailing support during the revision process.

Carol Simon Weinstein

Ingrid Novodvorsky

PART I

INTRODUCTION

When you hear the words, "a really good teacher," what comes to your mind?

We have asked our teacher education students this question, and invariably they talk about *caring*. A good teacher is a caring teacher, they say, someone who respects and supports students, who doesn't put them down, and who shows genuine interest in them as individuals. Our teacher education students also believe they have the capacity to be that kind of teacher. They envision themselves nurturing students' self-esteem, rejoicing in their successes, and creating strong bonds of affection and mutual respect.

And then these prospective teachers begin student teaching. Over the weeks, the talk about caring begins to fade away, replaced by talk of control and discipline, penalties and consequences, names on the board and detention. Our students lament the fact that they were "too nice" at the beginning and conclude that they should have been "meaner." Some even seem to believe that caring and order are mutually exclusive.

The tension between wanting to care and needing to achieve order is not uncommon among novice teachers. But showing care and achieving order are not irreconcilable goals. The two actually go hand in hand. Indeed, *one of the ways teachers create an orderly, productive environment is by treating students with warmth and respect.* Common sense tells us that students are more likely to cooperate with teachers who are seen as responsive, trustworthy, and respectful, and research consistently shows this to be true.

At the same time, *one of the ways to show students you care is by taking responsibility for keeping order.* Far from just being "warm and fuzzy," caring teachers are willing to assume the leadership role that is part of being a teacher. For such teachers, caring is not just about being affectionate and respectful; it's also about monitoring behavior, teaching and enforcing norms, and providing needed organization and structure. These teachers understand that students actually crave limits—even though they may protest loudly.

In the first chapter of this book, you will meet the four "good" secondary teachers whose experiences and wisdom form the basis for this book. As you will see, these teachers know how to combine warmth and caring with an insistence that students work hard, comply with classroom norms, and treat one another with consideration. This combination constitutes *authoritative classroom management.* Borrowing terminology from the literature on parenting, authoritative classroom managers are neither dictatorial and unresponsive ("authoritarian"), nor affectionate but undemanding ("permissive"). Instead, they are "warm demanders," a concept we will meet in many of the chapters that follow.

CHAPTER 1

CLASSROOM MANAGEMENT IN A CROWDED, COMPLEX ENVIRONMENT

For many prospective and beginning teachers, entering a middle or high school classroom is like returning home after a brief absence. So little has changed: desks with oversized arms are still arranged in straggly rows; bells still signal the end of classes; and bulletin boards still display faded copies of bell schedules and fire drill instructions. The familiarity of these sights and sounds makes us feel comfortable and at ease; in fact, it may lead us to conclude that the transition from student to teacher will be relatively easy. Yet, ironically, this very familiarity can be a trap; it can make it difficult to appreciate what a curious and demanding place the secondary classroom really is. Looking at the classroom as if we have never seen one before may help us recognize some of its strange characteristics and contradictions.

Viewed from a fresh perspective, the classroom turns out to be an extremely crowded place. It is more like a subway or a bus than a place designed for learning, and it is hard to think of another setting (except prison, perhaps) where such large groups of individuals are packed so closely together for so many hours. Nonetheless, amid this crowdedness, students are often not permitted to interact. As Philip Jackson (1990) has noted, "students must try to behave as if they were in solitude, when in point of fact they are not. . . . These young people, if they are to become successful students, must learn how to be alone in a crowd" (p. 16).

There are other contradictions in this curious place. Middle and high school students are expected to work together in harmony, yet they may be strangers— even rivals—and may come from very different cultural backgrounds. Students

[handwritten margin notes:] classrooms like prison

yet must succeed in environment

"I expect you all to be independent, innovative, critical thinkers who will do exactly as I say."

Figure 1.1   *Source:* Reprinted by permission of Warren.

are urged to help one another, but they are also told to keep their eyes on their own papers. They are encouraged to cooperate, but they are often in competition, especially if they are concerned about class rank and college admission. They are lectured about being independent and responsible, yet they are also expected to show complete, unquestioning obedience to the teacher's dictates. (This peculiar situation is captured in the cartoon that appears in Figure 1.1.) They are urged to work slowly and carefully, but they are often reminded that 42- (or even 84-) minute periods require adherence to a rigid time schedule.

In addition to these contradictions, Walter Doyle (2006) has pointed out six features of the classroom setting that make it even more complex. First, classrooms are characterized by *multidimensionality.* Unlike a post office or a restaurant, places devoted to a single activity, the classroom is the setting for a broad range of events. Within its boundaries, students read, write, and discuss. They work on projects, view DVDs, and listen to lectures. They also form friendships, argue, and evaluate last Saturday's basketball game. Teachers lead whole-class discussions, coordinate small-group activities, and administer tests. They also take attendance, settle disputes, and counsel students with problems. Somehow, the classroom environment must be able to accommodate all these activities.

Second, many of these activities take place at the same time. This *simultaneity* makes the classroom a bit like a three-ring circus. Secondary teachers tend to use whole-group instruction more than their elementary counterparts; nonetheless, it is not uncommon to see a cluster of students working on a project while a few individuals write at their desks or on computers and a small group meets

Classroom a place of contradictions

with the teacher about materials to include in their portfolios. Still other students may be text messaging about yesterday's soccer game. It is this simultaneity—this three-ring circus quality—that makes having "eyes in the back of your head" so valuable to teachers.

A third characteristic of classrooms is the rapid pace at which things happen. Classroom events occur with an *immediacy* that makes it impossible to think through every action ahead of time. An argument erupts over a perceived insult; a student complains that a neighbor is copying; a normally silent student makes a serious, but irrelevant, comment during a group discussion. Each of these incidents requires a quick response, an on-the-spot decision about how to proceed. Furthermore, classroom incidents like these cannot always be anticipated, despite the most careful planning. This *unpredictability* is a fourth characteristic of classrooms. It ensures that being a teacher is rarely boring, but unpredictability can also be exhausting.

A fifth characteristic of classrooms is the *lack of privacy.* Classrooms are remarkably public places. Within their four walls, each person's behavior can be observed by many others. Teachers talk of feeling as though they are always "on stage" or living in a "fishbowl" (Lortie, 1975). Their feelings are understandable. With 20 or 30 pairs of eyes watching, it is difficult to find a moment for a private chuckle or an unobserved groan. But the scrutiny goes two ways: Teachers constantly monitor students' behavior as well. And in response to this sometimes unwelcome surveillance, students develop an "active underlife" (Hatch, 1986) in which to pursue their own personal agendas. With skills that increase as they progress from grade to grade, students learn to doodle and draw, comb their hair, and do homework for another course, all—they hope—without the teachers ever noticing. Yet, even if they avoid the teacher's eyes, there are always peers watching. It is difficult for students to have a private interaction with the teacher, to conceal a grade on a test, or to make a mistake without someone noticing.

Finally, over the course of the academic year, classes construct a joint *history*. This sixth characteristic means that classes, like families, remember past events—both positive and negative. They remember who got yelled at, who got away with being late to class, and what the teacher said about homework assignments. They remember who was going to have only "one more chance" before getting detention, and if the teacher didn't follow through, they remember that too. The class memory means that what happens today affects what happens tomorrow. It also means that teachers must work to shape a history of shared experiences that will support, rather than frustrate, future activities.

Crowded, competitive, contradictory, multidimensional, fast-paced, unpredictable, public—this portrait of the classroom highlights characteristics that we often overlook. We have begun the book with this portrait because we believe that *effective organization and management require an understanding of the unique features of the classroom.* Many of the management problems encountered by beginning teachers can be traced back to their failure to understand the complex setting in which they work.

Past experiences with children and adolescents may also mislead beginning teachers. For example, you may have tutored an individual student who was having academic difficulties, or perhaps you have been a camp counselor. Although these are valuable experiences, they are very different from teaching in classrooms. Teachers do not work one-on-one with students in a private room; they seldom lead recreational activities that participants have themselves selected. Teachers do not even work with people who have chosen to be present. Instead, *teachers work with captive groups of students, on academic agendas that students have not helped to set, in a crowded, public setting.* Within this peculiar setting, teachers must carry out the fundamental tasks of classroom management.

PAUSE AND REFLECT

Before going any further, jot down the words that come to mind when you hear the phrase "classroom management." Then write the answer to this question: "What is the goal of classroom management?" After reading the next section, compare your goals statement with the statement in the book. Are they similar? Different?

[handwritten margin note: students have to be there → not like tutoring or camp]

GUIDING PRINCIPLES

Sometimes, we become so preoccupied with basic management issues (like getting everyone to sit down), we forget that classroom management is not about achieving order for order's sake. Indeed, classroom management has two distinct purposes: *It not only seeks to establish and sustain a caring, orderly environment in which students can engage in meaningful learning, it also aims to enhance students' social and emotional growth.* From this perspective, *how* a teacher achieves order is as important as *whether* a teacher achieves order (Evertson & Weinstein, 2006). Keeping this in mind, let us consider five principles that guide the content and organization of this book. (These are summarized in Table 1.1.)

The first principle is that *successful classroom management fosters self-discipline and personal responsibility.* Let's be honest: Every teacher's worst fear is the prospect of losing control—of being helpless and ineffectual in the face of unruly, anarchic classes. Given this nightmare, it's tempting to create a coercive, top-down management system that relies heavily on the use of rewards and penalties to gain obedience. Yet, such an approach does little to teach students to make

TABLE 1.1 Guiding Principles of Classroom Management

1. Successful classroom management fosters self-discipline and personal responsibility.
2. Most problems of disorder in classrooms can be avoided if teachers foster positive student-teacher relationships, implement engaging instruction, and use good preventive management strategies.
3. The need for order must not supersede the need for meaningful instruction.
4. Managing today's diverse classrooms requires the knowledge, skills, and predispositions to work with students from diverse racial, ethnic, language, and social class backgrounds. In other words, teachers must become "culturally responsive classroom managers."
5. Becoming an effective classroom manager requires reflection, hard work, and time.

(handwritten margin notes: teach + manage class using same set of principles → form good rel. → prevent, not punish)

good choices about how to act. Furthermore, as Mary McCaslin and Tom Good (1998) point out, "the success of a compliance model depends upon constant monitoring (if the teacher turns her or his back, students misbehave . . .)" (p. 170). An emphasis on external control is also inconsistent with current thinking about curriculum and instruction (McCaslin & Good, 1992, 1998). It doesn't make sense to design learning activities that encourage independence, problem solving, and critical thinking, and then use managerial strategies that encourage dependence on points, popcorn parties, and punishment. This is not to discount the importance of teachers' authority; clearly, in order to be effective, you must be willing to set limits and guide students' behavior. Nonetheless, what you are aiming toward is an environment in which students behave appropriately, not out of fear of punishment or desire for reward, but out of a sense of personal responsibility.

The second principle is that *most problems of disorder in classrooms can be avoided if teachers foster positive student-teacher relationships, implement engaging instruction, and use good preventive management strategies.* Let's look at each of these components in order. Extensive research demonstrates that when students perceive their teachers to be supportive and caring, they are more likely to engage in cooperative, responsible behavior and adhere to classroom rules and norms (Hoy & Weinstein, 2006). Similarly, when students find academic activities meaningful, engrossing, and stimulating, they are less inclined to daydream or disrupt. Finally, a pivotal study by Jacob Kounin (1970) documented the fact that orderly classes are more the result of a teacher's ability to *prevent* student misconduct than of particular ways of *handling* it. As a result of Kounin's work, we now distinguish between *discipline*—responding to inappropriate behavior—and *classroom management*—ways of creating a caring, respectful environment that supports learning.

(handwritten margin note: Classrm managemet shouldnot encompass "discipline" very! △)

Third, *the need for order must not supersede the need for meaningful instruction.* Although learning and teaching cannot take place in an environment that is chaotic, an excessive focus on quiet and uniformity can sometimes hinder instruction (Doyle, 2006). For example, a teacher may wish to divide the class into small groups for a cooperative learning activity, believing that her students will learn better by doing rather than by simply watching. Yet her anxiety about the noise level and her fear that students will not work well together could make her abandon the small-group project and substitute an individual worksheet assignment. In one respect, this teacher is correct: A collaborative activity will not only be more intellectually and socially challenging, it will also be more challenging from a managerial perspective. Yet, it is crucial that teachers not sacrifice the curriculum in order to achieve an orderly classroom. As Doyle (1985) comments, "A well-run lesson that teaches nothing is just as useless as a chaotic lesson in which no academic work is possible" (p. 33).

The fourth principle is that *managing today's diverse classrooms requires the knowledge, skills, and predispositions to work with students from diverse racial, ethnic, language, and social class backgrounds. In other words, teachers must become "culturally responsive classroom managers"* (Weinstein, Curran, & Tomlinson-Clarke, 2003; Weinstein, Tomlinson-Clarke, & Curran, 2004). Sometimes, a desire to treat students fairly leads teachers to strive for "color-blindness"

(Nieto, 2002), and educators are often reluctant to talk about cultural characteristics for fear of stereotyping. But definitions and expectations of appropriate behavior are culturally influenced, and conflicts are likely to occur if we ignore our students' cultural backgrounds. Geneva Gay (2006) provides a telling example of what can happen when there is a "cultural gap" between teachers and students. She notes that African Americans frequently use "evocative vocabulary" and "inject high energy, exuberance, and passion" into their verbal communication (p. 355). European American teachers may interpret such speech as rude or vulgar and feel compelled to chastise the students or even impose a punishment. Since the students see nothing wrong with what they said, they may resent and resist the teacher's response. As Gay notes: "The result is a cultural conflict that can quickly escalate into disciplinary sanctions in the classroom or referrals for administrative action" (p. 355).

(margin note: know cult. background of class members)

In order to avoid situations like this, we need to become aware of our own culturally based assumptions, biases, and values and reflect on how these influence our expectations for behavior and our interactions with students. By bringing our cultural biases to a conscious level, we are less likely to misinterpret the behaviors of our culturally different students and treat them inequitably. In addition, we must acquire cultural content knowledge. We must learn, for example, about our students' family backgrounds and their culture's norms for interpersonal relationships. Obviously, this knowledge must not be used to categorize or stereotype, and it is critical that we recognize the significant individual differences that exist among members of the same cultural group. Nonetheless, cultural content knowledge can be useful in developing *hypotheses* about students' behavior (Weiner, 1999).

The final principle is that *becoming an effective classroom manager requires reflection, hard work, and time*. Classroom management cannot be reduced to a set of recipes or a list of "how tos." As we have seen, the classroom environment is crowded, multidimensional, fast-paced, unpredictable, and public. In this complex setting, pat answers just won't work. Similarly, well-managed classrooms are not achieved by following "gut instinct" or doing "what feels right." Classroom management is a *learned craft*. That means that you must become familiar with the knowledge base that undergirds effective management. You must also be ready and willing to anticipate problems, analyze situations, generate solutions, make thoughtful decisions—and learn from your mistakes.

(margin note: Won't happen overnight! Tough to be a good classroom manager)

PLAN OF THE BOOK

Middle and Secondary Classroom Management focuses first on ways of creating a classroom environment that supports learning and self-regulation, such as designing an appropriate physical setting, building an atmosphere of caring and respect, and developing standards for behavior. It then moves to the managerial tasks directly related to instruction—for example, using time wisely, motivating students to learn, organizing group work, and managing student-centered discussions. Finally, the book examines the inevitable challenges associated with classroom management, such as responding to inappropriate behavior and preventing and coping with violence.

Throughout the book, concepts and principles derived from research are woven together with the wisdom and experiences of four real secondary teachers. You learn about the classes they teach and about the physical constraints of their rooms; you hear them reflect on their rules and routines and watch as they teach them to students. You listen as they talk about motivating students and fostering cooperation, and as they discuss appropriate ways to deal with misbehavior. In sum, *this book focuses on real decisions made by real teachers as they manage the complex environment of the secondary classroom.* By sharing their stories, we do not mean to suggest that their ways of managing classrooms are the only effective ways. Rather, our goal is to illustrate how four reflective, caring, and very different individuals approach the tasks involved in classroom management. And now, let's meet the teachers (in alphabetical order). Table 1.2 provides an overview of the teachers and the districts in which they teach.

MEETING THE TEACHERS

Fred Cerequas

Fred Cerequas ("Ser-a-kwas") works in a school district that has a reputation for innovation. This well-regarded school district currently has about 7,500 students and is gaining more than 400 a year. The student population is also becoming increasingly diverse; it is now 64 percent European American, 20 percent Asian American, 10 percent African American, and 6 percent Latino. More than 50 different first languages are spoken—in particular, Spanish, Gujarati, Hindi, Cantonese, and Arabic—and the socioeconomic range is striking. Although people think of the community as middle- to upper-middle-class, a sizable number of its children

TABLE 1.2 Overview of Featured Teachers and Their Districts

Name	Subject	District Size (students)	Students Qualified for Free/Reduced Lunch	District Ethnic/ Racial Diversity
Fred Cerequas	Social Studies	7,500	12%	predominantly European American
Donnie Collins	Mathematics	6,500	80%	approximately half Latino and half African American
Sandra Krupinski	Chemistry	1,650	26%	53% European American 17% African American 14% Latino 16% Asian American
Christina Vreeland	English	12,900	13%	predominantly European American

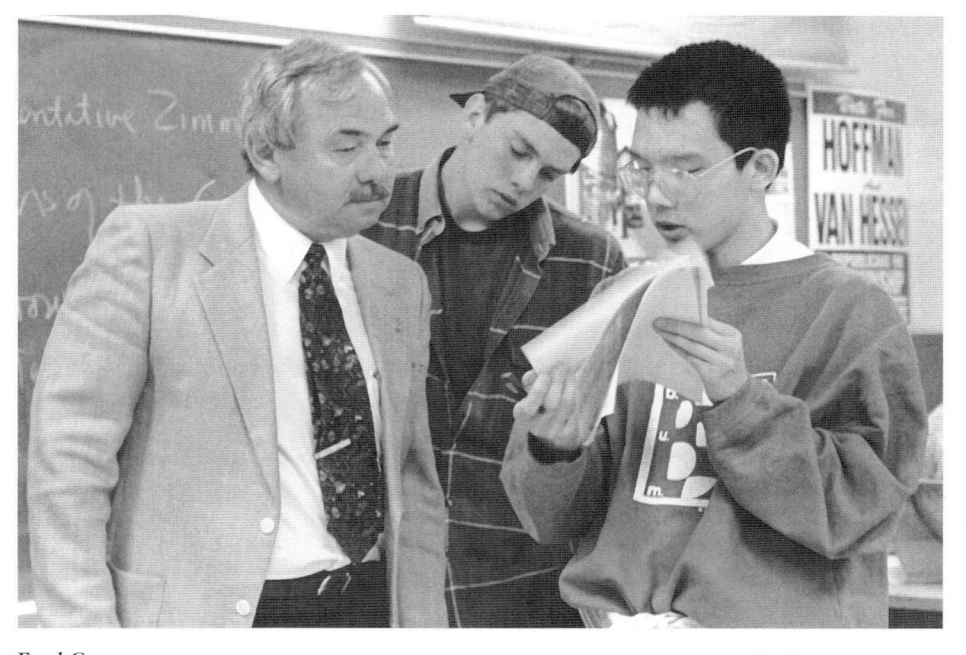

Fred Cerequas

live in low-cost mobile home parks. About 12 percent are eligible for the federal free or reduced-price lunch program.

A 58-year-old father of three, Fred is a member of the 10-person social studies department at the high school. The building currently houses 1,800 students (up from 1,200 only five years ago), but an addition is already needed because of the continuing population growth.

Fred's route to teaching was circuitous. As the son of factory workers who had to leave school for economic reasons, Fred went into the United States Army after high school. He worked as an information specialist in Alaska, where he had a radio and television show, narrated troop information films, and wrote for several army newspapers. When he was discharged, he began to work his way through college by driving a school bus for high school students. It was then that he discovered he was able to "connect with kids" and decided to earn a teaching certificate "just in case." A successful and gratifying student teaching experience led him to decide that this was the career he wanted to pursue. He's taught in the same district for his entire career—a total of 34 years. Far from being burned out, Fred still believes he learns as much from his students as they do from him.

Fred currently teaches five classes: two sections of U.S. History I (honors); one section of the Institute for Political and Legal Education (IPLE), a practicum in law, government, and politics for a heterogeneous group of seniors; and two sections of Contemporary World Issues, a non-Western history course for seniors (one honors and one "regular"). He articulates his goals for his students by telling the story of Tanida, a senior he had in class last year. After learning about the problems of women and children in the third world, Tanida arranged for her classmates to sponsor a little girl in Africa through the organization Save the Children—all without prompting from the teacher. To Fred, Tanida's efforts represent a combination of knowledge and compassion, and it is this combination that he strives for in his classes. He tells us:

 I believe real teachers are cultivators. They nurture the seeds of wisdom in their students by helping them become independent, eager learners who combine experience and knowledge with the genuine concern for others that gives life its meaning.

Fred admits that his goals are not easily achieved in today's typical high school, where an "Industrial Revolution mentality" dominates:

 Buildings like factories; seats in rows; rigid schedules; production quotas; quality controls. . . . The whole system seems geared to efficiency rather than humanity. At times, it seems to me that schools as they are designed actually inhibit education.

Despite the obstacles to learning that he sees in our current system of schooling, Fred is energetic and optimistic, and he demands a lot from his students. Early in the fall, for example, Fred led a discussion in Contemporary World Issues on the social institutions common to all cultures. Although students were generally cooperative, about one-half of the class wasn't fully engaged—a fact that did not escape his notice. Fred stopped the lesson and addressed the students' apathy in his characteristically direct, down-to-earth manner:

 Listen, we don't study junk in here. What we're doing in here is trying to understand processes of change. This affects us; this stuff can make a difference in your life. And if you can be more than just bored seniors, we can do some really important stuff in here.

After class, Fred sat in the teachers' room reflecting on the students' resistance. He reviewed the class roster, noting which youngsters had participated and which had remained silent. He spoke of the skepticism and detachment frequently displayed by students, particularly seniors; he acknowledged the difficulty of convincing them that what they were studying held meaning for their lives. Nonetheless, he vowed to "convert" them, and looked ahead to the day when he would actually have to chase them out after class. Given Fred's commitment and passion for teaching, there was little doubt that he would succeed. After all, according to Fred, "*Teacher* is not a word that describes what I do for a living; rather, it defines who I am."

Donnie Collins

Donnie teaches in a mid-sized urban district that serves 6,500 students in 10 schools; 54 percent of the students are Latino and 41 percent are African American.

Donnie Collins

Many of the children come from poor or low-income families, evidenced by the fact that 80 percent of the students qualify for the federal free or reduced-price lunch program. The socioeconomic conditions breed other problems—drugs, transiency, homelessness, teenage pregnancy, physical abuse.

The high school is a few miles from the heart of downtown, a low brick building set back from the street on a wide expanse of lawn. Built in the 1960s, the school currently accommodates 788 students in grades 9 through 12. On the second floor, in a corner classroom opposite the math department office, we find Donnie, a 9th- through 12th-grade mathematics teacher. A 56-year-old mother of one, Donnie began teaching math in Birmingham, Alabama, and then moved to her current district; she's been teaching there ever since, first on the junior high level and then at the high school. This year, since the high school is now on block scheduling (a topic we will discuss in Chapter 7), Donnie teaches two 80-minute classes at the high school—Algebra I and "SRA," a special review course for students who have failed the mathematics portion of the state exam required for graduation. She then drives to a nearby elementary school, where she teaches mathematics to eighth-graders in the gifted and talented program.

Being a teacher was Donnie's childhood dream. "As a child I always wanted to play school," she recalls, "and I always wanted to be the teacher, never one of the pupils." Reflecting on this early dream, Donnie acknowledges the influence of her grandmother, who had been an elementary teacher before she opened a beauty school and shop. Although Donnie's parents were farmers, they recognized that farming was not for her. As Donnie puts it, "My calling was to be a teacher."

Donnie was influenced not only by her grandmother but also by two of her own teachers. Her fifth-grade teacher, Mrs. Poole, was intimidating at first, but Donnie soon realized that she needn't be frightened. Mrs. Poole wasn't mean; she was just concerned about students' achievement and well-being. "From Mrs. Poole, I learned about the importance of maintaining discipline, about the need to be firm and fair, and the value of keeping in touch with parents." Later, in high school, Donnie encountered Miss Anchrum, a young math teacher fresh out of college, with lots of new ideas about how to make math exciting: "Miss Anchrum made math real, and she would accept nothing less than our best." From her, Donnie learned the importance of motivating students and holding high expectations.

Donnie eventually earned both a bachelor's degree and a master's degree in mathematics, along with certification to teach. But the impact of Mrs. Poole and Miss Anchrum has stayed with her, and her teaching reflects the lessons she learned from them. When asked about her goals, she answers without hesitation:

> I want the same things my teachers wanted. I want my students to become creative, independent thinkers; I want them to be able to function effectively in our everyday world; I want them to make a positive contribution to society. I continually stress that there is always more than one way to solve a problem and I encourage them to find alternative solutions. I believe strongly in the importance of group work and peer tutoring so that students can learn to work together and to take constructive criticism. When students say, "Oh, Ms. Collins, I don't need to know this; all I need to know is how to count my money," I tell them: "But first you have to make the money, and once you've made your money, you have to keep it." And you have to know math to do that.

Donnie's goals are not achieved easily. She is frustrated by those students "who can't see beyond today," who cause disruption, and who create problems for those who do want to learn. She is also concerned about a lack of parental involvement (a topic we will discuss in Chapter 6), and the problems that her students face. As she puts it, "Education is just not a priority for many of my students. *Survival* is the priority." Sometimes she has to forgo a math lesson in order to discuss the more immediate problems of her students: conflicts with families, pregnancy, parenting (the high school has a day care center for the children of its students), running away from home, violence in the community, drugs. With a certain amount of resignation, Donnie comments:

Sometimes it's okay to "roll" w/ class discussion

> If you try to go ahead with a math lesson when they're all riled up about something that has happened at home or in the neighborhood, you're doomed. There's just no point to it. It's better to put away the quadratic equations and *talk*.

Despite the difficulties of teaching in an urban district, Donnie is still enthusiastic and optimistic about her chosen career. Listening to her speak about the goals she has for her students and the satisfactions she derives from teaching, it is obvious that the legacy of Mrs. Poole and Miss Anchrum lives on in this secondary mathematics teacher.

Sandra Krupinski

Sandy Krupinski teaches in a small, extremely diverse community. The district's three schools serve children who live in large, expensive houses as well as those from low-income apartment complexes. The student population of 1,650 is 53 percent European American, 17 percent African American, 14 percent Latino, and 16 percent Asian American. About 26 percent of the children qualify for the federal free or reduced-price lunch program. The high school currently houses 650 students in grades 7 through 12.

In the science wing on the second floor is the chemistry classroom where Sandra Krupinski, a 50-year-old mother of two, teaches three classes of chemistry—two college prep and one advanced placement. This year, Sandy's classes are larger and

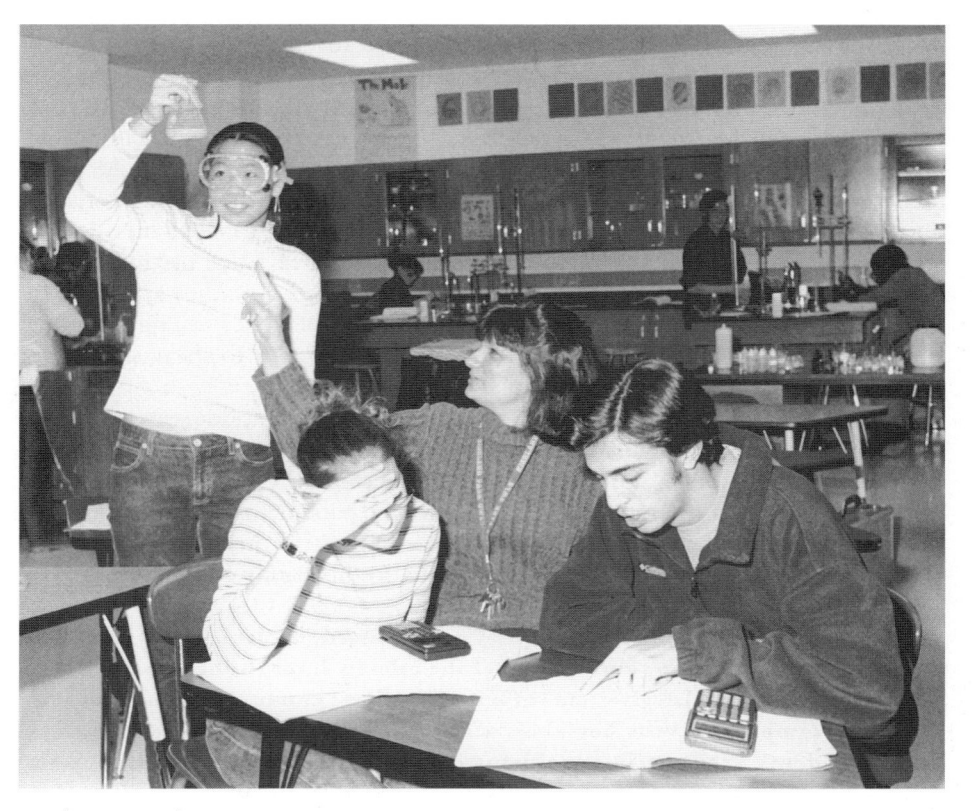

Sandra Krupinski

more diverse than in previous years. In her sixth-period class, for example, there are 25 students, including five African Americans, one Latino, one Asian American, and one whose family has come from India. The class also includes a student classified as emotionally disturbed.

Sandy's love of science was awakened when she herself was a student at the very same high school, and teaching seemed like the obvious, logical career. Her father, a construction worker, and her mother, an office manager for an insurance company, applauded the decision to be a teacher, proud that Sandy would be the first in her family to attend college.

Sandy is very clear about what she is trying to achieve with her students. She sees chemistry as a vehicle for helping students develop problem-solving skills, self-discipline ("a new experience for some"), and self-confidence:

 Chemistry is seen as a difficult subject, and some students begin the year thinking they'll never be able to master it. They'll come up to me with a blank paper and say, "I couldn't do this, Mrs. K." I can't stand that. My hope is that by the end of the year these students will have the confidence to attack problems and the ability to develop appropriate strategies. That's much more important to me than getting the right answers.

In order to achieve this goal, Sandy tries hard to create an accepting, non-threatening atmosphere in her class. On the first day of school, for example, she gives her students an index card and asks them to answer four questions: (1) How do you learn best? (2) What do you expect to be excited about in chemistry? (3) What do you expect to be nervous about? and (4) What can I do to help? Their responses are revealing, particularly to the third and fourth questions. One student shares his fear of talking in front of the class and asks her not to call on him. Several confide that they are anxious about the difficulty of the course, particularly the mathematics and the need to memorize "lots of itsy, bitsy facts"; they ask her to be patient and to take extra time. One girl with limited proficiency in English writes about the fact that her "language is not good," and asks Sandy to speak slowly and to "sometimes explain something for me."

When students return on the second day of class, Sandy addresses each concern that has been raised (telling students that these are the fears expressed by "two or more students"). She thanks them for sharing information that will help her to help them and reassures them that she will be patient, that they will proceed slowly, and that she will always be available for extra help outside of class. Afterwards, thinking about why she takes the time to do this, Sandy comments:

let students know they are not alone in their concerns

 As I talk about each fear they've expressed, I can actually see their shoulders drop, and I can feel the anxiety level in the class go down. Doing this also gives me information that I can use to help them. For example, take the boy who's afraid of speaking in front of the class. Today, students were putting problems on the board that they had done for homework. Normally, I don't particularly want people with the right answers to

put the problems up on the board, because I want them to see that what's important is developing a strategy, not just getting the correct answer. In this case, however, it was important for him to feel confident about going up to the board. So, as I walked around the room, I glanced at his paper and saw that he had a particular problem correct. I told him he had done a good job with it and asked him to put it on the board. Instead of getting anxious, he smiled at me! This couldn't have happened if I hadn't asked students to share their concerns with me.

always expect success

Sandy may be sensitive to students' anxieties about chemistry, but she still communicates high expectations and a no-nonsense attitude. This year, during an unexpectedly long "vacation" brought about by a fierce blizzard, Sandy e-mailed all of her Advanced Placement students to give them an assignment "so they wouldn't fall behind." Her students weren't surprised; one of them told her, "Oh, Mrs. K., we just *knew* you'd contact us!" Incidents like this have helped to build Sandy Krupinski's reputation as a teacher who is passionate about chemistry and fiercely committed to students' learning—a teacher who manages to be both demanding and caring.

Christina Lugo Vreeland

With 24 schools and 12,900 students, Christina's district is the largest of our four districts. The high school serves almost 900 students from 10 different towns. The student body is predominantly European American (61 percent), but the racial and ethnic diversity is steadily increasing (African American, 8 percent; Latino, 10 percent; Asian American, 20 percent; Native American, 1 percent), and 13 percent of the students qualify for the federal free or reduced-price lunch program.

In the English wing on the second floor, we find Christina Lugo Vreeland—24 years old, newly married, and in her second year of teaching English and journalism. Christina grew up in the community, the daughter of a truck driver whose family emigrated from Puerto Rico when he was three, and an office worker raised in a nearby town. She attended the state university, where she majored in English and minored in Spanish. After receiving her bachelor's degree, Christina continued on for a master's degree and certification in English Education.

Like Donnie and Sandy, Christina never really considered a career other than teaching (except for a time in eighth grade when she wanted to be a fashion designer). Even as a little girl, Christina "always had to be the teacher and tell everyone else what to do." But it wasn't until her junior year in high school that Christina began to think seriously about the kind of teacher she wanted to be:

I had an excellent teacher, Helaine Rasmussen. She was very strict, and we were afraid of her before we actually had her, but then we got to like her. She really enjoyed what she was doing. . . . We had to do a big term paper that year. . . . It seemed insurmountable—20 pages! But

Christina Lugo Vreeland

Mrs. Rasmussen had former students come in and talk about how they had done the project, and she took us through it step by step, so that . . . everything just seemed to fall into place. We were able to compose this paper we had never thought we would be able to do.

Then in my senior year, I had Angela Korodan for honors English. She started off by meeting with us at the end of junior year to give us the summer reading assignment. She gave us her address and opened the lines of communication. We had to mail her one of our assignments over the summer. She started teaching before she had to. And then the first two or three days of school, we sat in a circle, and talked about ourselves. These were people I had known for a long time, but I still learned things. She did the same; she told us about how she became a teacher, and how she had been a nun.

From Mrs. Rasmussen, Christina learned the importance of being rigorous and systematic. From Mrs. Korodan, she learned about the value of building communication and a sense of community. These are lessons that Christina tries hard to remember now that she is on the other side of the desk.

Like Donnie's high school, Christina's school uses block scheduling, so Christina meets three 84-minute classes a day, with one professional or "prep" period. Given the double periods, "year-long" classes last for half a year; this means that Christina gets new students and new courses every January. Her current schedule calls for two 10th-grade English classes, one with 29 students and one with

imp. to communicate w/ students ⤷ create sense of community

25 students, and one basic skills class for 11 students who have failed the state test required for graduation.

One of Christina's major goals is to help her students "make a place for reading and writing in their everyday lives." She explains:

> **I think that lots of times English teachers are so passionate about literature and analysis of literature that we forget that our students are not preparing to be English teachers. . . . The way I read and the way my students read is different, and that's okay. What I need to do is foster the kind of reading and writing that will be useful for them and to create the *desire* to read and write.**

To promote students' fluency in writing, Christina begins every class period with journal writing. As soon as the bell rings, students glance at the journal topic on the chalkboard, take out their journals, and begin writing. Sometimes journal entries serve as a lead-in to the day's lesson; for example, when students were about to discuss Antigone's decision to bury her brother, they wrote on a journal topic related to civil disobedience: "If you believed that what you were doing was right, would you break a law knowing that the penalty would be five years in jail?" Sometimes, journal entries are intended to stimulate thinking about the character traits we value in people ("Whom do you admire and why?" "What is patience, and who is the most patient person you know?"); sometimes, they're responses to music ("Describe the music you're listening to").

One day in midwinter, Christina reminisced about her first year and a half of teaching. She was still recovering from a bout of flu, and she was feeling upset about having missed several school days right at the beginning of the new term. She talked about feeling overwhelmed by the stacks of ungraded essays and the classes that were larger than usual. With an embarrassed smile, Christina expressed some of the doubts she had recently been feeling:

[handwritten margin note: Share your own experiences + difficulties]

> **For the last few days, I've been questioning, "Why do I want to be here? Why do I say I enjoy this?" And then today, we had a great discussion about the novel we're reading. The kids really understood things. They really got into it; they got excited about it. I had kids making important points—I didn't have to ask the leading questions each time. And they had the desire to discuss with each other and to read more. . . . At the end of the class [in the English Department office], the other teachers looked at me and saw me smiling. They knew I'd been feeling overwhelmed. And one of them asked, "Why are you so happy?" And I told them, "I just had an experience that renewed my faith in my ability to do this for the rest of my life."**

PAUSE AND REFLECT

Now that you've met the teachers, take a minute to think about their personalities and approaches to classroom management. Do you feel a special kinship with any of the four teachers? If your answer is yes, why do you feel this way? Next, reflect on your own middle and high school experiences. Were there any teachers that you would characterize as especially effective classroom managers? What did they do that made them especially effective? Are there any similarities between these teachers and the teachers you've just read about?

WHAT DO THE STUDENTS SAY?

While working with these four teachers, we became curious about the perceptions of the students in their classrooms. In particular, we were interested in why they thought students were cooperative and well behaved in some classes and uncooperative and ill behaved in others, as well as their views of the particular classes we were observing. In each class, the teacher left the room so that the students could talk more comfortably. We explained that we wanted the "student perspective" on classroom management and asked them to explain in writing "why kids behave in some classes," "why kids misbehave in some classes," and "how kids generally behave in this class and why." After students had a chance to write down their thoughts, they shared their responses.

Across classes, students demonstrated extraordinary consistency. Whether students were 8th-graders or 12th-graders, basic skills or honors students, their responses reflected three main themes. First, students stressed the importance of teachers' *relating to students with caring and respect.* They talked about teachers who "can relate to our teenage lifestyle," who "try to get to know us and understand us," who "create trust," who "help you and explain what they want," and "who work with you, not against you." A student in one of Fred's classes put it this way: "When a teacher takes some time to get to know students and shows some humor or shares a bit of their personal life, students may relate to them better." In Sandy's classes, students also echoed the importance of relationships: "The teacher must relate to the students. Understand when there is a problem and try to solve it. When the students see a teacher doing his/her best to make them feel comfortable with what they're learning, they behave well." And one of Christina's students wrote this:

> I want to cooperate in this class because she is not all serious, she can laugh, have fun, and still get all the work done. Students can tell when a teacher wants to help you and teach you, and when they just do it because they have to.

Clearly, not all teachers relate to students in this way. Students wrote about teachers "who put students down" and treat them like "little kids," about teachers who "don't care," and about teachers who are "beyond strict and just don't want to hear what we have to say." As one student wrote:

> Sometimes, if a teacher really demands the respect from day one, instead of earning it, a disliking developes [sic]. If a teacher doesn't think about what the students are feeling, they won't like him/her. Students can always detect those sort of things. Dislike = misbehave.

Many students used the word *respect* in both their written and oral comments, and we pressed them to tell us what "respecting students" looks like. They didn't have difficulty: Teachers respect students when they give them their grades privately, when they come prepared for class, when they don't tell students a question is dumb, when they "scold a student quietly instead of in class in front of others," when they take time to help kids who are confused, when they allow students to give their own opinions, when they make sure that students treat each other well (e.g., they don't allow kids to talk when another kid is talking), and when they show students that they *care.*

handwritten note: students want to know where the line is ⟶ want discipline

A second theme that students discussed was the need for teachers to *set limits and enforce them.* This was expressed in a number of different ways: "Teachers need to be a strong authority figure"; "teachers need to tell kids what they expect and give no second tries"; "teachers need to show strength"; "teachers need to be strict (but not mean)"; "teachers need to come off as someone who has control." What is clearly conveyed by these responses is students' lack of respect for teachers who are too permissive, who are "too cowardly to take charge," and who "let kids run all over them." One student wrote: "Kids misbehave when the teacher lets them pretty much do whatever they want. If they're disrupting class the teacher will try to go on with her class by maybe trying to speak above the person disrupting the class or ignoring it." This view was reiterated in another student's response: "Usually misbehavior happens in classes when teachers are too lenient. Every class needs to have some time to relax and fool around, but the teacher should know the limit." Still another summed it up this way:

> *Some teachers seem very insecure about misbehaving students. They tend to say "stop or I'll send you to the office" too much. When a teacher first meets his/her class they need to set down guidelines and go over them confidently and be sure of what he/she is doing.*

The final theme to emerge from students' comments was the importance of *teaching in a way that is motivating and interesting.* One of Donnie's students captured this widely shared perspective:

> *Teachers have to make the class fun, but organized. Have a lot of interaction between students and challenge them. . . . Sometimes teachers are boring. The class drags on and the students lose attention span towards the teacher and the class. If the teacher teaches in an old-fashion [sic] style, the kids become frustrated.*

These ideas were expressed in a number of ways: Teachers need to be knowledgeable and to *love* what they do ("kids can tell"); teachers need to teach in creative ways—not just out of the book; they need to get the whole class involved; they need to relate the material to students' lives. Although a lot of people used the word *fun,* one of Fred's students wrote, "Not everything can be fun; it doesn't have to be fun,

℘ PAUSE AND REFLECT

After listening to these students discuss the characteristics of effective classroom managers—caring and respect, teaching in a way that is motivating and engaging, and firmness (the ability to set and enforce limits)—take a moment to reflect on your own strengths and weaknesses in these three areas. What do you think will be your greatest challenge?

but there are ways teachers can make it more interesting and more challenging." For Christina's students, the "cool things Mrs. Vreeland picks for us to do" were especially important, since their classes are 84 minutes long. They clearly appreciated the fact that class sessions are "not just lectures and question and answer" and that Christina "uses different ways to teach us as opposed to 'open your book, read questions 1 to 5 and answer them.'"

handwritten note: even if you don't love a lesson, improve student understanding by teaching lesson as if you love it.

These themes—*relating to students with caring and respect, setting limits and enforcing them, and teaching in a way that is motivating and interesting*—characterize the behavior of the four teachers featured in this book. As we watched them teach, we were repeatedly struck by the caring and sensitivity they showed to students, by their authoritative, "no-nonsense" attitudes, and by their efforts to stimulate students' interest and engagement in lessons. The ability to combine these three characteristics is clearly recognized and appreciated by students.

We will address these themes in the three sections of the book that follow.

CONCLUDING COMMENTS

Fred, Donnie, Sandy, and Christina teach different subjects in different settings. Grade levels range from 8th to 12th. Sandy, Fred, and Christina teach classes that are predominantly White (although still quite diverse), while Donnie's classes are predominantly African American and Latino. Fred and Christina work in districts where about 10 percent of the children are eligible for free or reduced-price lunch, compared with the 26 percent figure in Sandy's district, and the 80 percent figure in Donnie's district. Sandy teaches an advanced placement class, while Donnie and Christina teach basic skills classes for students who have failed portions of the state test required for graduation. Donnie and Christina teach in schools that have adopted block scheduling, while Fred and Sandy's classes are about 45 minutes. All four teachers follow district curricula that reflect state standards, but Fred and Sandy have more flexibility than Donnie and Christina in terms of implementation and choice of materials. In order to be effective, our four teachers must be sensitive and responsive to these differences in age, race, culture, socioeconomic conditions, achievement levels, and district policies.

Despite these differences, Fred, Donnie, Sandy, and Christina are alike in many ways. Obvious similarities emerge when they talk about the tasks of classroom management. Interestingly, when these four teachers speak about classroom management, they rarely use the words *discipline* or *punishment, confrontation* or *penalty*. Instead, they emphasize mutual respect; they talk about the importance of being organized and well prepared; they stress the need to develop a "caring community," in which all individuals are contributing, valued members (Schaps, 2003; Watson & Battistich, 2006); they speak about involving students and helping them to achieve.

It's important to remember that Fred, Donnie, Sandy, and Christina are real human beings working in the complex, uncertain environment of the secondary classroom. Christina is only in her second year of teaching, and as she herself admits, she is "a novice when it comes to knowing what works." Fred, Donnie, and Sandy are experienced, skillful teachers who are extremely effective at preventing misbehavior, but even their classrooms are not free of problems. (In fact, Chapter 12 focuses specifically on the ways all four teachers deal with misbehavior.) Like all of us, these teachers make mistakes; they become frustrated and impatient; they sometimes fail to live up to their own images of the ideal teacher. By their own testimony, they are all still learning how to run more effective classrooms.

[handwritten margin note: Respect + resolve is better than conflict + punishment]

It is also important to remember that these four teachers do not follow recipes or prescriptions for classroom management, so their ways of interacting with students often look very different. Nonetheless, underlying the differences in behavior, it is often possible to detect the same guiding principles. The chapters that follow will try to convey the ways these four excellent teachers tailor the principles to fit their own particular contexts.

Finally, it is necessary to point out that these teachers do not work in schools where conditions are so bad that classes have to be held in stairwells or storage closets, where windows remain broken for years, and where 40 students in a class have to share a handful of books. Nor do they teach in schools that have installed metal detectors, where students regularly carry weapons, and where gang activity is common. In recent years, the districts in which the teachers work have all experienced an increase in serious problems, but violence is certainly not a common occurrence. Whether the strategies discussed here are generalizable to severely troubled schools is not clear. Nevertheless, we hope that *Middle and Secondary Classroom Management* will prove to be a useful starting point for teachers everywhere.

SUMMARY

This chapter examined some of the contradictions and special characteristics of classrooms. It argued that effective management requires an understanding of the unique features of the classroom environment and stressed the fact that teachers work with captive groups of students on academic agendas that students have not helped to set. Within this peculiar setting, teachers must work to accomplish the two major goals of classroom management—creating a caring, orderly environment for learning and enhancing students' social and emotional growth.

Contradictions of the Classroom Environment

- Classrooms are crowded, yet students are often not allowed to interact.
- Students are expected to work together harmoniously, yet they may not know or like each other.
- Students are urged to cooperate, yet they often work in individual or competitive situations.
- Students are encouraged to be independent, yet they are also expected to conform to the teacher's dictates.
- Students are instructed to work slowly and carefully, but they have to be aware of the "press of time" in a 42- (or an 84-) minute period.

Characteristics of the Classroom Environment

- Multidimensionality
- Simultaneity
- Immediacy
- Unpredictability
- Lack of privacy
- History

Guiding Principles of the Book

- Successful classroom management promotes self-regulation.
- Most problems of disorder can be avoided if teachers foster positive teacher-student relationships, implement engaging instruction, and use good preventive management strategies.
- The need for order must not supersede the need for meaningful instruction.
- Teachers must be "culturally responsive classroom managers."
- Becoming an effective classroom manager requires reflection, hard work, and time.

Meeting the Teachers

This chapter introduced the four teachers whose thinking and experiences will be described throughout the rest of the book. For an overview of the featured teachers and their districts, see Table 1.2.

- Fred Cerequas (social studies)
- Donnie Collins (mathematics)
- Sandra Krupinski (chemistry)
- Christina Vreeland (English)

Although these four teachers teach different subjects in very different settings, they are alike in many ways. In particular, they speak about classroom management in very similar terms: They emphasize the prevention of behavior problems, mutual respect, involving students in learning activities, and the importance of being organized and well prepared.

What Do the Students Say?

When asked why they behave well in certain classes and not in others, students consistently voiced three themes: relating to students with caring and respect; teaching in a way that is motivating and interesting; and setting limits and enforcing them. We will return to these three themes in subsequent chapters.

ACTIVITIES FOR SKILL BUILDING AND REFLECTION

In Class

1. In a group, discuss the six characteristics of classroom environments and share your ideas about how these characteristics will affect you as a classroom teacher.
2. Reflect on your past experiences with children and adolescents (e.g., tutoring, being a camp counselor). What did you learn from those experiences that might help you in the classroom?
3. Review the biographies of each teacher. Identify 3–4 major ways in which the teachers are similar.

On Your Own

Think about the questions that Christina was pondering: *"Why do I want to be here? Why do I say I enjoy this?"* What is it that *you* want in your classes? What do *you* find enjoyable (or *think* you will find enjoyable) about teaching? Then consider the implications for classroom organization and management. In other words, if you want students to participate enthusiastically, what will you do to encourage their participation? If you want them to treat one another with respect and kindness, what will you do to create that kind of atmosphere?

For Your Portfolio

Pretend you are a teacher being featured in this book. What is *your* story? Think about what motivated you to choose a career in teaching and what your goals are. Write down some of the key points you would want included in your own introduction. (This piece of writing can be a useful document to review before interviewing and can serve as inspiration during the often difficult first year of teaching.)

FOR FURTHER READING

Charney, R. S. (2002). *Teaching children to care: Classroom management for ethical and academic growth, K–8.* Greenfield, MA: Northeast Foundation for Children.

   This book provides a lively, practical guide to creating a respectful, friendly, academically rigorous classroom. Based on Charney's experiences as a teacher and informed by work on the Responsive Classroom approach (Northeast Foundation for Children), the book illustrates ways of managing classrooms to nurture students' social and intellectual growth. Although the book is geared to elementary school, it is also appropriate for teachers in middle school and junior high.

Cushman, K. (2003). *Fires in the bathroom: Advice for teachers from high school students.* New York: The New Press.

Cushman, K., & Rogers, L. (2008). *Fires in the middle school bathroom: Advice for teachers from middle schoolers.* New York: The New Press.

   For each of these books, the authors conducted extensive interviews of 40 students from urban areas across the country. Students were asked what they wished their teachers knew about them and about how they best learn. Their responses are presented in chapters on building positive relationships with students, helping them learn difficult academic material, being fair to all students, and reacting to misbehavior, among others. The middle school version of the book also includes advice on working with, rather than against, students' high energy levels, keeping parents involved, and preparing students for the transition to high school. A clear message in both books is that when students talk about instruction, what comes up first is how they feel about their teachers and how their teachers make them feel as learners.

Gregory, A., & Ripski, M. (2008). Adolescent trust in teachers: Implications for behavior in the high school classroom. *School Psychology Review, 37*(3), 337–353.

   This study examined the relationship between high school teachers' approaches to discipline and their students' behavior. Interviews and surveys were administered to 32 teachers and 32 students who had been referred to the office for disciplinary problems. Findings indicated that teachers who emphasized relationship-building were less likely to have students who exhibited defiance. Students seemed to pick up on their teachers' relational approach and to see them as trustworthy, legitimate authorities. This in turn increased their willingness to conform to their teachers' rules and requests.

Walker, J. M. T. (Ed.) (2009). A person-centered approach to classroom management. *Theory Into Practice, 48*(2).

> The articles in this theme issue of TIP are all built around the assertion that viewing classroom management as a person-centered endeavor is both humane and leads to better teaching practice. While the articles address classroom management at varying levels, from the individual classroom to the school to teaching about management in college classrooms, they all develop the idea that relationships are the heart of schools.

Weinstein, C. S. (Ed.) (2003). Classroom management in a diverse society. *Theory Into Practice, 42*(4).

> The articles in this special theme issue of *TIP* address different aspects of classroom management in a diverse society, but all of them reflect the idea that the fundamental task of classroom management is to create an inclusive, supportive, and caring environment. All the authors view classroom management in terms of human relationships—relationships between teachers and students and among students themselves.

ORGANIZATIONAL RESOURCES

REACH Center, 307 North Olympic Avenue, Suite 211, Arlington, WA 98223 (www.reachctr.org, 1-800-205-4932). The REACH center has developed school curricula to promote multicultural and global awareness for elementary, middle, and high school classrooms. The center provides training in the use of these curricula, along with books and teacher guides.

What Kids Can Do, Inc., P.O. Box 603252, Providence, RI 02906 (www.whatkidscando .org, 401-247-7665). This organization was founded to promote the perception of young people as valued resources, and to advocate for learning that engages students as knowledge creators and not simply test takers. It also works to bring youth voices to policy debates about school, society, and world affairs. The youth who concern WKCD most are those marginalized by poverty, race, and language. The website presents examples of students' work and their partnerships with adults both in and out of school, along with resources for teachers.

PART II

ESTABLISHING AN ENVIRONMENT FOR LEARNING

"Don't smile until Christmas."

When the two of us went through our respective teacher education programs, that bit of folk advice was all we learned about preventing inappropriate behavior. The idea was to refrain from smiling during the first few months of school so students would perceive you as stern and serious. Then they wouldn't dare act up.

Actually, our programs didn't talk much about student behavior at all; the overwhelming focus was on what to teach and how to teach it. When, on rare occasion we did discuss students' behavior, it was always in terms of *discipline*—what to do to individuals *after* an instance of misbehavior had occurred. When we graduated from our programs and entered teaching, our ability to create respectful, productive learning environments was more a matter of good instincts and luck than any real knowledge.

Fortunately, the situation has changed a great deal over the last 30 years. Teacher education students can now learn research-based principles, concepts, and practices for creating orderly classrooms—and smiling is definitely encouraged. The emphasis has shifted from what to do *after misbehavior occurs* (discipline) to how to *prevent it in the first place.* Discipline is still important since prevention sometimes fails, but educators now talk about the much broader concept of *classroom management* (of which discipline is only one part). As we discussed in Chapter 1, we define classroom management *as the tasks teachers must carry out to establish a learning environment that is caring, inclusive, and productive.*

This section of the book addresses "beginning-of-the year" tasks. Since most teachers are immediately faced with arranging classroom furniture, Chapter 2 focuses on the physical environment. The chapter is intended to help you design a classroom setting that supports your academic and social goals. In Chapter 3, we examine ways to create a classroom community in which individuals feel connected, respected, and cared for. Chapter 4 focuses on the task of establishing and teaching expectations for behavior. We stress the fact that shared behavioral expectations (or norms) are essential if classrooms are to be safe, comfortable, and productive environments. Chapter 5 emphasizes the importance of getting to know your students—understanding and appreciating their common characteristics, as well as their special needs. Finally, Chapter 6 discusses the benefits that accrue when teachers and families work together and suggests strategies for reaching out to families. Throughout the chapters, we learn about the beliefs and practices of our four teachers, as well as what research has to say on the topic.

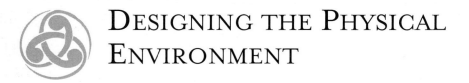

DESIGNING THE PHYSICAL ENVIRONMENT

Discussions of organization and management often neglect the physical characteristics of the classroom. Unless it becomes too hot, too cold, too crowded, or too noisy, we tend to think of the classroom setting as an unimportant backdrop for interaction. This general tendency to ignore the physical environment is especially prevalent in secondary schools, where many teachers are like nomads, moving from room to room throughout the day. In this unfortunate situation, it is difficult to create a classroom setting that is more than simply adequate. Nonetheless, it is important to recognize that the *physical environment can influence the way teachers and students feel, think, and behave.* Careful planning of this environment—within the constraints of your daily schedule—is an integral part of good classroom management. Moreover, *creating a comfortable, functional classroom is one way of showing your students that you care about them.*

PAUSE AND REFLECT

You have probably spent more than 13,000 hours as a student in elementary and secondary classrooms. Undoubtedly some of these rooms were much more attractive and comfortable than others. Think about what made them that way. For example, was it the bulletin boards or posters? The presence of plants? The type and arrangement of the furniture? The lighting? The size or location of the room? Think about the specific characteristics that made these rooms pleasant environments in which to learn and then reflect on which ones are under the teacher's control. Keep these characteristics in mind as you read this chapter.

Create a comfortable, inclusive environment

Environmental psychologists point out that the effects of the classroom setting can be both *direct* and *indirect* (Proshansky & Wolfe, 1974). For example, if
students seated in straight rows are unable to carry on a class discussion because
they can't hear one another, the *environment is directly hindering their participation*. Students might also be affected *indirectly* if they infer from the seating
arrangement that the teacher does not really want them to interact. In this case,
the arrangement of the desks is sending a message to the students about how
they are supposed to behave. Their reading of this message would be accurate if
the teacher had deliberately arranged the seats to inhibit discussion. More likely,
however, the teacher genuinely desires class participation, but has never thought
about the link between the classroom environment and student behavior.

This chapter is intended to help you develop *"environmental competence"*
(Martin, 2002; Steele, 1973): awareness of the physical environment and its impact
and the ability to use that environment to meet your goals. Even when they share
space or move from room to room, environmentally competent teachers are sensitive to the messages communicated by the physical setting. They plan spatial
arrangements that support their instructional plans. They know how to evaluate
the effectiveness of a classroom environment. They are alert to the possibility that
physical factors might contribute to behavioral problems, and they modify at least
some aspects of the classroom environment when the need arises.

As you read this chapter, remember that classroom management is not simply a matter of dealing with misbehavior. As we stressed in the first chapter,
successful managers *promote students' involvement in educational activities,
foster self-regulation, prevent disruption, and relate to students with care and
respect.* Our discussion of the classroom environment reflects this perspective:
We are concerned not only with reducing distraction and minimizing congestion
through good environmental design, but also with ways the environment can
promote students' security, increase their comfort, and stimulate their interest in
learning tasks.

Throughout this chapter, we will illustrate major points with examples from
the classrooms of the four teachers you have just met. Interestingly, Donnie, Fred,
and Sandy happen to teach their classes in one room this year, although they share
their room with other teachers. For Donnie and Fred, teaching in one room is a
substantial improvement from past years, when they had to move from room to
room. Last year was particularly difficult for Fred: He taught his five classes in four
different rooms! This year, it is Christina who has to move; another English teacher
uses her room during the first two blocks of the day, when Christina has prep
period and then teaches her state test class in another room.

FIVE FUNCTIONS OF THE CLASSROOM SETTING

Fred Steele (1973), a consultant in the field of organizational development, has suggested that all physical settings serve a number of basic functions. Five of Steele's
functions—security and shelter, social contact, symbolic identification, task instrumentality, and pleasure—provide a useful framework for thinking about the physical environment of the middle and secondary classroom. These functions make it

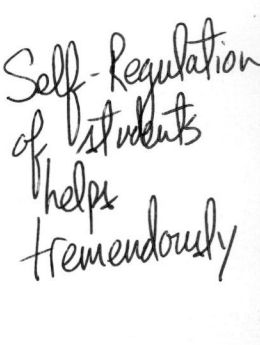

[handwritten margin notes:] phys. env. gives students clues how to act ⌐ also can actually limit their actions

[handwritten margin note:] Self-Regulation of students helps tremendously

clear that designing the physical setting is far more than decorating a few bulletin boards.

Security and Shelter

This is the most fundamental function of all built environments. Like homes, office buildings, and stores, classrooms should provide protection from bad weather, noise, extreme heat or cold, and noxious odors. Sadly, even this most basic function is sometimes not fulfilled, and teachers and students must battle highway noise, broken windows, and leaky roofs. In situations like this, it is difficult for any of the other functions to be met. Physical security is a *precondition* that must be satisfied, at least to some extent, before the environment can serve students' and teachers' other, higher-level needs.

Physical security is a particularly important issue in classes like science, home economics, woodworking, and art, where students come into contact with potentially dangerous supplies and equipment. It is essential that teachers of these subjects know about safety guidelines regarding proper handling, storage, and labeling of course materials. The National Science Teachers Association has established recommendations for safe storage, safety equipment, and effective layouts, as well as student/teacher and student/space ratios in science classrooms (Biehle, Motz, & West, 1999). In her classroom, Sandy tries to anticipate where accidents might occur and to arrange supplies in a way that minimizes risk. For example, when her students are doing a lab that involves two chemicals that are harmful when mixed together, she sets one chemical out and keeps one under her control. In this way, students have to ask her for it ("I'm ready for my nitric acid."), and she can double-check that they are following correct lab procedures.

Physical security is also a matter of special concern if you have students who use wheelchairs, leg braces, or crutches, or who have unsteady gaits. Navigating through crowded classrooms can be a formidable and dangerous task. Be sensitive to the need for wide aisles and space to store walkers and crutches when not in use. The physical or occupational therapists working in your school can provide consultation and advice.

Often, school environments provide *physical* security but fail to offer *psychological* security—the feeling that this is a good, comfortable place to be. Psychological security is especially crucial for youngsters who live in impoverished, unstable, or unsafe home environments. One way of enhancing psychological security is to make sure your classroom contains some "softness." With their linoleum floors, concrete block walls, and Formica surfaces, classrooms tend to be "hard" places. But youngsters (and adults) tend to feel more secure and comfortable in environments that contain items that are soft or responsive to their touch. In elementary classrooms, we sometimes find small animals, pillows, plants, beanbag chairs, and area rugs, but these are generally absent in middle and high school classrooms. If you are lucky enough to have your own classroom, think about ways that you can incorporate elements of softness into the environment. For example, a comfortable rocking chair and reading lamp can soften an English or social studies classroom, plants or an aquarium can provide softness in a science

use plush items to "soften" environment

classroom, and bright accents of varying textures can help to create an atmosphere of security and comfort.

Another way of increasing psychological security is to arrange classroom space so that students have as much freedom from interference as possible. In the crowded environment of the classroom, it is easy to become distracted. You need to make sure that students' desks are not too near areas of heavy traffic (e.g., the pencil sharpener, the bookcase, the front door). This is particularly important for students with attention-deficit hyperactivity disorder (ADHD), a neurobiological disability that interferes with an individual's ability to sustain attention. Students with ADHD have difficulty focusing attention, concentrating, listening, following instructions, and organizing tasks. They may also exhibit behaviors associated with hyperactivity: diffficulty staying seated, fidgeting, impulsivity, lack of self-control. (See Chapter 5 for additional information on ADHD.) You can help students with ADHD by seating them away from noisy, high-traffic areas, near well-focused students, and as close to you as possible so that it's easy to make eye contact (Carbone, 2001).

You can also enhance psychological security by allowing students to select their own seats. Often, students want to sit near their friends, but some individuals have definite spatial preferences as well (e.g., they prefer to sit in a corner, near the window, or in the front row). Donnie, Sandy, and Fred all allow students to sit where they wish—as long as they behave appropriately, of course (and Fred advises his students to "sit next to someone smart"). If you have your own room, you might also set up a few cubicles where students who want more enclosure can work alone, or provide folding cardboard dividers (three pieces of heavy cardboard bound together) that they can place on their desks. All of us need to "get away from it all" at times, but research suggests that opportunities for privacy are particularly important for youngsters who are distractible or have difficulty relating to their peers (Weinstein, 1982).

[handwritten margin note: let them select own seating as long as they behave ok]

Social Contact

Interaction among Students

As you plan the arrangement of students' desks, you need to think carefully about how much interaction you want among students, since different arrangements facilitate different amounts of contact. Clusters of desks promote social contact since individuals are close together and can have direct eye contact with those across from them. In clusters, students can work together on activities, share materials, have small-group discussions, and help each other with assignments. This arrangement is most appropriate if you plan to emphasize collaboration and cooperative learning activities. But it is unwise—even inhumane—to seat students in clusters and then forbid them to interact. If you do that, students receive two contradictory messages: The seating arrangement is communicating that it's okay to interact, while your verbal message is just the opposite!

In contrast to clusters, rows of desks reduce interaction among students and make it easier for them to concentrate on individual assignments (Bennett & Blundell, 1983). This appears particularly true for students who have behavior

[handwritten margin note: if sit in small groups, must allow + encourage interaction]

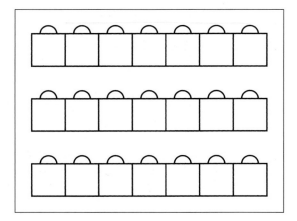

Figure 2.1   A Horizontal Arrangement

problems and learning disabilities. Researchers found that on-task behavior dropped by half and disruptive behavior increased by three times when "behaviourally troublesome" adolescents with moderate learning problems moved from rows to tables (Wheldall & Lam, 1987).

Rows also direct students' attention toward the teacher, so they are particularly appropriate for teacher-centered instruction. But there are a number of variations on this theme. For example, you might consider putting desks in horizontal rows. (See Figure 2.1.) This arrangement still orients students toward the teacher, but provides them with close "neighbors" on each side. Another variation is shown in Figure 2.2. Here, desks are arranged two-deep in rows that face each other, with a wide aisle down the middle of the classroom. Since this arrangement allows students to see each other and to interact more easily, it is particularly useful in

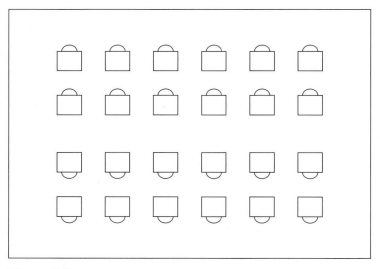

Figure 2.2   Rows Facing Each Other

Figure 2.3   Fredric Jones's Interior Loop Arrangement
Source: Jones, F. H., Jones, P., Lynn, J., Jones, F., Jones, B.T. (2007).
Tools for Teaching: Discipline, Instruction, Motivation. Santa
Cruz, CA: Fredric H. Jones & Associates. Reprinted with permission.

← focuses everyone's energy forward, but corners it on you

social studies or world language instruction. Still another row option, advocated by Fredric Jones and others (2007), is shown in Figure 2.3. Here, an "interior loop" places you "only a few steps from any student in the class" (p. 42).

Figures 2.4 to 2.6 illustrate the way Sandy, Fred, and Christina have arranged their classrooms. As you can see, Sandy's classroom is divided into whole-group instructional areas and laboratory or work areas (Figure 2.4). For presentations and homework review, students sit in a horizontal row arrangement. An aisle separates clusters of two and three trapezoidal desks (which Sandy hates because they take up so much room). Although she is unhappy that students are packed so closely together, Sandy wants to get as many students as possible in a row, so that all students are relatively close to the front of the room.

Fred and Christina have chosen to arrange their desks in rows (see Figure 2.5 for Fred's arrangement); however, both teachers regularly have students move into other configurations when appropriate. As Christina explains:

 I don't like them in rows . . . but it's a functional place to start, especially since I share the room. My philosophy is that I move them based on the activity. [Having the desks in rows] is a good starting point for journal writing, attendance, and whole-group presentations, and then I move them when I want to.

Both Fred and Christina have students rearrange their desks into clusters for small-group work, and—when classes are small enough—into a circle for class

Figure 2.4 Sandy's Room Arrangement

discussions. This year, Christina's large classes have led to experimentation with a new arrangement for discussion (see Figure 2.6):

> When we're going to have discussions, I stand in the center of the room, and I tell all the kids to turn their desks to a 45 degree angle, so that they're all facing the center. Then I sit outside the circle; it helps me to keep my mouth shut.

In Donnie's classroom, two-person tables have replaced the standard desks she used to have. Donnie started out by arranging the tables in groups of two, forming horizontal rows, but continues to try other arrangements as the need arises (see Figure 2.7 for one example). She even allows individual students to move their tables into configurations that they feel are more comfortable. Interestingly, although Donnie's tables are attractive and facilitate small-group work, she actually prefers desks, which she can more easily arrange in a horseshoe.

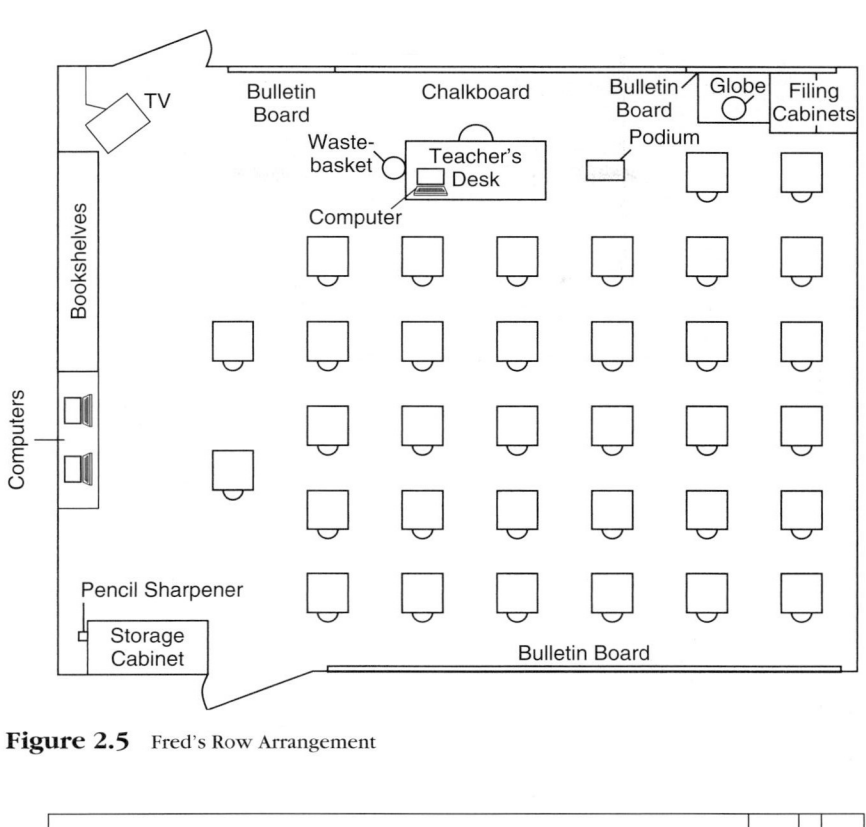

Figure 2.5   Fred's Row Arrangement

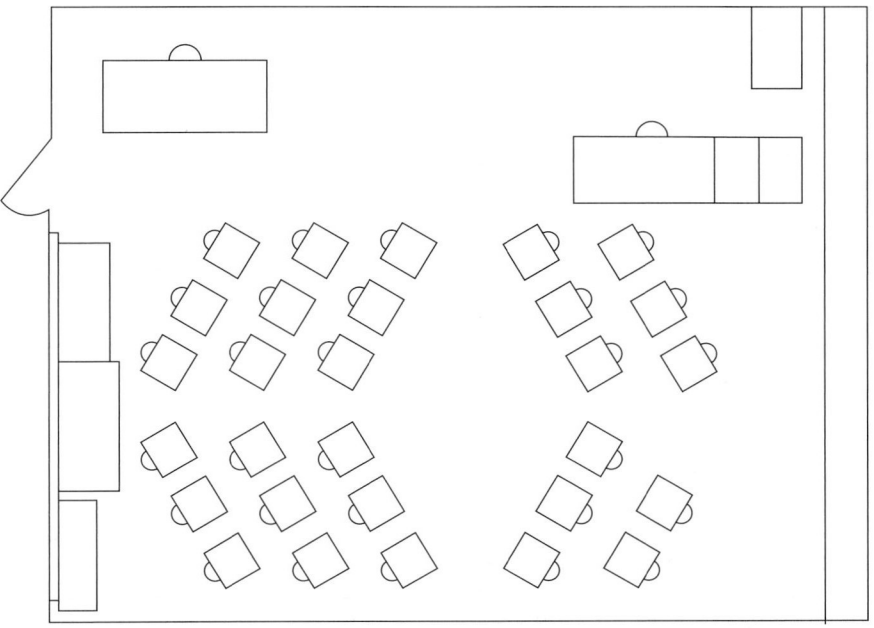

Figure 2.6   Christina's Arrangement for Whole-Class Discussions

Christina's arrangement for class discussions

Class discussions
→ great for S.S.
→ eye contact
→ face each
*   other*

Christina, Fred, and Donnie show a willingness to rearrange their rooms that is not typical. Indeed, a recent study found that teachers generally prefer to change the instructional format to fit the existing furniture arrangement, rather than changing the arrangement to fit the instructional format (Kutnick, Blatchford, Clark, McIntyre, & Baines, 2005). Thus teachers who have student desks in rows might opt for paired discussion rather than cooperative learning groups, as this will not require moving the furniture. We can understand this reluctance: Moving furniture can result in loss of instructional time, chaos, and confusion. But it doesn't have to be this way. Watching Christina, Fred, and Donnie's students move their desks or tables into new configurations makes it clear that students can learn to do this quietly and quickly—but they will need to be taught the procedures to follow. (See Chapter 4.)

Interaction between the Teacher and the Students

The way students are arranged can also affect the interaction between teacher and students. A number of studies have found that in classrooms where desks are arranged in rows, the teacher interacts mostly with students seated in the front and center of the classroom. Students in this "action zone" (Adams & Biddle, 1970) participate more in class discussions and initiate more questions and comments.

Educational researchers have tried to tease out the reasons for this phenomenon. Do students who are more interested and more eager to participate select

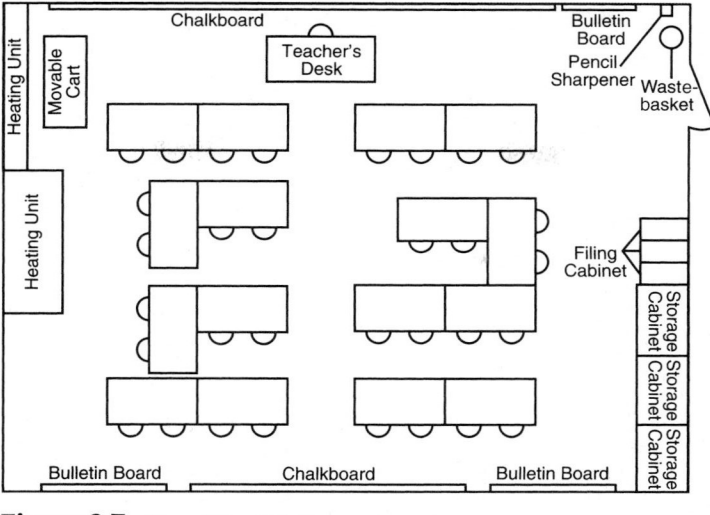

Figure 2.7   One of Donnie's Rearrangements

seats in the front, or does a front seating position somehow produce these attitudes and behaviors? This issue has not been fully resolved, but the weight of the
evidence indicates that a front-center seat does encourage participation, while a
seat in the back makes it more difficult to participate and easier to "tune out."
During a discussion with students in one of Sandy's classes, it was clear that they
were aware of this phenomenon. As one student said, "When we're all so close to
the front, you know that the teacher can see you real easily. That helps keep you
awake!"

Christina is also well aware of the influence that seating can have on participation and involvement. On the first day of school, she assigns seats alphabetically.
A few weeks later, however, she reassigns seats to maximize students' engagement
and participation:

> I try to evaluate their needs with respect to participation and my needs
> with respect to management. I look at problem areas; for example, I'll
> break up areas of too much talking. If students seem to need an extra
> push to participate, I'll put them in the front. If students are falling out
> of their chairs trying to participate, it's okay if they're farther back. If I can, I try
> to avoid seating people in the back corners; that's where they can get lost. But in
> my class of 29 students, someone has to be in the back corners. I try to remedy this
> by changing seats every few weeks and by having students reconfigure the seating
> arrangements for different activities.

Although research on the action zone has only examined row arrangements,
it is easy to imagine that the same phenomenon would occur whenever teachers
direct most of their comments and questions to the students who are closest to
them. Keep this in mind and take steps to ensure that the action zone encompasses

[handwritten margin notes: "Rows not good → limit my focus onto first, central rows"]

[handwritten margin notes: "use seating arrangements to aid certain students"]

To encourage students to sit in the front row,
Varsteen High equipped all of its classrooms
with electronic massage recliners.

Figure 2.8   *Source:* CLOSE TO HOME © 1999, John
McPherson. Reprinted with permission of
UNIVERSAL UCLICK. All rights reserved.

your whole class. Some suggestions are to (1) move around the room whenever
possible; (2) establish eye contact with students seated farther away from you;
(3) direct comments to students seated in the rear and on the sides; and (4) periodically change students' seats (or allow students to select new seats) so that all
students have an opportunity to be up front. See Figure 2.8 for a humorous suggestion on how to encourage students to sit in the front row!

Symbolic Identification

This term refers to the information provided by a setting about the people who
spend time there. The key questions are these: What does this room tell us about
the students—their classroom activities, backgrounds, accomplishments, and preferences? And what does the classroom tell us about the teacher's goals, values,
views of the content area, and beliefs about education?

Too often, classrooms resemble motel rooms. They are pleasant but impersonal, revealing nothing about the people who use the space—or even about the
subject that is studied there. This "anonymity" is exacerbated in middle and secondary school where six or seven classes may use the space during the day (and
then an adult class uses it in the evening, as in Fred's situation!). Nonetheless,
it's important to think about ways of personalizing your classroom setting. Before
using wall space or bulletin boards, however, be sure to negotiate "property rights"
with the other teachers who are using the room.

All four teachers attempt to personalize their classrooms, within the constraints
of their individual circumstances. In Christina's classroom, mobiles of drama masks
and literary genres hang from the ceiling. Five brightly colored bulletin boards
across the back wall are devoted to various aspects of English. The two nearest
the windows contain photographs of famous writers at their desks; quotations
describe the ways they approach—and conquer—the agonies of writing. Donnie
has the use of only two bulletin boards, but she tries to have them reflect her

have class personalize their classroom

students' activities and accomplishments. She watches the newspaper and regularly posts stories about her current and former students. One bulletin board is usually devoted to a "Math Honor Roll" (students who have received As or Bs for the marking period). Sometimes, she even takes photographs of the students in her classes and displays them in honor of special events (e.g., when a student does particularly fine work, when a student has had outstanding attendance, etc.).

Sandy also posts photographs of her students conducting laboratory investigations, although never without explicit permission. Occasionally, Sandy also displays students' outstanding work, but she offers words of caution:

> **High school students often don't want their work posted on the bulletin board, because they don't want to "stand out" from their peers in any way. If I do put work up, I make sure to put their names on the back of the paper.**

You can also personalize classroom space by displaying materials that reflect the cultural backgrounds of the students in your class, especially as they relate to your subject matter. For example, an art classroom could exhibit work by artists from your students' native countries, while a science classroom could display posters of scientists from around the world who have made significant contributions to scientific progress. In a math classroom, "ethnomathematical" displays could explore concepts such as number, graphs, topology, probability, and symmetry in the context of non-Western cultures (e.g., Africa, China, India, the Incas, the Mayans).

use cult. backgrounds as fodder for decorations

In addition, consider ways you can use the environment to communicate something about your *own* cultural background, experiences, and interests. You might want to hang your favorite art prints, display pictures of your family, or exhibit your collection of ceramic frogs. (You probably shouldn't display irreplaceable objects, as they may be inadvertently damaged.) Over Christina's desk is a mobile of wooden apples that she made during the summer before her first year of teaching. A teddy bear represents the collection of bears she has at home. On the front chalkboard, a framed poem, written by a former student, begins this way: "This is a poem/about the one who tried to teach us/Though sometimes we all were stubborn/She still managed to reach us."

Finally, look critically at commercial materials before posting them on your classroom walls and ask yourself if they really contribute to students' learning (Tarr, 2004). Bulletin boards are prime "real estate," so unless the materials are valuable, it might be better to display students' work or items that you have created.

make sure whatever you put up is useful

Task Instrumentality

This function concerns the many ways the environment helps us to carry out the tasks we need to accomplish. Think about the tasks and activities that will be carried out in your classroom. Will students work alone at their desks on writing assignments? Will they work cooperatively on activities and projects? Will you instruct the whole class from the chalkboard, whiteboard, overhead projector, or video projector connected to a computer? Will you work with small lab groups? Will students complete tasks on computers in the classroom?

For each of these tasks, you need to consider the physical design requirements. For example, if you plan to give whole-group instruction before students work independently (e.g., at lab tables), think about where to locate the instructional area vis-à-vis the work area. Do you want it near a chalkboard or the projection screen? In any case, its location should allow all students to see and hear your presentations without being cramped. You also want the work areas to be organized well so that individuals or small groups do not interfere with one another.

If you have a computer dedicated to noninstructional uses such as record keeping, you probably want to locate it on your desk; if you have a computer used for presentations, it will need to be located near the video projector or interactive whiteboard (Bolick & Cooper, 2006). If you have computers in your classroom for student use, you also need to think carefully about where to locate your computer workstations, although the placement may be dictated by the location of electrical outlets and wiring for Internet access. If students are going to work in pairs or in small groups, place the stations in an area where clusters of students can gather round without creating traffic congestion and distraction. Also be sure to keep the computers away from water and from chalkboards, since dust can cause a problem.

Whatever tasks will occur in your classroom, there are a few general guidelines you need to keep in mind. These are presented in the Practical Tips Box.

Pleasure

The important question here is whether students and teachers find the classroom attractive and pleasing. To the already overworked teacher preoccupied with covering the curriculum, raising test scores, and maintaining order, aesthetic concerns may seem irrelevant and insignificant (at least until parent conferences or open house night draw near). Yet given the amount of time that you and your students spend in your classroom, it is worth thinking about ways to create a pleasing environment. It is sad when students associate education with sterile, uncomfortable, unpleasant places.

In a classic study on environmental attractiveness, experimenters compared interviews that took place in an "ugly" room with those that took place in a "beautiful" room (Maslow & Mintz, 1956). Neither the interviewer nor the subject knew that the real purpose of the study was to assess the impact of the environment on their behavior. The researchers found that interviewers assigned to the ugly room complained of headaches, fatigue, and discomfort. Furthermore, the interviews *finished more quickly* in the ugly room. Apparently, people in the ugly room tried to finish their task as quickly as possible in order to escape from the unpleasant setting.

Additional studies have also demonstrated that aesthetically pleasing environments can influence behavior. For example, two college-level studies have indicated that attractive classrooms have a positive effect on attendance and feelings of group cohesion (Horowitz & Otto, 1973) and on participation in class discussions (Sommer & Olson, 1980). The classrooms in these studies had <u>specially designed</u>

seating, soft lighting, plants, warm colors, and carpeting, hardly the kinds of aesthetic improvements that can be implemented by most secondary school teachers. Nonetheless, it is worth thinking about the kinds of environmental modifications that *are* possible, especially if you have your own room. Try to be as creative as Roberta Jocius, a high school English teacher in Portage.

PAUSE AND REFLECT

We have heard middle and high school teachers comment that the five functions of the classroom setting are interesting, but more applicable to the elementary classroom. We disagree. Think about how a teacher can use the five functions of the classroom in planning and setting up a classroom environment that is developmentally appropriate for 6th- through 12th-grade students.

PRACTICAL TIPS FOR

ARRANGING A FUNCTIONAL CLASSROOM

- *Frequently used classroom materials should be accessible to students.* Materials like calculators, scissors, dictionaries, textbooks, staplers, tape, and rulers should be easy to reach. This will minimize the time spent preparing for activities and cleaning up. Decide which materials will be kept in locked or closed cabinets and which will be kept on open shelves. Think about whether materials are accessible to students who use wheelchairs, crutches, or walkers.

- *Shelves and storage areas should be well organized so that it is clear where materials and equipment belong.* It is useful to label shelves so that everyone knows where things go. This will make it easier to obtain materials and to return them. You should also have some sort of a system for the distribution and collection of students' work (e.g., in–out boxes). Materials that students should not access without permission should be stored in locked or closed cabinets.

- *Pathways throughout the room should be designed carefully to avoid congestion and distraction.* Paths to the pencil sharpener, supply closet, and trash can(s) should be clearly visible and unobstructed. These high-traffic areas should be as far from students' desks as possible. Are pathways wide enough for students who use wheelchairs?

- *The seating arrangement should allow students to have a clear view of instructional presentations.* If possible, students should be able to see instructional presentations without turning their desks or chairs around.

- *The location of the teacher's desk depends on where you will be spending your time.* If you will be constantly moving about the room, your desk can be out of the way, in a corner perhaps. If you will use your desk as a conference area or as a workstation, then it needs to be more centrally located. But be careful. With a central location, you may be tempted to remain at your desk for long periods of time, and this cuts down your ability to monitor students' work and behavior. Moreover, if your desk is in a central location, holding student conferences there may be distracting to other students.

- *Decide where to store your own personal teaching aids and supplies.* If you move from room to room, arrange to have a desk drawer or a shelf in a storage cabinet for your own personal use. At the very least, you will probably need storage for pens and markers, paper clips, a stapler, rubber bands, chalk or whiteboard markers, tape, tissues, attendance forms, and file folders. An alternative strategy is to carry your personal supplies with you, perhaps in a plastic organizer or a movable cart.

Indiana, who is passionate about creating an attractive, homey classroom (Schmollinger, Opaleski, Chapman, Jocius, & Bell, 2002). In one corner of Jocius's classroom is a rocking chair with an afghan and reading lamp, right next to a display of young adult novels. Lace curtains and an artificial fireplace with an electric log also enhance the feeling of warmth and homeness, along with a set of china teacups and teapots that she uses in conjunction with her students' study of *Great Expectations!*

THE TEACHER AS ENVIRONMENTAL DESIGNER

Steele's functions give you a way of thinking about the environment, but they don't provide you with an architectural blueprint. If you think about the various roles that settings play, you will realize that the functions not only overlap, they may actually conflict. Seating that is good for social contact may be bad for testing, as Donnie can attest: She often prepares two to three versions of a test, since students are sitting so close to one another! Similarly, room arrangements that provide students with privacy may be poor for monitoring and maintaining order. As you think about your room and your own priorities, you will have to determine which functions will take precedence over others. You also need to think about what is possible for you to achieve if you are a "nomad" who must move from room to room or share space with other teachers. This section of the chapter describes a process that you can follow as you design your classroom.

Think about the Activities the Room Will Accommodate

The first step in designing a classroom is to reflect on activities your room is to accommodate. For example, if you are teaching a lab science, you may need to accommodate whole-group instruction, hands-on lab work, media presentations, and testing. If you are teaching history, you may want to have small-group research projects, debates, simulations, and role plays in addition to teacher presentations, class discussions, and seatwork. If you are teaching a world language, you may want to facilitate conversation among students. List these activities in a column, and next to each activity note if it poses any special physical requirements. For example, small groups may need storage space for projects, and lab work may require access to gas lines or water. Also consider which activities involve objects that cannot be moved, such as the projection screen, equipment that needs an electrical outlet, or wiring for Internet access.

Next, consider which of these activities will *predominate* in your classroom and reflect on the physical arrangement that will be most suitable for the majority of the time. Will students most often be participating in whole-class discussion? If so, you may want to arrange the desks in a large circle. Will you generally be doing presentations and demonstrations at the board? If your answer is yes, then some sort of row arrangement may be best. In addition, consider how the furniture can be rearranged to accommodate the *other* activities you will be conducting. For example, Christina has desks arranged in rows, but as soon as students are done

what activities you do most often should influence class set-up with journal writing (the first activity of every period), they move into clusters of four or five to carry out small-group tasks.

Think about Whether the Students in Your Classroom Have Special Needs That Require Environmental Modifications

Also think about the characteristics of the students who will be using the room and whether you need to make any environmental modifications so the classroom is safe and comfortable. Will any students have orthopedic problems that require wide aisles or special equipment and furniture? (For example, Sandy has a portable lab table to accommodate a student who uses a wheelchair.) If any students have hearing impairments, it's desirable to minimize background noise by placing felt or rubber caps on chair and table legs. (Tennis balls work well!) Covering table surfaces with fabric and lining study carrels with acoustical tile or corkboard can also help cut down on noise (Mamlin & Dodd-Murphy, 2002).

Keep it quiet + comfortable

Also think about special needs when assigning students their seats. Will you have any students with attention difficulties who may need seats away from distractions? If you have any students with hearing impairments who need to lip-read, locate their seats so they can see your face at all times. If you have any students with visual impairments, they will need seats close to where you will present material (e.g., the projection screen or whiteboard). Make a list of the accommodations you may need to make in your classroom for each of these types of learners, and also what you might do to benefit all the students in your classroom.

Think about the Needs of Other Adults in the Room

As more and more students with special needs are educated in general education classrooms, it becomes increasingly likely that you will be working with other adults (e.g., special education teachers providing in-class support, paraprofessionals, instructional aides). In fact, a recent study of 18 elementary schools found that teachers were more likely to have at least one additional adult in their classrooms than to be alone with their students (Valli, Croninger, & Walters, 2007).

Resource teachers or instructional aides require, at a minimum, a place to store materials and equipment and a place to sit, so you will need to decide where these will be. One of Sandy's classes, for example, includes a student with a brain injury who has a full-time personal aide. In this particular case, Sandy prefers the aide to sit in the back of the room, rather than next to the student. She explains:

> My biggest challenge with James is to make him part of the community, and having the aide sitting right next to him, taking notes for him, makes it harder for him to get integrated into his group. I decided to have another member of his cooperative group take notes for him (on carbonless paper), and they have really begun to connect. The kids learned to listen to him and to accept his contributions, but that wouldn't have happened as easily if the aide had been right there. Sometimes an aide's protection doesn't

allow the student to grow, to become more independent, and to become a real, functioning member of the group.

(We will revisit these issues in Chapter 5, when we discuss co-teaching between general and special education teachers.)

Draw a Floor Plan

Before actually moving any furniture, draw a number of different floor plans and select the one that seems most workable. The classroom diagrams shown earlier contain some useful symbols, or you can create your own. In order to decide where furniture and equipment should be placed, consider the special requirements noted on your list of activities, as well as the room's "givens"—the location of outlets, chalkboards or whiteboards, permanently installed TV monitors or video projectors, windows, built-in shelves, computer wiring, cabinets, or lab tables. Also keep in mind our discussion of psychological security, social contact, and task instrumentality.

It may be helpful to begin by deciding where you will conduct whole-group instruction and the way students will be seated during this time. Think about where the teacher's desk should be, whether frequently used materials stored on shelves or in cabinets are accessible to you and your students, and whether pathways are clear. Remember, there is no one right way to design your classroom. The important thing is to make sure that your spatial arrangement supports the teaching strategies that you will use and the kinds of behaviors you want from your students.

Involve Students in Environmental Decisions

Although a great deal can be done before the start of school, some things can be left undone, so your students can be involved in the design process. If you teach four or five classes in one room, it is obviously impossible to involve everyone in all environmental decisions; however, you might solicit ideas for room design from your various classes, and then select those that seem most feasible. You might also rotate responsibility for some aspect of the environment among your classes (e.g., each class could have an opportunity to design a bulletin board display). Inviting students to participate in environmental decision making not only helps to create more responsive physical arrangements, it also prepares students for their roles as active, involved citizens who possess environmental competence.

Try the New Arrangement, Evaluate, and Redesign

In addition to being responsive to students' input on your room arrangement, you can use Steele's functions of the environment as a framework for evaluating your classroom design. For example, does the desk arrangement facilitate or hinder social contact among students? Do displays communicate information about the subject matter and students' work? Are frequently used materials accessible to students? Does the room provide pleasure?

As you evaluate the effectiveness of the classroom setting, stay alert for behavioral problems that might be caused by the physical arrangement. For example, if a student suddenly becomes inattentive when his seat is moved next to the pencil sharpener, it is likely that an environmental change is in order, rather than detention. If the classroom floor is constantly littered despite your appeals for neatness, the underlying problem may be an inadequate number of trash cans and/or inconvenient locations.

Improving your room does not have to be tedious and time consuming. In fact, small modifications can bring about gratifying changes in behavior. Billy, a middle school student in Queens, New York, refused to sit still and often deliberately tumbled out of his desk (Burke & Burke-Samide, 2004). It turned out that sitting on the hard chair caused him a great deal of discomfort, and his frequent position changes and falling out of his chair were ways to compensate. The authors suggest that providing Billy more comfortable seating is likely to increase his attention span and participation in class.

SOME THOUGHTS ON HAVING TO SHARE ROOMS

When we sat down as a group to discuss the role of the physical environment in classroom management, it became clear that all of the teachers feel frustrated by the need to share classrooms. Christina was blunt about having to teach in two different rooms: "I hate it!" Sandy emphasized the difficulties that are created when access to the classroom is limited:

When *I'm* not in my room, someone else is; that means that I can't get into the room during the school day to prepare labs—and we do six labs a week. I have to prepare labs before or after school, and that's also when I carry out the other responsibilities associated with being a chemistry teacher, like organizing materials, disposing of old chemicals, making sure all the equipment is in working order, and of course, working with kids who are having trouble. Although I'd like to pay attention to creating a more attractive environment, that's got to be a lower priority.

The teachers also expressed irritation over other common problems—for example, inadequate storage space (Christina likes to "hoard" things), inappropriate furniture, and insufficient numbers of desks. They traded war stories about materials that disappear (Fred's gone through three staplers this year) and the lack of personal work areas (it took Sandy three years to get a desk where she could sit during free periods to plan lessons and grade papers; when she finally got one, it was in a storage closet!). They also talked about the problems that arise when the other teachers sharing the room are inconsiderate "roommates" who fail to clean up adequately. Since this was a topic that clearly raised their blood pressure, it seems important to share a few of the lessons they have learned.

Being a Good Roommate

During our discussion, Donnie shared an anecdote that illustrates the kinds of problems that can occur when teachers have to share rooms.

> I share the room with a long-term substitute who's supposed to monitor a study hall in my room during second period. He thinks he doesn't really have to watch the kids, so they sit there and write all over the desks.
> Finally, I couldn't stand it anymore; I took a sponge and cleanser and cleaned all the tables before school began. I taught first period and then turned the room over to him. When I came back for third period, the desks were covered with writing again! I was furious!

Given the other teacher's status as a long-term substitute coming in the middle of the year, Donnie's situation was particularly difficult. In general, however, it is important to work out an explicit agreement at the very beginning of the year about how the classroom is to be initially arranged, which boards (bulletin, chalk, or white) are available to each of you, and what storage space you can each use. If, as a new teacher, you are assigned to share a room with an experienced teacher, be sure to have these discussions before you start rearranging the room or taking over board or storage space.

You should also discuss how the classroom should be left at the end of each class period. You and your roommate might agree that desks are to be returned to a standard arrangement, boards are to be erased, materials are to be put away, the floor is to be cleaned, no food is to be in the room, and (of course) no writing is to be on the desks or tables. You also need to agree on a procedure to follow if the agreement is violated, so you don't have to suffer in silence. As Sandy tells us, "It's not enough to have an agreement; you have to follow through. My roommate and I have agreed to hold the kids accountable for the condition of the room. If I come in and find a problem, I tell her about it, and she deals with it the next time she sees those students."

PAUSE AND REFLECT

Think about the problems that arise when teachers have to share rooms. If you are in that situation, what specific items would you want to include in an agreement about how the room is to be left? What procedure would you want to have in place if the agreement is violated?

CONCLUDING COMMENTS

All four teachers agree on the importance of thinking about the physical environment. Fred comments:

> Some of the ideas—like the action zone, for example—are important for teachers to know about even if they move from room to room and have little control over the classroom. On the other hand, some of the ideas—like psychological security—are hard to put into practice if you're a nomad like I was. But that's okay; thinking about these issues is important anyway.

We need to say to new teachers, "Listen, folks, you're going to have to be clever in dealing with this. If you can't add soft, warm fuzzies to your room, then you're going to have to compensate. You're going to have to find other ways of providing psychological security, like making sure your kids feel safe in your classroom because they know they're not going to get hammered."

As Fred suggests, it is not easy for secondary teachers to create their ideal classroom settings. Nonetheless, we hope this chapter has given you a greater awareness of the physical environment and its impact, along with a realistic sense of how you can use the environment to meet your goals. Remember, environmental competence is an integral part of effective classroom management.

Summary

This chapter discussed how the physical environment of the classroom influences the way teachers and students feel, think, and behave. It stressed the need for teachers to be aware of the direct and indirect effects of the physical environment. This awareness is the first step to developing "environmental competence." The chapter suggested ways to design a classroom that will support your instructional goals, using Steele's functions of the environment as a framework for discussion.

Security and Shelter
- Be aware of and implement safety guidelines for dangerous supplies and equipment.
- Be sensitive to the needs of students with physical disabilities and attentional problems.
- Add elements of softness.
- Arrange space for freedom from interference.
- Create opportunities for privacy by adding cubicles or folding cardboard dividers.

Social Contact
- Consider how much interaction you want among students.
- Think about whether you are making contact with *all* of your students; avoid a small action zone.

Symbolic Identification
- Personalize your classroom space so that it communicates appropriate information about you, your students, and your subject matter.

Task Instrumentality
- Make sure frequently used materials are accessible to students.
- Make it clear where things belong.
- Plan pathways to avoid congestion and distraction.
- Arrange seats for a clear view of presentations.
- Locate your desk in an appropriate place (off to the side helps to ensure that you will circulate).

Pleasure

- Create an aesthetically pleasing environment through the use of plants, color, and bulletin board displays.

Careful planning of the physical environment is an integral part of good classroom management. When you begin to design your room, think about the activities it will accommodate; if possible, invite your students to participate in the design process. Also reflect on whether any of your students have special needs that require environmental modifications. Be sure to provide the necessary seating and storage space for any other teachers or aides who will be in your classroom. Try your arrangement, evaluate it, and redesign as necessary. If you are sharing your room with other teachers, be sure to work out an explicit agreement about how you will share the space and how you and your students will be accountable for maintaining it in good condition.

ACTIVITIES FOR SKILL BUILDING AND REFLECTION

In Class

In small groups, consider the following seating arrangements. For each one, think about the types of instructional strategies for which it is appropriate or inappropriate. The first one has been done as an example.

Arrangement	Instructional Strategies for Which This Arrangement Is Appropriate	Instructional Strategies for Which This Arrangement Is Inappropriate
Rows	*Teacher or student presentations; audiovisual presentations; testing*	*Student-centered discussions; small-group work*
Horizontal Rows		
Horseshoe		
Small Clusters		
Circle		

On Your Own

Visit a middle or high school classroom, watch two to three class sessions in that classroom, draw a classroom map, and evaluate the physical layout in terms of Steele's functions of the environment. Use the bulleted items under each of the functions presented in the chapter summary to create a checklist. For example, to evaluate social contact, look for evidence that the classroom arrangement supports the appropriate amount of student interaction and that the action zone encompasses the entire class.

For Your Portfolio

Imagine for a moment that you have a classroom of your own: You don't have to change rooms, and you don't even have to share it with any other teacher! Draw a floor plan of your ideal classroom. In a brief commentary, explain why you are designing the room this way.

FOR FURTHER READING

Emmer, E. T., & Evertson, C. M. (2009). Organizing your classroom and materials. Chapter 1 in *Classroom management for middle and high school teachers* (8th ed.). Upper Saddle River, NJ: Pearson Education.

    This straightforward, easy-to-read chapter discusses "five keys to good room arrangement" and provides concrete suggestions for bulletin boards and displays, seating arrangements, computer workstations, centers, and storage.

Heiss, R. (2004). *Feng shui for the Classroom: 101 easy-to-use ideas.* Chicago: Zephyr Press.

    Feng shui (pronounced *fung shway*) is the ancient Chinese method of designing spaces to create balance and harmony. This book applies feng shui concepts to the school, "providing teachers with strategies and suggestions for improving harmony and positive energy in their classrooms." Even readers who are skeptical about the notion of arranging classrooms so that *chi* (energy) can move freely should find the suggestions regarding furniture arrangement, clutter, plants, calming sounds, color, and mobiles intriguing.

Schmollinger, C. S., Opaleski, K, Chapman, M. L., Jociu, R., & Sherri, B. (2002). How do you make your classroom an inviting place for students to come back to each year? *English Journal, 91*(6), 20–22.

    This article presents five English teachers' ideas about how to create an attractive, inviting, and stimulating environment for their students.

ORGANIZATIONAL RESOURCES AND WEBSITES

Learn NC K-12 Teaching and Learning, 140 Friday Center Drive, CB #7216, The University of North Carolina at Chapel Hill, Chapel Hill, NC, 27599-7216 (http://www.learnnc.org/lp/pages/BasicEnv1, 919-962-8888). The University of North Carolina at Chapel Hill School of Education finds the most innovative and successful practices in K–12 education and makes them available to teachers and students.

The site includes articles on the physical climate of the classroom, arranging for independence, working with available space, and sample classroom floor plans.

The National Clearinghouse for Educational Facilities, 1090 Vermont Avenue, NW, Suite 700, Washington, DC 20005-4905 (www.edfacilities.org/rl/classroom_design.cfm, 888-552-0624). This site includes an annotated bibliography of publications on classroom design.

The Science House, NC State University Centennial Campus, Box 8211, NC State University, Raleigh, NC 27695-8211 (www.science-house.org/resources/safety .htm, 919-515-6118). This site provides resources and information regarding science classrooms and lab safety.

BUILDING RESPECTFUL, CARING RELATIONSHIPS

Some years ago, we supervised a student teacher named Annie, who had been placed in a fourth-grade classroom. One of us had taught Annie in a course on campus, and we had some concerns about her organizational ability. Nevertheless, we weren't prepared for what we saw on the first visit to her classroom. Annie was teaching a lesson on quotation marks. Although it wasn't exactly captivating, it wasn't awful. But her students' behavior *was*. They chatted, rummaged through their desks, and completely ignored the lesson. Furthermore, throughout the period, a steady stream of students walked up to Annie, asked to go to the restroom, and left the room. We watched in disbelief as a student left about every three minutes; at one point, five or six students were out at the same time. Yet Annie never asked students to wait until she had finished teaching or until the previous person had returned.

When the period was over and we met with Annie to discuss the lesson, we asked her to talk about the students' behavior. We wondered how she interpreted the students' lack of interest in her lesson and their obvious desire to leave the room. We also wanted to know why she had never said "no" when a student asked to leave the room. We remember her answer clearly:

> *I want to show the children that I care about them. I don't want to rule this classroom like a dictator. If I say no when someone asks to go to the bathroom, that would be showing them that I don't respect them.*

Annie never did create the atmosphere of mutual respect she desired; in fact, she never completed student teaching. Her commitment "to care"—which she defined as "never say no"—led to a situation so chaotic and so confused that no learning, teaching, *or* caring was possible.

WHY IS SHOWING CARE IMPORTANT?

Over the years, we have thought a lot about Annie and her efforts to establish a respectful, caring environment. Although Annie was ultimately unsuccessful, we understand and applaud the high priority she placed on positive teacher-student relationships. Both common sense and research tells us that students are more likely to cooperate with teachers who are seen as caring, trustworthy, and respectful (Cornelius-White, 2007; Gregory & Ripski, 2008; Hoy & Weinstein, 2006; Osterman, 2000). This appears to be especially true for Black and Hispanic students, who frequently perceive that their teachers (generally European American) fail to understand their perspectives, accept them as individuals, honor their cultural backgrounds, or demonstrate respect (S. R. Katz, 1999; Nieto & Bode, 2008; Sheets, 1996). Indeed, Angela Valenzuela (1999) argues that the immigrant Mexican and Mexican American high school students she studied in Houston need to feel *cared for* before they can *care about* school.

Another study underscores the key role that positive student-teacher relationships play in classroom management (Cothran, Kulinna, & Garrahy, 2003). Interviews with 182 adolescents (grades 6–12), representing diverse socioeconomic, cultural, and academic backgrounds, revealed students' high regard for teachers who listen well, treat students with respect, and exhibit caring. Sonya made this comment: "If you have a relationship with your students, they're gonna trust you more and they're gonna respect you more and then they'll be nicer to you." When the researchers asked her to elaborate on what she meant by "be nicer to you," she responded this way:

> We like don't mouth off to her. We try not to talk when she is talking and we don't talk back. We try to listen and remember what she is telling us like directions and instructions and we don't talk back to her and we aren't whining about what she wants, what she has planned. (p. 439)

The researchers note that the importance of caring, respectful relationships "is not a common topic in classroom management discussions" (p. 441). They contend that this is unfortunate, since teacher caring is a key factor in gaining students' cooperation and their engagement in academic activities.

But gaining cooperation is certainly not the only reason for trying to develop positive relationships with students. If we want adolescents to be seriously engaged in learning, to share their thoughts and feelings, to take risks, and to develop a sense of social responsibility, then we need to organize classrooms so that students feel safe and cared for (Patrick, Ryan, & Kaplan, 2007). If we want students to feel a sense of connectedness and trust, then we must work to create classroom communities where students know that they are needed, valued members of the group (Roeser, Eccles, & Sameroff, 2000). Even achieving the most basic goal of having students stay in school depends on developing meaningful relationships: When youths were asked why they dropped out of high school, they frequently stated it was because no one cared about them (National Research Council, 2004).

PAUSE AND REFLECT

Before going any further, think about a teacher you had in middle or high school who showed caring and respect for students. In specific behavioral terms, what did this teacher do to communicate that he or she cared about you?

In retrospect, Annie's problem was not the high priority she placed on being caring and creating positive relationships with her students. *Her problem was the way she thought about caring.* Clearly, never saying "no" doesn't work. So what *does?* How can you show students that you care about them?

This chapter begins by considering ways of showing care and respect for students. We then turn to relationships among students themselves and discuss strategies for creating a caring community in which students feel respected, trusted, and supported by one another. As you read, keep in mind the characteristics of classroom groups that were discussed in Chapter 1. Recall that, unlike most other social groups, students do not come together voluntarily. They are a captive audience, often required to work on tasks they have not selected and in which they may have little interest. Remember, too, that classroom groups are formed somewhat arbitrarily; students do not usually choose their peers *or* their teachers, yet they are expected to cooperate with both. Recalling these special characteristics makes it easier to see why teachers must work to create cohesion, cooperation, and a sense of community.

WAYS OF SHOWING CARE AND RESPECT FOR STUDENTS

Be Welcoming

Beginning teachers are often told not to smile until Christmas, so students will perceive them as serious and tough. We don't agree. A smile is a simple, effective way to be welcoming. You can also welcome students by standing at the classroom door and greeting students at the beginning of the period. (This also helps to ensure that students enter the room in an orderly fashion.) If you have students who are not native English speakers, learn a few phrases in their native languages. It can mean a lot to students if you can welcome them to your class each day with a few words from their homeland.

Most importantly, learn students' names (and any preferred nicknames) as quickly as possible. You also need to learn the correct pronunciation, especially for names that are unfamiliar. In the classes of our four teachers, for example, there are Sriram ("Shree-rom"), Hrushita, Yili, Isha ("Eye-sha"), Hamzuh ("Hum-zuh"), Wei Hou ("Wee-how"), and Aisha ("Eye-ee-sha"). Christina finds that writing the phonetic pronunciations in her record book is a real help. She has also noted that some Asian American students are reluctant to correct mispronunciation, fearing that it would be disrespectful.

Watch how Donnie shows an interest in students' names as she welcomes students on the first day of school:

 After introducing herself and explaining how she got her name, Donnie asks the students to tell her about themselves in the same way: "Tell me your name, where you got it from or what it means, if you have a nickname you want me to use, and then choose an adjective to describe yourself. I'm going to write these down so I can learn your names as quickly as possible. But please be patient; it might take a little while."

Learn about Students' Lives

In addition to welcoming your students, another way of showing care and respect is to learn about their lives. For example, you might ask your students to complete an information sheet that asks about favorite school subjects, after-school jobs, hobbies, or pets, along with anything else they want you to know about them. Attending their sporting events, plays, and concerts is another way of getting to know your students.

Fred begins the process of learning about his students as he takes roll on the first day of school. After pronouncing each student's name, he asks a question (e.g., What is your favorite TV show? What's your favorite kind of music?). This not only allows him to learn about his students, but it gives them some confidence about speaking out in class. Fred also conducts class discussions in which he asks students to respond to questions such as:

- What are the best things about being a high school student in the 21st century?
- What are the most memorable world events in your life so far?
- If you were the superintendent of this district, what changes would you make in this high school?

Another idea comes from JoBeth Allen (2008), who was part of a teacher study group in Georgia that used photography to learn about students' families. With a small grant, the study group teachers bought three cameras for each classroom and invited students to photograph what was important to them in their homes and neighborhoods. Students took the cameras home on a rotating basis, and students and family members wrote personal stories, memories, poetry, and letters about the photos.

Be Sensitive to Students' Concerns

In essence, this means thinking about classroom events and activities from a student's point of view. On the first day of school, for example, Christina assigns seats alphabetically so that she can learn students' names as quickly as possible. Realizing that students may be unhappy about the location of their seats or their particular neighbors, she reassures them that seats will be changed periodically.

Sensitivity is also demonstrated by keeping grades a private matter between you and an individual student. Most adolescents don't want anyone to know they've gotten a failing grade; public announcements are less likely to increase motivation than to generate resentment. Even if you announce only the As, you can embarrass students. A fifth-grader we know was mortified when her teacher held her test up in front of the whole class and announced that "Laura was obviously the only one who studied!" And what does an announcement like that convey to the student who normally received Ds, but studied really hard and earned a C? When Sandy gives students' papers back, she tells them to keep their grades to themselves while they are in the room—"no asking, no telling." If they wish to divulge their grades once they've left the room, that's their prerogative.

Since secondary students have a tremendous need to save face, sensitivity also means discussing inappropriate behavior quietly and privately. Public reprimands are humiliating—and research consistently demonstrates that students view public humiliation as an *unacceptable* form of discipline (Hoy & Weinstein, 2006). Moreover, students consider it a very *severe* intervention—not something to be shrugged off lightly. A study of 300 junior high school students in Israel found that students viewed *"shaming or personally insulting a student" as severe as "permanent suspension from school,"* and more severe than detention, student-teacher conferences, reporting to the principal's office, and verbal reprimands (Zeidner, 1988). Students also rated public humiliation as significantly more severe than teachers did.

Not only will public humiliation poison your relationship with students, it can also have long-term negative effects. A recent Canadian study (Brendgen, Wanner, Vitaro, Bukowski, & Tremblay, 2007) found that elementary students, from kindergarten through fourth grade, who were "picked on" by the teacher (defined as behaviors such as scolding, criticizing, or shouting) were more likely to display behavior problems in young adulthood.

In order to preserve the student-teacher relationship, Donnie approaches misbehaving students quietly and sets up a time to meet:

 I'll tell them, "I don't want to take up class time and I don't want to embarrass you. Stop by after school so we can talk privately." If that's not possible, we'll meet during lunch or before school. It means giving up some of my own time, but it's much more effective than talking during class in front of everyone.

Sensitivity also means noticing if someone looks especially edgy, depressed, or angry, and privately communicating your concern. As Donnie puts it:

 Sometimes a student will come in and they just don't have the same glow. I'll go over and say, "Is everything OK?" And sometimes they'll say, "No, Miss, I'm having problems at home" or "I'm having trouble with my boyfriend." If they tell me that, I try to respect that and give them some space. I'll go a little easier on them that day, like I won't call on them as much.

In addition, it's important to take students' concerns seriously if they choose to confide in you. From your adult vantage point, breaking up with a girlfriend, having to be home by 1:00 A.M. on a Saturday night, or not making the track team might not be sufficient cause for depression. But Christina emphasizes how important it is to acknowledge the legitimacy of students' concerns:

 One of my 11th-grade students was absent for two days, and when he came back, he was falling asleep, wouldn't talk with anyone, was real cranky. I called him out in the hall while other students were working in small groups and asked him what the problem was. Of course he said, "Nothing." But I told him I was really concerned, and eventually, he told me his girlfriend had broken up with him. Later that day, I arranged for him to see the guidance counselor. She let him stay there, gave him tea. It really meant a lot to him. We can't just blow these things off, even if they don't seem that earth-shattering to us. He needed to know that we noticed and cared about how he was feeling.

Finally, be sensitive to anxiety or difficulty your students may be experiencing with course material or requirements. During a visit to Sandy's class after a severe blizzard that had closed school for several days, we watched students resume a lab activity they had begun before the "vacation." It required them to use pipettes, and several students expressed concern about having forgotten how to use them.

Sandy acknowledges their concerns: "I know that some of you are worried that you don't remember how to use the equipment. That's a valid concern, since it's been such a long time since you practiced. But don't worry. See if you remember, and if not, just call me over and I'll help you out." Later, when two students express confusion about the lab procedure, she comments: "Your confusion is understandable, because this is the first time we're doing this procedure. Next time we do it you'll know what to do. Remember when we were learning to use the balance, and you were so confused? The first time is always a challenge."

Establish and Enforce Clear Expectations for Behavior

Establishing and enforcing clear norms for behavior makes the classroom a safer, more predictable environment and communicates that you care about your students' well-being. With clear rules and routines, there is less likelihood of confusion, misunderstanding, and inconsistency—and more likelihood that teachers and students can engage in warm, relaxed interactions. As Christina puts it:

I feel like the more organized and the more structured the class is, the more I can show that I'm human, joke around, invite students to tell me things they would like to change. I can let my guard down, because they know what is expected.

Clear expectations also establish you as the classroom leader; this is especially important if you are working with African American students, who generally expect teachers to be authoritative—to speak in a firm voice, provide a no-nonsense atmosphere, to demand respect, and to convey high expectations (Brown, 2004; Gordon, 1998; Irvine, 2002; Milner, 2006; Obidah & Teel, 2001).

Research has demonstrated the *long-term benefits* to students of organized classrooms with clear norms. In one study (Catalano, Haggerty, Oesterle, Fleming, & Hawkins, 2004), elementary teachers from schools in high-risk neighborhoods were trained in the use of proactive classroom management techniques (e.g., establish consistent classroom expectations and routines at the beginning of the year; give clear, explicit instructions for behavior; recognize desirable student behavior and efforts to comply). Not surprisingly, the students of those teachers demonstrated a higher level of school bonding and fewer problem behaviors than students in a control group. What is even more noteworthy is the fact that when those same students were followed into high school, their levels of school attachment, commitment, and academic achievement were higher than those in the control group, and school problems, violence, alcohol abuse, and risky sexual activity were reduced. (Establishing clear norms for behavior will be addressed more fully in Chapter 4.)

Be Fair

It seems obvious that caring teachers must strive for fairness. For example, issues of fairness often arise in relationship to evaluation and grading. Jeffrey Smith, a colleague who specializes in assessment, emphasizes the need for communication:

> *If you know the criteria for good work, tell your students. Don't make them guess. Don't withhold information about how you're going to grade, and then play "gotcha." If you're going to count participation and effort as part of the grade, tell students that too, and tell them what you mean by participation.*

Christina earnestly follows Jeff's advice. Since she counts participation as one-third of students' grades, she provides her classes with a weekly "participation checksheet" that lists the behaviors she expects, and she spends considerable time explaining how it works. During one interview, she shared her reasoning:

> **Most teachers don't use participation as an actual portion of the grade; they use it as a tie-breaker (like if you're trying to decide between an A and a B). But I think it's one of the most important things. Participation is not just raising your hand and speaking out. It's also having your work done, being prepared for class, being engaged, staying on task. I know some kids are going to be more verbal and more confident, but everyone can make some contribution to class.**

In these instances, caring and fairness seem to go hand in hand. But it's not always so simple. Being fair generally involves "making judgments of students' conduct and academic performances without prejudice or partiality" (M. S. Katz, 1999, p. 61). In terms of classroom management, this translates into ensuring that rules apply to everyone, no matter what. On the other hand, being fair can also imply a recognition that people may need different, personalized treatment, and being caring certainly seems to demand that we acknowledge students' individuality. From this perspective, treating everyone the same is *unfair*. So what is a teacher to do?

Even experienced, masterful teachers who care deeply about students' well-being may have conflicting positions on this fundamental dilemma. Consider Sandy and Fred. Sandy observes:

> You can't have community in the classroom unless everyone feels that they'll be treated fairly, whether they're the student congress president or not. You're better off having a class with very few rules that apply to everyone, rather than a lot of rules that apply to only some people.

Sandy demonstrated this principle not too long ago, when three of her students, including a boy classified as having an emotional disorder, didn't have their homework and asked for permission to turn it in the next day:

> My answer was no. I don't accept late homework, and they know it. I want them to learn how to budget their time and to prepare. This was a 20-point homework assignment, due on Monday. I reminded them all week, and made a big point of it on Friday. Then they walk in on Monday without it. I said, "I believe you did it; your integrity is not in question. But it's not here." To my horror, Billy (the boy classified as emotionally disturbed) started to cry in front of the whole class. I got him out of the room and talked with him. I told him I understood that other things can interfere with doing homework, but the rule applies to everyone. I know this seems harsh, but I think this was a really significant event. It was important for Billy—and the rest of the class—to see that he has to meet the same expectations.

From Sandy's perspective, having the rules apply to everyone is both fair *and* caring. But Fred takes a somewhat different position:

> I try to treat kids fairly in that my decision is always based on what is best for the kid. At times that means you treat everyone the same, and that's the right decision. Other times you may treat everyone differently, and that's the right decision. There's no recipe for being fair that we can all follow. We have to constantly examine our decisions and ask, "Is this in the best interest of the kid?"

I gain some things by not always treating everyone the same. I have more flexibility this way. I can say, "This kid is having a really hard time, and I'm not going to give him a zero for the day, no matter what the rule says." I'm just going to throw out that rule. And I've never had a kid say, "That's not fair." But I lose some things too—namely, the consistency that comes when everyone knows exactly what's going to happen. So you have people who push the envelope. I have to be more on guard; I have to watch for people who are trying to take advantage.

In sum, being fair is certainly an essential component of being caring, but it's not always obvious what this means in terms of actual practice. Teaching is messy and uncertain, and we often don't know what the right decisions are until after we've made them. What *is* certain, however, is that teachers need to engage in ongoing reflection about these complex moral issues. (We return to these issues in Chapter 12, when we discuss the issue of consistency.)

Welcome Students' Input

Allow students to voice their suggestions and opinions about lessons, assignments, or grouping decisions. Interestingly, all four teachers begin the school year by asking students to talk or write about their expectations for the class. As we saw in Chapter 1, Sandy begins the school year by asking her students to write answers to four questions: (1) How do you learn best? (2) What do you expect to be excited about in chemistry? (3) What do you expect to be nervous about? and (4) What can I do to help? In similar fashion, Donnie also solicits students' expectations. On the first day of school, she has students write her a letter, focusing on their attitudes and feelings about mathematics, about the kinds of teaching and managerial strategies they like or dislike, and about their own responsibility in making the classroom a good place to be.

Christina not only asks students to write about their expectations, she also invites their continuing suggestions and feedback on the class:

"I want you to know that I really welcome your input. I'm sure you have good ideas, and I'm interested in hearing your suggestions for things we can do. Also, if you think something didn't work very well, I welcome your criticism too. For example, you might say, 'I know that you were trying to have a good discussion today, but a lot of people weren't responding because . . .' That kind of feedback would be very helpful." Christina points out her school e-mail address and encourages students to use it.

There is an interesting postscript to our first-day observations of Christina's request for suggestions and criticism. Several months later, it became clear that a few students were disgruntled by the amount of work they had been assigned. Christina tells it this way:

It was right after spring break, and there were a couple of kids who seemed upset and were complaining about work. So, wondering how widespread it was, I opened up a discussion. It was like opening Pandora's box. Out came all these complaints about how I was giving too much homework, and some of it was too difficult for them to do by themselves—they wanted partners. They kept saying it was like college work, and that they were only 15!

I was floored at first, but after everyone had their say, I tried to address their concerns. We made some changes. I postponed some assignments and promised to give them in-class time to work in groups on some of them. I explained why I was giving them challenging work, and I made it clear that I am here every day to work with anybody who needs help. But I also told them that what was most upsetting to me was the fact that they hadn't come to me about all this sooner.

Since the discussion, a lot of kids have been coming in for help, and things really seem to be better. But what I learned is that even if you invite kids to provide input, you still have to go back and check that it's working. You have to teach them that it's really okay to come to teachers and talk about these things. I just assumed my invitation was enough, but it wasn't.

Be a Real Person (as Well as a Teacher)

On the first day of school, Donnie takes a few minutes to explain how she got the name Donnie, that her husband is the principal of a nearby elementary school, and that they have a daughter who "is one year short of a quarter of a century." (When students look at her questioningly, she laughs and tells them, "Do your math!") Within the first few minutes of the very first class meeting, she has already communicated an important message: In addition to being a teacher, Donnie Collins is a real person with a life outside of school.

Beginning teachers often puzzle over the extent to which they should share information about their personal lives. We remember having teachers who refused to reveal their first names—as if that would somehow blur the boundary between teacher and student and diminish their authority. On the other hand, there are teachers who are extremely open. In an article on "Building Community from Chaos" (1994), Linda Christensen, a high school English teacher in Portland, Oregon, writes:

> Students have told me that my willingness to share stories about my life—my father's alcoholism, my family's lack of education, my poor test scores, and many others, opened the way for them to tell their stories. . . . And through their sharing, they make openings to each other. Sometimes a small break. A crack. A passage from one world to the other. And these openings allow the class to become a community. (p. 55)

As a new teacher, it's probably wise to find a happy medium between these two extremes and to share limited information (e.g., about families, vacations, cultural and athletic activities, hobbies, or pets). Before you start your first teaching job, be sure to review any online profiles you may have on sites like MySpace and Facebook. Make sure your profiles don't reveal more than you would want your students (and their parents) to know about you.

As you gain experience and confidence, you can decide if you want to follow Linda Christensen's example and share more information about your personal life. During an early visit to Christina's classroom, for example, we watched as she introduced a writing assignment on identity. She began by distributing copies of her own identity essay. In it, she reflects on her Puerto Rican father, her "all-American" mother (unable to "recount all of her various nationalities"), her "Asian eyes" (with eyelids that "kept escaping" the blue eyeshadow she tried to use), and the "curious ambiguity" of her skin. Four months later, near the end of the school year, Christina talked about her students' reactions to the essay:

> **I think it helped to build connections with the students. It stimulated all kinds of questions: What do you do for this holiday? Do you go to the Puerto Rican Day parade? They were able to see me as a real person. Just today, it came up again and led to a good discussion about the most appropriate terms for various ethnic and racial groups. It clearly made an impact on them.**

Another way of showing your humanity is to admit when you don't know something. Teachers sometimes feel that they have to be the "sage on the stage," but it can be beneficial for students to see that even "experts" don't know all the answers all the time. The best way to encourage students to take risks in the process of learning is to take risks yourself.

It's also important to admit when you make a mistake and to acknowledge that you are fallible. We recently visited a Spanish I class taught by a native Spanish speaker who told students that she would "give two points to the student who wins the *more*." When a boy corrected her in a respectful way ("It should be wins the *most*"), the teacher thanked him for helping her with her English. Her willingness to admit her mistake and to learn from a student certainly reinforced the lesson that she tries so hard to teach. As she told us later, "I constantly stress the fact that it's okay to make mistakes when you are talking and learning another language, and you don't have to be afraid of that."

Keep in mind that presenting yourself as a real person to your students doesn't mean that you should dress like them. Students, and also parents, tend to respect teachers who dress professionally. If you are coming straight from college, your clothes may be too casual for the classroom. Use other teachers as a model or ask the principal about expectations for professional dress. You should also learn about school policy or norms about piercings and tattoos.

Become Aware of Adolescent Culture

Positive relationships with students can be facilitated if you have what Robin Gordon (1997) calls "social insight"—knowledge of popular music, styles of dress, current movies, and other aspects of adolescent culture. Donnie also finds it helpful to sit quietly and listen to students' chatter right before homeroom:

> **That's when I learn all about the concerts they've attended or the deejays they like. We talk about today's music; I tell them I don't know what the groups are saying these days, and they explain. They also like to hear about the things that I did "back in the old days" and compare it with the things they're doing now.**

In particular, teachers need to be aware of the digital media that are so much a part of students' lives (and which may be a part of your life). Today's teenagers have been dubbed the *DIG Generation* for "digital immediate gratification" (Renard, 2005). They download information, podcasts, songs, and movies from the Internet; take photographs with digital cameras or cell phones and share their pictures online; communicate through e-mail, text and instant messaging; build online social networks (MySpace or Facebook, for example); and disclose their thoughts and experiences on blogs. Not only do you need to understand how digital technologies have changed the way adolescents live and think, you need to harness the engagement provided by these technologies to make academic activities more relevant and motivating (Prensky, 2005). For example, you can design a "WebQuest," an inquiry-oriented activity that asks students to explore a set of high-quality online information sources to complete a specific task. (WebQuests for all content areas and grade levels, as well as training for teachers interested in designing such activities, can be found at www.WebQuest.org.) You can create a class blog on which students reflect on assignments, exchange comments about one another's work, and share resources. (One resource for starting your own blog is www.edublogs.org.)

Promote Autonomy

Visiting kindergarten classes, we're always struck by how much more choice and control these young students have over their day than secondary students do. We see kindergartners making decisions about what they want to do and with whom they want to do it. Ironically, as students advance through the grades, becoming more capable of making decisions and more concerned about having autonomy, we offer fewer opportunities for choice and involvement in decision making (Nucci, 2006). At the junior high level, research has documented the decline in intrinsic motivation and interest in school that result from this mismatch between adolescents' increasing desire for greater autonomy and the schools' increasing emphasis on teacher control (e.g., Eccles, Wigfield, & Schiefele, 1998).

Think about ways the students in your classes could make decisions about their own behavior and class events. For example, you might sometimes allow students to choose their own groups for cooperative learning activities. You might give students responsibility for creating assignments, constructing questions for class discussions and tests, leading class activities, and evaluating their own progress and behavior (Ridley & Walther, 1995). You might also assign "block homework assignments" that require students to develop their own time line for completion. For example, Sandy usually assigns a certain amount of reading and 25 to 30 problems that are due in a week or so. She recommends that students do four or five problems a night, but she does not require them to show her their work on a daily basis. She realizes that this means some students will wait until the last night to do all the problems:

 High school teachers have to remember that students want to be treated like young adults, not like babies. It's important to give them some responsibility for their own behavior. They might make the wrong decisions and "fall and scrape their knees," but then they can see the

consequences. I think they're more likely to take responsibility for their mistakes if teachers don't dictate everything.

Sharing decision making can be difficult for teachers. When you're feeling pressured to cover the curriculum and to maximize learning time, it's easier to make the decisions by yourself. For example, assigning topics for a term paper is faster than allowing students to decide on their own topic; giving students a set of instructions for a laboratory activity is simpler than allowing them to develop their own procedures. Involving students can be messy and time-consuming, and allowing students to make decisions about their own behavior means that they'll sometimes make the wrong decisions. Nonetheless, a "short-term investment of time" can lead to "a long-term gain in decision-making ability and self-esteem" (Dowd, 1997).

Another way of increasing students' experience of autonomy is to decrease the use of extrinsic rewards and punishments. None of us like to feel controlled or manipulated, and we generally experience external regulation as alienating (Reeve, 2006; Ryan & Deci, 2000). Indeed, research has found a *negative* relationship between the use of external control and student engagement (Kim, Solomon, & Roberts, 1995); this is critical, since student engagement is, in turn, significantly related to sense of community. What seems clear is that the more students feel externally regulated, the less they show interest and effort and the more they tend to disown responsibility for negative outcomes (Ryan & Connell, 1989). This hardly makes for a caring community. (The impact of extrinsic rewards will be discussed further in Chapter 8.)

Be Inclusive

In recent years, *inclusive education* has been used to refer to the practice of placing students with disabilities in general education classrooms rather than segregating them in special classrooms or schools. But the term can also be used more broadly, to describe classes in which differences related not only to disability, but also to race, class, ethnicity, gender, cultural and linguistic background, religion, and sexual orientation are acknowledged, understood, and respected.

This, of course, is easier said than done. Before we can create a classroom community that acknowledges and respects differences, we need to recognize that we are often afraid and suspicious of those differences. As we mentioned in Chapter 1, sometimes we deny even *seeing* differences. It is not uncommon, for example, for our European American teacher education students to pride themselves on being "color-blind, that is, fair and impartial when it comes to judging people based on their race" (Nieto & Bode, 2008, p. 75). Yet, to deny cultural or racial differences is to deny an essential aspect of people's identity—and recognizing those differences does not make us racist. During one conversation, Fred spoke passionately about these issues:

So many times I hear teachers say things like, "I don't think of kids as Black or Hispanic or Asian—just as kids." But being Black or Hispanic or Asian is part of who those kids are—just like being Polish and Russian is part of who I am. . . . A part of the whole community-building thing

is acknowledging that these differences exist. We're not all the same. . . . To build community we also need to face the fact that racism and bias are part of the real world. People don't want to admit it's there. But it's everywhere; it's part of all of us. The question is not "Are you a racist?" but "How much of a racist are you, and how can you become less so?"

In addition to *acknowledging* differences, creating inclusive classrooms means learning about disabilities, or cultures, or races, or religions that we've never before encountered. For example, you can't acknowledge and respect behaviors that have cultural origins if you have no idea that the behaviors are rooted in culture. Teachers may be shocked when Southeast Asian students smile while being scolded if they are unaware that the smiles are meant not as disrespect but as an admission of culpability and an effort to show that there is no grudge (Trueba, Cheng, & Ima, 1993). Similarly, teachers who are not cognizant of the fact that Pacific Islanders value interpersonal harmony and the well-being of the group may conclude that these students are lazy when they are reluctant to participate in competitive activities (Sileo & Prater, 1998). Teachers who are unaware that the culture of most American Indians tends to emphasize deliberate thought may become impatient when those students take longer to respond to questions (Nieto & Bode, 2008).

A particularly heated debate about students' use of Ebonics or Black English illustrates the problems that occur when teachers are unaware of the cultural origins of language. Ernie Smith (2002), an African American linguist, notes that during his years of schooling, teachers often equated the use of Ebonics with deficiency:

> Teachers and other school officials often used such terms as "talking flat," "sloven speech," "corrupt speech," "broken English," "verbal cripple," "verbally destitute," "linguistically handicapped," and "linguistically deprived" to describe the language behavior of my Black classmates and me. They suggested that our language differences were deficiencies that were related to physical and/or mental abnormalities. Often during Parent-Teacher Conferences or at Open House Conferences, my teachers were not hesitant to suggest to my parents, and to parents of other children, that we should be assigned to the school speech clinic for speech therapy or to the school psychologist for a diagnostic examination, and treatment for possible congenital mental disorders. (pp. 17–18)

Not surprisingly, this negative reaction to children's home language frequently leads to alienation from school. As Lisa Delpit argues in *The Skin That We Speak* (2002), "language is one of the most intimate expressions of identity" so "to reject a person's language can only feel as if we are rejecting him" (p. 47). Rejection like this has no place in an inclusive classroom; instead, inclusive teachers honor students' home language while teaching them the importance of learning to speak Standard English—what Delpit (1995) calls the "language of the culture of power." In other words, our goal is to enable students to "code switch" according to the norms of the setting.

It's unrealistic to expect beginning teachers (or even experienced ones) to have familiarity with all of the cultures that might be represented in their extremely diverse classrooms. Certainly, developing this kind of "cultural literacy" takes time and effort. Some specific suggestions are listed in the Practical Tips box. Meanwhile, when you encounter behaviors that seem inappropriate and inexplicable, ask yourself whether these behaviors might, in fact, be culturally grounded. In addition, think about how you can use your students as a resource. Listen to Fred:

> If I have kids from other countries in my class, I'll ask about customs there, and how they compare with customs here. Not only do I learn something I didn't know before, but I can just see the "little lights go on." It's like, "Hey, here's someone who's interested in my experiences."

We don't have to be intrusive about it, but it's important that classrooms be a place where we can learn about one another. I can use my classroom like a textbook.

PRACTICAL TIPS FOR

DEVELOPING CULTURAL LITERACY

- **Examine your own taken-for-granted beliefs, values, and assumptions and reflect on how they are influenced by your cultural, racial, and socioeconomic identity.** As we mentioned in Chapter 1, many European Americans consider their beliefs and values to be normal, correct, and universal, not realizing that these are products of their particular cultural background. Developing cultural literacy begins by examining one's own cultural norms. For example, a White middle-class worldview emphasizes individual achievement, independence, and competition. This is in stark contrast to the worldview of more collectivist cultures (e.g., Asian, Latino, and Native American) that avoid displays of individual accomplishment and, instead, stress cooperation, harmony, and working for the good of the group. One worldview is not necessarily better than the other—but they are certainly different. Failing to appreciate and respect these differences can lead to misunderstanding and miscommunication.

- **Explore students' family backgrounds.** Where did the student come from? Was it a rural or urban setting? Why did the family move? How long has the student been in this country? How many people are in the family? What are the lines of authority? What responsibilities does the student have at home? What are parents' beliefs with respect to involvement in the school and in their child's education? Do they consider teachers to be experts and therefore refrain from expressing differences of opinion? Is learning English considered a high priority?

- **Explore students' educational background.** If students are new to this country, how much previous schooling have they had? What kinds of instructional strategies are they used to? In their former schools, was there an emphasis on large group instruction, memorization, and recitation? In students' former schools, what were the expectations for appropriate behavior? Were students expected to be active or passive? independent or dependent? peer-oriented or teacher oriented? cooperative or competitive?

- **Be sensitive to cultural differences and how they may lead to miscommunication.** How do students think about time? Is punctuality expected or is time considered to be flexible? Do students nod their heads to be polite or to indicate understanding? Do students question or obey authority figures? Do students put their needs and desires before those of the group or vice versa? Are expressions of emotion and feelings emphasized or hidden?

- **Use photographs to communicate without words.** Take pictures of the students engaged in various activities to take home to parents; display photographs around the room; invite students to bring in pictures of themselves and their families; use photographs for get-acquainted activities.

Sources: Kottler, 1994; Sileo & Prater, 1998; Weinstein, Tomlinson-Clarke, & Curran, 2004.

Just as we must learn to acknowledge and respect racial and cultural diversity, we must also learn to create an accepting classroom environment for other, less visible kinds of differences. Several years ago, *Newsweek* magazine featured a special report on "Gay today: How the battle for acceptance has moved to schools, churches, marriage, and the workplace." The article on the schools (Peyser & Lorch, 2000) described the efforts of two 17-year-olds, Leslie-Claire Spillman and Martin Pfeiffer, to establish a Gay-Straight Alliance in their Baton Rouge, Louisiana, high school. Like other gays and lesbians, Spillman and Pfeiffer had suffered through years of harassment and hatred. As a result, Pfeiffer had once been suicidal; Spillman had dropped out of school, become addicted to heroin, and spent five weeks in "detox." Such problems are all too common among homosexual youth; indeed, some researchers have found that gay and lesbian adolescents are two to three times more likely to attempt suicide than their heterosexual peers; they are also at increased risk for poor school performance, truancy, and dropping out (Nichols, 1999). It is essential that teachers work to create an atmosphere of tolerance for the "forgotten children"—those "whose needs have been ignored, whose existence has been whispered about, and whose pain is just beginning to surface" (Anderson, 1997, p. 65). You can take a step toward creating that atmosphere by making it clear that homophobic name-calling is absolutely unacceptable, by respectfully using the words *gay, lesbian,* and *bisexual,* and by referring to spouses or partners rather than husbands or wives (Edwards, 1997).

Search for Students' Strengths

In *The Culturally Responsive Teacher* (2007), Ana Maria Villegas and Tamara Lucas tell the story of Belki Alvarez, an eight-year-old girl from the Dominican Republic. As the oldest child in the family, Belki was responsible for getting her brother and sister ready for school and caring for them until her parents came home from work. On weekends, she joined her mother at a community street fair, selling products prepared at home, negotiating prices with customers, and handling financial transactions. She also served as an English language translator for her parents. But Belki's teachers didn't see this competent, responsible child. They saw only a youngster lacking in language and math skills and made no effort to tap into her life experiences. In other words, they focused on her deficits, rather than her strengths.

Searching for deficits makes a certain amount of sense. After all, if we can identify what students don't know or can't do, we can try to fix the problems. But responsible teaching also involves a search for strengths. In *Teaching to Change the World* (2007), Jeannie Oakes and Martin Lipton argue that when teachers and students have a caring relationship, they work together to find competence: "The student's search is his own discovery of what he knows and how he knows it. The teacher's search—an act of care and respect—is also discovering what the student knows and how he knows it" (pp. 266–267).

We thought of this perspective on caring during one meeting with the teachers, when Sandy talked about her conviction that "everyone needs their 15 minutes of fame":

> Chemistry lends itself to a variety of talents—the math problems, the writing, the spatial relations, the mechanical ability. So I can give different people a chance to shine. Take Adam. He's really good at spatial relationships so I know that I can call on him to do diagrams.

When we have student presentations, I always try to think who I want to call on so I can showcase kids' different strengths. For example, I told the class that I was going to randomly choose a lab group to present the lab to the rest of the class. Everyone had to think about how to teach this and to be prepared. It was a nice safe situation—a great opportunity to get these two quiet girls to shine. I knew they had done a good job on the lab. So I wrote their names 12 times and put the slips in a beaker, and had someone pull out a slip. Of course their presentation went very well. But it was important for the girls—and everyone else—to think it was a risky situation, that they had just gotten chosen by chance. When they got a great evaluation, they felt terrific.

> ### ✎ PAUSE AND REFLECT
>
> At the beginning of this chapter, we stressed the fact that students are more likely to cooperate with teachers who are perceived to be caring. Since a big part of showing care is being a good listener, it's important to think about exactly what that means. Before reading the next section on communication skills, think about a time when someone *really listened well* to a problem you were relating. What kinds of behaviors did this person display? How did you know they were *really* listening?

Develop Communication Skills

Another way of showing students that you care is by being a good listener. Sandy puts it this way:

> How come there are only certain teachers in the school that kids will go to [when they have a problem]? After all, most kids have six teachers a day. It's all about listening. When you're a high school teacher, you have to listen seriously to problems that might not be problems to you, but they are to them. And that's a way of gaining their trust. A kid is not going to come to you and say, "I want to commit suicide" if three weeks earlier you said, "Oh grow up, you'll get over her."

Being a good listener means being attentive, trying to understand students' feelings and concerns, asking appropriate questions, and helping students solve their own problems. In the following sections, we will examine each of these. As you read, keep in mind that as a teacher, you are required by law to report child abuse or neglect and sexual abuse or assault, so there may be times when you will need to go beyond merely listening. It's important to let your students know that if you do learn about any of these abuses, you will need to report the information to the appropriate child welfare agency.

Attending and Acknowledging

Giving a student your complete, undivided attention is the first and most basic task in being helpful (Kottler & Kottler, 1993). It is rare that individuals are fully attentive to one another. Have you ever tried to talk with someone who was simultaneously organizing papers, posting notices on the bulletin board, or straightening rows of desks? Divided attention like this communicates that the person doesn't really have time for you and is not fully paying attention.

Attending and acknowledging involve both verbal and nonverbal behaviors. Even without saying a word, you can convey that you are totally tuned in by orienting your body toward the student, establishing eye contact, nodding, leaning forward, smiling, or frowning. In addition, you can use verbal cues. Thomas Gordon (2003) recommends using "acknowledgement responses" or "empathic grunting"—the little "uh-huhs" and phrases (e.g., "Oh," "I see," "Mmmmm") that communicate, "I'm really listening." Sometimes, when a student needs additional encouragement to talk more, you can use an explicit invitation, what Gordon calls a "door opener": "Tell me more," "Would you like to say more about that?" "Do you want to talk about it?" "Want to go on?"

Active Listening

Attending and acknowledging communicate that you are totally engaged, but they do not convey if you really *understand.* Active listening takes the interaction one step further by having you reflect back what you think you heard. This feedback allows you to check out whether you are right or wrong. If you're right, the student knows that you have truly understood. If you're off target, the student can correct you, and the communication can continue. Examples of active listening appear in Table 3.1.

If you're new to active listening, you may find it useful to use the phrase, "You feel . . ." when you reflect back what you heard. Sometimes, novices feel stupid, as if they're simply parroting back what the person just said. As you gain more skill, however, you are able to *paraphrase* what you hear, and the interaction becomes far more subtle.

You can also use active listening to respond to the nonverbal messages contained in students' facial expressions and body language. For example, if you see that a student entering the room looks really angry, you might be able to ward off problems by recognizing that something is wrong. Here is a recent journal entry from a student teacher who did this without even knowing about active listening:

> *I was writing the "Do Now" on the marker board when all of a sudden I heard a loud crash behind me—the sound of a backpack crammed full of books hitting the floor. I turned around, and there was John sulking in the seat directly behind me. Obviously, I could not let this slide, so I quickly finished writing the "Do Now" for the rest of the class to begin while I attended to John. I came up to him, squatted down to his level, and asked, "What's wrong? You seem really upset"—not knowing at the time this was a communication strategy called Active Listening. His immediate response was, "Nothing." I paused, trying to come up with something "teacher-y" to say and in that pause of 10 seconds, John spoke! The problem was that he was*

mad at his parents. He had broken his book bag the day before, and since he had to use the same broken bag the next day, he was extremely embarrassed. We talked about his anger and he started to work once he had vented. The next day he came into class with a different book bag—an old one, but a functional one. I took notice, and even though he was mad that it was an old one, he was glad I paid attention to him and his problem.

TABLE 3.1 Examples of Active Listening

STUDENT:	Wait till my mom sees this test grade. She's gonna flip out.
TEACHER:	You think she'll be really mad at you?
STUDENT:	Yeah, she expects me to come home with all As.
TEACHER:	Sounds like you're feeling really pressured.
STUDENT:	Well, I am. You'd think that getting a B was like failing. My mom just doesn't understand how hard this is for me.
TEACHER:	So you think a B is an okay grade in a tough course like this, but she thinks that you can do better.
STUDENT:	Yeah, she has this thing that if I come home with a B I'm just not working.
TEACHER:	That's rough. I can see how that would make you feel like she doesn't appreciate the efforts you're making.
STUDENT:	I can't believe I have to be home at 12:00! It's crazy! All my friends have a later curfew—or they don't have any curfew at all!
TEACHER:	So you think your parents are a lot stricter than the other kids' parents.
STUDENT:	Well, they are! I mean, I know it's 'cause they care about me, but it's really a pain to have to be home earlier than everyone else. I feel like a dork. And besides, I think I'm responsible enough to have a later curfew.
TEACHER:	So you're not just embarrassed, you're mad because they don't realize how responsible you are.
STUDENT:	All along my boyfriend's been telling me how he'll stick by me if I get pregnant, and then it happens, and he's gone.
TEACHER:	You feel really abandoned.
STUDENT:	I don't want to go to School-Base [for mental health counseling]. Only crazy kids go to School-Base!
TEACHER:	Going to School-Base is kind of embarrassing . . .
STUDENT:	Yeah. My friends are going to give me a really hard time.
TEACHER:	You think they're going to say you're crazy.
STUDENT:	Yeah, I wanna go, but I don't want people to make fun of me.
TEACHER:	I can understand that. It's really rough when people make fun of you.
STUDENT:	I had the worst nightmare last night! I mean, I know it was just a dream, but I just can't get it out of my head. This bloody guy with a knife was chasing me down this alley, and I couldn't get away.
TEACHER:	Nightmares can be scary.
STUDENT:	Yeah, and I know it's babyish, but I just can't shake the feeling.
TEACHER:	Sometimes a bad feeling from a nightmare stays with you a long time . . .

Active listening is not always this easy. Student teachers with whom we work often want to reject it out of hand; many find it unnatural and awkward, and they would much prefer to give advice, not simply communicate that they understand. But knowing that someone really understands can be profoundly important, especially to teenagers who so often feel misunderstood. In addition, active listening provides an opportunity for students to express their feelings and to clarify their problems. It can also help to defuse strong feelings without taking the responsibility away from the student for solving the problem.

Questioning

When people tell us their problems, we often want to ask them questions in order to find out more information. As a teacher, you need to be careful about this practice:

> The problem with questions, as natural as they may come to mind, is that they often put the child in a "one down" position in which you are the interrogator and expert problem solver. "Tell me what the situation is and I will fix it." For that reason, questions are used only when you can't get the student to reveal information in other ways. (Kottler & Kottler, 1993, p. 42)

Sandy also warns beginning teachers about the use of questions:

 I don't ask too many questions. I prefer to let them talk themselves out. Questions can open up situations you're not prepared to deal with. After all, you're not a counselor; you're more like a *conduit*: You hear about problems and you try to put them in touch with someone who has the knowledge and the skill to help. Twenty years ago I didn't realize that. I was only three or four years older than my students and I thought I could help them solve their problems. But they don't need teachers to solve their problems for them. They need teachers who can help them solve their own problems or who can get them expert help for solving their problems.

If you must ask questions, they should be open-ended—requiring more than a one-word response. Like active listening, open-ended questions invite further exploration and communication, whereas close-ended questions cut off communication. Compare these questions:

What are you feeling right now? versus Are you feeling angry?
What do you want to do? versus Do you want to tell your boyfriend?

There is one notable exception to the rule of avoiding questions whenever possible: that is, when it is important to get very specific information in a potentially dangerous situation, such as when a student is discussing suicide (Kottler & Kottler, 1993). Then it would be appropriate to ask specific questions: Have you actually tried this? Will you promise not to do anything until we can get you some help?

Problem Solving

Instead of trying to solve students' problems, you can guide them through a process that helps them to solve their *own* problems. In problem solving, students define their problem, specify their goals, develop alternative solutions that might be constructive, narrow the choices to those that seem most realistic, and put the plan into action (Kottler & Kottler, 1993).

Not too long ago, Donnie used a problem-solving approach when a female student told her she was pregnant and asked if she should get an abortion.

First, the student needed to clarify the situation: Was her boyfriend available or not available? Were her parents supportive or not supportive? Was she using drugs or not using? Also, she needed to think about what resources were available to her. All of these factors play a role in making a decision about what to do.

Then, she needed to figure out what her values and priorities were—does she want to go to college? How does she feel about giving the baby up for adoption? Finally, I tried to help her figure out the alternatives—adoption, abortion, staying single and keeping the baby, getting married and keeping the baby.

I don't give advice in situations like this—I wouldn't know what kind of advice to give. But I *can* try to help kids clarify the situation. They're confused, and as an outside party who can think clearly, I can help them to see alternatives they haven't thought of, to talk about the resources that are available to them. My goal is to help them make the best possible decision for *themselves.*

Be Careful about Touching

In recent years, the fear of being accused of sexual harassment and physical abuse has made teachers wary of showing students any physical affection. This is a particularly salient issue for males (King, 1998). Indeed, one of our male student teachers recently wrote this entry in his journal:

> *I had occasion to talk to a student who had a death in the family. She was pretty upset. After explaining that she needn't worry about her class work for that day, I tried my best to comfort her. It's funny, under any other circumstances I would have put an arm around a person in that state, but in this case, I wasn't sure if that would be right.*

This student is not alone in his concern. A study of male teacher education students about to begin their teaching careers revealed a tension between their natural inclinations to be warm, caring, and affectionate to students and the fear that their behavior would be misconstrued as sexual (Hansen & Mulholland, 2005). Fortunately, the anxiety about showing physical affection decreased somewhat as the teachers became more experienced. The young male teachers also found other ways of expressing their affection—for example, by talking and listening with empathy.

Although our four teachers have all been told to avoid touching students, they do not want to forgo all physical contact. Listen to Fred:

I have colleagues who say they'll never touch a kid at all. I understand, but I think you have to touch people if you're going to be a teacher. There have to be rules, of course. I would never be alone with a kid,

because of the appearance of impropriety, but I'll hug kids. . . . It doesn't have to be any big demonstrative thing, but just touching somebody's hand or shoulder can mean a lot. If someone's getting antsy, I'll put my hand on their shoulder, and they'll settle down. If they're hurting, and they need a hug, I'll give them one. What kind of community is it if you can't give someone who's hurting a hug?

It's important to point out that Fred has been in his district for many years and has a solid reputation. As a new teacher, you are in a very different situation. Speak with your colleagues about the policy in effect in your school; some schools actually direct teachers to "teach but don't touch." Even if there is no explicit prohibition against touching students, you need to be cautious so that your actions are not misconstrued. Give your hugs in front of others. Give "high fives" instead of hugs (Jones & Jones, 2010). When a student stays after school, keep the door open, or make sure that other students or teachers are around.

Ask Students How They Feel about the Classroom Environment

In *Beyond Discipline: From Compliance to Community* (1996), Alfie Kohn suggests that teachers begin the school year by asking students about ways of building feelings of safety:

> A teacher might say, "Look, it's really important to me that you feel free to say things, to come up with ideas that may sound weird, to make mistakes—and not to be afraid that other people are going to laugh at you. In fact, I want everyone in here to feel that way. What do you think we can do to make sure that happens?" (pp. 110–111)

It's also a good idea to ask students to provide you with feedback about their perceptions of the classroom environment. "*What Is Happening in My Class?*" is a questionnaire to assess a variety of classroom dimensions, including student cohesiveness, teacher support, involvement, cooperation, and equity (Fraser, McRobbie, & Fisher, 1996). Some of the items from the questionnaire appear in Table 3.2. If you periodically administer these items, you can get a sense of how students are feeling about your classroom environment.

BUILDING CARING RELATIONSHIPS AMONG STUDENTS

A great deal has recently been written on ways of fostering supportive, trusting relationships among students. Unfortunately, much of the advice focuses on elementary classrooms, where teachers generally work with the same group of children for the entire day and there's more opportunity to build a sense of connectedness. The challenge of creating a safe, caring community is certainly more daunting when you teach three or four or five groups of students a day, for 42 or 45 or even 84 minutes. What can secondary teachers possibly do in the limited amount

TABLE 3.2 Items from the *What Is Happening in This Class?* Questionnaire

Student Cohesiveness

I know other students in this class.

Members of the class are my friends.

I work well with other class members.

In this class, I get help from other students.

Teacher Support

The teacher takes a personal interest in me.

The teacher considers my feelings.

The teacher helps me when I have trouble with the work.

The teacher talks with me.

The teacher is interested in my problems.

Involvement

My ideas and suggestions are used during classroom discussions.

I ask the teacher questions.

I explain my ideas to other students.

I am asked to explain how I solve problems.

Cooperation

I cooperate with other students when doing assignment work.

When I work in groups in this class, there is teamwork.

I learn from other students in this class.

Students work with me to achieve class goals.

Equity

The teacher gives as much attention to my questions as to other students' questions.

I have the same amount of say in this class as other students.

I am treated the same as other students in this class.

I receive the same encouragement from the teacher as other students do.

Items are scored 1, 2, 3, 4, and 5, respectively, for the responses *almost never, seldom, sometimes, often,* and *almost always.*

Source: Fraser, McRobbie, & Fisher, 1996.

of time—especially when there's so much pressure to cover the curriculum? We posed this question to our four teachers. Here are some of their suggestions, along with others from educational writers interested in students' social and emotional learning.

Model and Recognize Prosocial Behavior

Teachers frequently exhort students to treat one another with respect. Yet exhortation is unlikely to be effective unless teachers themselves are respectful. As Mary Williams (1993) tells us, "'Do as I say, not as I do' clearly does not work"

(p. 22). Williams was interested in learning how respect was taught and learned by students in middle school classrooms (grades six through eight). She found that respect was best taught through modeling. According to students, teachers "have to follow the values themselves" (p. 22). Students resented teachers who told them to be kind and to respect others, yet exhibited favoritism, treated students "like babies," didn't listen, and gave "busywork."

We thought a lot about the importance of modeling respect during a discussion we recently had with a teacher about her treatment of a "troublemaker" named Serena:

> *Serena was late to class today. She said it was because another student had been bullying her in the hallway on the way to class. I told her to go to the office to report it. When I told another teacher about the incident, she said, "You believe her?!" She looked at me like I was crazy. But I don't like the way Serena and some of the other kids are stereotyped. It's true, they're often troublemakers, but I wasn't in the hallway, so I don't know what happened. I want to treat Serena with the same respect I show to other students. I want to give her the benefit of the doubt. Kids shouldn't have to live the whole year with the same label and not have their improvements recognized.*

As this anecdote illustrates, teachers sometimes categorize students as troublemakers (or criminals, gang members, thieves, and prostitutes [S. R. Katz, 1999]) and fail to accord them the respect that they as teachers demand. But students are unlikely to be respectful of teachers who treat them in demeaning ways. This is certainly a case of "Do unto others. . . ."

Provide Opportunities for Students to Get to Know One Another

On the first day of school, Christina distributes a handout entitled "Find Someone Who." Students must find one person in the class who fits each of the 36 descriptions (e.g., someone who "has read at least three Stephen King novels," someone who "has the same favorite television show as you do," someone who "is a procrastinator," and someone who "would rather work alone than in groups") and have the person sign his or her name next to the appropriate statement. Students are allowed to sign their names only once per sheet, even if more than one item applies.

"Find Someone Who" can be especially useful if you include items relating to race, cultural and linguistic background, and disability and solicit information in addition to a signature. Consider these examples (Sapon-Shevin, 1995):

> Find someone who grew up with an older relative. What's one thing that person learned from the older relative?
>
> Find someone whose parents come from another country. What's one tradition or custom that person has learned from his or her parents?
>
> Find someone who has a family member with a disability. What's something that person has learned by interacting with the person with a disability?

In order to build community, we have to create opportunities for students to learn about one another and to discover the ways in which they are both different and similar. There are numerous getting-acquainted activities like the one Christina chose that teachers can use. Some of these are listed in the Practical Tips box. (Figure 3.1 shows one student's opinion of these activities.)

PRACTICAL TIPS FOR

HELPING YOUR STUDENTS TO GET ACQUAINTED

- **Guess Who?** Have students write a brief autobiographical statement (family background, hobbies, extracurricular activities, etc.), which they do not sign. Collect the statements, read each description, and ask students to write the name of the individual they believe wrote the description. (You can participate too.) After all the descriptions have been read, reread them and ask the authors to identify themselves. Ask students to indicate how many classmates they correctly identified. (Jones & Jones, 2010)

- **Two Truths and a Lie** (or **Two Facts and a Fiction**). Have students write down and then share three statements about themselves, two of which are true and one of which is a lie. For example, one of the authors (Carol) might write, "I once played the princess in *Once Upon the Mattress,* and one night during a performance I fell from the top of 15 mattresses and herniated a disk in my back," "I won third prize in the All-Alaska Logging Championship for the rolling pin toss," and "I trekked through Nepal on my honeymoon." Students guess which one is the lie, and then she tells the truth. (Carol didn't trek through Nepal; she backpacked through Colorado and Wyoming.) The activity can be done as a whole class or in small groups. In either case, since the activity allows students to select what to disclose about themselves, there is little chance of embarrassment. It also provides opportunities for students to discover common interests and experiences and to test assumptions and stereotypes. (No one looking at Carol today, for example, would ever guess that she had camped on her honeymoon!) (Sapon-Shevin, 1999)

- **Little Known Facts about Me.** This is a variation of the previous activity. Students write a statement about themselves that they think others won't know. The papers are folded, collected, put in a box, and shaken. Students take turns drawing a paper and reading the statement aloud. Everyone guesses who wrote the little known fact. (Sapon-Shevin, 1999)

- **Lifelines.** Each student draws a line on a piece of paper and then marks six to ten points representing important events in their lives that they are willing to share (e.g., the birth of a sibling, the death of a close family member, the time they starred in the school play, when they moved to this school). Students then get into pairs and share their life stories. Members of each pair could also introduce each other to the rest of the class, referring to points on the lifeline. (Sapon-Shevin, 1999)

- **Your Inspiration.** Have students bring in pictures of people or things that inspire them, along with an accompanying quotation. Post them on a bulletin board. (Schmollinger, Opaleski, Chapman, Jocius, & Bell, 2002)

- **What Are You Most Proud of Yourself For?** Have students write their individual responses to this question on paper in the shape of a footprint. Post these on a bulletin board in the shape of a path labeled "success." (Schmollinger, Opaleski, Chapman, Jocius, & Bell, 2002)

Figure 3.1   *Source:* FOXTROT © 2006, Bill Amend. Reprinted with permission of
UNIVERSAL UCLICK. All rights reserved.

It's important to note that one or two activities at the start of school are not sufficient to enable students to get to know one another, let alone to build community. Christina learned this lesson halfway through the school year:

Since my basic skills class only has 11 kids I figured that they had all gotten to know one another, especially since I had done getting-to-know-you activities at the beginning of school. But one day, when they were working in small groups, I found out that some kids didn't know other kids' names. I was astounded. The class was a combination of English language learners and native English speakers who were very low achieving, and I realized that these two groups of kids had never really gotten to know one another. Obviously, I should have done more team building throughout the year; once or twice at the beginning of school was just not enough.

Hold Class Meetings

During advisory or homeroom periods, middle school teachers can implement a type of class meeting called "Circle of Power and Respect" or "CPR" (Kriete, 2002). CPR is the middle school version of "Morning Meetings," with which many elementary teachers begin the day, and it contains the same four components. Sitting in a circle, students first *greet one another;* the greeting can be simple—a simple hello, a handshake, or a high-five. As students become more comfortable, the teacher can introduce variations (e.g., greeting one another in different languages). *Sharing* comes next; during this phase of CPR, a few students present news they wish to share, and others ask questions and comment. Sometimes teachers can generate a question for a "focused sharing" (e.g., "What's one accomplishment you feel proud of?" "If you could change one thing about school, what would you change and why?" "What person do you most admire? Why?"). After sharing, the class engages in a *group activity* to build team spirit and to encourage cooperation, participation, and inclusion. Group activities can include games (e.g., Twenty Questions, Charades, Telephone), puzzles, and choral readings of poems. Finally, students focus on a chart containing *news and announcements;* typically, the chart tells them

November 21, 2005

Good Morning, Everyone!

Today there will be an assembly program at
11:15 honoring Rosa Parks, who died last month.
Ms. Parks is known as the "mother of the civil
rights movement." In 1955, she changed the
course of American history by refusing to give up
her seat on a bus for a white man.

Write something you know about Rosa
Parks here:

Figure 3.2   An Example of a News and Announcements Chart

about class and school events and presents an "academic challenge" to develop and reinforce language, math, and other academic skills. (See Figure 3.2.)

Ideally, CPR should be done at least three times a week at the beginning of the day, although schedules do not always allow that. Implemented regularly, CPR allows middle school students to learn CARES—cooperation (rather than competition), assertion (rather than aggression), responsibility (rather than apathy), empathy (rather than self-absorption), and self-control (rather than lack of control). For detailed information about this type of class meeting, see Kriete (2002).

At the high school level, many schools are also incorporating a homeroom or advisory period into their daily schedules, to allow opportunities for class meetings. For example, at the Jefferson County Open School, near Denver, each middle and high school teacher is assigned 18–20 advisees and meets with those students twice each week (Baker, Basile, & Olson, 2005). These opportunities for groups of students to meet regularly with mentors is part of the philosophy of the Small Learning Communities movement, which focuses on establishing small communities, either in a stand-alone school, or within a larger school (Cotton, 2001). Even if your school schedule doesn't include regular time for class meetings, including team-building activities into your classes can help build caring relationships among students.

Two educators who emphasize the importance of class meetings are Jane Nelsen and Lynn Lott. See Box 3.1 for information on their ideas.

Use Cooperative Learning Groups

Research suggests that there are few opportunities for interaction among students during the school day (Osterman, 2000). These findings are disturbing in light of innumerable studies attesting to the power of cooperative learning to promote

MEET THE EDUCATORS   BOX 3.1

MEET JANE NELSEN AND LYNN LOTT

Jane Nelsen and Lynn Lott are therapists and educators who write, lecture, and conduct workshops for parents and teachers on Positive Discipline. Their work is grounded in the ideas of Alfred Adler (1870–1937) and Rudolf Dreikurs (1897–1972), two Viennese psychiatrists who advocated treating children respectfully and kindly, but firmly. Nelsen and Lott's collaboration began in 1988, with the book that is now entitled *Positive Discipline for Teenagers*. Since then, the Positive Discipline series has grown to include titles that address different age groups, settings (e.g., home, school, and child care), and types of families (e.g., single parents, blended families).

Some Major Ideas about Classroom Management

1. Methods of classroom management must be based on *caring and mutual respect*, with the goal of creating a climate that is nurturing to self-esteem and academic performance.
2. In order to convey caring, teachers need to be aware of five pairs of behaviors that affect their relationships with students. In each pair, the first behavior is a *barrier* to good relationships and the second is a *builder* of good relationships: (1) Assuming, rather than Checking; (2) Rescuing/Explaining, rather than Exploring; (3) Directing, rather than Inviting/Encouraging; (4) Expecting, rather

than Celebrating; and (5) Using "Adultisms" (when you forget that children are not mature adults) rather than Respecting.
3. *Class meetings* not only help to minimize discipline problems, they also help students develop social, academic, and life skills.
4. To ensure that class meetings are effective, teachers need to take time to teach students the *Eight Building Blocks:* (1) Form a circle; (2) practice compliments and appreciations; (3) create an agenda; (4) develop communication skills; (5) learn about separate realities; (6) recognize the four reasons people do what they do; (7) practice role-playing and brainstorming; and (8) focus on nonpunitive solutions.

Selected Books and Articles

Positive Discipline in the Classroom, Revised 3rd Edition: Developing Mutual Respect, Cooperation, and Responsibility in Your Classroom (Nelsen, Lott, and H. Stephen Glenn, Prima, 2000)

Positive Discipline for Teenagers, Revised 2nd Edition (Nelsen & Lott, Prima, 2000)

Positive Discipline: A Teacher's A–Z Guide, Revised 2nd Edition: Hundreds of Solutions for Every Possible Classroom Behavior Problem (Nelsen, Duffy, Escobar, Ortolano, & Owen-Sohocki, Prima, 1996)

Website: www.positivediscipline.com

---

the development of positive peer relations. More specifically, cooperative learning facilitates interaction and friendship among students who differ in terms of achievement, sex, cultural and linguistic background, and race; fosters the acceptance of students with disabilities; increases positive attitudes toward class; and promotes empathy (Good & Brophy, 2008).

David and Roger Johnson (1999), two prominent researchers in the field of cooperative learning, distinguish among three types of cooperative learning. In *formal cooperative learning,* teachers assign students to small heterogeneous groups that work together on carefully structured tasks; groups may stay together for one class period up to several weeks. In *informal cooperative learning,* students work together in temporary groups that might last from a few minutes to a whole period. For example, during a whole-class presentation, Donnie frequently tells her students to "turn to your neighbor and talk about how you'd tackle this problem." Finally, *cooperative base groups* are long-term, heterogeneous groups in which students support one another's academic progress and emotional well-being. Members of the base group can collect assignments for absent students and provide assistance when they return, tutor students who are having problems with the course material, check homework assignments, and provide study groups for tests. It's helpful to have base groups meet several times a week for 5 to 15 minutes. (See Chapter 10 for a more detailed discussion of cooperative learning.)

Teach Social-Emotional Skills

Consider the following scenario: An eighth-grade girl finds out that some of her peers have been spreading rumors about her. In response, does she corner them in a hallway and call them names, or does she realize she is angry and hurt, try to calm down, and decide to speak to them about how she is feeling? The answer depends on her "emotional competence"—the ability to understand and manage social-emotional situations (Elias & Schwab, 2006; Woolfolk, 2007). Individuals with emotional competence can identify and regulate their feelings, solve problems by generating alternative solutions and selecting the best action, show respect and empathy for others, and communicate effectively. There is now a raft of programs designed to foster skills such as these; indeed, all of our teachers work in districts that have implemented some kind of program to teach social-emotional learning (SEL). As a classroom teacher, you may not be involved in delivering these programs to your students; nonetheless, you should be aware of what programs are offered in your school, so that you can reinforce the skills students are learning when teachable moments arise.

Being able to resolve conflicts constructively is a key social-emotional skill that is the focus of numerous programs. There is great diversity in approaches, but generally the programs fall into two categories: those that train the entire student body in conflict resolution strategies and those that train a particular cadre of students to mediate disputes among their peers (Johnson & Johnson, 2004). An example of a program that targets the entire student body is Johnson and Johnson's *Teaching Students to be Peacemakers* (1995). The program spans grades 1 through 12; each year all students learn increasingly sophisticated negotiation and mediation procedures. Research conducted by Johnson and Johnson indicates that students trained in the peacemaker program are able to apply the negotiation and mediation procedures to a variety of conflicts—both in and out of the classroom. In addition, training results in fewer discipline problems that have to be managed by the teacher and the principal (Johnson & Johnson, 2004).

In a peer mediation program, selected students guide disputants through the problem-solving process. The advantage of using peers as mediators rather than adults is that students can frame disputes in a way that is age appropriate.

Generally working in pairs, mediators explain the ground rules for mediation and provide an opportunity for disputants to identify the problem from their differing perspectives, explain how they feel, brainstorm solutions, evaluate the advantages and disadvantages of each proposed solution, and select a course of action. These steps can be seen in the example of a peer mediation that appears in Figure 3.3.

Obviously, peer mediation is not an option when the conflict involves drugs, alcohol, theft, or violence, since these are criminal actions. But mediation *can* help to resolve disputes involving behavior such as gossiping, name calling, racial put-downs, and bullying, as well as conflicts over property (e.g., borrowing a book and losing it). Even then, mediation must be voluntary and confidential. In cases where school rules have been violated, mediation should not substitute for disciplinary action; rather, it can be offered as an opportunity to solve problems and "clear the air."

Curb Peer Harassment and Bullying

Efforts to promote prosocial behavior have to be matched with intolerance for antisocial behaviors that might threaten the safe and caring community. Every day, students suffer name calling, teasing, ridicule, humiliation, social exclusion, ostracism, and even physical injury at the hands of their peers. When this peer harassment is repeated over time (rather than being infrequent or incidental); is intended to cause harm, discomfort, or fear; and involves an imbalance in strength or power, it becomes *bullying* (Hyman, et al., 2006; Olweus, 2003). Boys bully other students more often than girls do, and their bullying tends to be physical. Girls typically use more subtle, "relational" bullying, such as excluding someone from the group and spreading rumors.

The problem of peer harassment and bullying is pervasive (although frequency rates vary a lot depending on the way bullying is measured). In one large-scale study of almost 16,000 students in grades 6 through 10 (Nansel, et al., 2001), about 30 percent of the sample reported moderate or frequent involvement in bullying. The primary targets tend to be girls who are unattractive, unstylish, or physically mature, and boys who don't fit the "stereotypic male mold" (Shakeshaft, et al., 1997). Especially at risk are teens who are lesbian, gay, bisexual, and transgender (LGBT). A study of school climate found that 86 percent of LGBT students had been verbally harassed during the past year, 44 percent had been physically harassed, and 22 percent had been physically assaulted (Kosciw, Diaz, & Greytak, 2008). Some 30 percent of LGBT students missed one class or one day of school in the past month because of feeling unsafe. In addition, almost 70 percent of teens frequently heard students say "that's so gay" or "you're so gay," where "gay" means something bad or devalued.

Despite its prevalence, teachers, counselors, and administrators generally underestimate the amount of bullying that exists in their schools. Barone (1997), for example, found that almost 60 percent of the students he surveyed reported having "been bothered by a bully or bullies" in middle school; in contrast, staff members believed that only 16 percent of the students had been victims of bullies.

Conflict: Billy and Juan sit next to each other during math class. While working independently on completing problems, Billy has the habit of humming as he figures out the equations. This makes it very difficult for Juan to concentrate and get his work done.

JUAN: Would you shut up with that humming?
BILLY: (Humming louder) What, did someone say something?
JUAN: Seriously, I'm going to come over there and make you be quiet.
BILLY: I'd like to see you try.

Teacher overhears and asks the boys if they would like to go to mediation. They agree.

Mediation Step 1:   Introductions and Explanation of Rules

MEDIATOR 1:   [Introduces self and other Mediator] We will serve as your peer mediators. What are your names? (Boys respond and Mediator writes them on form.)
MEDIATOR 2:   We are not here to judge or punish you, but to simply help you work through your conflict. Everything we say here will be held in confidence, unless something discussed is illegal, harmful, or a sign of abuse.
MEDIATOR 1:   We need you both to agree to some rules before we begin. They are:
               1) Allow others to speak without interruption.
               2) Treat others with respect and avoid put-downs.
               3) Take responsibility and be willing to solve the problem.
MEDIATOR 2:   Do both of you agree to the rules? (If both agree, move on to Step 2.)

Mediation Step 2:   Listening and Understanding the Problem

MEDIATOR 1:   Juan, please tell us your side of the story.
JUAN: I was trying to work and this loser is humming so loud I can't think!
MEDIATOR 1:   Please be respectful and refrain from putting him down or calling names.
JUAN: Sorry. I was trying to work and he was humming *very* loud.
MEDIATOR 1:   His humming was disrupting your work. How does that make you feel?
JUAN: I'm really mad because it happens every day.
MEDIATOR 1:   You are angry because you feel that he is intentionally humming loudly.
MEDIATOR 2:   Billy, what is your side of the story?
BILLY: I was working and minding my own business, and yes, I was humming.
MEDIATOR 2:   How do you feel about this situation?
BILLY: I'm frustrated because Juan is so sensitive!
MEDIATOR 2:   You would like to keep humming and you think Juan is overreacting. Is this correct? (Billy agrees.) Is there anything else either one of you would like to say? (If yes, continue taking turns. If no, go to Step 3.)

Mediation Step 3:   Brainstorming Solutions

MEDIATOR 1:   You've both heard the other's side of the story. Think about what you could do to solve this problem now or in the future. We're going to write down all your ideas and we can decide what to do later. (Juan suggests he can ask Billy to stop humming in a nicer manner; Billy suggests he can change seats; Juan suggests he could wear earplugs; Billy says he can hum in his head.)
MEDIATOR 1:   Any other ideas? (If none, go to Step 4.)

Mediation Step 4:   Reaching an Agreement

MEDIATOR 2:   Let's look at all the solutions you both suggested. Which ones might help solve this conflict? (The boys decide that moving seats is impractical, and it is unfair that Juan would have to wear earplugs. Juan suggests, and Billy agrees, that Billy should hum in his head, and Juan will remind him if he gets loud enough to be a distraction.)
MEDIATOR 2:   Is this conflict solved? (If both boys agree yes, they sign an agreement on the Peer Mediation form. If they disagree, they go back to Step 3 for more solutions.) Thank you for being willing to work out your conflict. We will check back with you in a few days to see how your new solution is working.

Figure 3.3   Peer Mediation Script

Unfortunately, even when teachers are aware of bullying, they do not always intervene, or they intervene in a minimal manner. A student in one study commented, "For name-calling, they'll [teachers] just say, 'I don't want to hear that,' and then that's it. They really don't do anything else. . . . I wish teachers would stop it right away; even if they hear only one thing" (Shakeshaft, et al., 1997, p. 25).

One reason for the lack of intervention may be the perception that bullying is "quasi-acceptable" (Hoover & Oliver, 2008). Bullies can be popular, and their behavior is often dismissed as normal. When the bullies are males, for example, it is not uncommon for adults to comment that "boys will be boys." Indeed, almost one-third of teachers in the United States perceive bullying as "normative behavior" that victims must learn to resolve (Hyman, et al., 2006). Another reason for not intervening may be the fact that a lot of peer harassment and bullying takes place in hallways and in the lunchroom, places where teachers may feel they don't have jurisdiction.

Taking peer harassment seriously and intervening to stop it—wherever it occurs— is crucial if teachers are to build safer, more caring classrooms. You need to be alert to hurtful comments about race and ethnicity, body size, disabilities, sexual orientation, unfashionable or eccentric dress, use of languages other than English, and socioeconomic status. You need to make it clear that disrespectful speech and slurs—even when used in a joking manner—are absolutely unacceptable. Stephen Wessler, director of the Center for the Prevention of Hate Violence at the University of Southern Maine, urges teachers to respond immediately to instances of peer harassment:

> Whether in the hallway or the classroom, teachers must speak up when students use degrading language or stereotypes. In a busy hallway, these interventions can be short. Making eye contact with a student and saying, "I heard that," "We don't talk like that here," or "That word is hurtful" sends the message that bias-motivated slurs and jokes are not acceptable. These low-key interventions break the pattern of escalation and stop some students from continuing to use degrading words. They also model for students what they can do to interrupt hurtful language themselves. And finally, when teachers speak up, they send a message of hope to those students who constantly hear slurs but feel that no one cares. (Wessler, 2008, p. 47)

Since much peer harassment and bullying occurs out of teachers' sight and hearing, it is important to teach students how to "stand up and speak up" when they witness unacceptable behavior (Wessler, 2008). Robert Marzano and colleagues (2005) suggest three simple rules for students to adopt to prevent bullying among students: (1) We will not bully other students. (2) We will help others who are being bullied by speaking out and getting adult help. (3) We will use extra effort to include all students in activities at our school. Some schools actually have students sign an anti-bullying pledge. (See Figure 3.4.)

It's also important to help students understand what behaviors constitute peer harassment and bullying. For example, teasing is the most frequent bullying behavior at all ages, but it can be difficult for students to draw the line between playful exchanges and hurtful harassment. During one discussion with Christina, she related a story that illustrated the pain that "friendly" teasing can cause.

This year I've got a freshman named Anita in one of my classes. Last year, I had her boyfriend, who's a junior. He's been in a lot of trouble; last year he was arrested. But he's been doing a really good job of turning his life

---

We, the students of the _____ school district, agree to join together to stop bullying.

BY SIGNING THIS PLEDGE I AGREE TO:

- Treat others respectfully.
- Try to include those who are left out.
- Refuse to bully others.
- Refuse to watch, laugh or join in when someone is being bullied.
- Tell an adult.
- Help those who are being bullied.

Signed by

_____

Date

_____

Figure 3.4   Anti-Bullying Pledge
Source: Harrison, 2005.

around. Anyway, one day I heard kids teasing Anita about him. They'd ask if he was on house arrest, or if he was in jail again. She looked unhappy about it, but she didn't say anything to me. After class, I told her that I had heard what the kids were saying, and I asked how she felt about it. She indicated that she didn't like it, but she didn't want to make a "big deal." She said she didn't want to get them in trouble. I offered to talk to the other kids—without indicating that I had spoken with her. I told her I'd make it clear that she hadn't asked me to intervene. The next day, I took the kids aside—there were two boys specifically—and said I had overheard them saying these things to Anita, and that I didn't think it was appropriate. They said they were "only teasing." I told them, "But teasing can hurt." I said that from the expression on Anita's face, it was clear that she didn't think it was funny. They looked surprised—as if they just hadn't given it any thought before. They promised to stop it, and they did.

Whether an exchange represents teasing or friendly banter may have to do with the social level or popularity of the individuals involved (Hoover & Oliver, 2008). If a higher-status student mocks a lower-status student, the exchange is likely to be seen as an attack. Teasing someone of the same status is more likely to be interpreted as playful. Here are some other guidelines (adapted from Hoover & Oliver, 2008) about teasing to help your students understand what is and isn't appropriate:

- Ask if teasing about a certain topic is hurtful and don't tease about that topic.
- Watch for body language that conveys that teasing bothers someone.
- Stand up for a student who is being teased.
- Speak up if teasing about a certain topic bothers you.
- Be careful about using humor, especially sarcasm.

- Avoid teasing someone you don't know well.
- Never tease people about sex, being a boy or girl, their bodies, or their family members.
- Refrain from teasing someone who seems to be having a bad day.
- Accept teasing that is meant in a friendly way.

To raise awareness, it's also useful to incorporate reflective activities into your curriculum whenever possible (Shakeshaft, et al., 1997). In literature classes, for example, students can read fiction that relates to the topic of harassment and bullying; in math classes, students can conduct surveys and analyze the results; in art classes, students can depict their feelings about name-calling and put-downs. In addition, students and faculty can work together to define the behaviors that are appropriate to inclusive, caring schools.

Be Alert for Instances of Cyber-Bullying

In the last few years, peer harassment and bullying have expanded from school grounds to cyberspace, as "cyber-bullies" use e-mail, cell phone text messages, instant messages, Web logs (blogs), and other social networking sites such as MySpace or Facebook to pursue their victims. For example, when eighth-grader Amanda Marcuson reported the fact that some of her classmates had stolen her makeup, she was immediately hounded by instant messages that began by calling her a tattletale and a liar and escalated to "increasingly ugly epithets" (Harmon, 2004). When 16-year-old Denise broke up with her boyfriend, he retaliated by posting her e-mail address and cell phone number on sex-oriented Web sites and blogs. For months, Denise was besieged with messages and calls that were embarrassing and frightening (Strom & Strom, 2005). And when a middle school student decided to do a survey on the top five "hated kids" in the sixth grade, he set up a Web site where students could vote (Lisante, 2005). Fortunately, the parents of one "winner" reported the survey to the principal, which prompted an in-school program on the damage that cyber-bullying can cause.

Online harassment is less visible to adults than "off-line" harassment, and adults who are unfamiliar and uncomfortable with the new technologies may have no sense of the nature or magnitude of the problem. At the same time, cyber-bullying can be vastly more humiliating to victims. Rumors, ridicule, embarrassing pictures, and hateful comments can be circulated among a huge number of peers with just a few clicks, and home no longer provides a safe haven from the taunting. Furthermore, youngsters may say things online they would never say in person, mainly because of the feeling of anonymity and the distance from the victim. As one student comments, "Over the Internet you don't really see their face or they don't see yours, and you don't have to look in their eyes and see they're hurt" (Leishman, 2002, cited in Shariff, 2004). Cyber-bullying also seems to have a particular appeal for girls, who prefer "relational aggression" rather than physical harassment and often try to avoid direct confrontation (Harmon, 2004).

Some strategies for dealing with cyber-bullying appear in the Practical Tips box.

PRACTICAL TIPS FOR

DEALING WITH CYBER-BULLYING

- Develop an explicit policy for acceptable in-school use of the Internet and include it in the school handbook (or your class rules). The policy should spell out what constitutes cyber-bullying and list consequences.

- Educate yourself about the technology tools used by your students. Don't give students the opportunity to exploit your ignorance.

- Make sure that students are aware that bullying will be dealt with seriously.

- Ensure that parents/guardians who express cyber-bullying concerns are taken seriously.

- Explain to students that they:
  - Should never share personal information online, such as address, school, or phone numbers.
  - Should not post identity-revealing photos of themselves online, or post photos of friends without their permission.
  - Should limit access to their online profiles (in Facebook or MySpace) to their friends, and be cautious about accepting friend requests, especially from people they don't know.
  - Should not delete messages; they do not have to read them, but they should show them to an adult they trust. Messages can be used to take action against cyber-bullies.
  - Should not open a message from someone they don't know.
  - Should *never* reply to the message.
  - Can block the sender's message if they are being bullied through e-mail or instant messaging.
  - Can forward the messages to their Internet service provider.
  - Should tell an adult.
  - Should show the message to the police if it contains physical threats.
  - Should speak out against cyber-bullying.
  - Should never send messages when they are angry.
  - Should never send messages they wouldn't want others to see.

- Make parents aware of the fact that all of the major Internet service providers offer some form of parental controls. For example, AOL has developed "AOL Guardian," which reports with whom youngsters exchange messages and what Web sites they visit, and monitors chat rooms for children 13 and under.

- Encourage parents to keep computers in a public room in the house.

- Invite members of the local police department to come to school to speak with parents and students about proper Internet use.

- Make sure ethics is included in any computer instruction given at your school.

Source: Adapted from Keith & Martin, 2005; Lisante, 2005; and the National Crime Prevention Council, 2009, at www.mcgruff.org.

Be Alert for Student-to-Student Sexual Harassment

On the way out of your classroom, a boy pats a girl on her bottom. She gives him an annoyed look and tells him to "quit it." Another girl comes to you in tears because a boy in the class is spreading stories about what they did on a date last weekend. You hear two girls in your class laughing and teasing a boy about what a "stud" he is. Are these instances of sexual harassment? And should you do anything about them?

Sexual harassment is generally defined as *unwanted and unwelcome sexual attention*. This includes a wide range of behaviors:

> leering, pinching, grabbing, suggestive verbal comments, pressure for sexual activity, spreading sexual rumors, making sexual or sexist jokes, pulling at another student's clothing, cornering or brushing up against a student in a sexual way, insulting comments referring to students' sexual orientation, date rape, sexual graffiti about a student, or engaging in other actions of a sexual manner that might create a hostile learning environment. (Hyman, 1997, p. 318)

Several studies (AAUW, 1993; National Council for Research on Women, 1994) have documented the fact that sexual harassment is an all too common occurrence in American high schools. One study, for example, found that 83 percent of girls and 60 percent of boys report unwanted sexual attention in school (Lee, Croninger, Linn, & Chen, 1996). And it's not a simple case of some students being perpetrators while others are victims: Over half of the students report that they have harassed their classmates *and* been harassed themselves.

It can sometimes be difficult for you—and your students—to distinguish between harmless flirting and sexual harassment. When you're faced with this situation, it's helpful to keep in mind the fact that whether harassment has occurred is truly in the "eye of the beholder." In other words, the determining factor is "how the person on the receiving end is affected by the behavior, not with what the other person means by the behavior" (Strauss & Espeland, 1992, p. 15). Kissing, touching, and flirting that the recipient likes or wants is *not* sexual harassment (although it may be inappropriate in school).

Our four teachers stress the importance of responding seriously when students complain that other students are making them feel "uncomfortable." Donnie tells about a first-year teacher in her school who failed to take action when a girl in his class complained that the boy sitting behind her kept touching her hair and "bothering" her:

 Her complaint was vague (I think she didn't want to spell out what was happening), and so even though she kept asking to be moved, he didn't do anything. He just kept saying she should ignore the boy or tell him to stop. Finally, the girl's mother e-mailed him, with a copy to the principal and the superintendent, saying that repeated requests to be moved had been ignored. It was a mess, but the teacher learned a good lesson: If kids are complaining that someone is bothering them, you have to take it seriously. People

need to feel comfortable in your classroom and they need to feel that they can trust you to keep them safe.

Given the importance of the recipient's feelings in determining whether sexual harassment has occurred, people can be nervous about whether signs of affection and compliments will be misunderstood. You can suggest that students ask themselves a few simple questions to guide their behavior (Strauss & Espeland, 1992):

Would I want my comments or behavior to appear in the newspaper or on TV?

Is this something I would say or do if my mother or father, girlfriend or boyfriend, sister or brother were present?

Is this something I would want someone else to say or do to my mother or father, girlfriend or boyfriend, sister or brother?

Is there a difference in power between me and the other person (e.g., in size or social status)?

In recent years, an increasing number of districts have written and distributed sexual harassment policies for both students and school personnel. These generally define sexual harassment, outline the procedures to follow when you learn about an incident of sexual harassment, and spell out the consequences. It's important that you obtain a copy of this policy and follow the specified procedures. Keep in mind that the Supreme Court has ruled that school districts can be found liable if they are "deliberately indifferent" to information about "severe, pervasive, and objectively offensive" harassment among students (Walsh, 1999).

A CAUTIONARY TALE

Building a caring classroom community is not an easy task, especially for secondary teachers who see students for such a limited amount of time. This lesson was brought home to us during a meeting in which Sandy ruefully described an incident that had just occurred in her classroom. We relate the incident here, not to discourage you, but to acknowledge the reality that building community is challenging work.

 My kids were going over homework, and they were in groups of three. I picked the groups. In one group, I had a girl who happens to be an honors student and a boy who had to be convinced to take chemistry. They finished reviewing the homework pretty quickly. Another group was in need of assistance, so I suggested that they get help from the first group. Mitchell, one of the kids in the second group, called over to the girl—the honors student—to come and help them. So Ryan—the kid who had to be convinced to take chemistry—says, "Wait a minute. Why did you just ask *her*, not *us*? Do you think we're stupid?"

Then he turns around to me and says, "See, Mrs. K., that's why I didn't want to take chemistry. Because all the smart kids know who they are and they know who's stupid. They think that kids who haven't done well in school could never do well in chemistry."

I'm standing there thinking, "How do I get out of this one? What do I say?" I had watched it all unfold in front of me. And 24 pairs of eyes are looking at me. Finally I said, "Well, I guess you certainly fooled *them*." I wish you could have seen it. Ryan's chest puffed up, and he says to Mitchell, "*Lucy's* not going to help you; *I'm* going to help you."

Here I thought that we had created a cohesive community, and then I find out there are all these little subgroups. The kids have these perceptions of one another, and they become barriers between them. Mitchell's perception was that Lucy would be best at explaining. Ryan's perception was that Mitchell thinks he's stupid. I'm always trying to demonstrate that people have multiple intelligences, multiple talents. I have them working in all these cooperative learning groups, and still, there are these barriers. *But I'll just keep trying to knock them down.*

CONCLUDING COMMENTS

Alfie Kohn (1996) suggests that it would be helpful if we all reflected on "what makes school awful sometimes" (p. 114). Then we might be more inclined to make sure that those kinds of experiences and situations don't happen for students in our classrooms. We recently followed his advice. With our students, we reminisced about the awful times we had experienced. Here are some of our students' memories:

> *As a high school junior, I took Algebra II and Trigonometry. Although I was a good student, the teacher and I did not hit it off for some reason. . . . Midyear, we had an exam on logarithms. I thought I understood it, but I made the same mistake reading the log charts for every problem and I failed the test. I came into class the next day thinking I had done OK on the test. The teacher held up my exam in front of the class and gloated that he had failed me. I hated going to that class for the rest of the year, and I hated that teacher for humiliating me.*

> *School was awful for me when I was switched from second track to first track in Spanish. . . . I wanted to be in that class because I wanted those students to like me and not think I was a dork. However, the guidance counselor went behind my back and called my parents. He did not inform them that I did not want to switch so they said it was OK. I did not even get a chance to talk to them before they switched my schedule. I felt powerless and betrayed.*

> *When I was a sophomore in high school, one of the girls would follow me around and torment me, call me names, and threaten to hurt*

me.... None of my teachers or any authority figure ever helped. I'm still curious why she hated me so much.

The worst was in junior high. . . . I was made fun of by the other girls, girls with whom I had been friends the year before. . . . I was tormented for not having money or clothes and for having a conscience (and by that I mean not breaking the law or hurting other people's feelings). It was the first year I didn't like going to school.

As a content-specialist eager to focus on academic instruction, you may be reluctant to put aside time to build caring relationships among students—especially in the era of high-stakes testing and pressure for academic excellence. And there is no doubt: Building a caring community takes time, especially in schools and classrooms where there are a lot of alienated, untrusting students. You obviously need to think about what is possible in your own situation, but remember—the time you take to build community will eventually lead not only to a more harmonious classroom, but also to greater motivation, academic engagement, and achievement (Watson & Battistich, 2006).

> ## Pause and Reflect
>
> For too many students, school is a place where they feel humiliated, threatened, ridiculed, powerless, and betrayed. Think about when school was awful for *you*. If you can keep those times in mind and try to ensure that they never happen to your students, you will be well on your way to creating a safer, more caring community.

Summary

This chapter began by discussing the key role that positive teacher-student relationships play in classroom management. The chapter then considered ways of showing students that you care about them and ways of building caring relationships among students.

Ways of Showing Care and Respect

- Be welcoming.
- Learn about students' lives.
- Be sensitive to students' concerns.
- Establish and enforce clear expectations for behavior.
- Be fair.
- Welcome students' input.
- Be a real person (as well as a teacher).
- Become aware of adolescent culture.
- Promote autonomy.
- Be inclusive.
- Search for students' strengths.
- Develop communication skills:

  - Attending and acknowledging
  - Active listening

- Open-ended questioning
- Problem solving
- Be careful about touching.
- Ask the students.

Building Caring Relationships among Students

- Model and recognize prosocial behavior.
- Provide opportunities for students to get to know one another.
- Hold class meetings.
- Use cooperative learning groups.
- Teach social-emotional skills.
- Curb peer harassment and bullying.
- Be alert for instances of cyber-bullying.
- Be alert for student-to-student sexual harassment.

Content-area specialists are often reluctant to take time away from academic instruction in order to focus on building community. Remember, time you take to build community will pay off in terms of a harmonious, respectful classroom and increased motivation and achievement.

ACTIVITIES FOR SKILL–BUILDING AND REFLECTION

In Class

1. Think about the teachers you had in middle and high school. Select one teacher who showed caring to students and one teacher who did not. Write a paragraph on each teacher, providing details and examples to illustrate what each teacher actually did. Share these in small groups.

2. In the following bits of conversation, students have confided in teachers about problems they are experiencing, and the teachers have responded in ways *not* suggested in this chapter. Provide a new response for each case, using the communication skills discussed in this chapter: acknowledging, active listening, asking open-ended questions, and problem solving.

> STUDENT: My parents won't allow me to go visit my boyfriend at college for the weekend. They say they trust me, but then they don't show it!
>
> TEACHER: Well, I'm sure they have your best interests at heart. You know, you really shouldn't gripe. After all, a lot of kids don't have parents who care about them. I see a lot of kids whose parents let them do anything they want. Maybe you think you'd like that, but I'm sure you wouldn't. . . .
>
> STUDENT: I can't stand my stepmother. She's always criticizing me and making me come home right after school to watch my sister, and making me feel really stupid.
>
> TEACHER: Oh, come on now, Cinderella. I'm sure it's not that bad.

STUDENT: My parents want me to go to college, but I really want to join the Marines. What do you think I should do?

TEACHER: Do what your folks say. Go to college. You can always join the Marines later.

On Your Own

1. Interview a few middle school or high school students about their definitions of caring teachers. Ask them to identify the ways in which teachers show caring to students.

2. Do some planning for the first week of school. First, think about how you will introduce yourself to your students. What will you tell them about yourself? Second, plan a way of showing students that you welcome their input. (Will you have students verbally share their suggestions and opinions about rules, lessons, assignments, or grouping? Write a letter to you? Answer specific questions?) Third, plan an introductory activity designed to help students become acquainted.

3. Visit a middle school or high school classroom that you have never been in before. Record your immediate thoughts when you walked into the room about how it feels to be a student in that room. Observe the class for a little while and jot down any ways that the teacher is promoting a safe and caring community, as well as your ongoing impressions about the tone of the classroom.

For Your Portfolio

Document the ways in which you work (or will work) to establish positive relationships with and among students. Include artifacts such as welcoming letters to students, lesson plans on conflict resolution, and getting to know you activities.

FOR FURTHER READING

Bondy, E., & Ross, D. D. (2008). The teacher as warm demander. *Educational Leadership, 66*(1), 54–58.

Teachers who are "warm demanders" demonstrate their caring for students by deliberately building relationships, learning about students' cultures, and communicating an expectation of success. Then they "relentlessly insist on two things": that students treat the teacher and one another respectfully, and that they complete the academic tasks necessary for successful futures.

Building classroom relationships. (2003). *Educational Leadership, 61*(1).

The entire September 2003 issue is devoted to this very important topic. Issues addressed include how to win students' hearts and minds, giving students what they need, personalizing schools, practicing democracy in high school, combating verbal harrassment , and building relationships with challenging children.

Creating caring schools. (2003). Theme issue of *Educational Leadership, 60*(6).

This entire issue of *Educational Leadership* is devoted to the topic of creating caring schools. Topics include bullying, teasing, creating community, social-emotional learning programs, student-led class meetings, collaborative learning, racial and ethnic tolerance.

Hoover, J. H., & Oliver, R. O. (2008). *The bullying prevention handbook: A guide for principals, teachers, and counselors* (2nd ed.). Bloomington, IN: Solution Tree.

The authors present an overview of bullying, along with ideas for bullying intervention, anti-bullying educational campaigns, and working with families to prevent bullying. This second edition includes new chapters on cyber-bullying and bullying of LGBT students. The book includes sample assessments to track anti-bullying efforts, and classroom activities and handouts designed to foster positive relationships among students and help them appreciate diversity.

Rodriguez, L. F. (2005). Yo, Mister! *Educational Leadership, 62*(7), 78–80.

Written by a teacher in an alternative urban high school, this article emphasizes the importance of positive teacher-student relationships. Rodriguez shows how he tries to acknowledge students as people, legitimize their knowledge and experiences, and engage with them personally and intellectually.

Sapon-Shevin, M. (2008). Learning in an inclusive community. *Educational Leadership, 66*(1), 49–53.

The author defines an inclusive classroom as one in which teachers acknowledge all the ways that students differ from each other, value this diversity, and design and implement sensitive responses. The article concludes with ten strategies to create a positive, inclusive classroom.

Stipek, D. (2006). Relationships matter. *Educational Leadership, 64*(1), 46–49.

Stipek argues that an era of high-stakes testing and accountability may be producing classroom conditions that undermine student learning. When teachers must focus their energies on preparing students for the test, they have less time to get to know students personally or make them feel valued, respected, and supported. The author reviews research showing that strong teacher-student relationships are crucial to student academic achievement at all grade levels, and provides suggestions for both classroom and schoolwide strategies that build strong student-teacher relationships.

ORGANIZATIONAL RESOURCES

The Anti-Defamation League (ADL), 823 United Nations Plaza, New York, NY 10017 (www.adl.org; 1-800-343-5540). Dedicated to combating anti-Semitism, hate crime, and bigotry through programs, services, and materials. (The *ADL Material Resource Catalog* is a wealth of resources, including lesson plans, curriculum guides, and lists of children's books.)

Collaborative for Academic, Social, and Emotional Learning (CASEL), Department of Psychology (M/C 285), University of Illinois at Chicago, 1007 West Harrison St., Chicago, IL 60607 (312-413-1008; www.casel.org). Dedicated to the development of children's social and emotional competencies and the capacity of schools, parents, and communities to support that development. CASEL's mission is to establish integrated, evidence-based social and emotional learning (SEL) from preschool through high school.

GroundSpark, 2180 Bryant St., Suite 203, San Francisco, CA 94110 (http://groundspark .org; 1-800-405-3322). Committed to a more just world, GroundSpark produces and distributes films and educational resources on issues ranging from environmental concerns to affordable housing to preventing prejudice. The Respect for All Project (RFAP), their landmark program, seeks to create safe, hate-free schools and communities. *Let's Get Real* is a film and curriculum guide on name-calling and bullying in middle school.

The Southern Poverty Law Center, 400 Washington Avenue, Montgomery, AL 36104 (www.teachingtolerance.org, 334-956-8200). The Teaching Tolerance project provides teachers at all levels with ideas and free resources for building community, fighting bias, and celebrating diversity.

CHAPTER 4

ESTABLISHING NORMS FOR BEHAVIOR

Middle and high school teachers sometimes contend that their students know how to behave, since they've been in school for many years. The argument goes like this:

> *My kids aren't babies. By middle or high school, students know the importance of coming to class on time, doing homework, respecting other people's property, and raising their hands to make a comment. Besides, there's so much material to cover, I can't waste time teaching rules to kids who should already know all this stuff.*

This reasoning has a certain appeal, particularly for teachers who are enthusiastic about their content area and eager to get started. Yet it's important to recognize that although your students have general notions about appropriate school behavior, they do not know *your specific expectations*. Your students probably see five different teachers each day, and specific expectations vary from class to class. A student's first-period teacher may not mind if everyone is milling around the room when the bell rings, while the second-period teacher insists that students be in their seats. In third period, the teacher wants students to put homework in the upper right-hand corner of their desks, but the fourth-period teacher has students drop homework in a basket at the front of the room.

Students need to know your specific expectations of behavior

What will *you* expect with regard to basic classroom routines like these—and how will your students know what to do if you don't tell them? It is unfair to keep students guessing about the behaviors you expect, and as we discussed in Chapter 3, it's actually an act of caring to explain your classroom norms to students. Not knowing the norms for appropriate behavior causes insecurity and misunderstandings, even among "school smart" adolescents. In contrast, *clearly defined classroom rules and routines help to create an environment that is predictable and comprehensible.*

Clear expectations for behavior have another major benefit. As Chapter 1 emphasized, classes are crowded, public, unpredictable places in which individuals engage in a variety of activities, often within the time constraints of a 42- or 45-minute period. *Clear rules and routines minimize confusion and prevent the loss of instructional time.* They enable you to carry out "housekeeping" tasks (e.g., taking attendance, distributing materials) smoothly and efficiently, almost automatically. They free you and your students to concentrate on the real tasks of teaching and learning.

This chapter describes research that demonstrates the importance of rules and routines. We then consider some principles to guide you in establishing rules for your own classrooms. We'll also learn how Donnie, Christina, Sandy, and Fred introduce rules and routines to their students and what they think about this central task of classroom management.

RESEARCH ON EFFECTIVE CLASSROOM MANAGEMENT

Prior to 1970, teacher preparation programs could offer only limited advice about classroom management to beginning teachers. Teacher educators shared useful "tricks of the trade" (e.g., flick the lights on and off for quiet), stressed the importance of firmness and consistency, and warned prospective teachers not to smile until Christmas. But research identifying the behaviors of effective managers was unavailable, and it was simply not clear why some classrooms function smoothly and others are chaotic.

That situation began to change in 1970, with the publication of Jacob Kounin's study of orderly and disorderly classrooms. In an effort to explain the differences, Kounin (1970) set out to compare teachers' methods of responding to misbehavior. To his surprise, he found that the reactions of good classroom managers were not substantially different from the reactions of poor classroom managers. What *did* differ were the strategies that teachers used to *prevent* misbehavior. Effective classroom managers constantly monitored students' behavior. They displayed what Kounin called *withitness:* They were aware of what was happening in all parts of the room, and they communicated this awareness to students. They also exhibited an ability to *overlap*—to do more than one thing at a time—certainly a desirable skill in a setting where so many events occur simultaneously! Furthermore, effective managers kept lessons moving at a brisk pace, so that there was little opportunity for students to become inattentive and disruptive.

Kounin's work led researchers to wonder how effective managers began the school year, and a series of studies was launched to investigate this topic. One project (Evertson & Emmer, 1982) involved observations of 26 mathematics teachers and 25 English teachers in junior high schools in an urban district. Each teacher was observed teaching two different classes. During the first three weeks of school, researchers observed extensively in each classroom and kept detailed records of what occurred. During the rest of the academic year, each teacher was observed once every three to four weeks (in both of his or her classrooms). On the basis of these latter data, the researchers identified six more and six less effective managers in mathematics and seven more and seven less effective managers in English. They then went back to the information collected at the beginning of the year and compared what the teachers had done during the first three weeks of school. Striking differences were apparent—even on the very first day of school!

Among the major differences was the way teachers handled rules and procedures. Although all of the teachers had expectations for behavior, and they all took time to present or discuss these with students, the more effective managers were more successful in *teaching* the rules and procedures. For example, the more effective teachers were more likely to distribute handouts stating their behavioral expectations or to have students copy them into their notebooks. They were also clearer and much more explicit about behaviors that are likely to cause problems—namely, those that occur frequently and that may vary from teacher to teacher (e.g., call-outs, movement through the room, student–student interaction, hand raising). Interestingly, for behaviors that occur infrequently per period (e.g., tardiness, bringing materials) and are fairly straightforward, no differences between the two groups of teachers were apparent.

Subsequent research has confirmed the importance of explicitly teaching students your expectations for their behavior. In one study, researchers videotaped two experienced and two inexperienced junior high school teachers (two in math and two in science) as they met with their classes for the very first time (Brooks, 1985). The contrast between the experienced and inexperienced math teachers is especially vivid.

The experienced math teacher, perceived by students and administrators as exceptionally clear and organized, began her presentation of behavioral expectations by distributing a copy of class rules that students were to keep in their folders. She first discussed schoolwide policies, but spent most of the time on classroom standards—how to enter the class, how to use materials, how to interact with the teacher and other students, what to do in the case of an emergency, and how to exit the class. In general, *she stated a rule, explained the rationale, provided an example of an appropriate behavior, and concluded with the consequences for noncompliance.* Interestingly, she rarely smiled during her presentation of rules and procedures (although she smiled a lot during her later introduction to the course). She spoke in a businesslike tone and continually scanned the classroom; no instances of disruption were observed during her presentation.

In contrast, the inexperienced math teacher was rambling and disorganized. Students were not given a copy of the rules, nor were they encouraged to write them down. Even as the teacher presented rules and procedures about talking in class, she tolerated students talking to each other. In addition, she repeatedly smiled during her presentation of the consequences for misbehavior, a nonverbal behavior that seems incompatible with a discussion of detention and calling home (and might have sent the message that she was not serious about imposing these consequences).

As the following excerpt from the transcript illustrates, the inexperienced math teacher provided few examples or rationales. In fact, she *never* used the experienced teacher's sequence of rule-rationale-example-consequence. Although many of the rules resembled those of the experienced math teacher, she presented rules she could not enforce (wanting students to respect all teachers), and she omitted discussion of some fundamental rules (listening while the teacher is talking). Furthermore, the rules did not appear to be prioritized or organized in any way:

> OK. I'm just going to tell you a few of my classroom rules. And, ah, so that you'll know these. The first thing I want you to know is I want, that I expect every student will obey any school policies that there are. . . . OK, all the school policies, if you haven't gotten it as of yet you will get it, this yellow sheet. It's got all the school policies on it. It explains everything to you. These apply in school and around school. . . . OK, another thing when you come in that door I expect you to walk through that door being prepared to start class. When you come in don't plan on going back out to get something out of your locker. . . . OK, when you come in you'll have a pencil, your paper, your folders, and a book. . . . OK, if you're fast at working you might bring something extra to do after you finish your work so that you can have something to keep you busy because I don't want any talking. . . . OK, and all times we'll use pencil . . . I don't want any ink on your homework papers or test papers. It should all be done in pencil . . . OK, we'll also have a folder that we'll do and I'll tell you about it later . . . OK, another thing is I expect you to be respectful. First, I want you to respect yourself, at all times respect yourself and then your classmates and also the teachers. Any teacher in the building should be respected by you and each student and if you see one anything they say goes. (Brooks, 1985, pp. 67–68)

Reading this transcript, it's impossible not to feel sympathy for this inexperienced teacher. After all, most beginning teachers, particularly those being observed, are nervous on the first day of school. But it is precisely *because* of this nervousness that you must (1) think about your expectations ahead of time and (2) plan the way you will present them to your students. Let's look at each of these steps separately.

DEFINING YOUR EXPECTATIONS FOR BEHAVIOR

Before the first student enters your classroom, you need to think about your expectations for behavior. Not only do you need to decide on *norms for students' general conduct* (commonly referred to as classroom rules), you also need to identify the *behavioral routines or procedures* that you and your students will follow in specific situations. For example, when students arrive at your classroom door, are they to go immediately to their seats, or may they congregate in small groups

[handwritten margin note: Think before you give presentation rules/regulations]

and socialize until you tell them to be seated? May they go to the storage cabinet and get the projects they've been working on, or should they wait for you to give out the projects one by one? When students need paper or rulers or protractors for an assignment, will they get them by themselves, will you have students distribute the materials, or will you distribute them yourself? If students have to leave your classroom to go to their lockers or to the library, must they have a pass? When students are working at their seats, may they help one another or must they work individually?

Because these seem like such trivial, mundane issues, it is easy to underestimate their contribution to classroom order. But lessons can fall apart while you try to decide how to distribute paper, and students feel anxious if they're unsure whether answering a classmate's question during an in-class assignment is considered helping or cheating. As we will see, rules and routines may vary from class to class, but no class can function smoothly without them.

PAUSE AND REFLECT

We have distinguished between norms for general conduct (*rules*) and the procedures that students will follow in specific situations (*routines*). In order to make sure that you grasp the distinction, consider the following expectations. For each one, decide if it is a rule or a routine: (1) At the end of the period, students are to wait until you tell them class is over before beginning to pack up. (2) Students are to be prepared. (3) Listen respectfully when people are talking. (4) Students are to turn in homework at the beginning of class in the basket for their class period. (5) During small-group work, students may talk quietly with their group members. We will review this list later in the chapter.

Planning Norms for General Conduct

Effective classroom managers typically have four or five general rules for student conduct (Akin-Little, Little, & Laniti, 2007). These describe the behaviors that are necessary if your classroom is to be a good place in which to live and work—for example, "come prepared," "follow directions," and "respect others." In Christina's class, the norms are contained in a "newspaper" that Christina writes and distributes on the first day of class. Here are some of her basic rules:

- **Respect every member of the class by using appropriate language, by paying attention when another person is speaking, and by raising [your] hand to speak.**
- **Complete all assignments on time and to the best of [your] ability.**
- **Come to class on time and be in [your] seat when the bell rings.**

As you reflect on rules for your own classroom, there are four guidelines to keep in mind. These are summarized in Table 4.1. First, *rules should be reasonable and necessary.* Think about the age and characteristics of the students you are teaching, and ask yourself what rules are appropriate for them. For example, it would be unreasonable to expect students to enter the classroom without greeting one another and chatting. Given adolescents' irresistible desire to interact, creating such a rule would only result in resentment, frustration, and subterfuge. It's far

TABLE 4.1 Four Guidelines for Planning Classroom Rules

Guideline	Questions to Think About
1. Rules should be reasonable and necessary.	What rules are appropriate for this grade level? Is there a good reason for the rule?
2. Rules need to be clear and understandable.	Is the rule too abstract for students to comprehend? To what extent do I want my students to participate in the decision-making process?
3. Rules should be consistent with instructional goals and with what we know about how people learn.	Will this rule facilitate or hinder students' learning?
4. Classroom rules need to be consistent with school rules.	What are the school rules? Are particular behaviors required in the halls, cafeteria, during assemblies, etc.? What is school policy with respect to electronic devices such as cell phones?

more sensible to establish a rule like "talk quietly," which specifies *how* the talk is to occur.

Also ask yourself whether each rule is necessary. Is there a compelling reason for it? Will it make the classroom a more pleasant place to be? Will it increase students' opportunity to learn? Can you explain the rationale to students, and will they accept it? Sandy stresses the importance of this guideline when she comments:

> **Rules have to have reasons. For example, one of my rules is about coming to class on time. Students know they'll get detention if they're late—even once. At the beginning of the year, students think I'm unnecessarily strict about that. But I'm not trying to be mean. I want students there on time because I always start class when the bell rings, and if they're not there, they miss important material. After a while, they begin to realize there's a real reason for the rule. I hear them say to their friends, "I have to get to class on time because they'll have started."**

Contrast this situation with that of a biology teacher we know who insists that students take notes in black pen only. Although the teacher is able to enforce the rule, she's unable to explain it with any conviction, and her classes perceive it as arbitrary and ridiculous. Similarly, an English teacher insists that students use cursive writing during spelling and vocabulary tests. Even to her student teacher, this seems like a unreasonable rule:

> *Being a printer myself whose cursive has not improved beyond the third grade, I am not a fan of mandated cursive writing. In the real world whenever I have filled out a form, I have been required to print so the words are legible to the reader. The only time cursive is required*

is when I sign my name and for vocabulary tests in my cooperating teacher's class. I can see why students are sometimes annoyed with our rules.

If rule would apply to you make it more reasonable.

It's easier to demonstrate that a rule is reasonable and necessary if it applies to *you* as well as your students. Although some rules may be intended only for students (e.g., raise your hand to speak), others are relevant for everyone (e.g., show respect for other people and their property). Sandy tells us, "If a rule is important for kids, it's important for you too. For example, I make sure that I get to class on time, and if I'm late, I owe them an explanation." Fred echoes this idea when he observes, "I try to make it clear to my students that we *all* have to follow the rules. After all, rules are not about power; they're what make civilized life possible."

Rules need to be clear & understandable

Second, *rules need to be clear and understandable.* Because rules are often stated in very general terms ("be polite"), they may be too abstract to have much meaning. When planning your rules, you need to think of specific examples to discuss with students. For example, one of Donnie's basic rules is "Be prepared." She makes sure that "preparation" is spelled out in precise, concrete behaviors: "Class preparation consists of having your homework, notebook, pen or pencil, and a covered textbook with you each day."

Some teachers believe that rules are more understandable and more meaningful when students are allowed to participate in the decision-making process. Participation, especially at higher grade levels, may increase students' willingness to "buy into" the rules, may make them more invested in seeing that rules are followed, and may help to prepare students for adult life. At the middle-school level, some teachers begin by asking students what their "hopes and dreams" are for that class (e.g., "What are your most important hopes and dreams for math this year? What would you really like to accomplish?"). Students then reflect on what they will need—from others as well as from themselves—in order to fulfill these hopes and dreams. Generating ideas for rules comes next. (For detailed information on this approach, see *Rules in School* by Brady, Forton, Porter, and Wood, 2003.)

As a beginning teacher, you may feel more comfortable presenting rules you have developed yourself. In fact, despite their many years of experience, neither Donnie, Sandy, nor Fred allows students to create classroom rules. They do, however, discuss the rationales for the rules they have established, and they solicit examples from students. If you do decide to involve your students in developing a list of norms for your classroom, you need to think carefully ahead of time about the norms that are important to you, and make sure those are on the final list. Also, be aware that this process might result in a different set of rules for each class period, and you will probably want to shape the students' lists so they can apply to all your classes.

 PAUSE AND REFLECT

Take a moment to reflect on the idea of having students generate the rules. Did any of your own secondary teachers ever use this approach? What do you see as the benefits? If you were to do this, what would you have to keep in mind and what pitfalls might you need to plan for?

A third guideline to keep in mind when planning classroom norms is that *rules should be consistent with instructional goals and with what we know about how people learn.* The first chapter discussed the principles underlying this book. One principle was that the need for order should not supersede the need for meaningful instruction. As you develop rules for your classroom, think about whether they will *facilitate or hinder the learning process.* For example, in the pursuit of order, some teachers prohibit talking during in-class assignments, and others refrain from using cooperative learning activities for fear that students will be too rowdy. Obviously, such restrictions are necessary at times (e.g., you may want students to work alone on a particular assignment so you can assess each student's comprehension of the material). It would be sad, however, if restrictions like this became the status quo. Educational psychologists who study the ways children learn stress the importance of their interaction. Much of this thinking is based on the work of the Soviet psychologist Lev Vygotsky, who believed that children's intellectual growth is fostered through collaboration with adults who serve as coaches and tutors and with more capable peers (Wertsch, 1985). Interestingly, studies on the use of small groups indicates that these interactions benefit the *tutor* as well as the person being tutored. Researchers found, for example, that junior high school students who provided explanations for their peers showed increased achievement themselves (Webb, 1985). Given the important role that interaction plays in young people's learning and cognitive development, it seems sensible not to eliminate interaction, but to spend time teaching students how to interact in ways that are appropriate. (We'll address this topic more fully in Chapter 10.)

Finally, *classroom rules need to be consistent with school rules.* The importance of this guideline can be illustrated by an excerpt from a student teacher's recent journal entry:

> *The first week of school I ejected a student from the room and told him he couldn't come back into the class until he had a note from his parents. Not only was the student back in class the next day without a note, but I was informed that (1) I was in violation of the school code when I ejected the student, and (2) only homeroom teachers communicate directly with the parents.*

Your school may hold an orientation meeting for new teachers where school rules, policies, and procedures are explained. In particular, find out about behaviors that are expected during assemblies, in the cafeteria and library, and in the hallways. You should also learn about the administrative tasks for which you are responsible (e.g., taking attendance, collecting field trip money, supervising fire drills, recording tardiness). If there is a school handbook, be sure to get a copy and use it as a guide for establishing your own rules and routines.

You also need to know if you are supposed to review the handbook with students. For example, Fred's students receive a booket explaining the school's "Rules, Regulations, and Policies," and teachers go over it with their first-period classes. The handbook addresses topics such as lateness, absenteeism, smoking, substance abuse, leaving school grounds, bias incidents, use of cell phones, MP3 players, and other electronics, fighting and physical assault, and possession of weapons. After reviewing the handbook, students sign a statement indicating that they agree to abide by the rules. The statement is then returned to the main office.

Reviewing the handbook with his students allows Fred to explain how his classroom rules and routines jibe with those of the school:

> OK, as you can see, the school rule is that you have to bring a note when you return to school after an absence. Let's talk about this a little more. When you're absent, it's your responsibility to call someone in class and make up the activity. So before you leave school today, get someone's phone number. [He smiles.] Try to get someone who is as smart or smarter than you. [The students laugh. He continues.] OK. With respect to lateness, the school rule is "Don't be late." If you're late three times, there's a penalty. I watch the lates pretty carefully, so I'll warn you if I think you're getting in trouble. Now, about cutting. I can't teach you if you're not in my class. [He speaks slowly and with emphasis.] *If you cut my class, I take it personally.* Now I'm a human being. I realize there are times when you need to not be here; you have to go to the bathroom or the library. But you need to come and ask and get a pass. If you don't, that's a cut. *And I'm death on that one. So don't cut.*

Planning Routines for Specific Situations

So many different activities occur in classrooms that trying to define behavior for specific situations can be daunting. Researchers at the Learning Research and Development Center at the University of Pittsburgh observed the behavior of effective classroom managers and categorized the routines they used (Leinhardt, Weidman, & Hammond, 1987). We have adapted their three-category system to provide you with a way of thinking about routines for your own classroom.

Class-Running Routines

These are *nonacademic routines* that enable you to keep the classroom running smoothly. This category of routines includes *administrative duties* (taking attendance, recording tardiness, distributing school notices), *procedures for student movement* (entering the room at the beginning of the period; leaving the room at the end of the period; leaving the room to go to the nurse, the library, or lockers; fire drills; moving around the room to sharpen pencils or get materials), and *housekeeping routines* (cleaning lab tables, watering plants, maintaining storage for materials used by everyone).

Without clear, specific class-running routines, these activities can consume a significant part of the school day. Research on the way time is used in fifth-grade classrooms has indicated that, on the average, these activities (transition, waiting, housekeeping) consume almost 20 percent of the time spent in the classroom—more than the amount of time spent in mathematics instruction (Rosenshine, 1980). This figure is undoubtedly higher in classrooms that are not well managed. (See Figure 4.1 for an example of a situation in which procedures are not clear and specific.)

Figure 4.1   *Source:* CALVIN AND HOBBES © 1995, Watterson. Distributed by UNIVERSAL UCLICK.

By defining how students are to behave in these specific situations, you can save precious minutes for instruction. You also enable students to carry out many of these routines without your direct supervision, freeing you to concentrate on instruction or other tasks. For example, Christina's students begin each class period by writing in their journals while Christina silently takes attendance. Students know that as soon as they enter the room, they are to get their journals, copy the journal topic from the board, and write silently for the allotted time. On the first day of school, Christina laid the groundwork for the smooth functioning of this activity. In the following vignette, we see her introduce the journals to her basic skills class.

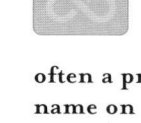
Before we start going over what this class is going to be about, I want to give you your journals, which you will keep on a daily basis. . . . Write your name on the cover—but open the journals first so you [can see which way is up and you] won't write your name upside down, which is often a problem. Then write English 3T, Block 2, then my name. [Points to her name on the board.] Open up your journals and write the date on the first page. I'm going to write a journal topic on the board, and I want you to copy it down, and then write a response to that topic. [Writes: *What do you expect from this class?*] When we do journals, you write until I say to stop writing, 5 to 10 minutes. Don't say you don't have anything to write about or that you can't think of anything else to say. If you run out of things to say about the topic I have given you, write about something else. OK, begin now.

Another important class-running routine involves what students are to do with electronic devices, such as cell phones and MP3 players. These devices are becoming ubiquitous on school campuses and, although students feel entitled to carry them, they can be extremely distracting. Unless your school has a specific policy forbidding their presence on campus, you will want to establish clear policies for your classroom. The most common classroom policy is to require that phones be turned off and put away while in class (unless, of course, you are having students use their phones for a class project or they are using the calculator function). Regarding MP3 players, a common classroom policy is to forbid their use except during individual work, and only if the music is not so loud that other students can hear it.

Lesson-Running Routines

These routines directly support instruction *by specifying the behaviors that are necessary for teaching and learning to take place.* They allow lessons to proceed briskly and eliminate the need for students to ask questions like "Do I have to use a pen?" "Should we number from 1 to 20?" and "What do I do if I'm finished?"

Lesson-running routines describe what items students are to have on hand when a lesson begins, how materials and equipment are to be distributed and collected, what kind of paper or writing instrument is to be used, and what should be done with the paper (e.g., folded into eight boxes; numbered from 1 to 10 along the left margin; headed with name, date, and subject). In addition, lesson-running routines specify the behaviors that students are to engage in at the beginning of the lesson (e.g., have books open to the relevant page, silently sit and wait for instructions from the teacher) and what they are to do if they finish early or if they are unable to finish the assignment by the end of the time period.

Clear lesson-running routines are especially important in classroom situations that are potentially dangerous, such as woodworking, auto mechanics, and cooking. When Sandy introduces chemistry labs, for example, she is very careful to specify the special safety procedures:

There are some special safety procedures for this lab. First, before working with the Bunsen burners, make certain that your hair is tied back. Second, make certain that your goggles are on. Third, I'll have a beaker on my desk where you can discard the metals. Everything else you can throw away in the sink.

Homework procedures can also be included among lesson-running routines, since the pace and content of a lesson often depends on whether students have done their homework assignments. You need to establish routines for determining quickly which students have their homework and which do not, as well as routines for checking and collecting assignments.

Also think about what routines will be followed when students are absent. How will you keep track of work for absent students? How will students learn what the day's assignments are? How will work get home to students who are absent? How many days will students have to complete work they missed?

Interaction Routines

These routines refer to the *rules for talk*—talk between teachers and students and talk among students themselves. Interaction routines specify *when talk is permitted and how it is to occur.* For example, during whole-class discussions, students need to know what to do if they want to respond to a question or contribute a comment. All four of our teachers, like many others, usually require students to raise their hands and wait to be called on, rather than simply calling out. In this way, the teachers can distribute opportunities to participate throughout the class and can ensure that the conversation is not dominated by a few overly eager individuals. The teachers can also check on how well the class understands the lesson by calling on students who do not raise their hands.

Often it's hard to keep track of which students have had an opportunity to speak. In order to avoid this problem, Donnie sometimes creates a pattern for calling on students, one that is more subtle than simply going up and down rows:

> I may start at the back corner of the room and call on students in a diagonal line. Or I might use the alphabetical list of students in my grade book, and alternate between students at the beginning of the list and those at the end. I try not to be obvious, but sometimes students figure out the pattern, and they'll say to me, "You missed so-and-so," or "I didn't get a question," so we'll go back and make sure that person has a turn.

Another way to keep track of which individuals have had a turn is to use the "popsicle stick system." One middle school Spanish teacher we know has a plastic glass for each of her classes; each glass contains popsicle sticks labeled with students' names. A student shakes the glass, pulls out a name, and then places the popsicle stick on the side until everyone has had a turn. The teacher explains why she uses this approach:

> *Sometimes kids are really afraid to talk in a language class; they look down at the floor and try to get real small, hoping that I won't notice them. But this course has been designed as a "proficiency development" course, where students learn how to use Spanish in "real world" situations. If they don't speak, they don't learn. Using the popsicle sticks is my way of making sure that I don't miss anyone.*

During some lessons, you may want students to respond chorally rather than individually. A simple signal can be used to indicate that the rules for talk have changed. For example, Donnie nods and extends her hands, palms up, in a gesture of invitation. Fred, with a background in music, literally conducts the group as if it were a chorus.

Sandy also suspends the normal rules for talk at times, but she adds words of caution for beginning teachers:

> If I'm at the board, with my back turned to the class, and a student wants to ask a question, I don't mind if he or she just calls out, "Mrs. K., I don't understand . . ." Or sometimes, during a whole-class discussion, someone will ask a question, and I'll ask other kids to help out. They'll turn to one another and start asking and answering questions as if I weren't even there. I can just stand aside and watch. It's great to see this kind of student–student interaction. But beginning teachers need to be careful about this. If things start to get unruly, I can just say, "Hey guys, use hands," and things settle right down, but I've seen situations like this get out of hand for beginning teachers.

Interaction routines also include *procedures that students and teachers use to gain each other's attention.* For example, if students are busy working, and you need to give additional instructions, how will you signal that you want their attention? Will you flick the lights, hold up your arm, or say, "Excuse me," the way Donnie does? Conversely, if you are busy working with a small group or an individual, and students need your assistance, how will they communicate that to you? Will they be allowed to call out your name or leave their seats and approach you?

Finally, you need to think about the rules that will govern *talk among students.* When 20 to 30 students sit so close to one another, it's only natural for them to talk. You must decide when it's all right for students to talk about the television show they saw last night (e.g., before the bell rings) and when their talk must be about academic work (e.g., during cooperative learning activities). You also need to think about times when students may talk quietly (e.g., during in-class assignments), and when you need to have absolute silence (e.g., when you are giving instruction or during a test). Table 4.2 summarizes the three types of routines we have just discussed.

TABLE 4.2 Summary of Classroom Routines

Class-Running Routines: Nonacademic routines that enable the classroom to run smoothly

Administrative routines
  Taking attendance
  Recording tardiness
  Distributing school notices

Routines for student movement
  Entering the room at the beginning of the period
  Leaving the room at the end of the period
  Going to the restroom
  Going to the nurse
  Going to the library
  Fire drills
  Sharpening pencils
  Using computers or other equipment
  Getting materials

Housekeeping routines
  Cleaning chalkboards or whiteboards
  Watering plants
  Storing personal items (book bags, cell phones, MP3 players)
  Maintaining common storage area

Lesson-Running Routines: Routines that directly support instruction by specifying the behaviors that are necessary for teaching and learning to take place
  What to bring to class
  Collecting homework

Recording who has done homework
Returning homework
Distributing materials
Preparing paper for assignment (heading, margins, type of writing instrument)
Collecting in-class assignments
What to do when assignments have been completed

Interaction Routines: Routines that specify when talk is permitted and how it is to occur.

Talk between teacher and students:
  During whole-class lessons
  When the teacher is working with a small group
  When the teacher needs the class' attention
  When the students need teacher's attention

Talk among students:
  During independent assignments
  Before the bell rings
  During transitions
  During loudspeaker announcements
  During cooperative learning activities
  During peer conferencing
  When a visitor comes to speak with the teacher

As we wrap up our discussion of planning for norms and routines, let's go back to the first "Pause and Reflect" box that asked you to identify if each expectation was a rule or routine. The first example, students waiting for you to indicate that class is over before they begin to pack up, would be an example of a class-running routine. This is a nonacademic routine that allows the class to run smoothly. The second example, "Students are to be prepared," would be a rule. As discussed earlier, Donnie uses this rule and explains to her students what they need to bring to class each day to be prepared. The third example, "Listen respectfully when people are talking," is also a rule that would allow the students and teacher to hear each other more clearly. Having students turn in homework in the basket for their class period, the fourth example, is a lesson-running routine that streamlines homework collection and allows more time for learning. Finally, the fifth example of students talking quietly during small-group work is an example of an interaction routine. It specifies one of the times when student-student talk is acceptable.

THE FIRST FEW DAYS OF SCHOOL: TEACHING STUDENTS ABOUT THE NORMS

In order to minimize confusion, you need to *teach students the rules for general conduct,* defining terms clearly, providing examples, and discussing rationales. As we indicated earlier in this chapter, Evertson and Emmer's (1982) research indicates that this is crucial for behaviors that are likely to occur frequently and where the appropriate behavior may be ambiguous (e.g., talking during an independent assignment). You also need to *teach the routines* you want students to follow for specific situations. Such thoroughness is particularly important in new situations, like science laboratories, wood shop, keyboarding, or ceramics studios, where students have had little prior experience. (See Box 4.1 for information on Harry and Rosemary Wong, who have written about the importance of teaching rules and routines during the first few days of school.)

Let's see what this looks like in action. On the morning of the first day of school, Donnie begins by introducing herself to her students and asking them to introduce themselves. Afterwards, she introduces the topic of "ground rules." Note that she also provides information on topics that are sure to be on students' minds—homework, notebooks, grading, and extra help:

 Today our main concern is to talk about how we're going to operate in here, what I expect of you in terms of behavior and what the consequences might be for some kinds of behavior. I want to discuss my ground rules or codes of behavior. I'll pass these out, and we'll discuss them. If you have any questions or problems, let me know. [She distributes a packet of handouts.] It looks like an awful lot, but it's not really. A lot will be familiar; I'm sure it will be similar to other teachers'.

OK, let's look at the first page. Here we have my ground rules. The first item on the page deals with general class procedures. *I expect you to be in your*

seat when the bell rings. [She says this slowly and firmly. Her tone is serious but pleasant.] Today several people were tardy. I can understand that. I recognize that today is the first day and you're running around, maybe lost. [She smiles.] But I anticipate that *there will be no late arrivals after this.* I'll talk about what happens for tardiness in a few minutes.

Donnie continues to elaborate on the printed statements, answering questions and inviting comments. She reviews the ground rules for notebooks, homework, extra help, paper headings, and participation, and goes on to explain the grading system. She then goes over an assignment sheet that students may use to record assignments and due dates, and elaborates on a checklist she will use to evaluate notebooks.

MEET THE EDUCATORS   BOX 4.1

MEET HARRY AND ROSEMARY WONG

Harry Wong, a popular educational speaker and consultant, taught middle school and high school science, garnering numerous teaching awards. Rosemary taught kindergarten through grade 8. The couple now has their own publishing company (Harry K. Wong Publications, Inc.), of which Rosemary is CEO. Together they wrote *The First Days of School,* which has sold over 3 million copies, making it the best-selling book ever in education. The Wongs have also produced the DVD series, *The Effective Teacher,* winner of the Telly Award for best educational video of the past 20 years and awarded the first place Gold Award in the International Film and Video Festival.

Some Major Ideas about Classroom Management:

- What you do on the first days of school will determine your success or failure for the rest of the school year.
- Effective teachers introduce rules (i.e., expectations of appropriate student behavior), procedures, and routines on the very first day of school and continue to teach them the first week of school.
- The number one problem in the classroom is not discipline; it is the lack of procedures and routines.

- A procedure is a method or process for how things are to be done in a classroom. When the procedure becomes automatic, it is a routine.
- Effective teachers have procedures for taking roll, exchanging papers, sharpening pencils, entering the classroom, starting class, leaving the classroom, etc.
- The three steps to teaching procedures are (1) explain clearly; (2) rehearse (until class procedures become class routines); and (3) reteach when necessary and reinforce (give specific praise).

Selected Books and Articles:

The First Days of School: How to be an Effective Teacher (Harry and Rosemary Wong, Harry K. Wong Publications, 2004)

Monthly columns by the Wongs can be found at http://teachers.net/wong. Some examples are listed here:
- An Amazing Kindergarten Teacher (May 2008)
- Schools That Beat the Academic Odds (Apr 2008)
- Wrapping the Year with Rap! (Dec 2007/Jan 2008)

Website: www.effectiveteaching.com

As this example illustrates, teaching students the rules for conduct doesn't have to be unpleasant or oppressive. In fact, some teachers don't even use the word rules. Sandy, for example, prefers to talk about "chemistry classroom guidelines" (see Figure 4.2), but like Donnie, she makes sure her expectations for behavior are explicit. Sandy defines terms ("Late means not being in the room when the bell rings."), provides examples wherever necessary, and stresses the reasons for each guideline. She explains why it's important for textbooks to be covered ("so they don't get chemicals on them"); why she has a "disclaimer" in her guidelines reserving the right to give unannounced quizzes ("That's there in case I see you're not doing the reading. But I really don't like to do this; I want kids to do well on tests."); why hats cannot be worn in class (for safety reasons); why she insists on promptness ("I start when the bell rings."); and why she lets them leave when the bell rings—even if she's in the middle of a sentence ("I will not keep you, because you'd be late to the next class and that's not fair to you

---

Chemistry Classroom Guidelines   Mrs. Krupinski

1. Always come to class prepared and ready to work. You must bring the following items with you each class period: a. notebook b. pen or pencil c. scientific calculator d. your textbook.

2. Be prompt to class. Tardiness will not be tolerated. You are considered to be late to class if you enter the room after the bell sounds. There is no penalty for the first tardy. Any further lateness is reported to the administration. Your third tardy to class will result in a call home.

3. When entering the classroom you will be expected to take your seat and begin working on the Do Now that will be on the board. Also on the board will be the homework assignment that will be due the next day. Copy it into your assignment pad.

4. Test and quizzes in this class will be based upon the information that you have received through class discussions, homework assignments, textbook readings, and laboratory work. It is imperative that you take notes during class discussions. All tests with the exception of the midterm and final are assigned a value of 100 points. Quizzes range in point value from 25–50. A quiz does not have to be announced. Quizzes and test make up 65% of your grade.

5. **You will have homework every night in chemistry!!!!!!** The assignment will be reading the text and/or assigned questions from the text or a worksheet. All written work will be collected at the beginning of the period and issued points. **NO LATE HOMEWORK WILL BE ACCEPTED. YOU ARE EXPECTED TO ATTEMPT AND COMPLETE ALL OF THE WORK ASSIGNED.** If you are out for a school activity and an assignment is due on that day you must leave the completed work in my mailbox or hand it to me personally **BEFORE** you leave for the activity.

6. If you are absent it is your responsibility to find out what was missed. Any lab missed due to an excused absence must be made up within one week of the absence. If you are absent 3 days or more, more time will be allowed for make-up. **If you are absent the day of a test or quiz and you were in class the day before, you will be required to make up the test the day you return to school.**

7. There are absolutely no extra credit points available in this class!!!!

8. **There will be no cutting of class!!!!!!!!!**

9. **I am available for extra help every day before or after school.**

Figure 4.2   Chemistry Classroom Guidelines (Mrs. Krupinski) or to the next teacher. But don't pack up books before the bell rings."). Sandy also discusses course requirements. In particular, she explains how homework is assigned and evaluated:

> **OK, people, let's talk about homework. You will have homework every night in this class! Please keep in mind that I will not accept late homework; it has to be in at the beginning of the period the next day. Part of the assignment is to get it in on time. I'll give you a reminder when you come in that homework is due, but if you don't hear and then you remember halfway through I don't want it. It's also important for you to understand that homework is not graded based on how correct it is. It's graded on the basis of your effort. Homework is not useless in my class. We go over every single item.**

Finally, Sandy stresses the need to come to class (in terms that are amazingly similar to Fred's):

> **OK, Number 8 is pretty clear ("There will be no cutting"); I don't really think this needs to be discussed. I want you here. I expect you to be here. *And I take it personally if you're not.***

In addition to going over her own class rules, Sandy also reviews the school's academic integrity policy. With an extremely serious demeanor, she explains the distinction between cooperating and cheating ("the ultimate disrespectful behavior"). She talks about the numerous behaviors that constitute cheating (e.g., giving or receiving test information, using "unauthorized written aids" or information from electronic devices during tests, claiming sole credit for work completed with other students, copying work that was supposed to be done independently, and fabricating laboratory data). She also gives students strategies for resisting peer pressure to cheat: "If someone asks you what was on the test, just tell them, "Oh, you know Mrs. K! You have to know everything!" Sandy also spends a lot of time talking about plagiarism. She tells students that "plagiarism is like someone behind you reaching into your backpack and taking your cell phone. Ideas belong to people, just like cell phones."

Like Sandy, Christina also talks about "guidelines" for behavior. On the first day of school she distributes a newspaper that she creates for each class she teaches. (See Figure 4.3.) Listen as Christina introduces the newspaper to English 10R:

> **Here's a page of information about this course. See the letter from the editor. That's me; I'm the editor. Read that silently, please. [She gives students a few minutes to read the letter.] There are a couple of things I want to point out. Let's look at the objectives for this class. [She goes over the objectives, clarifying terms and talking about some of the activities they'll be doing to fulfill the objectives.] OK, let's look at the "Guidelines for Student Conduct." [She goes through the list commenting on some of the bulleted points.]**

ENGLISH 10 R

Reading
Writing
Speaking
Listening
Viewing &
Media Literacy

Fall Semester   *Mrs. C. Vreeland*

A Letter from the Editor:

Dear Students,

Welcome to tenth grade English. I hope you had a pleasant summer and are ready for some exciting educational experiences. I am looking forward to working with you this semester.

I have been working hard to plan this course for you and I think you will learn a great deal and have some fun this semester. In order to make this class successful, I must ask for your cooperation. I will ask for your input frequently, and if you have any ideas you may feel free to share them at any time.

Please raise any questions or comments at an appropriate time during class or check my schedule on the classroom door to reach me during the school day. In addition, you can reach me through school e-mail. However, please note that I can not guarantee immediate response to your e-mail. Therefore, questions or comments that require immediate attention (i.e.homework concerns) should be addressed before you leave school.

Please read the rest of this introductory handout carefully and share it with your parents, as it will provide you with an overview of the course. You will learn about rules, procedures, grading policies, and course objectives; all of which will be helpful to you throughout the semester.

I wish you much success this semester and I know that you will achieve your goals if you approach this class with enthusiasm and dedication.

Sincerely,

Mrs. C. Vreeland

Guidelines for Student Conduct

The student will be responsible to:

- create a positive, comfortable learning environment in the classroom and on electronic classroom forums.
- respect every member of the class by using appropriate language, by paying attention when another person is speaking, and by raising his/her hand to speak.
- complete all assignments on time and to the best of his/her ability.
- obtain and complete make-up work on time — two days for each day absent.
- listen to and follow all directions given by the teacher, asking for clarification if he/she does not understand the directions. (NOTE: Refusal to follow directions constitutes interference with the educational process and will result in disciplinary action.)
- come to class on time and be in his/her seat when the bell rings.
- bring his/her textbook, notebook, a writing implement, a pen AND pencil, and any other required materials (as assigned by the teacher) to class each day.
- leave ALL food, drink and outerwear in his/her locker, and leave cell phones at home.
- LEARN and THINK independently as well as cooperatively.

Penalty Box

Students who do not listen to directions or obtain make-up work will not receive credit for missed assignments. Late work will be marked down ten points for each day late.

Students who are not in their seats when the bell rings will be marked late (six lates equal loss of credit).

Students who disrupt the learning of others or refuse to follow directions given by the teacher will lose participation credit. If disruption or refusal persists, students will be removed from the classroom. Appropriate disciplinary action will follow.

Objectives

After successfully completing this course, students will be able to:

1. recognize the act and importance of listening.
2. organize, prepare and present a spoken presentation clearly and expressively.
3. collaborate by sharing ideas, examples and insights productively and respectfully.
4. recognize that reading has many purposes and demonstrate an ability to choose an approach appropriate to the text and purpose.
5. experience and respond to print and non-print media.
6. use research skills to access, interpret and apply information from a variety of print and non-print sources.
7. compose a variety of written responses for different purposes and audiences.
8. use a variety of technologies as a tool for learning.
9. use their language arts skills for decision making, negotiating and problem solving.
10. develop a better understanding of themselves, of others, and of the world through literature and through language.

Grading Policy

Marking period grades are comprised of a major assessment mark and a minor assessment mark, each counting for 50% of the marking period grade. The average of the two marking period grades will count as 80% of the course grade. The final exam will count as 20% of the course grade.

Major Assessments include activities covering large blocks of material such as long-term projects and tests. Minor Assessments include classwork, homework, quizzes, group activities and class participation.

Figure 4.3 Christina's Introductory Newspaper

We're all working together to make this a positive, comfortable class. I can't do it by myself. There are 29 of you and only one of me. So you have to contribute to the environment—being nice to each other, not using put-downs, using appropriate language. You won't hear me using inappropriate language, so I don't expect you to use it either; I'm very strict about that. . . . "Obtain and complete make-up work." I expect you to be vigilant, to find out what you missed. You have two days to get the work in. "Come to class on time." On time means in your seat, not by someone else's desk. If you need to use the restroom, come to class first, put your books away, and let me know you're here. Then you can go. That way if you're 10 or 20 seconds late, I'll know where you are. Remember that coats, scarves, hats, food, and drink are not allowed in class; that's a school rule so you should all be familiar with that.

Let me point out the penalty box: You get one warning for disruptive behavior and then you're removed from the classroom. Take a minute to look over the grading policy. . . .OK, to make sure that we're all on the same page about rules and procedures, read this paper and then sign it. [She gives out the "Dear Student and Parent/Guardian" page.] Your first homework assignment is to take this home and get your parents to sign it too.

In contrast to Donnie, Sandy, and Christina, Fred introduces rules and routines in a relatively informal way. As we saw earlier, when he reviews the school handbook with his first-period class of sophomores, he uses the school rules as a jumping-off point for a presentation of his class rules. Even here, however, he distributes no handouts, nor does he post rules, and he interjects a degree of humor:

 [Fred finishes reviewing the handbook and has students sign the page acknowledging receipt and agreement. He then continues with his own rules for the class.] Do you know what an acronym is? It's letters that form a word and each letter stands for a word. PITA is an acronym. And it's the main rule we have in here: *Don't be a PITA.* What's a PITA, Suzanne? [She shakes her head.] You don't know? [He looks around to see if anyone else knows. There's silence.] A PITA is a . . . pain . . . in . . . the . . . neck! [There's some laughter as the class catches on.] I want you to inscribe PITA across your forehead. Don't forget: *Don't be a PITA.* Now, I have one rule for me, too: *I must make you laugh once every day.* If I don't, I go home in a suicidal mood. [Students laugh.] OK, let's talk about what you'll be learning in U.S. History I.

With his seniors, Fred prefers an even less systematic approach. On the first day of class, he introduces himself, takes attendance, and immediately launches into a description of the course. During the period, he explicitly teaches his students routines for specific situations that arise (e.g., how to pass in papers), but he does not teach rules for general conduct. Instead, he monitors the class carefully and immediately informs students about behavior he finds unacceptable. His interactions with individual students are watched carefully by the rest—and they quickly learn what he expects. When Fred asks one student to takes off his baseball cap, for example, another hears and takes off his own hat. To a student wearing sunglasses, Fred asks, "Is there is a medical reason for those glasses?" and the student immediately removes them.

As you can see, Fred communicates expectations for conduct to older students primarily by providing clear, immediate feedback when behavior is unacceptable. He recognizes that one reason this approach works for him is the reputation he has established during his years at the high school. Reflecting on this reputation, Fred's student teacher observes:

> *Everyone knows that he plays the "dumb old man," but that he's not. He has this incredible relationship with the kids; he knew everyone's name within two days. He works them hard, but he projects warmth, and the kids know he really cares. I've never seen a kid give him lip. One look is enough.*

CONCLUDING COMMENTS

Donnie, Christina, Sandy, and Fred all have well-defined expectations for student behavior, and they make these expectations absolutely clear. Nonetheless, the four teachers have somewhat different expectations, and they introduce rules and routines in different ways. These differences reflect their beliefs about what works best for their own particular students in their own particular contexts. Donnie, Christina, and Sandy teach rules and routines in a systematic, explicit fashion; they all spend considerable time explaining what they expect; and they distribute written copies of the rules for students to keep in their notebooks. Christina goes further: She requires her students to sign a statement that they have read and understood the information about student conduct, penalties, grading policies, and expected class procedures and to obtain their parents' signatures as well. In contrast, Fred is much more informal. With his sophomores, Fred explicitly teaches rules, but he neither posts them nor distributes copies. With his seniors, he teaches specific routines, but relies primarily on monitoring and feedback to communicate what he expects in terms of general conduct.

As a beginning teacher, you would be wise to adopt a deliberate, thorough approach to teaching rules and routines. If you have your own classroom, it is also a good idea to post your rules in the classroom, for example, on a front bulletin board, so your expectations are clear to your students. Once you've gained experience—and a reputation—you might try a less formal approach with your older students. Also keep in mind that rules and routines are not invented in a single year, polished and fully developed. Instead, they will evolve over time, products of your experience and creative efforts.

One final note from our own teaching experience: On the first day of school, at the beginning of fifth period, one of us (Ingrid) distributed copies of the classroom rules. An audible groan went through the classroom, and the students noted that this was how every previous class that day had started! Although we have emphasized the importance of establishing behavioral expectations early in the year, rules and routines should not be the *most salient* aspect of the first days of the school year. As you plan the first few days, make sure that you balance the teaching of rules and routines with a variety of learning activities that students will find meaningful, enjoyable, and memorable. We want our students to understand that they will learn more in our classes than simply how to behave.

SUMMARY

This chapter discussed two important functions of rules and routines in the classroom: (1) to provide a structure and predictability that help students to feel more comfortable; and (2) to reduce the complexity of classroom life, allowing you and your students to concentrate on teaching and learning. It then outlined two broad categories of behavioral expectations—rules for general conduct and routines for specific situations—and emphasized the need to teach these explicitly.

Decide on Norms for General Conduct That Are

- Reasonable and necessary.
- Clear and understandable.
- Consistent with instructional goals and with what we know about how people learn.
- Consistent with school rules.

Plan Routines for Specific Situations

- Class-running routines
    Administrative routines
    Routines for student movement
    Housekeeping routines
- Lesson-running routines
    Use and distribution of materials
    Assignment procedures
    Early completion procedures
- Interaction routines
    When and how talking is permitted
    How teachers and students get each other's attention

Teach Norms and Routines Explicitly

- Define terms.
- Discuss rationales.
- Provide examples.

Remember, developing good rules and routines is only the first step. For rules and routines to be effective, you must actively teach them to your students. Time spent on rules and routines at the beginning of school will pay off in increased instructional time throughout the year.

ACTIVITIES FOR SKILL BUILDING AND REFLECTION

In Class

1. Working together in small groups, develop a set of rules for general conduct. About five rules should be sufficient. For each rule, list a rationale and examples that you will discuss with students to make the rules more meaningful. Think about which rules are most important to you and why.

2. In a small group, refer to Table 4.2, which lists the areas for which you will need specific behavioral routines. First, share your ideas about the actual routines you might use in each category (e.g., what kind of routine can you establish for taking attendance in an efficient way?). Then, think about which routines need to be taught on the first day. In other words, decide on priorities so that you can teach routines when it is most appropriate (and most likely to be remembered).

On Your Own

If you are teaching, student teaching, or observing in another teacher's classroom, keep a reflective journal on developing and teaching rules and routines. Using the routines listed in Table 4.2, note which routines cause the most problems, the nature of the problems, and how you might respond to those problems. Also note which routines work particularly well.

For Your Portfolio

Write a brief statement on the rules that will guide behavior in your classroom. Will you develop and distribute them yourself? If so, what rules will you create? Will you generate rules with students? If so, how will you do this? Describe the specific approach you will take.

FOR FURTHER READING

Bicard, D. F. (2000). Using classroom rules to construct behavior. *Middle School Journal, 31*(5), 37–45.

   Arguing that "rules are one of the most cost effective forms of classroom management available to teachers," Bicard reviews the characteristics of positive, negative, and vague rules and discusses the keys to developing and implementing positive rules in classrooms. The article also discusses what to do when students violate rules.

Brady, K., Forton, M. B., Porter, D., & Wood, C. (2003). *Rules in school.* Greenfield, MA: Northeast Foundation for Children.

   One of the Strategies for Teachers Series, this book provides practical suggestions for involving K–8 students in generating classroom rules that grow out of their hopes and dreams. Chapter Six focuses specifically on middle school (grades 6–8) and includes a discussion of logical consequences to ensure accountability.

Marzano, R. J., with Marzano, J. S., & Pickering, D. J. (2003). *Classroom management that works: Research-based strategies for every teacher.* Alexandria, Virginia: Association for Supervision and Curriculum Development.

Chapter 2 focuses on rules and procedures. The authors first discuss research confirming the importance of classroom norms. They then outline a series of "Action Steps" that teachers can take to identify appropriate rules and procedures and to involve students in their design.

CHAPTER 5

KNOWING YOUR STUDENTS AND THEIR SPECIAL NEEDS

Getting your class lists at the beginning of the school year always brings a sense of anticipation, excitement, and curiosity: What are these students like? What do they know? How do they think? What strengths do they bring? What struggles do they face? Where do they come from? Over the first few weeks and months of school, you begin to formulate answers to these questions. Gradually, you gain an understanding of *who your students are*. This understanding allows you to tailor your teaching to their specific needs and to find ways of building connections. And *knowing your students is essential if you are to build an inclusive, caring environment for learning.*

Knowing your students means recognizing and appreciating the ways each is a unique individual, as well as understanding the common characteristics of adolescence. Undoubtedly, your class will be comprised of students with a wide range of abilities, social skills, and emotional maturity. In addition, your class will probably include students with "special needs." Although this term is generally used to refer to those with disabilities, students who are learning English as a second language also have special needs. Likewise, young people who are growing up in impoverished, unstable, or abusive circumstances may have physical, emotional, or psychological problems that must be addressed.

This chapter begins by looking at some of the common developmental characteristics of middle and high school students and considering the implications for classroom management. Then we discuss strategies for supporting students who are English language learners. Next, we examine ways of helping students with disabilities and attention-deficit/hyperactivity disorder, the most commonly diagnosed behavior disorder among children in the United States (Coles, 2000). We then consider the needs of students who are troubled—namely, those who suffer from the problems associated with substance abuse, child abuse and neglect, and eating disorders. Finally, we discuss approaches to working with students who are poor or homeless.

THE DEVELOPING ADOLESCENT

The middle school and high school years are marked by tumultuous physical, emotional, and social changes. During this period, adolescents may become confused, moody, short-tempered, and rebellious. They may alternate between confidence and high expectations on one hand and insecurity and anxiety on the other; indeed, middle-graders suffer from the lowest self-esteem of any age group (Charles & Charles, 2004). Adolescents increasingly turn to their peer group, trying hard to "fit in," and become extremely concerned about appearance, clothes, and body image. (See Figure 5.1 for an example of typical middle school concerns.)

According to Erik Erikson (1963), the major developmental task of adolescence (starting at age 13) is the development of identity. Young people must find the answer to the question, "Who am I?" or experience "role confusion" or "identity diffusion." As they work to forge an identity and "keep themselves together," adolescents experiment with different roles and temporarily "overidentify" with the "heroes of cliques and crowds" (Erikson, 1963, p. 262). During this phase, they can be "remarkably clannish," excluding all those who are different. Erikson cautions adults to understand (although not to condone) this intolerance as a "defense against a sense of identity confusion" (p. 262).

During early adolescence (middle school and the freshman year of high school), teens may also begin to question norms and social conventions (e.g., no running

Figure 5.1 *Source:* STONE SOUP © 2000, Jan Eliot. Reprinted with permission of UNIVERSAL UCLICK. All rights reserved.

in the hallways) that they readily accepted at an earlier age (Nucci, 2006). Viewing norms as the arbitrary dictates of those in power, early adolescents are more likely to violate school conventions. Fortunately, by middle adolescence (about 15 or the sophomore year), most American adolescents have moved on to the next stage of reasoning about social conventions, recognizing that they are necessary for ensuring orderly interaction among members of a society.

At the same time, changes are also occurring in the way adolescents view matters of personal prerogative and privacy. Domains in which convention touches on personal expression (hair, dress), personal associations (friends), or personal safety (sexuality) become "zones of dispute" over which adolescents want autonomy and control (Nucci, 2006, p. 725).

Together, the negation of convention and the extension of what is considered personal (and therefore off limits to interfering adults) makes the period of early adolescence a difficult time for parents and teachers trying to guide students' behavior.

Implications for Classroom Management

Since middle-graders tend to "push the limits," it is helpful to distinguish between norms that are absolutely necessary to create a safe, secure environment and those that are really only a minor threat. As Larry Nucci (2006) argues:

> To put it another way, it is important for teachers to realize that there are times when it makes more sense to say "yes" in response to student noncompliance than it is to simply say "no" in an effort to maintain consistency for its own sake. For example, marking a student tardy for being next to his seat rather than sitting in it as the bell rings may make the adult feel powerful, but it does little to enhance the student's appreciation of the norm of promptness. (pp. 725-726)

Nucci reminds us that this phase will pass and that teachers (and students) will benefit from patience: "Firm and fair enforcement of rules with a dash of humor will work better than rigid requirements for compliance" (p. 726).

Unfortunately, middle schools do not generally adopt this more sensitive, understanding approach. In fact, a number of educators have commented on the mismatch between schools and young adolescents around these issues. Despite the increased maturity of adolescents and their need to obtain greater autonomy, middle schools and junior high schools emphasize greater teacher control and discipline and offer fewer opportunities for student involvement in decision making, choice, and independence (Eccles, Wigfield, & Schiefele, 1998). Moreover, just when students face the task of constructing a firm sense of self, they move from an environment where they were the most mature and highest status students to being the babies in a large, impersonal middle school (Woolfolk, 2007). They go from close connection with one teacher to more impersonal relationships with many teachers. They go into a more competitive environment, with lots of social comparison, just at a time when they are very self-conscious and their self-concepts are particularly fragile. Not surprisingly, middle school students often show decreased motivation and interest in school (Nucci, 2006).

Obviously, all students can thrive when teachers are fair, encouraging, and willing to listen and when they provide opportunities for independence along with needed support. But the "developmental peculiarities" of adolescents (such as the struggle for identity, insecurity, fragile self-concept, self-consciousness, and concern about fitting in) make this even more critical (Emmer & Gerwels, 2006, p. 412). At this stage, it is essential not to put students down, not to embarrass them in front of their peers, and to show a sense of humor. When teachers are sensitive to the emotional stresses that characterize this stage and treat adolescents with respect and understanding, attachment to school is strengthened. This has far-reaching implications: Attachment to school significantly decreases the likelihood that students will become involved in dangerous behavior such as smoking, drinking, marijuana use, or violence (Emmer & Gerwels, 2006).

ENGLISH LANGUAGE LEARNERS

The past two decades have seen a significant increase in the language minority population of the United States. According to community surveys conducted from 2005 through 2007, 54 million people, or nearly 20 percent of the general population aged 5 and over, speak a language other than English at home (U.S. Census Bureau, 2008). This is up from 14 percent in 1990 and 11 percent in 1980. California has the largest percentage of language-minority speakers (42 percent), followed by New Mexico (36 percent), Texas (34 percent), New York (29 percent), Arizona and New Jersey (each about 28 percent), Nevada (27 percent), and Hawaii (24 percent). The 2000 U.S. census indicated that Spanish is the non-English language spoken most frequently at home, followed by Chinese, French, German, Tagalog, Vietnamese, Italian, Korean, Russian, Polish, and Arabic (Shin with Bruno, 2003).

The growth in the language minority population is reflected in public school enrollments. It has been estimated that in the 2005–2006 school year, over 5 million English language learners (ELLs) were enrolled in public schools (pre-K to 12th grade). This represents more than 10 percent of the total school enrollment, and a 57 percent increase from 1995–1996 (NCELA, 2007).

Federal legislation provides funding and encouragement for programs to assist ELLs; however, there are no federally mandated programs like those provided for students who have disabilities. The state in which you teach may mandate such services or merely permit them; it may even prohibit them! Despite the variability, state laws generally call for the identification and assessment of ELLs and describe options for special services. One option is a *bilingual education program,* which teaches students in their native language as well as in English, thus allowing them to learn academic subjects while they're learning English. In some states, if there is a given number of ELLs in a district, speaking

PAUSE AND REFLECT

Bilingual education programs are extremely controversial, and in some states, laws have been passed restricting bilingual education and substituting programs that stress the use of English. Even the parents of some English language learners oppose bilingual education, contending that they hinder children's learning of English. At the same time, scholars in bilingual education stress the importance of receiving instruction in a child's first language to build on his or her existing literacy skills. What do *you* think about this issue?

a common native language at approximately the same grade level, the district is required to provide bilingual programs.

When English language learners come from many different language backgrounds, bilingual education programs are impractical. In this case, schools typically place students in regular English-only classrooms and pull them out for instruction from a specially trained teacher in *English as a Second Language.* Since the focus is on learning English, students with different native languages can be in the same room.

In general education, English-only classrooms, ELLs will undoubtedly have problems if they are expected to "sink or swim," and if teachers are unwilling to make any modifications. ELLs may be able to function admirably, however, if you implement some of the environmental supports used in "sheltered instruction" or "Specially Designed Academic Instruction in English" (SDAIE). A comprehensive model of SDAIE includes five components (Diaz-Rico & Weed, 2009). First—and critical—is the *teacher's attitude*; unless the teacher is open and willing to learn from students, SDAIE cannot be successful. The second component is *content,* meaning that lessons must have both subject matter and language objectives, and lessons must be planned and implemented with language in mind. Third is an emphasis on *comprehensibility*; lessons must include explicit strategies that aid in students' understanding (e.g., modeling, frequent comprehension checks, adjustment in use of language). Fourth, *connections* refers to the importance of connecting curriculum to students' background and experiences. The final component is *interaction*; Students in a sheltered English classroom have frequent opportunities to work together, to clarify concepts in their native language, and to represent learning in a variety of ways. (See Diaz-Rico & Weed, 2009, for additional information on these five components.)

Having a number of English language learners in your class will add to the cultural richness and global understanding of your students. It may also be a source of stress, especially for new teachers. Questions are likely to arise about how to meet the needs of your ELLs while not shortchanging the rest of the class; however, incorporating some sheltered English strategies into your teaching and following the suggestions listed in the Practical Tips box should benefit *everyone.*

PRACTICAL TIPS FOR

HELPING ENGLISH LANGUAGE LEARNERS

- Provide a safe, welcoming environment for language risk taking. Be aware of your own biases toward cultures different from yours.

- Take time to learn about the discourse patterns of cultures besides your own, so you don't misinterpret students' words, gestures, or actions. (See Chapter 11 for some examples of discourse patterns.)

- Communicate the expectation that all students can succeed and show students that you are eager to help them.

- Increase time and opportunities for meaningful talk; small-group or whole-class discussions provide opportunities to practice language skills.

(continued on next page)

- Find ways for students to participate in group activities, giving them roles that are less dependent on language use (e.g., have them draw pictures or serve as timekeepers).

- Encourage English speaking while honoring students' first language and culture. Allow students to use their native language at appropriate times (e.g., when they need to process new material with another speaker of their language or need to construct meaning from a reading selection).

- Encourage children to tell about their culture. Listen carefully and ask questions. View ethnic and linguistic diversity within a classroom not as a problem, but as an asset from which both teachers and students can profit.

- Build on and utilize students' background knowledge and personal interests.

- Encourage students to write about topics of their choice and for real-world purposes.

- Encourage parents to develop and maintain their primary language at home.

- Learn and use some second language yourself with students.

- Emphasize collaborative over individual work.

- Emphasize doing rather than telling.

- Speak a bit more slowly and enunciate clearly, with your mouth in direct view of the students.

- Use gestures and body language to accompany your verbal messages to students.

- Make the language of the text comprehensible by interpreting it in simple, everyday language.

- Offer periodic summaries.

- Paraphrase questions and statements to allow for different levels of proficiency. Use synonyms to clarify the meaning of unknown words.

- Control vocabulary and sentence structure (e.g., if you use idioms like "It's raining cats and dogs," explain what they mean).

- Ask questions that require different degrees of English proficiency in responding (e.g., nonverbal signals to communicate agreement or disagreement, yes-no, single-word or short answers).

- When students respond to your questions, focus on the content, rather than on the form of the response.

- Use objects, video, pictures, or movement to increase comprehensibility and provide a context for learning.

- Apply Specially Designed Academic Instruction in English (SDAIE) strategies across the curriculum. Often known as "sheltered instruction," SDAIE focuses on core curriculum content and uses a rich variety of techniques and materials such as artifacts, visuals, video, storyboarding, movement, role plays, and collaborative learning.

- Think aloud and model a variety of reading comprehension strategies (e.g., making connections, predicting, inferring).

- Use a variety of reading supports such as text tours and picture walks (to preview material), graphic organizers (story maps, character analyses), and text signposts (chapter headings, bold print).

- Use a variety of writing supports, such as group composing, graphic organizers, and drawing-based texts.

Sources: Cary, 2007; Henning, 2008; Romero, Mercado, & Vazquez-Faria, 1987.

STUDENTS WITH DISABILITIES AND ADHD

 Matthew is a student in Sandy's last-period class who has been identified as emotionally disturbed. Although he's very quiet, he erupts
angrily when provoked and is prone to violent outbursts. Sandy says
that you can tell something is boiling just beneath the surface. She
makes sure to place him in groups with students who are cooperative and supportive; even so, he frequently gets tense and frustrated with group members
who he thinks are "wasting his time." According to Sandy, "Matthew is really
bright, and when students are quibbling over something he thinks is silly (like
how to write down an answer), he'll get a funny look on his face and turn his
back on the other group members. It's almost as if he's trying to block out
whatever's bothering him. When I see that look, I know to get over there and
intervene." Sandy has carefully reviewed Matthew's individualized education
program (IEP), but it's the close communication with his case manager and
the school psychologist that has allowed her to gain a deeper understanding of
Matthew's behavior. As she puts it, "Matthew's having a successful year in
chemistry—and that's due to the fact that many people are helping *me* to
help *him*."

Matthew's presence in Sandy's classroom is a direct result of the Individuals
with Disabilities Education Act (reauthorized as IDEA 2004, and also referred to
as the Individuals with Disabilities Education Improvement Act or IDEIA), federal legislation mandating a "free appropriate public education" for all children
with disabilities. According to the IDEA, disability is defined as mental retardation, a hearing impairment including deafness, a speech or language impairment, a visual impairment including blindness, serious emotional disturbance, an
orthopedic impairment, autism, traumatic brain injury, other health impairment
(e.g., limited strength or vitality due to chronic or acute health problems such
as asthma or diabetes), a specific learning disability, deaf-blindness, or multiple
disabilities.

The IDEA requires *students with disabilities to be educated with their
nondisabled peers to the maximum extent appropriate, with the supplementary aids and services needed to help them achieve.* The general education,
mainstream class needs to be consid-
ered as the "*least restrictive environment.*" However, the law also requires
schools to have available a *continuum
of alternative placements* (e.g., part-
time placement in a special education
classroom; full-time placement in a
special education classroom; placement in a special school; placement
in a residential school) if the nature or
severity of a student's disability precludes the possibility of a satisfactory education
in the general education setting.

 PAUSE AND REFLECT

What do you think about the inclusion of students with
disabilities in the general education classroom? Do your
views depend on the kind of disability (e.g., physical,
emotional, cognitive)? What are your specific concerns, if
any, about teaching in inclusive classrooms?

The next sections of the chapter summarize the characteristics of students with learning disabilities, emotional and behavior disorders, autism and Asperger syndrome, and ADHD, along with some strategies for effectively working with these students. We then discuss a variety of general strategies that may be useful as you work to achieve a classroom that is truly inclusive.

Learning Disabilities

More students are identified as having "specific learning disabilities" than any other type of disability. Of the 10 percent of school-age children identified as having disabilities, just over 50 percent of this group (or 5 percent of the total school-age population) is diagnosed as LD, and the number has been increasing dramatically (Vaughn, Bos, & Schumm, 2003). It is estimated that every public school classroom contains at least one student with a learning disability, and probably several more (Henley, Ramsey, & Algozzine, 2002).

It is difficult to get a satisfactory definition of LD because there are many types of learning disabilities and children diagnosed with LD are a heterogeneous group. The IDEA defines learning disabilities as a "disorder in one or more of the basic psychological processes involved in understanding or in using language, spoken or written," which results in learning problems that are not explained by some other disability (such as mental retardation). A diagnosis of LD is often made when there is a severe discrepancy between intellectual ability and academic performance. However, the discrepancy criterion is a source of concern to many parents and educators, since children have to struggle for several years before the disparity between achievement and ability is severe enough to allow diagnosis. This means that most students with LD do not qualify for services until late second or third grade—a practice that seems to set these children up for failure (Vaughn, Bos, & Schumm, 2003). Many educators now prefer an alternative called *response-to-intervention (RTI)*. In RTI, small-group, intensive instruction in the needed academic areas is provided early. If this early intervention fails to benefit the student, then he or she may qualify as having a specific learning disability.

Although it is difficult to list a set of characteristics that adequately describe all students with LD, Table 5.1 presents some signs that may indicate a learning disability. If a student displays a number of these problems, then teachers should consider the possibility of a learning disability and seek advice from special services personnel.

Reviews of research indicate that three teaching strategies are particularly powerful in promoting the academic success of students with LD (Vaughn, Gersten, & Chard, 2000). First, teachers need to match tasks to the student's abilities and skills, sequencing examples and problems to allow high levels of student success. Second, small group instruction with no more than six students appears to be especially beneficial. Finally, students with LD need to learn self-questioning strategies (i.e., to ask themselves questions while reading or working on an academic

TABLE 5.1 Possible Indicators of a Learning Disability

When a child has a learning disability, he or she

- may have trouble learning the alphabet, rhyming words, or connecting letters to their sounds.
- may have trouble blending sounds into words.
- may make many mistakes when reading aloud, and repeat and pause often.
- may not understand what he or she reads.
- may confuse similar letters and words, such as *b* and *d, was* and *saw.*
- may have real trouble with spelling.
- may have very messy handwriting.
- may have difficulty with fine motor activities.
- may have trouble remembering the sounds that letters make or hearing slight differences between words.
- may have trouble understanding and following directions.
- may have trouble organizing what he or she wants to say or not be able to think of the word he or she needs for writing or conversation.
- may confuse math symbols and misread numbers.
- may not be able to retell a story in order.
- may not know where to begin a task or how to go on from there.

Source: Adapted from Fact Sheet 7 of the National Dissemination Center for Children with Disabilities (2004).

task). Teachers can model this by thinking aloud about text being read or mathematics problems to be solved. These instructional practices are hardly revolutionary; unfortunately, they are too rarely implemented in classrooms (Vaughn, Gersten, & Chard, 2000).

Emotional and Behavioral Disorders

The terms *emotional disturbance* and *behavioral disorder* are often used interchangeably. While the IDEA uses the term "emotional disturbance," many professionals prefer the term "behavioral disorder," which they feel is less stigmatizing (Vaugh, Bos, & Schumm, 2003).

IDEA defines an "emotional disturbance" as a condition characterized by one or more of the following: an inability to learn that cannot be explained by intellectual, sensory, or health factors; an inability to build or maintain satisfactory interpersonal relationships with peers and teachers; inappropriate types of behavior or feeling under normal circumstances; a general pervasive mood of unhappiness or depression; or a tendency to develop physical symptoms or fears associated with personal or school problems. As you can see, like the term *learning disabilities,* the term "emotional disturbance" actually encompasses a variety of conditions, from conduct disorders to depression.

When teachers are asked to talk about "problem students," they tend to speak about those who are disruptive, aggressive, and defiant and whose behaviors interfere with others—students whose behavioral disorders are *externalizing* (Vaughn, Bos, & Schumm, 2003). Students like these have a *conduct disorder (CD),* characterized by a "repetitive and persistent pattern of behavior in which the basic rights of others or major age-appropriate societal norms or rules are violated" (American Psychiatric Association, 2000). It's easy to identify students who display this kind of behavior, but what do you do about it?

First, it's essential to be *proactive.* Too often, teachers react only to the student's negative behaviors, but students with CD must be taught how to behave more appropriately. This means monitoring students' behavior closely, so that you can prompt, recognize, and reward acceptable behaviors (i.e., "catch 'em being good") and anticipate and head off unacceptable behavior. Second, students with CD can benefit from *direct teaching of appropriate social behavior,* with rewards provided for the display of these behaviors, as well as a response-cost procedure in which points (or tokens) are lost for inappropriate behavior (Ostrander, 2004). Third, *exploring the intent or purpose of the unacceptable behavior* may reveal what a student needs in order to behave more appropriately and to learn, such as getting help with a difficult or frustrating assignment. Some additional suggestions are listed in the Practical Tips box. (Also refer to the section on defiance in Chapter 12 and the section on de-escalating potentially explosive situations in Chapter 13.)

PRACTICAL TIPS FOR

HELPING STUDENTS WITH CONDUCT DISORDER

- Make sure your classroom environment is organized, predictable, and structured.
- Plan and implement activities to promote a sense of community (see Chapter 3).
- Actively work on establishing positive relationships; provide consistent, positive attention and decrease negative comments.
- Closely monitor behavior and acknowledge and reward positive behavior.
- Directly teach social skills (e.g., anger management skills).
- Provide structured choices ("Would you prefer to do your math or your writing first?" "Do you want to do this alone or work in a group?").
- Have a plan for removing the student if he or she becomes disruptive.
- Learn to anticipate and de-escalate problem situations (see Chapter 13).
- Use self-management approaches (see Chapter 12) such as self-monitoring, self-evaluation, and self-instruction.
- Develop and implement contingency contracts (see Chapter 12).
- Make sure that instruction is appropriate for the student's level of ability, since frustration and academic failure can exacerbate the student's emotional/behavioral problems.

Children and adolescents with emotional disturbance may also show a pattern of *internalizing* behaviors, such as shyness, withdrawal, anxiety, and depression

(Vaughn, Bos, & Schumm, 2003). Consider the following journal entry written by a student teacher:

> *I'm really worried about one of my kids. She's unbelievably shy and withdrawn. It took me a long time to even notice her. She never participates in class discussions, never raises her hand, and never volunteers for anything. When I call on her, she looks down and doesn't answer, or her answer is so soft that I can't hear her. I've watched her during lunch time in the cafeteria, and she doesn't seem to have any friends. The other kids aren't mean to her—they act like she doesn't even exist—and that's sort of the way I feel too!*

Students like this, who act sad, reserved, withdrawn, or irritable, may actually be suffering from depression. Table 5.2 lists the signs that suggest depression in children and adolescents.

It is important to consult with a guidance counselor or school psychologist if you are concerned that a youngster is depressed (Schlozman, 2001). Journals, drawings, or essays that suggest suicidal or homicidal thoughts certainly warrant a formal referral. In addition, teachers need to understand that depressed students often feel as though they have little to contribute. To counter these feelings, you need to communicate respect and confidence in the student's abilities, minimize the possibility of embarrassment (e.g., by calling on depressed students to answer questions that have no clearly correct answer), and encourage them to assist younger or less able students. Most importantly, you need to forge a connection with the depressed student. Adults who suffered from depression when they were younger frequently remember a specific teacher as key to their recovery (Schlozman, 2001).

TABLE 5.2 Indicators of Depression

- Indecision, lack of concentration, or forgetfulness
- Change in personality, such as increased anger, irritability, moodiness, agitation, or whining
- Change in sleep patterns and appetite
- Loss of energy
- Lack of enthusiasm or motivation
- Loss of interest in personal appearance and hygiene
- Hopelessness, helplessness, and sadness
- Frequent physical complaints such as headaches and stomach aches
- Thoughts of suicide or death
- Low self-esteem, frequently expressed through self-blame and self-criticism
- Withdrawal from friends and activities once enjoyed
- Poor school performance

Pervasive Developmental Disorders: Autism and Asperger Syndrome

Autism and Asperger syndrome are two *pervasive developmental disorders (PDDs)* or *autism spectrum disorders (ASD),* a cluster of disorders characterized by marked impairments in the development of social interaction and communication skills. Biological and neurological in origin, autism and Asperger syndrome (AS) are generally evident by age 3. Just how frequently PDDs occur is not entirely clear, but the Centers for Disease Control and Prevention (2007) report that autism spectrum disorders affect an approximate average of one child in every 150. Furthermore, their prevalence appears to be increasing dramatically. Between 1993 and 1998, for example, there was an increase of 244 percent in identified cases of autism (Vaughn, Bos, & Schumm, 2003). Why this should be happening is unclear. Some educators hypothesize that the increase is due to better assessment measures, changes in diagnostic criteria, and growing awareness of PDDs among parents and professionals, rather than an actual rise in incidence (Hagin, 2004).

Children and adolescents with autism display a lack of responsiveness and unawareness of social situations; for example, they may make little or no eye contact, show little awareness of social situations, and exhibit a lack of interest in sharing enjoyable activities with other people. In addition, they may have little or no spoken language; those who do develop language may use it idiosyncratically (e.g., repeating sentences said to them, a condition known as *echolalia*). Finally, individuals with autism often exhibit restricted, repetitive patterns of behavior (e.g., body rocking or hand flapping; inflexible adherence to routines or rituals) and a consuming preoccupation with specific topics (e.g., train schedules). Hypersensitivity to sensory input such as noise, lights, and touch is also common. Autism is four times more common in boys than in girls (National Dissemination Center for Children with Disabilities, 2003).

There is ongoing debate about whether Asperger syndrome (AS) is an independent diagnostic category or a mild form of autism (Myles, Gagnon, Moyer, & Trautman, 2004). In fact, the Individuals with Disabilities Education Act (IDEA) does not recognize AS as a specific disability category, so that youngsters with Asperger syndrome are often served under the diagnostic labels of autism, behavior disorders, or learning disabilities. Like autism, AS is characterized by marked impairment in social interaction; however, individuals with AS often desire interaction—they just lack the skills and knowledge needed to initiate and respond appropriately in social situations. For example, they often demonstrate an inability to understand the perspectives of others and have difficulty understanding nonverbal social cues. Although individuals with AS have no clinically significant delay in cognition and do not have delayed language development, they have difficulty understanding the subtleties of language, like irony and humor (National Dissemination Center, 2003) and their voice quality may be flat, stilted, and "robotic." They also have a restricted range of interests or obsessions, developing an exhaustive knowledge of one topic (e.g., monsters, numbers, or movies) on which they give long-winded lectures. In addition, children and adolescents with AS tend to have poor motor skills and to be clumsy and uncoordinated. Like those with autism, individuals with AS show an "apparently inflexible adherence to specific, nonfunctional routines or rituals" (American Psychiatric Association, 2000, p. 84).

It is important to note that manifestations of autism and AS can range from mild to severe. Thus, two children with the same diagnosis may function very differently and require different kinds and amounts of support. Although there are no cures for PDDs, educational interventions can be effective in bringing about improvements. Students with autism can benefit from augmentative and alternative communication systems. For example, they can learn to point to a picture on a communication board to indicate preferences for academic work. Students with PDDs can also benefit from direct instruction in social skills and in reading social cues. Since students with autism and AS adhere rigidly to routines, it's also essential that you create and follow a consistent classroom schedule. If a change in the schedule is necessary, you need to provide plenty of warning. See the Practical Tips box for additional suggestions on helping students with AS; also refer to Kline and Silver (2004) for a comprehensive discussion.

PRACTICAL TIPS FOR

HELPING STUDENTS WITH ASPERGER SYNDROME

- *Establish a "home base,"* a safe area in which a student can calm down, away from the overstimulation of the classroom (e.g., a counselor's office, a resource room, the nurse's office). Home base should *not* be used for time-out or punishment.

- *Use "priming" to familiarize students with academic material prior to its use in school.* Priming can reduce the stress associated with new tasks and increase success. A typical priming session lasts 10–15 minutes and is held in a quiet space the evening or morning before the materials are to be used.

- *Modify the environment:*
  Seat the student in an area free of distraction.
  Keep the student's space free of unnecessary materials.
  Use checklists to help the student be organized.
  Provide opportunities for the student to move around.

- *Modify instruction:*
  Since fine motor skills can make handwriting difficult, let the student type or record responses.
  Since verbal information can be difficult to process, use visual supports whenever possible.
  Color-code assignments.
  Provide the student with a skeletal outline of the main ideas.
  Schedule short, frequent conferences with the student to check for comprehension.
  Break assignments into shorter tasks.
  Allow the student to use a computer or calculator.

Source: Myles, Gagnon, Moyer, & Trautman, 2004.

Attention-Deficit/Hyperactivity Disorder

Although teachers often find it particularly challenging to work with students who have attention-deficit/hyperactivity disorder (ADHD), this condition is *not* included in the IDEA's definition of children with disabilities. For this reason, students with ADHD are not eligible for services under IDEA unless they fall into other disability categories (e.g., learning disabilities, serious emotional disturbance, other health impairment). They may, however, be able to receive special services under

Section 504 of the Rehabilitation Act of 1973. Section 504 prohibits discrimination on the basis of disability by recipients of federal funds and requires that public schools receiving federal funding address the needs of children with disabilities. As defined in Section 504, a person with a disability is any person who has a physical or mental impairment substantially limiting a major life activity such as learning. Thus, students with ADHD may fit within that definition.

No diagnostic test for ADHD is currently available, but Table 5.3 lists the symptoms that suggest an individual has ADHD. Five conditions must be met for a positive diagnosis: (1) Six or more of the symptoms must be present; (2) the symptoms have to have persisted for at least six months; (3) the symptoms have to have appeared before seven years of age; (4) the symptoms must result in impaired functioning in at least two settings (e.g., home and school); and (5) the symptoms do not occur exclusively during the course of another pervasive developmental or psychotic disorder, and are not accounted for by another mental disorder. Keep in mind that any one of the behaviors can be normal. It is when a individual frequently displays a large number of these behaviors at a developmentally inappropriate age that the possibility of ADHD should be considered.

It is estimated that 3 percent to 5 percent of school-age children in the United States have ADHD, with far more boys than girls affected (Wodrich, 2000). The reason for the disparity is not clear. Some researchers believe the explanation lies in brain biochemistry or structure; others point to the way boys are socialized, which may make it harder to sit quietly and attend. Still others suggest subtle discrimination on the part of elementary teachers, who are predominantly women (Wodrich, 2000).

Students with ADHD often have difficulties in school. They may be underproductive or disorganized, failing to complete their work, or even losing it. They may also have problems with memory, language, visual perception, and fine motor control, which interfere with academic achievement. Indeed, as many as 35 percent of children and adolescents with ADHD may have learning disabilities, compared with 3 percent of all children (Wodrich, 2000). Finally—and not surprisingly—individuals with ADHD may have problems meeting behavioral expectations and getting along with their peers.

In order to help students with ADHD, your classroom needs to be predictable, secure, and structured. Behavioral expectations must be clear, and consequences must be fair and consistent. The Practical Tips box offers some more specific suggestions.

PAUSE AND REFLECT

In recent years, dramatic increases in the number of children who have been diagnosed and treated for ADHD have stirred debate not only about the possibility of overdiagnosis, but even whether the disorder really exists. Skeptics criticize teachers for wanting to suppress children's natural enthusiasm and energy, parents for failing to provide appropriate guidance and discipline, and physicians for overmedicating. What do you think about this?

General Strategies for Helping Students with Disabilities and ADHD

Implementing inclusion on the secondary level is especially challenging, since content area teachers generally feel pressure to "cover the curriculum"—pressure that has been heightened in this age of high-stakes testing. Teachers also expect

TABLE 5.3 Symptoms of Attention-Deficit/Hyperactivity Disorder

Either (1) or (2):

(1) Six (or more) of the following symptoms of inattention have persisted for at least 6 months to a degree that is maladaptive and inconsistent with developmental level:

Inattention

   (a) Often fails to give close attention to details or makes careless mistakes in schoolwork, work, or other activities.
   (b) Often has difficulty sustaining attention in tasks or play activities.
   (c) Often does not seem to listen when spoken to directly.
   (d) Often does no follow through on instructions and fails to finish schoolwork, chores, or duties in the workplace (not due to oppositional behavior or failure to understand directions).
   (e) Often has difficulty organizing tasks and activities.
   (f) Often avoids, dislikes, or is reluctant to engage in tasks that require sustained mental effort (such as schoolwork or homework).
   (g) Often loses things necessary for tasks or activities (e.g., toys, school assignments, pencils, books, tools).
   (h) Is often easily distracted by extraneous stimuli.
   (i) Is often forgetful in daily activities.

(2) Six (or more) of the following symptoms of hyperactivity-impulsivity have persisted for at least 6 months to a degree that is maladaptive and inconsistent with developmental level:

Hyperactivity

   (a) Often fidgets with hands or feet or squirms in seat.
   (b) Often leaves seat in classroom or in other situations in which remaining seated in expected.
   (c) Often runs about or climbs excessively in situations in which it is inappropriate (in adolescents or adults, may be limited to subjective feelings of restlessness).
   (d) Often has difficulty playing or engaging in leisure activities quietly.
   (e) Is often "on the go" or often acts as if "driven by a motor."
   (f) Often talks excessively.

Impulsivity

   (g) Often blurts out answers before questions have been completed.
   (h) Often has difficulty awaiting turn.
   (i) Often interrupts or intrudes on others (e.g., butts into conversations or games).

Source: Reprinted with permission from the *Diagnostic and statistical manual of mental disorders,* Text Revision, Fourth Edition, (Copyrighr 2000). American Psychiatric Association.

students to have independent study skills and to possess the prior knowledge required to master new material, something that may not be true of students with disabilities (Mastropieri & Scruggs, 2001). Nonetheless, research indicates that inclusion on the secondary level can be successful in terms of academic and social outcomes (Mastropieri & Scruggs, 2001; Wallace, Anderson, Bartholomay, & Hupp, 2002). The following section of the chapter delineates some of the ways to enhance the likelihood of such success.

PRACTICAL TIPS FOR

HELPING STUDENTS WITH ADHD

- Provide structure, routine, predictability, and consistency.
- Make sure that behavioral expectations are clear.
- Seat them close to you, among attentive, well-focused students.
- Make frequent eye contact.
- Make sure their desks are free of distractions; provide cardboard dividers to block out distractions.
- Provide a quiet work area or a "private office" to which students can move for better concentration.
- Provide headphones to block out noise during seatwork or other times that require concentration.
- Provide opportunities to move around in legitimate ways (e.g., exercise breaks, doing errands).
- Use physical contact to focus attention (e.g., a hand on a shoulder).
- Develop private signals to help focus attention.
- Ease transitions by providing cues and warnings.
- Use positive reinforcement and behavior modification techniques.
- Modify assignments:
    Cut the written workload.
    Break the assignment into manageable parts.
- Limit the amount of homework.
- Allow more time on assignments or tests.
- Assist with organization (e.g., assignment pads; checklists; color-coded notebooks for different subjects; accordion folders for loose papers).
- Try to give students at least one task each day that they can do successfully.
- Try to call on students when they are paying attention; use their first names before calling on them.
- Provide extra sets of books to keep at home so that students are not overwhelmed after an absence and to prevent problems caused by forgetting books.
- Provide access to a computer, along with keyboard and word processing instruction; do not remove access to the computer as a penalty.
- DO NOT PUNISH; DO NOT ASSUME STUDENTS ARE LAZY; DO NOT GIVE UP.

Source: Adapted from Rief, 1993 and CHADD Facts, 1993.

Become Familiar with the Student's IEP or 504 Plan

The IDEA requires that an individualized education program (IEP) be developed for each student with a disability. IEPs are developed by a team comprised of a representative of the local education agency (e.g., an administrator who can commit school district resources), one of the student's general education teachers, the special education teacher who will have primary responsibility for implementing the IEP, parents or guardians, a person who can interpret the instructional implications of the evaluation results, the student (when appropriate), and other individuals at the discretion of the parent or school.

Similarly, a student who is eligible for special services under Section 504 of the Rehabilitation Act will have a "504 plan" outlining the accommodations and services needed to ensure that the student receives an appropriate education. Like the IEP, a 504 plan is developed by a team, although its composition is not specified by law.

Unfortunately, at the middle and high school levels, general education teachers often do not participate in the IEP or 504 process; sometimes they do not even know which students in their classrooms have been identified as having special needs (Schumm & Vaughn, 1992). Moreover, obtaining access to students' IEPs and 504s is not always easy. Policies and procedures vary from school to school. Sandy reports that by the second day of school, her mailbox is filled with the IEPs and 504s of students in her classes, and she has to sign a form indicating that she's received them. In contrast, Christina never gets copies; instead, a special educator or the school nurse shows her the documents. However you're told, our teachers emphasize the fact that implementation is your responsibility. As Sandy comments: "Teachers need to realize that 504s and IEPs are not optional. You can't ignore them. And if no one shows you any IEPs or 504s (as sometimes happens), it's your responsibility to track them down and read them."

It's also important to reexamine IEPs every marking period and make sure that you are monitoring the progress of students with disabilities. In this regard, it's helpful to keep a folder of relevant work samples to document progress (Vaughn, Bos, & Schumm, 2003).

Create an Accepting Climate

Secondary teachers often display a less positive attitude toward inclusion than their elementary-level counterparts (Scruggs & Mastropieri, 1996). This is unfortunate, since the success of inclusion largely depends on a teacher's ability and willingness to create a positive atmosphere that is accepting of individual differences (Mastropieri & Scruggs, 2001). You can promote a positive climate by making it clear that all students are accepted, valued members of the class; establishing norms that emphasize belonging and respect; and implementing group activities that foster interaction between students with disabilities and their nondisabled peers (Soodak & McCarthy, 2006). Students with special needs may display significant social deficiencies and have difficulty establishing friendships (Meadan & Monda-Amaya, 2008); in this case, you can help students find common interests, regardless of their abilities or special needs (Grandin, 2007). If social interaction is fostered through commonalities, students may be more likely to accept each other as equal members of the classroom community. (Refer back to Chapter 3 for additional ideas to create an accepting classroom climate.)

Coordinate and Collaborate with Special Education Teachers and Paraprofessionals

In addition to following your students' IEPs and 504 plans, it is important to communicate regularly with special services personnel. For example, you can ask a special educator for suggestions about enhancing the learning of your students; you might also ask the special educator to demonstrate lessons or to come in and help you instruct students with special needs. You should also inform the special education teacher if you are concerned about a student's progress.

When approaching special services personnel, bring specific information about the student and about the interventions and accommodations you've already tried. Complaints like "He's driving me crazy," "She constantly demands attention," or "He just can't hack it in my class" are not helpful. The more detailed your information can be, the more likely you are to receive assistance. Here are some of our teachers' suggestions about the kinds of information to bring:

- An overall description of the student (both strengths and weaknesses)
- If the student exhibits problem behavior, a detailed description of the inappropriate behavior:

  When does the student exhibit the behavior?

  How frequently does the student exhibit the behavior?

  What antecedent events set off the behavior?

  What is the duration of the behavior?

  What is the reaction of other students in the class?

- If the student is having academic problems, a detailed description of the student's academic difficulties (with work samples to support your description)
- Efforts on your part to correct or deal with the problem
- How you'd like to be helped or what type of help you believe the student needs

As inclusion has become more widespread, so too has the practice of having content specialists co-teach with special educators in the general education classroom. Co-teaching is defined as two or more people sharing responsibility for planning, teaching, and evaluating some or all of the students in a class (Villa, Thousand, & Nevin, 2008). Co-teaching, also known as collaborative teaching or cooperative teaching, can take a variety of forms (Dieker, 2001). For example, in the "lead and support" model, one teacher takes responsibility for instruction while the other offers assistance and support to individuals or small groups. In "parallel teaching," teachers jointly plan instruction, but each delivers it to half the class, and in "team teaching," both teachers share the planning and instruction of students.

Although co-teaching can be very effective, it also poses challenges for both parties. Some of these difficulties stem from inadequate school supports (e.g., lack of common preparation time), personality conflicts, and a lack of clarity about roles and responsibilities in co-taught classrooms (Murray, 2004). None of our four teachers works in a co-teaching arrangement, but they have seen situations that are less than ideal. Christina comments:

> Regular ed teachers sometimes have a problem working with special ed teachers; they are very "territorial" and treat the special educator like an aide. They don't do collaborative planning; they just say, "Here's what we're doing." But sometimes the problem is the other way around. You have a regular ed teacher who really wants to collaborate with the special ed teacher, but the special ed teacher wants to sit in the back of the room and only help a couple of kids.

In order to avoid these problems, it is essential to discuss the roles that each teacher will have in the general education classroom. The Practical Tips box lists strategies for co-teaching at the secondary level.

Like co-teaching, using paraprofessionals or teaching assistants has become an increasingly popular method of supporting students with disabilities in general education classrooms. In fact, in many schools, having a paraprofessional accompany a student with disabilities to class is the "primary or exclusive" way in which inclusion is accomplished (Giangreco & Doyle, 2002, p. 2). Paraprofessionals can play a valuable, vital role in inclusive classrooms, but too often, they become the student's actual instructor, while the teacher becomes the delegator (Giangreco & Doyle, 2002). When this happens, we have a situation in which those who are least qualified to teach are responsible for instructing the students who present the most complex challenges.

PRACTICAL TIPS FOR

CO-TEACHING IN SECONDARY CLASSROOMS

- **Begin slowly.** Discuss your respective understandings of co-teaching; examine various models.

- **Involve an administrator.** Discuss the kinds of administrative support that is needed (especially with respect to common planning time). Find out if such support will be forthcoming.

- **Get to know your partner.** Discuss your expectations with respect to roles and responsibilities regarding
    Planning whole class instruction
    Planning modifications for individual students
    Conducting instruction
    Grading
    Parental contact
    Discipline

- **Create a workable schedule.** Decide how often co-teaching will occur (daily, a few times a week, for a specific unit). Decide on the model that will be used. Think about how to ensure that both teachers are actively involved and that neither feels over- or underutilized. Arrange for common planning time.

Source: Adapted from Murawski & Dieker, 2004.

If you have paraprofessionals in your classes, it is critical that you remain engaged with the students who have disabilities and not turn their education over to someone who may be uncomfortable and unknowledgeable about the subject matter. You also need to discuss explicitly what your respective roles and responsibilities will be with respect to instruction and behavior management. Paraprofessionals can provide support by carrying out a variety of noninstructional activities (e.g., preparing materials, taking attendance) as well as instructional tasks (e.g., assisting students during independent work, providing additional practice opportunities to reinforce previously taught material), but they should not have primary responsibility for a student's learning. It is also desirable to have paraprofessionals interact with *all* students, not just those with disabilities.

Examine your Classroom Environment for Possible Mismatch

It's important to remember that problems do not always reside exclusively within a student. Sometimes problems are the result of a discrepancy between a student's needs and the classroom environment. A student teacher shared this account of a mismatch:

> *Jason is an autistic student who has a full-time aide. While Jason is very intelligent and capable of completing assignments, he is often frustrated and agitated in class. The other students, including the teacher, often make inappropriate comments about his outbursts and seem to lack patience with him. And his aide doesn't try to educate them about his condition. Jason's teacher has placed him with a group of students who are not easily distracted, to prevent Jason's occasional outbursts from disturbing the group. However, the students in Jason's group rarely include him in their discussions and often completely ignore him. It's not surprising that Jason reacts by getting agitated.*

As this story illustrates, we sometimes think of a student as disabled, when actually the problem is the result of a *disabling situation* (Gearheart, Weishahn, & Gearheart, 1992). Before concluding that "the entire problem is the kid," examine your classroom situation and reflect on ways the environment may be contributing to the student's difficulties. Here are some questions that our teachers ask themselves:

- Where is the student sitting? Is the seat near a source of distraction? Is it too far from the teacher?

- Is sitting in groups too difficult for the student to handle? Should I move the student to a pair or to individual seating?

- What type of academic work am I providing? Are assignments too mechanical? Too dry? Too long? Do they require too much independence? Do I ever allow choice?

- How do I speak with the student? How do I praise the student? *Do* I praise the student?

- What rules and routines have I set up? Are they contrary to the student's ability to comply? Am I expecting quiet behavior too long? Am I setting the student up for failure?

- Am I allowing an appropriate amount of time for completing assignments? For transitions?

Don't Lower Your Expectations

Sometimes, in our efforts to be understanding and sympathetic, we lower our expectations so much that we teach students to accept less from themselves as well. We water down curriculum; we forgive inappropriate behavior; we place students in safe environments where they will never be asked to do things we are sure they can't do. And when, in fact, they cannot do them, when they behave inappropriately, and when they do not learn, our beliefs seem justified.

Last year, one of Sandy's classes included a student who had a brain tumor that caused permanent motor skill damage; an aide attended classes with him. As Sandy recounted:

I never lowered one standard nor did I lower my expectations for this wonderful young man. He had to do what everyone else in the class had to do but we had to be creative in some situations. Every year I give a major lab in which students must develop a plan and perform a series of experiments in order to identify an unknown solution. This young man obviously could not safely handle chemicals in the laboratory. I did not excuse him from the lab nor did I substitute a different activity (as his IEP suggested), but rather he developed a plan on his own and I became his hands the day of the lab. He told me step by step what he wanted me to do and I followed his instructions exactly.

I have to admit that while he was instructing me through his plan I really thought that he was on the wrong track. I couldn't see the direction in which he was heading because it certainly wasn't the way that I would have approached the unknowns. It wasn't until the end that I was able to see how this unique plan was going to result in a successful identification. He successfully identified his unknown in his own unique manner. Needless to say he was beaming! Having students like this young man in your classroom makes you grow as a teacher as you strive to help them reach their potential.

Use Peer Tutoring, Peer Assistance, and Cooperative Learning

Successful inclusion programs make effective use of peers. Students can serve as *tutors* on academic tasks, *buddies* who assist with difficult activities, or *advocates* who "watch out" for the welfare of those with special needs (Gearheart, Weishahn, & Gearheart, 1992). For example, Peer Buddies is a structured program of peer support in which a nondisabled high school student is paired with a student with disabilities for at least one period each day. The Buddies support their partners in a variety of ways and in a variety of settings. They may accompany them to a school pep rally, introduce them to other general education students during lunch, help them complete a lab project in a science class, or teach them to

TABLE 5.4 Ways That Peers Can Support Classmates with Disabilities

- Teach class room routines (e.g., where to put homework, what to do when you first get to class).
- Read a test and record answers.
- Read or record selections from a textbook, paraphrasing as needed.
- Take notes during a teacher lecture and spend time discussing the notes and answering questions at the end of the period.
- Help a classmate fulfill an assigned role during cooperative learning activities.
- Facilitate conversation with other general education students during free time.
- Keep track of assignments when students are absent.
- Provide tutoring in a specific skill.
- Provide assistance with organization (e.g., recording assignments, finding the relevant place in the textbook, organizing notebooks).

Note: Although peers can support classmates with disabilities, it is important to make sure that every student has an opportunity to be the tutor or supporter; in other words, students with disabilities should not always be relegated to the position of "helpee."

Source: Adapted from Copeland, et al., 2002.

set tables at a restaurant serving as a job training site. (See Table 5.4 for additional ways that peers can provide supports.) Copeland and her colleagues (2002) found that general and special educators involved in a Peer Buddies program reported both academic and social benefits; in particular, students who received support from peers seemed more independent, more self-confident, and more willing to participate in everyday high school activities.

Research has also demonstrated that cooperative learning can promote positive social relationships between students with disabilities and their peers. The use of cooperative learning can help to minimize the problem of students with special needs being isolated and rejected *socially,* even though they are included *physically* in the regular classroom. (See Chapter 10 for guidance on implementing successful small-group work.)

STUDENTS WHO ARE TROUBLED

During one meeting, the teachers talked about how they try to be alert to problems their students might be experiencing. Sandy told us how she tries to distinguish between problems that warrant immediate action and those that do not, and how she collects additional information:

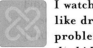

> I watch for changes in students' behavior. If I see anything that looks like drug abuse, I report it immediately. If it doesn't seem like a drug problem, I generally approach the student and ask what's going on. If the kid seems depressed, I'll say something like, "Hey, you seem a little down today. Are you having a problem? Do you want to talk?" We all have bad days, and adolescents have wide swings of mood; it's the nature of the beast. A day or two

of strange behavior doesn't necessarily mean there's a big problem. Adolescents aren't very good at masking their emotions, and most of the time they're upset because they had a fight with their mother, or the dog had to be put to sleep, or their boyfriend or girlfriend broke up with them. But if a kid is acting weird or seems depressed for longer than a few days, I check with other teachers to find out if they're seeing anything unusual too. If they've also noticed problems, I go to the principal or the vice principal; often they know if something is going on at home. If there appears to be a real problem, I'll report it.

As Sandy's comments illustrate, *you need to be alert to the indicators of potential problems.* As an adult immersed in adolescent culture, you will probably develop a good idea of what typical teenage behavior is like. This allows you to detect deviations or changes in a student's behavior that might signal the presence of a problem. Learn to ask yourself a series of questions when you notice atypical behavior (Kottler & Kottler, 1993):

- What is unusual about this student's behavior?
- Is there a pattern to what I have observed?
- What additional information do I need to make an informed judgment?
- Whom might I contact to collect this background information?
- What are the risks of waiting longer to figure out what is going on?
- Does this student seem to be in any imminent danger?
- Whom can I consult about this case?

Substance Abuse

In order to deal with problems rooted in drugs and alcohol, many schools have student assistance programs (SAPs) and student assistance counselors (SACs). Note that the initials "SA" do *not* stand for substance abuse. The wording is deliberate. Although SAPs focus on identifying and helping students at risk for alcohol and other drug problems, they generally adopt a broad-based approach. There are two good reasons for this strategy. First, drug problems usually occur in conjunction with other problems—depression, abuse, academic difficulties, family problems, pregnancy. Second, it's less stigmatizing to go to a student assistance counselor than a substance abuse counselor. Shirley Sexton, the SAC in Christina's school, emphasizes this point: "It's really important not to be known as the 'drug lady.' I try to make it clear that I'm available to talk about all kinds of problems that kids may be experiencing—from bereavement to divorce to communication problems with parents."

With respect to alcohol and drugs, SACs can provide help to students who are the *children of alcoholics/addicts (COAs) and students who are themselves substance abusers.* Let's turn first to the problems of COAs and consider the cases of Amanda and Eric (adapted from Powell, Zehm, & Kottler, 1995).

Amanda's father is an alcoholic who becomes aggressive and abusive when he drinks. At age 13, Amanda is her mother's primary source of support and works hard to make her family appear normal. She has assumed many adult responsibilities that would normally be carried out by the father of a household. At school, she is a very success-ful student; her teachers describe her as superdependable and motivated. They don't realize that she is filled with feelings of inadequacy and confusion, that her behavior is prompted by a compulsive need to be perfect. Nor do they notice that in between classes and at lunch time Amanda spends most of her time alone. Amanda avoids forming friendships because she is afraid of revealing the family secret.

Eric is a ninth grader whose teacher describes him as sullen, disrespectful, and obstructive. He frequently fights with other students and has been suspended several times for antisocial behavior. His mother claims not to understand his behavior; she reports that Eric never acts this way at home and implies that his teachers are the cause of his perpetual negative attitude. Yet he often has violent outbursts at home. At the core of Eric's behavior is anger: He is enraged by the rejection he feels from his alcoholic father and feels resentful that his mother spends so much time wallowing in self-pity. He soothes his pain by planning ways to leave home when he's old enough to drop out of school. He is on the verge of jumping into his own life of addiction.

Substance abuse touches secondary classrooms every time youngsters like Amanda and Eric enter the room—and their presence is not a rare occurrence. It is estimated that one in every four students sitting in a classroom comes from a family in which one or both parents are addicted to drugs or alcohol (Powell, Zehm, & Kottler, 1995). When these youngsters are angry and disruptive like Eric, it is relatively easy to recognize that a problem exists; it is far more difficult when students are compliant perfectionists like Amanda.

Leslie Lillian, a student assistance counselor in Fred's district, stresses that COAs can exhibit a wide variety of behaviors (see Table 5.5):

> *Some children become perfectionists and peacemakers. They want to prevent situations that might evoke their parents' anger because their parents' responses are so unpredictable. It's as if they think to themselves, "I'm not going to disturb anything; I'm not going to do anything wrong; I'll try and keep the peace, so that no one will be angry." Some children become class clowns; maybe they've found that making people laugh breaks the tension, or maybe they're seeking attention. Others become very angry; they may begin to lie, or steal, or cheat. Some become sad and melancholy; everything about them says, "Nurture me." We see a whole spectrum of reactions—and it's the same spectrum of behaviors that we see in kids from violent homes.*

It's important to understand that for COAs, family life revolves around the addiction. Rules are arbitrary and irrational; boundaries between parents and chil-dren are blurred; and life is marked by unpredictability and inconsistency. Leslie comments:

> *These kids never know what they're going home to. One day, they may bring a paper home from school that's gotten a low grade, and the parent might say, "That's OK, just do it over." Another day, they might get beaten up for bringing home a paper like that.*

One of the most frustrating aspects of working with COAs is the realization that you do not have the power to change the child's home life. Instead, you must

TABLE 5.5 Characteristics of Children of Alcoholics/Addicts

- Difficulty in creating and maintaining trusting relationships, often leading to isolation.
- Low self-esteem.
- Self-doubt.
- Difficulty in being spontaneous and open, caused by a need to be in control and to minimize the risk of being surprised.
- Denial and repression because of the need to collaborate with other family members in keeping "the secret."
- General feelings of guilt about areas for which the child had no responsibility.
- Uncertainty about his or her own feelings and desires caused by shifting parental roles.
- Seeing things in an "all or nothing" context, which sometimes manifests itself in a perfectionist fear of failure.
- Poor impulse control, which may result in acting-out behavior, probably caused by lack of parental guidance, love, and discipline.
- Potential for depression, phobias, panic reactions, and hyperactivity.
- Preoccupation with the family.
- Abuse of alcohol and/or drugs.

Source: Adapted from Towers, 1989.

concentrate on what you *are* able to do during the time the student is in your classroom. Many of the strategies are not different from those we have espoused for all students. (See the Practical Tips box.) For example, it is essential that you establish clear, consistent rules and work to create a climate of trust and caring.

In addition to using these strategies, you should find out if your school has student assistance counselors or other special services personnel who can provide help. Find out if support groups for COAs are available. For example, Tonia Moore, an SAC in Sandy's district, runs groups at school, sometimes alone and sometimes with the guidance counselor. Tonia speaks about the benefits that joining such a group can bring:

> *There's such a sense of relief. The comments are always the same: "I thought I was the only one." "I didn't know anyone else was going through this stuff." The shame is so great, even at a very young age, and the need to keep it all a secret is so hard. There's instant camaraderie.*

Unfortunately, COAs may be reluctant to join such groups. Shirley Sexton (the SAC in Christina's school) has recently started three groups at the high school, one on bereavement, one on divorce and separation, and one for COAs. Although students immediately signed up for the first two groups, thus far she's gotten little response to the third. Shirley is not surprised. "It'll take some time," she explains. "Talking about your parents' alcoholism or addiction is a touchy issue."

A second way that substance abuse can affect middle and high school classrooms is when students themselves abuse drugs and alcohol. Up-to-date information on adolescent drug and alcohol use comes from an annual study sponsored by the National Institute on Drug Abuse (Johnston, O'Malley, Bachman, & Schulenberg, 2008),

PRACTICAL TIPS FOR

HELPING CHILDREN OF ALCOHOLICS/ADDICTS

- **Be observant.** Watch your students not just for academic or behavior problems, but also for the more subtle signs of addiction and emotional distress. Remember that COAs can be overachieving, cooperative, and quiet, as well as disruptive and angry.

- **Set boundaries that are enforced consistently.** When chaos exists at home, some sense of order is crucial at school.

- **Be flexible.** Although it is necessary to set boundaries, classroom rules that are too rigid and unyielding may invite students to act out.

- **Make addiction a focus of discussion.** Find a way to deal with this subject. Incorporate addiction into literacy instruction, science, social studies, etc.

- **Make it clear you are available.** Communicate that you are eager and open to talk. Reach out to the troubled student in a gentle, caring way. "I notice you are having some difficulty. I just want you to know that I care about you. Call me any time you are ready to talk. And if you would rather speak to someone else, let me find you someone you can trust."

- **Develop a referral network.** Find out what services are available to help and refer the student for appropriate professional care.

- **Accept what you can do little about.** You can't make people stop drinking or taking drugs.

Source: Adapted from Powell, Zehm, & Kottler, 1995.

which surveys 50,000 students in grades 8, 10, and 12 located in about 400 schools nationwide. Results from the 2008 study show that the proportion of 8th-, 10th-, and 12th-grade students who reported using any illicit drug in the prior 12 months continued a gradual decline that began in 1996 for 8th-graders and in 2001 for 10th- and 12th-graders. Indeed, among the nation's 8th-graders, there has now been a two-thirds decline in annual use of illicit drugs (from 23.6 percent in 1996 to 7.4 percent in 2008). Specific drugs showing some decline in use are amphetamines, methamphetamine, cocaine, and crack. After reaching a low point in 2005, use of the drug ecstasy has increased and is now regarded as remaining steady. Other drugs with little change in usage in 2008 are LSD, heroin, and narcotics such as Oxycontin and Vicodin. Marijuana use had been in a gradual but steady decline since 1996 for 8th graders and since 2001 for the upper grades. In 2008, however, survey results indicate that this decline ended, with a slight usage increase in all grades. With respect to alcohol, there has been a decline in all measures of drinking at all three grade levels since 2001, and that gradual decline continued in 2008.

To a large extent, SACs rely on teachers to refer students who might be having problems with alcohol and other drugs or who might be at risk for such problems. But teachers may be particularly reluctant to make referrals about suspected drug use. Several different reasons for this reluctance emerged during conversations with teachers and counselors. First, some teachers think drug use is just not all that serious. According to Carol Lowinger, the SAC in Fred's school, "Some teachers have a tendency to minimize the situation—especially if it involves alcohol or pot. They just don't consider pot to be a 'real' drug. They think, 'Oh, all kids do this; it's not that big a deal.'"

In addition, Carol speculates that some teachers feel it's not their role to get involved, while others want to play the role of confidante:

> *Sometimes, teachers are overwhelmed by all the responsibilities of teaching. They feel like they have more than enough to do without getting involved in students' personal problems . . . . But other times, teachers don't refer because they want to try to help the kid themselves. You know, a lot of teachers really like the role of mediator, caretaker, trusted confidante. They like the fact that a student is confiding in them about a problem, and sometimes they make a pact of confidentiality with the student: "You can tell me your secret. I won't tell anybody." But if the kid is in serious trouble, that can be a problem. First of all, they don't really have the training to help the way a counselor could. Second, they might be sending a message to the kid that it's not okay to go to a counselor or a mental health professional—and that's not a message we want to send . . . . Third, they could actually be serving as a "professional enabler"—they're allowing the kid to continue behavior that could be self-destructive . . . . What you've got to do is say to the kid, "I care too much about you to allow this to continue. We've got to get help for you."*

Another reason for teachers' reluctance to refer is the belief that they are "turning kids in" when they would rather "give the kid a break" (Newsam, 1992). Sandy herself comments on this attitude:

> **Some teachers are afraid to report suspected drug use because they don't want to create a hassle for the kid. They don't want to get the kid in trouble. They may also be afraid that reporting kids will ruin their relationship with students. But I haven't found that to be the case. Sometimes, the kid will come back and say, "Why did you do that?" But I say, "This is too big for us. We need more help." Sometimes, I'll even have kids come to tell me about a problem with a friend. They know I'll find help.** *That's what they want.*

Finally, teachers may be reluctant to report suspected drug use because they are unsure about the indicators. Tonia is very sensitive to this problem:

> *Teachers tell me, "I have no idea what substance abuse looks like. It wasn't a part of my training. I wouldn't know when to refer a student." I tell them, that's okay. You can't tell substance abuse just by looking. There has to be a chemical screening. But you can see changes in behavior. You know enough about kids to know when somebody's behavior has changed, or if their behavior is different from all the other kids. You don't need to know the student is using; you just need to suspect that there may be drug use or a problem related to drug use.*

What are the behaviors that might lead you to suspect drug use and to make a referral? Figure 5.2 shows the behavior checklist used at Fred's high school. Many schools use forms that are very similar to this one. Keeping your school's behavior checklist handy can help you stay alert to the possibility that students are using drugs or living with addiction in their families.

Academic Performance
_____Drop in grades
_____Decrease in participation
_____Inconsistent work
_____Works below potential
_____Compulsive overachievement
_____Decrease in motivation

School Attendance
_____Change in attendance
_____Absenteeism
_____Tardiness
_____Class cutting
_____Frequent visits to nurse or counselor
_____Frequent restroom visits
_____Frequent requests for hall passes

Social Problems
_____Family problems
_____Job problems
_____Peer problems
_____Relationship problems
_____Run away
_____Constantly borrowing money

Physical Symptoms
_____Staggering/stumbling, poor coordination
_____Incoherent or slurred speech
_____Glossy, bloodshot eyes
_____Smelling of alcohol/marijuana
_____Vomiting, nausea
_____Deteriorating physical appearance
_____Sleeping in class
_____Physical injuries
_____Frequent physical complaints
_____Dramatic changes in musculature

Extracurricular Activities
_____Lack of participation
_____Possession of drugs/alcohol

_____Involvement in thefts and assault
_____Vandalism
_____Talking about involvement in illegal activities
_____Possession of paraphernalia
_____Increasing noninvolvement
_____Dropping out/missing practice(s)
_____Not fulfilling responsibilities
_____Performance changes

Disruptive Behavior
_____Defiance of rules
_____Irresponsibility, blaming, lying, fighting, cheating
_____Problem with authority figures
_____Sudden outbursts, verbal abuse
_____Obscene language or gestures
_____Attention-getting behavior
_____Frequently in wrong areas
_____Hyperactivity, nervousness
_____Lack of motivation, apathy
_____Extreme negativism

Atypical Behavior
_____Difficulty in accepting mistakes
_____Overly sensitive or defensive
_____Erratic behavior
_____Boasts about alcohol or drug use
_____Change of friends
_____Depression
_____Disoriented
_____Inappropriate responses
_____Withdrawn/difficulty relating
_____Sexual behavior in public
_____Unrealistic goals
_____Seeking adult advice without a specific problem
_____Rigid obedience
_____Constantly seeks approval

Figure 5.2   The Behavior Checklist Used in Fred's District

It's important to distinguish between situations in which a pattern of behavior problems suggests possible *drug use outside of school* and situations in which a student appears to be *under the influence of drugs during school, at school functions,* or *on school property.* When you see students who might be "under the influence," you cannot wait to fill out a behavior checklist; you need to alert the appropriate personnel as soon as you possibly can. Fred shares this experience:

A few years ago, I had this really bright kid in my first-period class . . . . But he got into drugs. I remember one day in particular when he came into class high. I didn't realize it at first, because he just sat down quietly and everything seemed okay. But then he got up to sharpen his pencil, and I could see that he was walking funny. He was actually leaning to one side. It looked like he was going to fall over . . . . I gave the rest of the class an assignment and asked him to come with me out into the hall. I tried to be really discreet; I didn't want everyone watching and talking about him. I planned to call the assistant principal, but the principal happened to be walking by just at that minute, so he took him to the nurse.

Tonia Moore explains one of the reasons for immediately alerting the appropriate personnel if you suspect a student is under the influence:

It used to be that teachers would come to me at the end of the day and say, "I was really worried about X today. I think he was really on something." That's no good. I need to know at the time. *After all, that student could fall down the stairs, or the student could leave the building during lunch time and get killed crossing the street.* We have to deal with the problem immediately. *It can really be a matter of life and death.*

Make sure you know to whom you're supposed to refer students who appear to be under the influence of drugs. In Fred and Christina's schools, teachers call an administrator, who comes to the classroom and accompanies the student to the nurse. In Sandy's school, teachers send students to the nurse, who then contacts the student assistance counselor. In Donnie's school, teachers call a security guard who takes the student to the nurse.

Since you cannot be sure that a student is using drugs just by looking, it's important not to be accusatory when you talk with the student. Sandy describes how she usually handles this situation:

If I see a kid with his head down on the desk, I'll go over and ask real quietly, "Do you need to see the nurse?" Usually they'll say, "No, I'm just tired," or "No, I'm bored." I'll tell them, "But this is chemistry! This is supposed to be fun." Usually, the head stays up after that. But if the head goes back down, I'll say, "I think you need to see the nurse. You don't seem to be feeling well." I'm not confrontational, and I try to show the kid that I'm acting out of concern. Sometimes I'm wrong, and it turns out that the kid just stayed up until 4:00 A.M. doing a term paper. That's fine. It's better to err on the side of caution.

Making a referral can be difficult, but you need to remember that turning away and remaining silent can send the message that you condone the behavior—or that you don't care enough to do anything.

One final note: If you suspect that a student is in possession of drugs or alcohol in school (e.g., in a purse or backpack), it's important to bring that person to the appropriate school official rather than undertake a search by yourself. In a landmark case (*New Jersey v. T.L.O.,* 1985), the United States Supreme Court ruled that a school official may properly conduct a search of a student "when there are reasonable grounds for suspecting that the search will turn up evidence that the student has violated or is violating either the law or the rules of the school" (Fischer, Schimmel, & Kelly, 1999). In other words, students in school have fewer protections than are normally afforded to citizens under the stricter "probable cause" standard (Stefkovich & Miller, 1998). Nonetheless, searching a student's belongings is best left to an administrator who is aware of the subtleties of the law. (We will discuss this further in Chapter 12.)

Abuse and Neglect

During one conversation with Donnie, she emphasized the difficulty of detecting abuse and neglect among older students:

 At the high school level, abuse and neglect are not as obvious as they are at the elementary level. Kids cover up more. But it's clear that a lot of them live in situations that are really awful. Teachers have to watch really carefully and listen to all the conversations that you're not supposed to hear. That way you can learn about what's going on in kids' lives and in the community.

As Donnie points out, abuse of adolescents is often well hidden. Furthermore, adolescents just don't seem as vulnerable as younger children: They may have as much strength or weight as adults; they seem able to run away from abusive situations; and they appear to have more access to potential help outside the family. For these reasons, it's easy to think that abuse and neglect are not problems at the high school level. But adolescents still need protection. During one meeting, Christina recalled a girl who had worn a short-sleeved shirt in December when temperatures were in the 20s:

 It was as if she was saying, "Please look at my arm." I did—and saw she had bruises all over it. As a new teacher, I was a little nervous about handling this the right way, so I went to consult with a more experienced teacher. We spoke with one of the school counselors, who took the student to the nurse.

It's also important to realize that girls are not the only victims of abuse. Consider this tale, shared by Donnie:

 A number of years ago, I had a 16-year-old football player in my class. I noticed that he seemed really quiet, which was unusual for him. I asked him to come see me after school. When he came in, I said, "You don't seem yourself. Is everything OK?" To my amazement, he started to cry. It turned out he had been seduced by a 35-year-old woman living next door. Obviously, she didn't tie him down, but having sex with a minor constitutes sexual abuse. It was the last thing I expected. I figured he had broken up with his girlfriend, or he was having a problem on the football team. I was really hit between the eyes, and I was furious. I kept thinking, "How could she do that? He's just a kid." I had difficulty thinking straight. I thought, "Now what do I do?" I was the first person he had told. It was after school, and the psychologist was gone, the counselor was gone. But I convinced him to go with me to the principal. The office took over from there.

The National Child Abuse and Neglect Data System reports that approximately 900,000 children were victims of maltreatment in 2006 (U.S. Department of Health and Human Services, 2008). In order to protect these youth, all states have laws requiring educators to report suspected abuse to the state's "child protective service." Although definitions of abuse vary, states generally include nonaccidental injury, neglect, sexual abuse, and emotional maltreatment. It is essential that you become familiar with the physical and behavioral indicators of these problems. (See Table 5.6.)

Teachers are often reluctant to file a report unless they have absolute proof of abuse. They worry about invading the family's privacy and causing unnecessary embarrassment to everyone involved. Nonetheless, it's important to keep in mind that *no state requires the reporter to have absolute proof before reporting.* What most states do require is "reason to believe" or "reasonable cause to believe or suspect" that abuse has occurred (Fischer, Schimmel, & Kelly, 1999). If you are uncertain whether abuse is occurring, but have reasonable cause, you should err in favor of the student and file a report. Waiting for proof can be dangerous; it may also be illegal. If a child is later harmed, and it becomes clear that you failed to report suspected abuse, both you and your school district may be subject to both civil and criminal liability. Also keep in mind that every state provides immunity from any civil suit or criminal prosecution that might result from the reporting of suspected child abuse or neglect—as long as you have acted "in good faith" (Fischer, Schimmel, & Kelly, 1999).

It's essential that you learn about the reporting procedures in your state *before* you are faced with a situation of suspected child abuse. Some states explicitly name the school personnel who are required to file the report. Other states have more general provisions that require reporting by "any person" who works with children; this would clearly include teachers, nurses, therapists, and counselors (Fischer, Schimmel, & Kelly, 1999). States also vary with respect to the form and content of reports required. Most states require an oral report, followed by a more detailed written report, and some states also have a 24-hour, toll-free hot line. Generally, you should be prepared to provide the student's name and address; the nature and extent of injury or condition observed; and your own name and address (Fischer, Schimmel, & Kelly, 1999).

TABLE 5.6 Physical and Behavioral Indicators of Child Abuse and Neglect

Type of Abuse or Neglect	Physical Indicators	Behavioral Indicators
Physical Abuse	Unexplained • bruises or welts • burns • fractures • lacerations or abrasions	Wary of adult contact Apprehensive when other children cry Behavioral extremes; aggressiveness or withdrawal Frightened of parents Afraid to go home Reports injury by parents
Physical Neglect	Consistent hunger, poor hygiene, inappropriate dress Consistent lack of supervision, especially in dangerous activities or for long periods Constant fatigue or listlessness Unattended physical problems or medical neglect Abandonment	Begging, stealing food Extended stays at school (early arrival and late departure) Constantly falling asleep in class Alcohol or drug abuse Delinquency States there is no caretaker
Sexual Abuse	Difficulty in walking or sitting Torn, stained, or bloody underclothing Pain or itching in genital area Bruises or bleeding in external genitalia, vaginal, or anal areas Venereal disease, especially in preteens Pregnancy	Unwilling to change for and participate in PE Withdrawal, fantasy, or infantile behavior Bizarre, sophisticated, or unusual sexual behavior or knowledge Poor peer relationships Delinquent or runaway Reports sexual assault by caretaker
Emotional Maltreatment	Habit disorders (sucking, biting, rocking) Conduct disorders (antisocial, destructive) Neurotic traits (sleep disorders, speech disorders, inhibition of play Psychoneurotic reactions (hysteria, obsession, compulsion, phobias)	Behavioral extremes; aggressiveness or withdrawal Inappropriately adult or infantile behaviors Developmental lags Attempted suicide

Source: Adapted from Governor's Task Force on Child Abuse and Neglect, 1988.

The variation among states underscores the importance of becoming familiar with the procedures and resources in your own school. The best way to do this is to speak with people who can provide guidance and direction—experienced teachers, the principal, the school nurse, and the student assistance counselor.

Eating Disorders

During a visit to one of Fred's honors classes in late April, we were shocked by the emaciated appearance of one of his female students, Sara. Her eyes and cheeks were sunken in, and her arms looked like twigs. We couldn't take our eyes off her. After class, Fred shared the story:

 This kid is a straight A student . . . . Everything she does is perfect. I don't think she's ever gotten less than 100 on any test or assignment I've given. And she's a fantastic soccer player . . . . To me, it looks like she couldn't even kick the ball. But I know that she practices every day, and she runs too.

A couple of Sara's friends have come to talk with me after school—they're worried about her too. They say that she insists she's fat and that she hardly eats. She seems to be particularly obsessed about not eating anything with fat in it—no pizza, no cheese, no cakes or cookies, and of course no meat of any kind. Apparently, all they ever see her eat is bagels and lettuce!

I've talked with Sara—I've told her that I'm really worried about her, but she insists that she's fine and that everyone's overreacting. I've also reported the situation to the school psychologist and the SAC [student assistance counselor], and I know that they've called Sara's parents. I even called her parents myself. But her parents don't acknowledge that there's a problem . . . .

Sara seems to suffer from anorexia nervosa, an eating disorder that generally begins during adolescence and primarily afflicts white females, although it's increasing among black females and does occur among males (Brodey, 2005; Gonet, 1994). Anorexic adolescents literally starve themselves; even so, they continue to feel fat and may actually perceive that they are becoming heavier. Sara's involvement in running and soccer is also typical; in an attempt to lose weight more quickly, anorexics may combine excessive physical exercise with dieting.

Another eating disorder is bulimia nervosa, in which individuals starve themselves, then binge (often on high-calorie or high-sugar foods), and finally purge themselves (by inducing vomiting). Individuals with bulimia may be underweight, overweight, or average, but they share an intense fear of gaining weight. They may also feel that they have lost control over their lives; thus, they seek to control their eating and their weight (Gonet, 1994).

Of the two eating disorders, bulimia is more common, while anorexia is more severe and can actually be fatal. But both are long-term illnesses that require treatment; they will not go away by themselves. This means that you need to be alert to the signs of eating disorders and report your concern to the appropriate person in your school. Too often, teachers overlook eating disorders since concern about weight is a "normal pathology" in our society. Furthermore, the young women who most frequently suffer from eating disorders are often high-achieving, compliant, perfectionist students who cause no problems in class.

STUDENTS LIVING IN POVERTY

More than one in six (13.3 million) children in the United States are considered poor, meaning they live below the federal poverty line for a family of four, which in 2008 was $21,200 (Children's Defense Fund, 2008). How many are homeless is not clear, since there are no regular surveys of homeless children in the United States; however, a frequently cited statistic is 1.3 million a year (National Law Center on Homelessness and Poverty, 2008). The economic crisis that began in 2008 has dramatically increased these numbers. Even as we write this, a growing number of newspapers articles and television newscasts are reporting on the surge of "tent cities" as people lose their jobs and homes (e.g., McKinley, 2009).

Children and adolescents living in poverty obviously face enormous challenges. They are far less likely than children from middle-class backgrounds to have access to adequate physical, dental, and mental health care. They may suffer from physical, emotional, and psychological problems, experience developmental delays, exhibit academic and behavioral difficulties, and be at risk for school failure. For homeless children, living arrangements are varied and far from adequate: Some double-up with other family members or friends; others live in shelters, emergency foster care, abandoned buildings, vehicles, or motels; still others are on the street (National Coalition of Homeless Children and Youth, 2008).

School can be a haven for children living in poverty. But what can you possibly do? First, *effective teachers are wary of claims about a "culture of poverty" whose members have shared (often negative) traits.* From this perspective, those who are poor are a homogeneous group with characteristics that differ starkly from those who are middle class. These characteristics include *language patterns* (casual rather than formal), *values* (money is to be spent rather than saved), *worldviews* (a focus on the present rather than the future), *ways of interacting with others* (physically rather than verbally), and *daily life* (noisy and chaotic rather than quiet and orderly). The idea of a culture of poverty has become popular among administrators and teachers, and numerous professional development workshops on this topic are offered throughout the country (e.g., Payne, 2005). Although these are intended to help teachers better educate poor children, some critics dispute the existence of a culture of poverty and contend that there is no research evidence to support this notion (e.g., Bomer, Dworin, May, & Semingson, 2008). They argue that traits like those listed above are undoubtedly true of *some* poor individuals (and some who are not poor!), but they do not define all poor people. Moreover, these critics warn that this characterization of poor people can lead teachers to engage in deficit thinking, a tendency to attribute school failure to internal deficiencies such as lack of motivation rather than to external factors such as inadequate funding to schools that serve poor students. Teachers who engage in deficit thinking are likely to overlook or dismiss the strengths of poor students, to "blame the victim," and to adopt negative stereotypes.

Second, *effective teachers of poor or homeless students are "bearers of hope"* (Landsman, 2006). They believe in the ability of all their students to learn, even if they're wearing dirty clothes or come to school hungry. They examine and monitor their assumptions. On one hand, they are careful not to assume that poor students will be unable to meet class expectations; on the other hand, they don't assume that students will be able to complete assignments in a comfortable, quiet room at a desk stocked with all needed materials. They do not lower their expectations in terms of class participation and work, but they show flexibility and compassion (e.g., by extending a due date). They try to give their students as much choice and control over assignments as possible, so that they can feel they have a say in their education.

Third, *effective teachers of poor or homeless adolescents work especially hard to build a supportive, trusting relationship.* They listen respectfully and respond empathically, using active listening skills to keep the lines of communication open. (See Chapter 3.) They are alert to opportunities to provide assistance. Donnie tells us, "Some of my students come early or hang around after school. They pretend that they need extra help, but they really don't. It's just that it's better than going home. And I always provide snacks or breakfast bars for them." Sandy also tries to help students in need:

I remember one girl who was around the age of my daughter. I had noticed that the winter coat she was wearing had a broken zipper. I waited until she was alone with me after school and was getting ready to leave my classroom. It was very cold outside and I said to her, "You are just like my daughter Jennifer. She always manages to break the zippers on her jackets on the coldest day of the year! It's a good thing she has an older cousin so I always have an extra coat around for her. She's already on her second coat this winter." I told her that I had an extra jacket in my office and wanted her to try it on and see if it fit her. Of course it did. After that I would bring in clothes (just a few pieces at a time) and just hand her the bag when we were alone. I would just say something like "Jennifer's cousin gave her too many," or "I have some extras," or "I thought that you might like these." I then gradually added some women's and men's clothing to the bag. I always tried to make it seem as if Jennifer was receiving clothes from other people and that it was no big deal. Of course it was all a lie (Jennifer does not have an older female cousin), but you do what you have to do to help someone maintain their dignity.

Some specific strategies for helping children who are poor or homeless are listed in the Practical Tips Box.

PRACTICAL TIPS FOR

HELPING STUDENTS WHO ARE POOR

Provide basic "survival" assistance:

- Keep granola bars and other healthful snacks on hand.
- If students live where things get stolen, allow them to leave school materials in school.
- Keep basic toiletries in your room for students who don't have access to personal hygiene items.
- Have extra school supplies on hand.

(*continued on next page*)

Be sensitive when disciplining:

- Think about whether students are purposefully misbehaving or whether they are behaving in ways that are acceptable in their home culture. Explain that their behavior may be all right at home but not at school, and explain why.

- Don't penalize students who are asleep without talking to them first; maybe they have no bed or quiet place to sleep.

- If students laugh when disciplined, recognize that this may be a way to save face. Teach other behaviors that are more appropriate.

- If students make inappropriate or vulgar comments, have them generate (or teach them) other phrases that are more acceptable for school and can be used to say the same thing.

- If students are physically aggressive, tell students that aggression is not an option in school. Have them generate (or teach them) other more appropriate options.

Encourage academic achievement:

- Examine what and how you're teaching. Do you assume that students living in poverty will not be going to college anyway, so it's okay if they're getting a watered-down curriculum?

- Give students as much choice and control over their assignments as possible so that they feel that they have a say in their education.

- Include topics that are familiar and relevant.

- Teach ways of keeping materials organized.

- Help students to set goals and to keep track of progress.

- Use rubrics that show levels of performance so students can begin to critique their own assignments.

- Maintain realistically high expectations.

Provide special help for students who are frequently changing schools:

- Assign a buddy who can show them the ropes.

- Explicitly welcome them to class.

- Have a special lunch with them.

- If you know they will be leaving, create a "memory book" for them to take.

- Coordinate with the homeless education liaison in your school.

Sources: Grossman, 2004; Landsman, 2006; Payne, 2005.

CONCLUDING COMMENTS

We strongly believe that teachers are responsible for all the students in their classes, including typical adolescents, English language learners, students with disabilities and ADHD, and students who are troubled or living in poverty. By keeping in mind the principles of effective classroom management, working to create an accepting climate for all students, and utilizing the strategies presented in this chapter, you can enhance the experience of schooling for all of your students.

Keep in mind, however, that there may be students whose problems are so great, you really cannot help a whole lot. As Fred reminds us,

There's failure in this business. Some problems transcend the classroom, and there's only so much an individual teacher or the school can do. Sometimes you just have to say, "I tried. Now I need to let go."

"Letting go" means recognizing that you may not be able to change a student's life; it *doesn't* mean abandoning your responsibility for making that student's time in school as productive and meaningful as possible. Carol Lowinger, the SAC at Fred's school, believes that, to some extent, teachers need to treat troubled students "like everyone else":

> *Sometimes teachers think, "These kids are going through a hard time; I'll give them a break." But out of this sense of caring, they give kids breaks they shouldn't get. Kids need to be held accountable. They have to learn to live in the real world where you can't hide behind your problems. You have to learn to cope, and you* mustn't *learn "I don't have to cope." I'm not saying that we shouldn't give them some leeway if their problems are really great; obviously, we need to be flexible and supportive. But they still need to be responsible for their current behavior. If we always bail kids out, we're enabling. That's not helpful—and it's even dangerous.*

When students have serious problems, it's more important than ever to create a classroom that is safe, orderly, and humane. You may not be able to change youngsters' relationships with their families, but you can still work to establish positive teacher-student relationships. You may not be able to provide students with control over unstable, chaotic home lives, but you can allow them opportunities to make decisions and to have some control over their time in school. You may not be able to do anything about the violence that permeates the neighborhoods in which they live, but you can structure classroom situations to foster cooperation and group cohesiveness. In Fred's words, "You can show them you care enough about them not to let them slough off. You can still keep teaching."

SUMMARY

Building a caring, inclusive classroom begins with knowing who your students are. Today's classrooms contain students at various stages in their physical and emotional development, and from a wide range of cultural and linguistic backgrounds. Many are learning English as a second language. Students with disabilities are frequently educated alongside their nondisabled peers. A greater number of young people are growing up in circumstances that put them at risk for physical, emotional, and psychological problems.

The Developing Adolescent

Students in middle and high school are:
- Developing their identity.
- Changing their thinking about and reaction to societal norms.
- Changing their views of personal prerogative and privacy.

Developmentally aware teachers:

- Help students find and develop areas of competence.
- Give students opportunities to make decisions.
- Affirm students' growing sense of self.

Ways of Helping English Language Learners

- Provide a safe environment for language risk taking.
- Avoid idioms and complex sentences.
- Ask questions that allow for different levels of proficiency in responding.
- Encourage English speaking while honoring students' first language.
- Offer periodic summaries and paraphrases.
- Emphasize collaborative over individual work.
- Emphasize process over product.
- Apply SDAIE strategies across the curriculum.
- Encourage students to write about topics of their choice and for real-world purposes.

Students with Disabilities and ADHD

- A diagnosis of LD is made when there is a "severe discrepancy" between intellectual ability and academic performance or when the student fails to respond to early, intense intervention.
- Emotional/behavioral disorders can be externalizing (e.g., conduct disorder) or internalizing (e.g., depression).
- Autism and Asperger syndrome are two "pervasive developmental disorders," a cluster of disorders characterized by marked impairments in the development of social interaction and communication skills.
- ADHD is not included as a disability in the IDEA; however, individuals may receive services under Section 504 of the Rehabilitation Act of 1973. ADHD is characterized by inattention, hyperactivity, and impulsivity.

Helping Students with Disabilities and ADHD

- Become familiar with students' IEPs or 504 plans.
- Create an accepting climate.
- Coordinate and collaborate with special education teachers and paraprofessionals.
- Examine your classroom environment for possible mismatch.
- Don't lower your expectations.
- Use peer tutoring, peer assistance, and cooperative learning.

Students Who Are Troubled

- Substance abuse:
  - Students may be children of alcoholics/addicts (COAs) and/or may be abusing drugs and alcohol themselves.
  - COAs can benefit from support groups.
  - Teachers must be watchful for students who may be abusing drugs and alcohol and refer students to the SAC or other appropriate persons.
  - Distinguish between situations in which drugs are being used outside of school and situations in which students are under the influence during school.
- Abuse and neglect:
  - Educators are required to report suspected abuse and neglect to the state's child protective service.
  - No state requires the reporter to have absolute proof before reporting.
  - Most states require "reason to believe" or "reasonable cause to believe or suspect."

- Eating disorders:
  - Students who suffer from eating disorders are often high-achieving, compliant, and perfectionist.

Students Living in Poverty

- Be wary of claims about a "culture of poverty" whose members have shared (often negative) traits.
- Strive to be a "bearer of hope."
- Work hard to build a trusting relationship.

Sometimes the problems that students bring to school can be overwhelming, especially for beginning teachers who are still learning the basics. And in fact, there may be students whose problems are so great, you just cannot help. Nonetheless, you can still try to create a classroom environment that is safe, orderly, and humane. You can show students you care by holding them accountable for their behavior and by continuing to teach.

ACTIVITIES FOR SKILL BUILDING AND REFLECTION

In Class

1. In a small group, read the following scenario and discuss the questions that are listed below.

    Joanne Wilson's second-period English class has 28 students. One has been identified with learning disabilities, and he struggles with the novels the class is reading, as well as the writing assignments. In addition, two students are recent immigrants with very limited English, and one student has ADHD. Although he is supposed to be on medication, he sometimes skips a dose; on days like that, he "bounces off the walls" and accomplishes very little in terms of academic work. Ms. Wilson is very concerned about these students' academic progress, and she doesn't know where to turn. An in-class support (ICS) teacher provides some assistance two days a week, but they have no planning time and so she functions more like an aide than a real teacher. Ms. Wilson is also painfully aware of the fact that the class is not a cohesive community; although there is no obvious disrespect, the other students generally ignore the students with special needs and are reluctant to work with them in cooperative groups.

Questions:

a. What strategies could Ms. Wilson use to help create a more inclusive, more accepting climate?
b. For each student with special needs (i.e., the student with LD, the two ELLs, and the student with ADHD), think of one strategy that Ms. Wilson could use to enhance his or her academic progress.
c. What kinds of help could Ms. Wilson ask for from the ICS teacher?

2. Working together in a small group, imagine that you are a general education teacher working in a co-teaching arrangement with a special education teacher. Generate a list of issues that you would want to discuss before beginning to teach together. In particular, consider what expectations you have with respect to planning and delivering instruction and with respect to classroom management. Then assume the role of the special education teacher and repeat the process.

On Your Own

1. In the school where you are observing or teaching, interview the principal or the director of special services to learn about the district's policies and procedures for supporting students with disabilities. Are any students with severe disabilities being educated in the general education classroom? If so, what kind of special supports are being provided for those individuals? Interview a teacher about his or her attitudes toward including a student with special needs who previously would have been educated in a special education classroom or sent to a special school.

2. In the school where you are observing or teaching, interview the principal or an ESL teacher about the district's policies and programs for supporting ELLs. How many languages are represented in the school? Interview a teacher in an English-only classroom who has English language learners in his or her classroom. How does the teacher provide supports for English language learners?

3. In the school where you are observing or teaching, interview the student assistance counselor, a guidance counselor, or the director of special services to determine the policies for reporting drug abuse. Get copies of the referral forms that are used and compare them with the form shown in this chapter.

For Your Portfolio

Reporting suspected abuse and neglect varies from state to state. Find out the policies used in your state. Also find out if your school has particular policies and procedures you are to follow. In particular, get answers to the following questions and compile your findings into a set of guidelines that you keep in your portfolio.

Who is required to report abuse and neglect?
When should you report child abuse? (When you have reasonable cause to suspect? Reasonable cause to believe?)
To what state agency do you report?
What information must be included in the report?
Do you have to give your name when reporting?

FOR FURTHER READING

Cary, S. (2007). *Working with second language learners: Answers to teachers' top ten questions* (2nd ed.). Portsmouth, NH: Heinemann.

    This book addresses teachers' "top ten" questions, chosen with four criteria in mind: veracity (meaning that they were asked by real teachers teaching real kids), frequency, relevancy, and difficulty (they needed to be challenging). Questions include: How do I assess a student's English? How do I find useful information on a student's cultural background? How do I make my spoken language more understandable? How do I get my reluctant speakers to speak English?

Gorski, P. (2008). The myth of the "culture of poverty." *Educational Leadership, 65*(7), 32–36.

In this reader-friendly, provocative article, Paul Gorski refutes "common and dangerous myths about poverty." Chief among them, he argues, is the "culture of poverty"—the idea that "poor people share more or less monolithic and predictable beliefs, values, and behaviors." Gorski looks at some of the stereotypes held about poor people and concludes that teachers must consider how their class biases affect their interactions with students.

Irwin, C. (2007). *Monochrome days: A firsthand account of one teenager's experience with depression.* New York: Oxford University Press.

The author has battled depression since the eighth grade, and this book recounts her dawning recognition of her condition, the treatment she has undergone, and the importance of supportive family, friends, and teachers. Although the book is aimed at teenagers suffering from depression, it's a useful resource for teachers who want to learn more about the impact of depression. Each chapter concludes with useful information, such as symptoms of depression, treatment options, and how to find help.

Kline, F. M., & Silver, L. B. (Eds.) (2004). *The educator's guide to mental health issues in the classroom.* Baltimore: Paul H. Brookes.

This book is dedicated to "general education classroom teachers who are charged with serving ALL students!" It is designed to serve as a reference for educators who work with students who have mental health issues and who need to collaborate with mental health workers. Chapters address biologically based disorders (e.g., ADHD), biologically based and/or psychologically based disorders (e.g., substance abuse), and behavioral disorders (e.g., oppositional defiant disorder).

Snell, M. E., & Janney, R. (2000). *Social relationships and peer support.* Baltimore: Paul H. Brookes.

This book is part of a series of reader-friendly teachers' guides to inclusive practices. This one focuses on ways of facilitating positive peer relationships in an inclusive classroom. Topics include creating a positive atmosphere, establishing peer support programs, teaching social skills, and building friendship groups.

Soodak, L. C., & McCarthy, M. R. (2006). Classroom management in inclusive settings. In C. M. Evertson & C. S. Weinstein (Eds.), *Handbook of classroom management: Research, practice, and contemporary issues.* Mahwah, NJ: Lawrence Erlbaum Associates.

This chapter reviews research-based practices that promote positive academic, social, and behavioral outcomes for students in inclusive classrooms. Practices include teacher-directed strategies (such as building classroom community and establishing programs that foster acceptance and friendship), peer-mediated strategies (such as cooperative learning and peer-tutoring), and self-directed strategies (such as self-monitoring). The authors stress the role of teachers in creating classrooms in which all students have greater access to the general education curriculum.

Villa, R. A., Thousand, J. S. & Nevin, A. I. (2008). *A guide to co-teaching: Practical tips for facilitating student learning* (2nd ed.). Thousand Oaks, CA: Corwin Press.

This book highlights the benefits and challenges of co-teaching and addresses both the NCLB requirement that all students have access to highly qualified teachers and the IDEA requirement that students with disabilities have access to the general education curriculum. The following four types of co-teaching models are described in detail: supportive, parallel, complementary, and team teaching.

ORGANIZATIONAL RESOURCES

Autism Society of America (ASA), 7910 Woodmont Avenue, Suite 300, Bethesda, Maryland 20814-3067 (www.autism-society.org, 800-328-8476). ASA exists to improve the lives of all affected by autism, by increasing public awareness about the day-to-day issues faced by people on the autism spectrum, advocating for appropriate services for individuals, and providing the latest information regarding treatment, education, research, and advocacy. Their website includes links to resources and local referrals.

Center on Addiction and the Family (COAF), 164 West 74th Street, New York, NY 10023 (www.coaf.org, 646-505-2060). COAF works to promote the healing of families affected by substance abuse. Their website includes information on the impact of substance abuse and how to work with children and families.

CHADD (Children and Adults with Attention-Deficit/Hyperactivity Disorder), 8181 Professional Place, Suite 150, Landover, MD 20785 (www.chadd.org, 800-233-4050). CHADD is a nonprofit organization serving children and adults with ADHD. It runs the National Resource Center on ADHD, a national clearinghouse for evidence-based information about ADHD.

The Council for Exceptional Children (CEC), 1110 North Glebe Rd., Suite 300, Arlington, VA 22201 (www.cec.sped.org, 888-232-7733). CEC is the largest international professional organization dedicated to improving educational outcomes for students with disabilities and those who are gifted.

CREDE (Center for Research on Education, Diversity, and Excellence), 1640 Tolman Hall, University of California, Berkeley, CA 94720-1670 (www.crede.org, 510-643-9024). CREDE is a federally funded research and development center focused on improving the education of students whose ability to reach their potential is challenged by language or cultural barriers, race, geographic location, or poverty. It offers a wide range of multimedia products.

Learning Disabilities Association of America (LDA), 4156 Library Road, Pittsburgh, PA 15234-1349 (www.ldanatl.org, 412-341-1515). LDA is the largest nonprofit volunteer organization advocating for individuals with learning disabilities. Its website includes links to information for teachers and parents.

National Center for Homeless Education, 1100 West Market St., Suite 300, Greensboro, NC 27403 (www.serve.org/nche, 800-308-2145). Serves as a clearinghouse for information and resources on the educational rights of homeless children and youth.

National Eating Disorders Association, 603 Stewart Street, Suite 803 Seattle, WA 98101 (www.nationaleatingdisorders.org, 206-382-3587). This organization is devoted to prevention of eating disorders, improved access to quality treatment, and increased research funding to better understand and treat eating disorders. It operates a toll-free helpline and provides resources for students, teachers, and families.

WORKING WITH FAMILIES

"I had no idea his mother lost her job and his father hasn't been around for a month. No wonder he's been so belligerent!"

"Her grandmother has been so good about making sure she's doing her homework. She's really working with me on this."

"His father has offered to chaperone the eighth-grade cookout and to organize the softball game! It will be terrific to have him along!

Comments like these can be heard in teachers' rooms all across the country. They reflect some of the benefits that accrue when teachers and families establish positive, productive relationships. A growing body of evidence shows that family involvement in schooling is linked to students' academic achievement (Anderson & Minke, 2007; Jeynes, 2007). But family-school relationships also have definite payoffs in terms of classroom management.

First, *knowing about a student's home situation provides insight into the student's classroom behavior.* Listen to Donnie:

It was the very first day of school—when everyone is still being really good—but this one girl was really loud and hyperactive. It was clear that everyone disliked her. She seemed completely unable to control herself. I checked into her home situation as soon as I had a free period. I found out that her mother had kicked her out of the house; she said she couldn't handle all the kids. The girl had tried to commit suicide, but now she was really trying to get her act together. She had gotten a part-time job, and she was living with an aunt. This girl had really been thrown out into the world, and school is her haven. Actually, when I think about what she's facing, I'm really impressed by how well she's doing.

As Donnie's example illustrates, it's easier to understand why Johnny sits with his head down on his desk if you're aware that he spent the night in a homeless shelter; Carla's apathy makes sense if you know that her mother is going through chemotherapy; and Jana's anxiety about getting all As is understandable if you appreciate how much her parents pressure her to succeed. Furthermore, insights like these can help you decide what course of action to take when dealing with a student's problems. You're better able to judge if a suggestion that a parent proof-read term papers is inappropriate because the parent can't read, or if a note home will lead to benefits or to beatings.

Second, *when families understand what you are trying to achieve, they can provide valuable support and assistance.* Most parents want their children to succeed in school and will do what they can to help. But they can't work in a vacuum. They need to know what you are trying to achieve and how you expect students to behave in your classroom. Familiarizing parents with your curriculum, routines, and policies minimizes confusion, misinterpretations, and conflict. For this reason, Christina requires parents to sign an acknowledgment form at the beginning of the course, indicating that they have read and understood the "news-paper" she sends home describing course objectives, policies, and procedures.

Third, *families can help to develop and implement strategies to change students' behavior.* Working together, parents and teachers can bring about improvements in students' behavior that would be impossible working alone. Fred shares this example:

> I had this kid in my U.S. History II class who wasn't doing any work at all. It was his senior year, and I think he just decided he didn't have to do anything anymore. His parents didn't have a clue about what to do. We all sat down and worked out a plan. They were to call me at 10:30 every Friday morning. If the report on their son was good, he got the car keys, got to go out with his friends, got to go to the ball game. If the report was bad, the weekend did not exist. We told him, "We really care about you and if this is what we have to do to get you through senior year, then so be it." The kid tested the plan once, and there was no weekend for him. After that, he really started to perform and ended up with a B for the year. Plus, there was an additional payoff. His parents were able to give him all kinds of good strokes because he started taking responsibility.

Finally, *parent volunteers can provide needed assistance in the classroom and the school.* Since schools are almost always short-staffed, parents can provide an extra pair of hands: They can work in libraries, computer centers, and homework programs; help make school safe by greeting visitors; accompany students on field trips; make phone calls to other parents; and join with school personnel to create, manage, and deliver special programs. They can also enrich the curriculum by sharing information about their hobbies, careers, travels, and ethnic backgrounds.

Despite the obvious benefits of close communication and collaboration, parents and teachers are often at odds with one another. Sometimes the relationship is detached and distant; sometimes it's distrustful and adversarial. What causes this adversarial relationship and what can teachers do to avoid it? In this chapter, we examine three challenges to close working relationships—teacher reluctance to involve parents, parent reluctance to become involved, and changes in the family and American society. We then turn to our teachers and to the literature on parent involvement in order to suggest ways that families and schools can work together to *overcome* the challenges.

 Pause and Reflect

Before reading on, think of three possible answers to each of the following questions:

- Why would teachers sometimes be reluctant to involve parents in their students' schooling?
- Why would parents sometimes be reluctant to become involved?
- How does the changing nature of the family affect parent-teacher collaboration?

Challenges to Family–Teacher Cooperation

Teacher Reluctance to Involve Families in Schooling

A primary reason for teachers' reluctance to work with families is the *extra time and energy that are required.* Teaching is physically and emotionally exhausting, and reaching out to parents is sometimes viewed as one more burdensome task. For example, telephoning 30 parents and talking for 10 minutes to each means five hours of work (Epstein & Becker, 1982, p. 103). And that's for just one class! Since this is obviously in addition to the normal workload, it's understandable if teachers wonder whether the extra time required is worth the trouble. For new teachers, the task of reaching out to parents may seem even more onerous. As Christina admits, "I'm always preparing materials and lessons, grading, or commenting on student papers. It takes time to be creative and effective—and that means there's less time for parent contact than I would like."

In addition, *teachers' perceptions of families* undoubtedly contribute to the reluctance to seek greater parental involvement. Many teachers recognize that time is often a scarce commodity for parents, limited by responsibilities at work, household chores, and caring for other family members. These teachers question whether it is fair to ask already burdened parents to spend time working with their teenage children on academic activities or assisting with behavior problems. As Sandy told us:

> Some parents are just overwhelmed. One poor, single mother I know just doesn't have the time or energy to become more involved. She's worried about keeping her job and making ends meet. Her plate is just too

full; she can't handle anything else. It's not that she doesn't care. But the fact that her kid is not doing his homework is just not her highest priority right now. Knowing this is important. Once you know you're not going to get parent involvement, you can figure out another approach.

Other teachers may see parents as too "ignorant" to be a resource (Eccles & Harold, 1993), while still others have been burned by encounters with angry, irresponsible, or apathetic parents. They would tend to agree with the statement that "far too many parents—and not just disadvantaged ones—simply don't give a damn. For them, school is a free babysitting service" (Walde & Baker, 1990, p. 322).

Another reason for teachers' reluctance to involve parents is *the worry that parents may not understand their role in the classroom.* Some parent volunteers intervene when they shouldn't (e.g., imposing their own punishments for inappropriate behavior instead of consulting the teacher); they may instruct students in ways that contradict what the teacher has demonstrated; or they may violate confidentiality by sharing student records and relating sensitive information. When situations like these occur, teachers may wonder if parent volunteers are more of a hindrance than a help.

Finally, teachers may be reluctant to involve parents because of the *authority and autonomy they enjoy within their classrooms.* Teachers are often exposed to criticism. Parents may blame them for children's problems or question their professional competence. It's not surprising that teachers sometimes become guarded and protective of their "turf," especially if they lack confidence in their skills and expertise. Indeed, research has shown that teachers with higher levels of "teacher efficacy" (teachers' beliefs that they can teach and that their students can learn) are more likely to reach out to parents (Hoover-Dempsey, Bassler, & Brissie, 1987).

Parent Reluctance to Become Involved in Schooling

It is well recognized that family involvement in schools declines as students move from elementary to middle school, and that by high school, it has practically disappeared (Rioux & Berla, 1993). Part of the decline may be due to the fact that, compared to elementary teachers, secondary teachers use fewer strategies to involve families (Pelco & Ries, 1999). Donnie offers an additional explanation for the decline:

Once kids leave elementary school, parents seem to feel it's time to cut the cord. They think the kids need to be on their own more, and that school should be the kids' responsibility. Also, they feel they can't help anymore because they don't know the content. They tell me, "I don't know algebra or geometry" or "I don't understand these new ways of teaching math." They're scared off by the content and feel they can't offer assistance.

There are also more general reasons why families across the grade levels may resist involvement. Clearly, the demands of work compete for parents' time and energy, especially in low-income households, which are more likely to have two parents who work full-time, parents who have two or more jobs, parents who have to work evenings and nights, and parents who have jobs with inflexible or unpredictable hours.

In addition, some adults have *unhappy, even traumatic, memories* of their own experiences as students. According to Sara Lawrence-Lightfoot (2003), parents' encounters with school are shaped by their own autobiographical stories—"their own childhood histories, their own insecurities, and their own primal fears" (p. xxii). These "ghosts" from the past may make parents nervous or even hostile to schools and teachers and less than eager to return for conferences or open houses. (A humorous example of these "ghosts" is illustrated in Figure 6.1.) Listen to this father describe his reasons for not participating more fully in his son's schooling:

> They expect me to go to school so they can tell me my kid is stupid or crazy. They've been telling me that for three years, so why should I go and hear it again? They don't do anything. They just tell me my kid is bad. . . . See, I've been there. I know. And it scares me. They called me a boy in trouble but I was a troubled boy. Nobody helped me because they liked it when I didn't show up. If I was gone for the semester, fine with them. I dropped out nine times. They wanted me gone. (Finders & Lewis, 1994, p. 51)

Other families may *feel guilty* when their teenage children have difficulties in school. They may become defensive and uncooperative when teachers try to discuss their youngster's problem or may be too embarrassed to disclose troubles they are having at home. Rather than deal with the child's problem, these families may try to deny what is occurring and to avoid communication with the teacher.

Still other families may be *unnerved and intimidated by schools.* This is particularly so when parents are poor, uneducated, or have limited proficiency in English. Some may find teachers and administrators unresponsive to their requests (Gutman & McLoyd, 2000); others may even fear teachers, viewing them as authority figures who must not be questioned (Lindeman, 2001). Consider the story of Sylvia, a parent involved in an Immigrant Parent Leadership class at Annandale High School in Virginia. Sylvia emigrated from Guatemala as a child

Figure 6.1   *Source:* Rose is Rose © Pat Brady & Don Wimmer. Reprinted with permission of United Features Syndicate. All rights reserved.

and attended U.S. schools from fourth grade on. She speaks English well and is committed to helping her stepdaughter, who recently arrived from Guatemala. According to Sylvia, "One of my stepdaughter's teachers thought someone else did her homework. But the reason she is doing so well is that I am working with her at home." When the leader of the class advised her to call the teacher and clear up the misunderstanding, Sylvia was amazed: "You mean I can talk to the teacher? I felt I would be insulting her if I did" (Sobel & Kugler, 2007, p. 62).

Finally, it is important to recognize that some families *do not view participation at school as part of their parental roles* (Hoover-Dempsey & Sandler, 1997). They may believe that schooling should be left to the professionals or that they are showing their support for teachers by not interfering. Immigrant families may not even realize that parental involvement is expected and valued: "In most countries outside the United States, the unspoken norm is that it's the teacher's job to educate a student and that participation from parents shows disrespect for the teacher's expertise" (Sobel & Kugler, 2007, p. 63). Asian American families, for example, generally hold high expectations for their children's academic success; nonetheless, they tend to view educational matters as the province of the school (Fuller & Olsen, 1998). Similarly, Latinos typically perceive their role as ensuring their children's attendance; instilling respect for the teacher; encouraging good behavior in school; meeting their obligations to provide clothing, food, and shelter; and socializing children to their family responsibilities (Chrispeels & Rivero, 2000; Trumbull, Rothstein-Fisch, Greenfield, & Quiroz, 2001). Parental presence at school is *not* a key component of this role.

A good example of how both the demands of work and parents' role-definition can affect involvement comes from a study of the Padillas, an immigrant, migrant family whose children were all very successful in school (Lopez, 2001). Their parental involvement, however, took the form of exposing their children to their hard work in the fields and teaching them that without an education they might end up in the same situation. Here is an excerpt from one interview:

INTERVIEWER: Now I want to know if you or your wife are involved in the schools in one way or another? For example, like volunteers or in the Parent's Committee.

MR. PADILLA: No sir. . . .

INTERVIEWER: Hmmm. Haven't you gone to a parents' meeting or something like that?

MR. PADILLA: No. Not really. It's just that we're always busy with work. We rarely go to the school.

INTERVIEWER: Not even to a conference with the teachers?

MR. PADILLA: Well, maybe once in a while. But it's really difficult. There's a lot of work.

INTERVIEWER: So how are you involved in your children's education?

MR. PADILLA: Well, I have shown them what work is and how hard it is. So they know that if they don't focus in their studies, that is the type of work they'll end up doing. I've opened their eyes to that reality. (Lopez, 2001, p. 427)

If the Padillas' "involvement" were defined by bake sales and back-to-school nights, they would appear to be uninvolved in their children's education. Yet they were *highly* involved in fostering their children's positive attitudes toward school. Clearly, we need to be cautious about assuming that parents who do not attend school events are unconcerned and uncaring. Teachers who equate parent involvement with presence at school are likely to overlook or underestimate the involvement that occurs at home (Anderson & Minke, 2007; Lee & Bowen, 2006).

Changes in the Family and American Society

In 1955, 60 percent of American households consisted of a working father, a homemaker mother, and two or more school-age children (Hodgkinson, 1985). Teachers sent letters home addressed to "Dear Parents," reasonably confident that two parents would read them, and schools scheduled "Parent Conferences" with the expectation that parents were the primary caregivers of their children.

Times have changed. The typical family of the 1950s is still called "normal" in everyday conversation, but less than one-quarter of all households conform to this model (Heilman, 2008). Today, about half of all marriages end in divorce (Heuveline, 2005), and about one-half of today's children will spend some portion of childhood in a single-parent family (Heilman, 2008), without the human or economic resources available to those growing up in two-parent families. In some cases, the significant adults in their lives are not their parents at all, but grandparents, aunts, uncles, brothers, sisters, or neighbors. The "stay-at-home" mother is vanishing; indeed, 65 percent of all preschoolers have mothers in the work force (Coontz, 2007). Between 8 and 10 million children are being raised in gay and lesbian families (Child Welfare Information Gateway, 2008), while some older students are emancipated minors living on their own. With a surge in immigration from Central and Latin America, the Middle East, Southeast Asia and the Pacific, and Russia and Eastern Europe, many students come from homes where a language other than English is spoken, and their families are unfamiliar with schools in the United States.

These changes in American society have made communication and collaboration more complicated than ever. Nonetheless, research has found that it is *teachers' attitudes and practices—not the educational level, marital status, or workplace of parents—that determine whether families become productively involved in their children's schooling* (Epstein, 2001; Griffith, 1998). In other words, it's the teacher that makes the difference. For this reason, you must not only understand the challenges to parent involvement, you must also be aware of the ways that families and schools can work together. (Note that in this chapter, when we refer to "parents," we are referring to all the various types of caregivers that your students may have in their lives, not just birth parents.)

OVERCOMING THE CHALLENGES: FOSTERING COLLABORATION BETWEEN FAMILIES AND SCHOOLS

Joyce Epstein and her colleagues at Johns Hopkins University have studied comprehensive parent involvement programs and have identified six different types of family-school collaboration. These are listed in Box 6.1. The first four of Epstein's categories

MEET THE EDUCATORS   BOX 6.1

MEET JOYCE EPSTEIN

Joyce Epstein is professor of sociology at Johns Hopkins University and director of the Center on School, Family, and Community Partnerships. She began research on parent involvement in elementary schools in 1981 and then extended her inquiries to middle schools and high schools. In 1996, Epstein and her colleagues established the National Network of Partnership Schools, which assists schools, districts, and states to use research-based approaches to develop programs of family involvement and community connections and to meet the requirements of No Child Left Behind for parent involvement. The Network now includes over 1,200 schools located in 21 states.

Some Major Ideas about Family, School, and Community Partnerships

1. Well-designed programs of school, family, and community partnerships benefit students, families, and schools.
2. There are six types of involvement for comprehensive partnership programs:
   - Type 1: Parenting—Help all families establish home environments to support children as students.
   - Type 2: Communicating—Design effective forms of school-to-home and home-to-school communication about school programs and children's progress.
   - Type 3: Volunteering—Recruit and organize parent help and support.
   - Type 4: Learning at Home—Provide information and ideas to families about how to help students at home with homework and other curriculum-related activities, decisions, and planning.
   - Type 5: Decision Making—Include parents in school decisions, developing parent leaders and representatives.
   - Type 6: Collaborating with the Community—Identify and integrate resources and services from the community to strengthen school programs, family practices, and student learning and development.

3. In order to create a lasting, comprehensive partnership program, each school needs an Action Team for Partnerships (ATP) to assess present practices and needs, develop options for action, implement selected activities, evaluate next steps, and coordinate practices.

Selected Books and Articles

Epstein, J. L. (2001). *School, family, and community partnerships: Preparing educators and improving schools.* Boulder, CO: Westview Press.

Epstein, J. L., Sanders, M. G., Simon, B. S., Salinas, K. C., Jansorn, N. R., & Van Voorhis, F. L. (2002). *School, family, and community partnerships: Your handbook for action* (2nd ed.). Thousand Oaks, CA: Corwin Press.

Hutchins, D. J., Greenfeld, M. D., & Epstein, J. L. (2008). *Family reading night.* Larchmont, NY: Eye on Education.

Website: www.partnershipschools.org

provide a framework for our discussion. For more information on the last two categories—including families as participants in school decision making and collaborating with the community—see Epstein and colleagues, 2002; Chapter 6 is specifically devoted to "Strengthening Partnership Programs in Middle and High Schools."

Helping Families to Fulfill Their Basic Obligations

This category refers to the family's responsibility to provide for children's health and safety, to supervise and guide children at each age level, and to build positive home conditions that support school learning and behavior (Epstein & Dauber, 1991).

Schools can assist families in carrying out these basic obligations by providing workshops on parenting skills; establishing parent support groups; holding programs on teenage problems (e.g., drug and alcohol abuse, eating disorders); and referring families to community and state agencies when necessary.

Asking teachers to assume responsibilities for the education of *families,* in addition to the education of *students,* may seem onerous and unfair. Not surprisingly, some teachers hesitate to become "social workers," a role for which they are untrained. Others feel resentful and angry at parents who do not provide adequate home environments. Although these attitudes are understandable, you need to remember that your students' home environments shape their chances for school success. As the number of distressed families grows, assisting families to carry out their basic obligations becomes increasingly critical.

What can you, as a teacher, realistically do to assist families in carrying out their basic obligations? Although you will probably not be directly involved in planning parent education workshops or leading support groups, you can play an important, *indirect* role. You can let families know about available materials, motivate and encourage them to attend programs, bring transportation problems to the attention of appropriate school personnel, and help families to arrange car pools (Greenwood & Hickman, 1991).

In Sandy's and Fred's districts, parent support groups enable families to get together to share concerns and to discuss topics like communicating with adolescents, discipline, resisting peer pressure, and home/school cooperation. A similar program, the Parent Involvement Corps (PIC), was established at Donnie's school some years ago. Designed for parents of ninth-grade students, the program was intended to welcome parents to school, to help them feel comfortable there, to teach parenting skills, and to inform parents of their rights. If programs like these exist in your school, you can make sure families are aware of them, even if you are not directly involved; if you see a family with special needs, you can alert school personnel involved in these programs about the situation.

You can also educate families about relevant community and state agencies. Donnie, for example, advises families who have no health insurance where they can obtain medical and dental attention. When it became clear that one of her students was bulimic (at prom time!), Donnie worked with the family to find an agency that could provide the necessary psychological and medical assistance.

In addition to playing this indirect assistance role, there are times when it may be appropriate to work *directly* with families. Fred reports that he often needs to provide parents with some perspective on "this unique creature called 'teenager'": "They haven't had 150 kids, and it's often a revelation for them to learn that they're not the only parents having problems." Similarly, Sandy tells us that a lot of her interactions with parents involve helping them to communicate more effectively with their teenage children:

Many times, I find that my discussions with parents begin with the problems their children are having in chemistry class, but move on to more general problems. You start talking about grades, and the next thing you know you're talking about curfews and dating. Many of the parents have no

control over their 15- and 16-year olds. They'll say to me, "I just don't know what to do. He or she is the same way at home. I'm at a loss." I acknowledge their frustration and the difficulty of working with teenagers. (It helps that I have teenagers too!) I tell them, "You're not alone. Many 15- and 16-year-olds behave this way, and many parents feel this way." I try to provide some perspective and give them some tips about communication. I try to encourage them to set some limits. I find that a lot of parents don't like to set limits; they don't want confrontations with their kids, and they need encouragement to monitor what their kids are doing.

Sometimes I encounter overbearing parents who put too much pressure on their kids. Their expectations are unrealistic. Ninety-five on a test is not good enough; they want their child to have the highest test grade in the class. I tell them, "Wait a minute, we both want what's best for your child; we want him to work to his utmost ability, but utmost ability is not perfection on every test." I remember one situation, where a girl in my class was putting out very little effort. She got a 79 on the first test, which was far below her ability. After I spoke with her, she started working a lot harder, and her grade on the next test was 89. I told her how proud I was of her, and said something like, "Your parents must have been delighted." She got this funny look on her face, and I knew something was wrong. I found out that they had made only one comment: "Why wasn't it an A?" They didn't give her any praise at all. I decided I needed to speak with them about the situation. I told them, "Look, your daughter went from doing no work and getting a 79 to working hard and getting an 89, and you didn't even acknowledge the improvement. She's going to figure out that she might as well do no work and get 79s, since working hard and getting 89s doesn't get her any approval." Parents like this need to understand the importance of acknowledging improvement, instead of holding out for the perfect grade.

 As you reflect on how to help families with parenting responsibilites, keep in mind that there are cultural differences in beliefs about child-rearing, and these differences may lead to cultural clashes between home and school—with students caught in the middle. Parents from collectivistic cultures, for example, may emphasize respect, obedience, helpfulness, and responsibility to the family, while teachers from individualistic cultures stress individual achievement, independence, and self-expression (Trumbull, Rothstein-Fisch, Greenfield, & Quiroz, 2001). Tonia Moore, a student assistance counselor at Sandy's school, provides additional examples of cultural clashes:

> *I see so many students who are caught between two cultures. At home, they're expected to follow a set of traditional values, but at school they really want to be American teenagers. It's so hard. We hold dances, but we have kids who are going to have arranged marriages. An Indian father wouldn't let his daughter go to Project Graduation [a boat trip the school organizes after graduation so that students will be in a safe, confined space without alcohol or drugs]. He said she couldn't stay out all night. An Iranian girl couldn't go to the prom; her father didn't believe in it. An Asian girl who just got 1400 on her SATs has to spend the summer taking review courses for college achievement tests. Her parents stress the need to achieve, while mainstream American culture stresses the importance of being well-rounded.*

If you have students whose families have recently immigrated to this country, you might also help them to understand the expectations and norms of American secondary schools. For example, teachers and administrators at Jericho High School, on Long Island, New York, made a concerted effort to reach out to Asian parents, who appeared reluctant to attend school events such as orchestra concerts, viewing them as unrelated to students' college aspirations. The goal of the project was to convey the message that parental involvement in all aspects of school life (not just worrying about test scores and college admission) is critical to help students become emotionally well adjusted and socially successful. As a result of these efforts, more Asian parents are attending school events and becoming part of the school community (Hu, 2008).

When families express values and goals that are different from those of the school, it is all too easy to dismiss them as "out-of-touch," "narrow-minded," or just plain "wrong." But attitudes like this only increase parents' resentment and suspicion. Awareness and respect are the keys to reaching cross-cultural understanding.

Communicating with Families

Epstein's second category of family–school involvement refers to the school's obligation *to communicate about school programs and students' progress.* Communications include electronic communication (e-mail and websites), phone calls, report cards and progress reports, and open houses and parent-teacher conferences. This is certainly the most commonly accepted way to work with parents, and there is no doubt that these communications are essential. The crucial question, however, is not only whether these communications occur, but *when they occur, whether they are being understood, and whether they lead to feelings of trust and respect or alienation and resentment.*

All of the teachers stress the importance of communicating with parents in a way that promotes a feeling of partnership. Donnie comments:

> Sometimes I see parents in the market, or in church, or downtown. When I do, I acknowledge them, and I invite them to call and talk about their children. I tell them, "We've got to work together. We're partners."

Fred echoes Donnie's message:

> Sometimes teachers don't invite contact. They'll only call if there is a problem. But some parents need that initial encouragement. If you can make that initial contact, then the parent will usually continue the contact. It's important to make parents understand that you're both working in the best interests of the kid. When you make that clear, even the most irate parent turns into a pussycat. I tell them, "Listen, everything I do is designed to be the best for your kid. But if you're concerned about something, let me know. Feel free to call." I tell my parents: "We need to work together as a team. And your kids need to know we're working together."

It is clear that Donnie, Sandy, Christina, and Fred are able to establish productive partnerships with families, and the next few sections of this chapter describe some of the ways they do this. In addition, the Practical Tips box lists some suggestions for communicating with parents who are particularly hard to reach.

Electronic Communication

In recent years, more and more teachers have begun using electronic mail and the Internet to facilitate communication with parents. For example, a class website can list assignments and due dates, the subject for the week, dates of quizzes and tests, news about current and upcoming events, and requests for supplies or assistance. A website can also provide links to related sites that might help students

PRACTICAL TIPS ON

REACHING "HARD TO REACH" PARENTS

Step 1: Try to figure out why parents are hard to reach. Ask yourself (or someone in the school or community who would know):

- Do parents speak English?
- Do parents come from cultures that do not identify parent involvement as a priority? Do they come from cultures that believe schooling should be left to the educators?
- Do parents have work schedules that conflict with conferences?
- Do parents live far from the school? Do they have transportation?
- Do parents have other children that would require babysitting during parent-teacher meetings?
- Do parents know where the school is?
- Are the parents homeless (and therefore have no good address for receiving written communications from school)?

Step 2: Develop outreach strategies to address the underlying issue. For example:

- Make sure that parents receive messages in their native language.
- Make sure that written communications are easy to read, warm, and friendly.
- Figure out how to get messages to parents who are homeless.
- Schedule conferences at flexible times to accommodate parents with conflicting work schedules.
- Provide child care for meetings, conferences, and events.
- See if neighbors or friends can be used as a liaison.
- Determine if meetings can be held in a more convenient, more familiar, more neutral location.
- Arrange for home visits (with appropriate security).
- Make it clear that you value the language, culture, knowledge, and expertise of parents and family members.

Source: Adapted from Swap, 1993.

to complete assignments. As an alternative to a class website, many schools have adopted student information management systems, which allow staff members to track attendance and tardiness, record grades and standardized test results, and generate reports, among other features. These systems typically provide parents with Web-based access to their child's records.

As one example of this, Sandy uses "ParentConnect," software that allows parents and guardians to visit a password-protected, read-only site to view their children's grades in her online grade book. (Note that parents have access for their child only.) Having grades online makes it easier for parents to track their children's academic progress, but teachers can't assume that all parents have Internet access (or that they use it even if they have it). As Sandy emphasizes, "Teachers still have to take responsibility for calling parents if their kid is not doing well in class."

Students' grades are the most frequent topic of e-mails from parents (Thompson, 2008), so convenient access to this information is clearly important to parents. In fact, one study documented an increase in overall parental involvement at a school in Israel that used an automated system to notify parents of academic or attendance problems (Telem & Pinto, 2006). Because they received early notification of problems and could respond quickly, parents also came to view the school personnel as more professional.

Like many teachers, Sandy and Christina communicate with parents and students via e-mail, and they have a few words of caution. First, keep in mind that many parents do not have or use e-mail as frequently as a teacher might hope. A recent study (Thompson, 2008) found that teachers communicated with only two to five of their students' parents on a regular basis via e-mail. Second, e-mail seems to encourage sloppiness and inaccuracy, so be sure to edit your e-mails for misspellings or grammatical errors. Third, be careful about using e-mail to discuss sensitive issues or problems. E-mail doesn't allow you to convey your message in a calm, quiet tone of voice or to "soften" it with smiles, gestures, or body language; nor can you see or hear parents' reactions. For this reason, e-mail may be more likely to lead to misinterpretations than face-to-face interactions or even phone calls. Further, e-mail can also be made very public with a simple touch of a few computer keys (intentional or not). You will want to keep this in mind as you compose e-mail messages to parents, and save sensitive or personal issues for phone calls or face-to-face interactions.

On the positive side, written messages (whether e-mail or snail mail) enable you to choose your words carefully and deliberately, an advantage you may not have when you're interacting with parents in "real time." So, don't fire off an e-mail in anger. Wait until you've calmed down and think carefully about what you want to say. Also be prepared for the fact that parents will not always follow this advice and will e-mail you when they are angry or upset about something. In cases like this, try not to let the tone detract from dealing with the issue.

Phone Calls

Given the hectic lives that people lead, one of the main problems about telephone calls is making the connection! At the beginning of the school year, all four teachers find out when and how to contact the families of their students. Some businesses have strict policies about employees' receiving phone messages, and a call during work hours may result in a reprimand. Some parents work at night, and a call in the morning will interrupt much-needed sleep; others may not have a phone at all, and you'll need to send a note home asking them to call you. (Donnie and Sandy both send notes home in plain, white envelopes—without the school's return address. This way there is less chance that a wary teenager will remove the letter from the pile of mail before the parent ever sees it!) All of the teachers also let parents know when they can receive telephone calls during the school day. Donnie even gives parents her home phone number; she says that no parent has ever abused the information.

To get the information she needs, Sandy has her students fill out a card with their parents' home and work numbers on the first day of school. She also asks students to indicate if their parents are permitted to get telephone calls at work. In addition, when Sandy has to call a parent, she'll often make a "precall," asking when it would be a convenient time to call and reassuring the parent that there's no earth-shattering problem. She's especially careful about checking the school personnel records to see which parent should be contacted:

 A majority of my students come from divorced homes. If the parents are not sharing joint custody, you cannot talk to the noncustodial parent. If the parents are sharing custody, then the record tells which parent the student is residing with, and I call that parent. Sometimes, the records will indicate if calls are to be made to both parents or if written communications are to be done in duplicate for both parents.

Before calling a parent about an academic or behavior problem, Sandy always gives her students notice:

 I say something like, "I know you want to be treated like an adult, but sometimes we need to work together with mom or dad to ensure your success. We need some help here. We can't solve this alone." I never use the telephone call as a threat or punishment. And I always wait 24 hours before calling. That way, the student can tell the parent that the call is coming (or about how the 75 they said they got on the test was really a 55!). When I talk with parents, I'm really careful about how I phrase things, so that I don't promote a negative reaction. Instead of saying, "Your son is disrupting the class," I'll say something like "We have to help your son control his behavior so that he can learn some chemistry." If the kid is disrespectful, I'll say, "I'm calling you about this because I know you wouldn't approve of this. I know you'd want to hear." In this way, you're conveying the idea that the parent will be supportive of you and that you don't think the kid comes from a family that would approve of such behavior.

During one meeting, we asked the four teachers to share some of the ideas they have for ensuring that telephone contacts with parents are productive. Their responses are listed in the Practical Tips box.

PRACTICAL TIPS ON

MAKING PRODUCTIVE TELEPHONE CONTACTS WITH PARENTS

- When the office receives a telephone call for you from a parent, and you're in class, have the staff member ask when would be a good time to call back.

- Even if a call comes during your free period, have the office take the message and say you'll call back. That gives you time to shift gears and prepare for the call. You can check your record book so that you are familiar with the student's progress.

- If a parent is calling with a complaint, try very hard not to get defensive. Listen and try to understand the parent's frustration. Respond by expressing your concern and assuring the parent that you are really committed to finding a solution.

- If a parent calls to complain that a child is upset about something ("He says you're picking on him" or "She says you're embarrassing her in front of the class"), acknowledge the student's perception. Convey your regret that the student has that perception. For example: "Gee, I'm really sorry that she has that perception. What specifically has she said, so that I can figure out what's going on? Help me to understand, because I don't want her to feel that way." Don't start out defensively: "I don't pick on kids."

- For chronic callers (parents who call three times a week) make it clear that it's important for you and the child to work the problem out. Explain that the frequent calls are embarrassing the student.

- If the telephone call is difficult, and there's a danger of your becoming defensive, have another person in the room to help monitor your tone of voice. He or she can tap you on the shoulder or make a face if you begin to get hostile or defensive.

- If a parent is out of control, suggest that you talk again at a later time, so that you both have a chance to calm down.

- If parents ask you to call every week with a report on their child's progress, suggest that they call you instead. (After all, you may have 150 students to think about, while they have only one!) Designate a day and time for them to call (e.g., on Fridays, during your prep period).

A few additional words of caution are in order. Although it's important to contact parents about serious problems, frequent phone calls about minor misbehaviors can be annoying. Furthermore, the practice can convey the message to both parents and children that the school can't deal with problems that arise; it's like saying, "Wait till your parents find out!"

It's also important to emphasize that phone calls should not be reserved for problems. As Donnie reminds us:

Teachers shouldn't just call when there's something bad. It's really important to call parents to give good news, to say "Your kid is really doing well," to tell them about something terrific that happened. Sometimes, when I do that, the student will come in the next day and say, "You called my house! And you didn't say anything *bad* about me!" And I'll tell them, "I had nothing bad to say!" I'll also let parents know what's coming up, the things that are going on. If you do that, then you've laid the foundation for a good relationship, and parents are more open later on. If you do have to call about a problem, they're less likely to be hostile or defensive.

Report Cards

Report cards have been the traditional way of communicating with families about a child's progress in school. Unfortunately, they are often not very informative. What exactly does it mean when a student receives a C in Spanish? Is she having problems with vocabulary, with comprehension, or with conversation? Is another student's D in mathematics due to difficulties with problem solving, or is it merely a result of careless computational errors? Since many high schools use computerized report cards, it is not always possible for the teacher to elaborate on grades with a personalized narrative. Donnie tells us:

On our report cards, you can pick from nine little statements, like "the student is disruptive," "comes late," "is doing well," "is working at or above grade level," "has missed tests." But you're only allowed to check two! And they're so impersonal, I'm not sure that they really communicate much of anything.

Another common problem with report cards is timeliness. If you rely solely on report cards to communicate with parents about a student's progress, two months might pass from the time a problem first appears until parents learn about it. In order to avoid this problem, some schools require teachers to send out progress reports midway through each marking period. Specific policies vary from district to district. Sandy explains what happens at her high school:

Progress reports have to be sent out mid-marking period for all seventh- and eighth-graders. In grades 9 through 12, we only have to send home a progress report if a student is in danger of receiving a D or an F for the marking period, but I send them out for other reasons too, like attendance or behavior or for commendable progress. I also tell students that I'm sending a progress report home, and I show it to them. I believe that they have the right to know.

Sometimes, showing students the progress reports encourages them to clean up their act. For example, Edward had a 75 average because he had two assignments missing. When I told him I was sending home a progress report, he asked me to just report the 75 average and leave off the part about the two missing assignments. He said his mother "would kill" him if she found out he wasn't doing his homework consistently. He promised he'd never miss another assignment. I decided he was serious, and so I agreed, but I told him that if she asked, I'd have to tell her. He never missed another assignment.

Although Sandy is conscientious about sending home progress reports, she also believes that any serious problem should be dealt with sooner:

Teachers should not rely on progress reports to tell parents about serious problems. Teachers need to contact parents if a problem develops. All of my students' parents know if their child has a D or an F before progress reports. I send progress reports because I have to, but my parents already know. Relying on progress reports is not very smart, since probably 50 percent of the kids take them out of the mail before their parents ever see them!

Back-to-School Night

For many parents, open house or back-to-school night is the first opportunity to meet you and to see the classroom. It's also the first opportunity *you* have to show parents all the great things you've been doing and to tell them about the plans you have for the future. As Fred says,

> I feel good about what happens in my room, and I want the parents to feel good about what's happening, too. I outline my objectives and the course syllabus; I describe my expectations for kids and for parents, and I talk about what they can expect from me. I usually talk about why I teach history; I give a little propaganda speech about what I'm trying to accomplish and how they can help. But it's always been a fun night. I believe that the parents have to laugh, just like the kids. The bell always rings when I'm halfway through; there's never enough time, but I talk with the parents at the coffee hour afterwards.

If you don't feel quite as enthusiastic as Fred, don't feel bad. Even teachers as experienced as Sandy sometimes feel nervous about back-to-school night. In fact, Sandy tells us: "I hate back-to-school night! The one good thing is that I always get so nervous that I talk really fast and finish early. That leaves plenty of time for people to ask questions."

As these comments suggest, back-to-school night usually involves a brief presentation to groups of parents who move from room to room, following their children's schedules. This is not always the case, however. In Christina's school, for example, teachers remain in their assigned rooms for 90 minutes, while parents visit teachers in any order they wish for brief, individual conferences. Since the time with each parent is so limited, Christina's goals are simply to attach a face to a name, to give parents a general sense of their children's progress, and to invite them to set up a longer conference. She also displays current class projects, so parents can look them over while they are waiting to see her.

Whatever format your school uses, keep in mind that first impressions *do* matter, so you need to think carefully about how you will orchestrate this event. The Practical Tips box contains some guidelines that emerged during discussions with Sandy, Fred, Donnie, and Christina. (Obviously, some of them apply only if you are giving group presentations.)

As a final comment about back-to-school night, it is important not to take low attendance personally. As noted earlier in this chapter, parents may have work schedules that prevent them from attending; they may feel just as nervous as you about the evening and decide not to come; or, if they have children of various ages, they may be at the back-to-school night of a younger sibling. Relax and enjoy meeting the parents who are there, and send follow-up e-mails to those parents who didn't attend.

PRACTICAL TIPS FOR

BACK-TO-SCHOOL NIGHT

- To increase attendance, consider sending e-mail invitations to the parents of your students, indicating that you are looking forward to meeting them. If you maintain a class website, include a prominent announcement about the night.

- Make sure your classroom looks especially attractive and neat. Display the books and materials that are used in your courses, as well as student projects from this year or previous years.

- Greet people at the door, introduce yourself, and find out who they are. *Do not assume that the student's last name is the same as the parents' last name, or that both parents have the same last name.*

- Make sure your presentation is succinct and well organized. Parents want to hear about your goals, plans, and philosophy, as well as the curriculum and policies about homework and absences. Create a PowerPoint presentation that incorporates photos of your students involved in class activities.

- Provide a handout, with a statement of goals, class schedules, homework policies, etc., for parents to take home. You can also e-mail this handout to parents who weren't able to attend back-to-school night.

- If parents raise issues that are unique to their child, let them know in a sensitive way that the purpose of open house is to describe the general program. Indicate that you're more than happy to discuss their concerns during a private conference. You may want to have a sign-up sheet available for this purpose.

- Listen carefully to questions that parents have. Provide an opportunity for parents to talk about *their* goals and expectations for their children in the coming school year. This can begin the two-way communication that is so crucial for family–school collaboration.

- Provide a sign-up sheet for parents who are able to participate in classroom activities (e.g., as a guest speaker or chaperone on field trips).

- If refreshments are being served after the class meetings, go down and join in conversations with parents. Clustering with the other teachers separates you from parents and conveys the idea that there is a professional barrier.

- RELAX AND HAVE FUN MEETING YOUR STUDENTS' PARENTS!

Parent-Teacher Conferences

Schools generally schedule one or two formal parent-teacher conferences during the school year. Interestingly, these meetings are often a source of frustration to both teachers and parents. Parents resent the formality of the situation (Lindle, 1989) and find the limited conference period frustrating. As one mother puts it, "Ten minutes is ridiculous, especially when other parents are waiting right outside the door. I need time to tell the teacher about how my child is at home, too" (Lindle, 1989, p. 14).

Teachers, too, are sometimes unhappy with these formal conferences. They agree with parents that the brief time allotted often precludes meaningful exchange. Furthermore, teachers complain about the lack of attendance: "The parents you *don't* need to see show up, while the ones you desperately *want* to talk with don't come."

Interestingly, Donnie doesn't mind that the parents of good students come to parent conferences:

> If there's a real problem, I've already contacted the parents by the time parent conferences come along. We've already met. So I think it's nice to see the ones whose kids are doing well. It's nice to be able to give positive reports. And parents want reassurance that all is going well.

Before a conference, it's important to prepare carefully. For example, Sandy looks over each student's grades, prints out a student progress sheet using a computerized grading program, notes any trends in academic performance or behavior, and jots down a few key words to use when she's talking to parents. It's also useful to have a few samples of students' work to show parents.

Conferences can be tense—especially if you're meeting with family members for the first time—so our four teachers begin by trying to put parents at ease. They suggest leading with something positive: "You son is a delight to have in class" or "Your daughter appears to be really interested in the topics we've been studying." You should be aware, however, that immigrant Latino parents (and others from collectivistic cultures) may be uncomfortable hearing extended praise of their children, since praise singles a person out from the group (Trumbull, Rothstein-Fisch, Greenfield, & Quiroz, 2001).

Next, problems or weaknesses can be broached—not as character flaws ("she's lazy"), but as problems that need to be solved ("She's having difficulty getting her assignments in on time. What can we do about this?"). Donnie puts it this way:

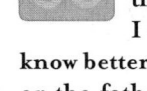

> I might tell parents, "We have a problem. Your son's performance is going down. Can you help me to understand? Is there anything going on that I should know about?" I stress that we have to work together. I explain that if I understand more about the home situation, then I'll know better how to approach the student. Maybe there's been a death in the family, or the father moved out, or a move is imminent. All this helps me to be more effective.

Sandy also tries to enlist parents' assistance in dealing with problems; however, she cautions teachers not to make demands that are impossible for parents to carry out:

> Don't say things like, "You have to get your child to participate more in class." Be reasonable. If you're talking about a 17-year-old senior, what are the chances that a parent can do that? On the other hand, you can say, "Joanne is very quiet in class. Is this her normal behavior?"

Although they try to provide parents with substantive information, our teachers emphasize the need *to listen*. All four teachers always allow time for parents to ask questions and to express their concerns, and they solicit parents' suggestions. A conference should be a two-way conversation, not a monologue. *It's also critical not to assume that poor parents, uneducated parents, or parents with limited English proficiency have nothing of value to offer.* One immigrant mother expressed her frustration this way: "Whenever I go to school, they want to tell me what to do at home. They want to tell me how to raise my kid. They never ask what I think. They never ask me anything" (Finders & Lewis, 1994, p. 53).

Ellen Kottler (1994) stresses the importance of encouraging families whose first language is not English to help you understand their children's educational and cultural background. For example, you might ask about past educational experiences, if their son or daughter is experiencing any cultural conflicts, what their educational goals for their child are, whether English is used at home, and if there are any special needs or customs you need to take into consideration. If you are meeting with parents who are using an interpreter, keep in mind that your conversation is with the parents, and not the interpreter. You should speak to and make eye contact with the parents. Speak no more than two or three sentences at a time, and then pause for the interpreter to speak.

You also need to be sensitive to cultural differences in communication styles. Cultures shape the nature of verbal interaction, providing norms for who can initiate conversation, whether it's all right to interrupt, and how long to pause between a question and its answer (Swap, 1993). If these norms are not shared, participants may feel uncomfortable. The following example of conversation between Athabaskan Indians and whites in Alaska illustrates how misunderstanding can arise because of different communication styles:

> [A] white speaker often will ask a question, then pause, waiting for the Indian speaker to reply; then, when it appears the listener has nothing to say, the white speaker will speak again. The Indian, who wishes to reply, but is accustomed to longer pauses between speakers, is not given an adequate opportunity to speak.
>
> On the other hand, when Indian speakers do have the floor, they are interrupted frequently because they take what are perceived by whites to be "lengthy" pauses between thoughts. As an Athabaskan woman said to one of us, "While you're thinking about what you're going to say, they're already talking." Hence, Indian speakers often say very little and white speakers seem to do all the talking. (Nelson-Barber & Meier, 1990, p. 3, as cited in Swap, 1993, p. 91)

In addition, you need to recognize that different cultures hold different views about appropriate classroom behavior. For example, a European American teacher may encourage students to participate actively in classroom discussions, to voice their opinions, and to ask questions. In contrast, some Latino and Asian American parents may expect their children to be quiet and obedient and not to contradict the teacher or ask questions (Scarcella, 1990). It's also important to understand that Latino immigrant parents may be primarily interested in the child's social and moral development:

> [B]eing a respectful contributor to group well-being rather than focusing on one's own achievement is highly valued. So when immigrant Latino parents come for a parent-teacher conference, their first question is likely to be, *"Como se porta mi hijo/hija?"* ("How is my son/daughter behaving?") A teacher may find it difficult to stifle her consternation after hearing the same question from 25 or 30 sets of

parents, believing that all the parents care about is their child's behavior, when the teacher's goal is to discuss the child's academic progress. (Rothstein-Fisch & Trumbull, 2008, pp. 14–15)

Finally, our teachers stress the importance of not closing doors to further communication. If a conference is not going well, you might suggest another meeting, perhaps with the department supervisor or a guidance counselor on hand to mediate the discussion.

Some schools have started to use three-way conferences that include the teacher, the parent or guardian, and the student (Bailey & Guskey, 2001). First, all participants, beginning with the student, share their perceptions of the strengths demonstrated in the student's work. They then discuss two areas on which the student needs to work, outline goals for the future, and agree on the kinds of support that each party will provide. Finally, the teacher answers questions and summarizes agreements.

Research indicates that the three-way conference has distinct advantages over the traditional parent-teacher conference. One study, for example, compared traditional parent-teacher conferences with conferences that included students as participants ("family-school conferences") (Minke & Anderson, 2003). Families chosen to participate in the project had children with mild learning or behavior problems. Two primary findings emerged with respect to traditional conferences. First, both teachers and parents agreed that conferences are important opportunities for an exchange of information; second, both groups approached conferences with trepidation. Parents used words like *worried, nervous, overwhelmed, angry,* and *apprehensive* to describe their emotions, and teachers described their feelings of "exhaustion and relief" when conference days were over (p. 59). In contrast, both parents and teachers felt that the family-school conference model increased trust and communication and provided greater opportunities to learn about one another and the child. Adults were particularly impressed by students' "unexpectedly mature behavior" and their "honest, insightful comments about their own learning" (p. 60). Indeed, "Teachers often noted that the child was the first one to bring up 'bad news,' which teachers saw as relieving them of a worrisome burden and greatly reducing parental defensiveness" (p. 60). Evidence also suggested that family-school conferences could be conducted in the same 15–20 minutes usually allotted to routine, two-party conferences. It should be noted, however, that three-way conferences like this require training and careful preparation. (See Bailey and Guskey, 2001, for practical strategies and suggestions.)

> ### PAUSE AND REFLECT
>
> We have already noted that family involvement in school drops off in middle and high school. Before reading the next section, think about the types of family involvement that could benefit your classroom and students, and the ways that you could encourage and nurture this involvement.

Family Involvement in School

At the high school level, most family involvement in school consists of attendance at student performances, athletic events, or other programs. Family involvement may also take place "behind-the-scenes"; for example, parents may engage in fund-raising activities, interview prospective teachers and administrators, prepare breakfast on "Teacher Appreciation Day," participate on committees developing discipline and attendance policies, and chaperone social events.

Participation in classroom activities is far less common, but involving even a few parents can provide considerable support and enrich the curriculum. When Fred's Contemporary World Cultures classes study religions, for example, parents of different faiths come in to explain their religious beliefs; in his Institute for Political and Legal Education (IPLE) class, parents who are lawyers sometimes share their expertise; and his history classes may be visited by survivors of Nazi concentration camps. In Sandy's chemistry classes, parents speak on scientific or environmental issues and parents who are faculty members at a nearby university have set up tours of the chemistry labs there. Donnie holds a "mini-career day," when successful former students share their career experiences and communicate the message, "You can do this too." In Christina's journalism classes, parents, friends of parents, former students, and local contacts speak about their careers as journalists.

If you decide to invite parents to participate in your classroom, you need to think carefully about how to recruit them. Sometimes parents don't volunteer simply because they're not sure what would be expected or how they could contribute. Back-to-school night offers a good opportunity to make a direct, in-person appeal and to explain the various ways parents can assist. If you do invite parents to make a presentation in your classroom, make sure you are clear about whether they will need to repeat the presentation in multiple classes. An engineer friend was surprised to learn that she would need to repeat her presentation in all three of the physics classes that one of us taught!

Another way of involving parents is in helping you get resources for your classroom. Perhaps one of your students' parents works in a laboratory and can arrange to donate surplus equipment to your science classroom. Or perhaps a parent who works in a bookstore can arrange to have slightly-damaged books donated to your literature classroom. (These sorts of donations to a school typically qualify as a charitable contribution at tax time.) You can use e-mail or a class website to distribute a "wish list" of resources for your classroom, as a further means of inviting parental involvement.

If you're teaching in a district where there has been little parent involvement in school, special efforts will be needed to change the situation. At Donnie's high school, a committee has been established to consider ways of making the school more "parent-friendly." As a result of the committee's efforts, teams of teachers have visited neighborhood churches on Sunday mornings to invite parents to the high school. As Donnie puts it,

Parents were complaining that they don't feel welcome. Well, the point of these trips is to say, "We want you to visit. This is your school; come in and see what's going on. If you can, volunteer, work in the library, help kids with homework. We welcome you."

Donnie's sentiment is echoed in research that found that increasing cultural programming in a school encouraged more American Indian parents to get involved (Powers, 2006), and that inviting Latino parents to become active in school government increased involvement of Latino families (Marschall, 2006).

Parents of Students with Special Needs

According to the Individuals with Disabilities Education Act (IDEA), parents of children with disabilities have a legal mandate to participate in the planning of their children's Individualized Education Program (IEP). Given the fact that inclusion is now widespread, you are likely to have contact with parents of children with disabilities and, hopefully, to be involved in the annual IEP meetings (at which a teacher must be present). But Sandy, who has an emotionally disturbed student in her class this year, cautions teachers not to wait for the formal, mandated meetings, or even for the regularly scheduled parent conferences:

Anytime I have a student with an IEP, I go to the case manager right away and say, "Tell me about this kid." Then I ask them to set up a time for us to meet with the parents, usually in the first week and a half of school. This shows parents that you're aware of the IEP; it gives them a sense of relief and confidence. They know that the IEP isn't just a piece of paper, that the teacher is already thinking about how to modify the course for the student. It starts you off on the right track, establishes the right tone.

At our initial meeting, we talk a lot about the IEP. You've got to remember that IEPs are open to interpretation, and that needs to be discussed. For example, an IEP may say that the student can have more time for tests. What does that mean? Is that an indefinite amount of time? Ten minutes? What?

I also want parents to educate me about their kid. This year, with an emotionally disturbed boy, it was important for me to know what sets him off. What will be stressful for him that might result in an outburst? Every kid is different, and I don't like surprises if I can avoid them. Sometimes it's as simple as "don't pair him with another male."

In addition to a meeting like this early in the year, Sandy keeps in close contact with parents throughout the year. Sometimes parents want a weekly report, and Sandy is happy to comply; however, she asks them to take the responsibility for calling or e-mailing: "With so many kids, it's just too hard for me to remember."

Family Involvement in Learning Activities at Home

Epstein's fourth type of involvement refers to the ways families can assist their children's learning at home. At the secondary level, this kind of involvement often creates considerable anxiety for parents. As Donnie mentioned earlier, some parents are scared off by the subject matter. Sandy agrees:

At the elementary level, parents often help with homework, read to their children, and monitor their studying. But at the high school level, the first thing out of a parent's mouth is "I can't do calculus. I can't do chemistry. There's no way I can help."

Parents are not the only ones who wonder how they can help with their teenagers' homework assignments. Some teachers also question whether parents can really be useful. In contrast, our four teachers believe that parents can play an extremely important role. Although parents may not have familiarity with the subject matter, they can still help by monitoring their children's schoolwork, providing support and encouragement, and setting limits. Fred tells us:

> I find that parents really want to help their kids, but they often don't have a clue about what to do. They're really receptive to suggestions. Sometimes I suggest that parents help by checking the spelling on their kids' papers. Maybe I'll suggest that they check that the kid has done the homework. Maybe I'll explain the requirements for a research paper, and suggest they check to see the requirements are met. I'll suggest they ask to see the kid's papers. A lot of times kids put their papers in the garbage and never show them to their parents.

Similarly, Sandy tells parents not to worry if they don't know chemistry; they can still help to structure their child's environment:

> If a kid is having trouble with chemistry, 99 percent of the time, the problem is not with the subject, but with the time spent on the subject. Parents can monitor the time spent on homework. They can say, "Doing chemistry in front of the TV is not working." They can say, "You have to do your homework before you go out." They can suggest that their child call a friend if they're having trouble. They can make sure that their child comes in for help after school. I'll tell them, "I want your child in here two days a week so I can help with the chemistry. But you have to see that they get here."

A recent review of research on parent involvement in homework (Patall, Cooper, & Robinson (2008) reinforces our teachers' beliefs. The review concluded that of all the various types of parent involvement, setting rules about when and where homework should be done may have the most beneficial effect on students' achievement. Moreover, this kind of involvement does not require years of higher education. A survey of middle-school students' homework practices (Xu and Corno, 2003) found that family members were especially helpful in arranging the environment (e.g., finding a quiet area, creating space for the child to work, turning off the television) and assisting children in controlling their emotions (e.g., calming a frustrated child, providing encouragement when a child is upset). The homework helper's educational level was unrelated to effective homework assistance

It is important to recognize that this view of the parental role may conflict with some families' beliefs about the importance of independence and self-sufficiency. For example, a mother in one study explains why she stays out of her daughter's schooling:

> It's her education, not mine. I've had to teach her to take care of herself. I work nights, so she's had to get up and get herself ready for school. I'm not going to be there all the time. She's gotta do it. She's a tough cookie. . . . She's almost an adult,

and I get the impression that they want me to walk her through her work. And it's not that I don't care either. I really do. I think it's important, but I don't think it's my place. (Finders & Lewis, 1994, p. 52)

Clearly, this mother is concerned for her child's well-being, but she sees independence as critical if her daughter is to survive and succeed.

> ### PAUSE AND REFLECT
>
> Homework is a controversial subject. For example, in *The End of Homework: How Homework Disrupts Families, Overburdens Children, and Limits Learning*, Etta Kralovec and John Buell argue that homework actually promotes discrimination. Children who are able to get support and assistance from their families (the "haves") can surge ahead while those who come from families that are unable to help them (the "have-nots") fall further and further behind. What do you think about this issue?

CONCLUDING COMMENTS

This chapter has described different ways that teachers can reach out to families. Our suggestions vary considerably in terms of how common they are and how much time and energy they demand. As you get to know your students and their family situations, you will be able to decide which practices are most appropriate and most feasible. Of course, you need to be realistic: As a beginning teacher, you may have to delay major efforts to facilitate communication and collaboration with families. Nonetheless, remember that family involvement can be key to students' success and extending specific invitations to participate has been shown to have a powerful impact on family involvement at home and in school (Deslandes & Bertrand, 2005).

This is an age of many single parents, of mothers who work outside the home, of grandparents, aunts, and neighbors who care for children, of increasing numbers of families whose cultural backgrounds differ from that of most teachers. Family–school collaboration has never been more difficult—but it has never been more important.

SUMMARY

This chapter began by discussing the benefits of working closely with families. It then outlined the challenges to family–teacher cooperation and stressed that teachers' attitudes and practices—not the educational level, marital status, or workplace of parents—determine whether families become productively involved in their children's schooling. Finally, the chapter presented strategies for overcoming the challenges and for fostering collaboration between families and schools.

Benefits of Working Closely with Families

- Knowing about a student's home situation provides insight into the student's classroom behavior.
- When families understand what you are trying to achieve, they can provide valuable support and assistance.
- Families can help to develop and implement strategies for changing behavior.
- Parent volunteers can provide assistance in the classroom and school.

Challenges to Family–Teacher Cooperation

- Teachers are sometimes reluctant to involve families in schooling because of:
   The extra time and energy that are required.
   Their perceptions that families are too overburdened, apathetic, and irresponsible or that they lack the skills needed.
   The level of authority and autonomy teachers enjoy within their classrooms.
- Parents are sometimes reluctant to become involved in schooling because they:
   Are overburdened by the demands of work.
   Have unhappy memories of school.
   Believe schooling should be left to the experts.
   Feel guilty if their children are having problems.
   Find schools intimidating and threatening places.
   Do not see involvement in school as part of their parental role.
- Changes in the family and American society:
   The number of single-parent families has increased.
   The "stay-at-home" mother is vanishing.
   The significant adults in children's lives may not be parents, but grandparents, neighbors, aunts, or uncles.
   Many children come from non-English-speaking homes.

Fostering Collaboration between Families and Schools

- Schools can assist families in carrying out their basic obligations by providing parent education, establishing parent support groups, and referring families to community and state agencies.
- Teachers need to communicate about school programs and students' progress through websites and e-mails, phone calls, report cards, progress reports, and face-to-face interactions (e.g., back-to-school night, parent conferences).
- Family members can serve as volunteers in classrooms and schools.
- Families can assist their children at home on learning activities:
   Supervising homework.
   Providing encouragement and support.
   Setting limits.

As a beginning teacher, you have to decide what you can realistically accomplish with respect to communication and collaboration with parents. Nonetheless, you need to remember that family involvement is critical to students' success. In this age of single parents, mothers who work outside the home, and students who come from diverse cultural backgrounds, meaningful family–school collaboration has never been more challenging, but it has never been more essential.

ACTIVITIES FOR SKILL BUILDING AND REFLECTION

In Class

Working in small groups, read the following vignettes (one per group) and do the following:

- Discuss the information provided in the vignette.

- Make a list of other information you might like to get and how you might get it.
- Make a list of possible ways you might address the issue aside from talking to the parent/guardian/family. What might some underlying issues be?
- Think about what you will do to prepare for the conference.
- Decide how you will structure the meeting so that you can state your information in a productive way without being defensive.
- Role-play the conversation that you might have with the family member about this issue.

Vignette 1:

You have stressed that research scientists work in teams, and you use a lot of cooperative learning activities in your seventh-grade general science class. Although students sit in rows, their seats are assigned so that they can quickly turn their desks around to form four-person "research groups" that are heterogeneous in terms of race, ethnicity, gender, and achievement level. At parent conferences, the father of a Pakistani girl in your class requests that you place his daughter in an all-girl group. As he explains, his culture frowns upon girls and boys sitting together, and he was extremely unhappy when he learned about his daughter's seat assignment and the composition of her research team.

Vignette 2:

Last week you conducted a parent conference with Mrs. Lewis, Joey's mother. During the conference you described his disruptive behaviors and what you've done to deal with them. You also explained that he is in danger of failing your class because he rarely does homework and has gotten poor grades on most quizzes and tests. Mrs. Lewis seemed to accept and understand the information; however, the next day, an irate *Mr.* Lewis called. He told you that he had never seen his wife so upset and that he wants another conference as soon as possible to get to the bottom of the problem. He also intimated that the problem might be due to a personality conflict between you and his son. Although the phone call caught you off-guard, you scheduled the conference for two days later.

Vignette 3:

You have a student in your 10th-grade class who is failing to complete her homework. She is an academically competent student in class; she does most of her class work and is friendly and easygoing. You have asked the student repeatedly to do her homework, yet she comes in almost daily with little or none of it complete. When you ask her why she has not done the work, she answers by saying, "I don't know." You have sent two letters home, and left one phone message for her family. Her mother shows up unexpectedly at the end of a school day, demands to speak with you, and tells you that her daughter is complaining that you are picking on her and do not like her.

Vignette 4:

Paul is an African American student in your sixth-grade class. You know his mother is very active in the PTA and is quite involved in school and district politics. Unfortunately, Paul is not doing well in class. He is an excellent reader and writer and he is quite intelligent, but you have documented his lack of class work, and you have anecdotal notes referring to his negative comments about the kinds of assignments you assign the class. He is getting more and more disengaged and disrespectful of you. You feel well prepared for the parent conference, because you have very thorough records and notes. When Paul's parents come to the conference, you carefully lay out your case. His father responds by explaining that in their home they encourage their children to question what they are taught and not to believe information just because it is presented in class. He explains that many students of color disengage from school because they are not represented in the Eurocentric curriculum. Paul's mother then suggests that as a European American teacher you need to learn about the history and culture of the students that you teach in order to fully engage them. She even goes on to suggest that you should listen to Paul's criticisms of your assignments and use that as a way to examine and evaluate what is essentially a biased curriculum.

On Your Own

1. In getting ready for the school year, you have decided to send a letter to the family of each student in your classes. The point of the letter is to introduce yourself, describe the curriculum, highlight a few upcoming projects, and explain your expectations in terms of homework, behavior, and attendance.

Select a subject that you might actually teach (e.g., American History, Algebra I, Spanish, Home Economics I, World Literature, Physical Education, etc.), and write such a letter. As you write, think about the need to create a warm tone, to be clear and organized, to avoid educational jargon, and to stimulate interest about school.

2. Anita is extremely "forgetful" about doing homework assignments. She has received innumerable zeros and regularly has to stay for detention to make up the work. You have called her mother to report on this behavior and to ask for assistance, but her mother does not want to get involved. As she puts it, "I've got all I can do to handle her at home. What she does with school work is your responsibility!"

Interview two experienced teachers about what they would do in a case like this, and then formulate your own course of action based on what you learn.

For Your Portfolio

Demonstrate your capacity to communicate with families by including two or three artifacts (e.g., newsletters; interactive homework; requests for parental help with homework; invitations to class events; student award certificates; checksheets to be used at parent conferences).

FOR FURTHER READING

Allen, J. B. (2007). *Creating welcoming schools: A practical guide to home-school partnerships with diverse families.* New York: Teachers College Press.
  This book contains many practical strategies for engaging families in schools, learning about diverse cultures, and building partnerships between school and home.

Bailey, J. M., & Guskey, T. R. (2001). *Implementing student-led conferences.* Thousand Oaks, CA: Corwin Press.
  In a student-led conference, students take the responsibility of communicating their progress, while teachers serve as facilitators. This very helpful book provides suggestions for preparing, conducting, and evaluating student-led conferences. It includes sample conference announcements and formats, portfolio planners, reproducible letters, and parent and student response forms.

Delgado Gaitan, C. (2004). *Involving Latino families in schools: Raising student achievement through home-school partnerships.* Thousand Oaks, CA: Corwin Press.
  Concha Delgado Gaitan provides strategies for including Latino parents in the goal of increasing student achievement. She stresses three conditions of increased parental

participation: connecting to families, sharing information with parents, and supporting continued parental involvement. Among the topics examined are Latino families' aspirations for their children; the communication systems needed between schools and Latino families; and techniques to foster Latino parent involvement.

Epstein, J., Sanders, M. G., Simon, B. S., Salinas, K. C., Jansorn, N. R., & Van Voorhis, F. L. (2002). *School, family, and community partnerships: Your handbook for action* (2nd ed.). Thousand Oaks, CA: Corwin Press.

This handbook provides a wealth of information on the six types of involvement, with "stories from the field" to show how schools are actually using the framework to implement partnership programs. It stresses the importance of taking an action team approach and provides practical strategies for conducting workshops and presentations, implementing interactive homework, organizing volunteers, and strengthening and evaluating partnership programs.

Lawrence-Lightfoot, S. (2003). *The essential conversation: What parents and teachers can learn from each other.* New York: Ballantine Books.

According to Lawrence-Lightfoot, "beneath the polite surface of parent-teacher conferences . . . burns a cauldron of fiery feelings." For parents, there is no more dreaded moment; for teachers, these meetings engender feelings of uncertainty, defensiveness, and exposure. This book focuses on the experiences of ten exemplary teachers in an effort to understand how parents and teachers "negotiate the treacherous and tender terrain" between them.

Trumbull, E., Rothstein-Fisch, C., Greenfield, P. M., & Quiroz, B. (2001). *Bridging cultures between home and school: A guide for teachers.* Mahwah, NJ: Lawrence Erlbaum Associates.

Researchers and teachers involved in the Bridging Cultures Project explain the ways that the individualistic values of American schools can conflict with the more collectivistic values of Latino students' home cultures. They provide research-based strategies for improving home-school relationships with immigrant Latino families.

ORGANIZATIONAL RESOURCES

The Family Involvement Network of Educators (FINE), Harvard Family Research Project, Harvard Graduate School of Education, 3 Garden Street, Cambridge, MA 02138 (www.hfrp.org, 617-495-9108). FINE brings together thousands of stakeholders committed to promoting strong partnerships among schools, families, and communities. FINE provides information about family involvement, including teaching tools, training materials, and research reports. Members can receive a free subscription to the FINE e-mail newsletter, which regularly highlights new resources for strengthening, family, school, and community partnerships.

The National Network of Partnership Schools, Johns Hopkins University, Center on School, Family, and Community Partnerships, 3003 North Charles Street, Baltimore, MD 21218 (www.partnershipschools.org, 410-516-8800). NNPS provides information on implementing comprehensive, goal-oriented programs of school, family, and community partnerships. Check out the interactive homework assignments (TIPS) and the collections of "Promising Partnership Practices" on their website.

The National Parent Teacher Association (PTA), National Headquarters, 541 N. Fairbanks Court, Suite 1300, Chicago, IL 60611-3396 (www.pta.org, 312-670-6782). The National Parent Teacher Association (PTA) and its state affiliates have produced a set of standards for family-community-school partnerships. Teachers, schools, and parents can use these standards to assess their own efforts. Additionally, the website provides materials for parents on how to help their children learn and how they can join their local PTA.

PART III

ORGANIZING AND MANAGING INSTRUCTION

Educators sometimes talk about classroom management and instruction as if the two were completely distinct and separate tasks of being a teacher. From this perspective, management and instruction occur in chronological sequence. First you establish rules, routines, and consequences, build positive relationships with students, and promote community. Then you begin to teach.

In contrast, we see these two tasks as closely entwined—even inseparable. As we pointed out in Chapter 1, in order to avoid problems of disorder, teachers must not only foster positive student-teacher relationships and use good preventive management strategies, they must also implement well-paced, organized, and engaging instruction. When students find academic activities purposeful and interesting, they are less likely to become inattentive and disruptive. In this section, we consider ways of managing instruction and instructional time to promote students' involvement and learning. Chapter 7 looks at the amount of time available for instruction and discusses ways to make sure you aren't wasting this precious resource. Chapter 8 argues that teachers are responsible for stimulating students' motivation and offers a variety of motivational strategies drawn from research, theory, and the practice of our four teachers. Chapters 9 through 11 examine four instructional situations common to middle and high school classrooms: independent work (also known as seatwork), small-group work (including cooperative learning), recitations (question-and-answer sequences), and discussions. For each of these, we describe the unique managerial challenges or "pit-falls" that teachers need to be aware of and then suggest ways to structure the instructional situation to increase the probability of success. We draw on the experiences and wisdom of our four teachers to illustrate how to effectively use these instructional modes.

Our discussion in Chapters 9 through 11 is based on the premise that what constitutes appropriate and orderly behavior varies across these types of instruction. For example, calling out may be perfectly acceptable in a student-centered discussion, but be inappropriate during a teacher-directed recitation. Similarly, students may be encouraged to work together during a cooperative learning activity, but be prohibited from helping one another during an independent writing assignment. Students have the right to know how you expect them to behave when they're participating in independent work, small-group work, recitations, and discussions. Thus, in addition to the rules for general behavior presented at the beginning of the year, you must think about the behaviors that are appropriate and desirable in each of these instructional situations and make your behavioral expectations absolutely clear.

MAKING THE MOST OF CLASSROOM TIME

On the first day of school, the academic year seems to stretch out endlessly. If you're a beginning teacher, you may wonder how you'll ever fill all the hours of school that lie ahead—especially if you're not even certain what you're going to do *tomorrow.* And yet, as the days go by, you may begin to feel that there's never enough time to accomplish all you need to do. With assemblies, fire drills, announcements over the intercom, standardized testing, snow days, holidays, and clerical tasks, the hours available for instruction seem far fewer than they did at first. Indeed, by the end of the year, you may view time as a precious resource—not something that has to be filled (or killed), but something that must be conserved and used wisely. (Of course, your students may not share this view—as Figure 7.1 illustrates!)

This chapter discusses issues of time and time management. Guiding the chapter is the premise that the wise use of time will maximize opportunities for learning and minimize opportunities for disruption. First, we look at the amount of school time that is actually available for teaching and learning. Then we consider strategies for using classroom time

PAUSE AND REFLECT

Keeping in mind that the average student spends 1,080 hours per year in school (180 days × 6 hours per day), estimate either the number of hours or the percentage of time that students are actually involved in productive learning (i.e., they are engaging in meaningful, appropriate academic tasks). Then read on to see what researchers have calculated and find out if you are on target.

Figure 7.1   *Source:* CALVIN AND HOBBES © 1993, Watterson. Distributed by UNIVERSAL UCLICK. Reprinted with permission. All rights reserved.

efficiently, focusing on three complementary approaches—maintaining activity flow, minimizing transition time, and holding students accountable. Finally, we examine block scheduling, a reform effort that replaces the traditional 42- or 50-minute period with fewer, longer classes of 85 to 90 minutes.

HOW MUCH TIME IS THERE, ANYWAY?

Although this seems like a straightforward question, the answer is not so simple. In fact, the answer depends on the kind of time you're talking about (Karweit, 1989). Most states mandate a school year of approximately 180 days. Let's suppose that you're teaching in a high school that has divided each of these days into 42-minute periods. This amounts to 126 hours of *mandated time* for each of your classes. But students are absent, and special assembly programs are scheduled, snowstorms cause delayed openings, and parent conferences require early closings. Factors like these immediately reduce the time you have for teaching, so the *time available for instruction* can be substantially less than mandated time. Listen to the reflections of a student teacher who has learned to deal with the constant interruptions and cancellations:

> *"Well, at least you're learning to be flexible!" If I heard that once, I heard it a million times. I believe every teacher that I've had contact with this semester has made this statement to me. A record snowfall, proficiency testing, marine biology field trips, half-day inservice days, pep rallies, assemblies . . . The actual time I have had a full class of students . . . for more than two consecutive days is minimal. Nowhere is the realization that I must be flexible more evident than in my lesson plan book. When I began student teaching, my lesson plans were typed and clipped into a binder (and labeled "Monday," "Tuesday," etc.). A short time later I began calling each day "Day One," "Day Two," "Day Three," and so on. A short time after that I began writing the lessons in a plan book in pencil. About halfway through my student teaching experience, I began doing my lessons on Post-it*

paper which I could arrange as needed. I only transferred the lesson to the blocks in the book as I became absolutely sure that they would not be disrupted. I have continued to use this practice with great success and have actually started one of my cooperating teachers on the same method.

Even when school is in session, students are present, and you have your class for the full 42 minutes, some portion of the available class time must be spent in noninstructional activities. This means that only part of the 42-minute period actually constitutes *instructional time.* In *A Place Called School* (1984), John Goodlad reports that the senior high school teachers he studied generally spent about 76 percent of available class time on instruction, 20 percent on routines, and 1.3 percent on behavior control; the remaining 2.2 percent was spent on socializing. Interestingly, the figures varied by subject area: Foreign language classes ranked first in terms of time spent on instruction (83 percent at the senior high level), while English ranked last (73 percent). School-to-school differences were also apparent, with instructional time varying from 68 percent to 84 percent at the senior high level. There was similar variation at the junior high level. At Crestview Junior High, for example, teachers spent 69 percent of class time on instruction and 25 percent on routines, while Fairfield Junior High teachers spent 87 percent on instruction and only 9 percent on routines.

Even within a school and a subject area, there can be considerable variation from teacher to teacher. In some classes, settling in at the beginning of the period, taking attendance, distributing materials, collecting homework, and reprimanding misbehaving students consume an inordinate amount of time. Karweit (1989) describes a "one-hour" math class, for example, in which the first 10 minutes were typically used to collect lunch money, and the last 10 were used to line up the students for lunch—leaving only 40 minutes for actual instruction.

Situations like this are not unusual in the classrooms of teachers who lack efficient strategies for carrying out routine, noninstructional tasks. Consider the difficulties encountered by one beginning teacher, Ms. Twain, as she attempted to check homework at the beginning of math class (Leinhardt & Greeno, 1986). Ms. Twain had two goals: to identify who had done the homework and to correct it orally. She began by asking, "Who doesn't have their homework?" In response, students did one of three things: They held up their completed work, called out that they didn't have it, or walked over to the teacher and told her whether they had done it or not. Ms. Twain then talked about the importance of homework and marked the results of this check on a posted sheet of paper.

Next, Ms. Twain chose students to give the correct answers to the homework problems:

She called out a set of problem numbers (1–10) and assigned a child to call out the answers as she called the problem number. The student slowly called out the answers in order. (The first child chosen was the lowest in the class, did not have her work done, and was doing the problems in her head.) Thus, for the first 10 problem answers, the teacher lost control of pace and correctness of answer; however, it was only when the child failed on the sixth problem that Twain realized the student had not done her homework. (Leinhardt & Greeno, 1986, p. 87)

Ms. Twain continued to call on students to give the answers, while the rest of the class checked their work. The last student chosen went through the sequence of problems quickly, but gave both the problem number and the answer, a situation that caused some confusion (e.g., "24, 27; 25, 64"). Ms. Twain's entire homework check took six minutes—and it was clear to the observers that she was never certain which students had done their homework.

In contrast, the researchers describe a homework check conducted by Ms. Longbranch, a successful, experienced teacher. Ms. Longbranch first gave a cue, "Okay, set 43," and then began to call the students' names. Those who had done the homework simply responded, "yes." Those who hadn't done the work got up and wrote their names on the chalkboard. In 30 seconds—with a minimum of fuss—Ms. Longbranch was able to determine who had completed the assignment.

The next goal was to correct the work:

> The students took colored pencils out and responded chorally with the correct answer, a fraction in lowest terms. As the teacher called the problem, "$\frac{1}{12} + \frac{1}{12}$," they responded "$\frac{2}{12}$ or $\frac{1}{6}$." Time to complete was 106 seconds. (Leinhardt & Greeno, 1986, p. 85)

Ms. Longbranch's homework check is not presented as a model to be copied in your classroom; indeed, her procedure may not be appropriate for your particular class. The important point is that Ms. Longbranch has established a routine that enables her to check homework efficiently, almost automatically, while Ms. Twain does not yet have a workable strategy. Although the difference in the time used by the two teachers is only about four minutes, it is probably symptomatic of the ways they managed class time in general.

Even when teachers are actually teaching, students are not necessarily paying attention. We must consider still another kind of time—*engaged time* or time-on-task. Let's suppose that while you are teaching, some of your students choose to text message about last Saturday night's party, do their homework for the next period, comb their hair, or stare out the window. In this case, the amount of time you are devoting to instruction is greater than the amount of time students are directly engaged in learning. This is not an atypical situation. Research documents the fact that students tend to be "on-task" about 70 percent of the time (Rosenshine, 1980). Again, there are sizable variations from class to class. A study of 30 middle and high school science teachers (McGarity & Butts, 1984) found that some classes had an engagement rate of 54 percent (i.e., the average student was attentive about one-half of the time), while in other classes the engagement rate was 75 percent.

To a large extent, variations like these reflect teachers' ability to manage classroom events and to get students involved in learning activities. But other factors also come into play—students' attitudes toward school and subject matter (Marks, 2000), time of day and day of week. And, despite the lack of empirical evidence, some teachers insist that attention falls off (and misbehavior increases) when there is a full moon!

There are also substantial differences in engagement from activity to activity. In one study, for example, high school students reported higher engagement (defined as interest, concentration, and enjoyment) during groupwork and individual work than while listening to lectures or watching television and videos (Shernoff, Csikszentmihalyi, Schneider, & Shernoff, 2003). It seems clear that instructional strategies requiring students to be active are more engaging than those in which students are passive. Students also reported more engagement when they perceived the task at hand to be relevant and appropriately challenging—which brings us to a final type of time.

This last type of time is the *amount of time students spend on work that is meaningful and appropriate.* We sometimes get so caught up in trying to increase students' time-on-task that we overlook the tasks themselves. We once saw students in a ninth-grade general science class spend 15 minutes coloring a worksheet that showed diagrams of flower parts. The students seemed absorbed; indeed, an observer coding time-on-task would have recorded a high engagement rate. But what was the purpose of the activity? In first grade, coloring may be useful for developing children's fine motor skills, but it is hard to imagine why it would be worthwhile in high school. Coloring flower parts is not science, and in this case, one-third of the science period was allocated to a nonscientific activity. It also makes no sense to have students spend time working on tasks they don't understand and are unable to complete successfully.

This chapter began by asking, "How much time is there, anyway?" Figure 7.2 depicts the answer to this question. The bar at the far left shows the number of hours that a typical 42-minute class would meet in the typical mandated school year—126 (180 days × 42 minutes). For the sake of argument, let's assume that student absences and assembly programs reduce this figure by 10 days or 7 hours (10 days × 42 minutes). Thus, the second bar indicates that available time is 119 hours. To be consistent with Goodlad's (1984) findings on the use of available class time, let's also assume that clerical and administrative tasks consume 20 percent of each class, leaving only 34 minutes each day for actual instruction. This yields 96 hours (bar 3). If students pay attention 80 percent of that time (an optimistic estimate), engaged time is 77 hours (bar 4). And assuming that students work on meaningful, appropriate tasks for 80 percent of the time they are engaged, we see that productive learning time is only 62 hours—*about one-half of the "mandated" school time for this typical secondary class* (bar 5).

Obviously, these figures are estimates. As we have stressed, there are substantial variations from subject to subject, school to school, and classroom to

PAUSE AND REFLECT

Most teachers are surprised when they see how little time is actually spent in productive learning. What are some practices that erode the amount of time? What are some practices that you could use to maximize the opportunity for productive learning? Keep both of these in mind as you read the next section of the chapter.

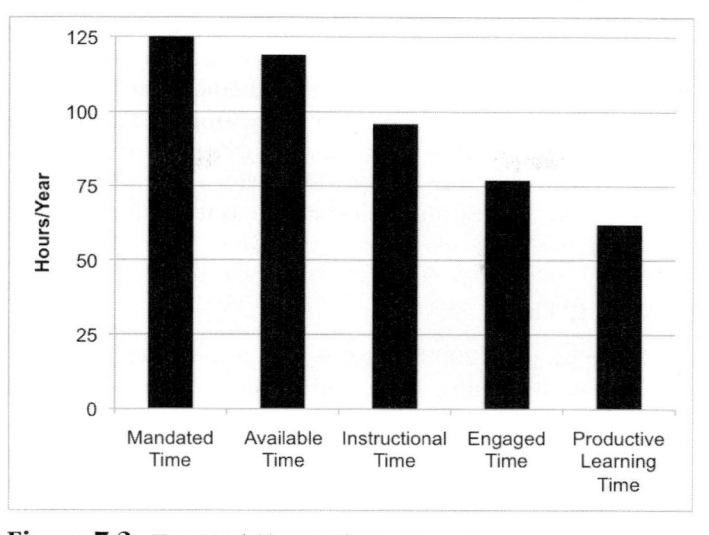

Figure 7.2   How Much Time Is There, Anyway?

classroom. Nonetheless, the graph illustrates the fundamental point: *The hours available for learning are far more limited than they initially appear.*

INCREASING OPPORTUNITY TO LEARN

Over the years, time has been a popular topic for reform-minded educators. In 1983, for example, the National Commission on Excellence in Education declared that we were "a nation at risk" because of "a rising tide of mediocrity" in our educational system. The report advocated a variety of reforms, including recommendations to extend the school day to seven hours and to lengthen the school year to 200 or 220 days. A decade later, the National Education Commission on Time and Learning (1994) also argued the need for more time. The commission characterized teachers and students as "prisoners of time" and paraphrased Oliver Hazard Perry's dispatch from the War of 1812: "We have met the enemy and they are [h]ours" (p. 1).

More recently, an education task force established by the Center for American Progress and the Institute for America's Future reached the same conclusions about the need for more time. In a report entitled *Getting Smarter, Becoming Fairer* (Brown, Rocha, & Sharkey, 2005), the task force observed that "the allocation and use of time today is still tied to an agrarian economy. . ., where children were needed to help in the fields during the after-school hours and summer months" (p. 15) and asserted that "abruptly thrusting American children out of the classroom door in the middle of the afternoon is a wasted opportunity" (p. 18). The first recommendation of the task force was to increase the amount of time that students spend in school by lengthening the school day and, in the case of low-performing schools, the school year.

Despite the cogency of the commissions' reports, the six-hour, 180-day school year is still the norm in the United States. For this reason, it is critical for teachers to manage the limited time available with skill and efficiency. The next sections of this chapter will discuss three strategies for increasing students' academic learning time: *maintaining activity flow, minimizing transition time, and holding students accountable.* (See Table 7.1 for a summary.) Of course, these strategies not only maximize time for learning, they also help to create and maintain classroom order.

Maintaining Activity Flow

Tom Good and Jere Brophy (2008) observe that "four things can happen" when students must wait with nothing to do, and "three of them are bad: (1) Students may remain interested and attentive; (2) they may become bored or fatigued, losing the ability to concentrate; (3) they may become distracted or start daydreaming; or (4) they may actively misbehave" (p. 79). Given the three-to-one odds that waiting will result in undesirable behavior and a loss of valuable learning opportunities, it's essential for teachers to learn how to maintain the flow of classroom activities.

Once again, we turn for guidance to the work of Jacob Kounin (1970). Kounin investigated differences in teachers' ability to initiate and maintain activity flow in classrooms. He then looked for relationships between activity flow and students' engagement and misbehavior.

Kounin's research identified many differences in the ways teachers orchestrated classroom activities. In some classrooms, activities flowed smoothly and

TABLE 7.1 Increasing Students' Learning Time

- *Maintain activity flow:*
  Avoid flip-flopping.
  Avoid "stimulus-bounded events" (being pulled away from the ongoing activity by an event or object that doesn't really need attention).
  Avoid overdwelling and fragmentation.

- *Minimize transition time:*
  Have clear beginnings and endings: bring first activity to a halt, announce the transition, monitor the transition, make sure everyone is attentive, begin second activity.
  Prepare students for upcoming transitions.
  Establish clear routines.

- *Hold students accountable:*
  Communicate assignments and requirements clearly.
  Monitor students' progress.
  Establish routines for collecting and checking classwork and homework.
  Maintain good records.

briskly, while in others, activities were "jerky" and slow. Kounin even developed a special vocabulary to describe the problems he observed. For instance, he found that some ineffective managers would terminate an activity, start another, and then return to the first activity. Kounin called this *flip-flopping.* It is illustrated by the following situation: A foreign language teacher finishes reviewing homework with the class and tells students to turn to the next chapter in their textbook. She then stops and says, "Wait a minute. How many got all the homework problems right? . . . Very good. . . . Okay, now let's talk about the imperfect tense."

Kounin also observed *stimulus-bounded events,* situations in which teachers are "pulled away" from the ongoing activity by a stimulus (an event or an object) that really doesn't need attention. Kounin describes the case of a teacher who is explaining a math problem at the board when she notices that a student is leaning on his left elbow as he works the problem. She leaves the board, instructs him to sit up straight, comments on his improved posture, and then returns to the board.

Sometimes, teachers slow down the pace of activity by *overdwelling*— continuing to explain when students already understand or preaching at length about appropriate behavior. Another type of slowdown is produced when a teacher breaks an activity into components even though the activity could be performed as a single unit—what Kounin called *fragmentation:*

> The teacher was making a transition from spelling to arithmetic as follows: "All right everybody, I want you to close your spelling books. Put away your red pencils. Now close your spelling books. Put your spelling books in your desks. Keep them out of the way." [There's a pause.] "All right now. Take out your arithmetic books and put them on your desks in front of you. That's right, let's keep everything off your desks except your arithmetic books. And let's sit up straight. We don't want any lazy-bones do we? That's fine. Now get your black pencils and open your books to page sixteen." (Kounin, 1970, p. 106)

Flip-flops, stimulus-boundedness, overdwelling, fragmentation—these are all threats to the flow of classroom activities. Not only do they result in lost learning time, they can have a significant impact on students' behavior. When activities proceed smoothly and briskly, students are *more involved in work and less apt to misbehave.* Indeed, as Kounin concluded four decades ago, *activity flow plays a greater role in classroom order than the specific techniques that teachers use to handle misbehavior.*

During one visit to Sandy's classroom, we watched the skillful way she maintained the flow of activity in her class. It was the end of October, and students were in the middle of a very intriguing lab that involved the production of silver. As you read the vignette, note how Sandy ensures that there will be no "down time" by preparing the board for the homework review before class begins, by starting class promptly, by having students put homework problems on the board during the lab activity, and by ensuring that students will have something to do if they finish the lab before others.

11:21   Sandy writes the numbers 4 through 11 on the chalkboard, evenly spacing them across the entire width.

11:22   She positions herself by the classroom door to greet students as they enter the room.

11:23   The bell rings. Sandy moves from the door to the front of the room. "Hats off, please. We have a lot to do today. First, we have to finish the lab. You need not wear your goggles. Second, I want to review the chemical equation sheet you did. You'll put the final balanced equations on the board. And third, you'll learn to solve problems associated with the balanced equations. So let's get going."

11:24   The students move to lab tables, get their equipment, and begin working. While students are doing the lab, Sandy moves around the room, assisting, questioning, and monitoring. The atmosphere is very relaxed. Sandy smiles, laughs, and jokes with students about the silver they're producing. While she circulates, she also notes which students are just about done with the lab and selects them to put the homework problems on the board: "Joe, are you finished? You have all your data? Okay, put number four up. Kim, you're done? Please put number five on the board." They leave their lab tables, get their homework, and put their assigned problems on the board. By the time the lab is over, numbers 4 through 11 are up on the chalkboard.

11:33   Sandy notices that students are nearing the end of the lab. She tells them: "When you're finished, take your seats so I know you're finished." One by one, students begin to move back to their seats; they take out their homework and begin to compare their answers to the work on the chalkboard.

11:37   The equipment is all put away, the lab tables have been cleaned, and the class is all seated.

11:38   Sandy introduces the problems on the chalkboard: "OK, let's turn to the equations on the board. Let me preface this by saying that you should not panic if you're having trouble writing formulas. You don't have to be able to write formulas until December. But what you do need to know now is how to balance the equations. All right, let's look at the first one." She turns to the first problem written on the board and begins the review.

12:00   All the problems have been discussed, and Sandy moves to the third activity of the morning. "Now I want you to listen very carefully. Do not take notes. I know this sounds strange, but I want you to be able to watch and listen and think. I'm going to show you a new type of problem." She writes a chemical equation on the board and challenges them to think about it. The students are stuck. Sandy lets them ponder the problem; she asks some easier questions to help them get started, and suggests they use paper if they want to. She walks around the room to see how they're doing, commenting on their efforts, encouraging them to consult with one another.

12:07   The bell rings. Students are still involved in trying to solve the problems. Sandy tells the class, "Think about this tonight, and come back with your ideas tomorrow."

Later, Sandy reflected on the day's lesson and talked about her very deliberate attempts to maintain the flow of activities:

> **Some people would regard this as obsessive. Many teachers have kids finish the lab, sit down, and then put all the problems on the board. But what do you do when students are sitting there and others are putting things on the board? Even during labs, if they have to boil something for 10 minutes, I'll give them a problem to do. Kids can't just sit and watch something boil for 10 minutes. That's when they'll start squirting water bottles. Maybe I'm strange, but I just can't stand any down time. There's so much to accomplish and so little time.**

Minimizing Transition Time

From the perspective of time management, transitions between activities can be very problematic. An analysis by Paul Gump (1982, 1987) helps us to understand the reasons. First, Gump observes, there may be difficulty "closing out" the first activity—especially if students are deeply engaged. (Ironically, the very involvement that teachers strive to achieve makes it more difficult to get students to switch activities!) Second, transitions are more loosely structured than activities themselves (Ross, 1985). Since there's usually more leeway in terms of socializing and moving around the room, there is also more opportunity for disruption. In fact, in a study of 50 classes taught by student teachers, Marshall Arlin (1979) found that there was almost twice as much disruption during transitions (e.g., hitting, yelling, obscene gestures) as during nontransition time.

Third, students sometimes "save up" problems or tensions and deal with them during the transition time (Gump, 1982). They may seek out the teacher to complain about a grade, ask for permission to retrieve a book from a locker, or dump out the contents of their bookbags in search of a lost homework assignment. Although these behaviors are legitimate—and help to protect the adjacent activities from disturbance—they also make transitions more difficult to manage. Finally, there may be delays in getting students started on the second activity (Gump, 1982). Students may have difficulty settling down, or teachers may be held up because they are dealing with individual students' concerns or are busy assembling needed materials.

Gump's analysis suggests that teachers can reduce the potential for chaos by *preparing students for upcoming transitions, by establishing efficient transition routines,* and *by clearly defining the boundaries of lessons* (Ross, 1985). These guidelines are especially important for students with attention-deficit/hyperactivity disorder (ADHD) and those with autism, who may have particular difficulty with transitions and changes in routine (McIntosh, et al., 2004).

Advance Preparation

Marshall Arlin's (1979) research revealed that transitions were far more chaotic when student teachers failed to warn students about the imminent change of activity. This often occurred at the end of the period because student teachers didn't even realize that time was up:

> The lesson was still continuing when the bell would ring. Not having reached any closure, the teacher, with some degree of desperation, would say something like "OK, you can go," and pupils would charge out of the room, often knocking each other over. (Sometimes, pupils did not even wait for the signal from the teacher.) The teacher might then remember an announcement and interject to the dispersing mob, "Don't forget to bring back money for the trip!" (Arlin, 1979, p. 50)

In contrast, other student teachers in Arlin's study were able to prepare students for the upcoming transition. If they were about to dismiss the class, they made sure that desks were in order and that students were quiet and ready to leave. They made announcements while students were still seated and then made sure students left the room in an orderly fashion.

Our four teachers are very diligent "clock watchers." They take care to monitor time and to inform students when the class period is drawing to a close. This is not as easy as it sounds, even for the three very experienced teachers. During one visit to Donnie's class, we watched both teacher and students get caught up in the lesson and lose track of time. When the bell rang, one girl actually blurted out, "Dang! That went fast!" Donnie laughingly agreed, broke off the lesson, and gave the homework assignment. Fortunately, she had taught her students early in the year that *she,* not the bell, dismissed them, so students stayed seated and attentive until she was finished.

In addition to warning students about the end of the period, it's also helpful to prepare them for changes in class activities during the period. In the following example, we see Fred explain to students what they will be doing that day and remind them periodically about how much time is left before they will be changing activities.

 The bell rings. Fred tells his students to take out paper and pencil while he distributes an article from *Newsweek* magazine regarding human rights and China. "While I meet with people one by one to go over grades, you will read and take notes on this article. You'll have about 12 minutes. At the end of that time, we will discuss these questions: What is the problem we're trying to solve between China and the United States? And is this just a case of Western arrogance? Take good notes—I'm going to collect them—and I will ask you to give an oral presentation of your views."

As students settle down to read, Fred gets out his grade book and sits at his desk. He quietly signals for individuals to come up to discuss their marking quarter grades. A few minutes later, he checks his watch. "Ladies and gentlemen, you have about seven more minutes to finish reading and taking notes."

Later, he issues another warning about the time: "About two more minutes, so you should be finishing up." At the end of 12 minutes, he gets up from his desk. "Okay, you've had enough time now to read the article and take some notes. At the bottom of the paper, please summarize in 25 words or less what the basic problem is between China and the United States."

The Use of Transition Routines

Chapter 4 talked about the importance of having clear, specific routines in order to keep the classroom running smoothly. At no time is the use of routines more important than during transitions. Well-established routines provide a structure to transitions that helps to prevent confusion and lost time.

In Christina's class, the routine for entering the room is very clear. Her students come in, take their seats, take out their journals, and begin writing on the journal topic posted on the board. According to Christina, using the journal achieves a number of objectives:

Using this routine allows me to have students engaged in a meaningful activity while I'm taking attendance, checking homework, etc. The journal is a timed writing exercise that encourages fluency in writing. I make it clear that students are not allowed to stop writing until I signal that time is up. . . . Also, the journal entries are often related to the literature we're studying so they help to introduce or extend the reading. And having a daily journal assignment creates a nice, quiet atmosphere in which I can give instructions for the next activity.

Similarly, Donnie begins every period with a "Do Now" activity that helps get students settled and gives her a few moments to take attendance. She stresses that the "Do Now" is not busywork that is disconnected from the lesson; rather, it assesses students' understanding of material covered the day before or provides a "kick off" for the current lesson.

In many classrooms, the transition routines are *implicit,* and students are expected to figure out what to do by picking up on subtle cues. This may be fine for the majority of students, but those with ADHD, autism, or other disorders may have trouble and end up getting reprimanded. If you have students like this in your classes, it is essential (and only fair) to spend time teaching them how to make efficient, orderly transitions. Kent McIntosh and his colleagues (2004) suggest that you teach routines explicitly, provide "precorrections" and positive reinforcement, and actively supervise. These techniques are described more fully in the Practical Tips box.

Clear Beginnings and Endings

Transitions proceed more smoothly if teachers bring the first activity to a halt, announce the transition, allow time to make sure that everyone is attentive, and then begin the second activity (Arlin, 1979). In other words, smooth transitions are characterized by well-defined boundaries.

In the following vignette, we see Christina implement a transition with well-defined boundaries. Watch the way she prepares her students for the transition from small-group work to a whole-class activity.

Students are seated in clusters of four or five, working on the poetry lessons they are creating for the rest of the class. Christina is circulating. She checks the clock and then moves to the front of the room. "May I

have your attention please? We are ready to move to the next part of the lesson. Please listen carefully to all of my instructions and do not move until I tell you to. First, you will have one member of your group hand in your assignment. This person will check to make sure each person's name is on the paper. Then you will return to your regular seats, take out your notebooks and textbooks and open your books to page 295. Also, have a pen out and on your desk. When you are settled, please begin reading the brief introduction on page 295. Are there any questions? Good. You may move now."

Later, when we commented on how quickly and efficiently her students had made the transition, Christina observed that it was sometimes difficult to get students to wait patiently for instructions:

 What I mean is, if the transition will require a series of movements, they want to move as soon as you give them the first direction. If you allow them to do this, they won't hear the rest of the directions. The transition time will actually be longer, since you'll have to spend time repeating everything. I've learned to tell them, "Don't move until I'm finished."

PRACTICAL TIPS FOR

TEACHING TRANSITIONS

- Think about the transitions that occur during the period, such as the following:
   Entering and leaving the classroom.
   Putting materials away and preparing for the next task.
   Cleaning up a work area.
   Moving from group to independent work.
   Turning in homework.
   Choosing partners for small-group activities.

- Explicitly teach the expected transition behavior:
   Model the behavior using both correct and incorrect examples.
   Provide opportunities for students to practice.
   Provide feedback.
   Reteach if needed.

- Provide precorrections (reminders of the expected behavior *before* the transition begins).

- Provide positive reinforcement for efficient, orderly transitions:
   Give specific praise or special privileges and activities.
   Use tangible rewards if necessary.

- Actively supervise the transition:
   Scan the room, looking for both appropriate and inappropriate behavior.
   Walk around the room, using proximity to encourage students to engage in the appropriate behavior.
   Interact with students during the transition, providing reminders and specific praise.

Source: McIntosh, Herman, Sanford, McGraw, & Florence, 2004.

Sometimes, in an effort to maintain activity flow, teachers rush into instructions and activities without checking that students are "with them." Arlin (1979) writes: "Several times I noticed over 15 children continuing the previous activity while the teacher was giving directions for the new activity" (p. 50). Needless to say, those teachers then became exasperated when students asked questions about what to do. On the other hand, Paul Gump (1982) warns that waiting *too* long can cause a loss of momentum: "Waiting for absolute and universal attention can sometimes lead to unnecessarily extended transition times" (p. 112). Gump reminds us that by keeping the instructional program going, teachers can often "pull in" students whose attention has momentarily wandered.

Holding Students Accountable

Walter Doyle (1983) has commented that students tend to take assignments seriously only if they are held accountable for them. Your own school experiences probably testify to the truth of this statement. Even as adults, it takes a good deal of self-discipline and maturity to put your best effort into work that will never be seen by anyone. And secondary students are *adolescents*. Unless they know that they will have to account for their performance, it is unlikely that they'll make the best use of class time.

Furthermore, students are *unable* to make good use of their time if they are confused about what they're supposed to be doing. Teachers sometimes tell students to "get to work" and are immediately bombarded by questions: "Can I use pen?" "Do I have to write down the questions or can I just put the answers?" "Do we have to show all our work?" "Can I work at the lab table?" When this happens, precious class time has to be spent clarifying the original instructions.

In order to help students use their time wisely, teachers must *communicate assignments and requirements clearly and monitor students' progress* (Emmer & Evertson, 2008). These practices minimize students' confusion and convey the message that schoolwork is important. Let's see what our teachers and the research have to say about these two practices.

Communicating Assignments and Requirements

Before students begin to work, it's a good idea to explain what they'll be doing and why, how to get help, what to do with completed work, what to do when they're finished, and how long they'll be spending on the task. You also need to make sure that students are familiar with your work standards—for example, what kind of paper to use, whether they should use pencil or pen, how to number the page, whether or not erasures are allowed, and what it means to "show all their work." Once you've given your instructions, have students explain what they will be doing in their own words and give them a chance to ask questions. Asking "Does everyone understand?" rarely yields useful information.

In addition to providing explicit directions for in-class activities, teachers need to communicate homework assignments in a clear, organized manner. This is particularly important if you are working with students who have difficulty remembering what they are supposed to do. Sandy has devised a routine for assigning homework that she first developed to help students with learning disabilities. She soon realized, however, that the routine was helpful for everyone:

When I first write a homework assignment on the board, I write it really big in the middle of the board and tell students to copy it down now. Then I move it to the left-hand corner of the board where it remains until the due date. Periodically, I remind students about it. I'm also really clear about the numbers of the problems that students have to do. For example, if the assignment is to do numbers 1 through 5, and then 7, 9, 11, and 13 through 16, I'll write out 1, 2, 3, 4, and 5, because some kids (especially my learning disabled students) don't see the difference between the comma and the dash.

Christina is also very diligent about writing out assignments and directions, especially for big projects. Sometimes, she provides a printed handout with detailed instructions. Other times, she'll have students copy the directions from the board or an overhead projector. During one meeting, she explained why she gives such explicit directions:

Not only does this help to alleviate the number of questions I need to answer—over and over again—it also makes students accountable for the details of the assignment. They can't say, "You didn't tell us we needed five sources" if they've copied it down from the overhead, or "You didn't say to use textual evidence to support our answers" if the written handout states this requirement. I've also learned that doing this is useful for meeting with parents because you have every assignment documented. I save all my handouts and overhead transparencies with the directions. This way, I can prove I stated the requirements to students (and to parents on the rare occasions when I'm questioned). And I also save myself from rewriting directions when I'm using an assignment again.

Monitoring Students' Progress

Once you've given directions for an assignment and your class gets to work, it's important to monitor how students are doing by circulating around the room (Fisher, et al., 1980). This practice enables you to keep track of students' progress, to identify and help with problems, and to verify that assignments are matched to students' ability. Circulating also helps to ensure that students are using their time well.

Observations of our four teachers revealed that they rarely sit down, unless they're working with a small group.

Donnie's class is working with rulers and protractors to discover the properties of parallelograms. As students work, Donnie continually circulates. She keeps up a steady stream of comments, questions, and praise: "Very good, Veronica." "Everybody finished with that first question?" "Answer the questions as you go, so you'll have all the answers when you finish." "Anyone need help?" "What does consecutive mean, José?" "Is there anyone who's having problems with the protractor?"

After class, Donnie talked about the fact that she is constantly on the move:

I don't see how a person can teach math and sit down. I just wouldn't feel comfortable sitting down. You have to write on the board, you have to guide students through the problems, you have to see they're on the right track. By walking around the room, I can catch mistakes. I can ask, "What were you doing here? Explain your reasoning." I can talk them through the problem. I have to be up and moving when I'm teaching.

In addition, it's essential to monitor whether students are regularly completing assignments. This requires you to *establish routines for collecting and checking classwork and homework.* For example, at the beginning of class, Donnie has students take out their homework and put it on their tables. While they review the assignment, she circulates around the room and notes in her grade book who has done the homework. The whole procedure takes just a few minutes and there's no loss of instructional time, since the class is simultaneously going over the homework problems.

Sandy uses a different system. She has a folder for each class that she keeps on the front table. Homework assignments are to be placed in the folder at the very beginning of class. She gives a "last call for homework," and then closes the folder. Sometime during the period, Sandy checks the papers to see if any assignments are missing. This allows her to verify immediately that she does not have an assignment from a particular student and to find out what happened. As she puts it, "This way I can avoid the situation where a student says, 'But I *did* do the homework. You must have lost it.' "

It's especially important to *keep track of students' progress on long-term homework assignments.* By establishing intermediate check points, you can help students develop a "plan of attack." For example, if they are writing a research paper, you can set due dates on which they have to submit each stage of the assignment (e.g., the topic; preliminary notes; a list of references; the first draft; the final draft). Not only does this allow you to monitor students' progress, it also helps to lessen the anxiety that adolescents sometimes feel when faced with a large assignment.

Fred tells an ironic story that points out the value of this approach:

Last year, my students did a long research paper. I had them turn in each piece to show me how they were coming along—a working outline, a bibliography, their notes, a rough draft, and then the final copy. I used a point system. The first four parts of the assignment were worth 10 points each; the final copy was worth 60 points.

This year, I decided it was babyish to do this, so I didn't do it. I told my classes, "I'm going to treat you like adults," and they said, "Great. We can do it." Well, they didn't get their papers in. They told me, "We messed up. We let it go, we procrastinated." They asked me to do what I had done last year! I trusted them to be mature, and they said, "We're not."

Finally, you need to *maintain records of what students are accomplishing.* In some districts, teachers can develop their own system for recording students' progress; others require teachers to follow a prescribed format. For example, Donnie's grade book has to reflect her weekly lessons plans and the "quarterly topic plans" she has to submit four times a year; following the district's objectives for her courses, these plans describe what she will be teaching day by day. For each marking period, Donnie must have two grades per week for homework and at least one test grade per objective. If five objectives are to be covered during a particular marking period, then Donnie would have to have at least five test grades.

In contrast, Fred is allowed to develop his own record-keeping system. Fred doesn't even have a regular grade book; instead he records his students' grades on the computer. Nonetheless, like Donnie, he is careful to keep up-to-date records of students' progress. He explained his record-keeping system to students at the very beginning of the year:

I want to take a minute or two to discuss grades with you. I don't have a grade book. I keep your grades on the computer. We can go anytime after school and check out your grades. What I use is homework, class work, projects, tests, and quizzes. Each in-class assignment is about four points. A big exam would be worth about five in-class assignments—about 20 points. The total point value for the marking period is 120–130 points. You can always find out what your point total is, what your grade is at any time. . . . It's important to me that everyone in here passes this class and does well. If you need me to get on your case, so you'll do okay in here, let me know. Remember, the grades are yours. You can see them at any time.

Checking or grading all the work that students do each day is an arduous, time-consuming task. One student teacher in English recently wrote about "the looming mountain of paperwork that a teacher must perpetually climb":

Sometimes I'm not sure if I'm a teacher or a certified [public] accountant! However, my experience . . . has enabled me to find ways to reckon with the ponderous load. Simple things like color-coordinated folders for each class, or writing the names of absent students on quiz sheets to keep track of make-up work, are "tricks" that I am extremely grateful to have been shown along the way.

Like this student teacher, you need to find ways to "make a molehill out of a mountain" (Shalaway, 1989). We asked Sandy, Donnie, Christina, and Fred how they handle the paperwork. Their ideas are listed in the Practical Tips box.

Practical Tips for

HANDLING PAPERWORK

Fred: Check that students do in-class assignments and routine homework, but don't spend a lot of time reading and grading these. Develop a simple system for keeping track of students' routine assignments (e.g., four points for full credit; 3.5 points for an almost-completed assignment, etc.).

Spend your time on the assignments that require higher-level thinking. These are harder to grade!

On tests, create structured essay questions. Construct your own answer to the essay. (Know what the essay is supposed to say.) Look for key words when grading.

Refuse to grade papers that contain more than three technical errors (spelling, punctuation, etc.). I tell students, "I have 100 of these to grade; it's not fair for me to sit here and correct your spelling mistakes. I'm not here to proofread. . . . Have someone who's good at this proofread your papers before you turn them in."

Sandy: With homework, grade on attempt/effort, not whether it's right or wrong.

For the first few assignments, read *everything* really carefully. Go over lab reports with a fine-tooth comb. That way, students come to see that you have really high expectations and that they have to be clear and thorough. Then, later, you can skim the first few pages (objectives, procedures, materials), and spend the bulk of your time on the data section.

Sometimes, in long labs, have students present their data in table form.

Donnie: Review homework every day, but have students check their own work. In your grade book, enter a check (as opposed to a grade) to show who has done the assignment.

Have students grade one homework assignment each week that you record in your grade book.

Collect one homework assignment each week to grade yourself.

Christina: Think of "time-spent-grading" as part of your lesson plans. Carefully plan activities and due dates to allow you enough time to grade assignments. For example, after I collect research papers, I plan for students to be primarily engaged in classwork assignments that I can monitor without collecting very much paperwork. This allows me to spend the majority of my grading time on the research papers.

Use detailed rubrics to provide detailed feedback without having to write the same comments over and over again.

Instruct students in proper editing, revision, and response procedures so they can provide feedback to one another. For example, I provide a detailed response on the first draft of the first section of a long research paper. Then students use a checklist with marking instructions to provide feedback to one another on the second and third sections of the paper.

THE USE OF BLOCK SCHEDULING

Many secondary schools have moved to block scheduling in an effort to maximize time for learning, to encourage the use of varied instructional strategies, and to allow teachers and students to explore topics in depth. There are two common scheduling configurations. On the *4 × 4 block schedule,* four 80- or 90-minute instructional blocks are scheduled each day, instead of the traditional six or seven. Since classes meet every day, a course that would normally last a year is completed in one semester or 90 days, and students take only four courses at a time. The *A-B or alternating day schedule* also offers four extended periods each day, but classes meet every other day for the entire school year. This means that students still take six or seven courses at one time.

Although one 80- or 90-minute block does not actually provide more contact time with students than two 42- or 50-minute periods, advocates of block scheduling contend that the extended class provides more *usable instructional time* (Fleming, Olenn, Schoenstein, & Eineder, 1997). Since classes meet half as many times, the time spent in routine tasks at the beginning of the period (e.g., taking attendance, getting students settled in, distributing materials) and at the end (e.g., talking about homework, getting packed up) is also halved. More importantly, instructional time is less fragmented.

At this point, research examining the effects of block scheduling on achievement is inconsistent, with some studies showing academic gains (e.g., Lewis, Dugan, Winokur, & Cobb, 2005; Nichols, 2005), some showing no difference (e.g., Bottge, Gugerty, Serlin, & Moon, 2003), and some actually finding negative effects (e.g., Gruber & Onwuegbuzie, 2001). On the other hand, block scheduling *does* seem to lead to a more relaxed school climate and a decline in discipline problems—possibly because it cuts down on hallway traffic (Shortt & Thayer, 1998/9; Zepeda & Mayers, 2006). On the 4 × 4 schedule, teachers have an additional benefit: They generally teach only *three* classes a day instead of four or five, so they are responsible for approximately 75–90 students at a time, rather than 125 or 150. Undoubtedly, this makes it easier to develop more attentive, caring relationships with students.

Unfortunately, block scheduling does not always result in the kind of innovative, varied instruction that proponents envision (Queen, 2000). Richard Elmore (2002), an expert on school restructuring, reports that he once asked a high school social studies teacher what he thought of block scheduling. The teacher replied that it was the best thing that had ever happened in his teaching career. When Elmore asked why, the teacher explained: "Now we can show the whole movie."

As this anecdote suggests, changing the *structure* of time doesn't always change the *use* of time. For example, in a study of 48 extended classes (Bush and Johnstone, 2000), teachers in all subject areas (algebra, biology, English, and U.S. history) spent the majority of time doing traditional, teacher-centered instruction. There was little individualization of instruction and little groupwork. These findings underscore the comments of one high school senior who observed that an 80-minute class does not necessarily lead to more active learning: *"Rather, it will*

simply create more time for students to daydream, scribble in their notebooks or catch up on sleep" (Shanley, 1999).

Although Christina recognizes the truth of this comment, she is an enthusiastic advocate of her school's 4 × 4 block schedule. During visits to her classroom, we observed the way she uses a variety of instructional formats—whole-group presentation, small-group work, student-led discussion, writing, student presentations—to maintain students' engagement and promote active participation. She may also include a variety of the content areas that comprise "English class." In the following excerpt, we see a class in which students write individually in their journals, work on reading strategy development in small groups, learn the format for a reference or "works cited" page in a mini-lesson, and act out a play they have been reading:

 11:35 Students enter, take their seats, read the journal entry written on the board, and begin to write on the day's topic: "Write about how your life would have been changed if one day in your past had come out differently. What actually happened that day?" While students write, Christina silently takes attendance.

11:50 Christina gives the agenda for the class: "First you're going to meet in your groups to practice making inferences. Then we'll have a mini-lesson on creating a works-cited page. On Wednesday, you'll be giving your speeches. I'll collect all the written components before you give your speeches, so I want to review what you'll need to turn in. Finally, we'll finish reading *Antigone.*"

11:52 Students get into their small groups to practice making inferences. Christina circulates and assists.

12:18 Christina announces that the groups have two more minutes to work.

12:20 Students move the chairs back into rows and return to their regular seats. Christina tells them to take out their notebooks and turn to the section on doing research. She moves the overhead projector to the front-center of the room, pulls down the shades, and announces that she wants to explain how to do the "works-cited" page for their research papers. She puts an overhead transparency on the projector and reviews the required format. Students are very attentive, taking notes and asking questions.

12:40 "Okay, guys, let's form the Greek Theater so we can finish reading *Antigone.*" Students get into a new configuration, roughly a circle, with the "chorus" at one end and an opening for the entrance to the "stage." "We left off on page 337. Chorus, take your places." Christina reads the stage directions, and students begin acting out *Antigone,* ending with the queen's death. A boy reads the last speech of the play.

12:58 "All right, everyone, move your desks back to where they belong and listen to what you're going to do next." After students are

PAUSE AND REFLECT

Would you prefer to teach on a block schedule or a traditional schedule? What are your reasons? Do you think the difference in the length of the period would make a difference in your instruction?

back in their regular seats, Christina announces the final activity of the period: "Open your journals and open your book. You have four minutes. Write about the last speech you just heard. What does it mean? Why is it important? Do you agree with it?"

1:02   Students finish their journal entries. The bell rings.

CONCLUDING COMMENTS

Tracy Kidder's book, *Among Schoolchildren* (1989), describes one year in the life of Chris Zajac, an elementary teacher who's feisty, demanding, blunt, fair, funny, and hard working. At the very end of the book, Kidder describes Chris's thoughts on the last day of school. Although she is convinced that she belongs "among schoolchildren," Chris laments the fact that she hadn't been able to help all her students—at least not enough:

> Again this year, some had needed more help than she could provide. There were many problems that she hadn't solved. But it wasn't for lack of trying. She hadn't given up. She had run out of time. (p. 331)

Like Chris, we all run out of time. The end of the year comes much too quickly, and some students' needs are much too great. Hopefully, the concepts and guidelines presented in this chapter will help you to make good use of the limited time you have.

SUMMARY

This chapter described time as a "precious resource." First, it considered the amount of school time that is actually available for teaching and learning. Then it described three strategies for increasing students' academic learning time—maintaining activity flow, minimizing transition time, and holding students accountable. The last section of the chapter examined the use of block scheduling.

Types of Time

- *Mandated time:* the time the state requires school to be in session.
- *Available time:* mandated time minus the time lost to absences, special events, half-days.
- *Instructional time:* the time that is actually used for instruction.
- *Engaged time:* the time a student spends working attentively on academic tasks.
- *Productive learning time:* the proportion of engaged time in which students are doing work that is meaningful and appropriate.

How to Increase Hours for Learning

- Maintain activity flow by avoiding:
    Flip-flopping.
    Stimulus-bounded events.

Overdwelling.
Fragmentation.
- Minimize transition time by:
    Defining boundaries to lessons.
    Preparing students for transitions.
    Establishing routines.
- Hold students accountable by:
    Communicating assignments and requirements clearly.
    Monitoring students' progress.
    Establishing routines for collecting and checking classwork and homework.
    Maintaining good records.

Block Scheduling

- Types of block scheduling
    4 × 4 block schedule: four 80- or 90-minute instructional blocks scheduled each day
        for one semester or 90 days; students take four classes at a time.
    A-B or alternating day schedule: 80- or 90-minute instructional periods every other
        day for the entire school year; students take six or seven courses at a time.
- Advantages:
    More usable instructional time.
    Less fragmented instructional time.
    More relaxed school climate.
    Decrease in hallway traffic.
    Opportunities for the use of varied instructional strategies.
- Problems:
    Block scheduling does not always result in the innovative, varied instruction that
        proponents envision.

By using time wisely, you can maximize opportunities for learning and minimize occasions for disruption in your classroom. Think about how much time is being spent on meaningful and appropriate work in your room, and how much is being eaten up by business and clerical tasks. Be aware that the hours available for instruction are much fewer than they first appear.

ACTIVITIES FOR SKILL BUILDING AND REFLECTION

In Class

Read the following vignette and identify the factors that threaten the activity flow of the lesson. Once you have identified the problems, rewrite the vignette so that activity flow is maintained OR explain how you would avoid the problems if you were the teacher.

Mrs. P. waits while her sophomore "A" level students take out the 10 mixed number addition problems she had them do for homework last night. Jack raises his hand. "I brought the wrong book by mistake, Mrs. P. My locker is right across the hall. Can I get my math book?"

"Be quick, Jack. We have 10 problems to go over, and the period is only 50 minutes long." Jack leaves, and Mrs. P. turns back to the class. "OK, this is what I want you to do. Switch papers with your neighbor." She waits while students figure out who will be partners with whom. She scans the room, trying to make sure that everyone has a partner. "OK, now write your name at the bottom of the page, on the right-hand side, to show that you're the checker. When I collect these papers, I want to know who the checkers were, so I can see who did a really accurate, responsible job of checking." She circulates while students write their names at the bottom of the page. "Ariadis, I said the right-hand side." Ariadis erases her name and rewrites it on the right side. "OK, now let's go over the answers. If your neighbor didn't get the right answer, put a circle around the problem and try to figure out what they did wrong so you can explain it to them. OK, number one, what's the right answer?" A student in the rear of the class raises his hand. "Billy?"

"I don't have a partner, Mrs. P. Can I go to the bathroom?"

"Jack will be right back, and then you'll have a partner. Just wait until we finish going over the homework." Jack returns. "Take a seat near Billy, Jack, and exchange homework papers with him."

Jack looks sheepishly at Mrs. P. "It's not in my book, Mrs. P. I must have left it on my desk last night. I was working on it pretty late."

"Class, go over the answers to problems one and two with your neighbors. See if you agree, and if you did the problems the same way. Jack, step outside."

Billy waves his hand again. "Mrs. P., can I please go to the bathroom now?"

"Yes, Billy. Fill out a pass, and I'll sign it. Just get back quickly." Billy leaves for the restroom. Leaving the door open so she can keep an eye on the other students, Mrs. P. follows Jack out of class. "You haven't had your homework done three times in the last two weeks, Jack. What's the problem?"

"Well, Mrs. P., my mother's been . . ." The office intercom phone buzzes.

"Want me to get that, Mrs. P.?" a student calls from the class.

"Yes, tell them I'll be right there."

"They said to just tell you that Billy has to go to the office if he's not doing anything right now."

"Go take your seat, Jack. I'll talk to you after class." Mrs. P. moves to the front of the room again. "I'm sorry, class, let's begin again. Did you all do numbers one and two?" The class murmurs assent. "OK, number three. Let's start with problem three. Joan?"

Joan gives the correct answer. Mrs. P. gets responses and explanations for three more homework problems. As the class reviews the homework, Mrs. P. wanders up and down the rows. As she passes Tanya's desk, she notices a pink slip of paper. "Class, I almost forgot to collect the slips for the Academic Fair. This fair is a chance for us to show how much progress we've made this year in math. How many of you remembered to fill out the slip, describing the project you're going to do?" Students proceed to hunt through their backpacks and flip through their math books. Those who find their pink slips give them to Mrs. P. She reminds the others to return them tomorrow. "OK, let's get back to problem . . . six, no, seven. We were on seven, right? Shakia." Shakia begins to respond. Then Billy returns. A student in a seat by the door reminds Mrs. P. that Billy has to go to the office. "Billy, go to Mr. Wilkins's office."

"Why, Mrs. P.? All I did was go to the john."

"I don't know, Billy. Just go and make it quick. We're trying to have a class." Billy leaves, and Mrs. P. turns to the class. "Pass your papers to the front. I'll check the rest for you and give you credit for your homework. We need to move on to subtraction with fractions. Who can think of a real-life problem where you would need to subtract fractions? Missy?"

"Can I go to the nurse, Mrs. P.? I don't feel good."

On Your Own

1. While you are visiting a class, carefully observe the way the teacher uses the time. Keep an accurate record for a complete period, noting how much of the available time is actually used for *instructional purposes.*

2. Observe a class that is on a block schedule. How is the extended time used? What instructional strategies are used (e.g. lecture, cooperative learning, discussion, simulations, etc.)? How long does each instructional strategy last? Does the teacher make use of the entire period? Do students seem able to sustain attention and involvement?

For Your Portfolio

Develop a transition routine for each of the following situations. Remember, your goal is to use time wisely.

a. Beginning class each day.
b. Taking attendance.
c. Checking homework.
d. Collecting papers.
e. Returning papers.
f. Moving from the whole group into small groups.
g. Ending class each day.
h. Leaving class at the end of the period.

FOR FURTHER READING

Gabrieli, C., & Goldstein, W. (2008). *Time to learn: How a new school schedule is making smarter kids, happier parents, and safer neighborhoods.* San Francisco, CA: Jossey-Bass.

Using common sense, experience, hard data, and personal observation, the authors of this book argue that the current school day is obsolete and out of step with the reality of working families without a stay-at-home parent. The additional one to two hours of the "new school day" allow students to master core academic subjects, receive individualized instruction and tutoring, and participate in the arts, music, drama, and sports.

Intrator, S. M. (2004). The engaged classroom. *Educational Leadership, 62*(1), 20–24.

Sam Intrator, a college professor, spent 130 days shadowing students in a diverse California high school in order to understand the "experiential terrain of students' class time." In this article he describes the different kinds of time that students experience: slow time, lost time, fake time, worry time, play time, and engaged time.

Shernoff, D. J., Csikszentmihalyi, M., Schneider, B., & Shernoff, E. S. (2003). Student engagement in high school classrooms from the perspective of flow theory. *School Psychology Quarterly, 18*(2), 158–176.

This study investigated how 526 high school students spent their time in school and the conditions under which they reported being engaged. Participants experienced higher engagement when the perceived challenge of the task and their own skills were high and in balance, when instruction was relevant, and when the learning environment was under their control. Participants were also more engaged in individual and group work versus listening to lectures, watching videos, or taking exams.

Smith, B. (2000). Quantity matters: Annual instructional time in an urban school system. *Educational Administration Quarterly, 36*(5), 652–682.

The official time policy of the Chicago public elementary schools is to provide students with 300 minutes of instruction per day for 180 school days per year. This adds up to 900 hours on instruction annually. But based on classroom observation records, field notes, teacher interviews, school calendars, and other documents, this report concludes that nearly half of Chicago students may be receiving only 40 percent to 50 percent of the recommended hours. The reasons for this erosion of instructional time are discussed, and recommendations are outlined.

ENHANCING STUDENTS' MOTIVATION

Sitting in the teachers' room of a large suburban high school, we overheard a conversation among members of the social studies department. One ninth-grade teacher was complaining loudly about his third-period class: "These kids don't care about school. I'm not going to waste my time trying to get them motivated. If they can't be responsible for their own learning by now, it's just too bad." As we reflected on the teacher's statement, it seemed that he was suggesting that motivation is entirely the student's responsibility; to be successful in school, students must arrive motivated, just as they must arrive with notebooks and pens. The statement also suggests that motivation is a stable characteristic, like eye color. From this perspective, some individuals come to school wanting to learn, and some don't. This can be a comforting point of view: If motivation is an innate or unchangeable characteristic, then we don't have to spend time and energy figuring out ways to motivate students.

On the other hand, some educators argue that motivation is an acquired disposition that is amenable to change. It can also be situation-specific, varying with the nature of the particular activity. Thus, students in world language classes can be enthusiastic about role-playing a visit to a restaurant, but can appear bored and uninterested when it's time to conjugate verbs.

According to this latter perspective, teachers are responsible for stimulating students' engagement in learning activities. It may be gratifying (and a lot easier) when students come to school already excited about learning; however, when this is not the case, teachers must redouble their efforts to create a classroom context that fosters students' involvement and interest. This year, for example, one of Fred's Contemporary World Issues classes has a large proportion of students who, according to Fred, are "just marking time." During one conversation, Fred shared both his frustration and his determination:

> **These kids are a constant struggle—the toughest kind of kids to work with. They're not dumb; they're not bad; they're just not intrinsically motivated when it comes to school. And they're used to taking it easy; for the last three years of high school, they've found that passive resistance works. They're so passive that teachers just leave them alone. But I refuse to give up on them. I look them in the face and say, "Tell me you want to stay home and be a slug and I'll leave you alone." And nobody's told me that. Actually, I think they're finally getting resigned to the fact that they can't coast in my class. And they can't even be mad at me, because they know that I'm on their side.**

As Fred's comment indicates, stimulating students' motivation is easier said than done, especially when dealing with adolescents. The downturn in motivation during the transition years from elementary to secondary school is well documented (Anderman & Maehr, 1994)—and it is often dismaying to beginning teachers, particularly those who are passionate about their subject fields. Consider this entry taken from the journal of a student teacher in English:

> *I began my student teaching with all of these grand ideas about how I was going to enlighten students to the beauty of literature and unlock all the insight and talent that had been buried. . . . I gave serious, complicated lectures and multitudes of homework assignments, sure that my students would all be grateful when they witnessed the emergence of their intellectual prowess. Somewhere in the middle of the third week, however, the truth came rearing its ugly head: Most of my students did not, and probably never would, approach literature with [as much] enthusiasm [as they feel for] a new computer game.*

To assist teachers who find themselves in this all too familiar situation, this chapter focuses on ways to enhance students' motivation. We begin by reflecting on what is realistic and appropriate with respect to motivating secondary students. We then examine the factors that give rise to motivation. Finally, we consider a variety of motivational strategies drawn from research, theory, and the practice of our four teachers.

PAUSE AND REFLECT

Think of a time when you were extremely motivated to learn. It might have been in preparation for your driver's license or the winter you learned to ski. Why were you motivated to learn? What supported you in your learning? What made it a successful experience? Try to relate your experiences to what you will be doing every day in your classroom.

What Is Realistic? What Is Appropriate?

Many of the teacher education students with whom we've worked believe that teachers motivate students *by making learning fun.* In fact, they frequently mention the ability to design activities that are enjoyable and entertaining as one of the defining characteristics of the "good teacher." Yet, as Jere Brophy (2004) reminds us, "schools are not day camps or recreational centers" (p. xii), and teachers are not counselors or recreational directors. Given compulsory attendance, required curricula, class sizes that inhibit individualization, and the specter of high-stakes standardized testing, trying to ensure that learning is always fun is unreasonable and unrealistic. Bill Ayers (1993), a professor of education who has taught preschool through graduate school, is even more blunt. Characterizing the idea that good teachers make learning fun as one of the common myths that plague teaching, Ayers writes:

> Fun is distracting, amusing. Clowns are fun. Jokes can be fun. Learning can be engaging, engrossing, amazing, disorienting, involving, and often deeply pleasurable. If it's fun, fine. But it doesn't need to be fun. (p. 13)

Probably all of us can remember situations in which we were motivated to accomplish an academic task that was not fun, but that nonetheless seemed worthwhile and meaningful. The example that immediately comes to our minds is learning a foreign language. Neither of us has ever been very good at languages, and we were anxious and self-conscious whenever we had to speak in language class. We found conversation and oral exercises painful; role-plays were excruciating. Yet, one of us took three years of French in high school and two more in college, while the other one took three semesters of Spanish well after finishing college. Both of us were determined to communicate as fluently as possible when we visited foreign countries.

Brophy (2004) refers to this kind of drive as *motivation to learn*—the "tendency to find academic activities meaningful and worthwhile and to try to get the intended learning benefits from them" (p. 15). He distinguishes motivation to learn from *intrinsic motivation,* in which individuals pursue academic activities because they find them pleasurable. At times, of course, you may be able to capitalize on students' intrinsic interests so that the learning activities will be perceived as fun. But it's unlikely that this will always be the case. For this reason, teachers need to consider ways of developing and maintaining students' motivation to learn.

An Expectancy × Value Framework

It is helpful to think about stimulating motivation to learn in terms of an expectancy × value (or expectancy-times-value model) (Brophy, 2004; Wigfield & Eccles, 2000). This model posits that motivation depends on *students' expectation of success* and *the value they place on the task* (or the rewards that it may bring—such as being able to speak fluent French). The two factors work together like a multiplication equation (expectancy × value): If either one is missing (i.e., zero), there will be no motivation.

The expectancy-times-value model suggests that you have two major responsibilities with respect to motivation. *First, you need to ensure that students can perform the task at hand successfully if they expend the effort.* This means creating assignments that are well suited to students' achievement levels. This may also mean helping students to recognize their ability to perform successfully. Consider the case of Hopeless Hannah (Stipek, 1993). During math class, Hannah frequently sits at her desk doing nothing. If the teacher urges Hannah to try one of the problems she is supposed to be doing, she claims she can't. When the teacher walks her through a problem step by step, Hannah answers most of the questions correctly, but she insists that she was only guessing. Hannah considers herself incompetent, and she interprets her teacher's frustration as proof of her incompetence. She is a classic example of a student with "failure syndrome" problems (Brophy, 2004).

Fortunately, extreme cases like Hannah's are uncommon (Stipek, 1993). But we've probably all encountered situations where anticipation of failure has led to avoidance or paralysis. A lengthy term paper assignment is overwhelming, so we procrastinate until it's too late to do it really well. Calculus is daunting, so we take general mathematics instead. If failure is inevitable, there's no point in trying. And if we rarely try, we rarely succeed.

A second responsibility of teachers is to help students recognize the value of the academic work at hand. For example, Satisfied Sam (Stipek, 1993) is the class clown. He earns grades of C+ and B−, although he's clearly capable of earning As. At home, Sam spends hours at his computer, reads every book he can find on space, loves science fiction, and has even written a short novel. But he displays little interest in schoolwork. If assignments coincide with his personal interests, he exerts effort; otherwise, he simply sees no point in doing them.

In order to help students like Sam, you need to enhance the value of class activities. For example, since Sam likes to interact with his peers, you might use small-group activities in class. To allow him to demonstrate his interests, Sam's English teacher might invite him to share excerpts from the novel he has written. Sam's biology teacher might ask him to explain the science in his favorite science-fiction novel. Another strategy is to communicate the value of the *rewards* that successful completion or mastery will bring. For example, Sam may see little value in learning history, but still recognize that a passing grade is required if he wishes to continue his study of science in college.

In accordance with the expectancy-times-value model, Brophy (2004) has reviewed relevant theory and research and derived a set of strategies that teachers can use to enhance students' motivation. The following sections of this chapter are based on Brophy's work. (See Table 8.1.) We begin with strategies that focus on the first variable in the model—students' expectations of success.

As you read, keep in mind *that none of these strategies will be very effective if you have not worked to create and sustain a safe, caring classroom environment* (Chapter 3). Before students can become motivated, they must feel safe from humiliation, understand that it's all right to take risks and make mistakes, and know that they are accepted, respected members of the class (Ryan & Patrick, 2001).

 PAUSE AND REFLECT

Now that you have read about the expectancy × value model, reflect on its implications for teachers. How would you use this model to motivate a disinterested student in a topic in your content area?

TABLE 8.1 Brophy's Strategies for Enhancing Motivation to Learn

Strategies for Increasing Expectations of Success

- Provide opportunities for success.
- Teach students to set reasonable goals and to assess their own performance.
- Help students recognize the relationship between effort and outcome.
- Provide informative feedback.
- Provide special motivational support to discouraged students.

Strategies for Increasing Perceived Value

- Relate lessons to students' own lives.
- Provide opportunities for choice.
- Model interest in learning and express enthusiasm for the material.
- Include novelty/variety elements.
- Provide opportunities for students to respond actively.
- Allow students to create finished products.
- Provide opportunities for students to interact with peers.
- Provide extrinsic rewards.

Source: Brophy, 2004.

In fact, Brophy considers a supportive environment to be an "essential precondition" for the successful use of motivational strategies (Good & Brophy, 2008, p. 148).

STRATEGIES FOR INCREASING EXPECTATIONS OF SUCCESS

Provide Opportunities for Success

If tasks appear too difficult, students may be afraid to tackle them. You may have to modify assignments for different students, make assignments open-ended so that a variety of responses can be acceptable, provide additional instruction, divide lengthy projects into shorter, more "doable" parts, or allow extra time. Fred calls this the "slanty rope theory" of class work: "If we set a rope across a room at four feet, some kids can get over it and some can't. But if we slant the rope, then everyone can find their way over at some point." According to Fred, "success is a better motivator than anything else I know. If I can get kids to feel success, then maybe I'll be able to get through to them."

When Christina teaches her students to write research papers, she tries to guarantee success by breaking the assignment into small sections—taking notes, constructing a bibliography, creating an outline, writing the introductory paragraph, using parenthetical documentation—and having students turn in each part before writing the final paper. This not only makes the task seem less overwhelming, it also enables Christina to correct mistakes and set students on the right course before it's too late.

Sometimes, it's necessary to go back and reteach material rather than simply plowing ahead. For example, during one class period when Donnie was explaining how to construct and bisect congruent angles, it became apparent that most students were lost. As they labored over their papers, frustrated comments began to be heard from all corners of the room: "I can't do it; you told me not to change the compass, but I had to"; "I need an eraser"; "Huh?"; "How you do this?"; "I don't get this." Circulating around the room, Donnie tried to help individuals who were having trouble. Finally, she moved to the front and center of the room and addressed the class: "Okay, let's start again. I see a lot of people are out in left field." She began to explain the procedure again, very slowly. After every step, she asked, "Does everyone have this?" before moving on to the next step. Students began to respond more positively: "Yeah"; "Uh-huh"; "Okay, we got it." One girl, who had been having particular difficulty, called out, "C'mere, Miss Collins, I wanna show you what I got." Donnie checked her work; it was correct. The girl turned to her neighbor and announced loudly, "You see, all I needed was a little help. Sometimes I gotta work step by step. I got it. I got it."

Sometimes, providing opportunities for success requires differentiated assignments for students of varying achievement levels. Consider this example:

> Seniors in Mr. Yin's government class are conducting research in groups of three to five. Their goal is to understand how the Bill of Rights has expanded over time and its impact on various groups in society.
>
> Mr. Yin has placed students in groups of somewhat similar readiness (e.g., struggling readers to grade-level readers, or grade-level readers to advanced readers). All research groups must examine an issue such as (1) how one or more amendments in the Bill of Rights became more inclusive over time; (2) societal events that prompted reinterpretation of one or more amendments in the Bill of Rights; (3) court decisions that redefined one or more of the amendments; (4) current interpretations and applications of one or more of the amendments.
>
> Students have a common rubric for the structure and content of appropriate writing, and they will be asked individually to develop a written piece that stems from what they have learned from their group's research. A wide range of print, computer, video, and audio resources are available to all groups.
>
> Mr. Yin has differentiated the work in two major ways. Some research groups will investigate society groups that are more familiar to them, areas where issues are more clearly defined, or areas where there is more information available on a basic reading level. Other groups will examine unfamiliar society groups, issues that are less defined, or issues where the library resources are more complex. In addition, students may choose to write an essay, parody, or dialogue to reflect their understandings. (Tomlinson, 1999, pp. 54–55)

Another way of enhancing the probability of success is to vary instructional approaches so that students with different strengths have equal access to instruction. Numerous schools have developed programs based on Howard Gardner's (1993, 1995) theory of "multiple intelligences" (MI). According to Gardner, people have at least eight types of intellectual capacities. (These are listed in Table 8.2.) Schools have traditionally emphasized the development of linguistic and logical-mathematical intelligences (and have favored those who are relatively strong in these), while they have neglected and undervalued the other intelligences. Although Gardner does not advocate one "right way" to implement a multiple intelligences education, he does recommend that teachers approach topics in a variety of ways, so that more students will be reached and more can experience "what it is like to be an expert" (1995, p. 208). For example, when teaching about photosynthesis, you might not only have students read the section of their textbook describing photosynthesis (linguistic intelligence), you might also have students do activities that tap different intelligences: paint the process of photosynthesis with watercolors (visual-spatial); write a journal entry that reflects on a personally transformative experience and compare it to photosynthesis (intrapersonal); create a timeline of the steps of photosynthesis (logical-mathematical); role play the "characters" involved in the process of photosynthesis (bodily-kinesthetic); or make predictions about the impact of different levels of light on plant growth (naturalist) (Campbell, Campbell, & Dickinson, 1999).

Obviously, in the real world of 42-minute periods and high-stakes standardized testing, incorporating all the intelligences into every topic is impossible. And Gardner himself claims that trying to do this is a waste of effort and one of the ways that MI theory is misused (Gardner, 1998). Nonetheless, the theory of MI can suggest varied ways of having students engage with academic content. By routinely integrating tasks involving two or three different intelligences into your planning, you can provide students with greater opportunities for success.

TABLE 8.2 Gardner's Multiple Intelligences

Type of Intelligence	Description
Linguistic	Capacity to use language to express and appreciate complex meanings; sensitivity to the sounds, rhythms, and meanings of words
Logical-mathematical	Capacity to reason and recognize logical and numerical patterns; to calculate, quantify, consider propositions and hypotheses
Spatial	Capacity to perceive the visual world accurately; to think in three-dimensional ways; to navigate oneself through space; to produce and understand graphic information
Musical	Sensitivity to pitch, melody, rhythm, and tone; to produce and appreciate different forms of musical expression
Bodily-kinesthetic	Capacity to use the body and to handle objects skillfully
Interpersonal	Capacity to understand and interact effectively with others; to discern accurately the moods and emotions of others
Intrapersonal	Capacity to understand oneself; perceptiveness about one's own moods, emotions, desires, motivations
Naturalist	Capacity to understand nature and to observe patterns; sensitivity to features of the natural world

Sources: Arends, 2008; Campbell, Campbell, & Dickinson, 1999.

One other consideration regarding student success is important to mention here. Keep in mind that the process of learning something new often involves temporary failure and possibly some frustration (Alfi, Assor, & Katz, 2004). It's important that you allow your students to experience temporary failure in the safety of your classroom, so that they can develop needed coping skills and a sense of mastery that will contribute to their motivation to continue learning.

Teach Students to Set Reasonable Goals and to Assess Their Own Performance

Some students think anything less than 100 on a test is a failure, while others are content with a barely passing grade. You may have to help students set goals that are reasonable and obtainable. At the very beginning of each course, Christina has students set the goals they hope to reach. (See Figure 8.1.) Then, based on these goals, students decide the criteria they will use to evaluate their work. They have to include four specific items that Christina requires and eight more that they devise for themselves. Throughout the marking period, students keep their work in a "collection folder," from which they then select work representing their progress in meeting the goals they set. For each selection, students also complete a "reflection sheet," which asks them to explain which goals and criteria the piece represents. The selected work, along with its reflection sheet, gets moved into a portfolio that both they and Christina assess.

Christina also gives her students a rubric that details how each major project will be scored and requires students to score their work before turning it in: "This way, students are aware of the score they will be receiving, and they can make a choice about whether they're happy with that or want to do more." Interestingly, Christina finds that students' self-evaluations are usually within a few points of her own assessments of their work.

We observed another example of helping students set goals when one of Fred's 11th-grade students turned in an appalling essay at the beginning of the year. Not only was it short, superficial, and vague, but both the handwriting and spelling were atrocious. When Fred investigated, he found out that the student had a learning disability; nonetheless, he told the student in no uncertain terms that his performance was inadequate: "Look, you can't write, you can't even print, and you can't spell. But you're not stupid. So what are you going to do to get better? Let's set some goals." With the assistance of the resource room teacher, they devised a plan for the student to learn keyboarding and to use a spell checker. When the next writing assignment was due, the student came to Fred complaining that it was too hard. Fred was sympathetic and supportive—but adamant that the student complete it. He did, and although it was far from adequate, it was a definite improvement over the first assignment. Reflecting on the student's problems, Fred comments:

 We can all feel sorry for him, but he can't go around like this; he has to be pushed to overcome his deficits. People have allowed him to stay a baby, but it's time for him to grow up. There are ways he can improve. My job is to teach him to set some reasonable goals and then work to achieve them.

Help Students Recognize the Relationship between Effort and Outcome

Like Hopeless Hannah, some youngsters proclaim defeat before they've even attempted a task. When they don't do well on an assignment, they attribute their failure to lack of ability, not realizing that achievement is often a function of effort. Other students may be overconfident—even cocky—and think they can do well without exerting much effort. In either situation, you have to make the relationship between effort and outcome explicit. Whenever possible, point out students' improvement and help them to see the role of effort: "See, you did all your math homework this week, and it really paid off. Look at how well you did on the quiz!"

Goals	
Your individual goals should represent what you wish to accomplish in this course. Choose goals that are directly relevant to your expectations for the course. For example, while it is valid to say that you want to be a millionaire, that goal is not specifically relevant to English class. Choose a more specific shorter-term goal. Once you have chosen your goals, explain your reasons for selecting them in the space provided. Then list 2 ways that you think you can reach these goals.	
Goal #1:	**Reason for selection of this goal:**
2 things you can do to help you reach this goal:	
Goal #2:	**Reason for selection of this goal:**
2 things you can do to help you reach this goal:	
Goal #3:	**Reason for selection of this goal:**
2 things you can do to help you reach this goal:	
Goal #4:	**Reason for selection of this goal:**
2 things you can do to help you reach this goal:	
Goal #5:	**Reason for selection of this goal:**
2 things you can do to help you reach this goal:	

Figure 8.1   Christina's Goal-Setting Handout

The relationship between effort and outcome became painfully clear to a student in Sandy's class who refused to take notes during class. When Sandy first noticed that he wasn't taking notes, she told him to take out his notebook and open it. He did, murmuring, "I'll open my notebook, but you can't force me to take notes." Later, he told Sandy he didn't need to take notes like the other kids, because he had a good memory. She explained that her years of experience had shown her that taking notes in chemistry was absolutely necessary; she suggested he keep his notebook out and open "just in case." When the first test was given, the boy's grade was 40. Sandy told him: "I know it's not because you're unable to do the work. So what do you think? What conclusion do you draw from this?" The boy responded, "I guess I gotta take notes."

Provide Informative Feedback

Sometimes turning in work to a teacher is like dropping it down a black hole. Assignments pile up in huge mounds on the teacher's desk, and students know that their papers will never be returned—graded or ungraded. From a student's perspective, it's infuriating to work hard on an assignment, turn it in, and then receive no feedback from the teacher. But a lack of academic feedback is not simply infuriating. It is also detrimental to students' motivation and achievement. The Beginning Teacher Evaluation Study (Fisher et al., 1980) documented the importance of providing feedback to students:

> One particularly important teaching activity is providing academic feedback to students (letting them know whether their answers are right or wrong, or giving them the right answer). Academic feedback should be provided as often as possible to students. When more frequent feedback is offered, students pay attention more and learn more. Academic feedback was more strongly and consistently related to achievement than any of the other teaching behaviors. (p. 27)

If you circulate while students are working on assignments, you can provide them with immediate feedback about their performance. You can catch errors, assist with problems, and affirm correct, thoughtful work. In the following vignette, we see Sandy help two girls having problems pouring a solution into a funnel. Only a clear, colorless solution was supposed to come out into the beaker, but the solution was yellow and had particles of the solid in it.

SANDY: **Why did this happen?**
TANYA: **Because I poured too fast and too much.**
SANDY: **Right. [She calls all the students over to see the problem that the two girls had.] So what happened?**
LISA: **The yellow stuff got over the filter paper, behind the fold.**
SANDY: **Okay, so what can you do?**
TANYA: **Pour it back in, but we're going to lose some.**
SANDY: **[To the other students] Can they pour it back in?**
STUDENT: **Yeah.**
SANDY: **Sure. It was good you washed the beaker.**

Sandy monitors the activity of lab groups.

Sometimes you're unable to monitor work while it's being done. In this case, you need to check assignments once they've been submitted and return them to students as soon as possible. You might also decide to allow your students to check their own work. Donnie believes this has numerous educational benefits:

> I like to go over the homework in class and have students check their own work. This gives them the chance to see how they're doing, where they're confused. If I just had them turn in the work and I graded it, they'd know which problems were right and which were wrong, but they wouldn't know why. Once a week, though, I do collect the homework and go over it myself. That way I can see for myself how students are doing.

As an English teacher, Christina finds that having students evaluate their own work and that of their peers is not only educational, it also allows them to receive feedback more quickly:

> I used to think it was an easy way out to have students grade their own papers or do peer editing, but experienced teachers told me it wasn't so, and I've come to agree. I couldn't have a writing-based classroom if I had to give all the feedback myself. My students write many drafts of their papers, and I simply cannot read them all quickly enough. . . . So I teach them to self- and peer-evaluate before revising. . . . They learn a lot when they do peer editing, and they can get instant feedback.

Whether you correct work while it's being done, at home over a cup of coffee, or together with your students, the important point is that students *need to know how they are progressing*. It's also important to give feedback in terms of *absolute standards or students' own past performance rather than peers' performance* (Brophy, 2004). Thus, instead of saying, "Congratulations! You received the sixth highest grade in the class," you could say, "Congratulations! You went from a 79 on your last quiz to an 87 on this quiz." Similarly, you can point out strengths and weaknesses and add a note of encouragement for further effort ("You've demonstrated a firm grasp of the perspectives of the slaveholders and the abolitionists, but not the slaves themselves. Check the chapter again, and add a paragraph to round out your presentation.")

Provide Special Motivational Support to Discouraged Students

For students with limited ability or learning disabilities, school may be a constant struggle to keep up with classmates and to maintain a sense of enthusiasm and motivation. Such students not only require instructional assistance (e.g., individualized activities, extra academic help, well-structured assignments, extra time), they may also need special encouragement and motivational support. For example, Donnie constantly exhorts students not to get discouraged if they're having trouble and reminds them that people work and learn at different paces. Often, she pairs low-achieving students with those she knows will be patient and helpful and encourages peer-assistance and peer-tutoring. Similarly, Sandy frequently reassures her students that they're in this together:

So many of my students are afraid of taking chemistry, and they find it harder than any subject they've taken. I spend the first five or six weeks of school reassuring them—"You're not alone, there's support, I'm here to help you, we'll do this slowly and systematically. . . . you don't have to learn it in three or four days; it may be a long haul but that's OK." If I can get them to trust me, and I believe they can do it, then eventually they develop more confidence and a sense of well-being.

Sandy also makes sure that she expresses concern and surprise when students don't do well on a test or assignment. She'll ask, "What happened here?" or "What's the problem?" so that students know she's not writing them off:

Too many times teachers will say "good job" to the person who's gotten the A, but nothing to the kid who got the D or F. But if you don't ask what happened, they think you expected it. Sometimes what you don't say is more powerful than what you do say.

Christina finds that students who have failed the standardized test required for high school graduation are particularly discouraged and anxious. Like Sandy, she makes it clear that she expects them to pass the next time around; at the very least, they will improve their scores. She cheers them on as they take numerous practice tests and analyze their performances. Then she has them think of one thing they will do differently when they take the test again. Responses vary—"I won't fall asleep"; "I'm going to read *all* the answer choices before I choose one"; "I'm going to figure out what kind of text I'm reading and mark it up"—but simply having a plan seems to help students to be more optimistic. Christina also gives her students a "care package" the day before the exam with granola bars and other healthful snacks (in case they don't have the makings for a good breakfast) and a page of test-taking tips, which encourages them to go to bed early and remember to set the alarm clock!

Unfortunately, teachers sometimes develop counterproductive behavior patterns that communicate low expectations and reinforce students' perceptions of themselves as failures. Table 8.3 lists some of the behaviors that have been identified.

As Brophy (2004) points out, some of these differences are due to the behavior of the students. For example, if students' contributions to discussions are irrelevant or incorrect, it is difficult for teachers to accept and use their ideas. Moreover, the boundary between *appropriate differentiated instruction and inappropriate differential treatment* is often fuzzy. Asking low achievers easier, nonanalytic questions may make instructional sense. Nonetheless, it's important to monitor the extent to which you engage in these behaviors and to reflect on the messages you are sending to your low-achieving or learning disabled students. If you find that you are engaging in a lot of the behaviors listed in Table 8.3, you may be "merely going through the motions of instructing low achievers, without seriously working to help them achieve their potential" (Brophy, 2004, p. 129).

Research on gender bias in the classroom has revealed that teachers also communicate low expectations to their female students, displaying some of the

---

TABLE 8.3 Ways That Teachers May Communicate Low Expectations

- Waiting less time for low achievers to answer a question before giving the answer or calling on someone else.
- Giving answers to low achievers or calling on someone else rather than helping the students to improve their responses by giving clues or rephrasing questions.
- Rewarding inappropriate behaviors or incorrect answers.
- Criticizing low achievers more often for failure.
- Praising low achievers less often for success.
- Paying less attention to low achievers.
- Seating low achievers farther away from the teacher.
- Demanding less from low achievers than they are capable of learning.
- Being less friendly in interactions with low achievers; showing less attention and responsiveness; making less eye contact.
- Providing briefer and less informative answers to their questions.
- Showing less acceptance and use of low achievers' ideas.
- Limiting low achievers to low-level, repetitive curriculum with an emphasis on drill and practice tasks.

Source: Brophy, 2004.

behaviors listed in Table 8.3 (Sadker, Sadker, & Zittleman, 2009). Again, it's important that you monitor your interactions with female and male students, to make sure you aren't sending an unintended message to your female students.

INCREASING THE PERCEIVED VALUE OF THE TASK

Recall that when we asked the students in the classes of our four teachers "why kids behave in some classes and not others," they stressed the importance of teaching in a way that is stimulating. As one student wrote, "Not everything can be fun. . ., but there are ways teachers can make [material] more interesting and more challenging." (See Chapter 1.) This student intuitively understands that motivation to learn depends not only on success expectations, but also on students' perceptions of the value of the task or the rewards that successful completion or mastery will bring. Remember Satisfied Sam? Seeing no value in his course assignments, he invests little effort in them, even though he knows he could be successful. Since students like Sam are unlikely to respond to their teachers' exhortations to work harder, the challenge is to find ways to convince them that the work has (1) *intrinsic value* (doing it will provide enjoyment), (2) *utility value* (doing it will advance their personal goals), or (3) *attainment value* (doing it will affirm their self-concept or fulfill their needs for achievement, understanding, skill mastery, and prestige) (Brophy, 2004; Eccles & Wigfield, 1985). Let's consider some of the strategies that teachers can use to enhance the perception of value.

Relate Lessons to Students' Own Lives

A study of the motivational strategies of first-year teachers demonstrated that students are more engaged in classrooms where teachers provide reasons for doing tasks and relate lessons to students' personal experiences (Newby, 1991). Unfortunately, *the study also found that first-year teachers use these "relevance strategies" only occasionally.* (See Figure 8.2.)

We thought about this study as we read a vignette about a seventh-grade teacher attempting to explain why an oxygen atom attracts two hydrogen atoms (Gordon, 1997). Jesse, a boy in the class, did not find this particularly engaging. However, by phrasing the concept in terms of the fact that two seventh-grade girls were attracted to him, the teacher was able to spark his involvement. As Gordon wryly observes, "metaphors involving sex immediately pique adolescents' interest" and can be particularly useful in generating attention and involvement—"as long as the metaphors do not cross the invisible boundary of propriety" (p. 58). A word of caution: Use metaphors like this sparingly, since they imply that all your students are heterosexual and will find this type of reference appealing.

When students are not from the dominant culture, teachers must make a special effort to relate academic content to referents from the students' own culture. This practice not only helps to bridge the gap between the two cultures, it also allows the study of cultural referents in their own right (Ladson-Billings, 1994). Two English teachers in a large multicultural, urban school in California provide a compelling

Figure 8.2   *Source:* ADAM @ HOME © 2008 by UNIVERSAL UCLICK. Reprinted with permission.
All rights reserved.

example (Morrell & Duncan-Andrade, 2002, 2004). Reasoning that hip-hop music could be used "as a bridge linking the seemingly vast span between the streets and the world of academics" (2002, p. 89), the teachers used hip-hop to develop the critical and analytical skills of their underachieving twelfth-grade students. First, the teachers paired famous poems with rap songs. They then divided their class into small groups and assigned one pair of texts to each group. Students were to interpret their poem and song and analyze the links between them. This curriculum unit illustrates the power of what Gloria Ladson-Billings (1994) calls *culturally relevant teaching*.

Our four teachers are well aware of the need to relate academic tasks to youngsters' lives. When Donnie teaches percents, for example, she has students do a project entitled "Buying Your First Car." Students work in small groups to determine how much a car they select will actually cost—a task that involves knowing and using interest formulas, calculating depreciation, learning about base prices and shipping fees, and figuring out if monthly payments will fit in their budgets. When Fred's students study the Bill of Rights, they debate whether wearing a T-shirt with an obscene slogan is protected free speech. Reflecting on the need for relevance, Fred comments:

> **You don't have to do it every day, but little bits and pieces help. Teachers always have to ask, "So what? What does this material have to do with me?" My brother always said, "If it doesn't make me richer or poorer then don't bother me with it." My brother was not a good student. So whenever I teach anything, I use "my brother Bob test." I ask myself, "So what? How will it make my kids richer or poorer in some way?"**

Provide Opportunities for Choice

One of most obvious ways to ensure that learning activities connect to individuals' personal interests is to provide opportunities for choice. Moreover, research has shown that when students experience a sense of autonomy and self-determination, they are more likely to be intrinsically motivated (Ryan & Deci, 2000) and to "bond" with school (Roeser, Eccles, & Sameroff, 2000). These opportunities are especially critical in middle schools, where students are typically faced with more teacher controls than elementary school and grades are used as extrinsic rewards (Urdan & Schoenfelder, 2006). During the transition to middle school, teachers can help students develop self-reliance and challenge-seeking behaviors by allowing them some autonomy in the classroom. While mandated curricula and high-stakes standardized testing thwart opportunities for choice, there are usually alternative ways for students to accomplish requirements. Think about whether students might (1) participate in the design of the academic tasks; (2) decide how the task is to be completed; and/or (3) decide when the task is to be completed (Stipek, 1993).

In one study, researchers asked 36 teachers about the types of instructional choices they gave to their students (Flowerday & Schraw, 2000). Although types of choices varied as a function of content areas and grade levels, all teachers agreed on six main types of choice: (1) topics of study (for research papers, in-class projects, and presentations); (2) reading materials (type of genre, choice of authors); (3) methods of assessment (exam versus final project); (4) activities (book report or diorama); (5) social arrangements (whether to work in pairs or small groups, choice of group members); and (6) procedural choices (when to take tests, what order to study prescribed topics, and when assignments were due). Teachers also expressed the belief that choice has a positive effect on students' motivation by increasing their sense of ownership and self-determination, interest, and enthusiasm.

Despite this belief, teachers tended to use choice as a *reward* for effort and good behavior, rather than as a *strategy for fostering* effort and good behavior. Thus, teachers were most likely to give choices to students who were already self-regulated. It's easy to understand why teachers would provide choice to students who have previously shown that they are responsible, motivated, and well behaved. (It certainly seems safer!) But if we think of choice as a motivational strategy rather than a reward, we can see that it might be useful to motivate students like Satisfied Sam.

There are many ways to build choice into the curriculum. To prepare for the state's high school graduation test, Christina's students have to complete various writing tasks, such as a persuasive letter or essay on a controversial topic, a cause/effect essay, and a problem/solution essay, but students often choose their own topics for all of these. When Fred's classes report on a historical figure, they are instructed to choose the figure who seems most like them (or whom they'd like to be). Donnie encourages students to "put their heads together" in small groups to identify the homework problems that caused the most difficulty; those are the ones they then review. And all four teachers sometimes allow students to choose their own groups for collaborative work.

Model Interest in Learning and Express Enthusiasm for the Material

To help keep your students interested in learning, it's important that you model an interest in learning. You can talk with your students about classes you are taking, books you are reading, or other ways that you continue to learn. When we were teaching in pre-college classrooms, we both made a point to share with our students things that we learned on vacation trips, or what we were doing to prepare for these trips, such as learning a foreign language or learning to scuba dive. Middle and secondary teachers are typically passionate about their content area, so you can also make sure your students know what you are doing to stay current in your field.

Research has shown that when teachers model an interest in learning, their students perceive that their classroom is focused on mastering the content rather than merely earning grades (Urdan & Schoenfelder, 2006). Christina often refers to her love of reading and the fact that she writes poetry. When Donnie gives students complex problems that involve a lot of skills and steps, she tells them, "I love problems like this! This is so much fun!" In similar fashion, Sandy frequently exclaims, "This is my favorite part of chemistry," a statement that usually causes students to roll their eyes and respond, "Oh, Mrs. K., *everything* is your favorite part!" When Fred is about to introduce a difficult concept, he announces: "Now please listen to this. Most Americans don't understand this at all; they don't have a clue. But it's really important, and I want you to understand it."

Include Novelty/Variety Elements

During a visit to Donnie's class, we watched as she introduced the "challenge problem of the day." Donnie distributed a photocopy of a dollar bill and told students to figure out how many $1 bills would be needed to make one mile if they were lined up end to end. The enthusiasm generated by the copies of the dollar was palpable. Fred also used money during one observation to make a point about choosing a more difficult, but more ethical course of action. He moved up an aisle and dropped a $5 bill on an empty chair. Turning to the girl sitting in the next seat, he commented, "You could just stick that in your pocket, walk out the door, and go to McDonald's, right? Take the money and run. That would certainly be possible, but would it be right?"

In Christina's basic skills class, we watched as students read and discussed *The Martian Chronicles* by Ray Bradbury. Then Christina explained how they were to create small illustrations of key incidents in the story, which would then be assembled in sequential order on large pieces of butcher paper and mounted in the library. As she assigned the incidents, it was clear that incorporating this art activity not only reinforced students' understanding of the story but also generated a great deal of enthusiasm.

Provide Opportunities for Students to Respond Actively

So often the teacher talks and moves, while students sit passively and listen. In contrast, our four teachers structure lessons so that students must be actively involved. When Fred's Institute for Political and Legal Education (IPLE) class studies the judicial system, students engage in a mock trial. In Christina's classes, where many students voice an entrenched dislike of poetry, Christina works hard to have students experience poetry in a way that is memorable and personal. She divides the class into groups to design a poetry lesson that requires each student in the class (1) to write a poem that uses a particular literary device (e.g., allusion, metaphor, simile, irony, alliteration, consonance, etc.) and (2) to study a poem. Instructing the groups to use as a model Mr. Keating (the Robin Williams character) from *Dead Poets Society,* Christina encourages students to design lessons that "appeal to the senses," that "are like games or sports with a lot of poetry added in," and that require students "to get up and move around." One group, for example, designed an impossible scavenger hunt for the class to attempt and then explained how the hunt related to Poe's poem "El Dorado."

Allow Students to Create Finished Products

Too much school time is devoted to exercises, drills, and practice. Students practice writing, but rarely write. They practice reading skills, but rarely read. They practice mathematical procedures, but rarely do real mathematics. Yet, creating a finished product gives meaning and purpose to assignments and increases students' motivation to learn.

After a fierce winter blizzard that closed school for seven days and left administrators trying to figure out how to make up the lost time, Fred's students wrote letters to state legislators offering various proposals. Since the task was

Fred and his students plan a mock trial.

real, the letters had to be suitable for mailing; motivation was far greater than it would have been if the task had been a workbook exercise on writing business letters. Similarly, Sandy's labs are not simply exercises in following a prescribed set of steps leading to a foregone conclusion. They are real investigations into real problems.

As an introduction to a multigenre project, Christina's students wrote children's books. First, a parenting-class teacher spoke with the class about writing for young children (e.g., how many characters would be appropriate; whether fantasy themes or something closer to children's own experiences would be most suitable; the importance of using simple vocabulary). Then students wrote their books, engaging in peer editing and revision. They read one another's books and chose six from each class. These were sent to the art classes, where they were illustrated and bound. Drama classes also got involved: They chose four of the books to act out to first-graders who came to the high school.

Provide Opportunities for Students to Interact with Peers

All four teachers firmly believe that motivation (and learning) are enhanced if students are allowed to work with one another. They provide numerous opportunities for peer interaction (a topic that will be explored further in Chapter 10).

Sometimes, groups are carefully planned; at other times, they are formed more casually. For example, one day we saw Donnie shuffle a deck of cards (admitting that she never learned how to do this really well) and then walk around the room, asking each student to pick a card. She then told students to get up and find the person or persons with the same number or face card that they had. Once students had found their partners, she proceeded to explain the group task.

Provide Extrinsic Rewards

Some effective managers find it useful to provide students with rewards for engaging in the behaviors that support learning (such as paying attention and participating) and for academic achievement. The use of rewards in classrooms is based on the psychological principle of *positive reinforcement:* Behavior that is rewarded is strengthened and is therefore likely to be repeated. Although rewards do not increase the perceived value of the behavior or the task, they link performance of the behavior or successful completion of the task to attractive, desirable consequences.

Rewards can be divided into three categories: social rewards, activity rewards, and tangible rewards. *Social rewards* are verbal and nonverbal indications that you recognize and appreciate students' behavior or achievements. A pat on the back, a smile, a thumbs-up signal—these are commonly used social rewards that are low in cost and readily available.

Praise can also function as a social reward. In order to be effective, however, praise must be *specific and sincere.* Instead of "Good paper," you can try something like this: "Your paper shows a firm grasp of the distinction between metaphor and similes." Instead of "You were great this morning," try, "The way you came into the room, took off your baseball caps, and immediately got out your notebooks was terrific." Being specific will make your praise more informative; it will also help you to avoid using the same tired, old phrases week after week, phrases that quickly lose any impact (e.g., "good job"). If praise is to serve as a reinforcer, it also needs to be *contingent on the behavior you are trying to strengthen.* In other words, it should be given only when that behavior occurs, so that students understand exactly what evoked the praise.

Donnie distributes a lab worksheet that asks students to draw a parallelogram and then work through five activities to discover the figure's properties. She stresses that students should write down their observations after each activity and then draw some final conclusions. As students work on the problems, she circulates through the room. When she sees Shaneika's paper, she tells her: "Shaneika, you are really following directions. You're writing the answers as you go along."

In addition to pats on the back and verbal praise, some teachers institute more formal ways of recognizing accomplishment, improvement, or cooperation. For example, they may display student work, provide award certificates, nominate students for school awards given at the end of the year, or select "Students of the Week." Whichever approach you use, be careful that this strategy of public recognition doesn't backfire by causing students embarrassment. As Sandy reminded us in Chapter 3, secondary students generally do not want to stand out from their peers. Moreover, individual public recognition may be upsetting to students whose cultures value collective over individual achievement (Trumbull, Rothstein-Fisch, Greenfield, & Quiroz, 2001).

In addition to social rewards, teachers sometimes use *special activities* as rewards for good behavior or achievement. In middle and high school, watching a DVD, listening to music, having free time, or having a night of no homework can be very reinforcing. One way of determining which activities should be used as rewards is to listen carefully to students' requests. If they ask you for the opportunity to listen to music or have a popcorn party, you can be confident that those activities will be reinforcing (at least for those particular students). It's also helpful to observe what activities students engage in when they have free time (e.g., do they read magazines? talk with friends? draw?)

Finally, teachers can use *tangible, material rewards* for good behavior—cookies, candy, key chains, pencils—although such rewards are used less in high school than in elementary school. For example, Donnie goes to a discount supermarket and buys a big supply of candy that she keeps in a back closet; when students have been especially cooperative, she'll break out the Twizzlers for an unexpected treat. Similarly, Fred sometimes gives prizes when students have to review factual information for tests, a task they usually find boring. He may have students play vocabulary bingo, telling them: "I have two prizes in my pocket for the winner—two tickets for an all-expense-paid trip to Hawaii or a piece of candy.

You get whichever one I pull out of my pocket first." Every now and then, Fred also uses candy to show his appreciation for good behavior. In his words,

> If someone has never given me grief, I may be moved to a spontaneous act of generosity. I'll say, "Here take this," and give them a Sugar Daddy or package of Sweet Tarts. It's amazing; kids go crazy over a little piece of candy.

Problems with Rewards

The practice of providing extrinsic rewards has been the focus of considerable controversy. One objection is that giving students tangible rewards in exchange for good behavior or academic performance is tantamount to bribery. Proponents of this position argue that students should engage in appropriate behavior and activities for their own sake: They should be quiet during in-class assignments because that is the socially responsible thing to do; they should do their homework so that they can practice skills taught during class; they should learn verb conjugations in Spanish because they need to know them. Other educators acknowledge the desirability of such intrinsic motivation, but believe that the use of rewards is inevitable in situations where people are not completely free to follow their own inclinations. Even Richard Ryan and Edward Deci, two psychologists who strongly endorse the importance of self-determination and autonomy, acknowledge that teachers "cannot always rely on intrinsic motivation to foster learning" since "many of the tasks that educators want their students to perform are not inherently interesting or enjoyable" (2000, p. 55).

Another objection to the use of rewards is the fact that they are attempts to control and manipulate people. When we dispense rewards, we are essentially saying, "Do this, and you'll get that"—an approach not unlike the way we train our pets. Indeed, Alfie Kohn, author of *Punished by Rewards: The Trouble with Gold Stars, Incentive Plans, A's, Praise, and Other Bribes* (1993), contends that rewards and punishments are "two sides of the same coin" (p. 50). Although rewards are certainly more pleasurable, they are "every bit as controlling as punishments, even if they control by seduction" (p. 51). According to Kohn, if we want youngsters to become self-regulating, responsible, caring individuals, we must abandon attempts at external control and provide students with opportunities to develop competence, connection, and autonomy in caring classroom communities. For more information on Kohn's work, see Box 8.1.

Another major concern is that rewarding students for behaving in certain ways actually *undermines their intrinsic motivation to engage in those behaviors.* This question was explored in an influential study conducted by Mark Lepper, David Greene, and Richard Nisbett (1973). First, the researchers identified preschoolers who showed interest in a particular drawing activity during free play. Then they met with the children individually. Some children were simply invited to draw with the materials (the "no-reward" subjects). Others were told they could receive a "good-player" award, which they received for drawing (the "expected-reward" subjects). Still others were invited to draw and were then given an unexpected

MEET THE EDUCATORS   BOX 8.1

MEET ALFIE KOHN

Alfie Kohn writes extensively on education, parenting, and human behavior. He is a frequent lecturer on topics such as "the deadly effects of 'tougher standards'"; the use of "A's, praise, stickers, and contests" to "bribe" students to learn; "the case against competition"; "teaching children to care"; and "the homework myth." *Time* magazine described Kohn as "perhaps the country's most outspoken critic of education's fixation on grades [and] test scores."

Some Major Ideas on Motivation:

- "How do I get these kids motivated?" is a question that reflects a "paradigm of control," and external control "is death to motivation" (Kohn, 1993, p. 199).
- "Do rewards motivate people? Absolutely. They motivate people to get rewards" (Kohn, 1993, p. 67).
- People who are trying to earn rewards generally end up doing worse on many tasks than people who are not. Like punishment, rewards are a form of control, designed to bring about compliance.
- In contrast, the three Cs create the conditions for "authentic motivation": *collaboration* (learning together), *content* (things worth knowing), and *choice* (autonomy in the classroom). When students have opportunities to work cooperatively on learning activities built around their interests, questions, and real-life concerns, and when they share responsibility for deciding what gets learned and how, there is no need for rewards.

Selected Books and Articles

The Homework Myth: Why Our Kids Get Too Much of a Bad Thing (Da Capo Press, 2006)

The Case Against Standardized Testing: Raising the Scores, Ruining the Schools (Heinemann, 2000)

The Schools Our Children Deserve: Moving Beyond Traditional Classrooms and "Tougher Standards" (Houghton Mifflin, 1999)

Beyond Discipline: From Compliance to Community (Association for Supervision and Curriculum Development, 1996/2006)

Punished by Rewards: The Trouble with Gold Stars, Incentive Plans, A's, Praise, and Other Bribes (1993/1999)

Website: www.alfiekohn.org

---

reward at the end (the "unexpected-reward" subjects). Subsequent observations during free play revealed that the children who had been promised a reward ahead of time engaged in the art activity half as much as they had initially. Children in the other two groups showed no change.

This study stimulated a great deal of research on the potentially detrimental effects of external rewards. Although the results were not always consistent, this research led educators to conclude that *rewarding people for doing something that is inherently pleasurable decreases their interest in continuing that behavior*. A common explanation for this effect is the *overjustification hypothesis*. It appears to work like this: Individuals being rewarded reason that the task must not be very interesting or engaging, since they have to be rewarded (i.e., provided with extra justification) for undertaking it. In other words, what was previously considered "play" is now seen as "work" (Reeve, 2006). Another explanation focuses on the possibility that external rewards conflict with people's need for autonomy and self-determination. This explanation argues that interest in a task decreases if individuals perceive rewards as attempts to control their behavior.

The detrimental effect of extrinsic reward on intrinsic motivation has been—and continues to be—hotly debated. In fact, reviews of the research (Cameron, 2001; Cameron, Banko, & Pierce, 2001; Cameron & Pierce, 1994; Deci, Koestner, & Ryan, 1999, 2001) have reached contradictory conclusions about the effects of expected tangible rewards. According to one researcher, it's all right to say, "If you complete the assignment with at least 80 percent accuracy, you'll get a coupon for something at the school store at the end of the period" (expected reward contingent on completion and level of performance), but it's *not* all right to say, "Work on the assignment and you'll get a coupon for something at the school store at the end of the period" (noncontingent reward) (Cameron, 2001). In contrast, other researchers contend that expected "tangible rewards offered for engaging in, completing, or doing well at a task" are *all* deleterious to intrinsic motivation (Deci, Koestner, & Ryan, 1999, p. 656; 2001). With respect to verbal rewards and unexpected tangible rewards, the reviews are more consistent: Both sets of researchers conclude that verbal praise can enhance intrinsic motivation and that unexpected tangible rewards have no detrimental effect. Further, most researchers acknowledge that external rewards can help develop intrinsic motivation when the initial interest level in the task is low (Williams & Stockdale, 2004). For example, if you are teaching Spanish verb conjugation, which high school students are not likely to find inherently interesting, providing rewards for successfully learning the conjugations at the beginning of the course can be phased out as students recognize the value of learning these conjugations in order to be successful in writing and reading assignments.

PAUSE AND REFLECT

Galvanized by No Child Left Behind, schools across the country are trying to improve attendance by offering students the chance to win cars, computers, iPods, shopping sprees, groceries—even a month's rent (Belluck, 2006). Having just read the section on providing extrinsic rewards, what do you think about this practice? Do you think such rewards are likely to bring about an increase in attendance?

At the present time, caution in the use of external rewards is still in order. As you contemplate a system of rewards for your classroom, keep in mind the suggestions listed in the Practical Tips box.

MOTIVATING UNDERACHIEVING AND DISAFFECTED STUDENTS

In *Building Community from Chaos* (1994), Linda Christensen, a high school teacher in Portland, Oregon, vividly portrays the challenge of motivating the academically unmotivated. Christensen writes about her fourth-block senior English class, a tracked class in which most of the students were short on credits to graduate but long on anger and attitude. Convinced that English class was a waste of time, her students made it clear that they didn't want "worksheets, sentence combining, reading novels and discussing them, writing about 'stuff we don't care

PRACTICAL TIPS FOR

USING REWARDS

- *Use verbal rewards to increase motivation to engage in academic tasks.* It seems clear that praise can have a positive impact on students' motivation to learn. But remember that teenagers may be embarrassed by public praise, and they are good at detecting phoniness. In order to be reinforcing, praise should be specific, sincere, and contingent on the behavior you are trying to strengthen.

- *Save tangible rewards for activities that students find unattractive.* When students already enjoy doing a task, there's no need to provide tangible rewards. Save tangible rewards for activities that students tend to find boring and aversive.

- *If you're using tangible rewards, provide them unexpectedly, after the task performance.* In this way, students are more likely to view the rewards as information about their performance and as an expression of the teacher's pleasure rather than as an attempt to control their behavior.

- *Be extremely careful about using expected tangible rewards.* If you choose to use them, be sure to make them contingent upon completion of a task or achieving a specific level of performance. If you reward students simply for engaging in a task, regardless of their performance, they are likely to spend less time on the task once the reward is removed.

- *Make sure that you select rewards that students like.* You may think that animal stickers are really neat, but if your high school students do not find them rewarding, their behavior will not be reinforced.

- *Keep your program of rewards simple.* An elaborate system of rewards is impossible to maintain in the complex world of the classroom. The fancier your system, the more likely that you will abandon it. Moreover, if rewards become too salient, they overshadow more intrinsic reasons for behaving in certain ways. Students become so preoccupied with collecting, counting, and comparing that they lose sight of why the behavior is necessary or valuable.

about'" (p. 51). Christensen knew she needed to engage them "because they were loud, unruly, and out of control" (p. 51), but she didn't know how. She eventually decided to use the novel *Thousand Pieces of Gold,* by Ruthann Lum McCunn, a book normally read by her college-level course in Contemporary Literature and Society:

> Students weren't thrilled with the book; in fact they weren't reading it. I'd plan a 90-minute lesson around the reading and dialogue journal they were supposed to be keeping, but only a few students were prepared. Most didn't even attempt to lie about the fact that they weren't reading and clearly weren't planning on it.
>
> In an attempt to get them involved in the novel, I read aloud an evocative passage about the unemployed peasants sweeping through the Chinese countryside pillaging, raping, and grabbing what was denied them through legal employment. Suddenly students saw their own lives reflected back at them through Chen whose anger at losing his job and ultimately his family led him to become an outlaw. Chen created a new family with this group of bandits. Students could relate: Chen was a gang member. I had stumbled on a way to

interest my class. The violence created a contact point between the literature and the students' lives.

This connection, this reverberation across cultures, time and gender challenged the students' previous notion that reading and talking about novels didn't have relevance for them. They could empathize with the Chinese but also explore those issues in their own lives. (pp. 51–52)

As Christensen's story illustrates, finding ways to enhance students' motivation is particularly daunting when students are disaffected, apathetic, or resistant. Such students find academic tasks relatively meaningless and resist engaging in them—even when they know they could be successful. Some may also be fearful that school learning "will make them into something that they do not want to become" (p. 205). This fear is apparent in some African Americans and other students of color who equate academic achievement with "acting White." In an influential paper published over two decades ago, anthropologists describe how bright Black students may "put brakes" on their academic achievement by not studying or doing homework, cutting class, being late, and not participating in class (Fordham & Ogbu, 1986). Not surprisingly, the existence of "acting White" has been the subject of heated debate ever since, but a recent study (Fryer, 2006) provides empirical evidence to support this phenomenon.

Motivating resistant, underachieving, or apathetic students requires "resocialization" (Brophy, 2004, p. 307). This means using the strategies described in this chapter in more sustained, systematic, and personalized ways. Extrinsic rewards may be especially useful in this regard (Hidi & Harackiewicz, 2000). By triggering engagement in tasks that students initially view as boring or irrelevant, "there is at least a chance" that real interest will develop (p. 159).

Resocialization also means combining high expectations for students with the encouragement and support needed to achieve those expectations—in short, showing students that you care about them as students and as people. As we mentioned in Chapter 3, a substantial body of research exists on students' perceptions of school and teachers (see Hoy & Weinstein, 2006). This research consistently demonstrates that when students perceive their teachers as caring and supportive, they are more likely to be academically motivated, to engage in classroom activities, and to behave in prosocial, responsible ways (e.g., Murdock & Miller, 2003; Ryan & Patrick, 2001; Wentzel, 1997, 1998, 2006).

Perceiving that teachers care appears to be especially important for students who are alienated and marginalized and those who are at risk of school failure. For example, Anne Locke Davidson (1999) interviewed 49 adolescents representing diverse socioeconomic, cultural, and academic backgrounds. Data revealed not only students' appreciation and preference for teachers who communicated interest in their well-being, but also students' willingness to reciprocate by being attentive and conscientious. This was particularly evident in the responses of "stigmatized" students who faced "social borders"—differences between their academic world (school) and their social world (home and community) in terms of values, beliefs, and expected ways of behaving. Describing Wendy Ashton, a teacher who prodded students to achieve, one student commented, "She won't put you down, she'll talk to you and she'll go, 'Yeah, you know I love you. You know I want you to make something out of yourself, so stop messing around in class" (p. 361). Davidson speculates that students who do not face social borders might be more accepting of teachers who are relatively distant and impersonal, because the students basically trust school as an institution; however, when students face the social divisions that can lead to alienation and marginalization, it is essential for teachers to be attentive, supportive, and respectful.

As the comment about Wendy Ashton suggests, this kind of caring is less about being "warm and fuzzy" and more about being a "warm demander"—someone who provides a "tough-minded, no-nonsense, structured, and disciplined classroom environment for kids whom society has psychologically and physically abandoned" (Irvine & Fraser, 1998, p. 56). Researchers identified a small group of teachers like this during a three-year study in two urban districts that served diverse student populations (Corbett, Wilson, & Williams, 2005). Both districts were desperately trying to find ways to close the achievement gap that existed between lower- and higher-income students. The researchers interviewed parents, students, teachers, and administrators and visited the classrooms of a sample of teachers from each grade level in each school. Their observations and interviews enabled them to identify a set of teachers who *simply refused to let students fail.* One of the teachers was Mrs. Franklin, an African American sixth-grade teacher whose school served mostly students of color. Mrs. Franklin believed that too many teachers had given up on students and didn't expect very much. As she put it: "Kids aren't the problem; adults are the ones finding the excuses" (p. 9). Mrs. Franklin didn't give her students an excuse not to do well. Her grading policy required any student work earning a grade lower than a C to be done over. Interestingly, interviews with students revealed that rather than resenting the strict grading policy, they appreciated it. As one student reported: "My teacher never let people settle for D or E; she don't let people get away with it. She give us an education. Other teachers don't care what you do. They pass you to be passing. Here, I pass my own self" (p. 10).

CONCLUDING COMMENTS

A while back, a professor of educational psychology remarked that learning about classroom management would be unnecessary if prospective teachers understood how to enhance students' motivation. Although this argument struck us as naive and unrealistic, we understood—and agreed with—its underlying premise; *namely, that students who are interested and involved in the academic work at hand are less likely to daydream, disrupt, and defy.* In other words, management and motivation are inextricably linked.

As you contemplate ways to increase your students' expectations for success and the value they place on academic tasks, remember that motivating students doesn't happen accidentally. Fred emphasizes this point when he contends that "how I will motivate my students" should be an integral component of every lesson plan. Fortunately, the motivational strategies discussed in this chapter are consistent with current thinking about good instruction, which emphasizes students' active participation, collaborative groupwork, and the use of varying assessments (Brophy, 2004).

Finally, remember the suggestions in Chapter 3 for creating a safer, more caring classroom. As we have stressed, students are more motivated when they perceive that teachers care about them. In Brophy's (2004) words: "You can become your own most powerful motivational tool by establishing productive relationships with each of your students" (p. 380).

SUMMARY

Although teachers are responsible for enhancing motivation, this chapter began by questioning the belief that "good teachers should make learning fun." Such a goal seems unrealistic and inappropriate given the constraints of the secondary classroom—compulsory attendance, required curricula, class sizes that inhibit individualization, and the specter of high-stakes standardized testing. A more appropriate, realistic goal is to stimulate students' *motivation to learn*, whereby students pursue academic activities because they find them meaningful and worthwhile.

An Expectancy-Times-Value Framework

- Motivation depends on:
    Students' expectation of success.
    The value they place on the task (or the rewards that it may bring).
- If either factor is missing, there will be no motivation.

Strategies for Increasing Expectations of Success

- Provide opportunities for success.
- Teach students to set reasonable goals and to evaluate their own performance.
- Help students recognize the relationship between effort and outcome.
- Provide informative feedback.
- Provide special motivational support to discouraged students.

Strategies for Increasing the Perceived Value of the Task

- Relate lessons to students' own lives.
- Provide opportunities for choice.
- Model interest in learning and express enthusiasm for the material.
- Include novelty/variety elements.
- Provide opportunities for students to respond actively.
- Allow students to create finished products.
- Provide opportunities for students to interact with peers.
- Provide extrinsic rewards:
    Keep in mind the different types of rewards: Social rewards, special activities, tangible rewards.

Be aware that rewarding people for doing something they already like to do may decrease their interest in continuing that behavior.

Think carefully about when and how to use rewards.

Motivating Underachieving and Disaffected Students

- Be sensitive to the possibility that students of color may fear accusations of "acting White" if they strive to achieve academically.
- Recognize that resistant, apathetic students need to know you care about them. Research on students' perceptions of "good teachers" demonstrates that they want teachers who make sure they do their work, maintain order, are willing to help, explain assignments clearly, vary instruction, and take the time to get to know them as people.
- Demonstrate care by using the strategies described in this chapter in more sustained and systematic ways.

By working to ensure that students are engaged in learning activities, you can avoid many of the managerial problems that arise when students are bored and frustrated. Management and motivation are closely intertwined.

ACTIVITIES FOR SKILL BUILDING AND REFLECTION

In Class

1. In the following two vignettes, the teachers have directed the activity. In a small group, discuss ways they could have involved students in the planning, directing, creating, or evaluating.

   a. Mrs. Peters felt that the unit her seventh-grade class completed on folk tales would lend itself to a class play. She chose Paul Bunyan and Pecos Bill as the stories to dramatize. The students were excited as Mrs. Peters gave out parts and assigned students to paint scenery. Mrs. Peters wrote a script and sent it home for the students to memorize. She asked parents to help make the costumes. After three weeks of practice, the play was performed for elementary students and parents.

   b. Mr. Wilkins wanted his 10th-grade World Civilization class to develop an understanding about ancient civilizations. He assigned a five-part project. Students had to research four civilizations (Egyptian, Mesopotamian, Indus Valley, and Shang); write a biography of Howard Carter, a famous archaeologist; describe three pyramids (step, Great Pyramid, Pyramid of Sesostris II); outline the reigns of five kings (Hammurabi, Thutmose III, Ramses II, David, and Nebuchadnezzar); and make a model of a pyramid. He gave the class four weeks to complete the projects and then collected them, graded them, and displayed them in the school library.

2. Working in small groups that are homogeneous in terms of discipline (i.e., English, world language, math, science), select a topic in your content area and design a lesson or activity that incorporates at least two of the strategies for increasing perceived value.

On Your Own

Interview an experienced, effective teacher about the motivational strategies he or she finds particularly effective with disaffected, resistant students.

For Your Portfolio

Design a "slanty rope assignment" in your content area that will enable students of varying achievement levels to experience success. For example, the task might vary in complexity; it might be open-ended, allowing a variety of acceptable responses; it might require the use of different reference materials; or it might allow students to choose the format in which they demonstrate their understanding (e.g., a report, poster, or role-play). (Use the example of Mr. Yin in this chapter as an example.)

FOR FURTHER READING

Brewster, C., & Fager, J. (2000). *Increasing student engagement and motivation: From time-on-task to homework.* Portland, OR: Northwest Regional Educational Laboratory (NWREL). Downloaded from www.nwrel.org/request/oct00/textonly.html.

This booklet, the 14th in a series of "hot topic" reports from the Northwest Regional Educational Laboratory, reviews research on motivation, provides strategies for motivating students to engage in class activities and to complete homework, and provides descriptions of three school systems that have made notable efforts to involve students. Included for each location is contact information, a description of the program, and observed outcomes.

Brophy, J. E. (2004). *Motivating students to learn* (2nd ed.). Hillsdale, NJ: Lawrence Erlbaum.

This excellent book is written explicitly for teachers and offers principles and strategies to use in motivating students to learn. It is not a "bag of tricks" but the product of the author's comprehensive, systematic review of the motivational literature.

Intrator, S. M. (2003). *Tuned in and fired up: How teaching can inspire real learning in the classroom.* New Haven: Yale University Press.

Sam Intrator spent a year in Mr. Quinn's academically and ethnically diverse fourth-period English class. He observed and recorded class sessions, repeatedly interviewed the teacher and students, and collected student writing, including "experience journals" in which students recorded the "peaks and valleys" of the school day. His goal: To capture "treasured moments" when teenagers "become immersed in their work" and experience a sense of energy and vitality. This book is about those moments of inspired learning.

Kohn, A. (1993). *Punished by rewards: The trouble with gold stars, incentive plans, A's, praise, and other bribes.* Boston: Houghton Mifflin.

Kohn argues that our basic strategy for motivating students ("Do this and you'll get that") works only in the short run and actually does lasting harm. Instead of rewards, Kohn suggests that teachers provide the "three Cs"—collaboration, content (things worth knowing), and choice. The result, he posits, will be "good kids without goodies."

Reeve, J. (2006). Extrinsic rewards and inner motivation. In C. M. Evertson & C. S. Weinstein (Eds.), *Handbook of classroom management.* Mahwah, NJ: Lawrence Erlbaum.

As Reeve notes, "Extrinsic rewards are ubiquitous in educational settings." For this reason, it's important for teachers to understand how rewards can be presented to students in ways that support, rather than interfere with students' inner motivational resources. This chapter discusses the different types of extrinsic rewards, whether they work, what their side effects are, and how rewards can be used to support autonomy.

Tomlinson, C. A. (2001). *How to differentiate instruction in mixed ability classrooms* (2nd ed.). Alexandria, VA: Association for Supervision and Curriculum Development.

Tomlinson explains what differentiated instruction is (and isn't), provides a look inside some differentiated classrooms, presents the "how tos" of planning lessons differentiated by readiness, interest, and learning styles, and discusses the complex issues of grading and record keeping. An appendix provides a useful summary of instructional and managerial strategies for differentiated, mixed-ability

MANAGING INDEPENDENT WORK

Independent work is a common instructional activity in secondary school. (Some would say it's *too* common, a position we'll discuss shortly.) In this situation, students are assigned to work at their desks with their own materials, while the teacher is free to monitor the total class—to observe students' performance, provide support and feedback, engage in mini-conferences, and prepare students for homework assignments. Independent work is often used to provide students with the chance to practice or review previously presented material. For example, in "direct instruction" or "explicit teaching" (Rosenshine, 1986), the teacher reviews previous material, presents new material in small steps, and then gives students the opportunity to practice, first under supervision ("guided practice") and then independently ("independent practice").

To be honest, this chapter almost didn't get written. Independent work is also referred to as *seatwork,* and this term has very negative connotations, particularly among educators who promote students' active participation and collaboration. Indeed, when we sat down with Donnie, Sandy, Fred, and Christina to discuss their views, we found heated differences of opinion on this particular instructional format. On one hand, Fred argued that seatwork could be a valuable activity:

I use seatwork to give kids the opportunity to practice skills like making predictions, valid inferences, generalizations. . . . Intellectual skills like these benefit from practice just like a backhand stroke in tennis. If

243

I have 27 kids doing an assignment in class, I can walk around, see immediately what they're doing, give individual critiques, catch them if they're having a problem. I can't give that individual, immediate feedback if the work is done as homework.

On the other hand, Sandy was vehemently negative: "I hate seatwork," she told us. "As far as I'm concerned, it's just a way of killing time." Similarly, Donnie claimed that she never used seatwork. We pointed out that we had frequently observed her using a pattern of direct instruction, beginning class with a review of the homework, then introducing a small segment of the new lesson, and having students do one or two problems at their seats while she circulated throughout the room. Donnie readily acknowledged her use of "guided practice," but argued that this was not seatwork:

It's not like elementary school, where you have different reading groups, and you have to find a way for kids to be busy for long periods of time while you're working with a small group. Most of my instruction is done with the whole group, so there's no need for all the kids to be sitting there quietly working on worksheets.

Finally, Christina admitted some ambivalence. She acknowledged that whenever she heard the word *seatwork,* she immediately thought of "bad teachers who sit at their desks grading papers, writing lesson plans, or even reading the newspaper, while their students do boring work designed to keep them in their seats and quiet." But she also recognized that independent work was sometimes useful:

Realistically, there are times when I need to confer with individuals, so I need the rest of the class to be meaningfully occupied. Or I might want students to do something in class so I don't have to give them additional homework (especially if they're already working on a long-term assignment). Or I might want the work to be preceded by some instruction and to be followed by an interactive activity. This necessarily situates the seatwork in the middle of the class period, rather than for homework. But because I'm so leery about seatwork, I always try to ask myself, "Does this work need to be done in the classroom, or should it be done as homework?"

We debated, we moralized, and we shared anecdotes about the awfulness or the usefulness of seatwork. Eventually, we came to realize that there was no fundamental difference of opinion among us. We all agreed that teachers sometimes need to assign work for students to do on their own but in class, with or without close teacher supervision. We agreed that seatwork didn't have to mean silence; in fact, all the teachers felt strongly that students should generally be allowed to help one another. But we also agreed that seatwork is too often busywork, that it frequently goes on for too long, and that too many teachers use it as a substitute for active teaching. As Donnie put it, "Some teachers think of seatwork as 'give them something to do all period so I can do something else.' They'll teach for 10 minutes, then give their students 30 minutes of seatwork, and sit down. That's not seatwork—that's a free period."

This chapter begins by discussing the problems that occur when independent work is misused—when teachers do not reflect on ways to organize the work so that it is appropriate and meaningful for students. We then go on to consider the ways Donnie, Sandy, Fred, and Christina try to avoid, or at least minimize, these problems. The intent is *not* to encourage you to spend large amounts of time in seatwork activities, but rather, to provide you with a way of thinking about seatwork so that you can make better decisions about when and how to use it. Throughout the discussion, the two terms—*independent work* and *seatwork*—are used interchangeably.

PAUSE AND REFLECT

The term *seatwork* has a negative connotation, and the question of whether or not to assign seatwork often arouses debate. What has your experience as a student been with seatwork, and what types of seatwork have you observed in classrooms? What do you think about the contention that seatwork is a "necessary evil"?

THE PITFALLS OF INDEPENDENT WORK

As Christina points out, the term *seatwork* conjures up images of bored, passive students doing repetitive, tedious worksheets while teachers sit at their desks calculating grades or reading the newspaper. Consider the following description of a typical seatwork situation. It was observed by Robert Everhart (1983), who spent two years conducting fieldwork in a junior high school. This scene takes place in Marcy's English class, where students are supposed to be learning about the proper form of business letters.

> First, Marcy asked the class to turn to the chapter on business letters in their grammar books and read that section. After five minutes Marcy asked the class, "How many have not yet finished?" Initially about one-third of the class raised their hands. Roy, sitting in the rear near where I was sitting, nudged John. John then spoke up, "I'm not finished."
>
> "I ain't finished either," Roy added, smiling. Needless to say, they both had finished; I had seen them close their books a few minutes earlier and then proceed to trade a *Mad* magazine back and forth.
>
> "Well, I'll give you a few more minutes, but hurry up," said Marcy. Those not finished continued reading while the rest of the class began engaging in different activities: looking out the window, doodling, and pulling pictures from their wallets and looking at them. Roy then pulled a copy of *Cycle* magazine from beneath his desk and began leafing through it. After a few minutes Marcy went to the blackboard and began outlining the structure of the business letter.
>
> "Ok, first thing we do is to place the return address—where, class?"

"On the paper," said one boy slouched in his chair and tapping his pencil.

"All right, comedian, that's obvious. Where else?"

"On the front side of the paper."

"Come on class, get serious! Where do you place the return address? Larry?" (Everhart, 1983, p. 47)

Marcy eventually gets through a description and explanation of the form of the business letter. She then informs students that they will be writing their own business letters, which will be due at the end of the following week. Today, they are to write the initial paragraph:

> After about 10 minutes of writing, Marcy asked, "How many are not finished with their paragraph?" About six students raised their hands. "OK, I'll give you a few minutes to finish up. The rest of you, I want you to read your paragraphs to each other because I want you to read them to the class tomorrow and they'd better be clear; if they aren't clear to you now they won't be clear to the class tomorrow."
>
> One of the students at the back of the room seemed somewhat surprised at this. "Hey, you didn't say anything about having to read these in front of the class."
>
> "Yeah, I don't want to read mine in front of the class," added Phil.
>
> Marcy put her hands on her hips and stated emphatically, "Now come on, class, you'll all want to do a good job and this will give you a chance to practice and improve your paragraphs before they're submitted for grades. And you all want to get 'As', I'm sure." There was a chorus of laughs from most of the class and Marcy smiled.
>
> "I don't care," I heard one girl say under her breath.
>
> "Yeah, I don't care either, just so I get this stupid thing done."
>
> After saying that, Don turned to Art and said, "Hey, Art, what you writing your letter on?"
>
> "I am writing the Elephant Rubber Company, telling them that their rubbers were too small."
>
> "Wow," Ron replied.
>
> "Don't think I'll write that letter though. Marcy will have a bird."
>
> "For sure," Art replied.
>
> The students continued talking to each other, which finally prompted Marcy to get up from her desk and say, "Class, get busy or some of you will be in after school." (Everhart, 1983, p. 48)

Analysis of this scenario allows us to identify five problems that are frequently associated with seatwork. (These are summarized in Table 9.1.) First, it is clear that *the assignment is not meaningful to students.* Don calls the business letter a "stupid thing," Art jokes about writing to the Elephant Rubber Company, and an unnamed girl mumbles that she doesn't care about getting an A. In Fred's terms, Marcy has given her students the kind of "garbage assignment" that is responsible for seatwork's bad reputation. "Garbage assignments" are not only a waste of precious learning time, they also foster boredom, alienation, and misbehavior. Clearly, if students do not perceive the value of a seatwork assignment, they are unlikely to become invested in it. That's when teachers have to resort to threats about

TABLE 9.1 The Problems with Seatwork

ALL TOO OFTEN:

- Assignments are not meaningful, educationally useful, or motivating.
- Assignments are not matched to students' achievement levels.
- Directions are not clear and thorough.
- Teachers do not circulate and monitor students' comprehension and behavior.
- Some students finish early, while others do not finish.

detention or extrinsic incentives like grades. Recall Marcy's words. First she tells her class, "And you all want to get 'As,' I'm sure." Later she warns, "Class, get busy or some of you will be in after school."

Second, it appears that Marcy's assignment *does not match students' varying achievement levels.* For some students, the reading assignment seems too easy; they finish reading quickly and fill their time by doodling, looking out the window, and reading magazines. Others seem to find the reading more difficult and need "a few more minutes." Similarly, writing one paragraph in 10 minutes doesn't seem like a particularly challenging assignment for most of Marcy's students, yet six students indicate they are not finished when Marcy checks their progress. (Of course, it's possible that they have just been wasting time.)

Assigning work that does not match students' achievement levels is typical of the behaviors exhibited by the less effective managers studied by Carolyn Evertson and Ed Emmer (1982; see Chapter 4 for a fuller description of this study). You may recall that Evertson and Emmer observed mathematics and English teachers at the junior high level and identified those who were more effective managers and those who were less effective. The observations led Evertson and Emmer to conclude that the more effective teachers had greater awareness of students' entering skills:

> An example of an activity showing low understanding was an assignment in one of the lower achieving English classes to "Write an essay from the perspective of an inanimate object." The problem was compounded by an unclear explanation of the term, perspective. Narratives noted more instances of vocabulary beyond some of the students' comprehension. As a consequence of being more aware of student skills . . ., the more effective teachers' classes had more success in participating in class activities and completing assignments. (p. 496)

A third problem is that Marcy *does not provide her students with clear, complete directions.* At the beginning of the period, Marcy tells the students to read the chapter on business letters, but she says nothing about why they are to read the chapter, how long they have, or whether they should take notes. In other words, she merely tells them to "do it"—without explaining the purpose for reading or suggesting strategies that might be used. Nor does Marcy explain that they will be writing their own letters later in the period. It is only after reviewing the form of the business letter that Marcy instructs her students to write the initial paragraph, and once again, she neglects to tell them what will be coming next—namely, that they will be reading the paragraphs aloud the following day. (Marcy might have made this decision at the last minute, in order to provide an activity for students who finished early.) Not surprisingly, some of the students react with displeasure. One complains, "Hey, you didn't say anything about having to read these in front of the class," while another protests, "Yeah, I don't want to read mine in front of the class."

Marcy's lack of clarity and thoroughness is also reminiscent of the less effective managers studied by Evertson and Emmer (1982). In addition to differing in their awareness of students' entering abilities, more and less effective teachers differed in terms of skill in communicating information. More effective English teachers were clearer in giving directions and stating objectives than less effective teachers. (Interestingly, this difference did not appear in comparisons of more and less effective math teachers.) According to Evertson and Emmer, more effective managers "were better able to segment complex tasks into step-by-step procedures and to help students understand their tasks, and how to accomplish them. When students knew what to do and had the skills to do it, they were more likely to stay on task" (Evertson & Emmer, p. 496).

A fourth problem evident in Marcy's class is her *lack of monitoring.* Although the vignette doesn't explicitly describe what Marcy is doing while her students are reading and writing, the last paragraph does state that Marcy gets up from her desk to admonish students who are talking. Furthermore, Marcy not only has to ask how many students have not yet finished, she also seems unaware that students in the rear of the room are reading *Mad* magazine. These are sure signs that Marcy is not circulating through the room, checking on students' progress, helping them with problems, and providing feedback. If Marcy is not going to provide this supervision and support, she might as well have her students do the assignment at home.

Finally, Marcy does not really plan for the fact that *students work at different paces.* They may *begin* seatwork at the same time, but they never *finish* at the same time. "Ragged" endings can upset a schedule that looked beautiful on paper. Students who cannot complete assignments in the allotted time may have to do the assignment for homework. Students who complete their work earlier than you expected need something to keep them occupied; if they must sit and wait with nothing to do, they may distract students who are still working. In Marcy's class, students who finish earlier than their peers are actually quite well behaved: They read *Mad* and *Cycle* magazines, look out the window, doodle, and look at pictures from their wallets. Nonetheless, they are wasting time that could be spent on more profitable activities.

DESIGNING AND IMPLEMENTING EFFECTIVE INDEPENDENT WORK

Analysis of Marcy's seatwork sheds light on the special problems associated with this particular instructional situation. In this section of the chapter, we consider ways to avoid or at least minimize these problems. (These are summarized in the Practical Tips box.)

PRACTICAL TIPS FOR

DESIGNING AND IMPLEMENTING EFFECTIVE INDEPENDENT WORK

- Assign work that is meaningful, useful, and relevant to students.
  Ask yourself:
  - What is the purpose of the task?
  - Does the task relate to current instruction? Are students likely to see the connection?
  - Are students likely to see the task as something worth doing or something boring and unrewarding?
  - Are the directions unambiguous and easy to follow?
  - Does the task provide students with an opportunity to practice important skills or to apply what they are learning?
  - Does the task provide students with the opportunity to think critically or to engage in problem solving?
  - Does the task require reading and writing, or does it simply ask students to fill in the blank, underline, or circle?
  - Does the task require higher-level responses or does it emphasize low-level, factual recall and "drill and kill" practice of isolated subskills?
  - Is there a reason the task should be done in school (e.g., the need for coaching by the teacher) rather than at home?
  - Will students be able to accomplish the task without assistance? If not, how will assistance be provided?
- Match assignments to students' varying achievement levels.
  - Make sure that written and oral directions are clear and thorough.
  - Monitor behavior and comprehension.
  - Plan for ragged endings.

Assign Work That Is Meaningful, Useful, and Relevant to Students

Secondary textbooks generally have questions, activities, and exercises at the end of each chapter, and some come with supplemental study guides, workbooks, or activity sheets. Since these materials may not always be meaningful and relevant to students, it is essential that you evaluate the activities you assign. As Fred observes:

The typical seatwork assignment is not well thought through. It's mindlessly designed and mindlessly done. "Read and answer the questions on page 287." "Fill in the blank." "Read and outline the chapter." What's really scary is when the kids don't even think assignments like that are so bad! That tells me that they're so used to that kind of thing, they don't realize it's a waste of time. But seatwork doesn't have to be that way.

In order to be sure that the independent work they assign is not "that way," Donnie, Christina, Sandy, and Fred carefully evaluate the tasks they give students to complete during class. The Practical Tips box lists some of the questions they ask themselves before they assign independent work.

Many teachers prefer to create their own assignments rather than to rely on commercially prepared materials. In this way, they are better able to connect the tasks with students' backgrounds and experiences, target particular problems that students are having, and provide greater individualization. For example, when Fred wants students to become familiar with the resources in the library, he asks them to do tasks like these:

- List three facts on one topic that interests you using the electronic database *Facts on File*.
- Use an almanac to find a country that begins with the first letter of your last name and tell the population of that nation.
- Use *The New York Times* electronic database (Internet or CD-ROM) to identify an important event that occurred on your last birthday.
- Locate a biography about a person whose last name begins with the same letter as your first name.

According to Fred, this simple way of individualizing the assignment has a very positive effect on students' motivation. (And there's an added bonus: Students have to do their own work.) Research on "situational interest" (Schraw & Lehman, 2001) suggests that teachers can also enhance interest in tasks by pointing out the relevance of the material, providing students with a greater sense of control (e.g., by providing choice about which problems to do), and giving reasons to persist in a task (i.e., explaining why the task is useful). (See Chapter 8 for related suggestions.)

Fred acknowledges that he can't always "be creative and wonderful five days a week, week after week," but he always tries to ensure that the independent work he assigns has a valid purpose. It's worth keeping his comments in mind:

 Look, I'm human. . . . There are times when I'll give kids seatwork assignments that are less than wonderful, assignments that I'm not especially proud of. But I really try to make that the exception, not the rule, and to come up with seatwork that's meaningful to kids and educationally useful.

Match the Work to Varying Achievement Levels

Fred also likes to use open-ended assignments that allow students working on a variety of levels to complete the work successfully. For example, when his students read a chapter in their texts, Fred often forgoes the end-of-chapter questions (which often have one correct answer); instead, he may ask students to create their own questions. At other times, he asks a question that is broad enough so that almost everyone in his extremely diverse class is able to respond—in some fashion—to the question, although answers obviously vary in terms of length, substance, and coherence. As mentioned in Chapter 8, Fred calls this the "slanty rope theory":

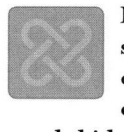 If we set a rope across a room at four feet, some kids can get over it and some can't. But if we slant the rope, then everyone can find their way over at some point. I firmly believe that people don't all want to go over at the lowest level. We can encourage kids to stretch—and once you teach kids to stretch, you've taught something more important than the subject matter.

In the following example (Tomlinson, 1999), we see how a foreign language teacher has created a "slanty rope assignment" that allows her heterogeneous class to pursue the same general topic, but at varying levels of difficulty and sophistication:

> Mrs. Higgins's German 1 class is studying the formation of past-tense verbs. One group of students will work with pattern drills in which much of a German sentence is supplied. However, each sentence uses an English verb, and students must supply the correct form of the past-tense German verb. Mrs. Higgins has ensured that the missing verbs are regular.
>
> A second, more proficient, group has a similar activity. But they will encounter a greater number and complexity of missing words, including a few irregular verbs. Another group of students works with the same sentences as the second group, but virtually all of the sentences are in English and must be translated into German. Two or three students don't need the skill drill at all; they are given a scenario to develop, with instructions about the sorts of grammatical constructions that must be included. (pp. 51–52)

For more about ways of differentiating assignments and responding to the needs of all learners, see Tomlinson (2001).

When working with students who have difficulty sustaining attention, it can be helpful to break large assignments into a series of smaller ones (Wallace, Cox, & Skinner, 2003) or to intersperse easy items between harder items. For example, researchers found that two middle school students with learning disabilities remained on task longer when they completed math worksheets containing easy problems interspersed among the harder problems (Calderhead, Filter, & Albin, 2006). Unfortunately, the students' accuracy was not affected.

Make Sure That Written and Oral Directions Are Clear

It is important to check that instructions provided in a text or on a worksheet are clear and precise. If you don't, you may encounter situations like this one, related by a student teacher in a foreign language class:

> *I decided to use this worksheet that listed in random order 10 statements from a short story we had read (e.g., "The gardener reported that the dandelions were growing furiously"). Underneath the list*

were 10 lines, numbered from 1 through 10, and students were instructed to put the statements or events in sequential order. A lot of the students thought that the numbers (1–10) referred to the order of events, so next to each number, they wrote the number of the statement. (So "1–7" was meant to indicate that the first thing that happened in the story was the seventh item in the list). Other kids figured that the 1 through 10 referred to the number of the statement. When they put "1–7," they meant that the first statement in the list occurred seventh. Needless to say, lots of kids "failed" the assignment! I couldn't understand how it could be, until we went over the papers. Then I realized how confusing it was. I learned a good lesson. Don't assume that everything printed on an "official" worksheet is clear!

Having had a number of experiences like this one, Christina now makes it a point to rewrite directions she thinks are confusing. For example, one district-wide assignment she gives requires students to read a book and write their reflections in a journal with at least 10 entries. Students are provided with 10 guiding questions, but it's not clear from the directions if students have to answer *one* question or *all* the questions for each journal entry. Actually, they have to do neither. So Christina adds a sentence specifying that students have to address each question *somewhere* in the journal, but not in any specific order and not in every entry.

Sometimes teachers think they don't have to explain orally what students are to do since there are written instructions in the textbook or on the worksheet. It's certainly important for students to read written instructions, but don't assume that they'll do this automatically; this may be a skill you'll have to teach. Consider the lesson learned by this student teacher:

These kids don't instinctively read something when it is given to them: They wait to have it explained. . . . I know that I'm supposed to state all the objectives and explain things carefully, but there are times when I want them . . . to be curious enough to take a look at what's in front of them. I try to pepper my handouts with cartoons and some of my own spectacular drawings just to make them more attractive and engaging. I'm so used to the college mentality—something is passed out and you read it rather than listen to it being explained. I have to remember it's usually the opposite in high school.

In addition to checking written directions for clarity, make sure your oral directions are clear and complete. Recall that one of the problems with Marcy's letter-writing activity was that she didn't tell students why they were to read the chapter on business letters or how long they would have; nor did she explain that they would be writing their own letters later in the period. Contrast this with the way Donnie introduces a brief seatwork assignment on rearranging equations to solve for different variables. Even though the assignment will take just a few minutes, she explains what students are to do, how much time they will have, and what they will be expected to do when they're finished:

> What I need you to do now is turn to page 178. Get out some paper and a pencil or pen. We're going to look at the chapter review, up through #15. I'm going to begin by making an assignment to each person. Problem #1, Ernest; Problem #2, Damika; Problem #3, Latoya; Problem #4, Jerome. [She continues until everyone has been assigned a problem to do.] Now I want you to solve the problem you were assigned. These are just like the homework problems we just reviewed. You're going to be rearranging equations to solve for the different variables. . . . I'll give you approximately two minutes to do this. When we come back, make sure you can give us the answer and explain the problem to the rest of the class.

Marcy also failed to tell students that they would be reading their paragraphs aloud the following day, an omission that upset a number of her students ("Hey, you didn't say anything about having to read these in front of the class."). This is a situation that Christina tries hard to avoid, especially since English class often involves having students write about personal experiences and feelings:

> Christina distributes copies of her own personal essay, which deals with her ethnic background. She explains that students should read her essay and then begin to jot down ideas and write a draft of their own personal essay on the topic of identity. They will have a total of 30 minutes. She cautions them to "select something that you will feel OK to share in small groups, and keep in mind that I'll be picking the groups." A girl in the front row nods and comments, "So we should write something we can share with anyone."

When you're presenting directions for seatwork assignments, you also need to make it clear whether or not students can ask peers for assistance. In some classes, teachers encourage students to work collaboratively, while in other classes giving or receiving help is tantamount to cheating. This latter situation can present a real dilemma for students. On one hand is their need to follow the teacher's directions and to stay out of trouble. On the other hand is their need to complete the assignment successfully and to assist friends who are having difficulty (Bloome & Theodorou, 1988).

Students' understanding and acceptance of the norms for helping peers can also be influenced by culture. Providing assistance may be especially valued by students with cultural roots in collectivist societies (e.g., African, Asian, Hispanic, and Native American). In collectivist cultures, people assume responsibility for one another's welfare, and the focus is on working toward the common good (Cartledge with Milburn, 1996). Thus, students from these cultures may resist teachers' directives to work independently. In contrast, those from individualistic cultures (e.g., English-speaking countries) may value individual effort.

In general, all of our four teachers not only allow, they *encourage* students to help one another. As Donnie puts it, "I can't possibly get around to everybody.

The kids would constantly be calling me to come over and help them. For my own sanity, I have to have students help one another. But I think they learn better that way anyway." Christina agrees. When she circulates around the room monitoring students' progress, she'll frequently refer students who are having problems to individuals she's already assisted:

 I do this for a few reasons. First, it's nice for the students I just helped to know that I now consider them to be "experts." Second, I think that having students teach others helps them to remember what I just explained. Third, it saves me having to repeat the same explanations. And finally I think it builds a helping community. But I always try to go back to the kids and check if the helpers were able to explain clearly and if the "helpees" now understand. I don't want kids to think I'm just pushing them off on others because I don't want to be bothered.

It's important to note that all of the teachers work hard to explain what "helping" really means. They take pains to explain to students that simply providing the answer or doing the task for someone else is not helping, and they stress the futility of copying. Donnie says she has "parasites" in her geometry class who don't want to do anything on their own; they just want someone to give them the answer. (This often irritates more diligent students, as Figure 9.1 illustrates.) In order to prevent this from happening, she'll sometimes assign different problems to students sitting next to each other; this allows them to help each other, but not to copy.

Although all the teachers firmly believe in the value of peer assistance, there are also times when they do *not* allow students to help one another. In these situations, they are careful to explain that the ground rules are different. Listen to Sandy:

 Most of the time, I stress that scientists do not work in isolation, that it's necessary to look at everyone's data and ask, "Did anyone else get these results?" But four or five times a year, I run "quiz labs" where students are individually responsible for listening to instructions, carrying out the procedures, and drawing conclusions. This is my way of making certain that every single person knows how to light the Bunsen burner, handle the equipment, etc. These are not discovery or inquiry lessons, but opportunities for students to apply what has been learned in class. During these lab activities, students cannot speak to one another. This is a real departure from regular lab activities, so I have to make it really clear that they are not to consult with one another—that the norms are different.

Monitor Behavior and Comprehension

Observers of classroom life have noted that students' engagement during independent work is often lower than their engagement during teacher-directed activities. Why should this be so? Apparently, even when they do find the activity meaningful and comprehensible, seatwork requires students to pace themselves through assignments. Since there are no external signals such as teachers' questions to

Figure 9.1   *Source:* CALVIN AND HOBBES © 1993, Watterson. Distributed by UNIVERSAL UCLICK. Reprinted with permission. All rights reserved.

push students along (Gump, 1982), they may begin to doodle, send text messages, comb their hair, and sharpen pencils—until the teacher reminds students to get back to work. In fact, research has shown that engagement in seatwork often follows a predictable cycle (deVoss, 1979): Students begin their assignments; attention wanes; the noise level increases; the teacher intervenes; the students return to the assignment. This cycle can repeat several times, until a final spurt when students rush to complete their tasks before the time is over.

In order to avoid the "mad rush" problem, Christina gives students a breakdown of the time that should be spent on each part of an assignment and periodically reminds students where they should be. She also monitors their behavior carefully by circulating around the room. In fact, none of our four teachers sits down while students are working, unless they are having individual conferences. In the following example, also taken from Donnie's lesson on rearranging equations, we see the way she circulates throughout the room while students are working. Notice how she is able to *overlap* (Kounin, 1970)—to monitor the behavior of students doing seatwork while she also works with an individual.

 Students are working on the problems Donnie has just assigned. She walks around the room, peering over students' shoulders, commenting, helping, prodding them along. Then she heads over to three students who were absent and are making up the assignment that everyone else did the day before. She checks what they are doing, and helps one girl who is having particular difficulty. While she is working with this student, she periodically looks up and scans the room to monitor the rest of the class. One boy appears to be doing nothing. "Jerome, are you finished with your problem?"

The purpose of circulating is not simply to monitor behavior. Roving around the room allows you to monitor students' *understanding of the assignment.* Recall the distinction between *engaged time* and *productive learning time* discussed in Chapter 7. Clearly, it's not enough for students to remain busy and on-task. They must also understand what they are supposed to do and carry out their tasks successfully. This requires monitoring. Sandy comments:

> When I give a seatwork assignment, I never sit at my desk doing paperwork. I give an assignment for an instructional reason, not just to keep kids busy while I grade papers. This means that I need to be moving around, seeing what they're doing. For example, at the end of the period, I might say, "Let's try problems 1, 2, and 3." I walk around and help. If I see that students are doing all right, then I know I can have them complete 4 through 6 for homework.

Watching our teachers monitor independent work, we were struck by the very quiet, discreet way they interacted with each student. This kind of discretion appears to have at least two advantages. First, audible comments may disturb everyone's concentration and progress; second, loud, public comments may be embarrassing and may have a negative effect on students' motivation or willingness to ask questions.

Fredric Jones (Jones, et al., 2007) offers additional advice for giving help to individual students during seatwork: "Praise, prompt, and leave" (p. 18). According to Jones, teachers should give help in 20 seconds or less for each student. Instead of questioning students ("What did we say was the first thing to do?") and providing individual tutoring, teachers should praise something the student has done correctly ("Good job up to here"), give a straightforward prompt ("Follow the model on the chalkboard"), and leave. In this way, teachers can circulate quickly and efficiently and minimize the time that students spend waiting for assistance.

PAUSE AND REFLECT

One aspect of management that beginning teachers often struggle with is circulating and monitoring all students during independent work while helping individuals who are having problems. Think of ways that you can increase your ability to *overlap* (i.e., addressing an individual student's question while still monitoring the rest of the class).

Plan for Ragged Endings

Although it's essential to plan activities for students who finish early, you need to think carefully about the approach you will take. If students learn they'll be given additional (perhaps tedious) work that others don't have to do, they may dawdle or pretend they haven't finished. In Marcy's class, for example, Roy and John both reported that they hadn't finished reading the chapter, when they had. Obviously, they wanted time to read *Mad* rather than move on to a new assignment about business letters.

In the classrooms of our four teachers, ragged endings are rarely a problem, since class activities are structured so that students rarely finish early. Listen to Sandy:

> Not only do students have to understand what to do and why they're doing it, they need to know what's expected upon completion. If you don't do this, some kids may rush through, thinking, "I'll finish real fast and then I'll have time to do my homework." If they know they'll have a follow-up related assignment, they keep going. I never make it a closed assignment. I'll say, "Today you're going to do an analysis of knowns. Once you've completed the analysis, formulate the flowchart for your unknowns." I know it usually takes a complete

double period to do this. When time is about to run out, I'll say, "If you're not done, do it tonight." If they know at the beginning that it's a homework assignment, they may relax, figure they'll just do it for homework. So I never let them know that they won't be able to finish. If they see that they have a lot to do, they'll say, "Wow, I really need to work." If it's a 10-minute task, they may drag it out. I suggest that teachers predict how long something will take and then tack on a related assignment.

Christina finds that ragged endings are a special challenge when students are doing writing workshop projects:

Some kids will say "I'm done" after only a few minutes. I tell them they can stop writing if they think they are finished, but they have to move to the next step of the writing process, revision. I give them specific strategies for content revision so they don't get stuck. Individual writing conferences and mini-lessons also help because I give them specific writing options to try out.

CONCLUDING COMMENTS

This chapter has highlighted the pitfalls and challenges associated with independent work and has provided suggestions for avoiding, or at least minimizing, these problems. Keep these in mind as you decide on the kinds of activities students will do during seatwork time, the way you will introduce assignments, and the rules and procedures you will establish to guide behavior.

It is important to note that the chapter focused almost exclusively on the situation in which the work is assigned to the entire class while the teacher circulates and assists students in accomplishing the tasks. But this is not the only way that seatwork can be used. One option is to assign independent work to the majority of the class while you work with individuals who need additional help or a more challenging assignment. Another option is to have students work on independent work while you have individual conferences with students about their grades. We saw an example of this from Fred's classroom in Chapter 7.

This use of seatwork is common at the elementary level. Most of us recall our primary teachers meeting with the "Cardinals," the "Butterflies," or the "Tigers," while the rest of the class worked independently. But independent seatwork combined with small-group instruction is far more unusual at the high school level, where instruction often tends to be conducted in a large group.

Research (Anderson, 1985; Fisher, et al., 1978) suggests that elementary students spend far too much time doing seatwork assignments that have questionable value, so we are certainly not suggesting that you replicate this situation at the secondary level. Nonetheless, there are times when it may be appropriate to have the majority of students work on an independent assignment, while you meet with individuals. This format may be particularly useful if you have an extremely heterogeneous class. But take heed: If you are going to be unavailable for circulating and assisting, your assignments need to be even clearer and more meaningful than usual. You also need to hone the skill of overlapping. This is a situation that truly requires you to have "eyes in the back of your head."

SUMMARY

This chapter examined independent work or seatwork, the situation in which students work individually on a given task at their own desks. Seatwork provides teachers with the opportunity to observe students' performance, to provide support and feedback, to engage in mini-conferences with individuals, and to prepare students for homework assignments. But it can also be misused. Too often, seatwork is synonymous with images of bored, passive students doing repetitive, tedious worksheets, while teachers sit at their desks calculating grades or reading the newspaper.

Problems with Seatwork

- The assignment is not meaningful to students.
- The assignment does not match students' varying achievement levels.
- The teacher does not provide students with clear, complete directions.
- The teacher does not monitor what students are doing.
- Students work at different paces, so that some finish early, while others do not finish.

Guidelines for Minimizing the Problems

- Provide assignments that are meaningful and relevant.
- Match the work to varying achievement levels.
- Make sure written and oral directions are clear.
- Monitor behavior and comprehension.
- Plan for ragged endings.

This chapter focused almost exclusively on the situation in which seatwork is assigned to the entire class, but it may sometimes be appropriate to give an assignment to the majority of the class while you work with individuals who need additional help or a more challenging assignment, or conference with students about their grades. This use of seatwork is rare at the secondary level; however, it may be a useful strategy if you need to work with small groups (e.g., if you have an extremely heterogeneous class). But be careful: If you are going to use seatwork this way, you truly need to have "eyes in the back of your head."

ACTIVITIES FOR SKILL BUILDING AND REFLECTION

In Class

1. Select a workbook page or obtain a handout (preferably in your content area), and bring four copies of it to class. In a small group, examine the worksheets, using the following questions as a guide. If you identify problems, suggest a way to improve the tions worksheet.
   - Are the directions clear?
   - Does the page organization facilitate students' understanding of the task?

- Does the activity reinforce the intended skill?
- Is the task meaningful?
- Are the pictures a help or a distraction?

2. Select a workbook page or obtain a handout (preferably in your content area), and bring four copies of it to class. Working in a small group, examine the pages that students have brought to class. For each page, note the topic, describe the format of the worksheet, identify the skill being practiced or extended, and generate an alternative activity that would accomplish the same goal. An example is provided.

Topic	Description of Worksheet	Skill	Alternative
Who fired the first shot at Lexington and Concord	*Three accounts by individuals who observed or participated in events at Lexington and Concord; students are to determine point of view for each account*	*Identifying point of view and bias*	*Choose two of the following characters (a British officer, an American militiaman, a French reporter, the minister's wife at Lexington, a maid at the inn in Concord) and tell the story of the events at Lexington and Concord from their respective points of view.*

On Your Own

1. Interview two to four middle or high school students to learn their perceptions about seatwork. If possible, select students who vary in terms of achievement level. Include the following questions in your interview:
   - In what classes is seatwork used most? Least?
   - To what extent is seatwork used in your academic classes?
   - Under what circumstances is seatwork useful/useless? Interesting/boring?
   - What do your teachers generally do when the class is doing seatwork? Are there consistent differences among teachers in this regard?
   - Are you generally allowed to ask for help from peers or do you have to work alone?

2. Observe a class, preferably in your content area, and note how much time is allocated to independent work during a typical period. During that time, observe three "target" students. Try to select a high-, average-, and low-achieving student. Note what activities each student is required to do during independent work time. (Are the activities the same across achievement levels?) Every two or three minutes, record if the students are on-task or off-task. If possible, ask the students to explain what they are doing and why.

For Your Portfolio

Select a topic in your content area and identify an instructional objective (e.g., "Students will be able to describe the process of photosynthesis"). Then design three independent work activities that all target that objective. Differentiate the activities, so that advanced students, average students, and struggling students can have an assignment well matched to their abilities. In a brief commentary, explain what the objective is and how you are differentiating.

FOR FURTHER READING

Tomlinson, C. A. (2001). *How to differentiate instruction in mixed ability classrooms* (2nd ed.). Alexandria, VA: Association for Supervision and Curriculum Development.

    Tomlinson explains what differentiated instruction is (and isn't), provides a look inside some differentiated classrooms, presents the "how tos" of planning lessons differentiated by readiness, interest, and learning styles, and discusses the complex issues of grading and record keeping. An appendix provides a useful summary of instructional and managerial strategies for differentiated, mixed-ability classrooms.

Tomlinson, C. A. (2005). Differentiated instruction. Special theme issue of *Theory Into Practice, 44*(3).

    This issue of *TIP* examines the concept of differentiated instruction from a variety of perspectives. Authors define the need for differentiated instruction, clarify some of the issues, and provide specific guidance for making classrooms more effective and efficient for all learners in today's schools.

MANAGING SMALL-GROUP WORK

Keep your eyes on your own paper.

Work without talking to your neighbor.

Pay attention to the teacher.

If you need help, raise your hand.

Do your own work.

These are the norms of the traditional classroom, a setting in which students have little opportunity to interact, assist one another, and collaborate on tasks. (See Figure 10.1.) Phrases like these are so much a part of the way we view classrooms that 4-year-olds who have never even attended kindergarten use them when playing school.

This lack of interaction is unfortunate, especially in today's heterogeneous classrooms. Letting students work together in pairs or small groups has many advantages. Donnie and Christina alluded to one advantage in Chapter 8: If students can help one another during classwork, they are less likely to "get stuck," to have to sit and wait for the teacher's assistance, and to become uninvolved and disruptive. In addition, working with peers on tasks can enhance students' motivation, especially for those students who have negative attitudes toward school and classroom work (Pell, et al., 2007). Small-group work can also have positive effects on achievement, as students debate and discuss, ask questions, explain, and evaluate the work of others (Walters, 2000). When students work in heterogeneous groups, they can develop relationships across gender, racial, and

"This class will stimulate your ideas and thoughts. And remember — no talking."

Figure 10.1   Source: Reprinted by permission of Warren.

ethnic boundaries (Ginsburg-Block, Rohrbeck, & Fantuzzo, 2006; Kutnick, Ota, & Berdondini, 2008; Oortwijn, Boekaerts, Vedder, & Fortuin, 2008). Group work can also help to integrate students with disabilities into the general education classroom (Johnson & Johnson, 1980; Madden & Slavin, 1983). Finally, as Rachel Lotan (2006) observes, group work can help teachers build more caring, equitable classrooms, in which "students serve as academic, linguistic, and social resources for one another and are accountable to each other individually and as members of a group" (p. 525).

Given all these benefits, why is there so little group work in secondary classrooms? Part of the answer has to do with the teacher's responsibility for keeping order and covering curriculum. In the crowded, complex world of the classroom, it's easier to keep order and cover curriculum when teachers do the talking, and students do the listening. Furthermore, if the school culture equates orderly classrooms with quiet classrooms, teachers may feel uncomfortable when group work raises the noise level. Consider this student teacher's journal entry:

Every time I read about group work it sounds so great I'm ready to use it everyday. Then I attempt it in the classroom and I start having second thoughts. I love the learning that comes out of it, but I never feel in control when it is happening. The part that really upsets me is that I really do not mind if the class gets loud. It's the other teachers and the principal I worry about. There have been a few times when I was using cooperative learning and someone has come in to ask if I need any help or they will take it upon themselves to tell my class to be quiet. This really makes me angry. I feel like the only acceptable noise level is no noise at all.

Finally, like seatwork, group work has its own set of challenges and potential pitfalls that can make it difficult for teachers to manage. This chapter examines those special pitfalls. It then discusses ways they can be minimized, drawing on the experiences of our four teachers, as well as the research and scholarly literature on group work.

THE PITFALLS OF SMALL-GROUP WORK

Let's begin by considering the recent experience of Ralph, a student teacher in social studies. During a recent meeting, Ralph recounted his first attempt to use group work with his third-period U.S. History I class:

> *We were working on sectional differences—the period from 1800 to 1850, when the Northeast, the West, and the South were like three different countries. I wanted my kids to research the views that each section of the country had on three topics—tariffs, slavery, and the role of the federal government. I didn't want to just lecture, or have them read out of the textbook and then discuss the material, and it seemed like this could be a great cooperative learning activity. My kids haven't had much experience working in groups, but my cooperating teacher is really good about letting me try new things, and he said, "Sure, go ahead and see what happens."*
>
> *I decided to do this over two days. On the first day, I planned to divide the class into the three sections of the country and have each group learn about its section's position on the three topics. I only have 20 kids in this class, so I figured that would be about six or seven kids in each group, which seemed about right. At the end of the first day, they were supposed to pick someone to be their section's spokesman— Daniel Webster from the Northeast, John C. Calhoun from the South, and Henry Clay from the West. The second day, these three spokesmen would debate the issues.*
>
> *So I come into class all fired up about this great thing we're going to do. It didn't seem important to have the groups be absolutely equal in size, and I figured if the kids could choose their own section they'd be more motivated. So I told them they could decide what section of the country they wanted to study. I told them, "If you want to do the Northeast move to this corner, and if you want to do the South move to that corner, etc. Ready, move." Well, it didn't work out. First of all, most of the kids wanted to be the West or the South—there were like nine people in the West and six people in the South and only four people in the Northeast. Plus—I couldn't believe it—the West was all girls (White and Asian American), the South was this really juvenile group of White*

boys (I just knew they would never get anything done), and the North-east was my three African American kids and Rick Moore, this White basketball player! And this really quiet, insecure kid just kind of stood there in the middle of the room, not knowing where to go. I had to start asking people to switch and they weren't very happy about that and started making comments about how I didn't know what I was doing and when was Mr. M going to come back and do some "real teaching."

Well, I finally got some of the girls from the West to move into the Northeast group so the sections were about the same size, and I explained what they were going to do. I told them to use their text, and I showed them all the resource materials I had gotten from the library, and told them to use them too. I explained that they were all supposed to help one another research their section's views on tariffs, slavery, and the role of the federal government. Then they were to work together to write a position paper outlining these views and choose someone to be Webster, Calhoun, or Clay for tomorrow's debate. By this time there's only about 25 minutes left, so I tell them to get to work right away. Well, most of them just sat there and stared and kept saying things like, "I don't understand what we're supposed to do." A few kids got up and went back to their desks to get their textbooks and pencils (of course, I had forgotten to tell them to take their books and stuff with them when they moved), and I went around giving out paper, but a lot of the kids just sat there.

I kept going around and trying to get them to work. When I'd come over, they'd begin to jot down notes, but I think they were really just act-ing like they were working, to get me off their back. Finally, some of the kids in the West and the Northeast began looking up stuff in their texts and taking notes, but they weren't helping each other much. I just could not get them to work together! And some of the kids never did anything—they just sat and let the other kids do it. I even heard comments like, "Let Allison be Clay—she's the smartest one in history." Meanwhile, the guys in the South spent most of the time fooling around and laughing. And they kept putting each other down, saying things like, "He's too dumb to be Calhoun.... We don't have any smart kids in this group," and yelling, "Hey Mr. G, we need some smart kids in this group." I kept asking them to be quiet and get to work but they just ignored me.

At the end of the period I told them they'd have to finish looking up their section's views for homework. Then I told them to decide on their spokesman, and of course nobody wanted to do it. In the West, they decided that this one kid who's really conscientious should do it. In the South, they fooled around a lot and then finally this real wise-guy says OK, he'll do it. Well, he was absent the next day, so there was no Cal-houn, which they seemed to think was really funny.

All in all, these were two of the worst days of my student teach-ing experience. After reading all these education theorists who say that cooperative learning is such great stuff, I had been real excited, but now I'm not so sure. Maybe if your class is really motivated to begin with, it would work, but my class is not all that great (the really smart kids are in Honors History), and maybe they just can't work together like this.

Unfortunately, Ralph's story is not unusual. It illustrates all too vividly what can happen when teachers don't understand the potential problems associated with group work and don't work to prevent them from occurring. Let's take a closer look at four of these problems.

First, as Ralph discovered, allowing students to form their own groups often leads to *segregation* among students in terms of gender, race, and ethnicity. Have you ever had lunch in the cafeteria of an ethnically diverse school? One glance is enough to see that members of each ethnic and racial group tend to sit together. It is important to recognize that strong forces operate against the formation of cross-ethnic friendships; left to their own devices, most students will choose to be with those they perceive as similar. An even greater barrier to friendship exists between students with disabilities and their nondisabled peers (Slavin, 1991). The Individuals with Disabilities Education Act (IDEA) requires the inclusion of students with disabilities in general education classrooms whenever possible, but mere physical presence is not enough to ensure that these individuals will be liked, or even accepted.

A second problem of group work is the *unequal participation of group members.* Sometimes, this is due to the "freeloader" phenomenon, where one or two students in the group end up doing all the work, while the others sit back and relax. We saw this happen in Ralph's class, when only a few of the students took the research assignment seriously, and one group decided to let Allison, the "smartest" history student, be her group's spokesperson. Although this might be an efficient approach to the task, it's not exactly a fair distribution of responsibility. And those who were freeloading were unlikely to learn anything about sectional differences.

Unequal participation can occur for other, more poignant, reasons as well. In a study of students' perceptions of doing mathematics in a cooperative learning group (King, Luberda, Barry, & Zehnder, 1998), Brett, an average achiever, reported that he often failed to understand the task; consequently, he either withdrew from participation or engaged in distracting, off-task behavior. Similarly, Peter, a low achiever, "was aware that the other students seldom asked for his ideas and if he suggested ideas they never listened to him" (p. 8). In order to save face, he engaged in "silly," "weird" behaviors.

Brett and Peter are good examples of the "discouraged" and "unrecognized" categories in Catherine Mulryan's (1992) typology of passive students (outlined in Table 10.1). It is worth keeping these categories in mind. Although a desire to freeload may be at the root of some students' passivity, it is also possible that uninvolved students are feeling discouraged, despondent, unrecognized, bored, or superior.

PAUSE AND REFLECT

You have just read Ralph's experiences and thoughts about group work. Ralph began with great intentions and optimism. Where did the lesson begin to fall apart? What did he do that contributed to the problems with his lesson? What suggestions might you give to Ralph? Is group work only for honors-level students, as Ralph suggests?

TABLE 10.1 Six Categories of Passive Students

Category	Description	Typical Achievement Level
Discouraged student	The student perceives the group task to be too difficult and thinks it better to leave it to others who understand.	Mostly low achievers
Unrecognized student	The student's initial efforts to participate are ignored or unrecognized by others, and he or she feels that it's best to retire.	Mostly low achievers
Despondent student	The student dislikes or feels uncomfortable with one or more students in the group and does not want to work with them.	High or low achievers
Unmotivated student	The student perceives the task as unimportant or "only a game," with no grade being assigned to reward effort expended.	High or low achievers
Bored student	The student thinks the task is uninteresting or boring, often because it is seen as too easy or unchallenging.	Mostly high achievers
Intellectual snob	The student feels that peers are less competent and doesn't want to have to do a lot of explaining. Often ends up working on the task individually.	High achievers

Source: C. Mulryan, 1992.

Just as some individuals may be passive and uninvolved in the group activity, others may take over and dominate the interaction (Cohen, 1994a, 1994b). Frequently, the dominant students are those with high academic status in the classroom—those who are recognized by their peers as successful, competent students. At other times the dominant students are those who are popular because they are good athletes or are especially attractive. And sometimes dominance simply reflects the higher status our society accords to those who are white and male. Indeed, research has shown that in heterogeneous groups, males often dominate over females (Webb, 1984), while Whites dominate over African Americans and Hispanics (Cohen, 1972; Rosenholtz & Cohen, 1985).

A third pitfall of group work is *lack of accomplishment.* In Ralph's class, a significant amount of instructional time was wasted while students formed groups, and most people didn't get much done even once the groups had formed. A number of students, particularly those in the group doing the South, seemed to view the opportunity to interact as an opportunity to fool around and socialize. Their behavior undoubtedly distracted students who were trying to work. Furthermore, the disruption was upsetting to Ralph, who repeatedly asked students to quiet down—without success.

Finally, a fourth problem associated with group work is students' *lack of coop-eration* with one another. Ralph tells us that the students tended to work alone, and the boys in the "juvenile" group spent a lot of time "putting each other down." Although these kinds of behavior are certainly disappointing, they are not surprising. As we have pointed out, most students have little experience working in cooperative groups, and the norms of the traditional classroom are dramatically different from the norms for successful group work.

Analysis of Ralph's experience demonstrates that *successful group work will not just happen.* If you want your students to work together productively, you must plan the groups and the tasks carefully, teach students new norms, and provide opportunities for them to practice the behaviors that are required. As Sandy comments:

 Sometimes, when beginning teachers do group work, they think, "I'll divide my students into groups and that's it. That's all I have to do." They don't plan the groups and they don't plan the group work. That's where they get into trouble. You not only have to think about how you're going to get your kids into groups, but what you're going to do after they're in the groups. You have to plan it so carefully, and it's not an easy thing to do.

DESIGNING AND IMPLEMENTING EFFECTIVE GROUP WORK

This section of the chapter presents some general strategies for avoiding the pitfalls of group work, based on research and the experiences of our four teachers. (These strategies are summarized in the Practical Tips box.)

Decide on the Type of Group to Use

Students can work together in a variety of ways. Susan Stodolsky (1984) has identified five different types of group work: helping permitted, helping obligatory, peer tutoring, cooperative, and completely cooperative. The first three types of groups can be considered "collaborative seatwork" (Cohen, 1994a). All of them involve students assisting one another on individual assignments. In a *helping permitted* group, individuals work on their own tasks, and they are evaluated as individuals; however, they are allowed—but not required—to help one another. *Helping obligatory* situations differ only in that students are now *expected* to offer mutual assistance. In *peer tutoring,* the relationship between the students is not equal: An

PRACTICAL TIPS FOR

**DESIGNING AND IMPLEMENTING EFFECTIVE
GROUP WORK**

- *Decide on the type of group to use:*
  - *Helping permitted*—students are allowed to assist one another on individual assignments.
  - *Helping obligatory*—students are expected to help one another.
  - *Peer tutoring*—a more skillful peer assists a less skillful peer.
  - *Cooperative*—students share a common goal or end; some division of responsibilities may occur.
  - *Completely cooperative*—students share a common goal and there is little or no division of labor; all members of the group work together to create the group product.

- *Decide on the size of the group:*
  - Partners are usually more appropriate for younger students.
  - Groups of 4–5 are generally recommended, and 6 is the upper limit.

- *Decide on group composition:*
  - Think carefully about achievement level, gender, cultural/linguistic background, race/ethnicity, ableness, and social skills.

- *Structure the task for positive interdependence by having students:*
  - Share materials.
  - Work toward a group goal, grade, or reward.
  - Share information.
  - Share talents and multiple abilities.
  - Fulfill different roles (materials person, timekeeper, recorder, facilitator, reporter, etc.).

- *Ensure individual accountability:*
  - Make sure that all group members are held responsible for their contribution to the goal.
  - Assess individual learning.
  - Differentiate responsibilities according to students' individual needs.

- *Teach students to cooperate:*
  - Help them to understand the value of cooperation.
  - Provide group skills training.
  - Provide the chance to evaluate their group-work experiences.

- *Monitor learning, involvement, and cooperative behavior:*
  - Monitor groups and intervene when needed.

"expert" is paired with a student who needs help, so assistance flows in only one direction. Peer tutoring is a particularly useful way of meeting the needs of students with disabilities and those who are learning English as a second language.

Cooperative groups differ from these helping situations in that students now share a common goal or end, instead of working on completely individual tasks. In a *simple cooperative group,* some division of responsibilities may occur. For example, a group researching the Civil War might decide that one student will learn about the causes of the war, while another learns about famous battles, and a third learns about important leaders. Tasks are carried out independently, but everyone's assignment has to be coordinated at the end in order to produce the final joint product.

More complex is a *completely cooperative group*. Here, students not only share a common goal, but there is little or no division of labor. All members of the group work together to create the group product. This was the type of group work that Ralph tried to implement when he directed his history students to research their section's views on tariffs, slavery, and the role of the federal government and then develop a position paper. (Of course, his students could have decided to divide up the research assignment, and then coordinate their findings, but Ralph did not direct them to do so.)

It is important to keep these distinctions in mind as you plan group work. *Different types of groups are suitable for different types of activities, and they require different kinds of skills.* (See Table 10.2.) In helping situations, for example, students are ultimately responsible for completing individual tasks. Although these students need to know how to ask for help, how to explain and demonstrate (rather than simply providing the right answer), and how to provide support and encouragement, they do not need the more complex skills required in truly cooperative situations where they share a common goal.

TABLE 10.2 Different Types of Groups

Type of Group	Skill Required	Example of an Activity

Helping permitted
Helping obligatory
	Ask for help
	Explain
	Provide support and
	  encouragement
		Creating clay sculptures:
		  Students ask each
		  other for assistance and
		  opinions, but everyone
		  completes an individual
		  sculpture.

Peer tutoring	Ask for help
	Explain
	Provide support and
	  encouragement
		Tutor helps tutee to
		  complete a set of
		  chemistry problems.

Cooperative group	Divide group task into
	  individual tasks
	Coordinate individual efforts
	  to produce final group
	  product
		Survey on what students do
		  after school: Each group
		  member interviews
		  students at one grade
		  level, then pool data to
		  make a group graph.

Completely cooperative	Take turns
	Listen to one another
	Coordinate efforts
	Share materials
	Collaborate on a single task
	Solve conflicts
	Achieve consensus
		Determining political party
		  affiliation: As a group,
		  decide if a hypothetical
		  person is a Democrat or
		  Republican.

As an example of a helping situation, let's consider the following activity that we observed in Christina's class:

Christina's students are working in small groups, sorting through work they have done, selecting items to include in their portfolios, and completing "portfolio selection sheets," where they explain why they chose that particular assignment and which criteria it demonstrates. Some of the talk is commentary on progress, not directed to anyone in particular: "I'm going to choose this piece. I finally understood the difference between metaphors and similes." "I love the alliteration in this poem." But there are also requests for assistance and opinions: "Which of these two would you choose?" "How many things are we supposed to select?" "Do you like this one or this one?" "I don't understand what it means here . . ."

In contrast to helping situations, cooperative groups require skills beyond requesting and giving appropriate assistance. Students must be able to develop a plan of action; they must be able to coordinate efforts toward a common goal; they must be able to evaluate the contributions of their peers and give feedback in a constructive way; they must monitor individuals' progress toward the group goal; they must be able to summarize and synthesize individual efforts. Consider the following example, provided by Donnie:

In my basic skills class, I work on collecting, analyzing, and depicting data. I have the students work in groups of four. Each group has to create a survey designed to learn what high school kids do after school—for example, how much they play computer games, watch TV, just hang around, play basketball, have an after-school job, do homework. Then, each group has to interview 80 students in the high school, and each person in the group is responsible for interviewing 20 students at one grade level (in other words, one person interviews all freshmen, one interviews all sophomores, and so on). Each person has to collect his or her own information, but then they have to come together to make a group graph showing how people at all four grade levels manage their time. Kids know that they can't complete the project unless everybody does their part, so they really get on each other's case if somebody isn't working.

Completely cooperative groups with no division of labor present even greater challenges. Not only must students be able to take turns, listen to one another carefully, and coordinate efforts, but they must also be able to collaborate on a single task, reconcile differences, compromise, and reach a consensus. During one visit to Fred's class, we observed a good example of a completely cooperative group activity. The class was divided into groups of four or five to consider profiles of eight hypothetical Americans (e.g., "A union member working in an automobile plant in one of the large factories located in the Industrial Belt that includes Buffalo, Cleveland, Toledo, Detroit, Chicago, and Milwaukee. He is a college graduate"; "A bank executive in a small county seat in Colorado. She is concerned about her career, is unmarried, and is about to buy her own home"). For each profile, students had to determine the probable party affiliation (or lack of one), the kinds of issues that would be important to the individual in a campaign, and whether the individual was likely to be a voter or a nonvoter. Although students were required to carry out individual tasks, they had to coordinate their individual efforts if the groups were to be successful:

 Fred hands out the worksheet describing the eight hypothetical American voters (or nonvoters). He explains that students will first do the task individually, taking notes for each profile. When everyone is finished, he divides the class into groups of four or five. Fred explains that students are to share their opinions, being sure to provide their reasoning. He encourages the groups to work toward consensus on each hypothetical voter and suggests that a different person serve as recorder for each voter. Each group will be expected to report on their results to the rest of the class.

Students begin to go through the eight profiles, sharing their responses. Fred circulates, asking students to explain their reasoning ("Why do you think he's a Democrat?"), commenting on their responses ("I can't believe how confident you people are!"), and checking on group process ("What number are you on? Has everyone had a chance to be a recorder for at least one profile?").

When the groups have finished, Fred announces that Group B will be the first group to report out. The four members of Group B stand in the front of the room. Sandra reports on the group's opinions about the first two profiles: "We think he's a Democrat. He definitely votes. We think he cares about auto safety." The reports continue, with Fred interjecting questions and comments.

Although this activity first required students to think through their responses as individuals, they then had to work together to construct a group report. They had to decide who would be the recorder and reporter for each profile, take turns explaining the reasons for their ideas, listen respectfully to one another, reject ideas without being destructive, and reach consensus on what to report. These are not easy skills to learn—even for adults.

As these three examples illustrate, the more interdependent students are, the more skills they need to cooperate successfully. It's a good idea to use simpler types of groups when you are just starting out. In Ralph's case, we can see that he began with the most complex kind of group work. He set up a situation in which students who were not even used to helping one another were expected to cooperate completely.

Spencer Kagan has developed a vast array of simple group structures that can be used at a variety of grade levels and in many content areas. Learn more about Kagan in Box 10.1.

Decide on the Size of the Group

To some extent, the size of the group you use depends on the task you assign. Pairs are appropriate when foreign language students are preparing a dialogue to role-play, or when home economics students are reviewing weights and measures in preparation for a test. Groups of two maximize students' opportunity to participate. They are also easier for beginning teachers to manage, and teachers of younger or less mature students often prefer pairs over larger groups that require more elaborate social skills. Even with high school students, Sandy makes sure to provide students with experiences in pairs before using cooperative groups.

MEET THE EDUCATORS   BOX 10.1

MEET SPENCER KAGAN

Spencer Kagan is a former clinical psychologist and professor of psychology and education. In 1989, he created Kagan Publishing and Professional Development, which offers materials, workshops, and graduate courses on topics such as cooperative learning, multiple intelligences, emotional intelligence, brain-friendly instruction, and classroom energizers. Dr. Kagan developed the concept of "structures," content-free ways of organizing social interaction among students. His structures are used in classrooms worldwide.

Some Major Ideas about Cooperative Learning

1. In a traditional classroom, teachers use structures such as "whole-class question-answer." In this structure, the teacher asks a question, students raise their hands to respond, and the teacher calls on one person. This is a *sequential structure,* in which each person participates in turn, giving little time per pupil for active participation. This structure also leads to competition among students for the attention and praise of the teacher.
2. Teachers can increase opportunity for student participation by following the *simultaneity principle.* For example, if all students pair up to discuss a question, half the class is talking at any given moment.
3. From a wide array, teachers select the structures that are most appropriate for their specific objectives. Some structures are useful for team building or for developing communication skills; others are most suitable for increasing mastery of factual material or for concept development.
   - "Numbered Heads Together" is appropriate for checking on students' understanding of

content. Students "number off" within teams (e.g., one through four). When the teacher asks a question, team members "put their heads together" to make sure that everyone on the team knows the answer. The teacher then calls a number, and students with that number may raise their hands to answer.
   - In "Timed Pair Share," students pair up to share their responses to a question posed by the teacher. First Student A talks for a minute, and then Student B has a turn. This simultaneous interaction allows all students to respond in the same amount of time that it would have taken for just two students if the teacher had used the more traditional "whole-class question-answer" structure.

Selected Books and Articles

Kagan, S. (1989/90). The structural approach to cooperative learning. *Educational Leadership, 47*(4), 14.

Kagan, S. (1994). Cooperative learning and the gifted: Separating two questions. *Cooperative Learning, 14*(4), 26–28.

Kagan, S. (2001). Teaching for character and community. *Educational Leadership, 59*(2), 50–55.

Kagan, S. (2006). Cooperative learning, the power to transform race relations. *Teaching Tolerance,* 53.

Kagan, S., & High, J. (2002). Kagan structures for English language learners. *ESL Magazine, 5*(4), 10–12.

Kagan, S., & Kagan, M. (2008). *Kagan cooperative learning.* San Juan Capistrano, CA: Kagan.

Website: www.kaganonline.com.

In the following vignette, we see Donnie use pairs of students in a helping situation:

Donnie is reviewing problems that involve different kinds of angles (supplementary, complementary, and vertical). After going through a number of problems on the board, Donnie announces that students will be doing the next set by themselves. She explains: "Please listen to what you're going to do next. On this assignment, you may confer with one other person. You're going to count off: one, two, three. [The students do so.] If you are a number one, you will start with problem number 19, and then go up by 3's (22, 25, 28, 31, 34, and 37). If you are a number two, your problems will start with 20, and go up by 3's. If you are a number three, your problems will start with 21, and go up by 3's. Pair yourself up with someone who has the same number that you have. Your job is to help one another understand the problems. You have 20 minutes to do these. Please have them ready to be passed in at the end of the period."

In situations where the task is an ambitious one that requires a division of labor (e.g., the survey on what high school students do after school), it makes sense to form groups larger than two. Groups of three are still relatively easy to manage, but you need to make sure that two students don't form a coalition, leaving the third isolated and excluded (Cohen, 1994a).

In general, educators recommend cooperative groups of four or five (Cohen, 1994a), and six is usually the upper limit (Johnson, Johnson, Holubec, & Roy, 1984). Keep in mind that as group size increases, the "resource pool" also increases; in other words, there are more heads to think about the task and more hands to share the work. It is also true, however, that the larger the group, the more difficult it is to develop a plan of action, allocate turns for speaking, share materials, and reach consensus.

Decide on Group Composition

In addition to deciding on the type and size of your groups, you must think carefully about group composition. As we mentioned earlier in this chapter, group work can provide opportunities for students to develop relationships with those who are different from themselves. For this reason, educators (e.g., Slavin, 1995) generally advise teachers to form groups that are heterogeneous with respect to gender, ethnicity, race, linguistic background, and ableness. On the other hand, it is important to be sensitive to the fact that trying to achieve heterogeneity can place a burden on students who must be separated from those with whom they feel most comfortable.

Let's consider a concrete example provided by Beth Rubin (2003), who studied two untracked ninth-grade classes in a diverse urban high school. The teachers of these classes were committed to using group work so that students could "learn about one another, appreciate differences, and develop the ability to work with others" (p. 553). However, since African American students were a racial minority, constructing groups that reflected the racial makeup of the class led to "one

Black kid in each group" (p. 553). Thus, when Tiffany and Christie, two African American students, wanted to be placed in the same group, their teacher said no. Instead, each was assigned to a group with three European American students they did not know well. As Rubin comments, "having one African American student in each group usually meant that that student did not have any close friends in that group" (p. 553).

Teachers also need to consider whether small groups will be heterogeneous or homogeneous with respect to achievement level. At times, homogeneous groups can be useful; for example, you may want to form a helping group of several students who are all working on a particular mathematics skill. In general, however, educators recommend the use of groups that are heterogeneous in terms of academic performance (Cohen, 1994a; Slavin, 1995).

One reason for this recommendation is that heterogeneous groups provide more opportunities for asking questions and receiving explanations. But keep in mind that creating academically heterogeneous groups does not guarantee that students will actually engage in these behaviors. Research indicates that students' interactions in groups appear to mirror the behavior of their teachers (Webb, Nemer, & Ing, 2006): If teachers model the role of the teacher as active problem-solver, with students as passive recipients of instruction, this is the behavior that students demonstrate in small groups. Research also suggests that the productivity of the group is more a function of the interactions among the students than their ability levels (Webb & Mastergeorge, 2003). Thus, preparing students for group work by modeling productive helping interactions appears to be more important than the academic heterogeneity of the group.

Another variable you need to consider when deciding on group composition is social skill. In fact, Fred focuses more on social skills and personalities than on academic ability:

First I think about who can't be in the same group, and I say, "Okay, he goes in Group 1, and she goes in Group 2, etc." Then I think about who the nicest people in the class are—the people who can get along with everybody—and I spread them out too. Then I separate the loudmouths—the kids who are not good listeners and who tend to talk a lot. Finally, I think about the kids who need "special handling." Maybe somebody who doesn't speak English, or maybe someone who's very sensitive or shy. I think, "Which group will not destroy this person?" and I try to put that kid in a group that will be most supportive.

As Fred's comments indicate, groups work better when students' personalities and social skills are taken into consideration. Some students have difficulty working with others—they may be unusually volatile, or angry, or bossy—and it makes sense to distribute them across the groups. On the other hand, some students have unusual leadership abilities; others are particularly adept at resolving conflicts; still others are especially alert to injustice and can help to ensure that everyone in the group has a chance to participate. When forming groups, it generally makes sense to disperse students like these too, so that each group has the benefit of their talents. All four teachers follow this practice; however, Sandy and Donnie occasionally find it useful to put all of the leaders in one group. Donnie explains:

> At first, the kids in the other groups say, "Oh, we don't have anybody good in our group. This isn't fair." They sort of sit there aimlessly, wondering what to do. But with encouragement, they begin to get their act together. It doesn't always work, of course, but sometimes this creates a chance for new leaders to emerge.

Teachers develop different systems for assigning students to groups. Some teachers write each student's name on a note card, along with information about achievement and interpersonal relationships (e.g., with whom the student doesn't get along). Then they rank students in terms of achievement level and assign a top-ranked student and a bottom-ranked student to each of the groups (although many teachers try to avoid extremes). Next, the average students are distributed. Having each student's name on a note card allows you to shuffle students around as you try to form equivalent groups that will work well together.

Trying to create the perfect groups can be a daunting challenge for teachers. Rachel Lotan (2006) suggests another approach—*controlled randomness*—in which teachers make group assignments in the students' presence. Using pocket charts on the wall to display group assignments, teachers shuffle students' names like a deck of cards, and then place the cards in the pockets. After distributing all the cards, teachers review the groups that emerge and make necessary changes. For example, an English language learner might need someone to translate, or two close friends who socialize might need to be separated.

All four teachers use controlled (or uncontrolled) randomness every now and then when they are forming groups. As mentioned in Chapter 8, we once observed Donnie take a deck of playing cards from her desk, walk toward a student, and ask him to help her shuffle:

> "I've never been very good at this. I never learned how." [A few students tease her about her inability to shuffle.] After the cards are shuffled, Donnie moves from student to student, directing each one to "pick a card." As she makes her way around the room, the students and I wonder what she is up to. When everyone has a card, Donnie tells the students to pay close attention. "Now, I need you to find the people with the same number or face card that you have. When you find your partners, choose a table and sit down in a group. Then I'll tell you what you're going to do and pass out the materials." The students get up and walk around the room to find their group members. Once the groups have all formed, Donnie proceeds to give directions for the problem-solving activity they are to do as a group.

After class, we talked about this strategy for forming groups:

> This was the first time I ever tried this. My main reason was to get them talking and working with people other than their normal neighbors. They're in seats they chose on the first day, and some of them are very quiet and shy. They don't like to move around or interact with new people. This made them get up and form some new groups.

Finally, there are times when Donnie, Fred, Sandy, and Christina allow their students to form their own groups, but only for certain kinds of tasks, and not until the students have had substantial experience working in various kinds of groups with almost everyone in the class. For example, Christina allows students to form their own groups for long-term assignments that require work to be done at home. As she comments, "It's just too difficult for students to get together with people other than their friends outside of school."

Structure Cooperative Tasks for Positive Interdependence

If you want to ensure that students cooperate on a task, you have to create a situation in which students perceive that they need one another in order to succeed. This is called *positive interdependence,* and it's one of the essential features that transforms a group work activity into true cooperative learning (Antil, Jenkins, Wayne, & Vadasy, 1998).

One simple strategy for promoting interdependence is to require group members to *share materials* (Johnson, Johnson, Holubec, & Roy, 1984). If one member of a pair has a page of math problems, for example, and the other member has the answer sheet, they need to coordinate (at least a little) if they are both to complete the problems and check their answers. By itself, however, sharing materials is unlikely to ensure meaningful interaction.

Another way to encourage interdependence is to create a *group goal.* For example, you might have each group produce a single product, such as a report, a science demonstration, a poem, or a skit. When Christina's students studied the play *Antigone,* she had students individually read Henry David Thoreau's essay, "Resistance to Civil Government," and then meet in groups to (1) define civil disobedience in their own words; (2) explain the purpose of civil disobedience; (3) list three to five real-life examples of civil disobedience; and (4) predict how the issue of civil disobedience is important in the play. Christina explained how group members were to discuss each part of the assignment, combine their ideas, and turn in one paper from the whole group. Although requiring a group product increases the likelihood that students will work together, Christina recognizes that this strategy is not foolproof: One person in the group can do all the work while the others remain uninvolved.

A stronger way to stress the importance of collaborating is to give a *group grade or group reward.* For example, suppose you want to encourage students to help one another with the symbols for chemical ions. You can do this by rewarding groups on the basis of the total number of ions correctly supplied by all the members of the group. You can also give bonus points to every group in which all students reach a predetermined level of accomplishment. Some teachers give each group member a number (e.g., one to four) at the beginning of class, and then spin a numbered spinner or toss a die to select the number of the group member whose homework or classwork paper will be graded (Webb & Farivar, 1994). Then everyone in the group receives that score. Such a practice clearly increases the pressure on group members to make sure that everyone's homework or classwork is complete and well done.

Another way of promoting collaboration is to structure the task so that students are dependent on one another for *information* (Johnson, Johnson, Holubec, & Roy,

1984). In Donnie's lesson on collecting and displaying information, for example, group members had to pool their individual data on adolescents' after-school activities. Since each student was responsible for collecting data on one grade level, they needed each other in order to construct a graph depicting the activities of freshmen, sophomores, juniors, and seniors.

Jigsaw, one of the earliest cooperative learning methods (Aronson, et al., 1978), is a good example of a group-work situation in which students need one another if they are to complete the task successfully. Here, heterogeneous teams are responsible for learning academic material (usually a narrative, such as a social studies chapter) that has been divided into sections. Each team member reads only one section of the material. The teams then disband temporarily, and students meet in "expert groups" with other people who have been assigned the same section. Working together, they learn the material in these expert groups and then return to their home teams to teach it to their teammates. Everyone is responsible for learning all the material, so successful task completion requires students to listen carefully to their peers. One note of caution is needed, however, as a recent study (Souvignier & Kronenberger, 2007) found that students tended to learn the section they were assigned, and were less inclined to learn the material their peers presented.

You can also foster interdependence by creating rich, complex tasks that require *multiple abilities* (e.g., reading, writing, computing, role playing, building models, spatial problem solving, drawing, creating songs, public speaking). By convincing your students that *every* member of the group is good at *some* of these and that *no* member of the group is good at *all* of them, you can reduce the differences in participation between high- and low-status students and enable those who are often left out to contribute (Cohen, 1994a, 1994b, 1998). Listen to Donnie:

> I have one girl who is not very good in math, but she's a great artist. When we were doing group projects on baking cookies, I put her in a group that I knew would be receptive and sensitive, and I structured the activity so there would be a need for artwork. I try to show them that we're not all good at the same things, but that we bring different strengths and weaknesses to the table.

Finally, you can assign *different roles* to group members, requiring each role to be fulfilled if the group is to complete the task. For example, Fred sometimes designates a recorder, a timekeeper, an encourager (to facilitate participation), a taskmaster (to keep people on track), a summarizer (to report out at the end of the group session), and an observer (to monitor group process). At times, the roles that Fred assigns are integral to the activity itself. In a social studies simulation on reconstruction, students form "Presidential Advisory Committees" to advise President Andrew Johnson on a program for the South after the Civil War. Groups have to provide guidance on weighty issues:

- Are the southerners who lately rebelled against us citizens? Shall they have the same rights and privileges as other loyal Americans?

- What shall we do with the leaders of the rebellion, especially General Lee and President Davis?

- How can I make sure that the South is governed by leaders loyal to the United States?
- Are the soldiers who fought against us traitors?
- What shall we do about the former slaves? Should they be given citizenship? Should they be allowed to vote? Should we pay former slave owners for the loss of their slave "property"?

Each Presidential Advisory Committee is composed of characters with very different backgrounds and points of view. Here are a few examples:

- The Reverend Harry (Harriet) Stone, 43 years old, deeply religious, attended college in Virginia, not very active in the Abolition Movement. Believed slavery is immoral but felt John Brown took things "too far."
- William (Mary) Hardwick, 52, a rich mill owner from Delaware, two sons fought in the war, the youngest was killed in the Wilderness while serving under Grant. Manufactures shirts and has profited from government war contracts, which have been canceled since Lee's surrender at Appomattox. Southern distributors still owe you $40,000 for purchases made before the war began.

Having a variety of roles ensures that everyone has a role to play and that all students have to participate if the group is to succeed.

Ensure Individual Accountability

As we discussed earlier in the chapter, one of the major problems associated with group work is unequal participation. Sometimes individuals refuse to contribute to the group effort, preferring to "freeload." Sometimes more assertive students dominate, making it difficult for others to participate. In either case, lack of participation is a genuine problem. Those who do not actively participate may not learn anything about the academic task; furthermore, the group is not learning the skills of collaboration.

One way to encourage the participation of all group members is to make sure that everyone is held responsible for his or her contribution to the goal and that each student's learning is assessed individually. *Individual accountability* is the second essential feature of cooperative learning—and it is one that teachers most often neglect (Antil, Jenkins, Wayne, & Vadasy, 1998).

There are several ways to establish individual accountability. You can require students to take individual tests on the material and receive individual grades; you can have each student complete an identifiable part of the total group project; or you can call on one or two students from each group to answer a question, explain the group's reasoning, or provide a demonstration. One morning in May, we watched Sandy explain that students were going to be working on understanding the idea of equilibrium. She divided the class into groups of three, explained the task, and reminded students that they needed to work together to discover the operative principle. Before she allowed them to begin work, however, she stressed that a group should not consider itself through until all group members understood, since everyone would eventually be taking an individual quiz. In other words, Sandy made it very clear that every student would be accountable for explaining the process of equilibrium.

Ensuring accountability does not always mean that every student has to perform the same activity or be responsible for the same material. Within a heterogeneous cooperative group, it is sometimes desirable or necessary to differentiate tasks by complexity and quantity (Schniedewind & Davidson, 2000). In other words, students can engage in tasks at different levels of difficulty or learn different amounts of material. The important point is that "every student learns something that he or she doesn't already know" and can "contribute to a common goal" (p. 24). For example, each student in a heterogeneous group might be responsible for reading a segment of a biography of Harriet Tubman. Students who are struggling readers might be assigned a relatively short portion of the book and review it with a resource teacher or an aide before the class activity, while more proficient readers read a more demanding section. But all students summarize their reading, report to one another, and are held accountable for knowing about all aspects of Tubman's life. According to Schneiedewind and Davidson, students do not appear to feel awkward or resentful about differentiated assignments like these. Indeed, they are well aware of one another's capabilities and seem to "feel more comfortable when teachers acknowledge and engage them in discussion about the tension-producing subject of academic difference" (p. 25). One teacher, for example, explained to her students that differentiated assignments helped her to fulfill her responsibility to challenge each student.

Teach Students to Cooperate

Recently, one of us read the following entry in a reflective paper written by a student teacher in English:

> *I have tried to use cooperative learning activities as much as possible but I'm not at all sure it's been beneficial. . . . Students spend more time goofing off than getting anything done. I'm not convinced that cooperative learning can work unless (1) students are mature enough to work without a teacher breathing down their necks and (2) they have the social skills to interact with peers.*

This student teacher has come to understand the fact that students' social skills can make or break a group work activity. What he fails to understand, however, is the role of the teacher in *teaching* these skills. Indeed, one research study compared students in groups that were taught to work cooperatively to students who were just placed in groups (Gillies, 2008). The students in the groups given instruction on cooperative work demonstrated more cooperative behaviors during group work, as well as more complex thinking and problem-solving skills, both during the group work and on a follow-up assessment of their learning.

As the classroom teacher, *it is your responsibility to teach students to work together.* This is not a simple process; students do not learn to cooperate in one 45-minute lesson. Indeed, we can think about the process in terms of three stages: learning to value cooperation, developing group skills, and evaluation. Let's consider each of these briefly.

Valuing Cooperation

Before students can work together productively, they must understand the value of cooperation. Sandy introduces cooperative group work early in the year by setting up a situation that students are unable to do alone:

 I tell the kids that they are to solve a particular chemical problem (it's different every year), and that they should go to the lab tables and get started. They look at me as if I'm crazy. They say, "But Ms. Krupinski, you didn't tell us what procedure to use." I tell them I forgot to write out the procedure for them. I say, "Let's see if you can come up with the procedure. You'll get five extra points if you can figure out a procedure by yourself. If you do it in pairs, you'll split the five points, etc." They all start out working alone—they want that five points for themselves. But as the period goes on, they begin to work in groups. They realize that they need each other, that they can really help one another and they don't care about the points. At the end of the period, I say, "Let's talk about what happened here. Why did you start out by yourself?" They tell me, "I wanted the five points, but I had to ask for help because I didn't know enough." We talk about how helpful it is to work together when you're learning something new, and how the points don't matter.

When students are going to work in the same groups over a period of time, it's often helpful to have them engage in a nonacademic activity designed to build a team identity and to foster a sense of group cohesion. For example, when Christina introduces group work, the first task that groups have is to write a summary about the group members. Then Christina calls on someone in each group and asks them to tell her what they learned about the members of the group. Another idea is to have each group create a banner or poster displaying a group name and a logo. In order to ensure that everyone participates in creating the banner, each group member can be given a marker of a different color; individuals can only use the marker they have been given, and the banner must contain all the colors.

Group Skills Training

Teaching a group skill is much like teaching students how to balance equations or use a pipette. It requires systematic explanation, modeling, practice, and feedback. *It's simply not enough to state the rules and expect students to understand and remember.* And don't take anything for granted; even basic guidelines like "don't distract others" and "speak quietly" may need to be taught. Introducing simple norms for group work (Cohen, 1994a) can give students helpful guidelines for what is expected of them:

Ask peers for assistance.

Help one another.

Explain material to other students.

Check that they understand.

Provide support.

Listen to your peers.

Give everyone a chance to talk.

It's helpful to begin by analyzing the group work task you have selected in order to determine the specific skills students need to know (Cohen, 1994a). Will students have to explain material? Will they have to listen carefully to one another? Will they have to reach a consensus? Once you have analyzed the task, select one or two key behaviors to teach your students. Resist the temptation to introduce all the required group skills at once; going too far too fast is sure to lead to frustration.

Next, explain to your students that they will be learning a skill necessary for working in groups. *Be sure to define terms, discuss rationales, and provide examples.* Johnson and Johnson (1989/90) suggest that you construct a "T-chart" on which you list the skill and then—with the class—record ideas about what the skill would look like and what it would sound like. Figure 10.2 shows a T-chart for "encouraging participation."

Finally, you need to provide opportunities for students to practice the skill and to receive feedback. You might have students role play, you might pair the skill with a familiar academic task so that students can focus their attention on using the social skill, or you might have students engage in exercises designed to teach particular skills.

Donnie sometimes teaches group skills in a more "devious" way. She secretly assigns individuals to act out different roles: the dictator, the nonparticipant, the person who tears down everybody else, and the facilitator who encourages participation and listens well. Students engage in some sort of nonacademic activity—perhaps the task of building a tower with pins and straws—and then debrief, sharing their reactions about the group process. An activity like this serves to heighten students' awareness of group skills—and they have fun at the same time.

Regardless of the type of practice you provide, you need to give students feedback about their performance. Fred has found that it's helpful to designate a "process person" or "observer" for each group. This individual is responsible for

Encouraging Participation

Looks Like	Sounds Like
Make eye contact.	What do YOU think?
Look and nod in person's direction.	We haven't heard from you yet.
Gesture to a person to speak.	Do you agree?
Make sure everyone's chair is in the cluster (no one is physically left out).	Anyone else have something to say? I'd like to know what you think. Let's go around to see what each person thinks.

Figure 10.2   A T-Chart for Encouraging Participation

keeping track of how well the group is functioning; for example, he or she may monitor how many times each person speaks. At the end of the group work session, the process person is able to share specific data that the group can use to evaluate its ability to work together.

Evaluation

In order to learn from their experiences, students need the chance to discuss what happened and to evaluate how successful they were in working together. This is especially important when norms for group work are first being established. For example, during one visit to Fred's classroom early in the year, we observed a lesson on U.S. policy toward Afghanistan. Students were working in groups of four or five, trying to reach consensus on a number of politically sensitive questions (e.g., Should the United States maintain a military presence in Afghanistan to train Afghani security and military forces? Should the United States build permanent bases in Afghanistan?). Before students began to work, Fred explained that students were to discuss each question and prepare a report for a special envoy advising the president on Afghanistan. The chairperson of each group was responsible for compiling the report and seeing that all members had an opportunity to participate. Fred made it clear that groups would not be evaluated solely on their reports, but also on how well they worked together—specifically, how quickly they got to work; how involved and engaged they looked; how well group members listened to each other; if members conducted themselves with maturity and decorum; and if all group members had a chance to express their views. During the activity, Fred roamed the room, watching and listening; in addition, the school's media specialist videotaped the entire class.

The following day, Fred spent about half the period evaluating the group activity his students had done. First, Fred talked about how difficult it is to work in groups and told a few "horror" stories about groups in which he had worked. Then he asked students to complete a self-evaluation of their group's interaction. (See Figure 10.3 for one student's evaluation.) Finally, he played the videotape, commenting on the things he had noticed:

[The tape shows students getting into groups, getting organized, and getting to work.] The first thing I did was watch you getting started. I actually timed you, from the moment you entered class to the time the last group was seated and working. It was less than three minutes. I think that was pretty good. [The camera zooms in on each group.] I also looked at how people were seated. [The tape shows a group where four people are clustered and one person is sitting away.] Your physical placement in the group is very important; if you have someone sitting outside the group, it's a good bet that person's not participating. I also tried to watch the way you took turns participating. Look at this. [William's group is shown on the tape.] William was a very organized chairperson. He went around to each person, asking "What do you think? What do you think?" It was very orderly, and everyone got a chance to speak. But what's a drawback? A drawback is you might be disengaged when you're not talking. [Camera shows Frank's group.] Now Frank here ran a more free-wheeling group. There was more arguing back and forth. What's a drawback here? [Student responds.] Yeah, someone can easily get left out. Now take a look at Jan's group. Jan really made an effort to draw people in. . . . I also tried to look at whether any people were dominating the discussion. It really ticks people off if you dominate the group. I'll say that again. It ticks people off. Now what did you people think about the composition of the groups? [Students comment.] I tried to put one person in each chair's group who I thought the chair could relate to. Instead of separating all the friends, I though it might make it easier to chair. Did it? What do you think about having friends in the group?

A far simpler approach to evaluation is to ask students to name three things their group did well and one thing the group could do better next time (Johnson & Johnson, 1989/90). You can also have students consider more specific questions, such as:

Did everyone carry out his or her job?

Did everyone get a chance to talk?

Did you listen to one another?

What did you do if you didn't agree?

After individual groups have talked about their experiences, you might want to have them report to the whole class. You can encourage groups to share and compare their experiences by asking, "Did your group have a similar problem?" "How many groups agree with the way they solved their problem?" "What do you recommend?"

Christina sometimes has students write letters to members of their group, noting the group's strengths and weaknesses, each member's contributions, and what areas need improvement. Afterwards, students pass the letters around their

Figure 10.3   One Student's Evaluation of the Group Work Activity

group, read what everyone has written, and briefly discuss the sentiments that were expressed. They then respond in writing to Christina.

Sometimes this process can be very encouraging for individuals. One very bright senior, for example, was gratified to learn that her less-proficient peers appreciated her patience, encouragement, and explanations. On the other hand, the process can sometimes lead to rancor. During one observation, we saw Christina meet with four students to discuss how they felt about having Nathan—who was now working by himself—rejoin their group. We were curious about what had happened, and after class, Christina explained:

 About a week ago, I had the students write letters to their group. Nathan's was really offensive; it was racist, sexist, and vulgar. The other kids were really upset, for good reason. He said it was all a joke, of course, but he got ISS [in-school suspension] for one day. I also removed him from the group for one week, and I told him we would then discuss whether or not he would go back. I know he's afraid to go back to the group. He knows they're mad. He asked me to check out how they feel about having him come back. They wanted to write their responses to me. Two said they don't want him, and two said they don't care. He's really bright and knows the material, but he's always telling everyone how great he is, and distracting everyone, and the kids get annoyed with him. And of course the letter was the last straw. But he's not learning any social skills sitting there by himself. I think I'm going to put him back in the group for a trial period and see what happens.

PAUSE AND REFLECT

Teachers sometimes use the terms *group work* and *cooperative learning* interchangeably. But although cooperative learning is a form of group work, group work is not always cooperative learning. It is important to be able to explain to students, parents, and yes, administrators the type of learning opportunities you will be using in your class. With this in mind, identify the key elements of cooperative learning that set it apart from other group work.

Obviously, this process can be very sensitive and cause a lot of hard feelings. Things like this don't usually happen, though, because students know that I'm going to collect the letters and that I expect them to give constructive criticism.

Monitor Learning, Involvement, and Cooperative Behavior

During cooperative learning activities, Donnie, Sandy, Christina, and Fred constantly circulate throughout the room, listening, assisting, encouraging, prodding, questioning, and in general, trying to ensure that students are involved, productive, and working collaboratively. For example, during the cooperative learning activity on equilibrium described earlier, Sandy was especially vigilant because she knew that the task was difficult and that students might become frustrated:

 Students are working in groups of three, trying to predict the molecular behavior of three chemical systems. Sandy notices that one group is particularly quiet. She moves over and places her hand on one boy's shoulder. He looks up and tells her: "I don't know what I'm doing." Sandy responds: "Why don't you talk to your group members?" He moves closer to the other individuals. As Sandy approaches another group, a girl indicates that she's "got it." Excitedly, she tries to explain the process to her group and to Sandy, but then collapses in confusion. "I'm just babbling," she says. Sandy decides it's time to intervene: "Okay, let's go back to the question. You have to understand what the question is asking first. What's the question?" In another group, a boy doesn't like the idea offered by a teammate: "I don't want to argue, but I don't think that's right." Sandy reaffirms his behavior: "That's okay. You're supposed to question one another." At one point, Sandy divides one group and sends its members to temporarily join two adjacent groups. "Mrs. K. says I should ask you my question," one boy says to his new group. While Sandy is working with a group on one side of the room, two groups on the other side begin to fool around. One boy has a bottle of correction fluid that he is tossing into the air with one hand and trying to catch with the other (which is behind his back). Sandy notices the disruption: "Excuse me, I don't think you're done, are you?" One group finally discovers the principle that is involved and erupts in a cheer. A girl in another group expresses frustration: "We're clueless over here and they're cheering over there." A few minutes later, Sandy joins this group to provide some assistance.

After class, during her free period, Sandy reflected on the importance of monitoring cooperative learning activities:

Since this was a difficult activity, I expected that there would be some frustration, so it was really important to keep close tabs on what the groups were doing. You can tell a lot just by watching students' physical positions. If kids' heads are down, or if they're facing away, those are good signs that they're not participating or interacting with other group members. Today, I could tell that Richard was going to try the problem as an individual; he was off by himself—until he got frustrated and joined the other students. But that group never really worked well. I thought that Sylvia would help the group along, but she never got completely involved.

I also try to listen closely to what they're saying to one another in terms of group process. Like Mark—he wasn't sure it was OK to disagree. I was glad I heard that so I could reassure him that he's supposed to do that. What's neat is to see how some kids begin to function as really good group leaders. For example, Sivan is really quiet, but she really listens, and she was able to bring in the other two boys she was working with.

You also have to monitor students' progress in solving the problem and try to prevent them from getting completely off track. Today I could see that one group got stuck; the kids were really in a rut, saying the same words over and over. So I split the group up and sent the kids to explain what they were thinking or to ask their questions to two other groups. Sometimes having them talk to other kids can help to move them forward. In this case, it seemed to work. By interacting with a different group, Roy got out of the rut and then he was able to go back and help the kids in his own group.

Research confirms that teacher monitoring helps to promote a high level of student involvement in group activities (Emmer & Gerwels, 2002). By monitoring, you are able to discern when an intervention into the group's activities is necessary. Chiu (2004) studied the way that two ninth-grade algebra teachers monitored small-group problem-solving activities and the impact of their interventions. He found that teachers typically intervened when students were more off-task than usual or had made little overall progress. In general, teacher interventions were beneficial to the group: Students were more likely to be on-task after an intervention from the teacher than before and were more likely to recognize their errors, develop new ideas, and explain ideas to one another. Unfortunately, such positive effects only persisted for about five minutes; eventually, students' attention wandered to other topics, such as events in their personal lives. Results like these underscore the importance of continuing to monitor students' progress.

Another way of monitoring what groups are actually achieving is to build in "progress checkpoints." For example, after two days of having his students try to rewrite the district's "Human Dignity and Affirmative Action" policies, Fred stopped the groups' activity and asked students to report on what they had accomplished and what problems they were having. Similarly, you can divide large assignments into components that are due every few days. This allows you to keep track of how well groups are functioning.

 PAUSE AND REFLECT

Now that you've read about managing group work, go back to your original suggestions for Ralph. What additional ideas might you offer him? What are some key changes he could make to ensure that his next attempt at cooperative learning will be more successful?

CONCLUDING COMMENTS

Although this chapter is entitled "Managing Small-group Work," we have seen that there are actually a number of different group work situations, each with its own set of uses, procedures, requirements, and pitfalls. As you plan and implement group work in your classroom, it's important to remember these distinctions. Too many teachers think that cooperative learning is putting students into groups and telling them to work together. They select tasks that are inappropriate for the size of the group; they use heterogeneous groups when homogeneous groups would be more suitable (or vice versa); they fail to build in positive interdependence and individual accountability; they fail to appreciate the differences between helping groups and cooperative learning. The following example (O'Donnell & O'Kelly, 1994) would be funny—if it weren't true:

> One of our colleagues recently described an example of "cooperative learning" in his son's school. The classroom teacher informed the students that [they] would be using cooperative learning. His son was paired with another student. The two students were required to complete two separate parts of a project but were expected to complete the work outside of class. A grade was assigned to each part of the project and a group grade was given. In this instance, one child received an "F" as he failed to complete the required part of the project. The other child received an "A." The group grade was a "C," thus rewarding the student who had failed to complete the work, and punishing the child who had completed his work. In this use of "cooperative learning," there was no opportunity for the

students to interact, and the attempt to use a group reward (the group grade) backfired. Although this scenario is not recognizable as cooperative learning to most proponents of cooperation, the classroom teacher described it as such to the students' parents. (p. 322)

This example illustrates the need for teachers to acquire an understanding of the intricacies of group work in general and cooperative learning in particular. We hope that this chapter has sensitized you to some of the problems that can arise and has provided you with some strategies for minimizing these problems. Group work is an extremely challenging instructional approach, and successful management requires careful planning and implementation. Despite the potential pitfalls, we believe group work should be an integral part of secondary classrooms—particularly as you work to establish a caring, supportive community.

SUMMARY

This chapter began by talking about the potential benefits of group work and about some of the special challenges it presents. It then suggested strategies for designing and implementing effective group work.

Benefits of Group Work

- Less idle time while waiting for the teacher to help.
- Enhanced motivation.
- Greater achievement.
- More involvement in learning.
- Decreased competition among students.
- Increased interaction across gender, ethnic, and racial lines.
- Improved relationships between students with and without disabilities.

Pitfalls of Small Group Work

- Segregation in terms of gender, ethnicity, and race.
- Unequal participation.
- Lack of accomplishment.
- Lack of cooperation among group members.

Designing and Implementing Effective Group Work

- Decide on the type of group to use (helping permitted, helping obligatory, peer tutoring, cooperative, completely cooperative).
- Decide on the size of the group.
- Decide on group composition.
- Structure the task for interdependence (e.g., create a group goal or reward).
- Ensure individual accountability.
- Teach students to cooperate.
- Monitor learning, involvement, and cooperative behavior.

Group work offers unique social and academic rewards, but it is important to understand the challenges it presents and not to assume that, just because a task is fun or interesting, the lesson will run smoothly. Remember to plan group work carefully, prepare your students thoroughly, and allow yourself time to develop experience as a facilitator of cooperative groups.

ACTIVITIES FOR SKILL BUILDING AND REFLECTION

In Class

1. In small groups that are homogeneous in terms of content area (e.g., math, science, social studies, etc.), choose a topic that you will be teaching and work together to create a completely cooperative activity. As you design the activity, keep in mind the following questions:

   How will you assign students to groups?

   How will you structure the activity to foster positive interdependence?

   What roles will you assign, if any?

   What forms of individual accountability will you build in?

   What are the social skills you need to teach, and how will you teach them?

   How will you monitor the group work?

   How will you provide an opportunity for students to evaluate the group process?

2. Consider the following situation: You regularly use small groups that are heterogeneous in terms of achievement because you believe that students can learn from one another. You also believe that learning to work cooperatively and to appreciate differences are important and valid goals. However, the parents of one of your high-achieving students contact you to complain that their son is not being appropriately challenged and is "wasting his time tutoring the slower kids." In a group, discuss what you might say in response.

3. In a group, read the following excerpt from a teacher-authored case on cooperative learning (Shulman, Lotan, & Whitcomb, 1998).

   Period 3 is one of the six eighth-grade social studies classes I teach each day. . . . [As an experienced proponent of cooperative groups,] I entered into group instruction this year with a good deal of confidence. I met my match with period 3. . . . This is one class in the district that merits a full time Resource Specialist Program teaching aide because we have nine—yes, nine—special education students. We also have 10 sheltered students who have recently left bilingual classes and are now making the transition to full-time English instruction. The makeup of this class creates a disturbing chemistry that is felt within 30 seconds of the starting bell. I usually place them in groups of four or five, then invariably watch in frozen amazement as they torment each other. I persist as I was trained to do, but find myself wondering whether group work is appropriate for this uncooperative classs of 28 students, skewed with a disproportionate number of emotionally needy individuals. . . .

   To sum it up, after 42 minutes with period 3, I feel like a giant, emotion-filled ball being slammed from one side of the room to the other. . . . Whether it's because they lack experience in small-group interaction or they lack self-esteem, or some combination of the two, creating a cooperative atmosphere is not something the students of period 3 seem to be able to accomplish.

At the end of the day I find myself wondering why I don't switch to the more traditional teacher-controlled setting with which these students are more familiar. Perhaps group work is not meant for every class. "It's okay to give up," I tell myself. Yet deep down I tell myself, "It's not okay. I know I need to do something." (pp. 21–23)

In your group, discuss what that "something" might be.

On Your Own

1. Observe a cooperative learning activity. In what ways has the teacher tried to promote positive interdependence and individual accountability?

2. Consider when you might use each of the following types of group work. List an example of an activity from your own content area.
    a.   Helping permitted
    b.   Helping obligatory
    c.   Peer tutoring
    d.   Cooperative group
    e.   Completely cooperative group

For Your Portfolio

Design a cooperative learning lesson on a topic of your choice. Write a brief commentary describing (a) the social skills that are required in this lesson and how you will teach them; (b) the way(s) in which you built in positive interdependence and individual accountability; and (c) how students will evaluate their group interaction.

FOR FURTHER READING

Gillies, R. M. (2007). *Cooperative learning: Integrating theory and practice.* Los Angeles: Sage.

> This book situates cooperative learning within the context of No Child Left Behind and high-stakes testing, arguing that cooperative learning has the potential to transform schools and lead to student success on standardized tests. Chapters in the book deal with establishing successful cooperative groups, promoting student discourse, and assessing small-group learning.

Lotan, R. (2006). Managing groupwork in the heterogeneous classroom. In C. M. Evertson & C. S. Weinstein (Eds.), *Handbook of classroom management: Research, practice, and contemporary issues.* Mahwah, NJ: Lawrence Erlbaum Associates.

> This chapter posits that group work is not only a useful pedagogical strategy for academically and linguistically heterogeneous classrooms, but that it also has the potential to help teachers build equitable classrooms. Lotan addresses the need to teach social skills, assign specific roles, delegate authority to students, and design interventions to combat unequal participation.

Rubin, B. C. (2003). Unpacking detracking: When progressive pedagogy meets students' social worlds. *American Educational Research Journal, 40*(2), 539–573.

> This article is based on a year-long study of two detracked ninth-grade classes, one in English and one in social studies, in a diverse urban high school. Rubin describes how the teachers used group work to facilitate both learning and social interaction across race and class lines and shows how the small groups "often proved to be sites of tension and discomfort where fractures of race and class came to the fore" (p. 541).

Schniedewind, N., & Davidson, E. (2000). Differentiating cooperative learning. *Educational Leadership, 58*(1), 24-27.

   This article provides "guiding tenets" and examples of how to differentiate assignments and responsibilities within heterogeneous cooperative groups.

Slavin, R. E. (1995). *Cooperative learning: Theory, research, and practice* (2nd ed.). Boston: Allyn & Bacon.

   This book provides an excellent introduction to cooperative learning methods, describes various approaches (e.g., Student Team Learning methods, Learning Together, Jigsaw, etc.), and summarizes the research on the effects of cooperative learning on achievement and social-emotional outcomes.

ORGANIZATIONAL RESOURCES

Cooperative Learning Center at the University of Minnesota, 60 Peik Hall, University of Minnesota, Minneapolis, MN 55455 (www.co-operation.org, 612-624-7031). Co-directed by Roger T. Johnson and David W. Johnson, the CLC is a research and training center focusing on how students should interact with each other as they learn and the skills needed to interact effectively.

The International Association for the Study of Cooperation in Education (IASCE), P.O. Box 390, Readfield, Maine 04355 (www.iasce.net, 207-685-3171). Established in 1979, IASCE is the only international, nonprofit organization for educators interested in cooperative learning to promote academic achievement and democratic, social processes. The website provides an annotated list of Web pages related to cooperative learning.

MANAGING RECITATIONS AND DISCUSSIONS

Much of the talk that occurs between teachers and students is unlike the talk you hear in the "real world." Let's consider just one example. In the real world, if you ask someone the name of a particular author, we can assume that you really need to know that information and will be grateful for a reply. The conversation would probably go something like this:

"Who wrote *The Grapes of Wrath?*"

"John Steinbeck."

"Oh, yes, thank you."

In contrast, if a teacher asks this question during a lesson, the dialogue generally sounds like this:

"Who wrote *The Grapes of Wrath?*"

"John Steinbeck."

"Very good."

Here, the question is not a request for needed information, but a way of finding out what students know. The interaction is more like a quiz show (Roby, 1988) than a true conversation: The teacher *initiates* the interaction by asking a question, a student *responds,* and the teacher *evaluates* the response or *follows up* in some way (Abd-Kadir & Hardman, 2007; Mehan, 1979). This pattern of interaction (I-R-E or I-R-F) is called *recitation,* and several studies (e.g., Stodolsky, 1988) have documented the substantial amount of time that students spend in this instructional activity.

The recitation has been frequently denounced as a method of instruction. Critics object to the active, dominant role of the teacher and the relatively passive role of the student. They decry the lack of interaction among students. They condemn the fact that recitations often emphasize the recall of factual information and demand little higher-level thinking. An example of this kind of recitation follows. In this excerpt, 12th-grade students have just finished reading the first act of Shakespeare's *Macbeth*.

MR. LOWE: OK, let's talk about the first act of this play. In the very first scene—which is very brief—three witches are on stage. What's the weather like, Sharon?

SHARON: It's thundering and lightning.

MR. LOWE: Right. What are the witches talking about, Larry?

LARRY: How they're going to meet Macbeth.

MR. LOWE: Good. When are they going to meet him? Jonathan?

JONATHAN: When the battle's done.

MR. LOWE: Right. Okay, let's jump to the third scene. The battle's done, and the three witches tell us that, "Macbeth doth come." So we meet Macbeth and Banquo, two generals in the king's army. They've just returned from the battle. Who were they fighting? Missy?

MISSY: Cawdor.

MR. LOWE: Very good. Now we know that Cawdor was a traitorous rebel, right? Who was he rebelling against, Tanya?

TANYA: King Duncan.

MR. LOWE: Good. What country is Duncan king of? Melissa?

MELISSA: Scotland.

MR. LOWE: Yes. Now, when the witches first speak to Macbeth, what do they call him? Eric?

ERIC: Thane of Glamis.

MR. LOWE: Right. That's his own title, so that makes sense. But then what do they call him?

SUSAN: Thane of Cawdor.

MR. LOWE: Right! So we know that Macbeth is going to be named the new thane of Cawdor. What happens to the old thane of Cawdor? Paul?

PAUL: He's killed.

MR. LOWE: Yes, he's put to death.

An additional criticism focuses on the public evaluation that occurs during recitation. When the teacher calls on a student, everyone can witness and pass judgment on the response. In fact, as Phil Jackson (1990) comments, classmates are sometimes encouraged to "join in the act":

Sometimes the class as a whole is invited to participate in the evaluation of a student's work, as when the teacher asks, "Who can correct Billy?" or "How many believe that Shirley read that poem with a lot of expression?" (p. 20)

Questions like these exacerbate the "negative interdependence" among students that recitations can generate (Kagan, 1989/90). In other words, if a student is unable to respond to the teacher's question, the other students have a greater chance to be called on and to receive praise; thus, students may actually root for their classmates' failure.

Despite the validity of these criticisms, recitations remain an extremely common feature of secondary classrooms. What is there about this instructional strategy that makes it so enduring in the face of other, more highly touted methods?

We thought hard about this question during one visit to Fred's classroom, and our observation of a recitation session that he conducted provided some clues. Students had just read about the controversy over granting China permanent "most-favored-nation" status, and Fred told them he wanted to hear what they thought about the basic issues described in the reading:

FRED: OK, Ms. Harnett, would you start, please?

HARNETT: I was really confused about this article. . . . I think it was talking about how in China there are a lot of political prisoners . . . and we don't like that . . . so we're trying to get them to change. . . . Oh, I don't know, it was confusing.

FRED: You really understand more than you thought. Let's hear from someone else. Jenny.

JENNY: Well, like the United States doesn't like it that China has all these political prisoners . . . but China says leave us alone, our people are doing OK.

FRED: OK, so China's saying that you have to look at the whole picture. You have to look at it from their perspective. [He calls on a student whose hand is raised.] Philip.

PHILIP: The Chinese are saying we keep talking about the dissidents, but they want to look at everyone. And like there's different ideas about human rights.

FRED: Hmmm. Let's talk about that. Let's talk about what we value as basic human rights in the United States. What are some of our basic human rights?

STUDENT: Equality.

FRED: What does that mean, equality? Come over here, Sally. [She comes up and stands next to him.] Are you my equal? Is she my equal?

STUDENT: Well, she's not as big as you are [laughter], and she's probably not as strong, but she's equal in terms of rights.

FRED: Hmmm. So we're not equal in terms of size or strength. Are we equal economically? [Murmurs of "No . . ."] Probably not. Are we equal in terms of power? You bet we're not. [More laughter.] But we have *legal* equality; we've got equal rights under the law. What are some of those rights?

STUDENT: Freedom.

FRED: To do what?

STUDENT: To speak . . . freedom of speech.

FRED: OK. What else?
STUDENT: Freedom of religion.
STUDENT: Freedom to vote.
FRED: OK. In the United States, human rights means individual rights. We emphasize personal freedoms—the right of individuals to follow their own religion, to vote for who they want. But in China, the group is the focus of human rights.

Fred's question-and-answer session helped us to identify five very useful functions of classroom recitations. First, the recitation allowed Fred to assess students' comprehension of the reading and to check their background knowledge on the issue of human rights and most-favored-nation status. Second, by asking intellectually demanding questions (e.g., "What do we mean by equality in the United States?"), Fred was able to prod his students to do some critical thinking and to guide them to some fundamental understandings. Third, the recitation permitted Fred to involve students in the presentation of material. Instead of telling students directly about most-favored-nation status and the debate over human rights, Fred brought out the information by asking questions. Fourth, the recitation provided the chance to interact individually with students, even in the midst of a whole-group lesson. In fact, our notes indicate that Fred made contact with eight different students in just the brief interaction reported here. Finally, through his questions, changes in voice tone, and gestures, Fred was able to maintain a

Fred leads a recitation.

relatively high attention level; in other words, he was able to keep most of his students "with him."

Later, Fred reflected aloud on some other useful functions of recitations:

> I'll use recitation a lot at the beginning of the year because it's a good way to get to know kids' names and to see how they handle themselves in class. It's also a tool for building self-confidence in a new class. They have a chance to speak in class, and I can provide them with opportunities for success early in the year. It's generally a pretty nonthreatening activity; since it doesn't ask for as much higher-level thinking as discussions, it's easier. I also try to emphasize that it's okay not to know, that we can figure out this stuff together. That's what education is.

As we can see, Fred's recitation session was hardly a "quiz show" in which passive students mindlessly recalled low-level, insignificant facts. On the other hand, both the pattern of interaction (I-R-E or I-R-F) and the primary intent (to assess students' understanding of the reading) set it apart from another type of questioning session: the *discussion.* (Table 11.1 summarizes the differences between recitation and discussion.)

TABLE 11.1 Differences between Recitations and Discussions

Dimension	Recitation	Discussion
Predominant speaker	Teacher (2/3 or more)	Students (half or more)
Typical exchange	Teacher question; student answer; teacher evaluation (I-R-E)	Mix of statements and questions by mix of teacher and students
Pace	Many brief, fast exchanges	Fewer, longer, slower exchanges
Primary purpose	To check students' comprehension	To stimulate variety of responses, encourage students to consider different points of view, foster problem solving and critical thinking, examine implications
The answer	Predetermined right or wrong, same right answer for all students	No predetermined right or wrong, can have different answers for different students
Evaluation	Right or wrong, by teacher only	Agree or disagree, by student and teacher

Source: Adapted from Dillon, 1994.

In order to make the distinction clear, let's consider another example from Fred's class. Here, students had been asked to read brief descriptions of hypothetical voters and determine if they were likely to be Democratic or Republican. (See Chapter 10 for a fuller description of this activity.) In this excerpt from the class, Fred was soliciting students' thoughts about the case of a retired school teacher living in New Jersey and dependent upon Social Security:

FRED: What are the indicators that the retired school teacher is left of center? Jeremy, what do you think?

JEREMY: She's from New Jersey.

FRED: Why would that affect her political views?

JEREMY: Well, New Jersey generally votes Democratic.

STUDENT: [Jumping in.] Wait a minute—what about Christie Whitman? She was a Republican governor.

JEREMY: Yeah, but there's a lot of diversity in NJ, and like, I don't know, but I think people tend to be more liberal.

FRED: Anything else here to indicate she might be liberal?

STUDENT: She's a teacher, so she's well educated.

FRED: Hmmmm . . . why would education be a factor that makes you more liberal?

STUDENT: Well it just seems like the more you know the more you understand about other people.

FRED: What other indicators might make you think that she's liberal?

STUDENT: Since she's a teacher, she probably cares about social issues. So that probably makes her more liberal.

STUDENT: Yeah, but she's older and she's retired. I think that would make her more conservative.

FRED: Let's consider that. Would age tend to make her more conservative?

STUDENT: Yeah. That happens.

FRED: Why? Why would age make her more conservative?

STUDENT: Older people are more set in their ways.

FRED: OK, I tend to be more skeptical because I've been around more. I've been dumped on more. But of course, we've got to remember that these are generalizations. I'm going to bring in an older guy who's a far left liberal and a young guy who's real conservative, just to defy the generalizations. OK, what other indicators are there that she's conservative?

STUDENT: She's living on Social Security, so she's probably real concerned about money.

FRED: So she's concerned about money. Why would that make her conservative?

STUDENT: She might vote against social programs that would cost her.

STUDENT: Yeah, like she'd probably vote against the school budget.

STUDENT: I don't agree with that. As a retired teacher, I can't see that she'd ever vote against a school budget.

Later in the interaction, after Fred and the students had decided that the retired teacher was probably a Democrat (but conservative on issues "close to the pocketbook"), Fred stressed the fact that there could be no right answers in this exercise:

> Are we right? I don't know. All we can make are informed generaliza-tions. If there's a right answer here, it's that there's no right answer. But this is not just an exercise in futility that we did. Lots of times in poli-tics, people are given tasks where they are required to make judgments and they don't have enough data to know the right answer. But people can make better judgments—in the absence of complete data—by being more attuned to the indicators. The indicators are useful for making predictions, which is really important in politics. And if it turns out your predictions are right, you're con-sidered a brilliant strategist; if you're wrong, you're fired.

As in the recitation presented earlier, Fred was still very much in charge of this interaction. In fact, we can characterize this as a *teacher-led discussion,* since Fred set the topic, posed the questions, and called on students to speak. Nonetheless, there are some obvious differences. In the discussion, Fred generally initiated the questions and students replied, but he often dispensed with an evaluation of their responses. Thus, the predominant pattern was not I-R-E, but I-R, even I-R-R-R. Fur-thermore, students occasionally initiated questions of their own, both to Fred and to each other, and sometimes they commented on or evaluated the contributions of their peers. Finally, the purpose of this interaction was not to review material or to elaborate on a text. Rather, the teacher-led discussion was intended to stimulate a variety of responses, to encourage students to consider different points of view, to foster problem solving, to examine implications, and to relate material to stu-dents' own personal experiences.

Although educational critics fre-quently decry the use of recitation and promote the use of discussion, both types of interaction have a legitimate place in the secondary classroom—if done well. This chapter begins by examining the managerial pitfalls associated with recita-tions and teacher-led discussions. Next, we consider what our teachers and the research have to say about minimizing these problems and implementing effec-tive recitations and teacher-led discus-sions. The final section of the chapter takes a brief look at yet another type of questioning session—the student-centered discussion—and offers some guidelines for managing this third pattern of interaction.

PAUSE AND REFLECT

Even if you are unfamiliar with the term *recitation,* you have most likely participated in many such question-and-answer sessions during your years in school. In contrast, your experiences with student-centered discussions may be far more limited. Reflecting on the differences between these two, consider the appropriateness of both instructional strategies for the content you plan to teach. Can you think of instances when a student-centered discussion would be appropriate? If so, when would you use such discussions?

THE PITFALLS OF RECITATIONS AND TEACHER-LED DISCUSSIONS

The first pitfall is *unequal participation.* Imagine yourself in front of a class of 25 students. You've just asked a question. A few individuals have their hands up, conveying their desire (or at least their willingness) to be called on. Others are sitting quietly, staring into space, their expressions blank. Still others are slumped down as far as possible in their seats; their posture clearly says, "Don't call on me."

In a situation like this, it's tempting to call on an individual whose hand is raised. After all, you're likely to get the response you want—a very gratifying situation! You also avoid embarrassing students who feel uncomfortable speaking in front of the group or who don't know the answer, and you're able to keep up the pace of the lesson. But selecting only those who volunteer or those who call out may limit the interaction to a handful of students. This can be a problem. Students tend to learn more if they are actively participating. Furthermore, since those who volunteer are often high achievers, calling only on volunteers is likely to give you a distorted picture of how well everyone understands. Finally, restricting your questions to a small number of students can communicate negative attitudes and expectations to the others (Good & Brophy, 2008): "I'm not calling on you because I'm sure you have nothing to contribute." Negative attitudes like this can be communicated even if you have the best of intentions. Listen to Sandy recall a situation in which she made a practice of not calling on a student who seemed painfully shy:

It was my second year of teaching, but I still remember it clearly. My kids did course evaluations at the end of the year, and one kid said I didn't care about students. I was devastated. I tracked her down and asked her why she thought I didn't care. She said it was because I hadn't required her to participate in class discussions. Here I had been trying to avoid causing her embarrassment. She seemed so afraid to talk, so I left her alone. And she interpreted my behavior as saying I didn't care. That taught me a good lesson!

Unequal participation can be a particular problem if you have English language learners (ELLs) in your classes. While ELLs can become proficient in conversations with their peers after about two years of exposure to English, it can take five to seven years for them to acquire grade-level proficiency in academic discourse (Cummins, 2000). Thus, it may be difficult or intimidating for them to take an active role in either recitations or discussions.

Another potential problem is the danger of *losing pace, focus, and student involvement.* In the early 1960s, a popular television program capitalized on the fact that *Kids Say the Darndest Things.* The title of the show aptly describes what can happen during a recitation or discussion. When you ask your question, you might receive the response you have in mind. You might also get answers that indicate confusion and misunderstanding, ill-timed remarks that have nothing to do with the lesson (e.g., "There's gum on my shoe"), or unexpected comments that momentarily throw you off balance. All of these threaten the smooth flow of a recitation or discussion and can cause it to become sluggish, jerky, or unfocused.

Threats like these require you to make instantaneous decisions about how to proceed. It's not easy. For example, if a student's answer reveals confusion, you need to determine how to provide feedback and assistance without losing the rest of the class. During recitations and discussions, you are frequently confronted with two incompatible needs: the need to stay with one person to enhance that individual's learning and the need to move on to avoid losing both the momentum and the group's attention. Donnie reflects on this common situation:

There always seems to be one person who doesn't understand! While you're trying to help that student, the rest of the class begins to mumble things like, "Why are we still doing this? We know this stuff already." Of course, they want you to stay with them when they don't understand, but they get restless if you spend too long on someone else.

When "kids say the darndest things" during a recitation or discussion, you also need to determine if the comment is genuine or if it is a deliberate ploy to get you sidetracked. Fred has had firsthand experience with this particular hazard:

I'll have kids try to get me off on a tangent by asking a question that's out of the blue. It's especially true with sharp kids. When that happens, I'll say, "What a great question. It's not what we're dealing with today, but I'd really like to discuss that with you. Is 2:30 okay or how about tomorrow?"

The third pitfall of recitations and teacher-led discussions is *difficulty monitoring students' understanding.* Recently, a high school teacher talked about a lesson taught by her student teacher, Adrian. The class had been studying the anatomy of various invertebrates, and halfway through the unit, Adrian planned to give his students a quiz. On the day of the quiz, he conducted a brief review of the material by firing off a series of questions on the anatomy of sea stars and sea urchins. Satisfied with the high percentage of correct answers, Adrian then asked, "Before I give out the quiz, are there any questions?" When there were none, he added, "So everybody understands?" Again, there was silence. Adrian told the students to close their books and distributed the quiz papers. That afternoon, he corrected the quiz. The results were an unpleasant shock—a large number of students received Ds and Fs. During a post-lesson conference with his cooperating teacher, he exclaimed, "How could this happen? They certainly knew the answers during our review session!"

This incident underscores the difficulty of gauging the extent to which all members of a class really understand what is going on. As we mentioned earlier, teachers sometimes get fooled because they call only on volunteers—the students most likely to give the correct answers. In this case, Adrian's cooperating teacher had kept a "map" of the verbal interaction between teacher and students and was able to share some revealing data: During a 15-minute review, Adrian had called on only *8* of the 28 students in the class, and all of these had been volunteers. Although this allowed Adrian to maintain the smooth flow of the interaction, it led him to overestimate the extent of students' mastery. Moreover, as Adrian's cooperating teacher pointed out to him, questions that try to assess comprehension by asking "Does everyone understand?" are unlikely to be successful. There's no accountability built into questions like this; in other words, they don't require students to demonstrate an understanding of the material. In addition, students who do not understand are often too embarrassed to admit it. (They may not even realize they don't understand!) Clearly, you need to find other ways to assess if your class is "with" you.

The final pitfall is *incompatibility with the communication patterns that children bring to school.* Although the I-R-E format of recitations is a staple of schools, it stems from White, middle-class values and represents a way of communicating that is not well matched with the discourse styles of many students from different cultural backgrounds (Arends, 2004). For example, recitation generally follows a "passive-receptive" discourse pattern: Students are expected to listen quietly during teacher presentations and then respond individually to teacher-initiated questions. African American students, however, may be accustomed to a more active, participatory discourse pattern ("call-response"). When they demonstrate their engagement by calling out prompts, comments, and reactions, European American teachers may interpret the behavior as rude and disruptive (Gay, 2000). Native Americans may also find the form of recitations unfamiliar and uncomfortable: "In Native-American culture, there is no naturally occurring situation in which a single adult authority regulates who speaks, when they speak, at what volume they speak, and to whom they speak" (Henning, 2008, p. 138). When Native American students are reluctant to participate, European American teachers may conclude that they are uninterested.

Another illustration of incompatibility comes from a teacher who explored students' experiences in her own discussion-intensive seventh-grade mathematics classroom (Lubienski, 2000). Committed to the idea that teachers should engage students in the exploration and discussion of mathematical ideas, she acted as a "facilitator who asked guiding questions instead of an authority figure who told students exactly what to think and do" (p. 398). But this pedagogical approach seemed to have different effects on her socioeconomically diverse group of 18 students. Focusing on the reactions of six European American female students, she found that high-socioeconomic-status (SES) students seemed comfortable with the open nature of the pedagogy; they felt confident to express and defend their own positions and generally perceived the discussions as a useful forum for exchanging ideas. In contrast, lower-SES students said they became confused when conflicting ideas were discussed, seemed afraid to say or believe the "wrong thing," and desired more teacher direction. The teacher speculates that although a discussion-intensive approach to mathematics may be well aligned with middle-class values and norms, it may actually disadvantage lower-SES students.

In addition to cultural and socioeconomic background, gender differences in discourse style may affect students' participation in recitations and discussions. As the linguist Deborah Tannen (1995) notes, boys and girls learn different ways of speaking as they are growing up:

> The research of sociologists, anthropologists, and psychologists observing American children at play has shown that, although both girls and boys find ways of creating rapport and negotiating status, girls tend to learn conversational rituals that focus on the rapport dimension of relationships whereas boys tend to learn rituals that focus on the status dimension. (p. 140)

According to Tannen, females learn to downplay status differences and to stress the ways everyone is the same. They also learn that sounding too sure of themselves will make them unpopular. At the same time, males generally recognize and expect differences in status; in fact, they learn to use language to negotiate their status in the group by displaying their abilities and knowledge. Males in leadership positions give orders, challenge others, and "take center stage by telling stories or jokes" (Tannen, 1995, p. 140). When we consider these very different styles of communication, it is easy to see that the I-R-E pattern of discourse, with its public display of knowledge and its inherent competition, is more compatible with males' communication styles than with those of females (Arends, 2004).

Research on gender and classroom talk has also indicated that "teachers demonstrate a clear bias in favor of male participation in their classes" (Grossman & Grossman, 1994):

> Teachers are more likely to call on a male volunteer when students are asked to recite; this is also true when they call on nonvolunteers. When students recite, teachers are also more likely to listen to and talk to males. They also use more of their ideas in classroom discussions and respond to them in more helpful ways. . . . This pattern of giving more attention to males is especially clear in science and mathematics classes. (p. 76)

Similarly, *How Schools Shortchange Girls* (1992), a study commissioned by the American Association of University Women (AAUW), reports that males often demand—and receive—more attention from teachers. In one study of 10 high school geometry classes (Becker, 1981), for example, males called out answers to teacher questions twice as frequently as females. The same result was obtained in a study of 30 physical science and 30 chemistry classes (Jones & Wheatley, 1990): Whereas the female students appeared "self-conscious and quiet," the males were "more aggressive in calling out responses and tended to use louder tones of voice when seeking the teacher's attention" (p. 867).

Why would teachers allow male students to dominate classroom interaction by calling out? There are three possible reasons: (1) The behavior is so frequent that teachers come to accept it; (2) teachers expect males to be aggressive; and (3) the call-outs may be perceived by teachers as indicators of interest (Morse & Handley, 1985). Whatever

> ## PAUSE AND REFLECT
>
> Reflect on your own experiences with respect to communication patterns that students bring to school. Have you noticed any gender differences in communication styles or differences between students from different cultural backgrounds in any of your classes? How have these differences affected participation in class recitations or discussions?

the reasons, Morse and Handley's study of junior high science classes found that the trend toward male dominance became even greater as students moved from seventh to eighth grade.

DESIGNING AND IMPLEMENTING EFFECTIVE RECITATIONS AND TEACHER-LED DISCUSSIONS

This section of the chapter considers six strategies for designing and implementing effective recitations and teacher-led discussions. As in previous chapters, research on teaching, discussions with our four teachers, and observations of their classes provide the basis for the suggestions. (The Practical Tips box provides a summary of the suggestions.)

Distributing Chances to Participate

Early in the school year, we watched Fred introduce the topics that his Contemporary World Issues class would be studying during the coming year. He explained that students would be examining a variety of cultures, looking at how people make a living in each culture.

> Okay, let's think about what goes into making a living. Make a list of the five most important elements in our economic system that have a bearing on your own life. I'm going to do this too. [Students begin to write. After a few minutes, Fred continues.] Okay, let's see if we can develop a good answer, a consensus. Let's go around the room and each person give one thing.

In this situation, Fred chose to use a "round-robin" technique, which allowed him to give everyone a chance to participate. Since he didn't have to deliberate each time he called on someone, this strategy also enabled him to keep the pace moving.

Sometimes, teachers prefer to use a pattern that is more subtle than the round-robin, so that students do not know exactly when they will be called on. Donnie uses this approach (described earlier in the section on interaction routines in Chapter 4):

> Sometimes I'll start in a front corner, and then go diagonally to the back of the room, then across, and down. I find that using a pattern like that helps me to keep track of who I call on, and it helps me make sure I get to everyone. And it's less obvious than just going up and down the rows. This way, kids are not so aware of who I'm going to call on next. So they don't sit there and try to work out the answer to the problem they know they're going to get. Sometimes, they'll try to figure out the pattern, and they'll say, "Wait a minute, you missed me," but it's like a game.

Instead of a pattern, some teachers use a list of names or a seating chart to keep track of who has spoken. Christina, for example, often records the names of all students who participate during a recitation or discussion, using tick marks to indicate how many times they contribute. When she has the time, she also uses different symbols to indicate types of participation (e.g., responding to a question; asking a question; great idea; adding to something somebody else said). Other teachers use the "popsicle stick system" (described in Chapter 4), pulling sticks labeled with students' names from a can or mug, and placing the sticks on the side after the student has responded.

Whichever system you choose, *the important point is to make sure that the interaction is not dominated by a few volunteers. Some students are just not*

PRACTICAL TIPS FOR

MANAGING RECITATIONS AND TEACHER-LED DISCUSSIONS

- *Distribute chances to participate*
  - Pick names from a cup.
  - Check off names on a seating chart.
  - Use patterned turn-taking.
- *Provide time to think*
  - Extend wait time to three seconds.
  - Tell students you don't expect an immediate answer.
  - Allow students to write a response.
- *Stimulate and maintain interest*
  - Inject mystery and suspense.
  - Inject humor and novelty.
  - Challenge students to think.
  - Incorporate physical activity.
- *Provide feedback to students*
  - When answer is correct and confident, affirm briefly.
  - When answer is correct but hesitant, provide more deliberate affirmation.
  - When answer is incorrect, but careless, make a simple correction.
  - When answer is incorrect but student could get answer with help, prompt or backtrack to simpler question.
  - If student is unable to respond, don't belabor the issue.
- *Monitor comprehension*
  - Require overt responses (e.g., have students hold up response cards, physically display answers with manipulative materials, put thumbs up or down).
  - Use a steering group (e.g., observe the performance of a sample of students, including low achievers, in order to know when to move on.
- *Support the participation of diverse learners*
  - Be conscious of your pattern of asking questions. Track who you call on, how often you call on them, and how you respond to their answers.
  - Become familiar with the discourse patterns characteristic of your culturally diverse students.
  - Consider whether some accommodation to students' discourse style is possible.
  - Teach explicitly about the discourse patterns that are expected in school.
  - Incorporate "alternative response formats" designed to engage all students rather than just one or two.

comfortable speaking in class and seek to avoid the risk of appearing foolish or stupid. Jones and Gerig (1994) examined verbal interaction between teachers and students in four sixth-grade classrooms. They identified *32 percent of the students as "silent."* During interviews, these students typically described themselves as shy (72 percent) and lacking in self-confidence (50 percent). Karen explained her silence by referring to an incident that happened *four years earlier:*

> I talk just a little in class. I'm afraid that what I say, someone won't like. When I was in the second grade, we were going to have a Thanksgiving dinner thing and students were going to be Pilgrims. I raised my hand and said I would like to be an Indian and would wear my hair in braids. Nobody said anything, and the teacher just went "Um hum," and it was embarrassing. (Jones & Gerig, 1994, p. 177)

Sometimes, distributing participation is difficult not because students are reluctant to speak and there are too *few* volunteers, but because there are too *many* volunteers. The more teachers stimulate interest in a particular lesson, the more students want to respond. This means greater competition for each turn, and "bidding" for a chance to speak can become loud and unruly. (See Figure 11.1 for an example of a student very eager to participate.)

Figure 11.1   *Source:* FOXTROT © 2006, Bill Amend. Reprinted with permission of UNIVERSAL UCLICK. All rights reserved.

One useful strategy is to allow several students to answer one question. In the following interaction, we see Christina increase participation by not "grabbing" the first answer and moving on to a new question. She has just focused students' attention on a passage from Edith Wharton's *Ethan Frome,* in which Ethan looks at a cushion his wife Zeena had made for him when they were engaged—"the only piece of needlework he had ever seen her do"—and then flings it across the room.

CHRISTINA: **He throws it across the room. What does this suggest about his feelings for her?**

STUDENT 1: **I think it shows that he really did hate her.**

STUDENT 2: **I think he was fed up, but I don't think he hated her. He had a lot of opportunities to leave her and he didn't.**

STUDENT 3:   I think he just felt so guilty. Guilt overpowered the hate. That's why he didn't leave her.

STUDENT 4:   He wouldn't know how to react to the freedom. I think he's afraid to leave.

CHRISTINA: Good point. Is he not leaving because he's used to the farm, or because of Zeena, or because he's afraid to be alone?

STUDENT 5:   Now that you said that, it made me think, maybe it's not Zeena who has the problem. Maybe it's Ethan. And maybe it would happen again with Mattie. . . .

STUDENT 6:   Yeah. He needs someone to rely on. First he relied on Zeena and his parents. Now she's getting sicker, and he can't rely on her, so he's turning to Mattie.

STUDENT 7:   But if he relied on her when he needed it, why can't she rely on him now that she needs it?

STUDENT 8:   He could slip something into her drink and get rid of her and marry Mattie.

STUDENT 9:   I don't think he hates her enough. He's just fed up with her.

Similarly, in the following vignette, Donnie distributes participation widely by specifying that each student should give only one possible answer to the problem:

DONNIE: Today we start a new adventure—equations with two variables. Our answers are going to be ordered pairs. I'm going to put this up here, $x + y = 3$. [She writes the equation on the board.] Now, if I ask you to give me all the possible answers, what would you say? [There are lots of hands up.] Okay, give me one, Shameika.

SHAMEIKA: (0, 3).

DONNIE: [She writes that on the board.] Okay, give me another. Sharif.

SHARIF: (1, 2).

DONNIE: Another. Tayeisha.

TAYEISHA: (2, 1).

Still another strategy is to have each student write a response and share it with one or two neighbors. This allows everyone to participate actively. You might then ask some of the groups to report on what they discussed.

One final thought: While you're thinking about ways to distribute participation, keep in mind the suggestions made in Chapter 2 for counteracting the action zone phenomenon: (1) Move around the room whenever possible; (2) establish eye contact with students seated farther away from you; (3) direct comments to students seated in the rear and on the sides; and (4) periodically change students' seats so that all students have an opportunity to be up front.

Providing Time to Think

Envision this scenario: You've just asked a well-formulated, carefully worded, higher-level question designed to stimulate critical thinking and problem solving.

And you're met with total silence. Your face begins to feel flushed, and your heart beats a little faster. What to do now?

One reason silence is so uncomfortable is that it's hard to interpret: Are students thinking about the question? Are they asleep? Are they so muddled they're unable to respond? Silence is also troubling to teachers because it can threaten the pace and momentum of the lesson. Even a few seconds of silence can seem like eternity. This helps to explain why many teachers wait less than *one second* before calling on a student (Rowe, 1974). Yet research demonstrates that if you extend "wait time" to three or four seconds, you can increase the quality of students' answers and promote participation. Extending wait time is also helpful to students with learning disabilities, who tend to process information more slowly than their peers.

Sometimes it's helpful to tell students that you don't expect an immediate answer. This legitimates the silence and gives students an opportunity to formulate their responses. During a visit to Fred's class, we saw him indicate that he wanted everyone to think for a while before responding:

We're been talking about how you can use indicators to decide if a person will be a liberal or conservative, a Republican or a Democrat, and some people came to me after school and said they thought that maybe I was encouraging you all to make stereotypes. I'm really glad they brought that up. You should not do an assignment in an unthinking, unquestioning way. So let's talk about this. First, these people obviously thought it was bad to stereotype people. Why? Why is it bad to stereotype people? Before you answer, think. [There's a long pause. Fred finally calls on a student to respond.]

Allowing students to write an answer to your question is another way of providing them with time to think. Written responses also help to maintain students' engagement, since everyone has to construct a response. In addition, students who are uncomfortable speaking extemporaneously can read from their written papers. In the following example, we see Sandy use this strategy:

Sandy is introducing the concept of chemical equilibrium. She has drawn a diagram on the board showing the relative concentrations of A + B and C + D over time. She asks, "Where is equilibrium established? At Time 1, Time 2, or Time 3? Jot it down and write a sentence explaining why you chose T1, T2, or T3." She walks around the room, looking at students' papers. With a little laugh, she comments: "I see a lot of correct answers, and then the word *because*."

During our conversation about her lesson, Sandy recalled an incident that underscored the value of having all students write a response to a question:

I had this girl in my honors class, who came to see me about the second week of school. She was obviously upset about how she was doing; she wanted to drop the class. She started to cry. "Everyone is so much smarter than I am." I asked her how she had come to that conclusion, and it was clear that she was equating response time with ability. I find that a lot of the girls do that. She says, "I'm just in the middle of figuring it out, and the other kids are already answering." She says, "I like it when you ask us to write our answers down first. But when I have to respond orally I'm intimidated."

Once you have selected someone to respond, it's also important to protect their opportunity to respond before allowing anyone else (you included) to jump into the interaction. Watch the way Donnie deals with this situation during a lesson on linear measurement:

DONNIE: Okay, so how are you going to figure this out? (Pause) Eugene.
EUGENE: You have to know how many inches are in a mile.
DONNIE: And how are you going to figure that out? [Eugene is silent, but Ebony is waving her hand.]
EBONY: Ooh, ooh, Miss, I know, I know how to do it.
DONNIE: [very softly] Wait a minute, Ebony, give him a chance. Let him think.

Stimulating and Maintaining Interest

In previous chapters, we have discussed Kounin's classic study (1970) of the differences between orderly and disorderly classrooms. One finding of that study was that students are more involved in work and less disruptive when teachers attempt to involve nonreciting individuals in the recitation task, maintain their attention, and keep them "on their toes." Kounin called this behavior *group alerting.* Observations of our four teachers reveal that they frequently use group-alerting strategies to stimulate attention and to maintain the pace of the lesson. For example, watch how Christina tries to generate interest in "parenthetical documentation"—a lesson that has the potential to be really deadly:

Today we're going to be talking about the next step in doing the research paper—how to cite sources in the body of the paper using MLA format. It's called parenthetical documentation. Now some of you have been asking why you have to learn this. Well, here's an example of a paper using parenthetical documentation. [She puts an excerpt from a paper on the overhead.] This is an excerpt from a 60-page paper [she waves it in the air] written by a friend of mine who works for a sales corporation. The paper doesn't have anything to do with literary analysis; it's a profitability analysis of one of my friend's $2.5 million clients. She's not in English, but we went to high school together, and we learned how to do this there, just like you're learning how to do it now. This is a skill that you'll use in lots of different situations, not just writing a literary analysis for English 10R.

Students' interest can also be stimulated and maintained if you inject some humor or novelty into the recitation itself. During a lesson on the difference between third-person limited narration and third-person omniscient narration, Christina uses Michaela, a student in the class, as an example:

CHRISTINA: Let's say that Michaela comes into the room, goes to her seat, does her journal entry, and then does her group task. We don't know anything at all about how she's feeling inside. That's an example of third-person, limited narration. All we know is what the narrator can see. Now, here's another version: Michaela comes into the room feeling tired, but then she sees the journal topic on the board and gets really excited. She enjoys writing her journal entry, and then enthusiastically moves to her group task. What would that be?

STUDENT: A fairy tale! [Everyone laughs.]

Challenges to students can also be a way of encouraging students to think and to pay attention. Here are a few examples:

FRED: Please listen to this now . . . most Americans don't understand this at all; they don't have a clue. I want you to understand this.

DONNIE: You need to fix this in your minds because we're going to use this later. . . . Now this is not really a trick question, but you'll have to think.

SANDY: This usually isn't covered in a first-year chemistry course. As a matter of fact, it's a problem that I asked on my honors chemistry test. But I know you guys can do it. I have confidence you can do it. Just take it apart, step by step.

These challenges are reminiscent of the behavior of "Teacher X," one of the subjects in Hermine Marshall's (1987) study of three teachers' motivational strategies. Marshall found that Teacher X frequently used statements designed to challenge students to think: "I'm going to trick you," "Get your brain started. . . . You're going to think," "Get your mind started," "Look bright-eyed and bushy-tailed" (stated, according to Marshall, "with enthusiasm and a touch of humor"). This frequent use of statements to stimulate and maintain student attention was in sharp contrast to the typical statements made by the other two teachers in the study (e.g., "The test will be on Thursday." or "Open your books to page 382."). In fact, Teacher Y and Teacher Z *never* used the strategy of alerting students to pay attention, and they rarely challenged students to think. The vast majority of their directives were attempts to *return* students to the task *after* attention and interest had waned.

Another way of engaging students is to make room for personal knowledge and experience. Bracha Alpert (1991) studied students' behavior during classroom recitations and discussions in three high school English classrooms. She found that in two classrooms, students tended to be resistant: They mumbled, refused to answer, and argued. In the third classroom, no signs of student resistance were apparent; instead, students in this class actively participated in discussions. Alpert concluded that the resistance was created by the teachers' tendency to emphasize factual, formal, academic knowledge, without any attempt to relate students' personal life experiences to what was being taught. She provides some examples of this approach: "What's the significance of the dream [in the poem]?" "What is the tone of the poem?" or "What's being implied [by the author] in that scene?" In sharp contrast, the third teacher encouraged students to relate their personal experiences to the literary works they read. For example, when discussing why the literary character is so angry, he asked students to think of things that made them angry. He also asked them questions that promoted their involvement with the literary works—for example, "Do you feel sorry for any of the characters?" "Do you want Eliza to marry Freddy?"

Although it may be easier to do this in subjects like English and social studies, observations indicate that Sandy and Donnie also try to relate topics to students' own personal experiences. For example, when Sandy is introducing acids and bases, she'll begin by inviting students to tell her everything they already know about the topic. Her invitation usually leads to a discussion about fish tanks and pools, and once, they talked about what could happen if a child for whom you were babysitting drank Drano (a base) and why you couldn't use vinegar (an acid) to neutralize it! Similarly, when Donnie teaches about circles in geometry, she talks in terms of bicycles; each spoke of the tire is a radius, and the place where the chain touches the gear is the point of tangency.

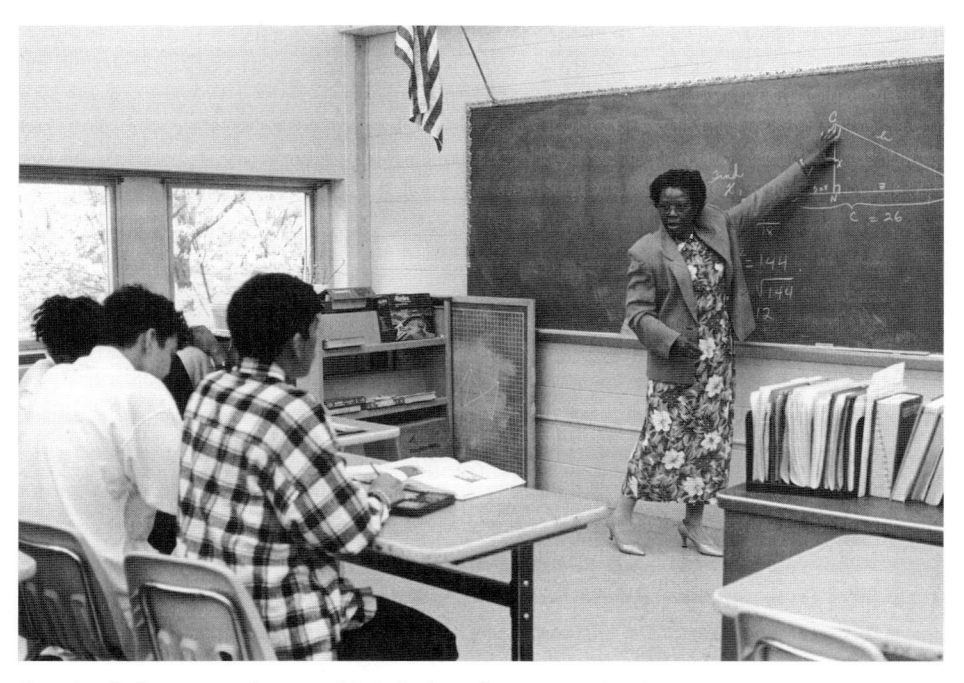

Donnie challenges students to think during a lesson on triangles.

Providing Feedback

Research has demonstrated the importance of providing feedback to students (Fisher, et al., 1980). But how can you provide appropriate feedback while maintaining the pace and momentum of your lesson? Barak Rosenshine (1986) reviewed the research on effective teaching and developed a set of guidelines that may be helpful. According to Rosenshine, when students give correct, confident answers, you can simply ask another question or provide a brief verbal or nonverbal indication that they are correct. If students are correct but hesitant, however, a more deliberate affirmation is necessary. You might also explain *why* the answer is correct ("Yes, that's correct, because . . .") in order to reinforce the material.

When students provide an incorrect answer, the feedback process is trickier. If you think the individual has made a careless error, you can make a simple correction and move on. If you decide that the student can arrive at the correct answer with a little help, you can provide hints or prompts. Sometimes it's useful to backtrack to a simpler question that you think the individual can answer, and then work up to your original question step by step. Watch Sandy:

Students are stuck on the question: "Given the following balanced equation, what volume of hydrogen gas can be produced from the decomposition of two moles of H_2O?" Their faces are blank, and there's absolute silence. Sandy asks: "Well, what is the volume of one mole of any gas at STP [standard temperature and pressure]?" All hands shoot up. Sandy calls on a student to respond. "22.4 liters." Sandy continues: "Do you know the relationship between moles of H_2O and moles of hydrogen gas produced?" Again, there are lots of hands, and a student replies: "It's a one-to-one relationship. The equation shows you that." Suddenly there is a lot of hand-waving, and students begin to call out, "Ooh, I see." "Oh, I got it." With a smile, Sandy motions for them to calm down and wait: "Okay, hold on, let's go back to the original question. Given the following balanced equation, what volume of hydrogen gas can be produced from the decomposition of two moles of H_2O?"

There are times when students are simply unable to respond to your question. When that happens, there's little point in belaboring the issue by providing prompts or cues; this will only make the recitation or discussion sluggish. Donnie sometimes allows students in this situation to "pass." This practice not only helps to maintain the pace, it also allows students to "save face." Meanwhile, she makes a mental note that she needs to reteach the material to the individuals having difficulty.

Donnie is reviewing homework problems on the Pythagorean theorem. "Okay, moving on to number 14." She moves over to Edward and looks as though she's going to call on him. He signals that he doesn't want to answer that question. "Don't call on you? Okay. I'll come back." She moves away and calls on someone else.

The most problematic situation for teachers is when students' answers are clearly incorrect. Saying "No, that's not right" can be uncomfortable, yet students deserve to have accurate feedback. As Sandy emphasizes: "It's really important to be clear about what's correct and what's not. The students have to know that the teacher will not leave them thinking the wrong thing." Rather than directly correcting students, however, Sandy prefers to help them discover their own errors:

I have difficulty saying "Your answer is wrong," but I usually don't have to. I can ask them to explain their reasoning. Or I can take the part of the answer that is correct and work with it. I can ask a question about their response. "How does the graph show that?" "So you're saying it would have to be like this. . . ." I like students to find their own mistakes and correct them.

Similarly, Fred will tell students: "That answer doesn't make sense to me. How did you figure it out?" Sometimes, he compliments students on making a "really good mistake": "I love mistakes. That's how we all learn."

Monitoring Comprehension

A simple way to determine how well your students understand the material is to have them respond overtly to your questions. For example, you can ask them to put their thumbs up or down to indicate agreement or disagreement with a particular statement. You can also have them physically display answers with materials or write down responses. Watch Donnie in this lesson on the properties of circles:

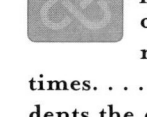

Donnie tells her students to take out a piece of unlined paper, a compass, a ruler, and a pencil. She tells the students: "Now I want to check on your ability to apply the terms that we've been going over, not just regurgitate the definitions. I will repeat the directions two or three times. . . . Draw a circle with a radius of two inches. [She pauses to give the students the chance to do so.] Call the center of the circle point P. . . . From the center, going due south, draw radius PA. Label it. . . . The next thing you're going to do is draw a chord, but listen, the chord you're going to draw is going to bisect PA and go in an east-west direction." As students work, Donnie circulates, checking on how individual students are doing.

Another way of checking on students' understanding is to observe a "steering group." This is a sample of students whose performance is used as an indicator that the class is "with you" and that it's all right to move on to a new topic (Lundgren, 1972). Be careful, however, about choosing students for the steering group. If you select only high achievers, their performance may lead you to overestimate the comprehension of the class as a whole.

During one discussion with Donnie, she explained that a boy in her algebra class was a key member of her steering group:

> I have this one boy who's average in ability. He generally sits in the back of the room, and when he doesn't understand, he gets a certain look on his face. I can tell he's confused. But when he does understand, the "light goes on." When I see the light is on with him, I can be sure most of the other kids understand.

Supporting the Participation of Diverse Learners

By understanding and appreciating the fact that students' home patterns of discourse may be mismatched with the discourse pattern used in recitation, you are better able to ensure that all students in your class—regardless of cultural background, socioeconomic status, or gender—will have equitable opportunities to participate. Although there are no simple solutions, several guidelines may be useful. (These are summarized in the Practical Tips box on recitations.) First, *teachers need to be conscious of their patterns of asking questions, using wait time, and providing praise* (Arends, 2008). This means tracking which students you call on, how often you call on them, and how you respond to their answers. (Since it is difficult to monitor your own questioning patterns, it's helpful to have someone do this for you.) Sandy is one science teacher who does not allow the boys to "grab the floor":

> I find that the boys are often faster at responding than the girls. Boys will call out the answers even if they're not sure, while the girls will sit and think before they give an answer. I really have to stay aware of that and make sure that the girls get an opportunity to respond.

Second, it is essential to become familiar with the discourse patterns characteristic of your culturally diverse students (Arends, 2008). Before assuming that students are being disrespectful by calling out, for example, it's a good idea to ask whether this behavior could represent a culturally learned style of discourse that is appropriate and normal in settings outside of school.

Third, consider whether some accommodation to students' discourse style is possible. For example, during recitations and discussions, "Mr. Appleby," a White, middle-class teacher of 17 low-achieving, predominantly Black students, encouraged his students to call out answers and make comments and did not expect them to raise their hands and speak one at a time. Observing this, Deborah Dillon (1989) reports:

> Appleby also allowed his students to interact with each other and with him, in the way they spoke to peers and adults in their family/community. In other words, within these lessons, Appleby allowed the interactions in his classrooms to be culturally congruent. . . . For example, students often talked sarcastically, interrupted Appleby, or overlapped the speech of other students as they presented their ideas. (p. 245)

Despite this "permissiveness," Dillon observed no disrespect. Students recognized that Appleby had high academic and behavioral expectations, and they met them. As LaVonne commented, "Students obey Appleby's wishes—we act crazy but we calm ourselves down and don't go overboard" (Dillon, 1989, p. 244).

Although accommodation to students' discourse patterns may be possible and appropriate at times, some educators (e.g., Delpit, 1995) argue that teachers need to be explicit about the discourse patterns that are expected (and usually implicit) in school. Indeed, the explicit teaching of this knowledge is considered a teacher's "moral responsibility," since it enables individuals to participate fully in the classroom community and the larger society (Gallego, Cole, & Laboratory of Comparative Human Cognition, 2001, p. 979). Thus, the fourth guideline is to provide explicit instruction on the discourse pattern of recitations (I-R-E) and to allow students to practice these communication skills.

Finally, teachers can incorporate "alternative response formats" designed to engage all students rather than just one or two (Walsh & Sattes, 2005). Some we've already mentioned—such as choral responses, overt responses (e.g., "thumbs up" or "thumbs down"), and work samples (e.g., students individually solve a prob- lem). While these all require students to answer individually, others allow students to work cooperatively before responding to the teacher's question; recall "Numbered Heads Together" and "Timed Pair Share" described in Chap- ter 10. These more active, participatory response formats may be more comfortable for students who find the traditional pattern of question-response-evaluation to be unfamiliar or intimidating.

> ### ◯ PAUSE AND REFLECT
>
> Think about the strategies for managing recitations described in the previous section. What are five of the most important things you will want to keep in mind as you plan a recitation?

FACILITATING STUDENT-CENTERED DISCUSSIONS

In both the recitation and the teacher-led discussion the teacher is in charge, determining the content, the participants, and the pacing. In contrast, the *student- centered discussion* provides an opportunity for students to interact directly with one another, while the teacher acts as a facilitator or moderator.

Consider this example observed in Fred's Institute for Legal and Political Education (IPLE) class. The topic was budget deficits, and Hope had just asked a key question: "Why can't the government just print more money to pay off a debt?" Fred noted that this was an important question, and he attempted to pro- vide an explanation. Hope wasn't convinced. Other students joined in:

SUSAN: I think I got it now. You know how they say that everyone can't be a millionaire. There's got to be some poor people? It's like that.

JOHN: Yeah, like when I play Monopoly. I buy every property, so I go into bankruptcy. So I take out a loan, and I'm ruining the game because I'm not playing with the money I'm supposed to have. It's like cheating.

LORIE: Yeah, that money doesn't really exist.

HOPE: What do you mean? If the government prints the money, it does exist. [A number of students begin talking at the same time.]

FRED: Hold on. Stuart, then Roy, then Alicia.

STUART: The money's worth a lot because there's only a little. If there were a lot, it would only be worth a little.

HOPE: I still don't understand. So what, if it's only worth a little.

ROY: Pretend there's this gold block sitting in Fort Knox and it's worth $10, but there's only one $10 bill. Now if we make up 10 $10 bills, each will only be worth $1.

HOPE: So what? I can still use it to buy stuff. [A few students start to jump in, but Fred intervenes.]

FRED: Alicia hasn't had her chance to talk.

ALICIA: I think I got it now. Let me try. There's this diamond, and we both want it. . . . [She continues to explain, but Hope is still confused.]

FRED: Let's see if I can help out here. . . .

As we can see from this excerpt, Fred essentially stays out of the interaction, except for making sure that students have an opportunity to speak when the interaction gets excited. In contrast to the recitation, or even many teacher-led discussions, students speak directly to one another. They comment on one another's contributions, they question, they disagree, and they explain.

Providing opportunities for student–student discussions means that teachers have to give up their role as *leader* and assume the role of *facilitator*. This can be difficult for teachers who are used to dominating or at least directing the conversation. But acting as a facilitator rather than a leader does not mean abdicating responsibility for guiding the interaction. This became very clear during a conversation with Fred, when he described some of the problems that he tries to anticipate and avoid:

First of all, a discussion like this can be an opportunity for some kids to show how smart they are and to get air time, so it's important to watch out that kids don't pontificate and monopolize. Second, you have to listen carefully and ask yourself, "Where is this going?" I often have an end goal in mind, and I try to make sure that the discussion doesn't get too far afield. Occasionally, I'll jump in and say something like, "I think we're losing the focus here" or "I think you're arguing over semantics." Also, a lot of times kids state opinions as fact, and I think it's important not to let them get away with that. I'll interject and ask them to provide supporting evidence. Or I'll ask for clarification: "Is that what you meant to say?"

Because student-centered discussions can be so difficult for both students and teachers, Christina has developed a strategy she calls "Post-It Note discussions." When students read an assigned text, they choose a passage that especially interests them—it can be a few words, a few pages, or anything in between. They place a Post-It Note near the passage they've chosen, and write responses to questions that Christina constructed (e.g., Why did you choose this passage? What does it

mean? What does it tell you about the rest of the text? What issues are raised here?)
Then they take a second Post-It Note and write a question for discussion. The following exchange is from a Post-It Note discussion on *Ethan Frome:*

> STUDENT 1: My passage is on page 95, beginning with "His impulses . . . ."
> [Students turn to page 95, and she reads the paragraph
> aloud, while everyone follows along.] I chose this passage
> because I think it's the most important in the chapter. It
> shows how Ethan is finally deciding to tell Zeena how he
> feels, but then he begins to change his mind and he's think-
> ing he can't do it. My question is, why do you think Ethan is
> having such a hard time about leaving Zeena?
>
> STUDENT 2: I think he feels it's wrong to leave her because she's sick and she's
> relying on him.
>
> STUDENT 3: I also think he's worried about the money, but it wouldn't stop him.
>
> STUDENT 4: But I do think it would stop him. He can't even afford the train ticket
> to leave her.
>
> STUDENT 3: But in the next sentence, he says he's sure he's going to get work.
>
> STUDENT 5: He's worried he won't be able to support Mattie.
>
> STUDENT 6: He wants to leave but he's afraid of change. . . .

As we can see, the students' role is to pose the discussion questions and to call on
classmates to respond—not a role to which students are accustomed. During the
previous discussion, in fact, a girl asked her question and then seemed paralyzed
in the face of her peers' raised hands. When she turned to Christina for assistance,
Christina quietly reminded her, "You're in charge, Renata." The girl laughed, "I'm
not used to this!"

Being "in charge" is certainly an unfamiliar role for students, but one that students gradually learn to assume with the Post-It Note strategy. After class, Christina
shared her thoughts on the importance of having students take responsibility for
class discussions:

> During my field experiences and student teaching, I often saw class
> "discussions," where the teachers did almost all the talking. I worried
> that I wouldn't be able to run an effective discussion because even the
> most experienced and talented teachers I observed were struggling to
> involve their students. It seemed like it would be torture to stand in front of a
> class and get no response. So I started thinking about how I could get students to
> take more responsibility for the discussion. I always write in the margins of my
> books when a passage interests me, but obviously kids can't do that with the school's
> books. So I hit upon the idea of Post-It Notes. I think it's working pretty well, and
> students' reactions have been overwhelmingly positive. This way, students really
> "own" the discussion. They talk about what interests them, rather than just what I
> think is important. They have to prepare for the discussion by putting their
> thoughts into writing, and that almost always makes it a better discussion. And all
> the students have to participate, at least to read their passage and ask their question.

The hardest part is being quiet. I purposely sit on the outside of the group, so I'm less likely to dominate, but I still have to remind myself a lot to stay out of it as much as possible.

When you're learning to lead a discussion, keep in mind three basic suggestions (Gall & Gillett, 1981). First, it may be wise to *limit the size of the group*. It's difficult to have a student-centered discussion with a large number of participants. Fred's IPLE class has only 12 students, so group size wasn't too much of a problem here, but in a class like Christina's, opportunities to speak are more limited. In his larger classes, Fred sometimes uses the "fishbowl" method, in which five or six students carry on the discussion in the middle of the room, while the rest of the class sits in a large circle around them and acts as observers and recorders. Another solution is to divide the class into small discussion groups of five, with one student in each group acting as a discussion leader.

Second, *arrange students so they can make eye contact*. It's difficult to speak directly to someone if all you can see is the back of a head. If at all possible, students should move their desks into an arrangement that allows them to be face-to-face. (See Figure 2.6 for an example of a room arrangement appropriate for a discussion.)

Finally, *prepare students for participating in a student-centered discussion by explicitly teaching the prerequisite skills:*

- Talk to each other, not just to the moderator.
- Don't monopolize.
- Ask others what they think.
- Don't engage in personal attack.
- Listen to others' ideas.
- Acknowledge others' ideas.
- Question irrelevant remarks.
- Ask for clarification.
- Ask for reasons for others' opinions.
- Give reasons for your opinions.

James Dillon (1994) also provides some extremely helpful guidelines for facilitating discussions. (See the Practical Tips box.) Note that Dillon advises against asking questions during a student-centered discussion for fear of turning the discussion into a recitation. Although his concern is well founded, other discussion experts believe that questions can be an appropriate and effective way to keep conversation going. In fact, Brookfield and Preskill (1999) identify several kinds of questions that are especially helpful in maintaining momentum:

Questions that ask for more evidence:
How do you know that?
What data is that claim based on?

What does the author say that supports your argument?

Where did you find that view expressed in the text?

What evidence would you give to someone who doubted your interpretation?

Questions that ask for clarification:

Can you put that another way?

What do you mean by that?

What's an example of what you are talking about?

Can you explain the term you just used?

Linking or extension questions:

Is there any connection between what you've just said and what Rajiv was saying a moment ago?

How does your comment fit in with Neng's earlier comment?

How does your observation relate to what the group decided last week?

Does your idea challenge or support what we seem to be saying?

Hypothetical questions:

What might have happened if Joey hadn't missed the school bus?

In the video we just saw, how might the story have turned out if Arnold had caught the ball?

If the author had wanted the teacher to be a more sympathetic figure, how might he have changed this conversation?

Cause-and-effect questions:

What is likely to be the effect of the name calling?

How might the rumor affect the school play?

Summary and synthesis questions:

What are the one or two most important ideas that emerged from this discussion?

What remains unresolved or contentious about this topic?

What do you understand better as a result of today's discussion?

Based on our discussion today, what do we need to talk about next time if we're to understand this issue better?

What key word or concept best captures our discussion today?

CONCLUDING COMMENTS

This chapter has focused on three different patterns of verbal interaction: recitations, teacher-led discussions, and student-centered discussions. It's important not to get them confused—to think that you're leading a discussion when you're actually conducting a recitation.

Teachers often say that they use discussion a great deal, when in fact they are conducting recitations. For example, in an observational study (Alvermann, O'Brien, & Dillon, 1990), 24 middle school teachers reported using discussion. Yet only 7 could actually be observed doing so; the others were using

PRACTICAL TIPS FOR

FACILITATING DISCUSSIONS

- Carefully formulate the discussion question (making sure that it is not in a form that invites a yes/no or either/or answer), along with subsidiary questions, embedded questions, follow-up questions, and related questions.

- Create a question outline, identifying at least three subquestions and at least four alternative answers to the main question.

- Present the discussion question to the class, writing it on the chalkboard or on an overhead transparency or on paper distributed to the class. After reading the question aloud, go on to give the sense of the question, identifying terms, explaining the relevance of the question, connecting it to a previous discussion or class activity, and so on. End with an invitation to the class to begin addressing the question.

- Initially, help the class focus on the question, rather than giving answers to it. For example, invite the class to tell what they know about the question, what it means to them.

- DO NOT COMMENT AFTER THE FIRST STUDENT'S CONTRIBUTION. (If you do, the interaction will quickly become I-R-E.) In addition, do not ask, "What does someone else think about that?" (If you do, you invite statements of difference or opposition to the first position, and your discussion turns into a debate.)

- In general, do not ask questions beyond the first question. Use instead nonquestion alternatives: statements (the thoughts that occurred to you in relation to what the speaker has just said; reflective statements that basically restate the speaker's contribution; statements indicating interest in hearing further about what the speaker has just said; statements indicating the relationship between what the speaker has just said and what a previous speaker has said); signals (sounds or words indicating interest in what the speaker has said); even silence. (Dillon acknowledges that deliberate silence is the hardest of all for teachers to do. To help teachers remain quiet, he recommends silently singing "Baa, baa, black sheep" after each student's contribution.)

- Facilitate the discussion by
  - Locating: "Where are we now? What are we saying?"
  - Summarizing: "What have we accomplished? Agreed on?"
  - Opening: "What shall we do next?"
  - Tracking: "We seem a little off track here. How can we all get back on the same line of thought?"
  - Pacing: "Just a minute, I wonder whether we're not moving a little too fast here. Let's take a closer look at this idea. . . ."

- When it is time to end the discussion, help students to summarize the discussion and identify the remaining questions.

recitation or lecture interspersed with questions. These findings are consistent with observations of 1,000 elementary and secondary classrooms across the country, in which discussion was seen only 4 to 7 percent of the time (Goodlad, 1984). Almost 20 years later, the amount of discussion does not appear to have changed: A study of 64 English/language arts classes in 19 middle and high schools found that discussion occurred for only 1.7 minutes per 60 minutes of class time—or 3.8 percent of the time (Applebee, Langer, Nystrand, & Gamoran, 2003). It is clear that real discussion is very rarely used in classroom. As Sandy comments:

> A lot of beginning teachers get these two mixed up. They've been told they're supposed to ask a lot of questions, so they do, but often the questions are yes/no questions or questions that elicit short answers without a lot of depth: What do all atoms have in common? How many protons are in this atom? In discussions, the majority of the questions are critical thought questions, and the response time is longer. You're trying to develop an idea or draw a conclusion. You're not just reviewing; you're working toward a conceptual goal.

Also keep in mind the criticisms that have been leveled against recitations, and reflect on how frequently you dominate the verbal interaction in your classroom. Ask yourself whether you also provide opportunities for student-centered discussion, during which you serve as a facilitator (rather than a questioner) and encourage direct student–student interaction. Reflect on the level of thinking that you require from students. The classroom recitation can serve a number of useful functions, but *overuse* suggests that your curriculum consists largely of names, dates, facts, and algorithms (Cazden, 1988).

SUMMARY

This chapter began by examining some of the major criticisms of recitation, as well as the useful functions it can serve. It then distinguished recitations from teacher-led discussions and considered the potential pitfalls of these two subsettings. Next, the chapter suggested a number of strategies for using recitations and teacher-led discussions successfully in your classroom. Finally, we looked at two examples of a student-centered discussion and briefly considered a number of guidelines for managing this type of verbal interaction.

Characteristic of Recitations

- I-R-E or I-R-F (teacher initiation, student response, teacher evaluation or follow-up).
- Quick pace.
- Used to review material, to elaborate on a text.

Criticisms of Recitations

- The teacher plays a dominant role, the student a passive one.
- There is a lack of interaction among students.
- Recall is emphasized over higher-level thinking skills.
- Recitation promotes public evaluation that can lead to negative interdependence.

Functions of Recitations

- Provides an opportunity to check on students' comprehension.
- Offers an opportunity to push students to construct more complete responses.
- Involves students in presentation of material.
- Allows for contact with individuals in a group setting.
- Helps to maintain attention level.

Characteristics of Teacher-Led Discussions

- I-R (or even I-R-R-R).
- Student-initiated questions.
- Student comments on contributions of peers.
- Slower pace.
- Intended to stimulate thinking, to foster problem solving, to examine implications.

Pitfalls of Recitations and Teacher-Led Discussions

- Unequal participation.
- Losing pace, focus, and student involvement.
- Difficulty in monitoring understanding.
- Incompatibility with communication patterns that students bring to school.

Strategies for Successful Recitations and Teacher-Led Discussions

- Distribute chances for participation:
    Use some type of patterned turn taking.
    Ensure that males and females have equal opportunity to participate.
- Provide time to think about answers before responding.
- Stimulate and maintain interest:
    Use group-alerting strategies.
    Use humor and novelty.
    Include challenges to students.
    Make room for personal knowledge and experience.
- Provide feedback without losing the pace.
- Monitor comprehension:
    Require overt responses.
    Observe a steering group.
- Support the participation of diverse learners:
    Be conscious of patterns of asking and responding to questions.
    Become familiar with discourse patterns of different cultures.
    Accommodate students' discourse styles where possible.
    Provide explicit instruction on discourse patterns of recitations.
    Use alternative response formats.

Facilitating Student-Centered Discussions

- Act as facilitator rather than questioner.
- Ensure that some students don't monopolize.
- Make sure the discussion stays on track.
- Ask students to provide supporting evidence for opinions.
- Limit group size.
- Arrange students so they have eye contact.
- Teach discussion skills.

When planning your lessons, think about the extent to which you use recitations, teacher-led discussions, and student-centered discussions in your classroom. Think about the level of the questions that you ask: Are all of your questions low-level, factual questions that can be answered with a word or two, or are your questions designed to stimulate thinking and problem solving? Ask yourself if you consistently dominate the interaction, or if you also provide opportunities for real discussion among students.

ACTIVITIES FOR SKILL BUILDING AND REFLECTION

In Class

1. Your colleague has asked you to help him figure out why his students are not paying attention in class. He would like you to observe him and offer feedback. What follows is a session you observed. In a small group, identify the trouble spots of his lesson and provide three specific suggestions for improvement. Use what you know about distributing participation, stimulating and maintaining interest, and monitoring comprehension.

    MR. B.: Who remembers what photosynthesis is? [No response.] Do you remember yesterday when we looked at green plants and we discussed how a plant makes its own food? [Mr. B. notices that Thea is nodding.] Thea, do you remember about photosynthesis?

    THEA: Yeah.

    MR. B.: Well, can you tell the class about it?

    THEA: It has something to do with light and chlorophyll.

    MR. B.: Good. Tom, can you add to this? [Tom was drawing in his notebook.]

    TOM: No.

    MR. B.: Tom, Thea told us that photosynthesis had to do with light and chlorophyll. Do you recall our discussion from yesterday when we defined photosynthesis?

    TOM: Sort of.

    MR. B.: What do you mean? Didn't you write down the definition with the rest of the class? Look in your notebook and tell me the definition. [Tom starts to page through his notebook. Many of the students have begun to whisper and snicker. Some are looking in their notebooks.] How many of you have found the page where we defined photosynthesis? [Seven students raise their hands.] Good. Would somebody read to me that definition? Thea.

    THEA: Photosynthesis is the process of forming sugars and starches in plants from water and carbon dioxide when sunlight acts upon chlorophyll.

    MR. B.: Excellent. Does everyone understand? [A few students nod.] Good. Tomorrow we will be having a quiz about plants and photosynthesis. Tom, will you be ready for the quiz?

    TOM: Sure, Mr. B.

    MR. B.: Okay, now let's all turn to page 135 in our science texts and read about the uses of plants.

2. Monitoring students' comprehension is sometimes problematic. In a small group, consider three of the following topics (or think of one in your own content area) and suggest two different ways a teacher could elicit overt participation in order to determine student understanding.

    a. Main characters and their traits.
    b. Characteristics of parallelograms.
    c. Symbols for chemical ions.
    d. Foreign language vocabulary words.
    e. Longitude and latitude.
    f. Types of clouds.
    g. Fat content of various products.

On Your Own

1. Visit a classroom and observe a recitation. On a seating chart, map the verbal interaction by placing a check or an x in the "seat" of each student who participates. (See the example in Figure 11.2.) Analyze your results and draw conclusions about how widely and fairly participation is distributed in this class.

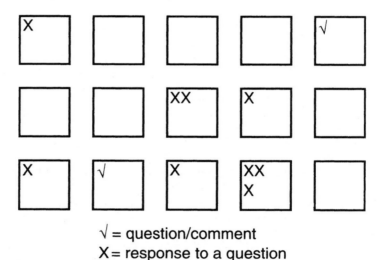

√ = question/comment
X = response to a question

Figure 11.2   An Example of a Seating Chart

2. We know that recitations and discussions are often confused. Observe and record 10 minutes of a class "discussion." Then, using the following checklist, see if the verbal interaction actually meets the criteria for a discussion or if it is more like a recitation.

    • Students are the predominant speakers.
    • The verbal interaction pattern is not I-R-E, but a mix of statements and questions by a mix of teacher and students.
    • The pace is longer and slower.
    • The primary purpose is to stimulate a variety of responses, to encourage students to consider different points of view, to foster problem solving, and the like.
    • Evaluation consists of agree/disagree, rather than right/wrong.

For Your Portfolio

Create two lesson plans, one that includes a recitation and one that includes a student-centered discussion. In sequence, list the questions that you will use for each. In a brief commentary, explain how these lessons differ from each other and why the chosen teaching strategy is appropriate for the content of the lesson.

FOR FURTHER READING

Brookfield, S. D., & Preskill, S. (2005). *Discussion as a way of teaching: Tools and techniques for democratic classrooms* (2nd ed.). San Francisco: Jossey-Bass.

    This book offers a wealth of practical information on how to plan, conduct, and assess classroom discussions. The authors describe strategies for starting discussions and maintaining their momentum. A chapter on discussion in culturally diverse classrooms provides valuable information on eliciting diverse views and voices.

Gambrell, L. B., & Almasi, J. F. (Eds.) (1996). *Lively discussions! Fostering engaged reading.* Newark, DE: International Reading Association.

    The first chapter of this book contrasts recitation and discussion and clearly explains the difference between the two in terms of the teachers' and students' roles. Other chapters offer practical strategies that teachers can use to foster discussions that promote literacy development. The book presents many examples of children collaboratively constructing meaning and considering alternative interpretations of a text in order to arrive at new understandings.

Henning, J. E. (2008). *The art of discussion-based teaching: Opening up conversation in the classroom.* New York: Routledge.

    This is a valuable text for K–12 teachers who want to foster more student-centered discussion in their classrooms. The book provides practical advice for asking questions, guiding discussions, and keeping students involved. A particularly helpful section focuses on ways to support culturally and linguistically diverse students.

Walsh, J. A., & Sattes, B. D. (2005). *Quality questioning: Research-based pracice to engage every learner.* Thousand Oaks, CA: Corwin Press.

    Based on the authors' QUILT framework (Questioning and Understanding to Improve Learning and Thinking), this book discusses preparing questions, presenting questions, prompting student response, processing student responses, teaching students to generate questions, and reflecting on questioning practice. Walsh and Sattes suggest strategies to engage all students in the teacher's questions and prompt students to generate their own questions.

PART IV

PROTECTING AND RESTORING ORDER

Newspaper headlines about crime, violence, and vandalism convey a grim, frightening image of classrooms, but in reality most of the misbehaviors that teachers encounter are far more mundane—inattention, talking to neighbors, not having homework done, calling out, and forgetting to bring supplies and books. Nevertheless, behaviors like these can be aggravating and wearing, take precious time away from teaching and learning, and threaten a caring community. Clearly, teachers must have a way of thinking about such problems and a repertoire of disciplinary strategies for dealing with them effectively.

The two chapters in this section focus on strategies for responding effectively to instances of problem behavior. Chapter 12 begins with a set of *principles* to guide your thinking about how best to respond in a constructive fashion. We then consider a hierarchy of strategies for dealing with a variety of problem behaviors, starting with strategies that are minimally obtrusive and easy to implement and concluding with those that require considerable time and effort. In Chapter 13, we turn to the issue of school violence. First we look at the frequency and severity of school violence. Then we consider approaches for preventing and coping with hostile, aggressive, and dangerous behavior. Throughout, we hear the voices of our four teachers describe how they handle problem behaviors and aggressive behavior.

Both chapters echo themes heard in earlier chapters—namely, the importance of building community and fostering positive teacher-student relationships. When students are inattentive, resistant, or disruptive, it's easy to fall back on punitive, authoritarian reactions—"Stop that or else!" "Because I said so!" "Go to the principal's office!" "That's three days of detention!" But responses like this destroy relationships with students. Resentment builds, defiance escalates, and an atmosphere of "us against them" begins to take hold. Moreover, such responses are usually ineffective, leading teachers to conclude that "nothing can be done with these kids."

As we have stated in earlier chapters, research consistently indicates that students are more likely to engage in cooperative, responsible behavior and adhere to classroom norms when they perceive their teachers to be supportive and caring. Thus, teachers who have positive relationships with students are able to *prevent* inappropriate behavior. But we believe that *teacher-student relationships also play a key role in a teacher's ability to respond effectively to problem behaviors.* If your students perceive you as fair, trustworthy, and "on their side," they are likely to comply more readily with your disciplinary interventions.

RESPONDING EFFECTIVELY TO PROBLEM BEHAVIORS

Not too long ago, we read an entry in the journal of a student teacher whose fourth- and fifth-period English classes were giving her a hard time. It was the middle of November, and Sharon was feeling frustrated by the disrespectful and disruptive behavior of her students. "They just won't sit still long enough to hear directions," she wrote. "I am spending more and more time on telling people to 'Shhh.' I don't understand why they are so rude, and I just don't know what to do." As we read more, it became clear that this student teacher's problem was not due to an absence of clear rules and routines or to boring, tedious instruction:

On the first day that I took over, we reviewed the rules my cooperating teacher had established (just like you suggested!): Come to class on time, don't call out, treat each other with respect, etc. They were really cooperative; I thought this was going to be great, but I guess they

*were just "psyching me out." Now they argue with me all the time.
I say "quiet" and they say, "But I was just telling him . . . ." I say, "Put
the newspaper/comic book/photo album away," and they say "Just
let me look, I have to see . . . ." There doesn't seem much else to do
except repeat myself. Sometimes it works, sometimes it doesn't. . . .
I'm really at my wits' end. If I can't gain some control, there's obviously no way I can teach anything. Sometimes I think I'd be better off
if I just forgot about trying to have interesting discussions, projects,
small groups, etc., and just gave out worksheets every day, lectured,
and didn't allow any talking. That's a far cry from the kind of classroom I wanted to have. I wanted to respect my students, to treat them
like adults, but I found I can't. I've always gotten along great with
kids, but not now. All these kids seem to understand is discipline
referrals and detention.*

This student teacher had learned a sad fact of classroom life: Having clear,
reasonable rules and routines doesn't automatically mean that everyone will follow
them. At the beginning of the school year, students work hard at figuring out the
teacher—determining teachers' expectations and requirements, the amount of
socializing they will tolerate, and how far they can be pushed. (See Figure 12.1.)
Most students will pursue their agendas within the limits the teacher sets, but
they need to know those limits. This underscores the importance of communicating your behavioral expectations to students (the topic of Chapter 4)—and then
enforcing those expectations. Listen to Donnie:

New teachers should not be fooled by the good behavior that students
exhibit at the very beginning of school. I usually find that on the first
day of school, everyone is really subdued. They're checking you out. It
isn't until the second week that they really start testing. That's when the
problems are going to start, and you have to make sure you hold students to the
expectations you set.

Figure 12.1   *Source:* ADAM @ HOME © 1997 by UNIVERSAL UCLICK. Reprinted with permission.

In this chapter, we consider ways of responding to the problems that you may encounter—from minor, nondisruptive infractions to chronic, more serious misbehaviors.

PRINCIPLES FOR DEALING WITH INAPPROPRIATE BEHAVIOR

There is little research on the relative effectiveness of disciplinary strategies (see Emmer & Aussiker, 1990), but six principles guide our discussion. (See Table 12.1.) First, *disciplinary strategies must be consistent with the goal of creating a safe, caring classroom environment.* You need to achieve order, but you also need to choose strategies that support your relationship with students, help them to become self-regulating, and allow them to save face in front of their peers. Richard Curwin and Allen Mendler (1988), authors of *Discipline with Dignity,* put it this way:

> Students will protect their dignity at all costs, even with their lives if pushed hard enough. In the game of chicken, with two cars racing at top speed toward a cliff, the loser is the one who steps on the brake. Nothing explains this bizarre reasoning better than the need for peer approval and dignity. (p. 27)

For more information about Curwin and Mendler, see Box 12.1.

In order to protect students' dignity and preserve your relationship with them, it is important to avoid power struggles that cause students to feel humiliated and ridiculed. (Remember our discussion of "when school was awful" in Chapter 3.) Fred, Donnie, Sandy, and Christina all make a real effort to speak with misbehaving students calmly and quietly. They don't bring up past sins. They take care to separate the student's *character* from the specific *misbehavior;* instead of attacking the student as a person ("You're lazy"), they talk about what the student has done ("You have not handed in the last two homework assignments"). When more than a brief intervention is necessary, they try to meet with students privately.

Table 12.1 Principles for Dealing with Inappropriate Behavior

---

Choose disciplinary strategies that are consistent with the goal of creating a safe, caring classroom environment.

Keep the instructional program going with a minimum of disruption.

Consider the context in deciding whether a particular action constitutes misbehavior.

Be timely and accurate when responding to behavior problems.

Match the severity of the disciplinary strategy with the misbehavior you are trying to eliminate.

Be "culturally responsive," since differences in norms, values, and styles of communication can have a direct effect on students' behavior.

During the first week of school, we witnessed a good example of disciplining with dignity in Sandy's classroom. Even though it was early in the school year,

MEET THE EDUCATORS   BOX 12.1

MEET RICHARD CURWIN AND ALLEN MENDLER

Richard Curwin and Allen Mendler are widely known authors, speakers, consultants, and workshop leaders who focus on issues of classroom management, discipline, and motivation. Curwin has been a seventh-grade teacher, a teacher of emotionally disturbed children, and a college professor. Mendler is a school psychologist who has worked extensively with children of all ages in general and special education settings. Together they developed the *Discipline with Dignity* program, first published in 1988.

Some Major Ideas about Classroom Management:

- Dealing with student behavior is part of the job.
- Management strategies must maintain the dignity of each student.
- Discipline plans should focus on teaching responsibility rather than obtaining compliance.
- In a typical classroom, 80% of the students rarely break rules and don't really need a discipline plan; 15% break rules on an occasional basis and need a clear set of expectations and consequences; 5% are chronic rule breakers. A good discipline plan controls the 15% without backing the 5% into a corner.
- Consequences for rule violations are not punishments. Punishment is a form of retribution; the goal is to make the violator pay for misconduct. Consequences are directly related to the rule; their purpose is instructional rather than punitive because they are designed to teach students the effects of their behavior. Consequences work best when they are clear, specific, and logical.
- Teachers should have a range of alternative consequences, so they can use discretion in choosing the best consequence to match the particular situation.
- Teachers need to teach the concept that "fair is not always equal."

Publications

Curwin, R. L., & Mendler, A. N. *Discipline with Dignity* (2nd ed). 1999. Alexandria, VA: Association for Supervision and Curriculum Development.

Mendler, A. N., & Curwin, R. L. (1999). *Discipline with Dignity for Challenging Youth*. Bloomington, IN: National Educational Service.

Mendler, A. N. (2001). *Connecting with Students*. Alexandria, VA: Association for Supervision and Curriculum Development.

Curwin, R. L. (2003). *Making Good Choices: Developing Responsibility, Respect, and Self-Discipline in Grades 4–9*. Thousand Oaks, CA: Corwin Press.

Website: www.tlc-sems.com

some students had already begun to test Sandy's adherence to the rules she had distributed a few days earlier:

Sandy stands by the door, greeting students as they come in. The bell rings; Sandy begins to close the door, when William breathlessly rushes up. "You're late," she tells him quietly. "Does that mean I have to come after school?" he asks. "I'll talk to you later," she replies and moves to the front of the room to begin the lesson.

Later in the period, students are working in small groups on a lab experiment. Sandy circulates through the room, helping students with the procedure. She goes over to William and pulls him aside. She speaks softly: "You owe me 10 minutes. Today or tomorrow?"

"What's today?"

"Tuesday."

"Uh-oh." William looks worried.

"Is it better for you to come tomorrow?" Sandy asks.

"Yeah—but will you remind me?"

"I certainly will," she says with a rueful smile. Sandy goes over to her desk, makes a note in her grade book, and then continues circulating. A few minutes later, she stands beside William again, helping him with a problem and encouraging his progress.

In this vignette, we see how Sandy tried to avoid embarrassing William by speaking with him privately; how she demonstrated concern for William by offering him a choice about when to come for detention; how she avoided accusations, blame, and character assassination; and how she showed William that she held no grudge by helping with the lab a few minutes later. In short, the vignette demonstrates the way a teacher can communicate clear expectations for appropriate behavior while preserving a positive teacher-student relationship.

The second principle for dealing with misbehavior is that it is essential to *keep the instructional program going with a minimum of disruption.* Achieving this goal requires a delicate balancing act. On one hand, you cannot allow inappropriate behavior to interrupt the teaching–learning process. On the other hand, you must realize that disciplinary strategies themselves can be disruptive. As Walter Doyle comments, interventions are "inherently risky" because they call attention to misbehavior and can actually pull students away from a lesson (1986, p. 421). In order to avoid this situation, you must try to anticipate potential problems and head them off; if you decide that a disciplinary intervention *is* necessary, you need to be as unobtrusive as possible.

Watching the four teachers in action, it is clear that they recognize the importance of protecting the instructional program. In the following incident, Christina sizes up a potentially disruptive situation and is able to maintain the flow of her lesson:

Christina is reviewing the difference between first-person and third-person narrative. In the back of the room, students are passing some photographs around. Christina continues to talk about narrative while she moves up the aisle. In between sentences, she gives the students a quizzical look, as if to say, "What are you folks doing?" Everyone returns the photographs to a girl who puts them in her backpack.

The third principle is that *whether or not a particular action constitutes misbehavior depends on the context in which it occurs* (Doyle, 1986). There are obvious exceptions to this notion—punching another person and stealing property are obvious violations that always require a teacher response. But other behaviors are not so clear cut. For example, in some classes, wearing a hat, sitting on your desk, chewing gum, and listening to your MP3 player are all misbehaviors, while in other classes these are perfectly acceptable. What constitutes misbehavior is often a function of a particular teacher's tolerance level or the standards set by a particular school. Even within a class, the definition of misbehavior is dependent upon the context. A teacher may decide that talking out of turn is acceptable during a class discussion, as long as students' comments contribute to the lesson and the situation doesn't turn into a free-for-all; at other times, this same teacher may feel that a more structured lesson is needed.

When determining a course of action, you need to ask yourself, "Is this behavior disrupting or benefiting the ongoing instructional activity? Is it hurtful to other students? Does it violate established rules?" If the answer to these questions is no, disciplinary interventions may not be necessary.

"I've got no control today," Fred announces with a grin. A glance around the room seems to confirm his assessment. Some students are sitting on their desks; others are standing in the aisles, leaning over other students who are writing. In the back of the room, four students are turned around in their seats and are having an animated discussion. One girl is standing by Fred's desk, loudly debating with a girl seated nearby. Just about everyone is talking. After a few moments, the topic of all this heated conversation becomes clear. Because of severe winter storms, the school district has exceeded the normal allotment of snow days. In order to meet the state mandate for 180 days of school, the board of education must now decide whether to eliminate spring break or extend the school year. Fred has seized the opportunity to teach a lesson on political activism. His students are to think about the issue, consider whether there should be a waiver from the 180-day mandate, and write to their state legislators. Today's assignment is to construct the first draft of the letter. After class, Fred thinks about the atmosphere in the class: "I know I could have exerted a lot more control over the situation. I could have told them to sit quietly, to jot down ideas, and then silently write a first draft. But what would I have gained?"

The fourth principle is to *be timely and accurate when responding to behavior problems.* Jacob Kounin (1970) identified two common errors that teachers make when attempting to handle misbehavior in the classroom: timing and target mistakes. A timing mistake is when a teacher waits too long to correct a misbehavior. For example, a teacher might not realize (or has ignored) that several students have called out responses without raising their hands, and sternly reprimands the next student to do so. Not only is this timing mistake unfair to that particular student, but calling out may have already become a habit for the students and much more difficult to curb than if it were corrected immediately.

Similar to timing mistakes, target mistakes call attention to one particular student when in fact one or more others are at fault. A student may kick the backpack of the girl in front of him and the girl gets reprimanded for yelling in class. The student who threw the paper airplane that hit the teacher may go unnoticed while a student closer to the teacher is blamed for the incident. Mistakes like these are understandable, since instances of inappropriate behavior are often ambiguous and occur when the teacher is looking elsewhere. For this reason, care must be taken to respond accurately and in a timely manner.

The fifth principle emphasizes the importance of *making sure the severity of the disciplinary strategy matches the misbehavior you are trying to eliminate.*

Research (e.g., Pittman, 1985) has indicated that some teachers think about mis-behavior in terms of three categories: *minor misbehaviors* (noisiness, socializing, daydreaming); *more serious misbehaviors* (arguing, failing to respond to a group directive); and *never tolerated misbehaviors* (stealing, intentionally hurting some-one, destroying property). They also consider whether the misbehavior is part of a pattern or an isolated event.

When deciding how to respond to a problem, it is useful to think in terms of these categories and to select a response that is congruent with the serious-ness of the misbehavior. This is easier said than done, of course. When misbe-havior occurs, teachers have little time to assess its seriousness, decide if it's part of a pattern, and select an appropriate response. Nonetheless, you don't want to ignore or react mildly to misbehavior that warrants a more severe response; nor do you want to overreact to behavior that is relatively minor. For example, a firm reminder to the class to lower the noise level is an appropriate response to this minor misbehavior, while your response to a student who has disrupted the class for the third time today might be to have a private conference with him.

Finally, the sixth principle stresses the need to be *"culturally responsive," since differences in norms, values, and styles of communication can have a direct effect on students' behavior.* Being culturally responsive means reflecting on the kinds of behaviors you judge to be problematic and considering how these might be related to race and ethnicity. For example, Gail Thompson (2004), an African American educator whose research focuses on the schooling experiences of students of color, notes that African American children are often socialized to talk loudly at home—a behavior that gets them into trouble at school. Listen to the mother of an eighth-grader who was starting to be labeled as a discipline problem at school for this reason:

> She's a loud person. My husband is a loud person, and when they get to explain themselves, they get loud. Their voices go up. Then, the teachers think she's being disrespectful. She's gotten a referral for that once. (Thompson, 2004, p. 98)

Similarly, African American youngsters tend to be more intense and confron-tational than European American youngsters; they are more likely to challenge school personnel since they see leadership as a function of strength and forceful-ness (rather than as a function of position and credentials); and they may jump into heated discussion instead of waiting for their turn (Irvine, 1990). Teachers who subscribe to the dominant culture are likely to see these behavioral patterns as examples of rudeness and disruptiveness, to respond with anger, and to invoke punitive measures. Alternatively, teachers who view the behaviors as reflections of cultural norms are better able to remain calm and nondefensive and to consider a variety of more constructive options (e.g., discussing classroom norms and the need for turn-taking in large groups). Indeed, they may actually come to see the benefits of allowing intensity and passion to be expressed in the classroom and broaden their definition of what is acceptable student behavior.

In addition, culturally responsive classroom managers are aware of the ways that race and ethnicity influence the use of disciplinary consequences. Research conducted over 30 years repeatedly shows that African American and Latino students, particularly males, are disproportionately referred for behavior problems compared to their majority counterparts (Skiba, et al., 2008). In fact, analyses have found out-of-school suspension rates for African American elementary school students that are between four and seven times greater than for European Americans (Raffaele-Mendez & Knoff, 2003).

What accounts for this disproportionality? One obvious explanation is that Black and Latino students violate class and school norms more often than their White peers. If this is the case, then disproportionate punishment is an appropriate response to inappropriate behavior, rather than an indicator of bias. Research on student behavior, race, and discipline, however, has yielded no evidence to support this explanation. In fact, studies suggest that African American students tend to receive harsher punishments for less severe behaviors (Skiba & Rausch, 2006). In addition, it appears that White students are referred to the office more frequently for "objective" offenses, such as vandalism, leaving without permission, and obscene language, while Black students are referred more often for "subjective" offenses—disrespect, excessive noise, and threat (Skiba, Michael, Nardo, & Peterson, 2002). In sum, it does not appear that racial disparities in school discipline are due to higher rates of misbehavior on the part of African American students. Instead, the evidence indicates that African American students are sent to the office and given punitive disciplinary consequences for less serious or more subjective reasons (Skiba & Rausch, 2006).

The implication is clear: In order to be a culturally responsive classroom manager, teachers need to acknowledge their biases and values and think about how these affect their interactions with students. Some useful questions to ask yourself are listed here (Weinstein, Curran, & Tomlinson-Clarke, 2003):

- Am I more patient and encouraging with some students?

- Am I more likely to reprimand other students?

- Do I expect certain students to be disruptive based on their race or ethnicity?

- Do I use hair style and dress to form stereotypical judgments of my students?

- When students violate norms, do I recommend equal treatment of all students?

With these six principles in mind—preserving a safe, caring classroom environment; protecting the instructional program; considering the context; responding in a timely and accurate manner; selecting a disciplinary strategy that matches the misbehavior; and being culturally responsive—we turn now to specific ways of responding to inappropriate behavior.

Pause and Reflect

Before reading about specific disciplinary interventions, think back to your own years as a student in elementary and high school. What disciplinary strategies did your most effective teachers use? What strategies did your least effective teachers use?

DEALING WITH MINOR MISBEHAVIOR

As mentioned in Chapter 4, Jacob Kounin's (1970) classic study of orderly and disorderly classrooms gave research support to the belief that successful classroom managers have eyes in the back of their heads. Kounin found that effective managers knew what was going on all over the room; moreover, *their students knew they knew,* because the teachers were able to spot minor problems and "nip them in the bud." Kounin called this ability *withitness,* a term that has since become widely used in discussions of classroom management.

How do "withit" teachers deal with minor misbehavior? How do they succeed in nipping problems in the bud? This section discusses both nonverbal and verbal interventions and then considers the times when it may be better to do nothing at all. (Suggestions are summarized in the Practical Tips box.)

Nonverbal Interventions

A while back, an 11-year-old we know announced that she could be a successful teacher. When we asked why she was so confident, she replied: "I know how to make *the look.*" She proceeded to demonstrate: her eyebrows slanted downward, her forehead creased, and her lips flattened into a straight line. She definitely had "the look" down pat.

The "teacher look" is a good example of an unobtrusive, nonverbal intervention. Making eye contact, using hand signals (e.g., thumbs down; pointing to what the individual should be doing), and moving closer to the misbehaving student

---

PRACTICAL TIPS FOR

DEALING WITH MINOR MISBEHAVIOR

- Use a nonverbal intervention such as:
  Facial expressions
  Eye contact
  Hand signals
  Proximity

- Use a nondirect verbal intervention:
  State the student's name.
  Incorporate the student's name into the lesson.
  Call on the student to participate.
  Use gentle humor.
  Use an I-message.

- Use a direct verbal intervention:
  Give a succinct command.
  Remind students about a rule.
  Give a choice between behaving appropriately or receiving a penalty.

- Choose deliberate non-intervention (but only if the misbehavior is minor and fleeting).

are other nonverbal ways of communicating withitness. Nonverbal interventions all convey the message, "I see what you're doing, and I don't like it," but since they are less directive than verbal commands, they encourage students to assume responsibility for getting back on task. Watch Donnie:

Donnie is at the board demonstrating how to construct congruent segments and congruent angles. Students are supposed to be following along, constructing congruent segments with rulers and compasses. Instead of working, two boys sit twirling their rulers on their pencils. Donnie notices what they are doing, but continues with her explanation. While she's talking, she gives the two boys a long, hard stare. They put down the rulers and get to work.

Nonverbal strategies are most appropriate for behaviors that are minor but persistent: frequent or sustained whispering, staring into space, calling out, putting on makeup, and sending text messages. The obvious advantage of using nonverbal cues is that you can deal with misbehaviors like these without distracting other students. In short, nonverbal interventions enable you to protect and continue your lesson with minimum disruption.

A nonverbal cue is sometimes all that's needed to stop a misbehavior and get a student back "on task." In fact, a study of six middle school teachers (Lasley, Lasley, & Ward, 1989) found that the *most successful responses to misbehavior were nonverbal.* These strategies stopped misbehavior 79 percent of the time; among the three "more effective managers," the success rate was even higher—an amazing 95 percent.

Verbal Interventions

Sometimes you find yourself in situations where it's just not possible to use a nonverbal cue. Perhaps you can't catch the student's eye, or you're working with a small group, and it would be too disruptive to get up and walk across the room to the misbehaving individual. Other times, you're able to use a nonverbal cue, but it's unsuccessful in stopping the misbehavior.

In cases like this, you might use a *nondirective verbal intervention.* These allow you to prompt the appropriate behavior, while leaving the responsibility for figuring out what to do with the misbehaving student. For example, *simply saying the student's name* might be enough to get the student back on task. Sometimes it's possible to *incorporate the student's name* into the ongoing instruction:

Shaheed is slouching down in his seat and appears inattentive. As Fred talks about respect for the elderly in China, he moves closer to him. "Let's say Shaheed was my son, and I beat him up because he was getting a failing grade in class. What happens to me?" Shaheed sits up and "tunes in."

If the misbehavior occurs while a group discussion or recitation is going on, *you can call on the student to answer a question.* Consider the following example:

The class is going over homework on isosceles triangles. As Donnie calls on students to do the problems, she walks through the room. "OK, we need someone to do number 14." Hands begin to go up. Donnie notices a girl in the back of the room who is gazing off into space. "Dominica, please do number 14." Dominica "comes back" from wherever she was, looks at the book, and answers correctly. Donnie smiles, "Good!"

Calling on a student allows you to communicate that you know what's going on and to capture the student's attention—without even citing the misbehavior. But keep in mind what we said earlier about preserving students' dignity. If you are obviously trying to "catch" students and to embarrass them, the strategy may well backfire by creating resentment (Good & Brophy, 2008). One way to avoid this problem is to alert the student that you will be calling on him or her to answer the *next question:* "Sharon, what's the answer to number 18? Taysha, the next one's yours."

The *use of humor* can provide another "gentle" way of reminding students to correct their behavior. Used well, humor can show them that you are able to understand the funny sides of classroom life. But you must be careful that the humor is not tinged with sarcasm that can hurt students' feelings.

It's near the end of the year, and Fred's students obviously have a case of "senioritis." They have just entered the room, and Fred is trying to get them to settle down. "Ladies and gentlemen, I know it's almost the end of the year, but could we make believe we're students now?"

An *"I-message"* is another way of verbally prompting appropriate behavior without giving a direct command. I-messages generally contain three parts. First, the teacher *describes the unacceptable behavior in a nonblaming, nonjudgmental way.* This phrase often begins with "when": "When people talk while I'm giving directions . . ." The second part describes the *tangible effect on the teacher:* "I have to repeat the directions and that wastes time . . ." Finally, the third part of the message states the *teacher's feelings* about the tangible effect: "and I get frustrated." Consider these examples of I-messages:

> "When you come to class without your supplies, I can't start the lesson on time, and I get really irritated."

> "When you leave your book bag in the middle of the aisle, I can trip over it, and I'm afraid I'll break a leg."

Although I-messages ideally contain all three parts in the recommended sequence, I-messages in any order, or even with one part missing, can still be effective (Gordon, 2003). We've witnessed the four teachers use "abbreviated" I-messages. For example, Fred communicates how strongly he feels about paying attention when he tells his class: "If you pass notes while I'm lecturing, I'll become suicidal." To a student who called him by his first name, he says, "I really feel uncomfortable when you call me by my first name in school."

There are several benefits to using this approach. In contrast to typical "you-messages" (e.g., "You are being rude," "You ought to know better," "You're acting like a baby"), I-messages minimize negative evaluations of the student. They make it easier to avoid using extreme (and usually inaccurate) words like "always" and "never" (as in "You *always* forget to do your homework" or "You're *never* prepared for class"). For these reasons, they foster and preserve a positive relationship between people. Since I-messages leave decisions about changing behavior up to students, this approach is also likely to promote a sense of responsibility and autonomy. In addition, I-messages show students that their behavior has consequences and that teachers are people with genuine feelings. Unlike you-messages, I-messages don't make students defensive and stubborn; thus, they may be more willing to change their behavior.

Most of us are not used to speaking this way, so I-messages can seem awkward and artificial. With practice, however, using I-messages can become natural. We once heard a 4-year-old girl (whose parents had consistently used I-messages at home) tell her nursery school peer: "When you poke me with that pencil, it really hurts, and I feel bad 'cause I think you don't want to be my friend."

In addition to these nondirective approaches, there are also *more directive strategies* that you can try. Indeed, several African American educators contend that these may be particularly well matched to the communication patterns of African American students (e.g., Delpit, 1995; Thompson, 2004). For example, Lisa Delpit, author of *Other People's Children: Cultural Conflict in the Classroom* (1995), observes that framing directives as questions (e.g., "Would you like to sit down now?") is a particularly mainstream, middle-class (and female) way of speaking, designed to foster a more egalitarian and nonauthoritarian climate. According to Delpit,

> Many kids will not respond to that structure because commands are not couched as questions in their home culture. Rather than asking questions, some teachers need to learn to say, "Put the scissors away" and "Sit down now" or "Please sit down now." (Valentine, 1998, p. 17)

As Delpit suggests, the most straightforward approach is to *direct students to the task at hand* ("Get to work on that math problem"; "Your group should be discussing the first three pages"). You can also *remind the student about the rule* or behavioral expectation that is being violated (e.g., "When someone is talking, everyone else is supposed to be listening"). Sometimes, if inappropriate behavior is fairly widespread, it's useful to review rules with the entire group. This is often true after a holiday, a weekend, or a vacation.

Another strategy is to *give students a choice between behaving appropriately or receiving a penalty* for continued inappropriate behavior (e.g., "If you can't handle working in your group, you'll have to return to your seats"; "You either choose to raise your hand instead of calling out, or you will be choosing not to participate in our discussion"). Statements like these not only warn students that a penalty will be invoked if the inappropriate behavior continues, they also emphasize that students have real choices about how to behave and that penalties are not imposed without reason. In the following example, we see how Fred embellishes this strategy with a little humor:

 The bell rings; Fred moves to the front of the room and tries to get his students' attention. They continue talking. "Ladies and gentlemen, if you want a zero for life, talk now. If you don't, listen." Students laugh and settle down.

Deliberate Non-Intervention

If misbehavior is extremely brief and unobtrusive, the best course of action may be *deliberate non-intervention.* For example, during a discussion a student may be so eager to comment that she forgets to raise her hand; or someone becomes momentarily distracted and inattentive; or two boys quietly exchange a comment while you're giving directions. In cases like these, an intervention can be more disruptive than the students' behavior.

One risk of overlooking minor misbehavior is that students may conclude you're unaware of what's going on. Suspecting that you're not "withit," they may decide to see how much they can get away with, and then problems are sure to escalate. You need to monitor your class carefully to make sure this doesn't happen.

Another problem is that occasional ignoring can turn into full-fledged "blindness." This was vividly demonstrated in a study of a student teacher named Heleen (Créton, Wubbels, & Hooymayers, 1989). When Heleen was lecturing, her students frequently became noisy and inattentive. In response, Heleen talked more loudly and looked more at the chalkboard, turning her back on her students. She did not allow herself to see or hear the disorder—perhaps because it was too threatening and she didn't know how to handle it. Unfortunately, Heleen's students seemed to interpret her "blindness" as an indication that noise was allowed, and they became even more disorderly. Heleen eventually recognized the importance of "seeing" and responding to slight disturbances, in order to prevent them from escalating.

DEALING WITH MORE SERIOUS MISBEHAVIOR

Sometimes, nonverbal cues or verbal reminders are not enough to convince students that you're serious about the behavioral expectations that you've established. And sometimes misbehavior is just too serious to use these kinds of low-level responses. In cases like these, it may be necessary to use more substantial interventions in order to enforce your expectations for appropriate behavior.

In some cases, teachers discuss penalties when they teach rules and procedures, so students understand the consequences of violating a rule from the very beginning. We saw Sandy do this with her students in Chapter 4, when she laid out the penalties for coming late to class. This practice prevents unpleasant "surprises," and should minimize protests of blissful ignorance—"But you didn't *tell* me that would happen!"

Selecting Penalties

It's often difficult for beginning teachers to decide on appropriate penalties. One student teacher in social studies vented his frustration in this way:

> *These two kids come to class every day and sit and do absolutely nothing. They don't create a big disturbance, and they're not really nasty or belligerent; they just won't do any work. They prefer to sit there and talk, and draw cartoons, and goof off. I keep telling them they're getting a zero for each day they just sit, and that they're going to fail for the marking period, but they just don't care. I've told them I'm going to call their parents, but they just laugh. I don't want to send them to the disciplinarian's office, because my cooperating teacher says I could get a reputation as a teacher who can't control the class, and I'd really like to get a job in this district. So I'm really at a loss. These kids are really smart, and I hate to see them fail. But what can I do?*

We posed this question to all four teachers and learned about the types of penalties that they typically use. As a general rule of thumb, our teachers try to implement penalties that are logically related to the misbehavior (Dreikurs, Grunwald, & Pepper, 1982). For example, when a student in Christina's class failed to work constructively in his small group, he had to work by himself until he indicated a readiness to cooperate. Similarly, if students make a mess in Sandy's chemistry lab, a logical penalty would be to make them clean it up. If an individual forgets her book and can't do the assignment, she must borrow someone's book and do the assignment during a free period. A student who hands in a carelessly done paper has to rewrite it.

Logical consequences differ from traditional punishments, which bear no relationship to the misbehavior involved. Examples are as follows: A student who continually whispers to her neighbor has to do an additional homework assignment (instead of being isolated). A student who forgets to get his parents' permission to go on a field trip has to serve detention (rather than writing a letter home to parents about the need to sign the permission slip). A student who continually calls out during a whole-class discussion gets an F for the day (instead of making a cue-card to post on his desk saying "I won't call out" or not being allowed to participate in the discussion.)

The specific penalties used by our teachers are described below. As you read about each one, keep in mind that these four teachers have worked hard to build caring, trusting relationships with students. Undoubtedly, these relationships increase the likelihood that students will interpret the penalties not as punishments imposed by a hostile, dictatorial adversary, but as reasonable consequences enacted by a teacher who cares enough to insist that students behave the best they can (Bondy & Ross, 2008; Gregory & Ripski, 2008).

Mandatory Private Conferences

When students do not respond to nonverbal cues or verbal reminders, our teachers generally call a private conference, often after school or during a free period.

During these conferences, they express their disappointment in the student's behavior. We normally don't think of this as a penalty, but since students in these classes really like their teachers, they feel bad when their teachers are upset. In serious, almost sorrowful tones, our teachers express their disappointment and surprise at the inappropriate behavior and direct students to think about the consequences of their actions. Sometimes, they will negotiate a plan for change, trying to get the students to take responsibility for their behavior. For example, when a student in Sandy's class failed a test, she held a private conference with him after school. Sandy shares this account of their meeting:

 We talked about how he had been doing in class, and what had happened in this particular exam. It turned out that he had gone clubbing until 11:30 the night before the test. I told him, 'Well, that was your choice, and this was the outcome. What do you think? Do you like this outcome?' Obviously he didn't. We agreed that the next time there was a test, he wouldn't stay out late the night before and see if it makes a difference. I really think it's important to approach teenagers this way—to put the responsibility back on them whenever possible."

Loss of Privileges

Sometimes, students lose the right to sit wherever they like, particularly if their behavior is having a negative impact on other students. Other privileges that can be taken away include working with a friend, free time, chewing gum, freely moving around the room, and joining in a class popcorn party.

Isolation from the Group

All four teachers will move students to an isolated or secluded area of the room if they are unable to work productively, but they try to be positive rather than negative about the move. Fred will signal a student to move to a place that's "less distracting." When Sandy covered a seventh-grade class, she sometimes had to tell a student, "Come with me. Let's go to the back of the class and see what you can do back here where you can concentrate better. This will be your own private office." This strategy can be particularly effective with students who suffer from attention-deficit/hyperactivity disorder (ADHD). These students have trouble dealing with the distraction and stimulation of the typical classroom environment; moving temporarily to a secluded area of the room can provide a much needed opportunity to refocus.

Exclusion from Class

All four teachers believe that "kicking kids out" is a strategy that should be reserved for major disruption. As Donnie points out, "Some students *want* to get out; they'll provoke a teacher just so they can leave the room. I know teachers who throw kids out all the time, but what's the point? Kids can't learn if they're in the office."

Despite their preference for handling problems within the room, the teachers recognize that there are times when this is just not possible. Sandy remembers how she sent a student to the "time-out" room when his behavior was so infuriating that she couldn't discuss it calmly: "I was so mad, I knew I was losing it. I was yelling, and the kid was yelling. So it was better for him to be out of the room. But 10 minutes later, I called and told him to come back. By then we had both cooled down and we were able to talk." Sandy has also worked out a system with another teacher so that she can send a student to his classroom if necessary. In the other room, the student must sit quietly and do chemistry work, ignored by both teacher and students.

Fred also sends students to the office if their behavior is really out of control. He recalls one student who was severely disturbed:

> I had it worked out with the office, so they knew what to do with him when he showed up. In the beginning, I had to kick him out three times a week, but slowly he got better about controlling his behavior, and we got it down to once every two weeks. But this only worked because class was a good place to be. He had friends there, we laughed every day, he got to do good stuff. If he hadn't liked it—and me—getting to leave would have been a reward.

Detention

For routine violations of rules (e.g., coming late to class), Donnie, Sandy, and Fred use regular school detention as a penalty. However, they are cautious about using this for "big" problems. As Sandy puts it, "If students are disrespectful, or really having problems controlling themselves, I prefer to talk privately with them. What's going to be learned from 45 minutes of detention?"

Written Reflections on the Problem

Sometimes, a situation is so complex that it warrants serious reflection in writing. Fred recalls this incident:

> My senior honors class was supposed to do a short research paper. When I began to grade the papers, it seemed to me that a lot of the citations were suspicious. I did some checking and found that some students had simply lifted material from the Web and made up the references. I went into class and told them how serious this was, and how they would all get zeros for their papers if they couldn't validate their references. But I gave them a way out: They could write a letter to me explaining what they had done and why, and they had to make "reparation" by doing two additional research papers with valid citations. The letters were really revealing. A lot of these kids were absolutely clueless about why it's important to reference accurately. One kid came in and thanked me for making a big deal about this. He said he really didn't know that what he was doing was dishonest.

Contacting Parents

Our four teachers all contact parents or guardians if a student shows a pattern of consistent misbehavior. For example, when a student in Sandy's class repeatedly "forgot" to do his homework, Sandy told him she would be calling his parents to discuss the problem. She tried to make it clear that she was calling not in anger but out of serious concern. She also wanted to convey the idea that "between all of us, maybe we can help you get it together."

These penalties illustrate the ways Christina, Donnie, Fred, and Sandy choose to deal with problems when they have a degree of flexibility. In addition, there are times when they are required to follow school policies mandating particular responses to specific misbehaviors. Consider the example of cutting class. In Christina's school, two instances of cutting a class result in no credit earned for that course. In Fred's school, one cut requires parental notification and a warning letter; two cuts result in "student/counselor contact" and "administrator/parent contact," a possible conference, and a warning letter. The third cut requires removal from class with a grade of AW (administrative withdrawal) and placement in study hall.

It's also important to note that under *No Child Left Behind,* schools must have a plan for keeping schools safe and drug free. These plans must include discipline policies that prohibit disorderly conduct, the illegal possession of weapons, and the illegal use, possession, distribution, and sale of tobacco, alcohol, and other drugs. As a result, almost all schools now have *zero tolerance* policies with predetermined consequences for such offenses. Zero tolerance may also be applied to other problems, like bullying and threatening. Such policies usually result in automatic suspension or expulsion, although there may still be wide variation in severity. Be sure to familiarize yourself with the zero tolerance policies in your school.

If you have students with disabilities in your classes, it's also essential that you consult with a special educator or a member of the child study team about appropriate intervention strategies. Serious behavior problems require a team effort, and parents, special education teachers, psychologists, social workers, and administrators can all provide valuable insights and suggestions. Also be aware that IDEA 2004 includes several stipulations about the rights of students with disabilities with respect to disciplinary procedures. For example, if the problematic behavior is "caused by" or has a "direct and substantial relationship" to the child's disability, removing the student for more than 10 school days may not be allowed.

PAUSE AND REFLECT

Review the various penalties that our four teachers generally use when dealing with inappropriate behavior. Which ones would you be most inclined to implement? Are there any with which you disagree?

Imposing Penalties and Preserving Relationships

It's frustrating when students misbehave, and sometimes we let our frustration color the way we impose penalties. We've seen teachers scream at students from across the room, lecture students on their history of misbehavior, insinuate that they come from terrible homes, and attack their personalities. Clearly, behavior like this destroys students' dignity and ruins the possibility of a good relationship. How can you avoid creating a situation like this?

First, if you're feeling really angry at a student, *delay the discussion.* You can simply say to the individual, "Sit there and think about what happened. I'll talk to you in a few minutes." During one observation in Fred's room, it was clear that he was becoming really annoyed at two students who were talking while he was introducing a film the class was about to watch. Twice during his comments he turned and told them to stop talking, but their conversation would begin again. We watched with curiosity to see if he would do anything further, but he continued the lesson. At the end of the period, however, he promptly went over and quietly spoke with the two offending students. Later, he reflected on their conversation:

> I told them I couldn't talk while they were talking, that it distracted me and made me really mad—especially since I was talking about Gandhi, who's one of my favorite guys. They apologized; they said they had been talking about some of the ideas that had come up in class. I told them I was really glad they were so excited, but they had to share their thoughts with the whole class, or wait until after class to talk. I think they got the message. Talking with them after class had three advantages: It allowed me to continue with my lesson, it gave me a chance to calm down, and it made it possible to talk to them privately.

As Fred's comments point out, by delaying discussion, you have a chance to calm down and to think about what you want to say. You'll also be more able to separate the student's character from the student's behavior. Your message must be: "*You're* okay, but your *behavior* is unacceptable."

Second, it's a good idea to *impose penalties privately, calmly, and quietly.* Despite the temptation to yell and scream, the softer your voice and the closer you stand, the more effective you tend to be (Bear, 1998). Remember, students are very concerned about saving face in front of their peers. Public sanction may have the advantage of "making an example" out of one student's misbehavior, but it has the disadvantage of creating resentment and embarrassment. Numerous studies have found that students view public reprimand as the *least acceptable method* of dealing with problems (Hoy & Weinstein, 2006). Furthermore, the ability to be firm without using threats and public humiliation appears to be particularly important for students who are already disaffected or alienated from school. For example, interviews conducted with 31 "marginal" junior high school students judged to be at risk of school failure found that teachers were perceived as uncaring and unfair adversaries if they "engaged in public acts intended to convey an impression of authority: making examples of specific students, sending students from the room, and ordering compliance" (Schlosser, 1992, p. 135).

Our four teachers agree. Sandy observes:

> Let's say you've just given back some paper you graded. A student looks at his or her paper, crumples it up, and throws it on the floor. If you yell, "Pick that paper up," you've created a confrontational situation. It's a

lot better to go over and talk privately and calmly. If you say something like, "If you have a problem with your grade, we can talk about it," then the kid doesn't lose face. It's really important not to back students into a corner; if you do, they'll come out fighting and create an even bigger problem than before.

Finally, after imposing a penalty, it's a good idea to get back to the student and *reestablish a positive relationship.* At the beginning of this chapter, we saw how Sandy made a point of helping William with his lab experiment after giving him detention. Similarly, complimenting a student's work or patting a back communicates that there are no hard feelings.

Another way to reestablish a positive relationship is to implement the Two-by-Ten strategy (Wlodkowski, 1983). For two minutes each day, for ten days in a row, have a personal conversation with the misbehaving student (or any one of your most difficult students) about anything of interest to the student. Teachers who have tried this strategy report a remarkable improvement in the behavior of the target student, as well as the entire class. In fact, the most difficult students can become your allies when there is a strong personal connection.

Being Consistent

Beginning teachers are constantly told to "be consistent," and research certainly supports this advice. Recall Evertson and Emmer's (1982) study of effective classroom management on the junior high level (discussed in Chapter 4). This study showed that more successful managers responded in a consistent, predictable fashion, often invoking the rules or procedures in order to stop the disruptive behavior. In contrast, the ineffective managers were more likely to act inconsistently: Sometimes they ignored the behavior; sometimes they invoked a pre-stated consequence (e.g., detention); sometimes they warned students of penalties, but then didn't act on their warnings. Inevitably, behavior problems increased in frequency and severity.

Although the importance of being consistent is obvious, teachers sometimes feel trapped by the need for consistency. (See the discussion in Chapter 3 about being fair.) When a normally conscientious student forgets a homework assignment, it seems unreasonable to send the same note home to parents that you would send if a student repeatedly missed assignments. In order to get out of this bind, it's desirable to develop a *hierarchy of consequences* that can be invoked if rules are violated. Some teachers develop a graduated list of generic consequences that can be applied to all misbehaviors. The following hierarchy is an example:

First violation:	Verbal warning
Second violation:	Name is written down
Third violation:	Conference with teacher
Fourth violation:	Call parents

Another approach is to develop a graduated list of consequences for individual classroom rules. Sandy used this approach when she developed her graduated list

[handwritten margin note: not as rigid → gives you + its some leeway]

of consequences for coming late (see Chapter 4), and she makes sure to enforce the consequences no matter who is involved. She tells us:

> **Kids have got to see that you're fair. If my best student walks through that door late, I have to give the same detention that I'd give to my worst student. If I don't give detention, the kids will see that and think to themselves, "She's playing favorites. She's letting him get away with coming late." That's the end of my relationship with them.**

Although all four teachers are absolutely consistent when dealing with straightforward behaviors like coming late, they consider these the "little problems." With the "big things," they prefer to talk privately with students and to develop a plan of action that is tailored to the individual student. By holding "mandatory private conferences," the four teachers can show students they are consistent in terms of enforcing class rules and dealing with problem behavior, but they can remain flexible with respect to the solution.

Penalizing the Group for Individual Misbehavior

Sometimes teachers impose a consequence on the whole class even if only one or two individuals have been misbehaving. The hope is that other students will be angry at receiving a penalty when they weren't misbehaving and will exert pressure on their peers to behave. Our four teachers are unanimous in their negative response to this practice. Donnie observes, "If you even attempt to do this, students will be furious. You'll alienate the whole class." And Fred puts it this way: "I do this when I'm teaching about the causes of revolutions. It's a great way to foment a rebellion!"

DEALING WITH CHRONIC MISBEHAVIOR

Some students with persistent behavior problems fail to respond to the routine strategies we have described so far: nonverbal cues, verbal reminders, and penalties. What additional strategies are available? In this section, we consider two basic approaches. First, we examine a *problem-solving strategy,* which views inappropriate behavior as a conflict to be resolved through discussion and negotiation. Next, we take a look at strategies *based on principles of behavioral learning.* We examine *self-management approaches* (self-monitoring, self-evaluation, self-instruction, and contingency contracting) and then turn to *positive behavioral supports* (PBS), interventions designed to replace problem behaviors with new behaviors that serve the same purpose for the student.

Using a Problem-Solving Approach

Most teachers think in terms of winning or losing when they think about classroom conflicts. According to Thomas Gordon, author of *T.E.T.—Teacher Effectiveness Training* (2003),

> This win–lose orientation seems to be at the core of the knotty issue of discipline in schools. Teachers feel that they have only two approaches to choose

from: They can be strict or lenient, tough or soft, authoritarian or permissive. They see the teacher–student relationship as a power struggle, a contest, a fight. . . . When conflicts arise, as they always do, most teachers try to resolve them so that they win, or at least don't lose. This obviously means that students end up losing, or at least not winning. (2003, p. 185)

A third alternative is a "no-lose" problem-solving method of conflict resolution (Gordon, 2003) consisting of six steps. In Step 1, the teacher and the student (or students) *define the problem.* In Step 2, everyone *brainstorms possible solutions.* As in all brainstorming activities, suggestions are not evaluated at this stage. In Step 3, the *solutions are evaluated:* "Now let's take a look at all the solutions that have been proposed and decide which we like and which we don't like. Do you have some preferences?" It is important that you state your own opinions and preferences. Do not permit a solution to stand if it is not really acceptable to you. In Step 4, you and the students involved *decide on the solution that you will try.* If more than one student is involved, it is tempting to vote on the solution, but that's probably not a good idea. Voting always produces winners and losers unless the vote is unanimous, so some people leave the discussion feeling dissatisfied. Instead, try to work for consensus.

Once you have decided which solution to try, you move to Step 5 and *determine how to implement the decision:* who will do what by when. Finally, in Step 6, *the solution is evaluated.* You may want to call everybody together again and ask, "Are you still satisfied with our solution?" It is important that everyone realize that decisions are not chiseled in granite and that they can be discarded in search of a better solution to the problem.

During one meeting, Donnie explained how she used problem solving when some of her students were not sitting in their assigned places during assemblies:

Whenever there's an assembly program, we're supposed to walk together to the auditorium and sit together. But it's crowded in the halls on the way to the auditorium, and everyone "loses" kids; someone has darted here or there, joined another class, faded into the crowd. By the time we get to the auditorium, the kids are scattered all over. They sit with other classes, and they act up. The teachers don't really know who they are, and sometimes the kids even give wrong names when the teachers ask. The behavior in assembly programs can be really bad. I decided this was a problem that we had to deal with before another assembly program was held.

I told the class that I felt this was a problem, and they agreed. Then I explained that we were going to brainstorm solutions. Boy, these kids can really be hard on each other! They came up with about eight different solutions:

Kick the offenders out of the assemblies.

Don't let past offenders go to assemblies at all.

Suspension.

Kids have to get permission to sit with another class.

Bring your friend to sit with you and your class (your friend would have to have special permission from his/her teacher).

Invite parents to assemblies (kids would act better).

Take attendance once you get to the assembly.

Have a buddy system.

The next day, we talked about each of these possible solutions, focusing on how they would affect everyone. I told them I didn't like the one about kicking people out of the assemblies because assembly programs were part of their education. I also explained that teachers don't have the right to suspend students, and if we chose that one, we'd have to get the disciplinarian involved. The kids said they could live with getting permission, and they also liked the buddy system. They said buddies should also have the responsibility of telling the person next to them to stop if he or she was disruptive. So we agreed to try those two. We also agreed that I would use the "teacher look" technique if I saw kids acting up and then write up a referral to the disciplinarian if they didn't stop.

We haven't had an assembly program yet, so I don't know how this is going to work, but I think it was good to get the kids involved in trying to solve the problem. Maybe they'll be more interested in trying to improve the situation.

Using a Behavioral Learning Approach

Behavioral learning principles emphasize external events (rather than thinking or knowledge) as the cause of changes in behavior (Woolfolk, 2007). Applied behavior analysis (also known as behavior modification) is the application of behavioral learning principles to change behavior; it involves the systematic use of reinforcement to strengthen desired behavior. Probably more research has focused on the effectiveness of applied behavior analysis than on any other classroom management approach, and dozens of books are available for teachers (e.g., Alberto & Troutman, 2006; Zirpoli, 2005).

Because traditional behavior modification techniques emphasize external control by the teacher, rather than trying to foster internal control by the student, some educators recommend behavioral approaches that involve the student in *self-management:* self-monitoring, self-evaluation, self-instruction, and contingency contracting. Self-management strategies have been reported to be effective with children from preschool through secondary school, with and without identified disabilities, and for a wide variety of problem behaviors, both academic and social (Shapiro, DuPaul, & Bradley-Klug, 1998; Smith & Sugai, 2000). The goal of self-management is to help students learn to regulate their own behavior. The perception of control is crucial in this process: When we feel in control, we are much more likely to accept responsibility for our actions.

In the next sections of the chapter we describe these self-management strategies. Then we turn to a relatively new behavioral approach that focuses on teaching students appropriate behavior through positive behavioral supports.

Self-Monitoring

Some students may not realize how often they're out of their seats or how frequently they sit daydreaming instead of focusing on their work. Others may be unaware of how often they call out during class discussions or how many times they make nasty comments to other members of their small group. Students like this may benefit from a self-monitoring program, in which they learn to observe and record a targeted behavior during a designated period of time. Interestingly, self-monitoring can have positive effects even when students are *inaccurate* (Graziano & Mooney, 1984).

Before beginning a self-monitoring program, you need to make sure that students can identify the behaviors targeted for change. For example, some students may not be able to accurately describe all the component parts of "working independently." You may have to model, explicitly noting that "When I work independently, I am sitting down (without tilting back in my chair), I am looking at the paper on my desk, and I am holding my pencil in my hand".

Students then learn how to observe and record their own behavior. Recording can be done in two ways. The first approach has individuals tally each time they engage in the targeted behavior. For example, students can learn to chart the number of math problems they complete during an in-class assignment, the number of times they blurt out irrelevant comments during a discussion, or the number of times they raise their hand to speak. For middle school students, the tally sheet might contain pictures of the appropriate and inappropriate behaviors. (See the "countoon" suggested by Jones and Jones, 2010, in Figure 12.2.) In the second approach, individuals observe and record the targeted behavior at regular intervals. At the designated time, for instance, students can mark a recording sheet with a "1" or a "2," depending on whether they are engaged in appropriate or inappropriate behavior.

There has been some debate about whether self-management can be helpful for students diagnosed with ADHD, since "the lack of self-management skills can be viewed as a core deficit among individuals with this disorder" (Shapiro, DuPaul, & Bradley-Klug, 1998). Recent research, however, supports the use of these strategies. For example, researchers investigated the practicality and efficacy of self-monitoring for five middle school students with ADHD (Barry & Messer, 2003).

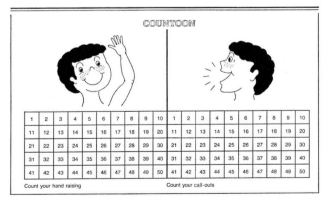

Figure 12.2   An Example of a "Countoon"
Source: Jones & Jones, *Comprehensive classroom management,* © 2010. Reproduced by permission of Pearson Education, Inc.

According to their teacher, all five boys had limited attention spans, rarely completed in-class assignments, frequently wandered around the room, and engaged in loud, disruptive behavior. Students were taught to ask themselves a series of questions written on a data-collection sheet: "Was I in my seat or where I needed to be to complete my class work? Was I paying attention by working on the assignment or listening to the teacher? Did I complete my assignments? Did I play or fight with my classmates in the classroom? Did I talk loudly or make noise in class?" In individual conferences, the teacher went over each question and asked the student to describe an example of his behavior that would indicate occurrence or nonoccurrence. The teacher also modeled the on-task behaviors that were described and had the students practice recording data. Initially, the boys had to respond to the questions every 15 minutes, but this interval was gradually increased. Goals were set (e.g., 75 percent or more 15-minute intervals on task), and students earned simple reinforcers from the teacher such as snacks and increased computer time. The researchers reported that the use of self-monitoring was effective in increasing students' on-task behaviors and academic performance and decreasing disruptive behaviors. Moreover, the intervention was relatively easy to implement. The teacher's initial meeting with each student took only about 20 minutes; although some additional time was spent checking for accuracy and providing feedback to students, this time was gained back as students' behavior and academic work improved.

Self-Evaluation

This self-management approach goes beyond simple self-monitoring by requiring individuals to judge the quality or acceptability of their behavior (Hughes, Ruhl, & Misra, 1989). Sometimes self-evaluation is linked with reinforcement, so that an improvement in behavior brings points or rewards.

A study of three seventh-grade inclusive language arts classrooms provides a good example of how self-evaluation strategies can be used to reduce off-task, disruptive behavior in a general education classroom (Mitchem, Young, West, & Benyo, 2001). The classes were all taught by the same teacher; there were 31 students in the second-period class, and 33 each in the fourth- and seventh-period classes. From the three classes, ten students were identified as target students based on a history of referrals for disruptive and/or off-task behavior, poor social skills, and poor grades. Using lesson plans and materials provided by the investigators, the teacher taught all students procedures for a ClassWide Peer-Assisted Self-Management (CWPASM) program, in which students evaluated their behavior using a rating system based on the school's citizenship grades: "H" (honors), "S" (satisfactory), "N" (needs improvement), and "U" (unsatisfactory). Training required from two to three periods, depending on the class. The teacher also assigned every student a partner based on her knowledge of students' personalities and preferences. During the implementation of the CWPASM program, students rated their own behavior and that of their partner every 10 minutes. Partners then compared their ratings and earned points for perfect or near-perfect ratings. The initial 10-minute interval was later lengthened to 20 minutes; eventually students did the ratings just once at the end of the period. The CWPASM program had an immediate and marked effect on both the classes as a whole and the ten target students. The researchers write:

> Before CWPASM was introduced, it was rare to see the entire group on task at the same time for even one minute during the entire period. The teacher spent a substantial portion of the class period managing students, redirecting them to get on task, and repeating instructions. After CWPASM was introduced, group on-task behavior across all target classes increased from near zero levels to almost 80%. In practical terms, this meant that all students were on task at the same time for approximately 32 minutes of the 40 minute observation. Group on-task behavior continued to increase the longer the intervention was in effect. (Mitchem, Young, West, & Benyo, 2001, p. 133)

Recently, Fred decided to try a self-evaluation procedure with a boy in his Contemporary World Issues class. Daniel was in serious danger of failing the course; although he was not disruptive, Daniel was consistently inattentive and rarely completed assignments. Fred and Daniel discussed self-evaluation, and Daniel was enthusiastic about trying it. Together, they designed a simple sheet, which they agreed that Fred would keep and give to Daniel to fill out at the end of each class period. As you can see from Figure 12.3, the form requires Daniel to describe and evaluate his behavior. Fred describes how the self-evaluation procedure worked out:

> **We did it faithfully for three weeks, and it really worked. Sometimes I forgot to give Daniel the self-evaluation sheet at the end of the period, and he actually reminded me. I took that as a sign of his commitment.**
> **His behavior really improved; he started paying attention and complet**ing assignments for the first time all year. At the end of three weeks, Daniel was

```
┌──────────────────────────────────────────────────────────┐
│                 WHAT DID YOU DO IN CLASS?                  │
│                                                            │
│  1. How well did you behave?                               │
│          Were you attentive?                               │
│          Did you complete assignments?                     │
│          Did you contribute to class discussion?           │
│          Did you think?                                    │
│          Did you learn something?                          │
│                                                            │
│  2. What score would be accurate?    1    2    3    4      │
│                                  (Excellent)    (Poor)     │
│                                                            │
│  Monday:                                                   │
│                                                            │
│  Tuesday:                                                  │
│                                                            │
│  Wednesday:                                                │
│                                                            │
│  Thursday:                                                 │
│                                                            │
│  Friday:                                                   │
└──────────────────────────────────────────────────────────┘
```

Figure 12.3   Daniel's Self-Evaluation Form

out for several days. When he got back, we didn't pick it up again, and I didn't push it. He was doing what he was supposed to be doing, without any monitoring.

Self-Instruction

The third self-management approach is self-instruction, in which students learn to give themselves silent directions about how to behave. Most self-instruction strategies are based on a five-step process of cognitive behavior modification: (1) An adult performs a task while talking aloud about it, carefully describing each part; (2) the student performs the task while the adult talks aloud (overt, external guidance); (3) the student performs the task while talking aloud to self (overt self-guidance); (4) the student performs the task while whispering (faded, overt self-guidance); (5) the student performs the task while thinking the directions (covert, self-instruction) (Meichenbaum, 1977). This approach has been used to teach impulsive students to approach tasks more deliberately, to help social isolates initiate peer interaction, to teach aggressive students to control their anger, and to teach defeated students to try problem solving instead of giving up (Brophy, 1983).

There is evidence that even seriously emotionally disturbed adolescents can learn to engage in self-instruction. In a study conducted in a self-contained special education class (Ninness, Fuerst, Rutherford, & Glenn, 1991), three teenage males who displayed high rates of off-task and inappropriate behaviors (running, fighting, fondling, spitting, throwing objects, jumping, or inappropriate language) were given formal instruction in social skills and self-management for one hour a day. Students were taught to raise their hands to ask questions, to avoid distractions of other students, and to talk politely to teachers and students. While others played the role of distractors, students rehearsed overt statements such as "I'm not going to let him or her bother me. I'm going to keep doing my work," and they practiced avoiding eye contact with those who annoyed them. In addition, students were taught to evaluate their own on-task and socially appropriate behavior, using a scale ranging from one to four. A bonus point was awarded on any occasion in which a student's self-assessment was within one point of the teacher's assessment.

The results of the study demonstrated that training in self-management can dramatically improve students' behavior. Prior to the training, off-task and socially inappropriate behavior in the classroom averaged 92 percent, 95 percent, and 76 percent for Subjects 1, 2, and 3, respectively. All three subjects improved substantially during the course of the five-week self-management training—and all three demonstrated *near-zero off-task or socially inappropriate behavior during the experimental situations.*

Before we leave the discussion of self-monitoring, self-evaluation, and self-instruction, it is important to note that these strategies hold particular promise for students with disabilities in general education settings. Only a handful of studies have been conducted in inclusive secondary classrooms, but they indicate that students with disabilities can be taught to use self-management to improve both their social and academic performance (McDougall, 1998). On the other hand, this training requires time and expertise that general education teachers may not have (McDougall, 1998). If you decide to try one of these self-management strategies, you should consult with your school's psychologist, a counselor, or a special education teacher.

Contingency Contracting

A contingency or behavior contract is an agreement between a teacher and an individual student that specifies what the student must do to earn a particular reward. Contingency contracts are negotiated with students; both parties must agree on the behaviors students are to exhibit, the period of time involved, and the rewards that will result. To be most effective, contracts should be written and signed. And, of course, there should be an opportunity for review and renegotiation if the contract is not working. An example of a typical contract appears in Figure 12.4.

Positive Behavioral Support and Functional Behavioral Assessment

Positive behavioral support (PBS) is based on the behavioral principle that behavior occurs for one of two reasons. It either enables individuals to obtain something they desire (positive reinforcement) or it enables individuals to avoid something they find unpleasant (e.g., negative reinforcement). In other words, behavior happens for a reason, although the individual may not be conscious of this. Given this principle, PBS begins by investigating *why* a problem behavior occurs (i.e., what *function* or purpose it serves); teachers can then design an intervention to eliminate the challenging behavior and replace it with a socially acceptable behavior that serves the same purpose.

Date_____

After discussion between Mr. Schroeder (social studies teacher) and Justin Mayer
(student), the following decisions were reached:
During the next marking period, I, Justin Mayer, agree to:

1. Be on time for U. S. History I, with book, notebook, and writing utensil.
2. To complete all homework assignments and to turn them in on time.
3. To meet with Mr. Schroeder after school on Thursdays to check on the progress of my
   quarterly project.
4. To sit on the other side of the room from Sam Holloway.
5. To pay attention during class.

If I meet these conditions, I will pass this class with a C or better for this marking period.

Student_____

Teacher_____

Parent_____

Figure 12.4   An Example of a Contract

The process of investigating why the problem behavior occurs is known as *functional behavioral assessment* (FBA). FBA procedures have historically been used in cases of severe behavior disorders, and in fact, IDEA 2004 mandates schools to conduct FBAs of a student with disabilities if he or she is to be removed more than 10 consecutive school days or if the removal constitutes a change in placement. In recent years, however, FBA has also been widely recommended for use in general education classrooms with typically developing students and those with mild disabilities (Robinson & Ricord Griesemer, 2006).

FBA is comprised of several steps. First, it is necessary to *describe the problem behavior* in precise, measurable, observable terms so that two or more persons could agree on the occurrence. This means that instead of saying that "Michael is aggressive," you need to say "Michael curses at other kids, puts his foot out to trip people, and throws his books on the floor when angry." In the second step, *information is collected regarding the environmental events that occur before and after the student's behavior.* This is generally referred to as an A-B-C assessment, where A represents the antecedents of the behavior, B represents the behavior, and C represents the consequences. (Figure 12.5 shows a sample ABC recording sheet.) Since it's generally not feasible to collect this information while you're teaching, you will probably have to arrange for someone else (e.g., a collaborating teacher, a teaching assistant, a school counselor) to do the assessment while you provide instruction (or vice versa). It's also essential to conduct observations across several days, so that you can be confident you are getting a representative sample of the student's behavior. Finally, make sure to observe times when the target behavior typically occurs and times when it typically does *not* occur. If you carry out this step carefully, you should then be able to answer the following questions (Kerr & Nelson, 2006):

Does the behavior occur in the presence of certain persons?

During what activities is the behavior more likely to occur?

During what activities is the behavior less likely to occur?

What happens to the student following the behavior?

How do others respond to the behavior?

Does the surrounding environment change in any way following the behavior?

In the third step of the FBA, *hypotheses are developed about the purpose of the behavior;* in other words, this is when you try to figure out what the student stands to gain. For example, let's assume that as a result of gathering information in step 2, it has become clear that Ronald, a student in a middle school English/language arts class, is disruptive only during writing workshop (the antecedent), when he annoys the students sitting nearby by uttering silly comments, making noises, and dropping books on the floor (the behavior). In response to this behavior, the teacher repeatedly tells him to "settle down and get to work" (one consequence). When this doesn't bring about a positive change, the teacher tells him to take a seat in the back of the room and think about how students are supposed to behave during writing workshop (another consequence). On the basis of this

Student Ronald   Date 10/11

Observer Mr. Green   Time 9:15

Setting/Activity Language Arts Class

Target Behavior(s) Noncompliance/aggression

Time	Antecedents (What happened before the behavior?)	Behavior (What did the student do?)	Consequences (What happened after the behavior?)
9:15	Teacher tells class to take out the stories they are writing and work on revising them.	Ronald sits slumped in seat. He doesn't open his notebook to work on his story. He starts to make comments about other students' stories.	Teacher tells Ronald to get to work. He continues to sit slumped in seat. He pushes several books off his desk onto the floor.
9:17	Teacher goes over to Ronald; quietly tells him to settle down and get to work.	Ronald says he doesn't want to write a "stupid" story.	Teacher tells Ronald that he needs to work on his story or will need to move to the back of the rook. She walks away. Ronald starts to make noises but doesn't open his notebook.
9:20	Teacher tells Ronald to move to the back of the room and think about how he is supposed to behave during writing workshop.	Ronald throws his notebook on the floor, yells at teacher: "who cares about a f_____ story?!" and walks toward the door.	Teacher follows Ronald; tells him to go with her out into the hallway where they can talk.

Figure 12.5   A Sample ABC Recording Sheet

information, we can hypothesize that Ronald's behavior enables him to avoid something he seems to find aversive—namely, writing workshop.

The fourth step is to *test the hypotheses you have developed* by creating a behavior intervention plan (BIP). This involves modifying some aspect of the environment and observing the effect. In Ronald's case, since the writing task appears to be frustrating, the teacher might provide him with additional support such as his own personal dictionary, allow him to seek assistance from a "writing buddy," and provide encouragement and additional instructional guidance as needed. In addition, the teacher might stop responding to the inappropriate behavior and instead respond to appropriate behavior with smiles and praise. If *monitoring* (the fifth step) shows the BIP is successful (i.e., the inappropriate behavior ceases), then the FBA is done. If the inappropriate behavior continues, you need to go back to the third step and develop some new hypotheses. Remember, however, that long-standing behavior does not change overnight; you may need to follow the plan for two or three weeks before deciding whether it is making a difference (Friend & Bursuck, 2002).

Although FBA is an extremely useful tool, it is not simple, and identifying the underlying function of a behavior may require the assistance of well-trained observers (Landrum & Kauffman, 2006). Therefore, teachers need to consult with special services personnel.

DEALING WITH THORNY PROBLEMS

Some problem behaviors seem to plague teachers regardless of where they are teaching. It's impossible to generate recipes for dealing with these problems, since every instance is unique in terms of key players, circumstances, and history. Nonetheless, it is helpful to reflect on ways to deal with them *before* they occur and to hear some of the thinking that guides the actions of our four teachers. In this section of the chapter, we will consider four behaviors that keep teachers awake at night wondering what to do.

Defiance

Some years ago, Claire came to seminar looking shaken and upset. When we inquired what was wrong, she shared this story:

> *My ninth-graders were really rowdy today. I'm not sure what was going on, but they just wouldn't stop talking and laughing and calling out. One boy in particular, Jamal, was really annoying me. He wouldn't stay in his seat; he kept going to the back corner of the room where his buddies sit. I kept telling him to sit down, and he'd slowly saunter over to his desk. But then a few minutes later, I'd see he was up again. Finally, I got so mad, I just yelled across the room, "Jamal, I've had it with you. Get out! Go to the office!" And he looked at me and in this real slow, mocking voice he said, "Make me." I just froze. This kid is more than six feet tall and really strong. He towers over me. I had no idea what to do. Finally, I said something stupid like, "I'm not going to make you, but you just better sit down." Then I just ignored him for the rest of the period. I felt like a complete jerk, and he knew it.*

Claire's interaction with Jamal was traumatic for her and unfortunate for him, but it gave our seminar group an opportunity to examine ways of dealing with defiance. As we pondered alternative strategies, it became obvious that *the best course of action would have been to avoid the situation in the first place.* For example, after she had repeatedly told him to sit down without success, she might have approached him and quietly, but firmly, let him know that he had the choice of getting to work or facing one of the consequences for inappropriate behavior (e.g., "Jamal, here are your choices. You can sit down and begin working or you can go to Ms. Rosen's classroom for time out"; "Jamal, you can sit down and begin working now or you can work on it after school"). Unfortunately, by shouting across the room, Claire created a public power struggle. She backed Jamal into a corner with no "graceful exit," and Jamal was forced to challenge her if he wanted to save face with his peers.

Having said that, we still need to consider Claire's options once Jamal defied her order to get out. When we recounted this episode to our four teachers, they gave several suggestions for dealing with defiance. (These are listed in the Practical Tips box.)

PRACTICAL TIPS FOR

HANDLING DEFIANCE

- **Don't lose your cool.** Stay in control of yourself. Even though your first inclination may be to shout back, don't. (It may help to take a few deep breaths and to use self-talk: "I can handle this calmly. I'm going to speak quietly.")

- **Direct the rest of the class to work on something** (e.g., "Everyone do the next three problems" or "Start reading the next section").

- **Move the student away from peers.** Talk to the student in an area where you can have more privacy. This eliminates the need for the student to worry about saving face.

- **Stand a few feet away from the student (i.e., don't get "in his face").** A student who is feeling angry and defiant may interpret closing in on him as an aggressive act (Wolfgang, 1999).

- **Acknowledge the student's feelings.** "I can see that you're really angry. . ."

- **Avoid a power struggle.** Do not use assertions like "I'm the boss in here and I'm telling you to . . ."

- **Offer a choice:** In Jamal's case, the confrontation was no longer about doing the work, but about going to the office. So the choices should focus on this issue: "Jamal, I can see that you're really upset, and we'll have to talk later. But meanwhile, here are the choices. You can go to the office, or I'll have to send for someone to come and get you."

Interestingly, as the teachers discussed ways of responding to defiance, we began to understand that this was not a major problem for any of them. When Sandy commented that she could "count on one hand the cases of insubordintation" she had encountered in a lifetime of teaching, the others nodded in agreement. So we asked why they thought that students in their classes were rarely defiant. The teachers were unanimous in their response: They don't allow minor problems to escalate into major ones. Donnie put it this way:

> I sometimes see students in the office, and I ask them, "Why are you down here?" They'll tell me, "I was thrown out for chewing gum." But you know that couldn't be the whole story. It probably started out with gum chewing, but escalated into a real power struggle. And for what? We need to make sure that we don't blow up situations way out of proportion.

And Fred had one last suggestion for new teachers: "If defiance is *not* a rare thing in your classroom, then it's time to think seriously about what you're doing with those kids. Some examination of your own practice is clearly in order." (See Chapter 13 for a related discussion of defusing potentially explosive situations.)

Failure to Do Homework

When students consistently fail to do homework assignments, you need to consider just how valuable those assignments are and if you have communicated that value to students. Fred comments:

> I am convinced that if teachers were evaluated on the basis of the amount and quality of their homework assignments, students would have much less homework and would do more of it! I never give homework assignments unless I can explain the reason to my students. Having students understand the importance of doing a particular task at home cuts down dramatically on the number of missing assignments.

In a similar vein, Sandy tells her students "there's a reason for every assignment I give":

> I tell them, "I will not insult your intelligence by giving you garbage assignments that waste your time. Every assignment is necessary for what we're currently working on; you have to do it to meet with success."

It's also important to reflect on how much homework you're assigning, if it's too difficult for students to complete independently, and whether the time allotted is sufficient. Recall that in Chapter 3, Christina talked about an instance when students had been disgruntled by the amount and difficulty of the homework she had assigned: "They kept saying it was like college work and . . . they were only 15!" Together, Christina and her students forged an agreement that was mutually satisfactory. Some due dates were postponed, in-class time was provided so that students could work in groups on some of the work, and Christina made sure she was available for help after school.

In addition to monitoring the amount and difficulty of homework, you need to make sure that your students will be able to understand the assignments. One way of assuring this is to ask a colleague to review the assignment and give you feedback (Darling-Hammond & Ifill-Lynch, 2006). Another way is to have students start the homework in class under your supervision, so you can address any confusion before students attempt the assignment at home.

The Practical Tips box lists some additional strategies that can help increase the likelihood of students completing homework.

Despite your best efforts, some students will still not turn in homework. In this case, you need to meet individually to discuss the problem, generate possible solutions, and decide on an action plan. This might include contacting parents and asking for their cooperation and assistance, writing a contingency contract, or assigning a "homework buddy" to help the student remember and complete homework. Listen to Fred:

> Many teachers have hard and fast rules about homework, with serious consequences if homework is not turned in on time. But I've come to believe that this kind of rigidity often does more harm than good. I try

PRACTICAL TIPS FOR

INCREASING THE LIKELIHOOD THAT STUDENTS WILL DO THEIR HOMEWORK

- **Review, collect, or grade assignments.** If you assign homework and then fail to check that students have done it, you're conveying the message that the homework just wasn't that important. Not all homework has to be graded, or even collected, but it's wise to check that students have done it and to record that fact in your grade book.

- **Give "homework quizzes."** Since Donnie finds that getting some students to do homework is a "constant struggle," she gives students a daily quiz with one or two problems that are just like those assigned the night before for homework. In addition, she gives a "homework quiz" every week or two. She selects five problems that were previously given for homework and allows students to refer to their homework papers, but not their books.

- **Require a "product" in addition to reading.** When Christina assigned 17 pages of *The Martian Chronicles* for homework, she discovered that fully one-half of the class had not done the reading—despite the fact that she had warned them about having a quiz. According to Christina, "students just don't count reading as homework." She has learned that they are far more likely to do the reading if she also has them do something *with* it (e.g., use Post-it notes to mark your three favorite passages; list 10 words or phrases the author uses to give clues about the protagonist's character; generate three questions about the reading to ask your classmates).

- **Accept no excuses.** Sandy warns new teachers: "There are valid reasons for not doing homework. But if you start judging what's valid and what's not, that leads to a host of problems. My students know that I don't accept late homework. Period. If they don't have it, they come in and do it after school, because it's necessary for going on. But they get no credit for it."

- **Provide in-school support.** Sometimes, students' home circumstances may interfere with doing homework. They may be in the midst of a family crisis. They may be living in an abusive situation. They may have after-school jobs or other responsibilities that leave little time for schoolwork. Donnie shares this incident: "Just last week I was visiting a friend in the hospital and ran into one of my students—a girl who often dozed off in class and frequently didn't have her homework. It turned out that she worked at the hospital every day from 3:00 to 11:00! This explained a lot! She's got a full-time job in addition to going to high school." In situations like this, you might work with the student to develop a plan for getting homework done in school. Perhaps the student can do her homework during lunch or during a study hall. (If lunch is 40 minutes, a student can eat in 20 minutes and still have time to get started on homework.) Perhaps she can stop by your room before or after school for 15 minutes.

to work individually with kids who seem to be "irresponsible" with regard to homework. Together, we develop a plan for improving in this area.

Cheating

A number of studies suggest that cheating is more prevalent than we like to think. A 2008 national survey conducted by the Josephson Institute of Ethics asked nearly 30,000 high school students about their behavior during the last 12 months. Nearly two-thirds (64 percent) reported that they had cheated on a test, 36 percent said they'd copied an Internet document, and 82 percent admitted they'd copied a classmate's homework. Despite these admissions, 93 percent said they were "satisfied with my own ethics and character," and 77 percent agreed with the statement, "When it comes to doing what is right I am better than most people I know."

Obviously, cell phones, e-mail, and online searches make it easier than ever before to distribute information to friends and to plagiarize. Websites offer research papers for sale or give them away; often the papers are not well written and contain spelling and grammatical errors—a fact that can actually help students avoid suspicion (Ditman, 2000). Furthermore, many students don't consider copying and pasting from a website to be cheating (Ma, Lu, Turner, & Wan, 2007).

Once again, it's better to prevent the problem than to deal with it after the fact. This means finding ways to *diminish the temptation to cheat.* Research indicates that students are more likely to report cheating when they perceive the teacher as emphasizing performance over mastery (i.e., when it's more important to get an A on a test than to really learn the material) (Anderman, Griesinger, & Westerfield, 1998). Similarly, students report more cheating when the teacher relies on extrinsic incentives to stimulate motivation (e.g., giving homework passes to students who get As on a test) rather than trying to foster genuine interest in academic tasks. In light of this research, you need to make sure that the work you assign and the tests you give are fair and worthwhile and that you use the information they provide to help students master the material (Savage, 1999). You can also help students avoid the temptation to cheat by not basing students' grades on one or two "high-stakes" tasks (Savage, 1999). Although students may complain about frequent testing or assignments, they are less likely to cheat if they know that no one task will determine success or failure in the course.

At the beginning of the year, our four teachers also take the time to define cheating and to discuss how they feel about it. As we mentioned in Chapter 4, Sandy elaborates on the distinction between helping one another with homework and cheating. She emphasizes that cheating is "the ultimate disrespectful behavior," talks about the numerous behaviors that constitute cheating, gives students strategies for resisting peer pressure to cheat, and reviews the school's academic integrity policy, which students and parents have to sign. Similarly, Fred gives what he calls his "cheating sermonette": "Listen, you can lie and cheat and you may not be caught. . . . But if you don't cheat, you will be admirable."

In addition to reducing temptation, you can also take a number of simple precautions to *minimize opportunity.* When giving tests, for example, it's helpful to circulate throughout the room, use new tests each year, and create different forms of the same test for students seated in different rows. (With the help of a computer program, Donnie actually makes up four different forms for each test she administers.) We recently heard about a teacher who let four students take a make-up test out in the hallway. Not only was the test the same as the one the rest of the class had taken two days before (and which these students had heard about), the four students were allowed to sit together—unsupervised—to complete the test. Even the most ethical of students would find it hard to resist an opportunity like this!

If you are assigning papers, make sure that you give realistic deadlines and provide enough preparation so that students feel comfortable. Make it clear to students that you know about websites that offer papers for sale or for free; also make it clear that you know how to detect plagiarism by using a search engine like Google to search for words and phrases that don't sound like student writing. (You might even demonstrate!) Christina has students turn in bits and pieces of their research papers all along the way (e.g., notes, an outline, the first paragraph, a first draft), making it far more difficult for students to use a research paper obtained from a website.

Obviously, despite all your precautions, incidents of cheating will occur. It then becomes necessary to confront the students involved. The Practical Tips box lists some suggestions for handling those encounters.

Inappropriate Use of Electronic Devices

As we discussed in Chapter 4, cell phones and MP3 players are ubiquitous on school campuses, and students feel entitled to carry them. Thus, the inappropriate use of these devices during classes can become an issue. Students send and receive text messages (many can send messages without even looking at their phones!), or try to hide their earphone buds under a hood so they can listen to their MP3

PRACTICAL TIPS FOR

DEALING WITH CHEATING

- **Talk privately.** Once again, avoid creating a situation where the student may be publicly humiliated. This is likely to lead to a series of accusations and denials that get more and more heated.

- **Present your reasons for suspecting cheating.** Lay out your evidence calmly and firmly, even sorrowfully. (If you suspect plagiarism, get help from www.plagiarism.org.)

- **Express concern.** Make it clear that you do not expect this kind of behavior from this student. Try to find out why students cheated (e.g., Were they simply unprepared? Are they under a lot of pressure to excel?)

- **Explain consequences.** A common response to cheating is to give the student a low grade or a zero on the assignment or test. This seems like a sensible solution at first glance, but it confounds the act of cheating with the student's mastery of the content (Cangelosi, 1993). In other words, a person looking at the teacher's grade book would be unable to tell if the low grade meant the student had violated the test-taking procedures or if it indicated a failure to learn the material. We prefer using a logical consequence; namely, having the student redo the assignment or test under more carefully controlled conditions. But some schools have predetermined consequences for cheating, such as detention and parental notification. If so, you need to follow your school's policy.

- **Discuss the consequences for subsequent cheating.** Alert the student to the consequences for additional cheating incidents. Emphasize that you are available for assistance if cheating was the result of academic difficulties (i.e., there is no need to cheat because of problems with the material). If the student is under pressure at home to succeed, you may want to talk with parents. If students have no appropriate place to study at home, you might explore alternatives (e.g., studying at school or the public library).

players. Many schools are adopting schoolwide policies to deal with this issue, such as Sandy's school:

Students can have cell phones at school as long as you don't see them and they're turned off. They can't be used during the school day (not even between classes in the halls). If a cell phone goes off in a classroom, the teacher confiscates it, and a parent has to come pick it up. If a cell phone goes off during a test, the student earns a zero for the test. Sometimes kids don't know what turning off a cell phone means; they think that silencing your cell phone means it's off. I say to my students, "If you don't trust your cell phone, put it on my desk. If it beeps while it's there, it's okay." So today I had 24 cell phones on my desk!

If your school does not have a policy regarding cell-phone use, you will want to have a clear classroom policy. As Christina commented, "Cell phones are just electronic note passing. If you always watched your students to make sure they aren't passing notes, it's the same thing." The teachers we've worked with state the need for a clear and consistent expectation that phones will be silenced during class and stored in a backpack, unless they are being used in class work. To discourage students from taking their cell phones out during class, they require that backpacks be placed on the floor, and they continually move around the classroom. Moving around also allows them to spot headphones, and they can quietly remind students to turn off MP3 players if they aren't doing independent work.

In addition to having a classroom policy, don't underestimate the value of a schoolwide reputation. A teacher we know shared this story:

My school has a strict "no cell phones in the building" policy but it is difficult to enforce. I try to handle the issue in my classroom and not get the administration involved. I found a hammer in my room a few years ago and I joke with my kids that it is my "phone fixer." Not long after I found the hammer, a student gave me an old cell phone and we "fixed" it, leaving the pieces lying on my desk for my classes to discover. Within about a week and a half there was a wonderful rumor going around the school that I smash cell phones when I see them. It was pretty easy to keep the rumor going because it was a student's phone and I did smash it with a hammer. Just before the holiday break, I had a student approach me about staging a scene to take his old phone during my third hour and smash it in front of the class. The performance was Oscar worthy! I have been meaning to hang my hammer on the wall with a sign above it that reads "PHONE FIXER" and the pieces of a broken phone next to it with the sign "FIXED PHONE."

Pause and Reflect

Before reading the next section, consider the following scenario: A student in one of your classes comes to school wearing a T-shirt with a picture of former President Bush above the caption, "International Terrorist." You tell him to turn the shirt inside out or to cover it with a jacket because it's inappropriate for school and because other students think it is disrespectful. Are you acting within your rights—or are you violating your student's freedom of expression? Reflect, and then read on.

When Discipline Violates Students' Constitutional Rights

Before leaving the topic of disciplinary interventions, it's important to examine three types of situations in which well-meaning teachers may unknowingly violate students' constitutional rights. The first situation involves students' *freedom of expression.* Consider the case of Tim Gies, a sophomore at a Michigan high school when the United States was preparing to go to war in Iraq. Passionately anti-war and anti-Bush, Gies painted symbols and slogans onto T-shirts and sweatshirts. School administrators repeatedly told him to remove the clothing, but Gies refused; as a result, he was suspended for weeks at a time and eventually threatened with expulsion. That's when he called the local American Civil Liberties Union (ACLU), which notified the school that it was infringing on Gies's First Amendment rights (Juarez, 2005). In April 2005, right before graduation, administrators rescinded their prohibition on his anti-war clothing.

Conflicts like this occur on all points of the political spectrum. In 2001, Elliot Chambers, a high school student in Minnesota, wore a T-shirt to school bearing the slogan, "Straight pride." The principal prohibited his wearing the shirt, and Chambers's parents filed a lawsuit on his behalf. A federal judge ruled in their favor. And in 2005, Daniel Goergen's Minnesota high school refused to allow him to wear his sweatshirt with the words "Abortion is homicide." When a Christian law center warned of legal action, the school retreated (Juarez, 2005).

According to David Schimmel (2006), an expert on law and education, "despite decades of judicial decisions reaffirming the free speech rights of students, teachers and administrators continue to restrict controversial expression that they think might be offensive" (p. 1007). In 1969, the U.S. Supreme Court ruled that the First Amendment applies to public schools and that a student's right to freedom of expression "does not stop at the schoolhouse gate" (*Tinker v. Des Moines,* 1969, p. 506; cited by Schimmel, 2006). In that groundbreaking case, schools in Des Moines, Iowa, fearing disruption, had forbidden students to wear black armbands protesting the Vietnam War. The Court rejected the schools' argument, concluding that schools cannot prohibit expression just "to avoid the discomfort and unpleasantness that always accompany an unpopular viewpoint" (p. 509). Although subsequent Supreme Court decisions have narrowed *Tinker,* the basic principle remains intact, "that is, a student's nondisruptive personal expression that occurs in school is protected by the First Amendment even if the ideas are unpopular and controversial" (Schimmel, 2006, p. 1006). And this protection isn't limited to ideas expressed on clothing. In 1997, the Supreme Court ruled that speech on the Internet (just like speech in print) is entitled to the highest degree of protection under the First Amendment (Haynes, et al., 2003). Given these judicial rulings, you need to be careful about disciplining students for controversial expression, whether in speech or writings, on clothing, on websites, or in chat rooms. The Court acknowledged that schools can prohibit student expression that causes "substantial disruption or interferes with the rights of others" (Schimmel, 2006), but this judgment is not easy to make. Without question, you need to consult with a school administrator or the district's legal counsel before taking disciplinary action.

The second situation is when educators' actions conflict with students' Fourth Amendment rights against search and seizure. For example, suppose you suspect that a student is in possession of drugs or alcohol in school (e.g., in a purse or backpack). Do you have the right to search the student's belongings or not? The answer derives from a landmark case (*New Jersey v. T.L.O.,* 1985), in which the U.S. Supreme Court ruled that a school official may properly conduct a search of a student "when there are reasonable grounds for suspecting that the search will turn up evidence that the student has violated or is violating either the law or the rules of the school" (Fischer, Schimmel, & Kelly, 1999). In other words, students in school have fewer protections than are normally afforded to citizens under the stricter "probable cause" standard (Stefkovich & Miller, 1998).

Although the Supreme Court ruling in *T.L.O.* was issued 25 years ago, searches are still a subject of debate and litigation. Indeed, while we were working on this chapter, the Supreme Court was hearing the case of *Safford Unified School District v. Redding* (Liptak, March, 2009). In this case, an assistant principal ordered the school nurse and a secretary to strip-search an eighth-grade honor student suspected of possessing prescription-strength ibuprofen tablets. No drugs were found, and the girl's mother, represented by the ACLU, filed suit against the school district. Although a district court in Arizona ruled *for* the school district, stating that the search was justified, a Court of Appeals in San Francisco ruled that the school had violated the student's Fourth Amendment rights. The Supreme Court subsequently ruled that the strip search *did* violate the student's constitutional rights (Liptak, June, 2009). Writing for the majority opinion, Justice Souter stated that "the pills in question . . . did not justify an embarrassing, frightening and humiliating search" (p. A16). However, the Court's decision did not provide clear guidance to school personnel on searches, instructing them only to take into account the danger of the suspected contraband and the likelihood of it being hidden on the student's person. The majority opinion in this case noted that school personnel only need "a moderate chance of finding evidence of wrongdoing" to justify a search (p. A16). Given the difficulty of determining what constitutes a "moderate chance" of finding evidence, it's best to leave that decision up to personnel familiar with the subtleties of the law.

Finally, another situation involving students' Fourth Amendment rights involves a form of time-out called "seclusion time-out," in which a student is removed from the classroom environment and placed alone in a room designated for this purpose. In recent years, several lawsuits have been brought by parents contending that school districts had violated their children's rights by improperly using seclusion time-out. In the *Peters v. Rome City School District* (2002) decision, for example, a jury in New York awarded $75,000 to a family whose second-grade child had been placed in a time-out room for over an hour with the door held shut (Ryan, Peterson, & Rozalski, 2007). If current advocacy efforts are successful, this form of time-out may be entirely prohibited; meanwhile seclusion time-out should be used only as a last resort, and only after checking carefully on school or district policies and procedures.

CONCLUDING COMMENTS

As real human beings working in different school contexts, our four teachers some-times differ from one another in terms of the strategies they select for dealing with problem behaviors. Fred, for example, uses pointed humor more often than the other teachers; Sandy more readily imposes detention for lateness; Donnie more frequently uses proximity and a gentle touch on a student's shoulder. Nonetheless, these teachers share two important characteristics of effective classroom manag-ers. *First, they are clearly willing to take responsibility for the behavior of their students.* They rarely refer students to the office. They recognize that they are "in charge" and that they are accountable for what happens in their classrooms. This willingness to take responsibility distinguishes more effective managers from less effective managers, who tend to disclaim responsibility and refer problems to other school personnel, such as the principal or the guidance counselor (Brophy & Rohrkemper, 1981).

Second, all four teachers can be characterized as "warm demanders" (Bondy & Ross, 2008). They have deliberately built supportive, trusting relationships with their students. At the same time, they insist that students meet high expectations for behavior (as well as academics). Our teachers accept the fact that problem behaviors will occur, but they believe in students' ability to improve. They make it clear that they demand appropriate, respectful behavior not to be mean, but because they care about their students. As Fred says: "It's important to remem-ber that the goal of a penalty is not to hurt kids, but to help them change their behavior. It's not to put kids down; it's to bring them up."

SUMMARY

This chapter discussed ways of responding to a variety of problems—from minor, nondis-ruptive infractions to chronic, more serious misbehaviors.

Guidelines for Dealing with Misbehavior

- Use disciplinary strategies that are consistent with the goal of creating a safe, caring classroom environment.
- Keep the instructional program going with a minimum of disruption.
- Consider the context of students' actions. Behavior that is acceptable in one context may be unacceptable in another.
- Be timely and accurate when responding to behavior problems.
- Match your disciplinary strategy to the misbehavior.
- Be culturally responsive, since differences in norms, values, and styles of communication can have a direct effect on students' behavior.

Strategies for Dealing with Minor Misbehavior

- Nonverbal interventions.
- Verbal interventions.
- Deliberate non-intervention for misbehavior that is fleeting.

Strategies for Dealing with More Serious Misbehavior

- Select penalties:
    Mandatory private conferences.
    Loss of privileges.
    Isolation from the group.
    Exclusion from the group.
    Detention.
    Written reflection on the problem.
    Parental contact.
- Impose penalties while preserving relationships.
- Be consistent.
- Don't penalize the group for individual misbehavior.

Strategies for Dealing with Chronic Misbehavior

- Use a problem-solving approach:
    Step 1: Define the problem.
    Step 2: Brainstorm possible solutions.
    Step 3: Evaluate solutions.
    Step 4: Decide on a solution to try.
    Step 5: Determine how to implement the decision.
    Step 6: Evaluate the solution.
- Use a behavioral learning approach:
    Self-monitoring.
    Self-evaluation.
    Self-instruction.
    Contingency contracting.
    Positive behavioral supports and functional behavioral assessment.

Dealing with Thorny Problems

- Defiance.
- Failure to do homework.
- Cheating.
- Inappropriate use of electronic devices.

When Discipline Violates Students' Constitutional Rights

- The First Amendment protects students' freedom of expression, unless it causes substantial disruption or interferes with the rights of others.
- The Fourth Amendment protects students from unreasonable search and seizure; however, school searches are permitted if there are "reasonable grounds" for suspecting that the student violated the law or school rules.
- Be very cautious about using "seclusion time-out" since this is a very restrictive, controversial intervention that may also violate students' Fourth Amendment rights against unreasonable seizure.

Effective teachers are willing to take responsibility for managing students' behavior. They can also be characterized as "warm demanders"—teachers who establish trusting, supportive relationships with students, but also insist on respectful, appropriate behavior.

ACTIVITIES FOR SKILL BUILDING AND REFLECTION

In Class

1. When a misbehavior occurs, there usually isn't much time for careful consideration of logical consequences. We've listed a few typical misbehaviors for your practice. In a small group, think of two logical consequences for each example.

    a. As part of a small group, Lou monopolizes the discussion and tells everyone what to do in an authoritarian manner.
    b. At the end of the year, Arianna returns her book with ripped pages and the cover missing.
    c. Shemeika yells out answers throughout your class discussion, even though you have instructed students to raise their hands.
    d. Whenever you're not looking, Tom practices juggling with three small bean bags he has brought to school.
    e. Instead of working on the class activity, Tanya examines the contents of her cosmetic kit.

2. In a small group, discuss what would you do in the following situation. You are reviewing homework from the night before. You call on James to do number 5. He slumps in his seat and fidgets with the chain around his neck. You tell him the class is waiting for his answer to number 5. Finally he mutters, "I didn't do the f____homework."

On Your Own

1. Beginning teachers sometimes overreact to misbehavior or take no action at all because they simply don't know what to do or say. First, read the examples. Then consider the situations that follow and devise a nonverbal intervention, a verbal cue, and an I-message.

Example	Nonverbal	Verbal	I-Message
A student writes on the desk	Hand the student an eraser.	"We use paper to write on."	"When you write on the desk, the custodian complains to me and I get embarrassed."
A student makes a big show of looking through her book bag for her homework, distracting other students and delaying the start of the lesson.	Give the "look."	"We're ready to begin."	"When you take so long to get your things out, I can't begin the lesson, and I get very frustrated about the lost time."

a. A student is copying from another student's paper.

b. A student takes another student's notebook.

c. A student sharpens his pencil during your presentation.

d. A student calls out instead of raising her hand.

2. One common misbehavior in many classrooms is students being off task (e.g., talking to other students while the teacher is presenting a lesson, or trying to distract other students).

a. What might be some of the reasons for the students' off-task behavior?

b. What might you conclude about the classroom norms or the classroom activities if this misbehavior is common?

c. Given your responses to a and b, what would be a reasonable teacher response?

For Your Portfolio

Develop a behavior modification plan (such as self-monitoring or a contingency contract) to deal with the following problems:

a. Arthur is a seventh-grader who exhibits aggressive behavior. Hardly a day goes by that another student hasn't come to you complaining of Arthur's pushing, teasing, or name-calling. You've talked to his parents, but they are at a loss about what to do.

b. Cynthia, an eleventh-grader, rarely completes her work. She daydreams, socializes with others, misunderstands directions, and gets upset when you speak to her about her incomplete work. The problem seems to be getting worse.

FOR FURTHER READING

Bear, G. G. (1998). School discipline in the United States: Prevention, correction, and long-term social development. *School Psychology Review, 27*(1), 724–742.

This article reviews strategies used by highly effective classroom teachers to achieve the short-term goal of order and the long-term goal of self-discipline. Bear argues that effective teachers can be characterized by an authoritative style that combines stratgies for preventing behavior problems, operant learning strategies for short-term management, and decision-making and social problem-solving strategies to achieve the long-term goal of self-discipline.

Gordon, T. (2003). *Teacher effectiveness training: The program proven to help teachers bring out the best in students of all ages.* New York: Three Rivers Press.

In this updated edition of his 1974 classic, Gordon contends that both authoritarian and permissive approaches to dealing with young people in schools are destructive, "win-lose," power-based approaches. Instead, he advocates a "no-lose" approach to solving problems that protects the teacher-student relationship and promotes communciation and caring. He explains the concept of "problem-ownership" so that they can respond in appropriate ways.

Kottler, J. A., & Kottler, E. (2009). *Students who drive you crazy: Succeeding with resistant, unmotivated, and otherwise difficult young people* (2nd ed.). Thousand Oaks, CA: Corwin Press.

This book gives teachers a model to assess, understand, and respond to challenging students. The authors cover a range of potential misbehaviors that are prevalent in teaching, and provide advice and support from teachers, counselors, and administrators who have had previous experience in handling such issues in practice.

Obidah, J. E., & Teel, K. M. (2001). *Because of the kids: Facing racial and cultural differences in schools.* New York: Teachers College Press.

      Jennifer Obidah is Black; Karen Mannhein Teel is White. Together, they conducted a three-year study to explore the impact of racial and cultural differences on Karen's relationship with her primarily African American middle school students. In the process, the two teachers also had to learn to communicate with each other across racial and cultural boundaries. This book describes the challenges they faced as they tried to generate specific ways that Karen could more effectively educate her African American students.

Thompson, G. L. (2004). *Through ebony eyes: What teachers need to know but are afraid to ask about African American students.* San Francisco: Jossey-Bass.

      Written in lively, conversational language, this book provides information and strategies to help teachers increase their effectiveness with African American students. Thompson talks about why some African American students misbehave in class and how teachers often unwittingly contribute to their misbehavior.

PREVENTING AND RESPONDING TO VIOLENCE

By the year 2000 all schools in America will be free of drugs and violence and the unauthorized presence of firearms and alcohol, and offer a disciplined environment that is conducive to learning. (HR 1804: *Goals 2000: Educate America Act,* 1994, Sec. 102)

In the late 1990s, a series of school shootings in Mississippi, Kentucky, Arkansas, Pennsylvania, Tennessee, and Oregon made it clear that this laudable national goal, adopted by Congress and signed by then President Clinton, was certainly out of reach. But nothing prepared the country for the events of April 20, 1999. On that day, two seniors at Columbine High School in Littleton, Colorado, shot and killed 12 students and a teacher before turning their guns on themselves. Overnight, the topic of school violence catapulted to the front page. Copycat shootings, bomb scares, and threats of violence created unprecedented terror and upheaval during the final weeks of the school year. Parents agonized about sending their children to school. Politicians, policy makers, and pundits talked about youth violence as a "national epidemic" and speculated on the causes. School officials across the country worried that "their schools could become the next Columbine High" and increased security measures (Drummond & Portner, 1999). Five years later the country was jolted again when a high school student went on a shooting rampage on the Red Lake Indian Reservation in northern Minnesota, killing his grandparents, five fellow students, a teacher, a security guard, and himself. Since then, additional school shootings by students have occurred in Wisconsin, Washington, Ohio, Tennessee, California, and Florida.

But just how widespread is school violence? Were Columbine, Red Lake, and these more recent shootings symptomatic of a growing epidemic, or horrible but isolated incidents? Let's look at some facts and figures.

HOW MUCH VIOLENCE IS THERE?

Information on the frequency and severity of school violence comes from the U.S. Departments of Education and Justice (Dinkes, Cataldi, & Lin-Kelly, 2007). The data show that from 1992 to 2005 crime in the nation's schools actually *decreased*—from 50 violent incidents per 1,000 students to 24 violent incidents. From 1993 to 2005, the percentage of high school students who said they had been in a fight on school property declined from 16 percent to 14 percent. Similarly, the percentage of students who reported carrying a weapon such as a gun, knife, or club on school property within the previous 30 days also declined, from 12 percent to 6 percent.

Despite the decreasing percentages, violence remains a problem that must be confronted. In 2005, 129,000 students from ages 12–18 were victims of serious violent crimes at school, and an additional 74,000 students were victims of theft at school (Dinkes, Cataldi, & Lin-Kelly, 2007). Moreover, *perceptions* of violence are widespread and produce a great deal of anxiety. (See Figure 13.1.) After the Red Lake shootings, a Gallup/CNN poll reported that close to three-quarters of the American public believed such school shootings were likely to happen in their communities, and 60 percent did not think events like these could be prevented (Astor & Benbenishty, 2005). When asked to name the biggest problem that their school had to deal with, students from ages 13–17 mentioned violence, fighting, and school safety nearly twice as frequently as any other problem (Gallup Poll, 2005). Clearly, teachers and administrators

Figure 13.1   *Source:* BALDO © 2001, Baldo Partnership. Distributed by UNIVERSAL UCLICK.
Reprinted with permission. All rights reserved.

must work to decrease students' fears and anxiety, as well as actual incidents of school violence.

Many strategies for preventing violence have already been addressed in earlier chapters of this book. Getting to know your students, building respectful relationships, establishing orderly classrooms, curbing peer harassment and bullying, and working to meet students' learning needs all reduce the potential for violence. In this chapter we discuss additional strategies for preventing violence and then examine ways to react to violence if it occurs.

> ## PAUSE AND REFLECT
>
> With the issue of school violence so prevalent in the media, anxiety around this issue is normal for all teachers, but for novice teachers in particular. What are your fears associated with school violence? Talk to teachers in the school where you are observing or teaching about the procedures in place to deal with issues of violence. Knowing what to do in a crisis situation will not only ease anxieties, but may make a significant difference in the outcome.

STRATEGIES FOR PREVENTING VIOLENCE

Improve Security Systems

In the wake of Columbine, school officials all across the country reexamined their safety and security measures. Schools installed metal detectors and surveillance cameras, stationed police officers in high schools, introduced photo identification cards, practiced "lock-downs" and safety drills, and required clear plastic backpacks or banned them completely. Although enhanced security is a logical reaction to the threat of violent crime, studies suggest that measures like these may actually make students feel *less* safe and may not reduce incidents of violent crime (Barton, Coley, & Wenglinsky, 1998; Portner, 2000). Furthermore, some educators worry that security measures create a negative environment, turning schools into prisonlike, oppressive institutions (Astor, Meyer, & Behre, 1999; Berreth & Berman, 1997; Noguera, 1995).

It is clear that enhanced security systems alone will not solve the problem of school violence, nor will they allay students' fears and anxieties. Creating safer schools—and schools that *feel* safer—requires a collaborative effort to reach out to students (especially those on the margins) and build a climate of tolerance.

Build Supportive School Communities

Although we focused on creating safer, more caring classrooms in Chapter 3, it's important to revisit this topic in relation to violence prevention. Numerous educators argue that violence prevention has to focus on the creation of more humane environments in which students are known and feel supported (Astor, Meyer, & Behre, 1999; Noguera, 1995). The superintendent of Sandy's district echoes this sentiment:

> *A safe school is one that is responsive to students, where the staff knows the kids, where you can get help for troubled kids right away. . . . We*

don't talk much about metal detectors or security measures here. Our approach to violence prevention emphasizes connecting to kids and addressing their social-emotional needs. We try hard to make sure that one group isn't elevated over another. . . . and to respect differences among kids.

Creating a supportive school community is not easy, especially in large high schools, where feelings of anonymity, alienation, and apathy are leading causes of problems. Doing so, however, is perhaps more important than ever. Given the changing nature of families and economic conditions that require both parents to work outside the home, many students spend more time in the company of peers than adults. Since these peer relationships are not an adequate substitute for adult attention, it is critical that teachers develop and nurture caring relationships with their students (Laursen, 2008).

Be Alert to Signs of Hate

According to a report from the Southern Poverty Law Center (2004), the number of hate crimes by youngsters has risen sharply since 9/11:

> [A] disproportionate number of assaults on Muslim-Americans were committed by teenagers. The same appears to be true for attacks against sexual and gender minorities, Hispanics and the homeless. And hate activity is no longer the province of white boys, though they are still the main offenders. Not only are more Hispanic and African-American kids getting involved in hate, but more girls as well. . . . [Furthermore,] in another demographic shift, the bulk of hate activity now bubbles up in the suburbs—among reasonably well-off youth. (p. 1)

As a teacher, you need to take note if book reports, essays, or journal entries convey messages of hate or violence, and report your concerns to the principal, a school counselor, or the district's affirmative action officer. Be aware of online hate sites and recruitment by hate groups. (The Southern Poverty Law Center's Intelligence Project can help you stay informed about this.) Help students recognize hate literature containing swastikas, derogatory references to race or ethnicity, and caricatures of racial/ethnic groups, and discuss what students can do if they find or someone gives them a hate flier. At Halloween time, discourage costumes that involve negative stereotyping (e.g., "Gypsy" costumes or "homeless person" outfits) or organizations that promote hate (e.g., Ku Klux Klan robes).

Examine the Ways Your School Recognizes Student Achievement

Traditions that contribute to a sense of superiority among some students may lead to feelings of frustration or inadequacy in others. Are athletes disciplined less severely for offenses? Are their achievements highlighted more than the achievements of other students? Do honors students and student leaders enjoy special privileges? Recognition and special privileges may seem far removed from the issue of school violence. However, an investigation of conditions at Columbine High School prior to the 1999 shooting revealed rampant favoritism toward student athletes (Adams & Russakoff, 1999). Athletes convicted of crimes were allowed to continuing participating in their sports, and they were not disciplined for physically abusing other students. Sports trophies were displayed in the front hallway, while student artwork was relegated to a back hallway. While this certainly does not excuse the actions taken by the two shooters, there was ample evidence that the school's "cult of the athlete" contributed to their actions. Given this, it is important that teachers take action to avoid institutionalized favoritism, and find ways to recognize and celebrate different kinds of achievement.

Ask Students to Contribute to Violence Prevention Efforts

It is critical to learn what students' views are with respect to violence and violence prevention strategies—and to include not just the "good ones," but also "the toughies, the gangbangers, the disruptive, the withdrawn, and the unmotivated" (Curwin, 1995, p. 75). Encourage students to organize their own antiviolence events. Solicit their perceptions of the school's high-conflict areas (e.g., hallways, cafeterias, restrooms) and their ideas about how to make these safer. Invite students to develop an antibullying campaign.

A good example of the way students can become meaningfully involved is by becoming peer mediators. As discussed in Chapter 5, these programs are becoming increasingly popular in schools across the country. Sandy's school has had a peer mediation program for many years, and Tonia Moore, the student assistance counselor, believes that it has definitely helped to reduce incidents of violence:

> *Before we had peer mediation, we had lots of kids getting suspended for fighting; now we rarely have fights. Kids will tell the peer mediators when something is brewing, and they can prevent the problem from erupting into a physical fight. Peer mediation gives kids a structure they may not have developed yet for dealing with emotional issues.*

Thus far, anecdotal evidence supports Tonia's conviction that peer mediation programs can substantially reduce violent incidents. Some researchers contend that peer mediation actually has more impact on the *mediators* than on the disputants, since they acquire valuable conflict resolution skills and earn the respect of their peers (Bodine & Crawford, 1998; Miller, 1994). If this is so, it means that high-risk students—not just the "good kids"—must be trained and used as mediators.

Know the Early Warning Signs of Potential for Violence

In 1998, the U.S. Department of Education and the Department of Justice published a guide to assist schools in developing comprehensive violence prevention plans (Dwyer, Osher, & Warger, 1998). The guide contains a list of "early warning signs" that can alert teachers and other school staff to students' potential for violence, as well as signs that violence is imminent. These appear in Tables 13.1 and 13.2.

TABLE 13.1 Early Warning Signs of Potential for Violence

- Social withdrawal.
- Excessive feelings of isolation and being alone.
- Excessive feelings of rejection.
- Being a victim of violence.
- Feelings of being picked on and persecuted.
- Low school interest and poor academic performance.
- Expression of violence in writings and drawings.
- Uncontrolled anger.
- Patterns of impulsive and chronic hitting, intimidating, and bullying behaviors.
- History of discipline problems.
- Past history of violent and aggressive behavior.
- Intolerance for differences and prejudicial attitudes.
- Drug use and alcohol use.
- Affiliation with gangs.
- Inappropriate access to, possession of, and use of firearms.
- Serious threats of violence.

It's important to remember that the early warning signs are not an infalli-ble predictor that a child or youth will commit a violent act toward self or oth-ers (Dwyer, Osher, & Warger, 1998). Also keep in mind that potentially violent students typically exhibit multiple warning signs. Thus, be careful about overre-acting to single signs, words, or actions, and don't be biased by a student's race, socioeconomic status, academic ability, or physical appearance. Lindy Mandy, a counselor in Fred's school, acknowledges the tension between needing to identify students who may pose a risk for violence and *social profiling:*

> *We have kids who wear the gothic look, and after Columbine, we wanted to reach out to them. But you have to be so careful about stereotyping, thinking that everyone who dresses in gothic must be potentially violent or alienated. It really made us think about our process. At what point does identifying kids who might be violent become social profiling?*

The difficulty of distinguishing between a real threat to safety and harmless student expression is underscored by a 2000 federal court ruling in Washington State (Walsh, 2000). In this case, a high school junior submitted a poem to his English teacher about a lonely student who roamed his high school with a pounding heart. The poem contained this passage:

> As I approached the classroom door,
> I drew my gun and threw open the door.
> Bang, Bang, Bang-Bang.
> When it was all over, 28 were dead,
> and all I remember was not felling [sic] any remorce [sic],
> for I felt, I was, cleansing my soul.

TABLE 13.2 Imminent Signs of Violence

- Serious physical fighting with peers or family members.
- Severe destruction of property.
- Severe rage for seemingly minor reasons.
- Detailed threats of lethal violence.
- Possession and/or use of firearms and other weapons.
- Other self-injurious behaviors or threats of suicide.

The student's teacher alerted administrators, and the poem was reviewed by a psychologist, who determined that the student was unlikely to cause harm to himself or others. Nonetheless, the district decided to expel him on an emergency basis. After the student was examined by a psychiatrist, the district rescinded the expulsion, and the student completed his junior year. The boy's parents then sued the district, claiming that the school had violated his First Amendment right to free speech and asking that the expulsion be removed from their son's record. On February 24, 2000, a federal district judge ruled for the family, maintaining that the district had overreacted in expelling the student. She suggested that there were less restrictive ways the district could have ensured the safety of students and school personnel, such as imposing a temporary suspension pending psychiatric examination.

Stories like this can discourage teachers from reporting essays or artwork that contain threatening messages or behavior that suggests a potential for violence. But it's better to alert school officials about what you have learned than to ignore indicators and be sorry later. Find out what the reporting procedures are in your school: Do you report your concerns to the principal? The school nurse? A counselor? Do you notify parents? Remember that parental involvement and consent are required before personally identifiable information is shared with agencies outside the school (except in case of emergencies or suspicion of abuse). The Family Educational Rights and Privacy Act (FERPA), a federal law that addresses the privacy of educational records, must be observed in all referrals to community agencies (Dwyer, Osher, & Warger, 1998).

Be Observant in "Unowned" Spaces

In addition to knowing the early warning signs, teachers can help prevent violence by being observant in hallways, cafeterias, stairwells, and locker rooms—"unowned" spaces where violence is most likely to erupt (Astor, Meyer, & Behre, 1999). Chester Quarles, a criminologist who specializes in crime prevention, suggests that teachers attempt to make eye contact whenever they pass students in the halls:

> The subliminal message being exchanged is that "I know who is here and I know who you are. I can remember your features. I can identify you." The influence of careful observation is a strong criminal deterrent for everyone that you observe. . . . Observant teachers . . . can decrease the probability that any of the people they encounter will commit a delinquent act against another that day. (1989, pp. 12–13)

Be Attentive to Whispers and Rumors

The high-profile school shootings that we have witnessed in the last several years are what the Secret Service calls *targeted violence*—incidents in which the attacker selects a particular target prior to the violent attack. As part of the Safe School Initiative of the U.S. Secret Service and the U.S. Department of Education, researchers studied 37 school shootings involving 41 attackers who were current or recent students at the school (Vossekuil, et al., 2002). Here are some of their findings:

- Incidents of targeted violence at school are rarely sudden or impulsive. Typically, the attacker *planned* the attack in advance.
- In most of the cases, other people knew about the attack before it occurred. In over three-quarters of the cases, at least one person knew; in nearly two-thirds, more than one person knew. Some peers knew details of the attack, while others just knew that something "big" or "bad" was going to happen in school on a particular day.
- Most attackers engaged in some behavior prior to the incident that caused others concern or indicated a need for help.

These findings contradict the common perception that students who commit targeted acts of violence have simply "snapped." Nor are they loners who keep their plans to themselves. In a follow-up study, researchers interviewed 15 students who had known about potential threats of violence at their schools (Pollack, Modzelski, & Rooney, 2008). They found that the school climate affected whether or not these students reported the threats of violance. One student who knew of a weapon on school property was reluctant to come forward because he expected a negative reaction: "When you say something, you get in trouble or interrogated by teachers" (Pollack, Modzelski, & Rooney, 2008, p. 7). Additionally, many of the bystanders did not believe that the threats would be carried out, and so told no one. This means that school staff must be attentive to whispers that something is afoot and create a climate that encourages students to report rumors of potential violence. As Tonia Moore puts it, "You have to have your radar out all the time."

De-Escalate Potentially Explosive Situations

Explosive situations often begin benignly. You make a reasonable request ("Would you join the group over there?") or give an ordinary directive ("Get started on the questions at the end of this section"). But the student is feeling angry—maybe he has just been taunted and humiliated in the hallway; maybe her mother has just grounded her for a month; maybe the teacher in the previous class has ridiculed an answer. The anger may have nothing to do with you at all, but it finds its outlet in your class. In a hostile mood, the student fails to comply immediately and may even respond defiantly. Unfortunately, at this point, teachers often contribute to the escalation of a conflict by becoming angry and impatient. They issue an ultimatum: "Do what I say or else." And now teacher and student are combatants in a potentially explosive situation neither of them wanted.

Let's consider an example (adapted from Walker, Colvin, & Ramsey, 1995) of a teacher–student interaction that begins innocuously enough, but quickly escalates into an explosive situation:

> Students are working on a set of math problems the teacher has assigned. Michael sits slouched in his seat staring at the floor, an angry expression on his face. The teacher sees that Michael is not doing his math and calls over to him from the back of the room where she is working with other students.

TEACHER: Michael, why aren't you working on the assignment?

MICHAEL: I finished it.

TEACHER: Well, let me see it then. [She walks over to Michael's desk and sees that he has four problems completed.] Good. You've done 4 but you need to do 10.

MICHAEL: Nobody told me that!

TEACHER: Michael, I went over the assignment very clearly and asked if there were any questions about what to do!

MICHAEL: I don't remember that.

TEACHER: Look at the board. I wrote it there. See, page 163, numbers 11–20.

MICHAEL: I didn't see it. Anyway, I hate this boring stuff.

TEACHER: OK, that's enough. No more arguments. Page 163, 11 through 20. Now.

MICHAEL: It's dumb. I'm not going to do it.

TEACHER: Yes you are, mister.

MICHAEL: Yeah? Make me.

TEACHER: If you don't do it now, you're going to the office.

MICHAEL: F———you!

TEACHER: That's enough!

MICHAEL: You want math? Here it is! [He throws the math book across the room.]

At first glance, it appears that the teacher is being remarkably patient and reasonable in the face of Michael's stubbornness, defiance, and abuse. On closer examination, however, we can detect a chain of successive escalating interactions, in which Michael's behavior moves from questioning and challenging the teacher to defiance and abuse, and for which the teacher is also responsible (Walker, Colvin, & Ramsey, 1995). Could the teacher have broken this chain earlier? The probable answer is yes.

First, the teacher should have been sensitive to Michael's angry facial expression and the fact that he was slouching down in his seat. Facial expression, flushing, squinty eyes, clenched fists, rigid body posture, pacing and stomping—these all suggest an impending eruption (Hyman, 1997). Second, teachers can usually avoid defiant situations if they do not corner a student, do not argue, do not engage in a power struggle ("I'm the boss in this classroom, and I'm telling you to . . ."), and do not embarrass the student in front of peers. The Practical Tips box summarizes specific recommendations.

With this background, let's go back to Michael and see how the teacher might have dealt with the situation to prevent it from escalating.

Students are working on a set of math problems the teacher has assigned. Michael sits slouched in his seat staring at the floor, an angry expression on his face. The teacher notices Michael's posture and realizes that he is feeling upset about something. She goes over, bends down so that she is on eye-level with Michael, and speaks very quietly.

TEACHER: Are you doing OK, Michael? You look upset. [Teacher demonstrates empathy.]

MICHAEL: I'm OK.

TEACHER: Well, good, but if you'd like to talk later, let me know. [Teacher invites further communication.] Meanwhile, you need to get going on this assignment.

MICHAEL: I already did it.

TEACHER: Oh, good. Let me see how you did. [She checks the paper.] OK, you've done the first four, and they're fine. Now do the next four problems and let me see them when you're done. [She walks away, giving the student space.]

Be Alert for the Presence of Gang Activity

A report issued by the U.S. Departments of Education and Justice (Chandler, Chapman, Rand, & Taylor, 1998) found that the presence of gangs in schools nearly doubled between 1989 and 1995, when approximately one-third of the 10,000 students surveyed (aged 12 to 19) reported gang presence. In 2005, 24 percent of students reported that there were gangs at their schools (Dinkes, Cataldi, & Lin-Kelly, 2007). Since gang presence is strongly linked to the presence of guns, drugs, and violence (Howell & Lynch, 2000), teachers need to be alert to the presence of gang activity in schools.

It's not easy to identify a gang, since teenagers frequently "run in packs" and try to look and act just like everyone else. However, a group of teenagers does not constitute a gang. A widely accepted definition of gangs includes these variables: group, permanence, symbols of membership, acknowledgement of membership, and involvement in crime (Naber, et al., 2006). Kenneth Trump, president of the National School Safety and Security Services, reminds us that the key to gang activity is negative behavior:

> Kids who sit together in the lunch room don't constitute a gang. But when groups start assaulting other students or creating an atmosphere of fear and intimidation, they become a gang. In short, groups of students reach gang status when their behavior, either individually or collectively, is disruptive, antisocial, or criminal. (1993, p. 40).

To determine the extent to which gangs are present in your school, you need to be familiar with the indicators summarized in Table 13.3. Keep in mind, however, that indicators of gang affiliation such as clothing style or colors change frequently, especially as school personnel learn what signifies gang affiliation and outlaw those clothing items (Struyk, 2006). Gang members simply adopt subtler indicators, such as belt buckles engraved with gang symbols, or earrings worn in combination with other accessories.

According to Donnie, gang activity in her city was intense about five years ago, when adolescents were divided into "uptown" and "downtown" gangs:

What you saw was that the kids who lived in the projects stayed together and kept up a feud with the kids on the other side of town. They'd fight about drugs, about somebody from one side of town going out with a girl from the other side of town, about somebody "ratting" on somebody else. Whenever there was a gang fight over the weekend or at night, the kids would all come in buzzing the next day. One year, a kid got killed in a gang fight, and

TABLE 13.3 Signs of Gang Presence

Gathering or hanging out	Gang members may establish territory (e.g., in the lunch room, on playing fields, and in bleachers). Once these areas are claimed, other students will stay away.
Nonverbal and verbal signs	Gang members often have special ways of signaling one another and conveying messages:
	"Flashing"—the use of finger and hand signs.
	"Monikers"—nicknames emphasizing a member's particular attribute.
Graffiti	Signs, symbols, and nicknames on notebooks, papers, clothing, and walls; graffiti advertises the gang and its members and may contain challenging messages to other gangs; when graffiti is crossed out, that constitutes a direct challenge from a rival gang.
Stance and walk	Unique ways of standing and walking that set them apart.
Symbols	Tattoos, earrings, colors, scarves, bandannas, shoelaces, caps, belts (change over time).

Source: Adapted from Lal, Lal, & Achilles, 1993.

 PAUSE AND REFLECT

How prevalent is gang activity in the school where you are observing or teaching? What schoolwide rules are in place to restrict gang activity on campus? Think about how the presence of gangs in a school may impact your classroom. How might you attempt to defuse any tension between rival gang members who happen to be in one of your classes?

there was a tremendous amount of tension that spilled over into the school. It would simmer down, and then every year, there'd be a big memorial to him that would rekindle all the trouble. But it seems as if the main kids who were involved have moved on. Things have been a lot quieter the last few years.

The presence of gang activity in schools can seem like a problem too complex for a classroom teacher to address. Remember, however, that students join gangs to satisfy needs that aren't being met elsewhere—namely, to belong to a group that is powerful and whose members stick up for each other. Although you may not be able to influence the "hard core" members of gangs, you may be able to provide potential gang members with the personal connection and sense of belonging that they need to resist gang membership.

 PAUSE AND REFLECT

Imagine an incident of aggressive behavior occurring in your classroom (e.g., a student explodes in anger and throws a book at another student). Think about the steps you would take to stop the aggression from escalating and to restore calm. What words would you use? Then, continue on to the next section and see how Sandy handled an outburst that occurred in her classroom.

RESPONDING TO VIOLENCE

Coping with Aggressive Behavior

Despite your best efforts at prevention, there are times when students erupt in hostile, aggressive behavior. A girl screams profanities and knocks a pile of dictionaries to the floor. A boy explodes in anger and throws a chair across the room. Someone yells, "I'll kill you," and hurls a notebook at another student. In situations like this—every teacher's nightmare—it's easy to lose self-control and lash out. As Fred puts it,

> The *normal* reaction is to become angry and aggressive and to get in the kid's face. But *teachers can't react normally*. That will only make things worse, and your responsibility is *to make things better*.

In order to "make things better," you need to think carefully about what you will do to defuse the aggression and protect yourself and your students. Let's consider an episode that occurred in Sandy's classroom.

> As usual, I was standing at the doorway as the kids were coming into the classroom. I noticed Robert come in without his backpack or any books. That didn't look right, and I watched him cross the room and go over to Daniel, who was sitting at his desk. Robert picked up the desk and the leg of Daniel's chair and overturned them, cursing and screaming the whole time. I ran over. The first thing I said was "Daniel, don't raise your hands." He was on the floor on his back, and Robert was standing over him screaming. I kept saying, "Robert, look at me, look at me, look at me." Finally, he made eye contact. Then I said, "You need to come with me." We began to walk toward the door, but he turned back and started cursing again. Very quietly and firmly I told him, "You need to come with me now." He followed me to the door, and as I reached the door I picked up the phone and called the office and said there was a problem and to send someone up. Then we stepped out into the hallway. Robert was angry and was going to leave, and I asked him to please stop and talk to me about what was going on, what was bothering him. I didn't yell, I didn't say, "How could you do something so stupid?" (even though that's what I felt like saying). I said, "Obviously you're upset about something. Tell me about it." It turns out that these two were friends, but Robert found out that Daniel was sleeping with his [Robert's] girlfriend. I heard a lot I didn't really want to hear, but it kept him occupied until the vice-principal came up.
>
> Once the vice-principal took Robert, I got Daniel out into the hallway and asked him if he was OK, and if he needed to go to the nurse, or needed to be out of the classroom. He said no, he was OK. I told him, "You were very smart for not raising your hands against Robert." He returned to his seat, and all the kids started saying, "Daniel, are you OK?" and crowding around him. I told them, "Robert's in the office. Daniel's OK. Let's get started on chemistry." At the end of

the period, the office called for Daniel to go to the peer mediation room to have the dispute mediated.

In addition to going to peer mediation, Robert was suspended for three days. But the day he was suspended, he came back after school hours (something he wasn't supposed to do) to apologize for his language. I accepted his apology, but I said that there were other ways to handle the situation and to express anger. It was a very low-key discussion. I didn't make light of what had happened, but I told him I was glad he realized the danger of the situation.

After the suspension, Daniel came to me before homeroom to say he was feeling frightened about coming to class that day. It was going to be his first meeting with Robert, and Robert sits right in front of him. I said that I had already changed both their seats. I told him, "Don't worry, I'll be watching." When they came in, I told them each "You have a new seat," and showed them where to sit. There was no problem from that point on.

Analysis of Sandy's response to Robert's outburst reveals some important guidelines for dealing with aggression in the classroom. Let's examine her behavior more closely and consider the lessons to be learned.

1. Although Sandy admits that she wanted to respond with anger ("What is wrong with you?!"), she remained outwardly calm and in control. By doing so, she was able to *prevent the situation from escalating.* She lowered the level of emotion in the class and decreased the chance of becoming a victim herself. She then directed Daniel not to raise his hands against Robert. This prevented Robert's aggressive actions from escalating into a full-scale physical fight. Next, she issued quiet, firm, repetitive instructions for Robert to look at her. This created a lull in the altercation, during which she was able to separate the two boys ("You need to come with me."). Since Daniel was lying on the floor under the desk, it was easier for her to have Robert move away. In other cases, however, it may be advisable to remove the targets of the aggression. You can direct them to go to a nearby teacher's classroom, preferably with a friend, since they are bound to be angry and upset ("Take Scott and go to Ms. Thomson's room so we can get this sorted out") or have them move to a far corner of the room, out of the aggressor's line of sight.

2. Sandy's next action was to report that there was a problem in her room and *to summon help.* Never send angry, aggressive students to the office alone: You cannot be certain they will actually get there, nor do you know what they will do on the way. If you do not have a telephone or intercom, quietly instruct a responsible student to go for assistance.

    Who should be summoned will vary, so it's important for you to check on the procedures in your own school. Fred would call one of the two SROs—security resource officers—who patrol the hallways. Christina and Sandy would call the main office. Donnie would contact one of the security guards.

3. While Sandy waited for someone from the office to provide assistance, she spoke privately and quietly with Robert in an attempt to *defuse the aggression.*

She did not rebuke or threaten punishment. Instead, she acknowledged his anger and showed her willingness to listen.

Again, it's critical that you resist the temptation to "react normally" and lash out at the student. You need to speak slowly and softly and to minimize threat by not invading the student's space and keeping your hands by your side. Allow the student to relate facts and feelings, even if it involves profanity, and use active listening ("So you were really furious when you found out what was happening . . ."). Do not disagree or argue.

If, despite your efforts to restore calm, the student's aggression escalates, it is best to move away unless you are trained in physical restraint techniques. Even then, don't use restraint unless you are strong enough and there are no other options. As Hyman (1997) emphasizes, "The last thing you ever want to do is to physically engage an enraged student who may be out of control" (p. 251).

4. When Robert came to see Sandy after school, he gave her the opportunity to discuss what had happened, to reinforce alternative ways to handle anger, and to accept his apology. He also gave her the chance to *reestablish a positive relationship*. Fred emphasizes how important this is:

Suspending a violent kid isn't the end of the situation. At some point, the kid is going to come back, and then it's your job to rebuild the relationship. You need to reassure them that they're still a member of the class. You need to tell them, "OK, you messed up. But I'm on your side. You can learn from this."

5. Once Robert was on his way to the office and Daniel was back in his seat, Sandy scanned the room in order to *determine how the other students were feeling* and what to do next. She decided that her best course of action was to provide them with the basic facts ("Robert is in the office. Daniel's OK.") and to begin the lesson ("Let's get started on chemistry"). She certainly did not want to explore with her class the reasons behind Robert's aggressive actions.

Sometimes, however, your students may be so upset and frightened that it's impossible to continue working. Tonia Moore suggests that it's important to allow them to express their feelings:

If the students are upset, you have to give them the opportunity to talk about what happened and to acknowledge their fear. You don't want to pretend nothing happened and then send them on to the next class all churned up inside.

Responding Effectively to Physical Fights

Physical fights are more likely to occur in hallways and cafeterias than in classrooms. But what do you do if you're on the scene when a fight erupts? We

> ## Practical Tips for
>
> ### RESPONDING EFFECTIVELY TO PHYSICAL FIGHTS
>
> - **Quickly appraise the situation.** Is this a verbal altercation? Is there physical contact? Does anyone have a weapon?
> - **Send a responsible student for help.** Send for the nearest teacher and for the principal or vice-principal. Once other people are there to help, it's easier—and safer—to get the situation under control.
> - **Tell students to stop.** Often, students don't want to continue the fight, and they'll respond to a short, clear, firm command. If you know the combatants' names, use them.
> - **Disperse other students.** There's no need for an audience, and you don't want onlookers to become part of the fray. If you're in the hallway, direct students to be on their way. If you're in the classroom, send your students to the library or to some other safe place.
> - **Do not intervene physically**—unless the age, size, and number of combatants indicates that it's safe to do so, there are three or four people to help, or you have learned physical restraint.

asked the teachers that question one evening, as we talked about the problem of violence in schools. They were unanimous in their response, listed in the Practical Tips box. As we discussed the issue of fighting in school, the teachers repeatedly stressed the fact that fights are fast. They can erupt quickly—so you don't have a lot of time to think through a response—and they're usually over in less than 30 seconds (although that can seem like a lifetime). There was also amazing unanimity among the teachers on the issue of fights among girls versus boys. As Donnie put it: "Teachers shouldn't think that fighting is only going to happen among boys. Girls fight too—and girl fights are terrible. Girls kick, pull earrings, bite, scratch, and when you try to stop it, they turn on *you.*"

It's important to remember that you must report violent acts. Every school system needs to have a violent incident reporting system that requires you to report what happened, when and where it happened, who was involved, and what action was taken (Blauvelt, 1990).

CONCLUDING COMMENTS

Using data from the National Longitudinal Study of Adolescent Health, the largest study ever conducted of teenagers in the United States, researchers set out to identify factors that predict whether adolescents will commit acts of violence (Resnick, Ireland, & Borowsky, 2004). They identified several factors that make violence more likely, such as carrying a weapon, experiencing problems at school, and using alcohol and marijuana. They also identified factors that decrease the likelihood of involvement in violence. Of particular relevance to this chapter is their finding that *feeling connected to school is a key protective factor;* in other words, both males and females are less likely to perpetrate violence when they feel part of the school community.

Installing metal detectors and state-of-the-art security systems can only go so far in creating a more peaceful school. The challenge for teachers and administrators is to reach out to young people and help them feel connected. In the final analysis, it is the presence of caring adults that holds the greatest promise for preventing school violence.

Summary

Although data on the frequency and severity of school violence indicate a decrease, students, teachers, and parents are fearful, and the perception that violence is increasing is widespread. This chapter presented a variety of strategies for preventing and responding to violence.

Prevention Strategies

- Improve security systems.
- Build supportive school communities:
    Be alert to signs of hate.
    Examine the ways your school recognizes student achievement.
    Ask students to contribute to violence prevention efforts.
- Know the early warning signs of potential for violence.
- Be observant in "unowned" spaces.
- Be attentive to whispers and rumors.
- De-escalate potentially explosive situations.
- Be alert for the presence of gang activity.

Responding to Violence

- Coping with aggressive behavior:
    Prevent escalation.
    Summon help.
    Defuse the aggression.
    Reestablish a positive relationship with the aggressor.
    Determine how the other students are feeling.
- Responding effectively to physical fights:
    Quickly appraise the situation.
    Send a responsible student for help.
    Tell the students to stop.
    Disperse onlookers.
    Do not intervene physically unless it is safe.

Metal detectors and security systems can only go so far. It's essential to build connections with students. In the final analysis, it is the presence of caring adults that holds the greatest promise for preventing violence.

ACTIVITIES FOR SKILL BUILDING AND REFLECTION

In Class

Consider the following situations. In small groups, discuss what you would do in each case.

a. As students enter your classroom, you overhear a girl teasing Annamarie about the boy Annamarie's dating. They go to their seats, but the taunts continue. Suddenly, Annamarie stands up, turns to the girl, and shouts, "You shut up, bitch. Just shut up, or I'll get you!"

b. Your students are taking a brief quiz on the homework. Those who have finished already are reading. As you circulate throughout the room, collecting the finished papers, you notice that James is looking at a catalog of weapons. He makes no attempt to conceal it.

c. Jesse comes to your first-period class wearing a T-shirt with a Celtic cross surrounded by the words "White Pride World Wide."

d. You ask Carla where her textbook is. She mutters something under her breath. When you tell her you didn't hear what she said, she shouts, "I left the f____book in my locker!"

On Your Own

Interview an experienced teacher, the student assistance counselor, the school nurse, or a guidance counselor about the school's efforts to prevent violence. Find out answers to the following questions:

If you think a student exhibits some of the early warning signs of potential for violence, to whom do you report?

Is there an official form to file?

Do you contact parents?

Are school personnel aware of gang activity?

What are the indicators of gang membership and gang activity?

For Your Portfolio

Document how you will establish a classroom climate in which students are comfortable telling you about threats of violence at school. Modify any of the artifacts you created after Chapter 3 to incorporate this chapter's material. Write a brief commentary explaining how you will help your students understand the importance of reporting threats.

FOR FURTHER READING

Colvin, G. (2004). *Managing the cycle of acting-out behavior in the classroom.* Eugene, OR: Behavior Associates.

This book provides practical strategies for managing and preventing acting-out behavior such as defiance, tantrums, threats, resistance, avoidance, and classroom disruption at various levels. It presents a model of acting-out behavior that consists of seven phases. The characteristics of each phase are described using examples and case studies. Strategies are then presented for interventions that can be used for each phase.

Noguera, P. (1995). Preventing and producing violence: A critical analysis of responses to school violence. *Harvard Educational Review, 65,* 189–212.

    In this article, Pedro Noguera asks whether the strategies that schools adopt in response to "disciplinary problems," including violence, actually perpetuate violence. Noguera argues that "get-tough" disciplinary measures produce prison-like schools, interrupt learning, and produce an environment of mistrust and resistance. He offers alternative strategies for humanizing school environments and encouraging a sense of community.

Teaching Tolerance is a magazine that is mailed twice a year at no charge to educators. It is published by the Southern Poverty Law Center, a nonprofit legal and educational foundation. (See listing below.) The magazine provides a wealth of information and resources on all aspects of promoting tolerance and respect and eliminating bias, oppression, and bullying (www.teachingtolerance.org).

ORGANIZATIONAL RESOURCES

The Anti-Defamation League (ADL), 823 United Nations Plaza, New York, NY 10017 (www.adl.org, 212-885-7970). Dedicated to combating hate crime and promoting intergroup cooperation and understanding.

Drug Strategies, 1616 P Street, Suite 220, Washington, DC 20036 (www.drugstrategies .com, 202-289-9070). Publishes a guide on conflict resolution and violence prevention curricula.

National School Safety Center, 141 Duesenberg Dr., Suite 11, Westlake Village, CA, 91362 (www.nssc1.org, 805-373-9977). Resource for school safety information, training, and violence prevention.

Office of Safe and Drug-Free Schools, 550 12th Street, SW, 10th Floor, Washington, DC 20202-6450 (www.ed.gov/offices/OESE/SDFS/news.html, 202-245-7896). Provides reports and articles on school safety and school violence.

The Southern Poverty Law Center, 400 Washington Avenue, Montgomery, AL 36104 (www.teachingtolerance.org, 334-956-8200). The Teaching Tolerance project provides teachers at all levels with ideas and free resources for building community, fighting bias, and celebrating diversity.

Students Against Violence Everywhere (SAVE), 322 Chapanoke Rd., Suite 110, Raleigh NC, 27603 (www.nationalsave.org, 866-343-SAFE). This student-driven organization helps students learn about alternatives to violence and encourages them to practice what they have learned through school and community projects.

REFERENCES

The AAUW Report: How schools shortchange girls. (1992). Washington, DC: The AAUW Educational Foundation and National Education Association.

Abd-Kadir, J., & Hardman, F. (2007). Whole class teaching in Kenyan and Nigerian primary schools. *Language and Education, 21*(1), 1-15.

Adams, L., & Russakoff, D. (1999, June 12). Dissecting Columbine's cult of the athlete, *Washington Post,* p. A-1.

Adams, R. S., & Biddle, B. J. (1970). *Realities of teaching: Explorations with video tape.* New York: Holt, Rinehart, & Winston.

Akin-Little, K. A., Little, S. G., & Laniti, M. (2007). Teachers' use of classroom management procedures in the United States and Greece: A cross-cultural comparison. *School Psychology International, 28*(1), 53-62.

Alberto, P. A., & Troutman, A. C. (2006). *Applied behavior analysis for teachers* (7th ed.). Upper Saddle River, NJ: Pearson Prentice Hall.

Alfi, O., Assor, A., & Katz, I. (2004). Learning to allow temporary failure: Potential benefits, supportive practices, and teacher concerns. *Journal of Education for Teaching, 30*(1), 27-41.

Allen, J. (2008). Family partnerships that count. *Educational Leadership, 66*(1), 22-27.

Alpert, B. (1991). Students' resistance in the classroom. *Anthropology and Education Quarterly, 22,* 350-366.

Alvermann, D., O'Brien, D., & Dillon, D. (1990). What teachers do when they say they're having discussions of content area reading assignments. *Reading Research Quarterly, 25,* 296-322.

American Association of University Women [AAUW]. (1993). Hostile hallways: The AAUW survey on sexual harassment in America's schools. Washington, DC: AAUW.

American Psychiatric Association (2000). *Diagnostic and statistical manual of mental disorders* (4th ed., text rev.). Washington, DC: Author.

Anderman, E. M., Griesinger, T., & Westerfield, G. (1998). Motivation and cheating during early adolescence. *Journal of Educational Psychology, 90*(1), 84-93.

Anderman, E. M., & Maehr, M. L. (1994). Motivation and schooling in the middle grades. *Review of Educational Research, 64*(2), 287–309.

Anderson, J. D. (1997). Supporting the invisible minority. *Educational Leadership, 54*(7), 65–68.

Anderson, K. J., & Minke, K. M. (2007). Parent involvement in education: Toward an understanding of parents' decision making. *The Journal of Educational Research, 100*(5), 311–323.

Anderson, L. (1985). What are students doing when they do all that seatwork? In C. W. Fisher and D. C. Berliner (Eds.), *Perspectives on instructional time* (pp. 189–202). New York: Longman.

Antil, L. R., Jenkins, J. R., Wayne, S. K, & Vadasy, P. F. (1998). Cooperative learning: Prevalence, conceptualizations, and the relation between research and practice. *American Educational Research Journal, 35*(3), 419–454.

Applebee, A. N., Langer, J. A., Nystrand, M., & Gamoran, A. (2003). Discussion-based approaches to developing understanding: Classroom instruction and student performance in middle and high school English. *American Educational Research Journal, 40*(3), 685–730.

Arends, R. I. (2008). *Learning to teach* (8th ed.). New York: McGraw-Hill.

Arlin, M. (1979). Teacher transitions can disrupt time flow in classrooms. *American Educational Research Journal, 16,* 42–56.

Aronson, E., Blaney, N., Stephan, C., Sikes, J., & Snapp, M. (1978). *The Jigsaw classroom.* Beverly Hills, CA: Sage.

Astor, R. A. (2005, July 27). Zero tolerance for zero knowledge. *Education Week, 24*(43), 52–42.

Astor, R. A., & Benbenishty, R. (2005). Zero tolerance for zero knowledge. *Education Week, 24*(43), 52.

Astor, R. A., Meyer, H. A., & Behre, W. J. (1999). Unowned places and times: Maps and interviews about violence in high schools. *American Educational Research Journal, 36*(1), 3–42.

Ayers, W. (1993). *To teach: The journey of a teacher.* New York: Teachers College Press.

Bailey, J. M., & Guskey, T. R. (2001). *Implementing student-led conferences.* Thousand Oaks, CA: Corwin Press.

Baker, H. B., Basile, C. G., & Olson, F. J. (2005). Teachers as advisors: Fostering active citizens in schools. *Kappa Delta Pi Record, 41*(4), 167–171.

Barone, F. J. (1997). Bullying in school: It doesn't have to happen. *Phi Delta Kappan, 79,* 80–82.

Barry, L., & Messer, J. J. (2003). A practical application of self-management for students diagnosed with attention-deficit/hyperactivity disorder. *Journal of Positive Behavior Interventions, 5*(4), 238–248.

Barton, P. E., Coley, R. J., & Wenglinsky, H. (1998). *Order in the classroom: Violence, discipline, and student achievement.* Princeton, NJ: Educational Testing Service.

Bear, G. G. (1998). School discipline in the United States: Prevention, correction, and longterm social development. *School Psychology Review, 27*(1), 724–742.

Becker, H. J., & Epstein, J. L. (1982). Parent involvement: A survey of teacher practices. *The Elementary School Journal, 83*(2), 85–102.

Becker, J. R. (1981). Differential treatment of females and males in mathematics classes. *Journal for Research in Mathematics Education, 12*(1), 40–53.

Belluck, P. (Feb. 5, 2006). And for perfect attendance, Johnny gets a car. *The New York Times,* pp. A1, A20.

Bennett, N., & Blundell, D. (1983). Quantity and quality of work in rows and classroom groups. *Educational Psychology, 3,* 93–105.

Berreth, D., & Berman, S. (1997). The moral dimensions of schools. *Educational Leadership, 54*(8), 24–26.

Biehle, J. T., Motz, L. L., & West, S. S. (1999). *NSTA guide to school science facilities.* Arlington, VA: NSTA Press.

Blauvelt, P. D. (1990, Fall). School security: "Who you gonna call?" *School Safety Newsjournal,* 4–8.

Bloome, D., & Theodorou, E. (1988). Analyzing teacher–student and student–student discourse. In J. E. Green & J. O. Harker (Eds.), *Multiple perspective analyses of classroom discourse* (pp. 217–248). Norwood, NJ: Ablex.

Bodine, R. J., & Crawford, D. K. (1998). *The handbook of conflict resolution education: A guide to building quality programs in schools.* San Francisco: Jossey-Bass.

Bolick, C. M., & Cooper, J. M. (2006). Classroom management and technology. In C. M. Evertson & C. S. Weinstein (Eds.), *Handbook of classroom management: Research, practice, and contemporary issues* (pp. 541–558). Mahwah, NJ: Lawrence Erlbaum Associates.

Bomer, R., Dworin, J. E., May, L., & Semingson, P. (2008). Miseducating teachers about the poor: A critical analysis of Ruby Payne's claims about poverty. *Teachers College Record, 110*(12), 2497–2531.

Bondy, E., & Ross, D. D. (2008). The teacher as warm demander. *Educational Leadership, 66*(1), 54–58.

Bottge, B. J., Gugerty, J. J., Serlin, R., & Moon, K. (2003). Block and traditional schedules: Effects on students with and without disabilities in high school. *NASSP Bulletin, 87,* 2–14.

Brady, K., Forton, M. B., Porter, D., & Wood, C. (2003). *Rules in school.* Greenfield, MA: Northeast Foundation for Children.

Brendgen, M., Wanner, B., Vitaro, F., Bukowski, W. M., & Tremblay, R. E. (2007). Verbal abuse by the teacher during childhood and academic, behavioral, and emotional adjustment in young adulthood. *Journal of Educational Psychology, 99*(1), 26–38.

Brodey, D. (2005, Sept. 20). Blacks join the eating-disorder mainstream. *New York Times,* p. F5.

Brookfield, S. D., & Preskill, S. (1999). *Discussion as a way of teaching: Tools and techniques for democratic classrooms.* San Francisco: Jossey-Bass.

Brooks, D. M. (1985). The teacher's communicative competence: The first day of school. *Theory into Practice, 24*(1), 63–70.

Brophy, J. (2004). *Motivating students to learn.* Mahwah, NJ: Lawrence Erlbaum.

Brophy, J. E. (1983). Classroom organization and management. *The Elementary School Journal, 83*(4), 265–285.

Brophy, J., & Rohrkemper, M. (1981). The influence of problem ownership on teachers' perceptions of and strategies for coping with problem students. *Journal of Educational Psychology, 73,* 295–311.

Brown, C. G., Rocha, E., & Sharkey, A. (2005). *Getting smarter, becoming fairer: A progressive education agenda for a stronger nation.* Washington, D.C.: Institute for America's Future. Retrieved August 27, 2009 from http://www.ourfuture.org

Brown, D. F. (2004). Urban teachers' professed classroom management strategies: Reflections of culturally responsive teaching. *Urban Education 39*(3), 266.

Burke, K., & Burke-Samide, B. (2004). Required changes in the classroom environment: It's a matter of design. *The Clearing House, 77*(6), 236–239.

Bush, M. J., & Johnstone, W. G. (2000, April). *An observation evaluation of high school A/B block classes: Variety or monotony?* Paper presented at the annual meeting of the American Educational Research Association, New Orleans.

Calderhead, W. J., Filter, K. J., & Albin, R. W. (2006). An investigation of incremental effects of interspersing math items on task-related behavior. *Journal of Behavioral Education, 15*(1), 53–67.

Cameron, J. (2001). Negative effects of reward on intrinsic motivation—A limited phenomenon: Comment on Deci, Koestner, and Ryan (2001). *Review of Educational Research, 71*(1), 29–42.

Cameron, J., Banko, K. M., & Pierce. W. D. (2001). Pervasive negative effects of rewards on intrinsic motivation: The myth continues. *The Behavior Analyst, 24*(1), 1–44.

Cameron, J., & Pierce, W. D. (1994). Reinforcement, reward, and intrinsic motivation: A meta-analysis. *Review of Educational Research, 64,* 363–423.

Campbell, L., Campbell, B., & Dickinson, D. (1999). *Teaching and learning through multiple intelligences* (2nd ed.). Boston: Allyn & Bacon.

Carbone, E. (2001). Arranging the classroom with an eye (and ear) to students with ADHD. *Teaching Exceptional Children, 34*(2), 72–81.

Cangelosi, J. S. (1993, April). *Cheating: Issues in elementary, middle, and secondary school classrooms.* A paper presented during the symposium, "Psychometric taboo: Discussions on cheating" (other participants: G. J. Cizek, W. H. Angoff, W. M. Haney, D. Pullin, E. A. Wynne, & R. L. Brennan) at the annual meetings of the American Educational Research Association and the National Council for Measurement in Education, Atlanta.

Cartledge, G., with Milburn, J. E. (1996). *Cultural diversity and social skills instruction: Understanding ethnic and gender differences.* Champaign, IL: Research Press.

Cary, S. (2007). *Working with second language learners: Answers to teachers' top ten questions* (2nd ed.). Portsmouth, NH: Heinemann.

Catalano, R. F., Haggerty, K. P., Oesterle, S., Fleming, C. B., & Hawkins, J. D. (2004). The importance of bonding to school for healthy development: Findings from the social development research group. *Journal of School Health 74*(7), 252–261.

Cazden, C. B. (1988). *Classroom discourse: The language of teaching and learning.* Portsmouth, NH: Heinemann.

Centers for Disease Control and Prevention. (2007). *Surveillance summaries.* MMWR 2007; 56(SS-1).

CHADD. (1993). *Attention deficit disorders: an educator's guide (CHADD Facts #5).* Plantation, FL: Children and Adults with Attention Deficit Disorders.

Chandler, K. A., Chapman, C. D., Rand, M. R., & Taylor, B. M. (1998). *Students' reports of school crime: 1989 and 1995.* Washington, DC: U.S. Department of Education, Office of Educational Research and Improvement, National Center for Education Statistics, and U.S. Department of Justice, Office of Justice Programs, Bureau of Justice Statistics.

Charles, C. M., & Charles, M. G. (2004). *Classroom management for middle-grades teachers.* Boston: Pearson/Allyn & Bacon.

Child Welfare Information Gateway. (2008). Gay and lesbian adoptive parents. Retrieved August 27, 2009 from http://www.enotalone.com/article/9874.html

Children's Defense Fund (2008). *The state of America's children 2008.* Washington, DC: Children's Defense Fund. Retrieved January 25, 2009 from http://www. childrensdefense.org

Chiu, M. M. (2004). Adapting teacher interventions to student needs during cooperative learning: How to improve student problem solving and time on-task. *American Educational Research Journal, 41*(2), 365–399.

Chrispeels, J. H., & Rivero, E. (2000, April). Engaging Latino families for student success: Understanding the process and impact of providing training to parents. Paper presented at the annual meeting of the American Educational Research Association, New Orleans.

Christensen, L. (1994). Building community from chaos. In B. Bigelow, L. Christensen, S. Karp, B. Miner, & B. Peterson (Eds.), *Rethinking our classrooms: Teaching for equity and justice.* Milwaukee, WI: Rethinking Schools Limited, pp. 50–55.

Cohen, E. G. (1972). Interracial interaction disability. *Human Relations, 25,* 9–24.

Cohen, E. G. (1994a). *Designing groupwork: Strategies for the heterogeneous classroom* (2nd ed.). New York: Teachers College Press.

Cohen, E. G. (1994b). Restructuring the classroom: Conditions for productive small groups. *Review of Educational Research, 64*(1), 1–35.

Cohen, E. G. (1998). Making cooperative learning equitable. *Educational Leadership, 56,*(1) 18–21.

Coles, A. D. (June 14, 2000). Lately, teens less likely to engage in risky behaviors. *Education Week,* 6.

Coontz, S. (May 13, 2007). Motherhood stalls when women can't work. Hartford Courant. Retrieved February 5, 2009 from http://www.contemporaryfamilies.org

Copeland, S. R., McCall, J., Williams, C. R., Guth, C., Carter, E. W., Fowler, S. E., et al. (2002). High school peer buddies: A win-win situation. *Teaching Exceptional Children, 35*(1), 16–21.

Corbett, D., Wilson, B., & Williams, B. (2005). No choice but success. *Educational Leadership, 62*(6), 8–12.

Cornelius-White, J. (2007). Learner-centered teacher-student relationships are effective: A meta-analysis. *Review of Educational Research, 77*(1), 113–143.

Cothran, D. J., Kulinna, P. H., & Garrahy, D. A. (2003). "This is kind of giving a secret away. . .": Students' perspectives on effective class management. *Teaching and Teacher Education, 19,* 435–444.

Cotton, K. (2001). *New small learning communities: Findings from recent literature.* Portland, OR: Northwest Educational Research Library.

Créton, H. A., Wubbels, T., & Hooymayers, H. P. (1989). Escalated disorderly situations in the classroom and the improvement of these situations. *Teaching & Teacher Education, 5*(3), 205–215.

Cummins, J. (2000). *Language, power and pedagogy: Bilingual children in the crossfire.* Clevedon, UK: Multilingual Matters.

Curwin, R. L. (1995). A humane approach to reducing violence in schools. *Educational Leadership, 52*(5), 72–75.

Curwin, R. L., & Mendler, A. N. (1988). *Discipline with dignity.* Alexandria VA: Association for Supervision and Curriculum Development.

Darling-Hammond, L., & Ifill-Lynch, O. (2006). If they'd only do their work! *Educational Leadership, 63*(5), 8–13.

Davidson, A. L. (1999). Negotiating social differences: Youths' assessments of educators' strategies. *Urban Education, 34*(3), 338–369.

Deci, E. L., Koestner, R., & Ryan, R. M. (1999). A meta-analytic review of experiments examining the effects of extrinsic rewards on intrinsic motivation. *Psychological Bulletin, 125*(6), 627–668.

Deci, E. L., Koestner, R., & Ryan, R. M. (2001). Extrinsic rewards and intrinsic motivation in education: Reconsidered once again. *Review of Educational Research, 71*(1), 1–27.

Delpit, L. (1995). *Other people's children: Cultural conflict in the classroom.* New York: The New Press.

Delpit, L. (2002). No kinda sense. In L. Delpit & J. K. Dowdy (Eds.), *The skin that we speak: Thoughts on language and culture in the classroom* (pp. 31–48). New York: The New Press.

Deslandes, R., & Bertrand, R. (2005). Motivation of parent involvement in secondary-level schooling. *Journal of Educational Research, 98*(3), 164–175.

deVoss, G. G. (1979). The structure of major lessons and collective student activity. *Elementary School Journal, 80,* 8–18.

Diaz-Rico, L. T., & Weed, K. Z. (2009). *The crosscultural, language, and academic development handbook. A complete K-12 reference guide* (4th ed.). Boston: Allyn and Bacon.

Dieker, L. A. (2001). What are the characteristics of "effective" middle and high school co-taught teams for students with disabilities? *Preventing School Failure, 46*(1), 14–23.

Dillon, D. R. (1989). Showing them that I want them to learn and that I care about who they are: A microethnography of the social organization of a secondary low-track English-reading classroom. *American Educational Research Journal, 26*(2), 227–259.

Dillon, J. T. (1994). *Using discussion in classrooms.* Philadelphia: Open University Press.

Dinkes, R., Cataldi, E. F., & Lin-Kelly, W. (2007). *Indicators of school crime and safety: 2007.* (NCES 2008-021/NCJ 219553). National Center for Education Statistics, Institute of Education Sciences, U.S. Department of Education, and Bureau of Justice Statistics, Office of Justice Programs, U.S. Department of Justice. Washington, DC. Retrieved November 15, 2008 from http://nces.ed.gov

Ditman, O. (July/August 2000). Online term-paper mills produce a new crop of cheaters. *Harvard Education Letter, 16*(4), 6–7.

Dowd, J. (1997). Refusing to play the blame game. *Educational Leadership, 54*(8), 67–69.

Doyle, W. (1983). Academic work. *Review of Educational Research, 53*(2), 159–200.

Doyle, W. (1985). Recent research on classroom management: Implications for teacher preparation. *Journal of Teacher Education, 36*(3), 31–35.

Doyle, W. (1986). Classroom organization and management. In M. C. Wittrock (Ed.), *Handbook of research on teaching* (pp. 392–431). New York: Macmillan.

Doyle, W. (2006). Ecological approaches to classroom management. In C. M. Evertson & C. S. Weinstein (Eds.), *Handbook of classroom management: Research, practice, and contemporary issues* (pp. 97–126). Mahwah, NJ: Lawrence Erlbaum Associates.

Dreikurs, R., Grunwald, B. B., & Pepper, F. C. (1982). *Maintaining sanity in the classroom: Classroom management techniques* (2nd ed.). New York: Harper & Row.

Drummond, S., & Portner, J. (May 26, 1999). Arrests top 350 in threats, bomb scares. *Education Week,* pp. 1, 12–13.

Dwyer, K., Osher, D., & Warger, C. (1998). *Early warning, timely response: A guide to safe schools.* Washington, DC: U.S. Department of Education.

Eccles, J. S., & Harold, R. D. (1993). Parent-school involvement during the early adolescent years. *Teachers College Record, 94*(3), 568–587.

Eccles, J., & Wigfield, A. (1985). Teacher expectations and student motivation. In J. Dusek (Ed.), *Teacher expectancies* (pp. 185–226). Hillsdale, NJ: Erlbaum.

Eccles, J. S., Wigfield, A., & Schiefele, U. (1998). Motivation to succeed. In W. Damon (Series Ed.) & N. Eisenberg (Vol. Ed.), *Handbook of child psychology: Vol. 3, Social, emotional, and personality development* (5th ed., pp. 1017–1095). New York: John Wiley.

Edwards, A. T. (1997). Let's stop ignoring our gay and lesbian youth. *Educational Leadership, 54*(7), 68–70.

Elias, M. J., & Schwab, Y. (2006). From compliance to responsibility: Social and emotional learning and classroom management. In C. M. Evertson & C. S. Weinstein (Eds.), *Handbook of classroom management: Research, practice, and contemporary issues* (pp. 309–342). Mahwah, NJ: Lawrence Erlbaum Associates.

Elmore, R. F. (2002). The limits of "change." *Harvard Education Letter.* Retrieved August 22, 2009 from http://www.hepg.org/hel/article/195

Emmer, E. T., & Aussiker, A. (1990). School and classroom discipline programs: How well do they work? In O. C. Moles (Ed.), *Student discipline strategies* (pp. 129–165). New York: SUNY Press.

Emmer, E. T., & Evertson, C. M. (2008). *Classroom management for middle and high school teachers.* Boston: Allyn & Bacon.

Emmer, E.T., & Gerwels, M. C. (2002). Cooperative learning in elementary classrooms: Teaching practices and lesson characteristics. *The Elementary School Journal, 102*(1), 5–91.

Emmer, E. T., & Gerwels, M. C. (2006). Classroom management in middle and high school classrooms. In C. M. Evertson & C. S. Weinstein (Eds.), *Handbook of classroom management: Research, practice, and contemporary issues* (pp. 407–438). Mahwah, NJ: Lawrence Erlbaum Associates.

Epstein, J. L. (2001). *School, family, and community partnerships: Preparing educators and improving schools.* Boulder, CO: Westview Press.

Epstein, J. L., & Becker, H. J. (1982). Teachers' reported practices of parent involvement: Problems and possibilities. *The Elementary School Journal, 83*(2), 103–113.

Epstein, J. L., & Dauber, S. L. (1991). School programs and teacher practices of parent involvement in inner-city elementary and middle schools. *The Elementary School Journal, 91*(3), 289–305.

Epstein, J. L., Sanders, M. G., Simon, B. S., Salinas, K. C., Jansorn, N. R., & Van Voorhis, F. L. (2002). *School, family, and community partnerships: Your handbook for action* (2nd ed.). Thousand Oaks, CA: Corwin Press.

Erikson, E. H. (1963). *Childhood and society* (2nd ed.). New York: W. W. Norton.

Everhart, R. B. (1983). *Reading, writing, and resistance: Adolescence and labor in a junior high school.* Boston: Routledge and Kegan Paul.

Evertson, C. M., & Emmer, E. T. (1982). Effective management at the beginning of the school year in junior high classes. *Journal of Educational Psychology, 74*(4), 485–498.

Evertson, C. M., & Weinstein, C. S. (2006). Classroom management as a field of inquiry. In C. M. Evertson & C. S. Weinstein (Eds.), *Handbook of classroom management: Research, practice, and contemporary issues* (pp. 3-16). Mahwah, NJ: Lawrence Erlbaum Associates.

Finders, M., & Lewis, C. (1994). Why some parents don't come to school. *Educational Leadership, 51*(8), 50-54.

Fischer, L., Schimmel, D., & Kelly, C. (1999). *Teachers and the law.* New York: Longman.

Fisher, C. W., Berliner, D. C., Filby, N. N., Marliave, R., Cahen, L. S., & Dishaw, M. M. (1980). Teaching behaviors, academic learning time, and student achievement: An overview. In C. Denham & A. Lieberman (Eds.), *Time to learn* (pp. 7-32). Washington, DC: U.S. Department of Education.

Fisher, C. W., Filby, N. N., Marliave, R. S., Cahen, L. S., Dishaw, M. M., Moore, J. E., et al. (1978). *Teaching behaviors, academic learning time and student achievement. Final report of Phase III-B, Beginning Teacher Evaluation Study.* San Francisco: Far West Laboratory for Educational Research and Development.

Fleming, D. S., Olenn, V., Schoenstein, R., & Eineder, D. (1997). *Moving to the block: Getting ready to teach in extended periods of learning time.* (An NEA Professional Library Publication.) Washington D.C.: National Education Association.

Flowerday, T., & Schraw, G. (2000). Teacher beliefs about instructional choice: A phenomenological study. *Journal of Educational Psychology, 92*(4), 634-645.

Fordham, S., & Ogbu, J. U. (1986). Black students' school success: Coping with the "burden of 'acting white.' " *The Urban Review, 18*(3), 176-206.

Fraser, B. J., McRobbie, C. J., & Fisher, D. L. (1996, April). *Development, validation and use of personal and class forms of a new classroom environment instrument.* Paper presented at the annual meeting of the Amercian Educational Research Association, New York.

Friend, M., & Bursuck, W. D. (2002). *Including students with special needs: A practical guide for classroom teachers.* Boston: Allyn & Bacon.

Fryer, R. G., Jr. (2006, Winter). Acting white. *Education Next,* 52-59.

Fuller, M. L., & Olsen, G. (1998). *Home-school relations: Working successfully with parents and families.* Boston: Allyn & Bacon.

Gall, M. D., & Gillett, M. (1981). The discussion method in classroom teaching. *Theory Into Practice, 19,* 98-103.

Gallego, M. A., Cole, M., & The Laboratory of Comparative Human Cognition (2001). Classroom cultures and cultures in the classroom. In V. Richardson (Ed.), *Handbook of research on teaching* (4th ed., pp. 951-997). Washington, DC: American Educational Research Association.

Gallup Poll. (2005). *Teens say safety issues top problem at school.* Retrieved January 22, 2009 from http://www.gallup.com

Gardner, H. (1993). *Multiple intelligences: The theory in practice.* New York: Basic Books.

Gardner, H. (1995). Reflections on multiple intelligences: Myths and messages. *Phi Delta Kappan, 77*(3), 200-209.

Gardner, H. (1998). Reflections on multiple intelligences: Myths and messages. In A. Woolfolk (Ed.), *Readings in educational psychology* (2nd ed., pp. 61-67), Boston: Allyn & Bacon.

Gay, G. (2000). *Culturally responsive teaching: Theory, research, and practice.* New York: Teachers College Press.

Gay, G. (2006). Connections between classroom management and culturally responsive teaching. In C. M. Evertson & C. S. Weinstein (Eds.), *Handbook of classroom management: Research, practice and contemporary issues* (pp. 343–370). Mahwah, NJ: Lawrence Erlbaum Associates.

Gearheart, B. R., Weishahn, M. W., & Gearheart, C. J. (1992). *The exceptional student in the regular classroom* (5th ed.). New York: Macmillan.

Giangreco, M. F., & Doyle, M. B. (2002). Students with disabilities and paraprofessional supports: Benefits, balance, and band-aids. *Focus on Exceptional Children, 34*(7), 1–12.

Gillies, R. M. (2008). The effects of cooperative learning on junior high school students' behaviours, discourse, and learning during a science-based learning activity. *School Psychology International, 29*(3), 328–347.

Gonet, M. M. (1994). *Counseling the adolescent substance abuser: School-based intervention and prevention.* Thousand Oaks, CA: Sage.

Good, T. L., & Brophy, J. E. (2008). *Looking in classrooms* (10th ed.). Boston: Pearson Education.

Goodlad, J. I. (1984). *A place called school.* New York: McGraw-Hill.

Gordon, J. A. (1998). Caring through control: Reaching urban African American youth. *Journal for a Just and Caring Education, 4*(4), 418–440.

Gordon, R. L. (1997). How novice teachers can succeed with adolescents. *Educational Leadership, 54*(7), 56–58.

Gordon, T. (2003). *Teacher effectiveness training: The program proven to help teachers bring out the best in students of all ages.* New York: Three Rivers Press.

Governor's Task Force on Child Abuse and Neglect. (1988, October). *Child abuse and neglect: A professional's guide to identification, reporting, investigation, and treatment.* Trenton, NJ: Author.

Grandin, T. (2007). Autism from the inside. *Educational Leadership, 64*(5), 29–32.

Graziano, A. M., & Mooney, K. C. (1984). *Children and behavior therapy.* New York: Aldine.

Greenwood, G. E., & Hickman, C. W. (1991). Research and practice in parent involvement: Implications for teacher education. *The Elementary School Journal, 91*(3), 279–288.

Gregory, A., & Ripski, M. (2008). Adolescent trust in teachers: Implications for behavior in the high school classroom. *School Psychology Review, 37*(3), 337–353.

Grossman, H. (2004). *Classroom behavior management for diverse and inclusive schools* (3rd ed.). Lanham, MD: Rowman & Littlefield.

Grossman, H., & Grossman, S. H. (1994). *Gender issues in education.* Boston: Allyn & Bacon.

Gruber, C. D., & Onwuegbuzie, A. J. (2001). Effects of block scheduling on academic achievement among high school sudents. *The High School Journal, 84*(4), 32–42.

Gump, P. (1982). School settings and their keeping. In D. L. Duke (Ed.), *Helping teachers manage classrooms* (pp. 98–114). Alexandria, VA: Association for Supervision and Curriculum Development.

Gump, P. V. (1987). School and classroom environments. In D. Stokols & I. Altman (Eds.), *Handbook of environmental psychology* (pp. 691–732). New York: John Wiley & Sons.

Gutman, L. M., & McLoyd, V. G. (2000). Parents' management of their children's education within the home, at school, and in the community: An examination of African-American families living in poverty. *The Urban Review, 32*(1).

Hagin, R. A. (2004). Autism and other severe pervasive developmental disorders. In F. M. Kline & L. B. Silver (Eds.), *The educator's guide to mental health issues in the classroom* (pp. 55–74). Baltimore: Paul H. Brookes.

Hansen, P., & Mulholland, J. A. (2005). Caring and elementary teaching: The concerns of male beginning teachers. *Journal of Teacher Education, 56*(2), 119–131.

Harmon, A. (2004, August 26). Internet gives teenage bullies weapons to wound from afar. *The New York Times,* pp. A1, A23.

Harrison, M. M. (Fall 2005). Bully on the bus. *Teaching Tolerance, 28,* 39–43.

Hatch, J. A. (1986, March). Alone in a crowd: Analysis of covert interactions in a kindergarten. Presented at the annual meeting of the American Educational Research Association, San Francisco. ERIC Document Reproduction Service No. ED 272 278.

Haynes, C. C., Chaltain, S., Ferguson Jr., J. E., Hudson Jr., D. L., & Thomas. O. (2003). *The first amendment in schools.* Alexandria, VA: Association of Supervision and Curriculum Development.

Heilman, E. (2008). Hegemonies and "transgressions" of family: Tales of pride and prejudice. In T. Turner-Vorbeck & M. Miller Marsh (Eds.), *Other kinds of families: Embracing diversity in schools* (pp. 7–27). New York: Teachers College Press.

Henley, M., Ramsey, R. S., & Algozzine, R. F. (2002). *Characteristics of and strategies for teaching students with mild disabilities* (4th ed.). Boston: Allyn & Bacon.

Henning, J. E. (2008). *The art of discussion-based teaching.* New York: Routledge.

Heuveline, P. (2005). *Estimating the proportion of marriages that end in divorce.* A research brief prepared for the Council on Contemporary Families. Retrieved August 27, 2009 from http://www.contemporaryfamilies.org

Hidi, S., & Harackiewicz, J. M. (2000). Motivating the academically unmotivated: A critical issue for the 21st century. *Review of Educational Research, 70*(2), 151–179.

Hodgkinson, H. (1985). *All one system: Demographics of education, kindergarten through graduate school.* Washington, DC: Institute for Educational Leadership.

Hoover, J., & Oliver, R. (2008). *The bullying prevention handbook: A guide for teachers, principals and counselors.* Bloomington, IN: Solution Tree.

Hoover-Dempsey, K. V., Bassler, O. T., & Brissie, J. S. (1987). Parent involvement: Contributions of teacher efficacy, school socioeconomic status, and other school characteristics. *American Educational Research Journal, 24*(3), 417–435.

Hoover-Dempsey, K. V., & Sandler, H. M. (1997). Why do parents become involved in their children's education? *Review of Educational Research, 67*(1), 3–42.

Horowitz, P., & Otto, D. (1973). *The teaching effectiveness of an alternate teaching facility.* Alberta, Canada: University of Alberta. ERIC Document Reproduction Service No. ED 083 242.

Howell, J. C., & Lynch, J. P. (2000). *Youth gangs in schools.* Washington, DC: Office of Juvenile Justice and Delinquency Prevention, U.S. Department of Justice. Retrieved August 26, 2009 from http://www.ncjrs.org/html/ojjdp/jjbul2000_8_2/contents.html

Hoy, A., & Weinstein, C. S. (2006). Student and teacher perspectives on classroom management. In C. M. Evertson and C. S. Weinstein (Eds.), *Handbook of classroom management: Research, practice, and contemporary issues* (pp. 181–219). Mahwah, NJ: Lawrence Erlbaum Associates.

HR 1804: Goals 2000: Education America Act, 103rd Congress, 2nd session. 1994.

Hu, W. (2008, November 12). A school district asks: Where are the parents? *The New York Times.* p. A25.

Hughes, C. A., Ruhl, K. L., & Misra, A. (1989). Disordered students in school settings: A promise unfulfilled? *Behavioral Disorders, 14,* 250-262.

Hyman, I. A. (1997). *School discipline and school violence: The teacher variance approach.* Boston: Allyn & Bacon.

Hyman, I., Kay, B., Tabori, A., Weber, M., Mahon, M. & Cohen, I. (2006). Bullying: Theory, research, and interventions. In C. Evertson & C. Weinstein (Eds.), *Handbook of classroom management: Research, practice, and contemporary issues* (pp. 855-884). Mahwah, NJ: Lawrence Erlbaum Associates.

Irvine, J. J. (1990). *Black students and school failure: Policies, practices, and prescriptions.* New York: Greenwood.

Irvine, J. J. (2002). *In search of wholeness: African American teachers and their culturally specific classroom practices.* New York: PALGRAVE.

Irvine, J. J., & Fraser, J. (May 13, 1998). Warm demanders: Do national certification standards leave room for the culturally responsive pedagogy of African-American teachers? *Education Week, 17*(35), 56.

Jackson, P. W. (1990). *Life in classrooms.* New York: Teachers College Press.

Jeynes, W. H. (2007). The relationship between parental involvement and urban secondary school student academic achievement: A meta-analysis. *Urban Education, 42*(1), 82-110.

Johnson, D. W., & Johnson, R. T. (1980). Integrating handicapped students into the mainstream. *Exceptional Children, 47*(2), 90-98.

Johnson, D. W., & Johnson, R. T. (1989/90). Social skills for successful groupwork. *Educational Leadership, 47*(4), 29-33.

Johnson, D. W., & Johnson, R. T. (1995). *Teaching students to be peacemakers* (3rd ed.). Edina, MN: Interaction.

Johnson, D. W., & Johnson, R. T. (1999). The three Cs of school and classroom management. In H. J. Freiberg (Ed.), *Beyond Behaviorism: Changing the Classroom Management Paradigm* (pp. 119-144). Boston: Allyn & Bacon.

Johnson, D. W., & Johnson, R. T. (2004). Implementing the "Teaching Students to be Peacemakers Program." *Theory Into Practice, 43*(1), 68-79.

Johnson, D. W., Johnson, R. T., Holubec, E. J., & Roy, P. (1984). *Circles of learning: Cooperation in the classroom.* Alexandria, VA: Association for Supervision and Curriculum Development.

Johnston, L. D., O'Malley, P. M., Bachman, J. G., & Schulenberg, J. E. (2008, December 11). Various stimulant drugs show continuing gradual declines among teens in 2008, most illicit drugs hold steady. Ann Arbor, MI: University of Michigan News Service. Retrieved February 23, 2009 from http://www.monitoringthefuture.org

Jones, F. H., Jones, P., Lynn, J., Jones, F., & Jones, B.T. (2007). *Tools for teaching: Discipline, instruction, motivation.* Santa Cruz, CA: Fredric H. Jones & Associates.

Jones, M. G., & Gerig, T. M. (1994). Silent sixth-grade students: Characteristics, achievement, and teacher expectations. *The Elementary School Journal, 95*(2), 169-182.

Jones, M. G., & Wheatley, J. (1990). Gender differences in teacher-student interactions in science classrooms. *Journal of Research in Science Teaching, 27,* 861-874.

Jones, V. F., & Jones, L. S. (2010). *Comprehensive classroom management: Creating communities of support and solving problems.* Upper Saddle River, NJ: Pearson.

Josephson Institute of Ethics. (2008). *2008 report card: The ethics of American youth.* Retrieved February 8, 2009 from http://charactercounts.org/programs/reportcard

Juarez, V. (Oct. 4, 2005). They dress to express. *Newsweek.* Retrieved August 26, 2009 from http://www.msnbc.msn.com/id/6098629/site/newsweek

Kagan, S. (1989/90). The structural approach to cooperative learning. *Educational Leadership, 47*(4), 12-15.

Karweit, N. (1989). Time and learning: A review. In R. E. Slavin (Ed.), *School and classroom organization* (pp. 69-98). Hillsdale, NJ: Lawrence Erlbaum.

Katz, M. S. (1999). Teaching about caring and fairness: May Sarton's *The Small Room.* In M. S. Katz, N. Noddings, & K A. Strike (Eds.), *Justice and caring: The search for common ground in education* (pp. 59-73). New York: Teachers College Press.

Katz, S. R. (1999). Teaching in tensions: Latino immigrant youth, their teachers, and the structures of schooling. *Teachers College Record, 100*(4), 809-840.

Keith, S., & Martin, M. E. (2005). Cyber-bullying: Creating a culture of respect in a cyber world. *Reclaiming Children and Youth, 13*(4), 224-228.

Kerr, M. M., & Nelson, C. M. (2006). *Strategies for addressing behavior problems in the classroom* (5th ed.). Upper Saddle River, NJ: Pearson Prentice Hall.

Kidder, T. (1989). *Among schoolchildren.* Boston: Houghton Mifflin.

Kim, D., Solomon, D., & Roberts, W. (1995, April). *Classroom practices that enhance students' sense of community.* Paper presented at the annual convention of the American Educational Research Association, San Francisco.

King, J. R. (1998). *Uncommon caring: Learning from men who teach young children.* New York: Teachers College Press.

King, L., Luberda, H., Barry, K., & Zehnder, S. (1998, April). A case study of the perceptions of students in a small-group cooperative learning situation. Paper presented at the Annual Conference of the American Education Research Association, San Diego, CA.

Kline, M. & Silver, L. B. (Eds.). (2004). *The educator's guide to mental health issues in the classroom.* Baltimore: Paul H. Brookes.

Kohn, A. (1993). *Punished by rewards: The trouble with gold stars, incentive plans, As, praise, and other bribes.* Boston: Houghton Mifflin.

Kohn, A. (1996). *Beyond discipline: From compliance to community.* Alexandria, VA: Association for Supervision and Curriculum Development.

Kosciw, J. G., Diaz, E. M., & Greytak, E. A. (2008). *The 2007 national school climate survey: The experiences of lesbian, gay, bisexual and transgender in our nation's schools.* New York: Gay, Lesbian, and Straight Education Network. Retrieved February 20, 2009 from http://www.glsen.org

Kottler, E. (1994). *Children with limited English: Teaching strategies for the regular classroom.* Thousand Oaks, CA: Corwin Press.

Kottler, J. A., & Kottler, E. (1993). *Teacher as counselor: Developing the helping skills you need.* Newbury Park, CA: Corwin Press.

Kounin, J. S. (1970). *Discipline and group management in classrooms.* New York: Holt, Rinehart & Winston.

Kriete, R. (2002). *The morning meeting book* (2nd ed.). Greenfield, MA: Northeast Foundation for Children.

Kutnick, P., Blatchford, P., Clark, H., McIntyre, H., & Baines, E. (2005). Teachers' understandings of the relationship between within-class (pupil) grouping and learning in secondary schools. *Educational Research, 47*(1), 1-24.

Ladson-Billings, G. (1994). *The dreamkeepers: Successful teachers of African American children.* San Francisco: Jossey-Bass.

Lal, S. R., Lal, D., & Achilles, C. M. (1993). *Handbook on gangs in schools: Strategies to reduce gang-related activities.* Newbury Park, CA: Corwin Press.

Landrum, T. J., & Kauffman, J. M. (2006). Behavioral approaches to classroom management. In C. M. Evertson & C. S. Weinstein (Eds.), *Handbook of classroom management: Research, practice, and contemporary issues* (pp. 47-72). Mahwah, NJ: Lawrence Erlbaum Associates.

Landsman, J. (2006). Bearers of hope. *Educational Leadership, 63*(5), 26-32.

Lasley, T. J., Lasley, J. O., & Ward, S. H. (1989, April). Activities and desists used by more and less effective classroom managers. Paper presented at the annual meeting of the American Educational Research Association, San Francisco.

Laursen, E. K. (2008). Respectful alliances. *Reclaiming Children and Youth, 17*(1), 4-9.

Lawrence-Lightfoot, S. (2003). *The essential conversation: What parents and teachers can learn from each other.* New York: Random House.

Lee, J., & Bowen, N. K. (2006). Parent involvement, cultural capital, and the achievement gap among elementary school children. *American Educational Research Journal, 43*(2), 193-215.

Lee, V. E., Croninger, R. G., Linn, E., & Chen, X. (1996). The culture of sexual harassment in secondary schools. *American Educational Research Journal, 33*(2), 383-417.

Leinhardt, G., & Greeno, J. G. (1986). The cognitive skill of teaching. *Journal of Educational Psychology, 78*(2), 75-95.

Leinhardt, G., Weidman, C., & Hammond, K. M. (1987). Introduction and integration of classroom routines by expert teachers. *Curriculum Inquiry, 17*(2), 135-175.

Leishman, J. (2002). Cyberbullying: The Internet is the latest weapon in a bully's arsenal. Toronto: CBC News. Retrieved August 26, 2009 from http://www.cbc.ca/news/background/bullying/cyber_bullying.html

Lepper, M., Greene, D., & Nisbett, R. E. (1973). Undermining children's intrinsic interest with extrinsic rewards: A test of the "overjustification" hypothesis. *Journal of Personality and Social Psychology, 28,* 129-137.

Lewis, C. W., Dugan, J. J., Winokur, M. A., & Cobb, R. B. (2005). The effects of block scheduling on high school academic achievement. *NASSP Bulletin, 89*(645), 72-87.

Lindeman, B. (2001). Reaching out to immigrant parents. *Educational Leadership, 58*(6), 62-66.

Lindle, J. C. (1989). What do parents want from principals and teachers? *Educational Leadership, 47*(2), 12-14.

Liptak, A. (March 23, 2009). Strip-search of girl tests limit of school policy. *The New York Times,* pp. A1, A19.

Liptak, A. (June 25, 2009). Supreme court says child's rights violated by strip search. *The New York Times,* p. A16.

Lisante, J. E. (June 6, 2005). *Cyber bullying: No muscles needed.* Retrieved August 27, 2009 from http://www.connectforkids.org

Lopez, G. R. (2001). The vallue of hard work: Lessons on parent involvement from an (im)migrant household. *Harvard Educational Review, 71*(3), 416–437.

Lortie, D. (1975). *Schoolteacher.* Chicago: University of Chicago Press.

Lotan, R. (2006). Managing groupwork in the heterogeneous classroom. In C. M. Evertson & C. S. Weinstein (Eds.), *Handbook of classroom management: Research, practice, and contemporary issues* (pp. 711–731). Mahwah, NJ: Lawrence Erlbaum Associates.

Lubienski, S. T. (2000). A clash of social class cultures? Students' experiences in a discussion-intensive seventh grade mathematics classroom. *The Elementary School Journal, 100*(4), 377–403.

Lundgren, U. (1972). *Frame factors and the teaching process.* Stockholm: Almqvist and Wiksell.

Ma, H., Lu, E.Y., Turner, S., & Wan, G. (2007). An empirical investigation of cheating and digital plagiarism among middle school students. *American Secondary Education, 35*(2), 69–82.

Madden, N. A., & Slavin, R. E. (1983). Cooperative learning and social acceptance of mainstreamed academically handicapped students. *Journal of Special Education, 17,* 171–182.

Mamlin, N., & Dodd-Murphy, J. (2002). Minimizing minimal hearing loss in the schools: What every classroom teacher should know. *Preventing School Failure, 46*(2), 86–93.

Marks, H. M. (2000). Student engagement in instructional activity: Patterns in the elementary, middle, and high school years. *American Educational Research Journal, 37*(1), 153–184.

Marschall, M. (2006). Parent involvement and educational outcomes for Latino students. *Review of Policy Research, 23*(5), 1053–1076.

Marshall, H. H. (1987). Motivational strategies of three fifth-grade teachers. *The Elementary School Journal, 88*(2), 135–150.

Martin, S. H. (2002). The classroom environment and its effects on the practice of teachers. *Journal of Environmental Psychology, 22,* 139–156.

Marzano, R. J., Gaddy, R. J., Foseid, M. C., Foseid, M. P. & Marzano, J. S. (2005). *A handbook for classroom management that works.* Alexandria, VA: Association for Supervision and Curriculum Development.

Maslow, A. H., & Mintz, N. L. (1956). The effects of esthetic surroundings: I. *Journal of Psychology, 41,* 247–254.

Mastropieri, M. A., & Scruggs, T. E. (2001). Promoting inclusion in secondary classrooms. *Learning Disability Quarterly, 24,* 265–274.

McCaslin, M., & Good, T. L. (1992). Compliant cognition: The misalliance of management and instructional goals in current school reform. *Educational Researcher, 21*(3), 4–17.

McCaslin, M., & Good, T. L. (1998, Summer). Moving beyond management as sheer compliance: Helping students to develop goal coordination strategies. *Educational Horizons,* 169–176.

McDougall, D. (1998). Research on self-management techniques used by students with disabilities in general education settings: A descriptive review. *Remedial and Special Education, 19*(5), 310–320.

McGarity, Jr., J. R., & Butts, D. P. (1984). The relationship among teacher classroom management behavior, student engagement and student achievement of middle and high school science students of varying aptitude. *Journal of Research in Science Teaching, 21*(1), 55–61.

McIntosh, K., Herman, K., Sanford, A., McGraw, K., & Florence, K. (2004). Teaching transitions: Techniques for promoting success *between* lessons. *Teaching Exceptional Children, 37*(1), 32–38.

McKinley, J. (March 25, 2009). Cities deal with a surge in shantytowns. *New York Times,* p. A1.

Meadan, H., & Monda-Amaya, L. (2008). Collaboration to promote social competence for students with mild disabilities in the general classroom: A structure for providing social support. *Intervention in School and Clinic, 43*(3), 158–167.

Mehan, H. (1979). *Learning lessons: Social organization in a classroom.* Cambridge, MA: Harvard University Press.

Meichenbaum, D. (1977). *Cognitive behavior modification.* New York: Plenum.

Miller, E. (1994). Peer mediation catches on, but some adults don't. *Harvard Education Letter, 10*(3), 8.

Milner, H. R. (2006). Classroom management in urban classrooms. In C. M. Evertson & C. S. Weinstein (Eds.), *Handbook of classroom management: Research, practice, and contemporary issues* (pp. 491–522). Mahwah, NJ: Lawrence Erlbaum Associates.

Minke, K. M, & Anderson, K. J. (2003). Restructuring routine parent-teacher conferences: The family-school conference model. *The Elementary School Journal, 104*(6), 49–69.

Mitchem, K. J., Young, K. R., West, R. P., & Benyo, J. (2001). CWPASM: A classwide peer-assisted self-management program for general education classrooms. *Education & Treatment of Children, 24*(2), 111–140.

Morrell, E., & Duncan-Andrade, J. M. R. (2002). Promoting academic literacy with urban youth through engaging hip-hop culture. *English Journal, 91*(6), 88–92.

Morrell, E., & Duncan-Andrade, J. (2004). What they do learn in school: Using hip-hop as a bridge between youth culture and canonical poetry texts. In J. Mahiri (Ed.), *What they don't learn in school: Literacy in the lives of urban youth* (pp. 247–268). New York: Peter Lang.

Morse, L. W., & Handley, H. M. (1985). Listening to adolescents: Gender differences in science classroom interaction. In L. C. Wilkinson & C. B. Marrett (Eds.), *Gender influences in classroom interaction* (pp. 37–56). Orlando, FL: Academic Press.

Mulryan, C. M. (1992). Student passivity during cooperative small groups in mathematics. *Journal of Educational Research, 85*(5), 261–273.

Murawski, W. W., & Dieker, L. A. (2004). Tips and strategies for co-teaching at the secondary level. *Teaching Exceptional Children, 36*(5), 52–58.

Murdock, T. B., & Miller, A. (2003). Teachers as sources of middle school students' motivaitonal identity: Variable-centered and person-centered analytic approaches. *The Elementary School Journal, 103*(4), 383–399.

Murray, C. (2004). Clarifying collaborative roles in urban high schools: General educators' perspectives. *Teaching Exceptional Children, 36*(5), 44–51.

Myles, B. S., Gagnon, E., Moyer, S. A., & Trautman, M. L. (2004). Asperger syndrome. In F. M. Kline & L. B. Silver (Eds.), *The educator's guide to mental health issues in the classroom* (pp. 75–100). Baltimore: Paul H. Brookes.

Naber, P. A., May, D. C., Decker, S. H., Minor, K. I., & Wells, J. B. (2006). Are there gangs in schools? *Journal of School Violence, 5*(2), 53–72.

Nansel, T. R., Overpeck, M., Pilla, R. S., Ruan, W. J., Simons-Morton, B., & Scheidt, P. (2001). Bullying behaviors among US youth: Prevalence and association with psychosocial adjustment. *Journal of the American Medical Association, 285*(16), 2094–2100.

National Coalition of Homeless Children and Youth. (2008). *Fact Sheet #10, June 2008.*

National Commission on Excellence in Education. (1983). *A nation at risk: The imperative for educational reform.* Washington, DC: Government Printing Office.

National Council for Research on Women. (1994). Teen-on-teen sexual harassment. *Issues Quarterly, 1*(1), 1–6.

National Crime Prevention Council. (2009). *What parents can do about cyberbullying.* Retrieved August 7, 2009 from http://www.ncpc.org/topics/cyberbullying/stop-cyberbullying

National Dissemination Center for Children with Disabilities. (2003). *Pervasive developmental disorders.* Fact Sheet 20. Retrieved August 8, 2009 from http://www.nichcy.org/Disabilities/Specific/Pages/Autism.aspx

National Dissemination Center for Children with Disabilities. (2004). *Learning disabilities.* Fact Sheet 20. Retrieved August 8, 2009 from http://www.nichcy.org/Disabilities/Specific/Pages/LD.aspx

National Education Commission on Time and Learning. (1994). *Prisoner of time.* Washington, DC: Government Printing Office.

National Law Center on Homelessness & Poverty. (2008). *Homelessness and poverty in America: Overview.* Washington, DC: The National Law Center on Homelessness & Poverty.

National Research Council Committee on Increasing High School Students' Engagement and Motivation to Learn. (2004). *Engaging schools: Fostering high school students' motivation to learn.* Washington, DC: National Academies Press.

NCELA. (2007). The growing numbers of LEP students, 2005–2006 Poster. Washington, DC: U.S. Department of Education. Retrieved August 26, 2009 from http://www.ncela.gwu.edu/files/uploads/4/GrowingLEP_0506.pdf

Nelson-Barber, S., & Meier, T. (1990, Spring). Multicultural context a key factor in teaching. *Academic Connections,* Office of Academic Affairs, The College Board, 1–5, 9–11.

New Jersey v. T.L.O., 105 S. Ct. 733 (1985).

Newby, T. (1991). Classroom motivation: Strategies of first-year teachers. *Journal of Educational Psychology, 83,* 195–200.

Newsam, B. S. (1992). *Complete student assistance program handbook.* West Nyack, NY: The Center for Applied Research in Education.

Nichols, J. D. (2005). Block-scheduled high schools: Impact on achievement in English and language arts. *The Journal of Educational Research, 98*(5), 299–309.

Nichols, S. (1999). Gay, lesbian, and bisexual youth: Understanding diversity and promoting tolerance in schools. *The Elementary School Journal, 99*(5), 505–519.

Nieto, S. (2002). *Language, culture, and teaching: Critical perspectives for a new century.* Mahwah, NJ: Lawrence Erlbaum Associates.

Nieto, S., & Bode, P. (2008). *Affirming diversity: The sociopolitical context of multicultural education* (5th ed.). Boston: Allyn & Bacon.

Ninness, H. A. C., Fuerst, J., Rutherford, R. D., & Glenn, S. S. (1991). Effects of self-management training and reinforcement on the transfer of improved conduct in the absence of supervision. *Journal of Applied Behavior Analysis, 24*(3), 499–508.

Noguera, P. A. (1995). Preventing and producing violence: A critical analysis of responses to school violence. *Harvard Educational Review, 65*(2), 189-212.

Nucci, L. (2006). Classroom management for moral and social development. In C. M. Evertson & C. S. Weinstein (Eds.), *Handbook of classroom management: Research, practice, and contemporary issues* (pp. 711-731). Mahwah, NJ: Lawrence Erlbaum Associates.

Oakes, J., & Lipton, M. (1999). *Teaching to change the world.* Boston: McGraw-Hill.

Obidah, J. E., & Teel, K. M. (2001). *Because of the kids: Facing racial and cultural differences in schools.* New York: Teachers College Press.

O'Donnell, A., & O'Kelly, J. (1994). Learning from peers: Beyond the rhetoric of positive results. *Educational Psychology Review, 6*(4), 321-349.

Olweus, D. (2003). A profile of bullying at school. *Educational Leadership, 60*(6), 12-17.

Osterman, K. F. (2000). Students' need for belonging in the school community. *Review of Educational Research, 70*(3), 323-367.

Ostrander, R. (2004). Oppositional defiant disorder and conduct disorder. In F. M. Kline & L. B. Silver (Eds.), *The educator's guide to mental health issues in the classroom* (pp. 267-286). Baltimore: Paul H. Brookes.

Patall, E. A., Cooper, H., & Robinson, J. C. (2008). Parent involvement in homework: A research synthesis. *Review of Educational Research, 78*(4), 1039-1101.

Patrick, H., Ryan, A. M., & Kaplan, A. (2007). Early adolescents' perceptions of the classroom social environment, motivational beliefs, and engagement. *Journal of Educational Psychology, 99*(1), 83-98.

Payne, R. K. (2005). *A framework for understanding poverty* (4th rev. ed.). Highlands, TX: aha! Process.

Pelco, L. E., & Ries, R. (1999). Teachers' attitudes and behaviors towards family-school partnerships: What school psychologists need to know. *School Psychology International, 20*(3), 265-278.

Pell, T., Galton, M., Steward, S., Page, C., & Hargreaves, L. (2007). Promoting group work at key stage 3: Solving an attitudinal crisis among young adolescents? *Research Papers in Education, 22*(3), 309-322.

Peters v. Rome City School District, 7M N.Y.S.2d 867 (N.Y. A D 4 Dept. 2002).

Peyser, M., & Lorch, D. (2000, March 20). Gay today: The schools. High school controversial. *Newsweek,* 55-56.

Pittman, S. I. (1985). A cognitive ethnography and quantification of a first-grade teacher's selection routines for classroom management. *The Elementary School Journal, 85*(4), 541-558.

Pollack, W. S., Modzelski, W., & Rooney, G. (2008). *Prior knowledge of potential school-based violence: Information students learn may prevent a targeted attack.* U.S. Secret Service and Department of Education. Washington, DC: U.S. Government Printing Office. Retrieved February 20, 2009 from http://www.ed.gov

Portner, J. (April 12, 2000). School violence down, report says, but worry high. *Education Week,* 3.

Powell, R. R., Zehm, S. J., & Kottler, J. A. (1995). *Classrooms under the influence: Addicted families/addicted students.* Thousand Oaks, CA: Corwin Press.

Powers, K. M. (2006). An exploratory study of cultural identity and culture-based educational programs for urban American Indian students. *Urban Education, 41*(1), 20–49.

Prensky, M. (2005). Engage me or enrage me: What today's learners demand. *EDUCAUSE Review, 40*(5), 60–64.

Proshansky, E., & Wolfe, M. (1974). The physical setting and open education. *School Review, 82,* 557–574.

Quarles, C. L. (1989). *School violence: A survival guide for school staff, with emphasis on robbery, rape, and hostage taking.* Washington, DC: National Education Association.

Queen, J. A. (2000). Block scheduling revised. *Phi Delta Kappan, 82*(3), 214–222.

Raffaele-Mendez, L. M., & Knoff, H. M. (2003). Who gets suspended from school and why: A demongraphic analysis of schools and disciplinary infractions in a large school district. *Education and Treatment of Children, 26,* 30–51.

Reeve, J. (2006). Extrinsic rewards and inner motivation. In C. M. Evertson & C. S. Weinstein (Eds.), *Handbook of classroom management: Research, practice, and contemporary issues* (pp. 645–664). Mahwah, NJ: Lawrence Erlbaum Associates.

Reeve, J. (2006). Teachers as facilitators: What autonomy-supportive teachers do and why their students benefit. *Elementary School Journal 106*(3), 225–236.

Renard, L. (2005). Teaching the DIG generation. *Educational Leadership, 62*(7), 44–47.

Resnick, M. D., Ireland, M., & Borowsky, I. (2004). Youth violence perpetration: What protects? What predicts? Findings from the National Longitudinal Study of Adolescent Health. *Journal of Adolescent Health, 35*(5), 424.e1–424.e10.

Ridley, D. S., & Walther, B. (1995). *Creating responsible learners: The role of a positive classroom environment.* Washington, D. C.: American Psychological Association.

Rief, S. F. (1993). *How to reach and teach ADD/ADHD children.* West Nyack, NY: The Center for Applied Research in Education.

Rioux, J. W., & Berla, N. (1993). *Innovations in parent and family involvement.* Princeton Junction, NJ: Eye on Education.

Robinson, S., & Ricord Griesemer, S. M. (2006). Helping individual students with problem behavior. In C. M. Evertson & C. S. Weinstein (Eds.), *Handbook of classroom management: Research, practice, and contemporary issues* (pp. 787–802). Mahwah, NJ: Lawrence Erlbaum Associates.

Roby, T. W. (1988). Models of discussion. In J. T. Dillon (Ed.), *Questioning and discussion—A multidisciplinary study* (pp. 163–191). Norwood, NJ: Ablex.

Roeser, R. W., Eccles, J. S., & Sameroff, A. J. (2000). School as a context of early adolescents' academic and social–emotional development: A summary of research findings. *The Elementary School Journal, 100*(5), 443–471.

Romero, M., Mercado, C., & Vasquez-Faria, J. A. (1987). Students of limited English proficiency. In V. Richardson-Koehler (Ed.), *Educators' handbook: A research perspective* (pp. 348–369). New York: Longman.

Rosenholtz, S. J., & Cohen, E. G. (1985). Status in the eye of the beholder. In J. Berger & M. Zelditch, Jr. (Eds.), *Status, rewards, and influence* (pp. 430–444). San Francisco: Jossey Bass.

Rosenshine, B. (1980). How time is spent in elementary classrooms. In C. Denham and A.Lieberman (Eds.), *Time to learn* (pp. 107-126). Washington, DC: U.S. Department of Education.

Rosenshine, B. V. (1986). Synthesis of research on explicit teaching. *Educational Leadership, 43*(7), 60-69.

Ross, R. P. (1985). *Elementary school activity segments and the transitions between them: Responsibilities of teachers and student teachers.* Unpublished doctoral dissertation, University of Kansas.

Rothstein-Fisch, C., & Trumbull, E. (2008). *Managing Diverse Classrooms.* Alexandria, VA: ASCD.

Rowe, M. B. (1974). Wait-time and rewards as instructional variables, their influence on language, logic, and fate control: Part 1: Wait time. *Journal of Research in Science Teaching, 11,* 291-308.

Rubin, B. C. (2003). Unpacking detracking: When progressive pedagogy meets students' social worlds. *American Educational Research Journal, 40*(2), 539-573.

Ryan, A., & Patrick, H. (2001). The classroom social environment and changes in adolescents' motivation and engagement during middle school. *American Educational Research Journal, 38*(2), 437-460.

Ryan, J. B., Peterson, R. L., & Rozalski, M. (2007). State policies concerning the use of seclusion timeout in schools. *Education and Treatment of Children, 30*(3), 215-239.

Ryan, R. M., & Connell, J. P. (1989). Perceived locus of causality and internalization. *Journal of Personality and Social Psychology, 57,* 749-761.

Ryan, R. M., & Deci, E. L. (2000). Intrinsic and extrinsic motivations: Classic definitions and new directions. *Contemporary Educational Psychology, 25,* 54-67.

Sadker, D., Sadker, M., & Zittleman, K. (2009). *Still failing at fairness: How gender bias cheats girls and boys in school and what we can do about it.* New York: Simon & Schuster.

Sapon-Shevin, M. (1995). Building a safe community for learning. In W. Ayers (Ed.), *To become a teacher: Making a difference in children's lives* (pp. 99-112). New York: Teachers College Press.

Sapon-Shevin, M. (1999). *Because we can change the world: A practical guide to building cooperative, inclusive classroom communities.* Boston: Allyn & Bacon.

Savage, T. V. (1999). *Teaching self-control through management and discipline* (2nd ed.). Boston: Allyn & Bacon.

Scarcella, R. (1990). *Teaching language minority students in the multicultural classroom.* Upper Saddle River, NJ: Prentice Hall Regents.

Schaps, E. (2003). Creating a school community. *Educational Leadership, 60*(60), 31-33.

Schimmel, D. (2006). Classroom management, discipline, and the law: Clarifying confusions about students' rights and teachers' authority. In C. M. Evertson & C. S. Weinstein (Eds.), *Handbook of classroom management: Research, practice, and contemporary issues* (pp. 1005-1020). Mahwah, NJ: Lawrence Erlbaum Associates.

Schlosser, L. K. (1992). Teacher distance and student disengagement: School lives on the margin. *Journal of Teacher Education, 43*(2), 128-140.

Schlozman, S. C. (2001). Too sad to learn? *Educational Leadership, 59*(1), 80-81.

Schmollinger, C. S., Opaleski, K. A., Chapman, M. L., Jocius, R., & Bell, S. (2002). How do you make your classroom an inviting place for students to come back to each year? *English Journal, 91*(6), 20-22.

Schniedewind, N., & Davidson, E. (2000). Differentiating cooperative learning. *Educational Leadership, 58*(1), 24-27.

Schraw, G., & Lehman, S. (2001). Situational interest: A review of the literature and directions for future research. *Educational Psychology Review, 31*(1), 23-52.

Schumm, J. S., & Vaughn, S. (1992). Planning for mainstreamed special education students: Perceptions of general classroom teachers. *Exceptionality, 3,* 81-98.

Scruggs, T. E., & Mastropieri, M. A. (1996). Teacher perceptions of mainstreaming/inclusion, 1958-1995: A research synthesis. *Exceptional Children, 63,* 59-74.

Shakeshaft, C., Mandel, L., Johnson, Y. M., Sawyer, J., Hergenroter, M. A., & Barber, E. (1997). Boys call me cow. *Educational Leadership, 55*(2), 22-25.

Shalaway, L. (1989). *Learning to teach . . . not just for beginners.* Cleveland, OH: Instructor Books, Edgell Communications.

Shanley, M. (October 22, 1999). Letter to the editor. *The New York Times,* A26.

Shapiro, E. S., DuPaul, G. J., & Bradley-Klug, K. L. (1998). Self-management as a strategy to improve the classroom behavior of adolescents with ADHD. *Journal of Learning Disabilities, 31*(6), 545-555.

Shariff, S. (2004). Keeping schools out of court: Legally defensible models of leadership. *The Educational Forum, 68,* 222-232.

Sheets, R. H. (1996). Urban classroom conflict: Student-teacher perception: Ethnic integrity, solidarity, and resistance. *Urban Review, 28*(2), 165-183.

Shernoff, D. J., Czikszentmihalyi, M., Schneider, B., & Shernoff, E. S. (2003). Student engagement in high school classrooms from the perspective of flow theory. *School Psychology Quarterly, 18*(2), 158-176.

Shin, H. B., with Bruno, R. (2003). *Language use and English-speaking ability: 2000.* Washington, D.C.: U.S. Census Bureau. Retrieved February 24, 2009 from www.census.gov/prod/2003pubs/c2kbr-29.pdf

Shortt, T. L., & Thayer, Y. V. (1998/99). Block scheduling can enhance school climate. *Educational Leadership, 56*(4), 76-81.

Shulman, J. H., Lotan, R. A., & Whitcomb, J. A. (Eds.). (1998). *Groupwork in diverse classrooms: A casebook for educators.* New York: Teachers College Press.

Sileo, T. W., & Prater, M. A. (1998). Creating classroom environments that address the linguistic and cultural backgrounds of students with disabilities: An Asian Pacific American perspective. *Remedial and Special Education, 19*(6), 323-337.

Skiba, R., Horner, R., Gung, C. G., Rausch, M. K., May, S. L., & Tobin, T. (2008, March). *Race is not neutral: A national investigation of African American and Latino disproportionality in school discipline.* Paper presented at the Annual Meeting of the American Educational Research Association, New York.

Skiba, R. J., Michael, R. S., Nardo, A. C., & Peterson, R. (2002). The color of discipline: Sources of racial and gender disproportionality in school punishment. *Urban Review, 34,* 317-342.

Skiba, R. J., & Rausch, M. K. (2006). Zero tolerance, suspension, and expulsion: Questions of equity and effectiveness. In C. M. Evertson & C. S. Weinstein (Eds.), *Handbook of classroom management: Research, practice, and contemporary issues* (pp. 1063-1089). Mahwah, NJ: Lawrence Erlbaum Associates.

Slavin, R. (1991). *Student team learning: A practical guide to cooperative learning* (3rd ed.). Washington, DC: National Education Association.

Slavin, R. E. (1995). *Cooperative learning: Theory, research, and practice* (2nd edition). Boston: Allyn & Bacon.

Smith, B. W., & Sugai, G. (2000). A self-management functional assessment-based behavior support plan for a middle school student with EBD. *Journal of Positive Behavior Interventions, 2*(4), 208–217.

Smith, E. (2002). Ebonics: A case history. In L. Delpit & J. K. Dowdy (Eds.), *The skin that we speak: Thoughts on language and culture in the classroom* (pp. 15–30). New York: The New Press.

Sobel, A., & Kugler, E. G. (2007). Building partnerships with immigrant parents. *Educational Leadership, 64*(6), 62–66.

Sommer, R., & Olson, H. (1980). The soft classroom. *Environment & Behavior, 12*(1), 3–16.

Soodak, L. C., & McCarthy, M. R. (2006). Classroom management in inclusive settings. In C. M. Evertson & C. S. Weinstein (Eds.), *Handbook of classroom management: Research, practice, and contemporary issues* (pp. 461–490). Mahwah, NJ: Lawrence Erlbaum Associates.

Southern Poverty Law Center. (September 2004). Hate among youth becomes widespread. *SPLC Report, 34*(3), 1.

Souvignier, E., & Kronenberger, J. (2007). Cooperative learning in third graders' jigsaw groups for mathematics and science with and without questioning training. *British Journal of Educational Psychology, 77*, 755–771.

Steele, F. I. (1973). *Physical settings and organization development.* Reading, MA: Addison-Wesley.

Stefkovich, J. A., & Miller, J. A. (1998, April). *Law enforcement officers in public schools: Student citizens in safe havens?* Paper presented at the conference of the American Educational Research Association, San Diego, California.

Stipek, D. J. (1993). *Motivation to learn: From theory to practice* (2nd ed). Boston: Allyn & Bacon.

Stodolsky, S. S. (1984). Frameworks for studying instructional processes in peer work groups. In P. L. Peterson, L. C. Wilkinson, & M. Hallinan (Eds.), *The social context of instruction* (pp. 107–124). New York: Academic Press.

Stodolsky, S. S. (1988). *The subject matters: Classroom activity in math and social studies.* Chicago: University of Chicago Press.

Strauss, S., with Espeland, P. (1992). *Sexual harassment and teens: A program for positive change.* Minneapolis, MN: Free Spirit.

Strom, P.S., & Strom, R.D. (2005). Cyberbullying by adolescents: A preliminary assessment. *The Educational Forum, 70*(1), 21–36.

Struyk, R. (2006). Gangs in our schools: Identifying gang indicators in our school population. *Clearing House, 8*(1), 11–13.

Swap, S. M. (1993). *Developing home-school partnerships: From concepts to practice.* New York: Teachers College Press.

Tannen, D. (1995). The power of talk: Who gets heard and why. *Harvard Business Review, 73*(5), 138–148.

Tarr, P. (2004). Consider the walls. *Young Children, 59*(3), 88–92.

Telem, M. & Pinto, S. (2006). Information technology's impact on school-parents and parents-student interrelations: A case study. *Computers & Education, 47*(3), 260–279.

Thompson, B. (2008). Characteristics of parent-teacher e-mail communication. *Communication Education, 57*(2), 201–223.

Thompson, G. L. (2004). *Through ebony eyes: What teachers need to know but are afraid to ask about African American students.* San Francisco: Jossey-Bass.

Tomlinson, C. A. (1999). *The differentiated classroom: Responding to the needs of all learners.* Alexandria, VA: Association for Supervision and Curriculum Development.

Tomlinson, C. A. (2001). *How to differentiate instruction in mixed-ability classrooms* (2nd ed.). Alexandria, VA: Association for Supervision and Curriculum Development.

Towers, R. L. (1989). *Children of alcoholics/addicts.* Washington, DC: National Education Association.

Trueba, H. T., Cheng, L. R. L., & Ima, K. (1993). *Myth or reality: Adaptive strategies of Asian Americans in California.* Washington, DC: Falmer Press.

Trumbull, E., Rothstein-Fisch, C., Greenfield, P. M., & Quiroz, B. (2001). *Bridging cultures between home and school: A guide for teachers.* Mahwah, NJ: Lawrence Erlbaum Associates.

Trump, K. (1993). Tell teen gangs: School's out. *American School Board Journal, 180*(7), 39–42.

U.S. Census Bureau. (2008). *Language spoken at home. American Community Survey.* Washington, DC: US Census Bureau. Retrieved February 24, 2009 from http://factfinder.census.gov/home/saff/main.html?_lang=en

U.S. Department of Health and Human Services, Administration of Children, Youth, and Families. (2008). *Child Maltreatment 2006.* Washington, D.C.: U.S. Government Printing Office. Retrieved February 25, 2009 from http://www.acf.hhs.gov/programs/cb/stats_research/index.htm#can

Urdan, T., & Schoenfelder, E. (2006). Classroom effects on student motivation: Goal structures, social relationships, and competence beliefs. *Journal of School Psychology, 44*(5), 331–349.

Valentine, G. (Fall 1998). Lessons from home (an interview with Lisa Delpit). *Teaching Tolerance, 7*(2), 15–19.

Valenzuela, A. (1999). *Subtractive schooling: U.S.–Mexican youth and the politics of caring.* Albany: State University of New York Press.

Valli, L., Croninger, R. G., & Walters, K. (2007). Who (else) is the teacher? Cautionary notes on teacher accountability systems. *American Journal of Education, 113*(4), 635–662.

Vaughn, S., Bos, C. S., & Schumm, J. S. (2003). *Teaching exceptional, diverse, and at-risk students in the general education classroom.* Boston: Allyn & Bacon.

Vaughn, S., Gersten, R., & Chard, D. J. (2000). The underlying message in LD intervention research: Findings from research syntheses. *Exceptional Children, 67*(1), 99–114.

Villa, R.A., Thousand, J. S. & Nevin, A. I. (2008). *A guide to co-teaching: Practical tips for facilitating student learning* (2nd ed.). Thousand Oaks, CA: Corwin Press.

Villegas, A.M., & Lucas, T. (2007). The culturally responsive teacher. *Educational Leadership, 64*(6), 28–33.

Vossekuil, B., Fein, R., Reddy, M., Borum, R., & Modzeleski, W. (2002). *The final report and findings of the Safe School Initiative: Implications for the prevention of school attacks in the United States.* Washington, DC: U.S. Secret Service and the U.S. Department of Education. Retrieved November 15, 2008 from www.secretservice.gov/ntac/ssi_final_report.pdf

Walde, A. C., & Baker, K. (1990). How teachers view the parents' role in education. *Phi Delta Kappan, 72*(4), 319-320, 322.

Walker, H. M., Colvin, G., & Ramsey, E. (1995). *Antisocial behavior in school: Strategies and best practices.* Pacific Grove, CA: Brooks/Cole.

Wallace, M. A., Cox, E. A., & Skinner, C. H. (2003). Increasing independent seatwork: Breaking large assignments into smaller assignments and teaching a student with retardation to recruit reinforcement. *School Psychology Review, 32*(1), 132-142.

Wallace, T., Anderson, A. R., Bartholomay, T., & Hupp, S. (2002). An ecobehavioral examination of high school classrooms that include students with disabilities. *Exceptional Children, 68*(3), 345-359.

Walsh, J. A., & Satates, B. D. (2005). *Quality questioning: Research-based practice to engage every learner.* Thousand Oaks, CA: Corwin Press.

Walsh, M. (1999, June 2). Harassment ruling poses challenges. *Education Week, 18*(38), 1, 22.

Walsh, M. (2000, March 8). Law update: A fine line between dangerous and harmless student expression. *Education Week,* 14.

Walters, L. S. (2000). Putting cooperative learning to the test. *Harvard Education Letter, 16*(3), 1-6.

Watson, M., & Battistich, V. (2006). Building and sustaining caring communities. In C. M. Evertson and C. S. Weinstein (Eds.), *Handbook of classroom management: Research, practice, and contemporary issues* (pp. 253-280). Mahwah, NJ: Lawrence Erlbaum Associates.

Webb, N. M. (1984). Sex differences in interaction and achievement in cooperative small groups. *Journal of Educational Psychology, 76,* 33-44.

Webb, N. M., & Farivar, S. (1994). Promoting helping behavior in cooperative small groups in middle school mathematics. *American Educational Research Journal, 31*(2), 369-395.

Webb, N. M., and Mastergeorge, A. M. (2003). The development of students' helping behavior and learning in peer-directed small groups. *Cognition and Instruction, 21*(4), 361-428.

Webb, N. M., Nemre, K. M., & Ing, M. (2006). Small group reflections: Parallels between teacher discourse and student behavior in peer-directed groups. *The Journal of the Learning Sciences, 15*(1), 63-119.

Weiner, L. (1999). *Urban teaching: The essentials.* New York: Teachers College Press.

Weinstein, C. S. (1982). Privacy-seeking behavior in an elementary classroom. *Journal of Environmental Psychology, 2,* 23-35.

Weinstein, C. S., Curran, M., & Tomlinson-Clarke, S. (2003). Culturally responsive classroom management: Awareness into action. *Theory into Practice, 42*(4), 269-276.

Weinstein, C. S., Tomlinson-Clarke, S., & Curran, M. (2004). Toward a conception of culturally responsive classroom management. *Journal of Teacher Education, 55*(1), 25-38.

Wentzel, K. R. (1997). Student motivation in middle school: The role of perceived pedagogical caring. *Journal of Educational Psychology, 89*(3), 411-419.

Wentzel, K. R. (1998). Social relationships and motivation in middle school: The role of parents, teachers, and peers. *Journal of Educational Psychology, 90*(2), 202–209.

Wentzel, K. R. (2006). A social motivation perspective for classroom management. In C. M. Evertson & C. S. Weinstein (Eds.), *Handbook of classroom management: Research, practice, and contemporary issues* (pp. 619–644). Mahwah, NJ: Lawrence Erlbaum Associates.

Wertsch, J. V. (1985). *Vygotsky & the social formation of mind.* Cambridge, MA: Harvard University Press.

Wessler, S. (2008). Civility speaks up. *Educational Leadership, 66*(1), 44–48.

Wheldall, K., & Lam, Y. Y. (1987). Rows versus tables. II. The effects of two classroom seating arrangements on classroom disruption rate, on-task behaviour and teacher behaviour in three special school classes. *Educational Psychology, 7*(4), 303–312.

Wigfield, A., & Eccles, J. S. (2000). Expectancy-value theory of achievement motivation. *Contemporary Educational Psychology, 25*(1), 68–81.

Williams, M. (1993). Actions speak louder than words: What students think. *Educational Leadership, 51*(3), 22–23.

Williams, R. L., & Stockdale, S. L. (2004). Classroom motivation strategies for prospective teachers. *The Teacher Educator, 39*(3), 212–230.

Wlodkowski, R. J. (2003). *Motivational opportunities for successful teaching (Leader's guide).* Phoenix, AZ: Universal Dimensions.

Wodrich, D. L. (2000). *Attention-deficit/hyperactivity disorder: What every parent wants to know* (2nd ed.). Baltimore, MD: Paul Brookes.

Wolfgang, C. H. (1999). *Solving discipline problems: Methods and models for today's teachers* (4th ed.). Boston: Allyn & Bacon.

Woolfolk, A. E. (2007). *Educational Psychology* (10th ed.). Boston: Pearson Education/ Allyn & Bacon.

Xu, J., & Corno, L. (2003). Family help and homework management reported by middle school students. *The Elementary School Journal, 103*(5), 503–517.

Zeidner, M. (1988). The relative severity of common classroom strategies: The student's perspective. *British Journal of Educational Psychology, 58,* 69–77.

Zepeda, S. J., & Mayers, R. S. (2006). An analysis of research on block scheduling. *Review of Educational Research, 76*(1), 137–170.

Zirpoli, T. J. (2005). *Behavior management: Applications for teachers* (4th ed.) Upper Saddle River, NJ: Pearson Education.

NAME INDEX

Subject Index

Note: Page numbers in *italic* type indicate figures or tables.